ENCYCLOPEDIC
ATLAS
OF THE
WORLD

ENCYCLOPEDIC
ATLAS
OF THE
WORLD

GENERAL EDITOR KEITH LYE FRGS

CARTOGRAPHIC EDITOR

SHIRLEY CARPENTER MA FRGS

NEW
BURLINGTON
BOOKS

A QUARTO BOOK

PUBLISHED BY
NEW BURLINGTON BOOKS
6 Blundell Street
London N7 9BH

ISBN 0 948872 80 2

Reprinted 1990, 1991

Typeset in Britain by Norman Ellis, Lintron, Watford
Colour origination in Hong Kong by Hong Kong Graphic Arts
Printed in Hong Kong by Lee Fung Asco Ltd

This book was designed and produced by
Quarto Publishing plc

Text Keith Lye FRGS, Theo Rowland-Entwistle MA FRGS FZS
Editorial Director Christopher Fagg
Art Director Alastair Campbell
Art Editor Nick Clark
Editors David Girling, Deirdre McGarry, Michelle Newton,
Stephen Paul, Fiona St. Aubyn
Designer Hazel Edington
Illustrators Marilyn Clark, Chris Forsey, Elaine Keenan, Abdul
Aziz Khan, Simon Roulstone, Sue Worth
Paste Up Leaper and Gard Ltd, Bristol

Contents

Earth and the solar system

Planet Earth is one of the nine planets in the Solar System. It is the third planet from the Sun and the fifth largest, although the mass of the Sun is 333,434 times greater than that of the Earth. Like Mercury, Venus, Mars and probably Pluto, the Earth is a terrestrial planet – that is, it is a dense, rocky body. The giant planets – Jupiter, Saturn, Uranus and Neptune – are low-density balls of gas, though they may contain small rocky cores.

The Earth moves in three ways. First, it spins in a west–east direction on its axis, which is tilted by 23.45 degrees, although the tilt varies periodically between about 21.8 degrees and 24.4 degrees. At the Equator, the Earth is spinning at a speed of 1,031.5 mph (1,660 km/h), but the speed diminishes towards the poles.

One complete rotation of the Earth, a mean solar day, lasts 24 hours. But the sidereal day, measured by the apparent motion of stars around the Pole Star is 23 hours, 56 minutes and 4 seconds. The difference between the two occurs because the Earth is also moving forward along its orbit around the Sun. Hence it takes ⅟₃₆₅th of a revolution more than a sidereal day before the same point on the Earth's surface exactly faces the Sun.

The time of day at any place is determined by the height of the Sun in the sky. When the Sun reaches its highest point, the local, or solar, time is noon. Because the Earth rotates through 360° every 24 hours, local time changes by 4 minutes for every degree of longitude. To avoid inconvenience, however, the world is divided into time zones that correspond roughly to 15° of longitude, which represents one hour in time. In practice, the boundaries between the time zones are modified to prevent a small country having two separate times. Time zones are measured east and west of the Greenwich, or Prime, Meridian, 0° longitude. As a result, at longitude 180° East (or West), there is a time difference of 24 hours. This is the International Date Line.

The Earth takes one year to complete one orbit around the Sun, moving at a speed of 65,991 mph (106,200 km/h). The solar year is 365 days, 5 hours 48 minutes and 46 seconds. Leap years of 366 days every four years prevent the solar and calendar years becoming out of step.

Because the Earth's axis is tilted, the northern and southern hemispheres lean towards and away from the Sun in turn. As a result, the latitude at which the Sun is directly overhead at noon constantly changes as the Earth orbits the Sun. On June 21, the Sun is overhead at the northern Tropic of Cancer and on December 21 it is overhead at the southern Tropic of Capricorn. These are the solstices. At the equinoxes, on March 21 and September 23, the Sun is overhead at the Equator. The apparent migration of the overhead Sun explains why the lengths of daylight vary throughout the year, and why areas north of the Arctic and south of the Antarctic circles have at least one day a year when the Sun does not set. (The poles themselves have six months of continuous daylight and six months of darkness.)

The Earth also moves in a third way. Together with the rest of the Solar System, it is moving around the spiral Milky Way galaxy once every 200 million years, at a speed of 42,380 mph (68,200 km/h). The Milky Way galaxy, which measures about 100,000 light-years across, contains about 100,000 million stars, of which our Sun is an average-sized, middle-aged example. If this fact does not make us feel insignificant, we should recall that the Milky Way galaxy is only one of millions of galaxies observable from Earth.

Russian astronomers recently estimated that there are probably 130 solar systems like our own within the observable part of the Milky Way galaxy. And the American astronomer Carl Sagan has suggested that perhaps a million planets within our galaxy have intelligent life forms.

Special conditions are required for life as we know it to exist. If a planet is too close to the Sun, it is too hot for life. The surface temperature on Mercury, the planet nearest the Sun, ranges from 662°F (350°C) during the day to −274°F (−170°C) at night. But on Mars, which is about 48.78 million miles (78.5 million km) farther from the Sun than the Earth, the surface temperature is −58°F (−50°C).

The Earth's atmosphere is also important, not only because it is breathable and filters out harmful ultra-violet radiation from the Sun, but also because it stops heat escaping into space. Our satellite, the Moon, has no atmosphere, and surface temperatures reach 212°F (100°C) by day only to plummet to −238°F (−150°C) at night.

Right From space, our planet Earth resembles a perfect sphere. But it is really an oblate spheroid, because it bulges slightly at the equator and is correspondingly flattened at the poles. The equatorial diameter of the Earth, which measures 7,926.4 miles (12,756 km) across, is, therefore, longer than the polar diameter of 7,900 miles (12,713 km). Similarly, the equatorial circumference is 24,902 miles (40,075 km), as compared with the polar circumference of 24,860 miles (40,007 km). The surface area of the Earth is about 196,938,000 sq miles (510,066,000 km²).

Sun
Mercury
Venus
Earth
Moon
Mars
Jupiter
Saturn
Uranus
Neptune
Pluto

88 days
225 days
365 days
687 days
11.9 years
29.5 years
247.7 years
84 years
164.8 years

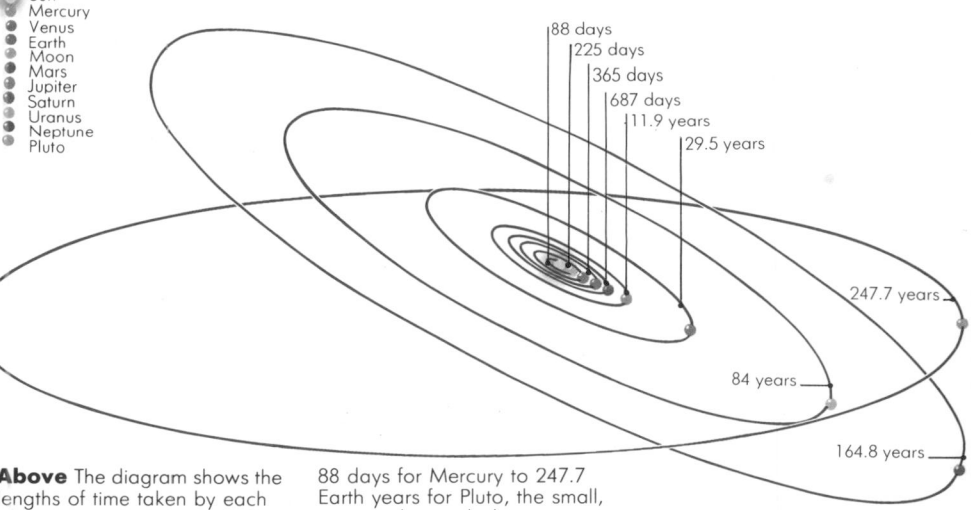

Above The diagram shows the lengths of time taken by each of the planets to complete one orbit of the Sun, ranging from 88 days for Mercury to 247.7 Earth years for Pluto, the small, remote planet which was discovered as recently as 1930.

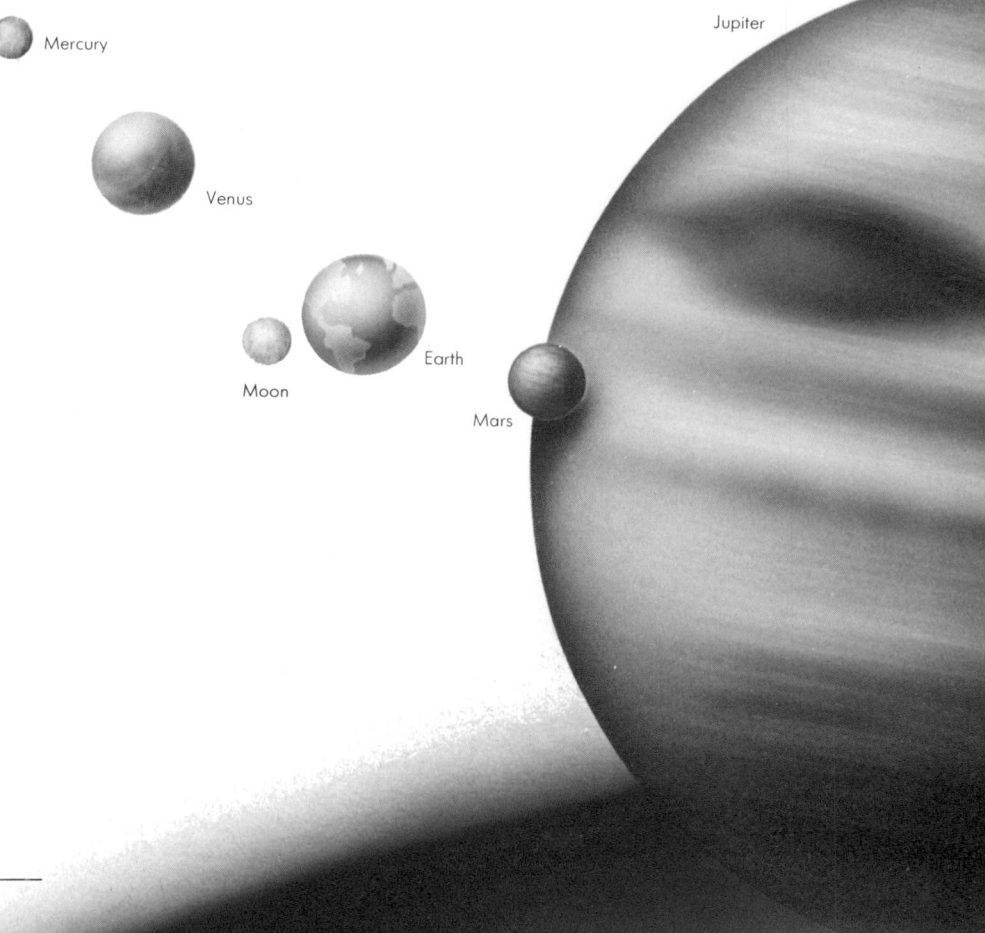

Mercury

Venus

Moon

Earth

Mars

Jupiter

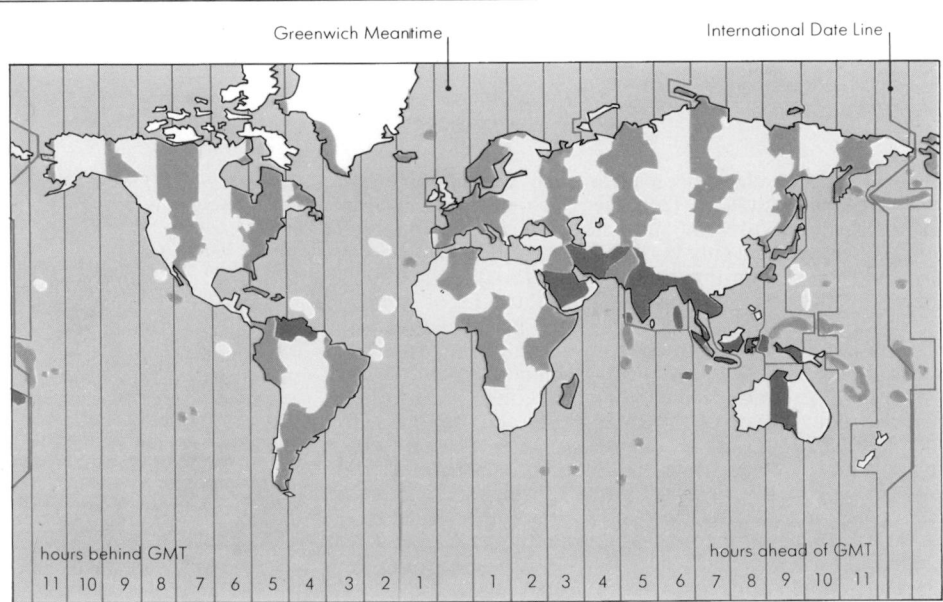

hours behind GMT

| 11 | 10 | 9 | 8 | 7 | 6 | 5 | 4 | 3 | 2 | 1 |

hours ahead of GMT

| 1 | 2 | 3 | 4 | 5 | 6 | 7 | 8 | 9 | 10 | 11 |

Below The Earth takes a year to complete one orbit of the Sun. Because the Earth's axis is tilted, the amount of insolation experienced at any place varies throughout the year. At the equinoxes (March 21 and September 23), the Sun is overhead at the equator. At the solstices (June 21 and December 21), the Sun is overhead, respectively, at the Tropics of Cancer and Capricorn. The apparent migration of the overhead Sun accounts for the four seasons experienced in the middle latitudes. In the tropics, the seasons are not so clearly differentiated.

Right The Earth is divided into time zones which cover roughly 15 degrees of longitude, the equivalent of one hour as the Earth rotates on its axis. To use local time would be extremely inconvenient, because a difference of one degree of longitude, or just over 69 miles (111 km) on the equator, represents a time difference of 4 minutes. Adjustments are made in the borders of the time zones to avoid anomalies, such as two times in one small country. Time is measured east and west of the prime meridian (0° longitude). The International Date Line corresponds roughly to longitude 180° East or West.

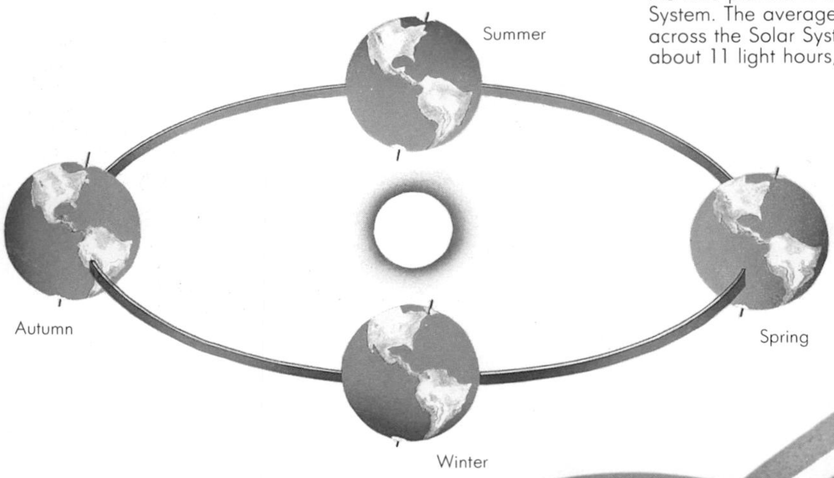

Summer

Autumn

Spring

Winter

Below The diagram shows the nine planets in the Solar System. The average distance across the Solar System is about 11 light hours, as compared with an average distance from the Earth to the Sun of eight light-minutes. The diagram also shows the main moons in the Solar System, although recent space probes to Saturn have revealed more moons, raising the total for Saturn to about 17 and the total in the Solar System to around 40. The smallest planet is Pluto, with an equatorial diameter of about 1,864 miles (3,000 km), as compared with Mercury, 3,014 miles (4,850 km), Mars, 4,219 miles (6,790 km), and Venus, 7,521 miles (12,104 km). The largest planets are huge balls of gas. Jupiter has an equatorial diameter of 88,610 miles (142,600 km), Saturn, 74,567 miles (120,000 km), Uranus, about 32,312 miles (52,000 km), and Neptune, about 29,827 miles (48,000 km). The Sun's diameter is about 864,972 miles (1,392,000 km). The Solar System also contains rocky bodies called asteroids, whose diameters range from about six to 500 miles (10–805 km); comets, collections of frozen gas, dust and rock particles revolving around the Sun; and meteors, which are small lumps of rock and metal (mainly iron and nickel).

Pluto

Neptune

Uranus

Saturn

The story of Earth

Several theories have been advanced to explain the origin of the Solar System. One suggests that a passing star tore material from the Sun and this material condensed into the various heavenly bodies. Another theory proposes that the rotating Sun threw out a disc of material. A third theory is that the Sun formed at the centre of a huge revolving cloud of gas and dust. After its formation, the other heavenly bodies formed from the remaining matter.

The Solar System is about 4,600 million years old. At first, the Earth may have resembled one of the giant planets, though most of the gases were later removed. In the molten Earth, denser elements, such as iron, sank towards the centre, while lighter elements rose to the surface. Eventually, a crust formed, which rested on a denser mantle. In turn, the mantle enclosed an extremely dense core. The early crust was constantly cracked and re-melted. As a result, the oldest rocks as yet discovered are not much more than 3,700 million years old.

Through incessant volcanic action, gases and water vapour were released from the rocks to form a primitive atmosphere. As the Earth cooled, water vapour in the atmosphere condensed into raindrops and water collected on the surface, forming lakes and seas. The first simple, one-celled organisms may have formed in pools which were rich in the chemical building-blocks of life. The first life forms may have appeared as early as 4,000 million years ago, although the oldest known fossils – traces of bacteria – are about 3,500 million years old.

Advanced oxygen-producing plants evolved around 1,800 million years ago. They slowly added oxygen to the poisonous atmosphere which had hitherto contained little. Some oxygen was converted into a layer of ozone in the upper atmosphere. This layer is of great importance, because it filters out ultraviolet radiation, which would make life on land impossible.

Right The geological timescale shows the main periods and epochs in the last 570 million years. The Pre-Cambrian consists of nearly 4,000 million years. Life forms first became abundant in the Cambrian period. The Cambrian to the Permian period makes up the Palaeozoic era. The Triassic, Jurassic and Cretaceous periods together form the Mesozoic era. The Tertiary and Quaternary periods make up the Cenozoic era.

Right Some 200 million years ago, towards the end of the Triassic period, the world's continents were grouped together in a single landmass, which geologists call Pangaea. By 100 million years ago, the plates which supported the land areas were moving steadily apart. By 50 million years ago, the modern oceans had all come into being, and the Himalayas had started to rise as a plate carrying the Indian subcontinent collided with Eurasia. Around 26 million years ago, the African plate pushed a small plate bearing Italy against Europe, making the Alps rise.

200 million years ago

100 million years ago

25 million years ago

today

Pre-Cambrian

570

Cambrian

530

Ordovician

440

Silurian

410

Devonian

345

Carboniferous

280

Permian

225

Triassic

195

Jurassic

136

Cretaceous

65

Tertiary

2 Quarternary

Palaeocene

Eocene

Oligocene

Miocene

Pliocene

The figures in italics indicate millions of years ago.

8

section through the crust

layers of sedimentary rock

ocean

land

mountain range

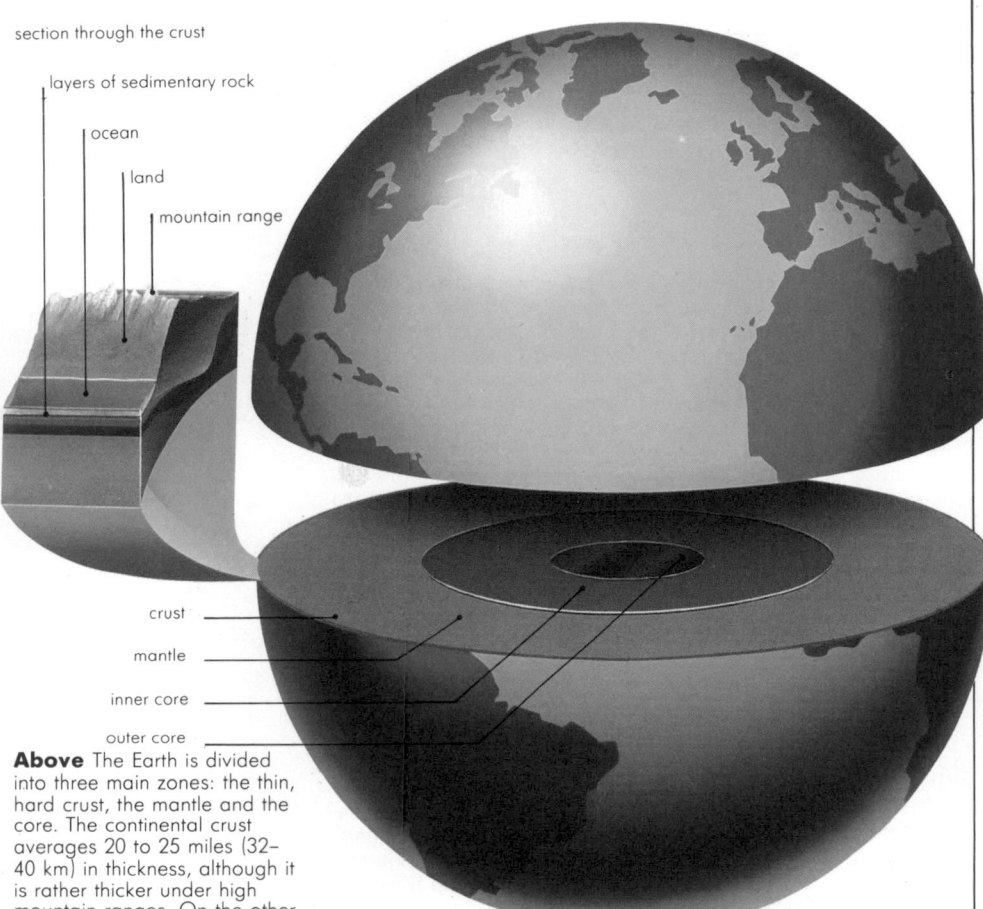

Fossils are rare in ancient rocks, probably because the plants and animals were soft and decayed quickly after death. But at the start of the Cambrian period, the first in the Palaeozoic era, some 570 million years ago, life was abundant and many life forms, such as animals called trilobites, had hard parts which left fossil traces in the rocks.

The earliest fishes, the first vertebrates, appeared in the late Cambrian period. At the end of the Silurian period, around 424 million years ago, plants spread from the sea on to land. They were followed in the Devonian period, about 370 million years ago, by vertebrates, namely amphibians which had evolved from bony fishes with lungs.

The later Carboniferous period (known in the United States as the Pennsylvanian period) saw another breakthrough, the evolution of the first true land animals, the reptiles. Reptiles developed quickly during the Permian period (the last in the Palaeozoic era). In the Mesozoic era (comprising the Triassic, Jurassic and Cretaceous periods), reptiles dominated the Earth. However, at the end of the Cretaceous period, the dinosaurs and most other large reptiles, excluding the crocodiles, became extinct. The reasons for their disappearance are still hotly debated by modern geologists.

The Cenozoic era (comprising the Tertiary and Quaternary periods) saw the rise of mammals. Ape-like creatures evolved about 35 million years ago and types of near-men appeared in East Africa between about 3.5 and 1.5 million years ago. Modern Man appeared towards the end of the Pleistocene epoch. In an incredibly short time, Man has spread across the Earth, displacing many other creatures. We have even begun to reach beyond Earth into space.

From space, the Earth seems stable enough. But it is changing in several ways. The theory of continental drift was first advanced in the early twentieth century, when studies of similar rocks, rock structures and fossils in distant landmasses suggested that the continents had once been joined together.

crust

mantle

inner core

outer core

Above The Earth is divided into three main zones: the thin, hard crust, the mantle and the core. The continental crust averages 20 to 25 miles (32–40 km) in thickness, although it is rather thicker under high mountain ranges. On the other hand, the average thickness of the oceanic crust, which underlies the continental crust, is only 4 miles (6 km) thick. The oceanic crust is called sima, after its two most important constituents, silicon and magnesium. The continental crust is called sial, being rich in silicon and aluminium. The oceanic crust has a density of

3.0 grams per cubic centimetre, and is denser than the continental crust, which has a density of 2.7 g/cm^3. Beneath the crust is the mantle, which has a density ranging from 3.4 g/cm^3 near the top to 4.5 g/cm^3 near the bottom. The mantle is about 1,802 miles (2,900 km) thick. Plates consist not only of the crust but also of

the top part of the mantle. Plate movements extend down to 45 to 62 miles (72–100 km). At these depths there is a semimolten layer in the mantle called the asthenosphere. The Earth's core has a diameter of 4,188 miles (6,740 km). The core's density ranges from 10 to 13 g/cm^3. It consists mainly of iron and nickel.

volcanic zone

earthquake zone

Right The map shows the zones where earthquakes and volcanoes are most common. Although earthquakes can occur anywhere, the most intense ones result from plate movements and so they occur on or near plate edges. Many volcanoes also occur alongside subduction zones. Hence, the bands on the map contain active plate margins.

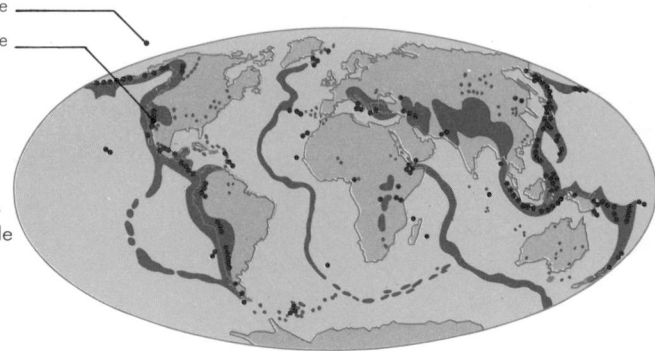

The late 1960s brought the theory of plate tectonics, according to which the Earth's crust and the top part of the mantle are split into rigid, moving blocks, called plates. The continents rest on these plates. The plates move because heat in the mantle sets up convection currents in the semi-fluid rocks of the upper mantle. The study of ocean ridges, long mountain ranges on the sea floor, supported this idea. Beneath the ridges, molten material is welling upwards and then spreading sideways before eventually sinking again. The centres of these ridges are plate edges. As the lateral movement below pulls the plates apart, molten rock wells up to fill the gap.

The ocean ridges are called 'constructive plate margins', because new crustal rock is being formed along them. The youngest rocks, therefore, are in the centres of the ridges. Farther away, in both directions, the rocks become progressively older. This process of 'ocean spreading' can be seen on the surface in Iceland, a volanic island straddling the Atlantic oceanic ridge.

'Destructive plate margins' occur where crustal rock is being destroyed. They occur along the ocean trenches, the deepest parts of the oceans. Here, the advancing edge of one plate is descending beneath another along a subduction zone. As the plate descends, in jerky movements, earthquakes occur and the friction generated creates magma which may reach the surface as lava through volcanoes alongside the trenches.

A third kind of plate edge is the transform fault, such as the San Andreas Fault in California. Here, two plates move alongside each other in occasional, jerky movements. Plate margins are zones of great earthquake activity, and the theory of plate tectonics has shed much light on earthquakes, volcanoes and the formation of mountains. Fold mountains are formed when rocks are squeezed together by plate collisions. Block mountains are formed when blocks of land are pushed upwards between huge faults formed by tugging plate movements.

Plate tectonics has also shed light on how landmasses have moved together and apart in the past. We now know that around 200 million years ago there was only one continent, Pangaea. But in the last 180 million years, Pangaea has broken up and plates have carried the continents to their present positions.

1

2

3

4

sea

ocean ridge

land

plate boundary

volcanoes at plate margin

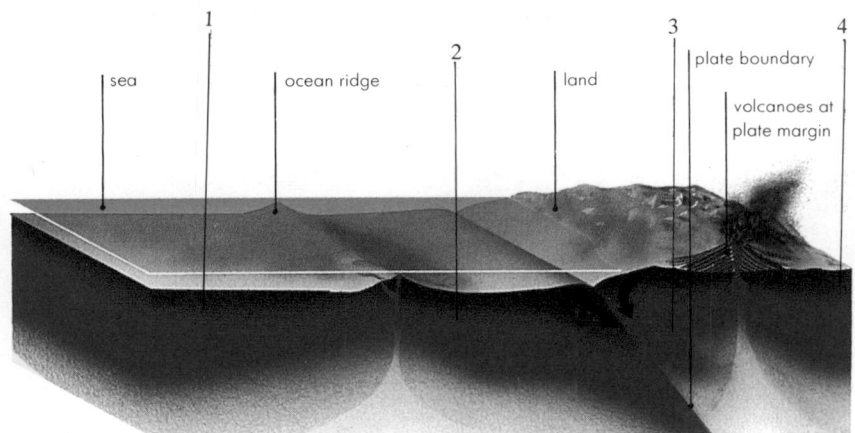

Above The stylized diagram shows how plate movements occur. Plates 1 and 2 and plates 3 and 4 are being pulled apart by convection currents in the upper mantle. The plate edges run through ocean ridges. These are

spreading ridges, or constructive plate margins, because new crustal rock is being formed in the gaps made as the plates move apart. Lateral movements occur along transform faults roughly at right angles to the ridges.

Plates 2 and 3 are colliding. The front edge of Plate 2 is pushed beneath Plate 3 in a subduction zone along a deep ocean trench. This is a destructive plate margin, because the descending plate is melted.

The Oceans

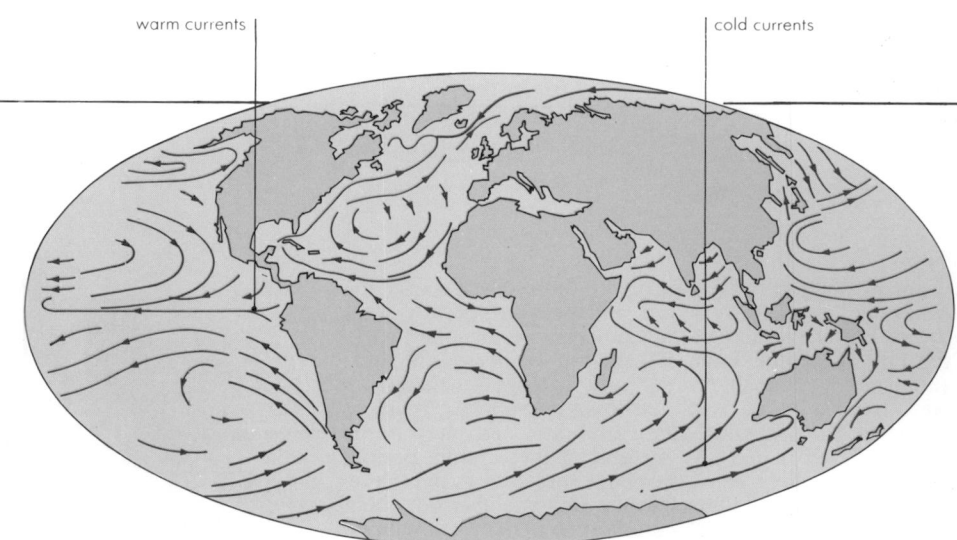

Water covers nearly 71 percent of the Earth's surface. Oceans account for four-fifths of the southern hemisphere and three-fifths of the northern. The oceans contain 97.2 percent of the world's total water.

Seawater is a complex substance, containing in solution 73 of the 93 elements which occur in nature. Of these, sodium and chlorine, the elements that form salt, are the most abundant. The saltiness, or salinity, of seawater is generally around 3.5 percent, although wide variations can occur. For instance, in the Baltic Sea, the salinity drops to 0.72 percent, while in the Red Sea it reaches 4.1 percent. One pound (0.45 kg) of seawater contains 0.56 ounces (15.8 g) of dissolved elements, of which chlorine and sodium make up about 85 percent. Another 13 percent is composed of sulphate, magnesium, potassium and calcium.

The salinity and temperature of seawater affect its density. The higher the salinity and the lower the temperature, the greater is the density. The temperature of seawater ranges from 28°F (−2°C), the freezing point of seawater, to about 84°F (29°C) or more in shallow, tropical seas. The temperature of seawater has a marked effect on marine life, because cold water can hold more oxygen than warm water.

The density of seawater affects ocean currents and the general circulation of the oceans. For example, cold, dense water will flow beneath warm, less dense water. Hence, cold bottom currents from the polar regions often flow in a reverse direction to warm surface currents flowing from the tropics towards the poles. But the chief factor causing surface currents is the wind.

Winds are also responsible for waves. But waves do not move water particles horizontally. It is the shape of the wave that passes through the water, while the water particles rotate in a circular orbit.

Tides are rises and falls in sea-level which occur twice every 24 hours and 50 minutes – the time it takes for the Moon to complete one orbit of the Earth. This is because tides are caused mainly by the gravitational pull of the Moon, and to a lesser extent the Sun, on the ocean waters. When the Moon is overhead at any point, the water is drawn towards it, creating a bulge, which is balanced by another on the far side of the Earth.

In the open sea, the sea-level changes by little more than 3 feet (0.9 metres), but high tides may occur in coastal waters, especially in bottlenecks, such as narrow estuaries. The highest, or spring, tides occur when the Sun, Moon and Earth are in a straight line. The lowest, or neap, tides occur when these three bodies form a right angle, and the gravitational pull of the Moon and Sun are opposed.

Beneath the waves is a landscape as varied as any on dry land. Around most landmasses are gently sloping continental shelves of varying widths. These shelves are flooded parts of the continents. They end at the continental slope, where the gradient changes markedly in a steep slope that leads down to the abyss. The top of the continental slope is the true edge of the continents.

The abyss contains large plains covered by oozes. But there are also abyssal hills and volcanic seamounts, some of which form islands. The oceans also contain massive oceanic ridges, parts of which reach the surface as islands. Along the centres of these ridges are rift valleys, where new rock is being formed as the plates on either side drift apart at rates of 0.5 to 4 inches (1–10 cm) a year. Equally dramatic features are the ocean trenches, where the advancing edge of one plate is being pushed down beneath another.

No rocks in the ocean crust are more than 200 million years old. This shows that the oceans are much younger features than the continents, where rocks around 3,700 million years old have been found. The youthfulness of the oceanic crust demonstrates that the oceans were formed during the last 200 million years.

The study of oceanography has progressed greatly in recent years. Echo-sounders have speeded the mapping of the ocean floor and such instruments as corers, dredges and underwater cameras have supplied much information about the ocean floor and the dark waters at considerable depths. Today, oil and natural gas are extracted from wells in the continental shelves, such as those in California and the Gulf of Mexico. Mining on the floor of the abyss is also possible. Some areas contain many potato-shaped manganese nodules, which contain not only manganese, but also cobalt, copper, iron and nickel.

Above The map shows the main surface currents and the general circulation of oceanic waters. The chief cause of these currents is the wind. The effect of the surface currents is felt only in the top 1,200 feet (366 m). But there are other, often strong countercurrents which flow in a reverse direction at greater depths. In no part of the oceans is the water completely still.

Right If the world's oceans were drained, a landscape as varied as that of the continents would be revealed.

Below Before the 1920's, when echo-sounders came into regular use, the mapping of the ocean floor was laborious and often inaccurate. There was a widespread belief that the ocean floor was a featureless plain. But we now know that the ocean waters conceal a considerable variety of landscapes. Around the continents are gently sloping continental shelves, which are flooded parts of the continents. Much of this area is masked by terrigenous oozes, consisting of silt, mud and other material worn from the land. The shelves end at the continental slopes, which descend steeply to the abyss. These slopes are the true edges of the continents. In places, the continental slopes are cut by massive submarine canyons, which may have been worn out by turbidity currents. At the foot of the continental slopes are flat abyssal plains and rolling abyssal hills. Other striking features include volcanoes, some of which reach the surface as islands. There are also ocean trenches, the deepest and darkest parts of the oceans. They occur in places where one plate is being pushed beneath another. The movements are jerky, so the trenches are earthquake zones. The ocean ridges are huge submarine mountain ranges. In the centres of these ridges, new crustal rock is being formed as the plates on either side move apart. The ocean ridges are also earthquake zones, with much volcanic activity. For example, the volcanic island of Iceland straddles the Mid-Atlantic ridge.

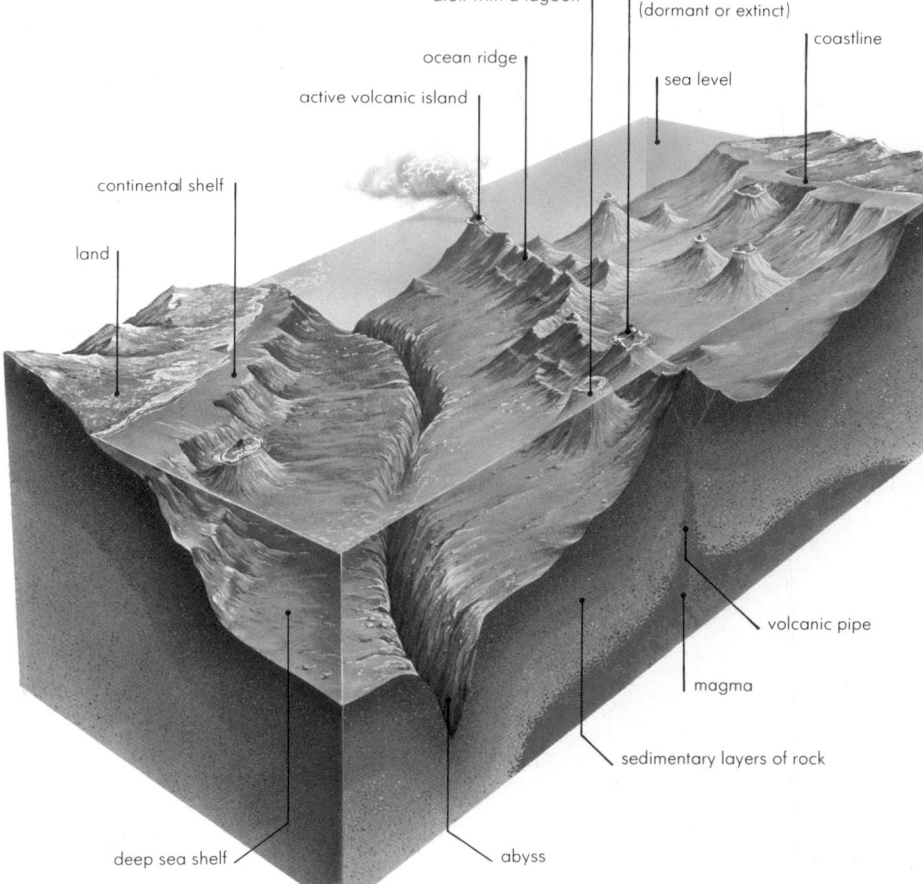

atoll with a lagoon

ocean ridge

active volcanic island

volcanic islands (dormant or extinct)

sea level

coastline

continental shelf

land

volcanic pipe

magma

sedimentary layers of rock

deep sea shelf

abyss

Pacific Ocean

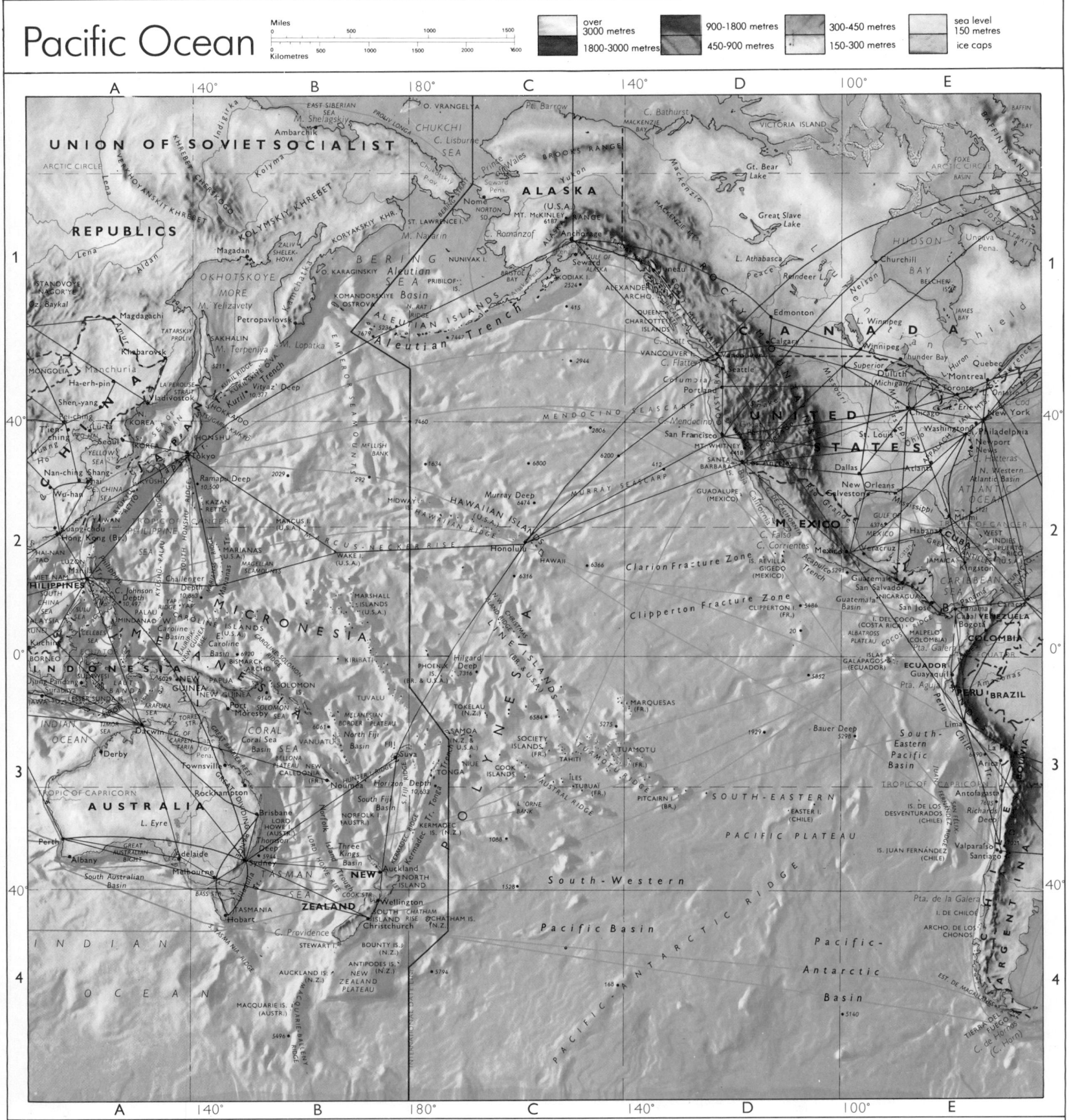

The Pacific Ocean, with an area of about 64 million sq miles (165.76 million km²), is by far the largest of the oceans. This is substantially more than the combined area of all the continents. The Pacific Ocean was named by the Portuguese explorer Ferdinand Magellan. But the ocean is less peaceful than its name suggests. Tropical cyclones, called typhoons in the China Seas, can cause great destruction, as can tsunamis, which are fast-moving waves triggered off by earthquakes, volcanic eruptions or landslides on the ocean floor. Tsunamis have caused great loss of life in coastal regions in such countries as Indonesia and Japan.

An oceanic ridge running southwards from Central America separates two plates in the southeast from the vast Pacific plate proper. The smaller of these plates, the Cocos plate, is moving against Central America, which accounts for the string of active volcanoes extending from Mexico through Central America. To the south is the larger Nazca plate which is moving against the South American plate. The subduction zone off the South American coast is responsible for the earthquakes which shake western South America and the volcano eruptions in the high Andes. In the north and west, the Pacific plate is bordered by deep trenches, extending from Alaska and the Aleutians to the Kamchatka peninsula, Japan, the Philippines and Indonesia. In the southwest, the edge of the Pacific plate extends to New Zealand. The margins of the Pacific are justly called the 'ring of fire'.

The Marianas trench in the northwestern Pacific contains the deepest point in all

the oceans, 36,198 feet (11,033 m). The Marianas trench was the site of the greatest man-made oceanic descent, when the Swiss-built US Navy bathyscaphe *Trieste* reached a depth of 35,817 feet (10,917 m) in 1960. It was manned by Dr Jacques Piccard and Lt Donald Walsh of the US Navy.

The Pacific islands are divided into the Melanesian, Micronesian and Polynesian groups (see pages 190–1 and 196–7). The islands are either volcanic and mountainous, or they are low coral islands which have formed on the continental shelves or on submerged volcanic mountains. Sea temperatures range from 81°F (27°C) near the Equator to just above freezing in the far north and south. The average salinity of Pacific waters is low, being between 3 and 3.5 percent.

The currents of the North Pacific, including the warm Japanese current and the North Pacific Drift (the equivalent of the Gulf Stream in the Atlantic), circulate in a clockwise direction, while the waters of the South Pacific circulate in the opposite direction. The first European to approach the Pacific from the Atlantic was Vasco Núñez de Balboa, who saw the Pacific after crossing the Isthmus of Panama in 1513. The navigator Ferdinand Magellan sailed through the Strait of Magellan in October-November, 1520. But, after successfully crossing the ocean, he was killed in the Philippines in April 1521. Magellan was followed in 1577–80 by Sir Francis Drake. In the wake of the explorers came traders and colonizers. Although the Pacific never became as important an ocean highway as the North Atlantic, the opening of the Panama Canal in 1914 greatly increased the ocean's commercial importance. There are now oilfields off the American and Asian coasts.

Atlantic Ocean

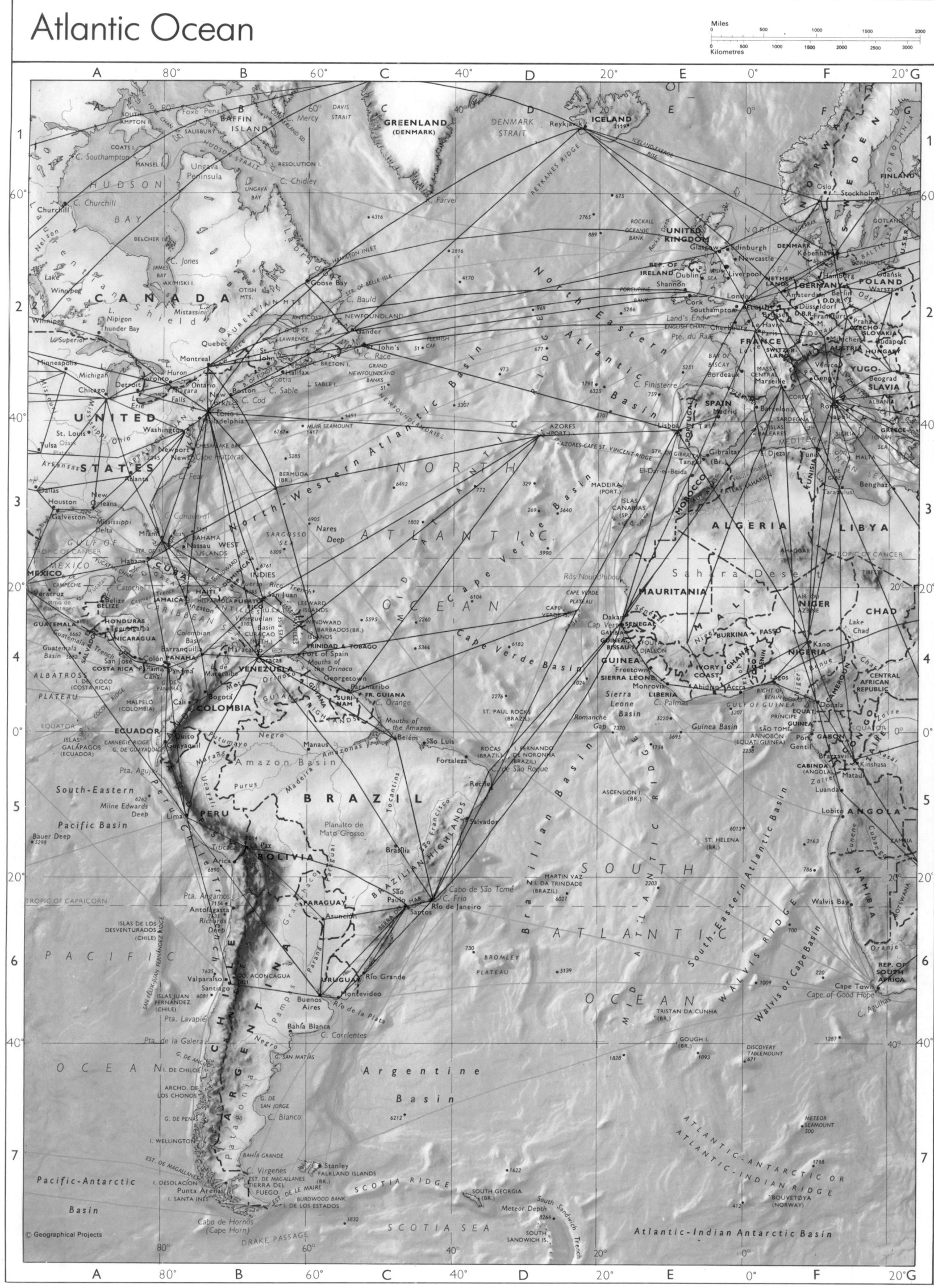

Indian Ocean

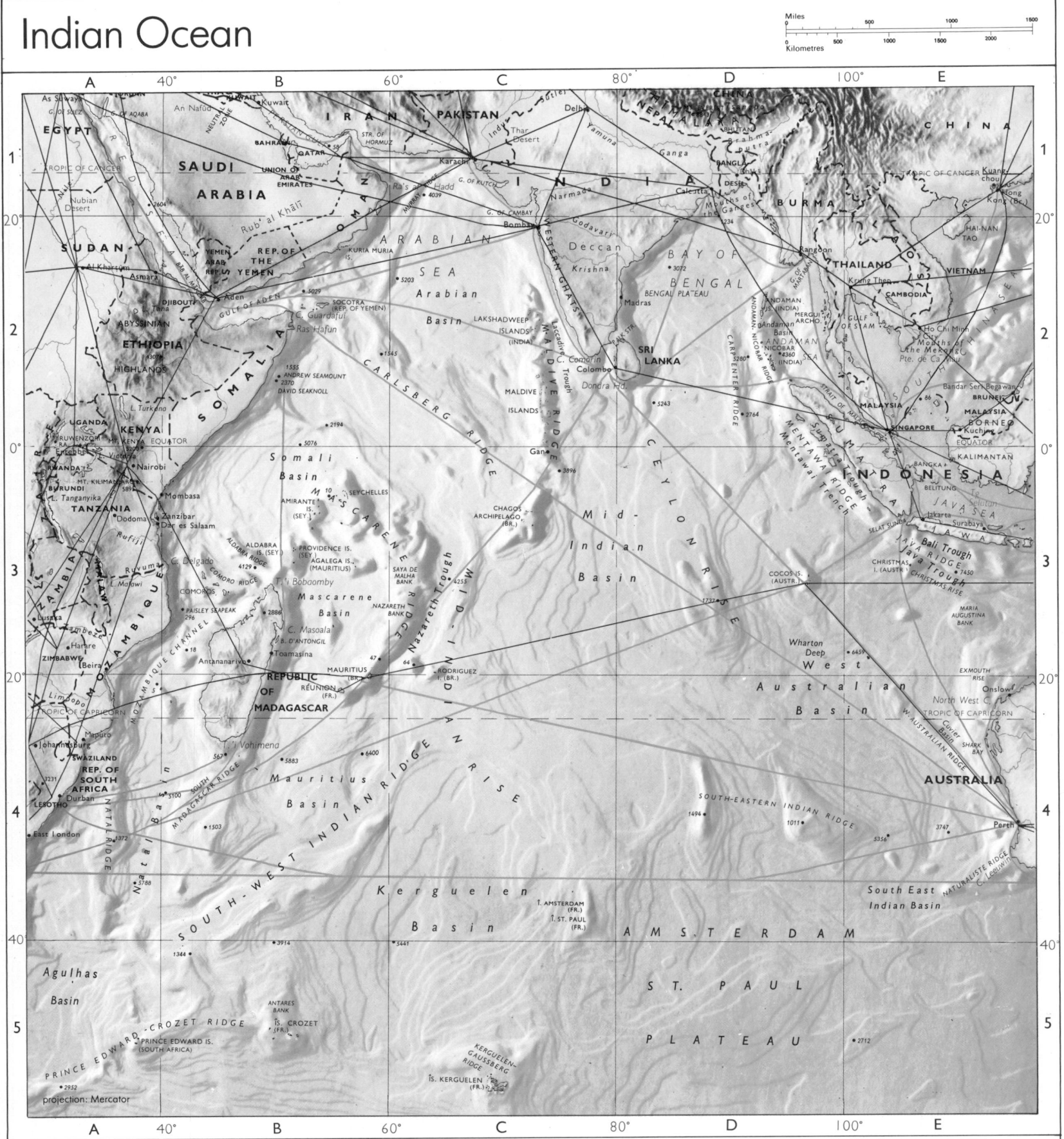

projection: Mercator

The Atlantic Ocean, including the Mediterranean and Caribbean seas, covers about 32 million sq miles (82.88 million km²). This makes it the second largest ocean after the Pacific. It is named after the Atlas Mountains of North Africa.

The area covered by the Atlantic is divided into four main plates: the Eurasian and North American in the north and the African and South American plates in the south. The Mid-Atlantic ridge is a plate boundary. A subduction zone lies off the West Indian islands, and the Puerto Rico trench contains the greatest depth in the Atlantic, 27,497 feet (8,381 m). This subduction zone and the Mid-Atlantic ridge are both unstable regions with much earthquake and volcanic activity.

Many islands in the Atlantic are of volcanic origin, although others near the continents are raised parts of the continental shelves. The average temperature of the Atlantic is 39°F (4°C), which makes it the warmest ocean, although the north and south extremities are cold. It is also the saltiest ocean, with an average salinity of about 3.5 percent. The ocean currents of the North Atlantic follow a clockwise pattern. They include the Gulf Stream and its extension, the North Atlantic Drift. These warm currents, which originate in the Gulf of Mexico, greatly moderate the climate of the coastlands of northwest Europe. In the south-western North Atlantic is the Sargasso Sea. In the South Atlantic, the oceanic circulation is counter-clockwise. The Brazil Current is a warm, southward-flowing current, while the cold Benguela Current flows up the southwest coast of Africa.

The Indian Ocean, the third largest ocean, has an area of about 28 million sq miles (72.5 million km²). Its greatest depth of 24,442 feet (7,450 m) is in the Java Trench in the northeast, although the average depth is about 13,000 feet (3,962 m). The eastern Indian Ocean is part of the Indo-Australian plate. It is separated from the African plate by the Carlsberg and Mid-Indian oceanic ridge, a zone of earthquake activity. In the south, the Mid-Indian ridge divides into two sections, one turning southwest and the other southeast. Ocean-spreading is still pushing the Indian peninsula against the Eurasian plate. There are subduction zones in the trenches along the coasts of Malaysia and Indonesia.

The largest island is Madagascar, and there are also volcanic and coral islands. Surface temperatures reach about 86°F (30°C) in shallow parts of the Persian Gulf. The average salinity is about 3.5 percent, but parts of the Red Sea are much saltier. North of the Equator, the water circulation is generally clockwise, although the directions of the currents in the Arabian Sea and the Bay of Bengal are reversed by the southwest summer monsoon. South of the Equator, the West Australian Current is weakened in winter. Its continuation, the South Equatorial Current, divides at Madagascar and part becomes the warm Mozambique Current. The northern part of the ocean is important for ships using the Suez Canal. The coastal waters contain some rich fishing grounds and there are offshore oilfields, particularly in the Persian Gulf.

Arctic

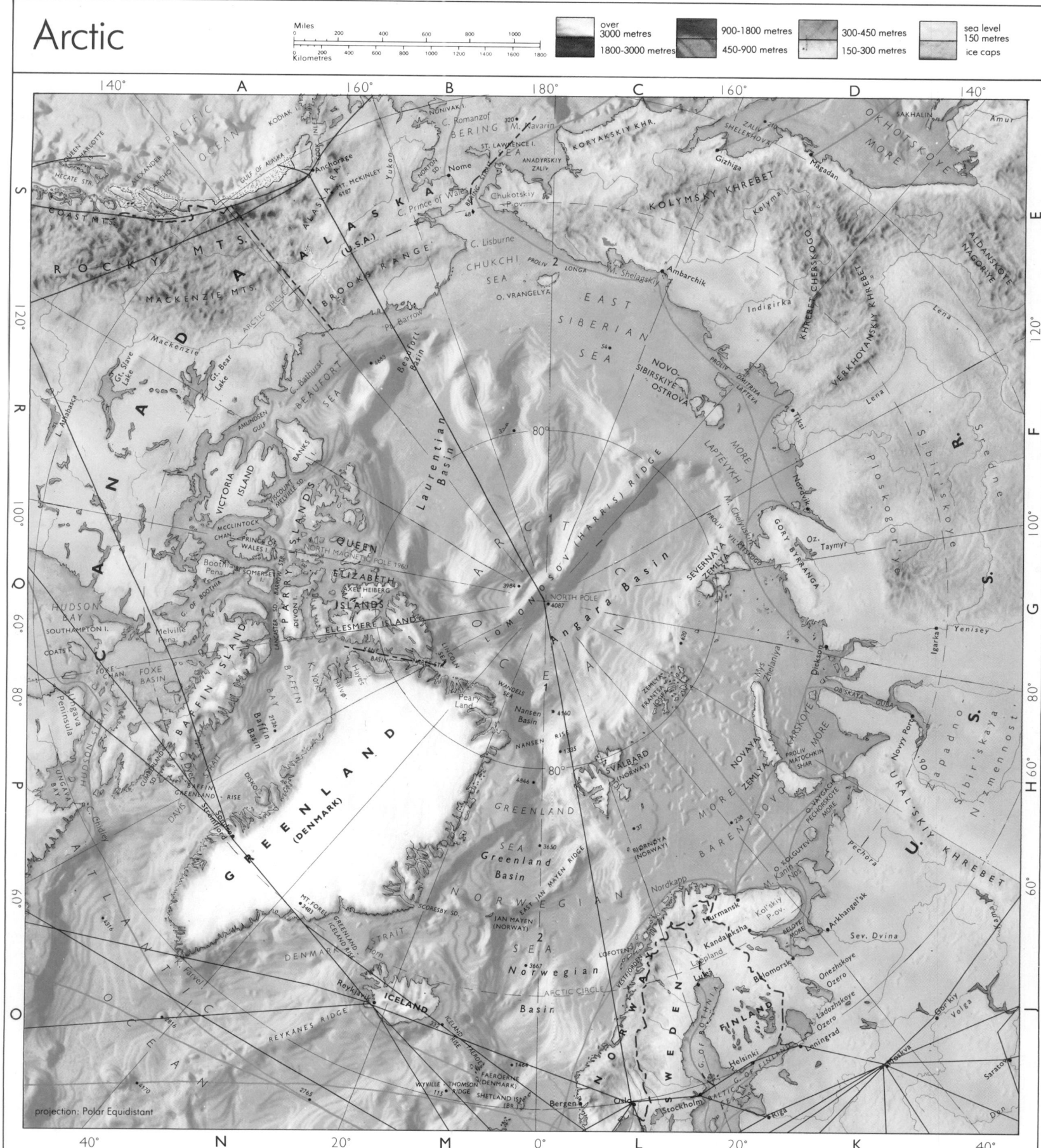

Miles
0   200   400   600   800   1000
0   200 400 600 800 1000 1200 1400 1600 1800
Kilometres

over 3000 metres	300-450 metres
1800-3000 metres	150-300 metres
900-1800 metres	sea level 150 metres
450-900 metres	ice caps

projection: Polar Equidistant

The Arctic Ocean, the smallest of the world's oceans, covers an area of about 5,500,000 sq miles (14,244,445 km²). Surrounding the ocean, which is mostly covered by pack-ice throughout the year, are parts of North America and Eurasia, which lie within the Arctic Circle (latitude 66° 33" North).

Within the Arctic Circle are some ice caps and the world's largest ice sheet, covering most of Greenland. In summer, nine-tenths of the lands in the Arctic are free from snow and ice. This is the tundra. Mosses, lichens and some flowering plants grow, although permafrost (permanently frozen subsoil) and the long winters prevent tree growth. Some ground-hugging dwarf shrubs are found.

Polar bears roam the pack-ice and feed on the seals. The richest marine life occurs where Arctic and Atlantic waters mix. Migrating animals, such as caribou and reindeer, graze on the tundra in summer. Other Arctic animals include bears, ermine, hares, foxes, lemmings, martens, sables and voles. There are also large numbers of birds, which breed in the tundra in summer when insects, including mosquitoes in marshy areas, are abundant.

The first man to reach the North Pole was Commander Robert E. Peary of the US Navy on April 6, 1909.

Antarctica, the southernmost continent, covers an area of about 5,100,000 sq miles (13,208,000 km²). Most of it is under ice, which totals about 7 million cubic miles (29 million km³). In places, the ice is nearly 3 miles (4.8 km) thick.

Parts of the coast are ice-free and bare mountain peaks (nunataks) jut through the ice in some areas. The highest peak is the Vinson Massif, 16,864 feet (5,140 m) above sea-level. Mount Erebus, near the American McMurdo station, is an active volcano.

Antarctica is the coldest continent. Soviet scientists reported a record low screen temperature of −128.6°F (−89.2°C) in 1983. The average temperature at the South Pole is −58°F (−50°C), though the coasts are much milder. The average annual precipitation in many places is only 2 inches (51mm). But there is much loose surface snow, blown around by high winds during blizzards.

The continent has little wildlife besides penguins, various bird migrants and seals, but the waters around Antarctica are rich in life, including whales.

The Norwegian explorer Roald Amundsen reached the South Pole on December 14, 1911. Argentina, Australia, Chile, France, Norway, New Zealand and the United Kingdom have all made territorial claims in Antarctica, but no claims are internationally agreed.

Antarctic

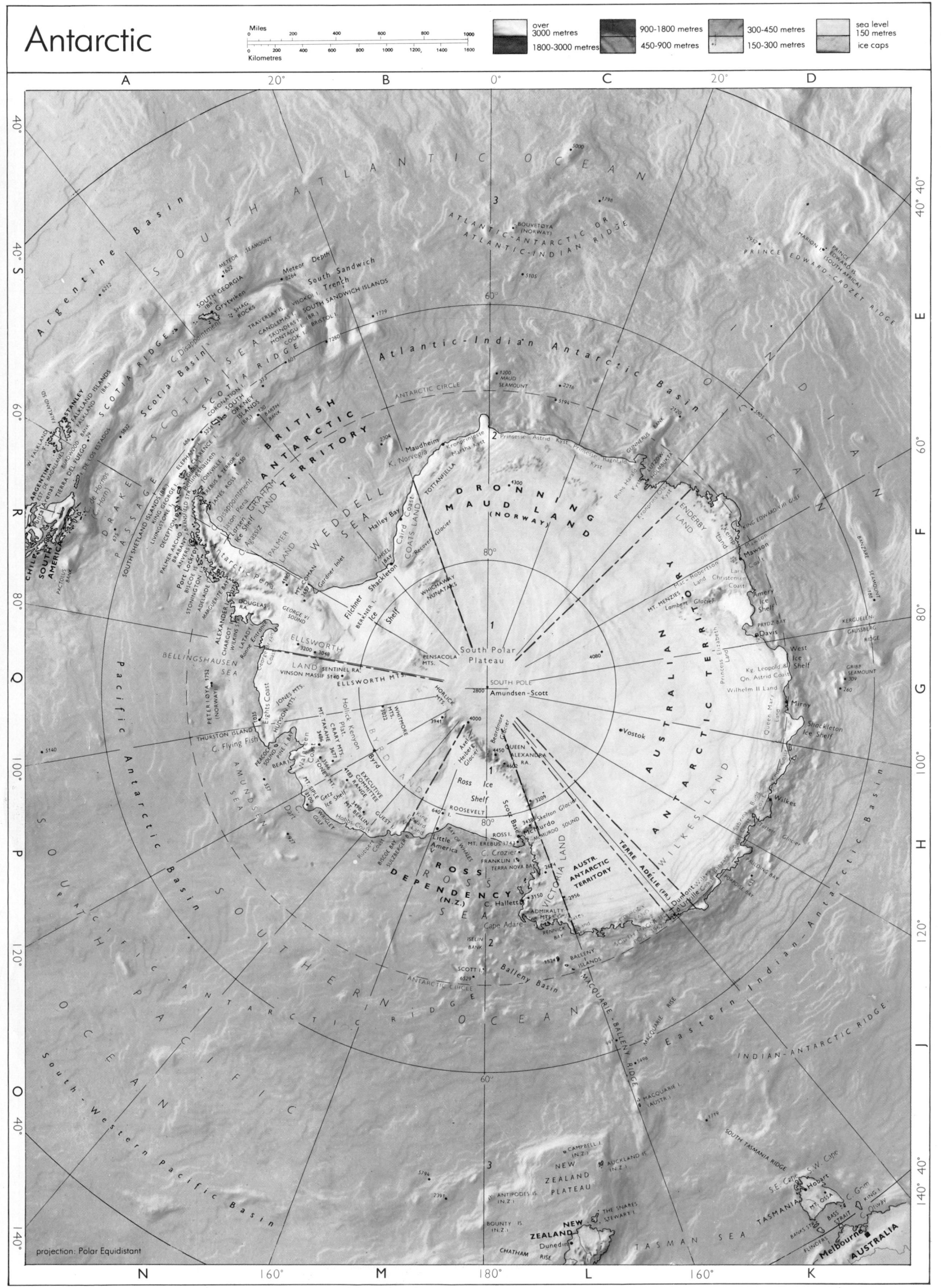

Miles
0 · 200 · 400 · 600 · 800 · 1000
0 · 200 · 400 · 600 · 800 · 1000 · 1200 · 1400 · 1600
Kilometres

over 3000 metres
1800-3000 metres
900-1800 metres
450-900 metres
300-450 metres
150-300 metres
sea level 150 metres
ice caps

projection: Polar Equidistant

Atmosphere, weather and climate

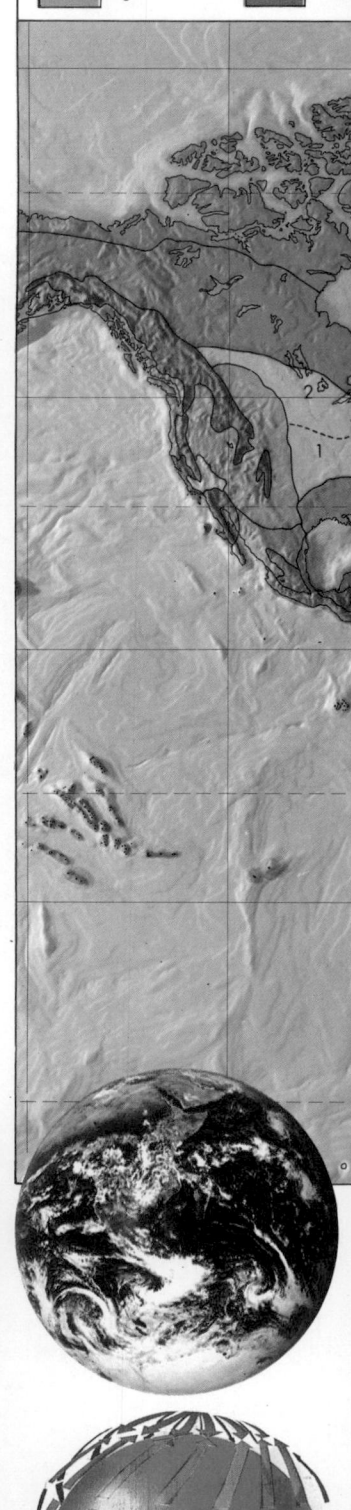

Weather is the day to day or hour to hour condition of the air. Nearly all the weather conditions we experience on Earth occur in the troposphere, the lowest layer of the atmosphere.

The troposphere extends to about 11 miles (18 km) above the Equator, 6 to 7 miles (10–11 km) above the middle latitudes, and 5 miles (8 km) above the poles. Temperatures decrease with height through the troposphere until they become stable at about −71°F (−57°C). The level at which temperatures stabilize is called the tropopause, and it is the upper limit of the troposphere. The troposphere contains 80 percent of the mass of the atmosphere and nearly all its water vapour.

Above the tropopause is the stratosphere, which contains the ozone layer that filters out most of the Sun's ultraviolet radiation. The rarefied ionosphere starts about 31 miles (50 km) above ground level. It is divided into two zones: the mesosphere and the thermosphere. The upper level of the thermosphere is about 310 miles (499 km) up. Beyond lies the exosphere which merges into space.

Air consists mainly of three gases: nitrogen (78.09 percent); oxygen (20.95 percent); and argon (0.93 percent). The remaining 0.03 percent consists of carbon dioxide, which is used by plants in photosynthesis, and minute amounts of neon, helium, ozone and hydrogen, with traces of krypton, methane, xenon and other gases. Air also contains water vapour, which makes up 4 percent of the atmosphere by volume, together with specks of dust, smoke and salt. Air has weight. The average air pressure at sea-level is about 15 pounds per square inch (1 kg per cm²). But variations in air pressure are an important element in weather. When air is heated, it expands and rises, and this has the effect of lowering air pressure. But cold dense air tends to sink and sinking air raises the air pressure.

Differences in temperatures and pressures keep the atmosphere moving. At the Equator, the Sun's heat makes air rise, creating a permanent low air pressure zone at the surface. This is called the doldrums. The rising air finally cools and spreads out north and south. It sinks back to the surface around 30° North and South, creating high pressure zones, called the horse latitudes. At the surface, some air flows from the horse latitudes towards the Equator, forming the trade winds, while some flows polewards to form the westerly wind belts. The westerlies eventually meet the polar easterlies, which are cold, dense air currents from the polar regions, along the polar front. The trade winds, westerlies and polar easterlies are the world's prevailing winds.

Cyclones or depressions form along the polar front. These rotating low-pressure weather systems are made up of warm, light air and cold, dense air. The boundaries between them at ground level are the cold and warm fronts. These fronts form bands of stormy weather. While changeable weather is associated with depressions, stable weather characterizes anticyclones, which are high-pressure weather systems. The development and movements of depressions and anticylcones are linked with the movements of jet streams, the strong winds that blow in the upper troposphere and lower stratosphere in the middle latitudes.

The two elements of weather which most concern people are temperature and rainfall. All air contains invisible water vapour, but warm air can hold more vapour than cold air. When warm air rises, it gradually cools and some of its vapour condenses around specks of dust or salt. These form minute water droplets or ice crystals, masses of which become visible as clouds. Mist, fog and frost form in a similar way. Eventually moisture in clouds coalesces to form raindrops or snowflakes.

Rain is a feature of storms. An average of about 45,000 thunderstorms occur every day somewhere in the world. Less common are tropical cyclones, or hurricanes, which form over the oceans north and south of the Equator. Hurricanes are the most destructive storms. On average, 11 strike the coasts of North America every year. The most intense storms are tornadoes, many of which form in the southeastern United States as warm air from the Gulf of Mexico flows north beneath cooler and denser air flowing south. But tornadoes are seldom more than 1,300 feet (396 m) across at ground level. Storm warnings and weather forecasts have been much improved in recent years with the use of sophisticated weather satellites and computers, which speed up the analysis of weather data at forecasting centres.

Climate is the usual weather of a place, based on data collected over a long period. The main factors used to define climates are temperature and rainfall. Latitude has a great effect on climate, because the Sun's radiation is most intense on the Equator and least effective at the poles. But a simple division of the world into latitudinal zones is unsatisfactory, because other factors complicate the picture.

First, temperatures decrease with height, and so polar conditions are experienced on mountain tops on the Equator. The nearness of a place to the sea also affects climate. This is because the sea heats up and cools down more slowly than land. This has the effect of moderating the climates of many coastlands. Places far from large bodies of water have continental climates, with colder winters and hotter summers than coastal regions in the same latitude. Ocean currents also play a part. For example, the warm North Atlantic Drift moderates the climate of places far to the north of the Arctic Circle.

Right The diagram shows a section through the lower part of the atmosphere. Most of the features which make up weather occur in the troposphere, the lowest part of the atmosphere. Nearly all clouds form within this bottom zone. Stratus, a grey layer cloud, and cumulus, a white heap cloud, are examples of low clouds, which form within about 8,200 feet (2,499 m) of the surface. Cumulonimbus, or storm clouds, may have a depth of about 15,000 feet (4,572 m) or more. They form when upcurrents of warm air rise swiftly through the troposphere. They often have a dark, ragged base not far from the surface and a high, anvil-shaped top. The highest clouds include cirrus clouds which are often drawn into long strands by jet streams. Cirrus clouds, composed of ice crystals, are often signs of an approaching depression. Mother of pearl clouds are rare. They occur occasionally in the lower stratosphere. To avoid the turbulence which often occurs in the troposphere, jet airliners usually fly around the top of the troposphere or in the lower stratosphere.

weather balloon
30,500 metres

mother of pearl cloud
21,000 metres

cirrus cloud
6,100-18,300 metres

jet airliner
15,000 metres

helicopter
10,970 metres

bird
8,200 metres

cumulus cloud
up to
13,700 metres

25

15

10

5

0

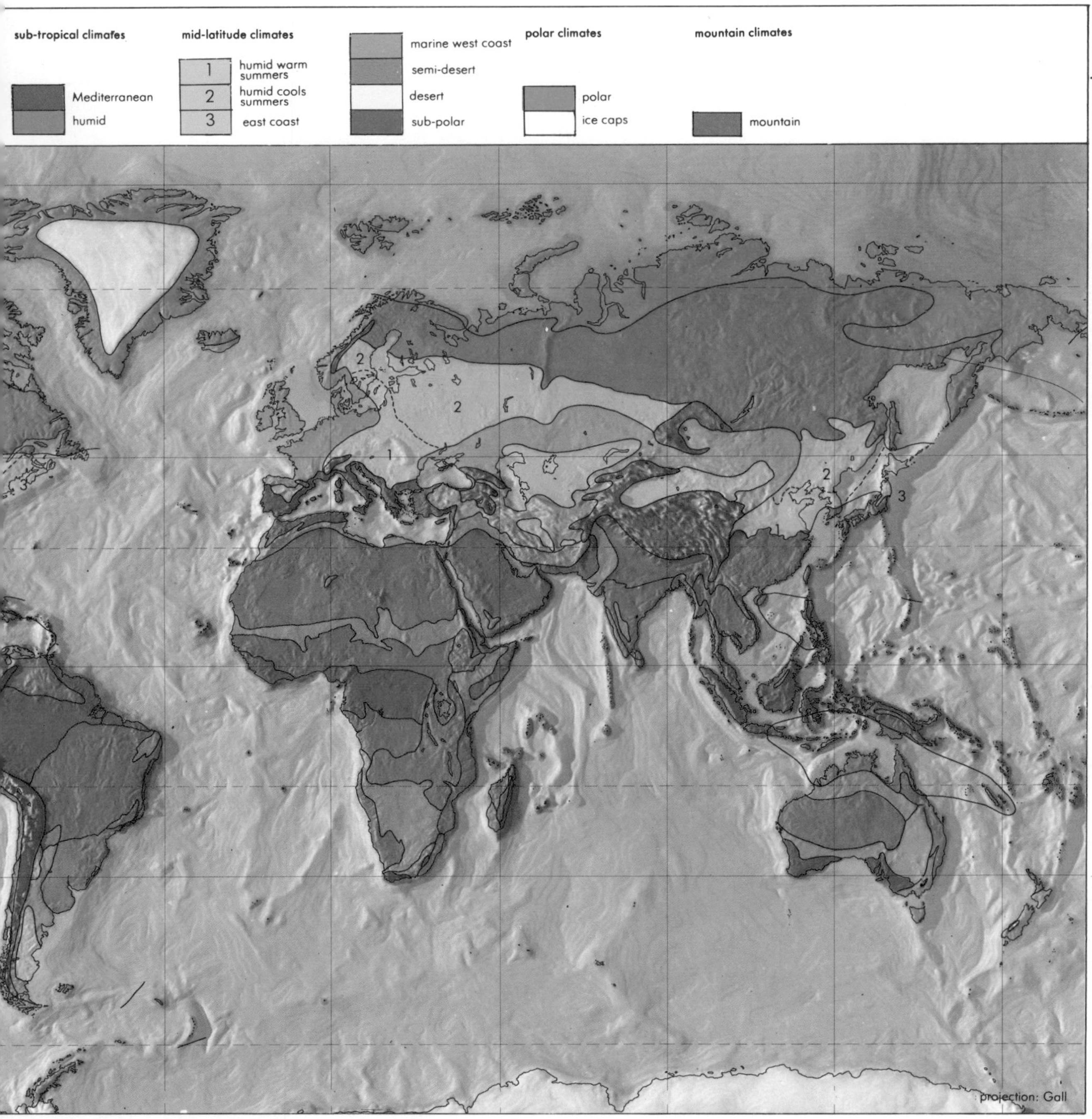

sub-tropical climates

Mediterranean

humid

mid-latitude climates

1 humid warm summers

2 humid cools summers

3 east coast

marine west coast

semi-desert

desert

sub-polar

polar climates

polar

ice caps

mountain climates

mountain

Left This map classifies the world's five main climatic types: polar, mid-latitude, subtropical, tropical, and the special mountain climates. These groups are organized into subgroups based on factors like rainfall and seasonal changes. Some groupings treat the hot deserts of the tropics and the cooler deserts of the middle latitudes as a sixth climatic type.

projection: Gall

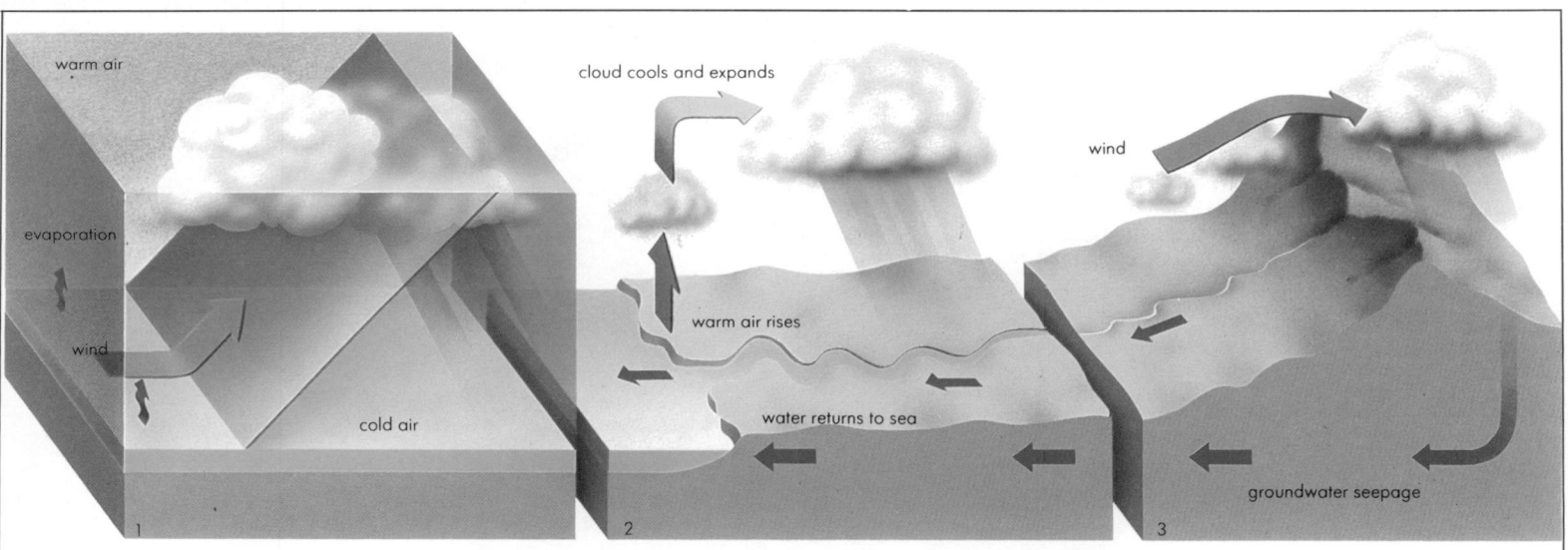

warm air

evaporation

wind

cold air

cloud cools and expands

warm air rises

water returns to sea

wind

groundwater seepage

1 2 3

Above Rain clouds form when moist air is forced to rise. Because cold air can hold less water vapour than warm air, cooling causes water vapour to condense into water droplets, which eventually coalesce into raindrops. Air is forced to rise in three main ways. Cyclonic rain is formed when warm air is forced to rise above cold air in cyclones (or depressions), as shown in the diagram. Orographic rain is formed when moist winds from the oceans rise over inland mountain ranges. Convectional rain occurs when intense heating of the land by the Sun sets up strong upcurrents of air. High cumulonimbus clouds form as the ascending air cools and the invisible water vapour is changed into water droplets.

Soil and vegetation

The Sun evaporates about 120,000 cubic miles (500,000 km³) of water from the oceans every year. This water becomes invisible water vapour. Much of this is converted into clouds, which winds carry over land areas, ensuring that they get a regular supply of fresh water. The water eventually makes its way back to the sea, much of it flowing through rivers, or seeping through rocks as ground water. The continual interchange of water between the oceans and the land, which is kept going by the Sun's heat and gravity, is called the water cycle. Without it, life would not exist on land.

Outside deserts, running water and glaciers (formed from compacted snow) are the main agents of erosion. Running water and glaciers carry away the products of weathering. Weathering, which is the breakdown or decay of rocks, takes two forms: mechanical and chemical weathering. Mechanical weathering includes frost action, which occurs in cold mountain areas when water collects in cracks during the day and freezes at night. Because ice occupies 9 percent more space than the same volume of water, the conversion of water into ice exerts pressure which widens cracks and eventually splits rocks apart. Chemical weathering occurs in several ways. For example, rocks are weakened by oxidation which occurs when oxygen combines with minerals. Rust is a product of oxidation. Hydration occurs when water combines chemically with certain minerals in rocks. For example, hydration 'rots' potassic feldspars in tough granite outcrops turning them into soft clays. Loose material formed by weathering is broken down into finer and finer particles as they are transported towards the sea. The fine aluvial silt which forms the fertile soils in many flood plains is often the product of weathering and erosion in distant mountains.

Weathering continues all the time and is a major factor in soil formation. Soils not only contain particles of worn rock, but also organic material called humus, the remains of dead plants, animals and animal excretions. Humus is important, because it both binds rock particles together and enriches the soil. Soils also contain bacteria, fungi, earthworms and other animals which constantly modify the soil.

Most soils are only a few feet deep. They normally contain three distinctive layers, called horizons. The top A horizon usually contains most of the organic material and the living organisms. The B horizon consists mainly of fine mineral grains, while the C horizon contains larger particles, which increase in size until they merge into the bedrock.

Heavy rainfall upsets this pattern. In wet regions, mineral and organic matter is leached (dissolved) out of the A horizon and redeposited in the B horizon. Heavily leached soils are, therefore, infertile unless deep ploughing brings the more fertile material from the B horizon to the surface. Heavily leached soils include latosols (tropical red earths) and podsols in the coniferous forest regions. The soils of tundra regions are also heavily leached, although the remains of dead plants, which are slow to decompose in the cold conditions, often form a dark, peaty surface. A few inches down, the subsoil is often frozen permanently.

mediterranean forest and scrub

savanna

tropical rain forest

monsoon forest

dry tropical scrub

desert

scrub, steppe and semi-desert

deciduous and broadleaf forest

coniferous forest

tundra and ice

The map shows the average annual rainfall throughout the world. Rainfall depends on two main factors: a supply of moist air and some means whereby the air can be cooled so that clouds will form. In equatorial regions, the rainfall is heavy, much of it being convectional in type. In some tropical areas, moist monsoon winds are drawn in summer into regions of low air pressure. High temperatures and heavy rainfall together enable a great variety of plants to flourish. By contrast, the hot deserts of the horse latitudes are regions of high air pressure, where air is sinking. Moist oceanic winds seldom penetrate into these areas and so rain-storms are rare. But even in deserts, the few plant and animal species show remarkable adaptations to their environment. This is also true of polar and tundra regions, which also have comparatively little rainfall.

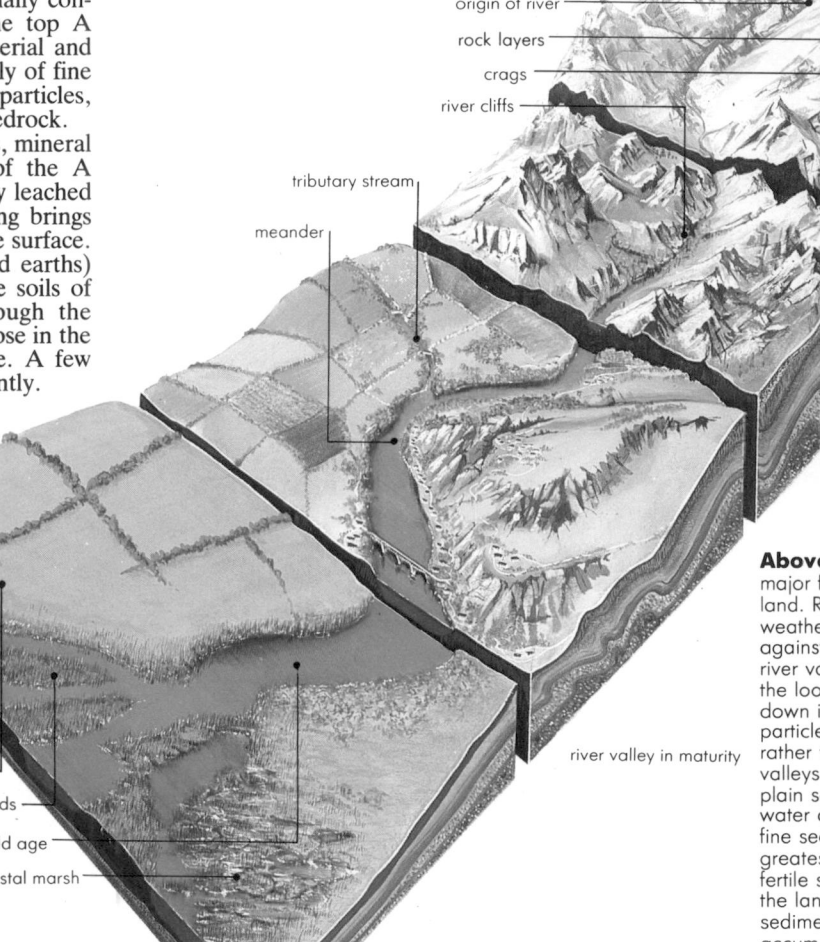

origin of river
rock layers
crags
river cliffs
tributary stream
meander
youthful valley section
flood plains
islands
river in old age
coastal marsh
river valley in maturity
flood plain section

Above Running water is a major force in shaping the land. Rivers transport weathered rocks which scrape against and deepen youthful river valleys. Through attrition, the loose material is ground down into smaller and smaller particles. Mature rivers widen rather than deepen their valleys. In the old age or flood plain section, the volume of water and the river's load of fine sediment are at their greatest. When floods occur, fertile sediment spreads over the land. In some places, sediment piles up in deltas or it accumulates on the seabed to form new sedimentary rocks.

Soils in arid and semiarid regions are not greatly leached. Such regions include grasslands, where decayed grass has given the soil a dark colour. Such soils include the chernozems (black earths) of the Russian steppes. Desert soils, however, contain little humus and are usually brown, red or yellow in colour.

Climate is, therefore, extremely important in determining the nature of soils. Climate and soils together determine the climatic climax vegetation – that is, the community of plants which is best adapted to a particular region which has not been disturbed by human activity.

Vegetation zones, like climatic zones, are broadly related to latitude. Polar ice-sheets blanket most of Antarctica and much of Greenland. These regions are almost without plant life. However, the cold polar seas are mostly rich in fish and so there are animals which feed on fish. The largest predator, the polar bear, preys on seals, which in turn eat fish.

South of the Arctic Ocean in the northern hemisphere is the tundra, which supports a variety of living things. The snow cover melts in summer when algae, mosses, lichens, such flowering plants as bilberries and cranberries, and dwarf shrubs grow quickly. Migratory animals, such as caribou, musk-oxen and reindeer, graze on the tundra in sum-

Above tropical forests are the most luxuriant on Earth. The tall trees often reach more than 100 feet (30 m) in height. They are often swathed in creepers and, at the higher levels, by parasitic plants, called epiphytes. Animal life is also most abundant in the upper, sunlit levels.

Left Tropical grasslands have a marked dry season. As a result, thick forests occur only along rivers. But there are large areas with scattered shrubs and trees, such as the acacia of the East African savanna. In regions where the rainfall is low, the grasslands become more open. Tropical grasslands have various local names, such as the llanos of Venezuela and the campos of Brazil. Tropical grasslands differ from the mid-latitude temperate grasslands, including prairies, pampas and steppes.

Below Coniferous forests include such trees as fir, pine and spruce. The largest of these forests sprawl across the northern hemisphere, south of the tundra. Conifers also grow on mountain slopes below the treeline, and others are found in regions with hot, dry summers, such as Mediterranean lands.

Below Deciduous forest was once the dominant vegetation of moist temperate regions. But these areas have proved attractive to human settlement and so the forests have been largely replaced by farmland and cities. Deciduous trees, including beech, elm, maple, oak, sycamore and willow, annually shed their leaves, which conserves moisture in winter. Most deciduous trees need at least six months every year when the temperatures are above the minimum needed for tree growth.

mer, and because insects are abundant, many birds nest and breed in the tundra in summer also. Other animals of the tundra include foxes, hares, lemmings, stoats and voles.

South of the tundra are the vast coniferous or boreal forests. This region is the taiga. Coniferous trees are specially adapted to cold winters. For example, their conical shapes prevent overloading and damage by snow, their thick barks are protection against the cold, and their shallow roots can obtain moisture even when the subsoil is frozen. Most conifers are evergreens, which begin to grow as soon as the long winter ends. The taiga is the winter home of many migrant animals which summer in the tundra. Bears, mink and wolves are other taiga animals.

The taiga merges in the south into mixed and then deciduous forest. Deciduous trees shed their leaves in autumn and so they save energy by being dormant in winter. Deciduous forests are much favoured for human settlement. As a result, the forests have been largely cleared to make way for farmland and urban areas, and the animal populations have also been much depleted.

Semiarid temperate grassland, including the American prairies, the Eurasian steppes, the South African veld, the Australasian downs and the South American pampas, have also been largely converted into farmland, with a consequent decimation of the wildlife. But tropical grasslands, including the savanna of Africa, still contain in some areas, a magnificent range of animals, including antelopes, giraffes, hyenas, leopards, lions, rhinoceroses and zebras.

Deserts contain specialized plants adapted to withstand droughts. Cacti characterize the deserts of the southwestern United States, while many plants in the Sahara and elsewhere germinate, flower and scatter their seeds within two weeks of a freak storm. These seeds may survive for years before another storm makes the desert bloom.

The tropical forests of Asia, Africa and Central and South America contain an enormous variety of plant species, many of which have never been classified. However, forest clearance is now proceeding so rapidly that many species are being lost. Most of the wild animals live in the trees, rather than on the damp, dark forest floor. They include primates, superbly coloured birds, varied reptiles, and vast numbers of insects. Like the plants many species are close to extinction.

Mountains, where temperatures fall with height, contain bands of varying vegetation and wildlife. In the tropics, mountain vegetation may range from dense rain forest at the bottom to tundra and polar conditions at the top.

Ecology and conservation

A group of plants and animals living together in a particular environment is called an ecosystem. Ecosystems may be as small as the corner of a garden or as large as a biome. The main biomes on land are the polar regions, the tundra, the taiga, the deciduous forests, temperate grasslands, tropical grasslands, dry scrublands, deserts and tropical forests. Within each biome, each of the living things shows special adaptations to its environment.

Food chains can be identified within ecosystems. A simple example of a food chain is as follows: grass is eaten by rabbits and rabbits are eaten by foxes. In practice, food chains are more complicated, because most animals eat several kinds of food. Complex food chains, called food webs, can be thought of as pyramids, consisting of several layers. At the base are the 'primary producers', which are plants. The second 'primary consumer level' consists of herbivores. The third layer, the 'secondary consumer level', contains small carnivores, and the top 'tertiary consumer level' contains large carnivores. Should changes occur in one level of the pyramid, then the other levels are affected.

For example, the use of pesticides to kill insects led to the extermination of many birds which ate sprayed insects. Interference in food chains can have disastrous cumulative effects. In Peru, overfishing of anchovies in coastal waters led to a decline in the populations of the cormorants which feed on them. Fewer cormorants meant that there was less guano (cormorant droppings) to enrich the coastal waters where plankton live. The reduced volume of plankton meant less food for the anchovies, whose numbers declined.

Ecosystems change naturally, as when a volcanic eruption buries land in ash. But this area is soon recolonized by plants and animals which undergo a series of changes until the climax community is established. On a much larger scale, whole biomes were obliterated during the Pleistocene

Above Wheat, one of the most important staple foods, grows mostly in areas with mild, moderately wet winters and warm, fairly dry summers. Rice is the other leading staple food. In recent times, new strains of these other crops have been developed so that yields might rise, especially in poor nations where the increasing population is outstripping food supplies.

Above Forestry is an important industry. The top producers of softwoods are the USSR, the USA and Canada. The top producers of hardwoods are India, Brazil and Indonesia. Wood is used as a fuel and in the construction and paper industries. A successful industry requires elaborate conservation policies.

Ice Age. But when the ice melted, the barren lands of the northern hemisphere were rapidly recolonized.

People have caused rapid and large-scale changes in biomes. For example, early pioneers in the United States cut down the deciduous forests in the northeast and ploughed up the grasslands of the arid midwest. The land was exposed to the weather. In humid areas, the forest soils were leached and robbed of their nutrients and natural cohesion. Imperceptibly at first, grains of soil were washed into rivers, and in some areas flash floods wore out deep gullies thus creating badlands.

Similarly, the winds that blew across the ploughed land on the central plains lifted grains above the surface, breaking them down into fine dust. Soon the grasslands became dust bowls and dust was carried by winds into the Atlantic Ocean. In barely 100 years, some 60 percent of the country was affected by soil erosion. In the 1930s, studies were made of soil erosion and of conservation techniques. Farmers were taught new methods suitable for restoring fertility to badly damaged land.

Above Natural rubber is made from latex, the sap of rubber trees which originated in Brazil. Today, however, the leading producers are Malaysia and Indonesia. And the development of synthetic rubber has led to a decline in the world production of rubber.

Below Natural processes take millions of years. Igneous rocks form from magma either on the surface (basalt) or underground (granite). Eroded fragments of these rocks form sedimentary rocks, such as conglomerates. The sedimentary rocks limestone and shale are sometimes metamorphosed by pressure and heat to form marble and slate.

limestone

conglomerate of sedimentary rock

slate

basalt

granite

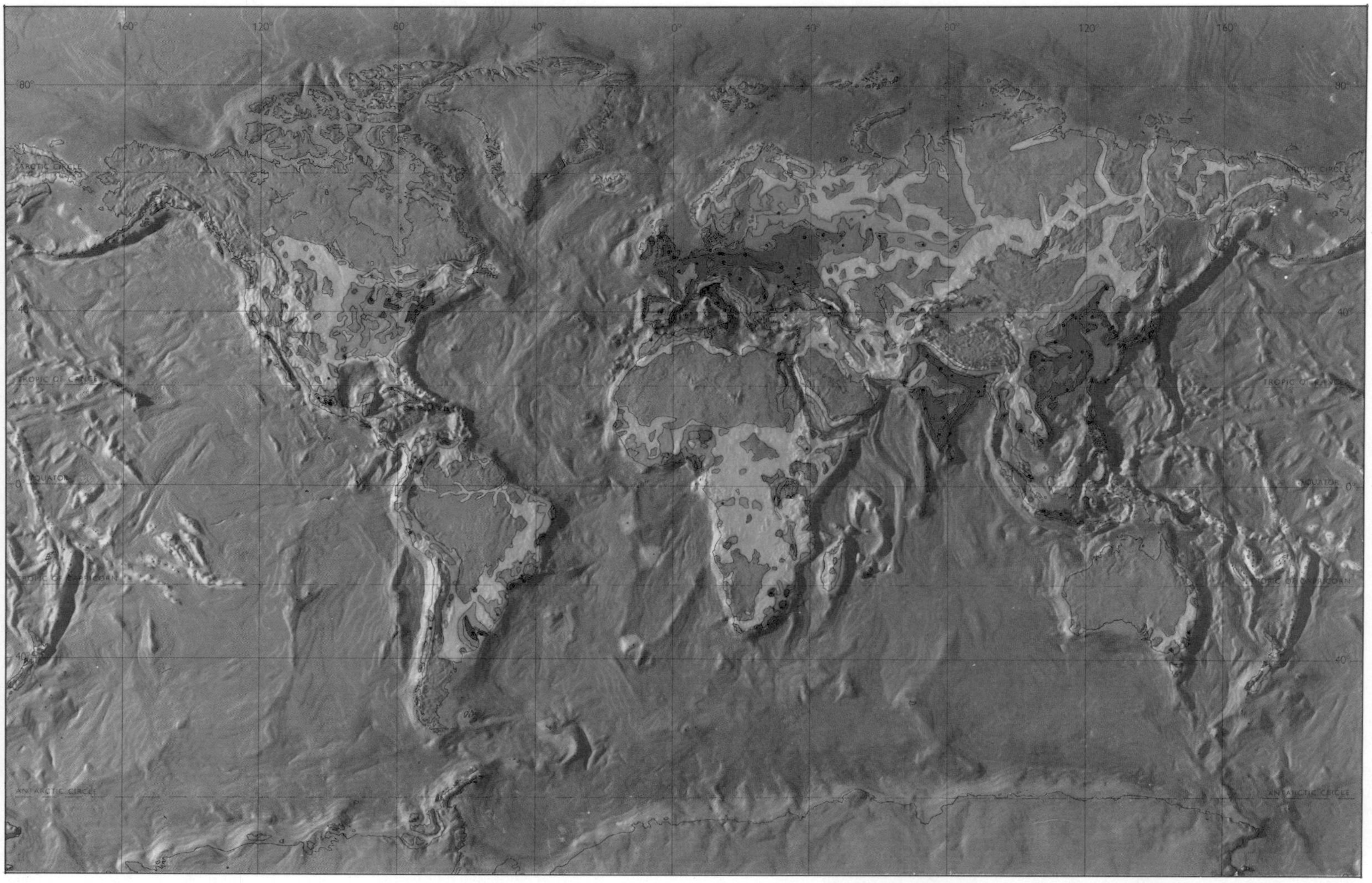

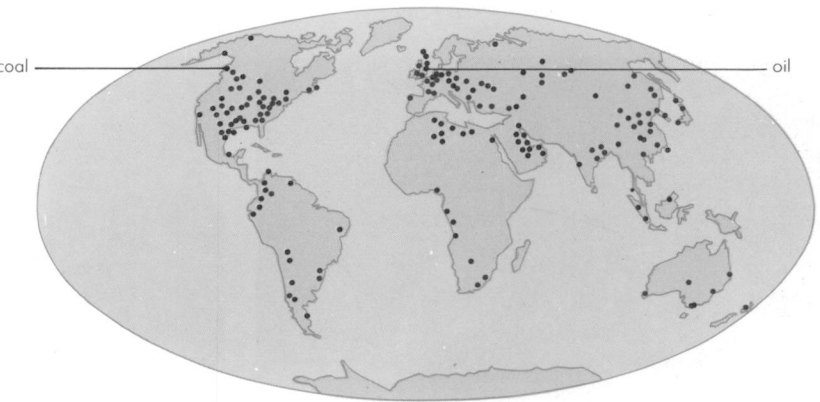

Above The map shows the uneven distribution of the world's population. The greatest concentrations of people are in areas with favourable soils and climate. But much of the land surface, including ice-covered regions, dense rain forests, hot and cold deserts and rugged highland regions are almost empty of people.

less than 2 per sq. mile
less than 1 per sq. km

2 to 25 per sq. mile
1 to 10 per sq. km

25 to 60 per sq. mile
10 to 25 per sq. km

60 to 125 per sq. mile
25 to 50 per sq. km

125 to 250 per sq. mile
50 to 100 per sq km

over 250 per sq. mile
over 100 per sq. km

• **Towns:**
over 1,000,000 population

Soil erosion is partly a consequence of population increases and the need for more food to feed the extra mouths. The fast annual growth of population has also led to industrial pollution. Industrial wastes and untreated sewage can kill all life in rivers and lakes. Edible freshwater and marine life can absorb poison until they become a danger to health. For example, acetaldehyde in industrial wastes pumped into Minamata Bay, Japan, accumulated in the bodies of marine animals which were eaten by local fisherfolk. About 10,000 people were poisoned before the source of pollution was identified. Oil pollution at sea can greatly damage marine ecosystems. Even farm fertilizers are hazards. In water, they stimulate the growth of plants, which use up the oxygen and kill off aquatic animals.

Air pollution includes the creation of smog from industrial smoke, soot and gases, and photochemical smog formed from car exhaust fumes. Rain also dissolves air pollutants from factories and cars, such as sulphur dioxide and nitrogen oxides. These substances turn the rain into acid. Acid rain has killed off nearly all living things in many lakes in northern Europe and northern North America. The killing of plants and animals by acid rain also affects the food chains of the regions. Radioactive particles released in nuclear bomb tests are another form of air pollution.

Above The map shows reserves of coal and oil, two fossil fuels formed from organic matter. The known reserves of oil are being used up rapidly, and coal reserves are also finite and will be exhausted if the rate of extraction continues to exceed the slow rate of natural renewal. Existing resources must be conserved and alternative energy resources must be developed.

The steady increase of the amount of carbon dioxide in the atmosphere, caused by the burning of fossil fuels, is also causing anxiety. Before the Industrial Revolution, carbon dioxide made up between 275 and 285 parts per million of the atmosphere. By 1980, it constituted 338 parts per million. Carbon dioxide has a 'greenhouse effect' because it absorbs some of the Sun's heat which is reflected off the Earth's surface. If the current rate of increase continues, the amount of carbon dioxide in the atmosphere will probably double in the next 50 years. This, it is estimated, might have the effect of raising temperatures by an average of 3.5°F (2°C). This could melt ice sheets and the sea-level would rise, flooding coastal plains and many great cities.

In recent years, much has been done to control pollution, especially in the richer, developed nations, and the establishment of national parks and reserves is halting the pace of animal extinctions. But the UN Environment Programme estimated in the early 1980s that tropical forests are disappearing at 124 acres (50 hectares) a minute.

It is clear that we must not interfere with the basic processes at work on our planet. In exploiting natural resources, we must ensure that we do not destroy them. It is also our responsibility to preserve the diversity of plant and animal life on Earth. Once a species is extinct, it is lost for ever.

The World in space

Perhaps the most unforgettable images of the Space Age are photographs of the blue, white and brown Earth against an empty black background. Such pictures emphasize the Earth's finite nature, making us even more aware that, if we continue to exploit the Earth's resources faster than the slow rates at which they are naturally renewed, then we will inevitably face shortages of essential raw materials, such as fossil fuels. They also remind us that if we render part or all of our planet uninhabitable by pollution or by a nuclear holocaust, there is nowhere else for us to go.

Space photographs, like world maps, show that land covers only about 29 percent of the world's surface, and that vast areas are too arid or too cold for any appreciable human settlement. Arable land covers only about 10 percent of the Earth's land areas and pasture another 20 percent. As a result, there is now on average about three-quarters of an acre (0.3 ha) of cultivated land per person. But as the population increases, so the amount of cultivated land per person decreases. At the same time food requirements will increase.

In about 8000 BC, before agriculture was invented, an estimated 8,000,000 people lived on Earth. The population steadily expanded as agrarian and early urban communities developed. By AD 1000, the world population stood at just over 300 million. The rate of population increase then began to accelerate. The 1,000 million mark was passed in the mid-nineteenth century, and the 2,000 million mark in the 1920s. In the next 50 years, the population doubled again, passing the 4,000 million mark in 1975. By 1981, it had risen to 4,508 million.

Left Photographs taken by artificial satellites have confirmed the accuracy of modern cartographers. Satellites are now used in several ways by map makers and surveyors to fix their latitude and longitude.

Below Satellites are also used in communications, in navigation, in scientific research and in meteorology. Weather satellites can record the birth, growth and movements of hurricanes so that forecasts can be made.

Above Views of the world from space remind us that we live on a planet whose resources are finite. If we squander those resources faster than they are renewed naturally, then we endanger present and future generations.

From 1975 to 1980, the average rate of population increase was 1.7 percent per year. Should this rate continue, the world's population would double in 42 years. However, there are indications that the rate of increase is declining. For example, the annual rate in 1970–75 was 1.8 percent. Declining rates of population increase are a feature of wealthier, developed nations, although some countries, such as China, have reduced their rates by a variety of birth control policies. In China, in 1975–81, the annual rate of population increase was 1.4 percent. But this rate is still high by comparison with Europe, excluding the USSR, where the rate in 1975–80 was 0.4 percent per year. At this rate, it would take 174 years for Europe's population to double.

The trend in Europe is in stark contrast to that in Africa, Latin America and southern Asia. For instance, in Africa, the population growth rates have risen in recent years, reaching 2.9 percent in 1981. At this rate, Africa's population would double in only 25 years. In Latin America, the annual rate in 1975–80 was 2.5 percent, which would double the population in 29 years. The effect of such massive population explosions is that a high proportion of the population is too young to contribute to the economy. Instead, with 40 percent or more of the population being under 15, large amounts of money have to be found to finance educational and health services. By contrast, in developed countries, the proportion of retired people over 65 years of age is steadily increasing.

There are other striking contrasts between the mainly developed continents of North America, Europe and Oceania (or Australasia), which contain about 23 percent of the world's population, and the mainly developing continents of Africa, Latin America and Asia.

The degree of economic development is indicated by the proportion of people employed in agriculture. In 1980,

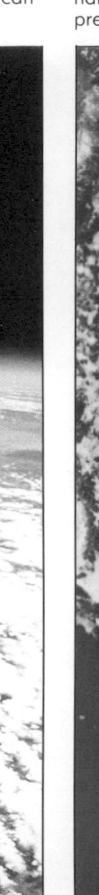

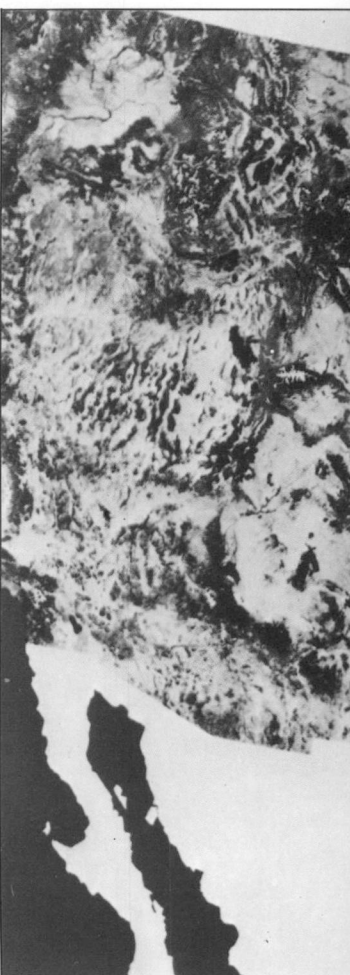

Above A picture of London recorded by a survey satellite, Landsat 1, gives a wealth of detail. Landsat satellites view the ground at four separate wavelengths and provide data which is not easily available on the ground. The coding includes 17 shades each of red (vegetation) and green (fallow fields), accompanied by dark brown for coniferous woodland and light brown for deciduous trees. Peaty soils are dark green, while chalky soils are bright green or yellow. The runways are also identifiable.

Below This photo mosaic of the United States by day is composed of 569 Landsat images. It took several months to get these cloud-free scans.

some 44.7 percent of the world's workforce was engaged in farming. But in North America and western Europe, where farming is mechanized and scientific, some 2.3 percent and 10.1 percent, respectively, were farm workers. In Asia and Africa, where there are great numbers of subsistence farmers, the comparable percentages are 57 and 64.7, respectively.

In economic terms, North America had a per capita GNP in 1980 of $11,460. Excluding Japan, Asia's only truly industrialized nation, the oil-rich countries of the Middle East, and the USSR, the rest of Asia had the low average per capita GNP of $330.

A person living in the developed world may well find it difficult to translate economic statistics into human terms. But the World Bank estimated that, in the late 1970s, about 40 percent of the people in the developing world, particularly in Africa and Asia, have incomes which are insufficient to secure the basic necessities of life. It also declared that there are probably more than 800 million people who are destitute. Some live in squalor in shanty towns around fast-growing cities. But even more wretched are the poor subsistence-farming communities, who are subject to starvation or death every time the harvest fails.

As the world moves towards the twenty-first century, it faces many dangers. There is the ideological divide between the democratic West and the Communist East, and the economic gulf between the developed North and the impoverished South (a useful synonym for the developing world providing one remembers to exclude Australia and New Zealand). But the Space Age has given us a new perspective on our world and new methods of monitoring man-made damage to the fragile environments on Earth.

There is today a deeper understanding of ecology and a greater emphasis on conservation than at any time in human history, and modern technology continues to improve agricultural and industrial efficiency in the developed world. The Report of the Independent Commission on International Development Issues (1980), also called the Brandt Commission after its chairman Willy Brandt, has pointed out that the problems of the rich and poor nations are interlocked. The developing world needs help to grow at an adequate pace, but the developed world cannot prosper or ultimately improve its position unless the developing world advances. Progress in the developing world would stimulate international trade and enable the developed world to utilize its spare capacity, which will increase as its industries are increasingly computerized. Mutual interest rather than altruism may, therefore, lead to a 'new deal' between the rich and poor nations.

How to use the Atlas

Introduction It is more important now than ever before to be informed about parts of the world other than our own. In an age of jet travel and fast communications, events move with a rapidity more startling than at any period in the world's long history. An incident of political or economic importance in some remote part of the world can rapidly develop to the point where it profoundly affects international and commercial relationships and our own everyday lives. The *Encyclopedic Atlas of the World* gives the reader the background information against which the possible consequences of the changing scene can be set. There is a wealth of relief and political maps, aerial and satellite photographs, colour photographs of cities, landscapes and people, and detailed information on all the world's countries. All these are combined in a way that enables the reader to explore the colourful variety of our modern world.

Maps This Atlas is sectionalized into continents for ease of reference. Each section begins with a map of the continent. Further maps focus on specific areas of the continents, for example Northern South America. Both relief colouring and natural colouring are used. Where necessary maps of individual countries and political maps of whole continents are included.

Relief Colour Key Shades of green denote low ground — shades of brown denote high ground. Areas on the maps below sea-level are indicated by the darkest green — the highest areas, such as mountain peaks, are indicated by the darkest brown.

Relief Maps The relief maps used in this atlas have all been reproduced from three-dimensional scale models. Using the latest geographical information the models were built to a high degree of accuracy. The shadow effect on the maps was produced by photographing the models under special lighting conditions. The maps enable the reader to picture the land with a greater insight into the relation of artificial and natural features to the land.

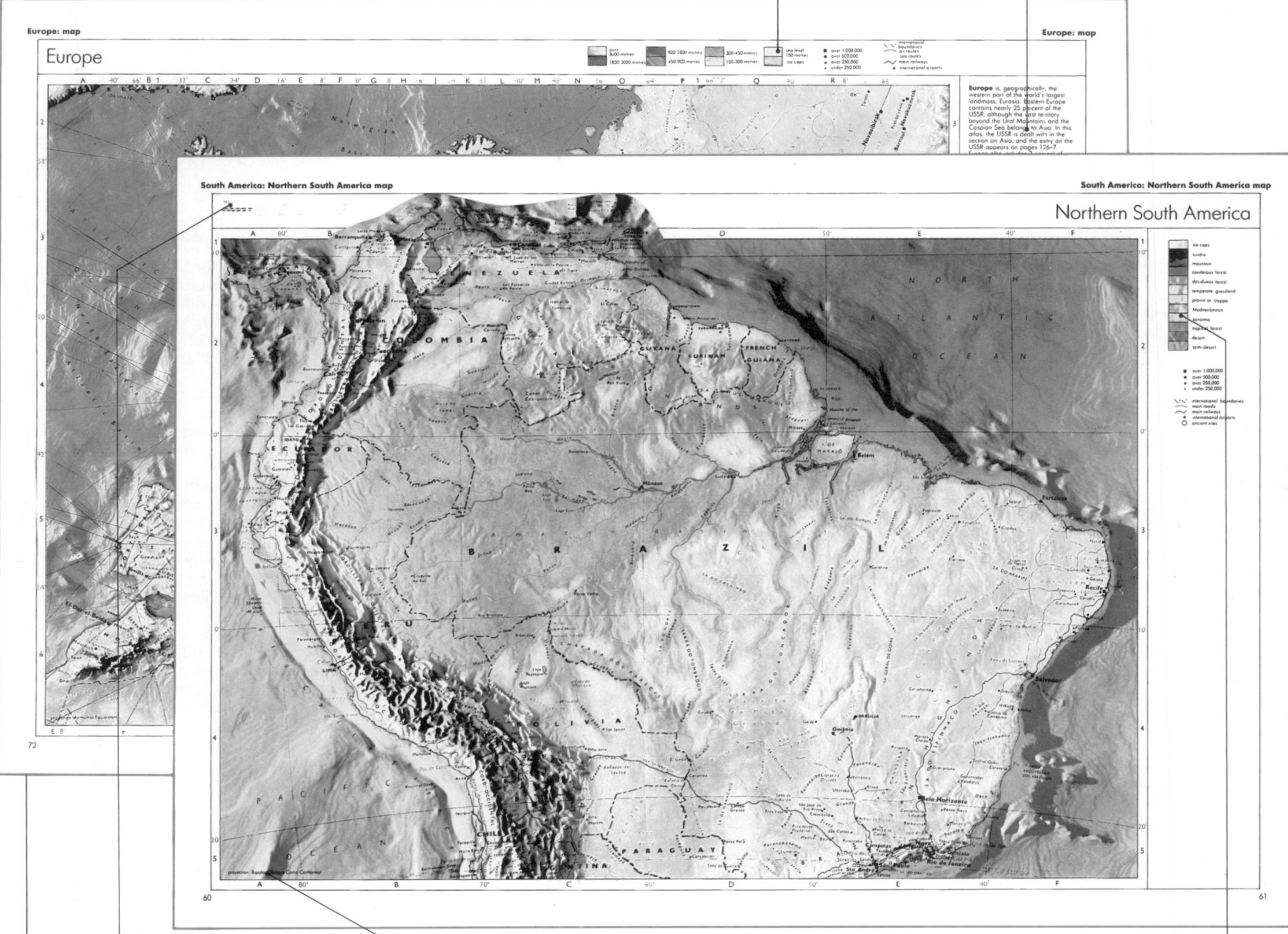

Scale Every map has a scale in miles and kilometres for easy reference.

Map Projections To represent the lines of latitude and longitude on a flat surface a 'projection' must be used. The choice of projection for any given map is determined by the purpose of the map. Individual projections are characterized by the geographical properties they preserve. These properties are area, shape, scale and bearing. Where the purpose of

the map demands a degree of compromise as to which properties are preserved a 'mathematical projection' may be used.

Natural Colour Key Natural colouring is used on maps to denote the nature of the climate and the predominance of types of vegetation — ie whether the land is hot or cold, wet or dry, desert or lush forest. There are 12 divisions in all — however, individual maps do not necessarily have all 12 divisions.

Political Maps All countries have been colour coded so as to clearly define their political boundaries.

Text Most continents are introduced with a detailed explanation of the land and climate, flora and fauna, people and languages, religions and economic and demographic trends. This is followed by a detailed analysis of each country in geographical order — again for ease of reference. Sources for the statistical informaton include the *World Bank Atlas 1983*, the *Statesman's Yearbook 83-84*, the *UN Demographic Yearbook 1981* and the *UN Development Report 1983*. (Unless otherwise indicated, population figures in this Atlas are for 1984.)

Fact Boxes Details of area, population, population growth rate, capital city, language, religion and currency are given in information fact boxes at the beginning of each country's entry.

The World

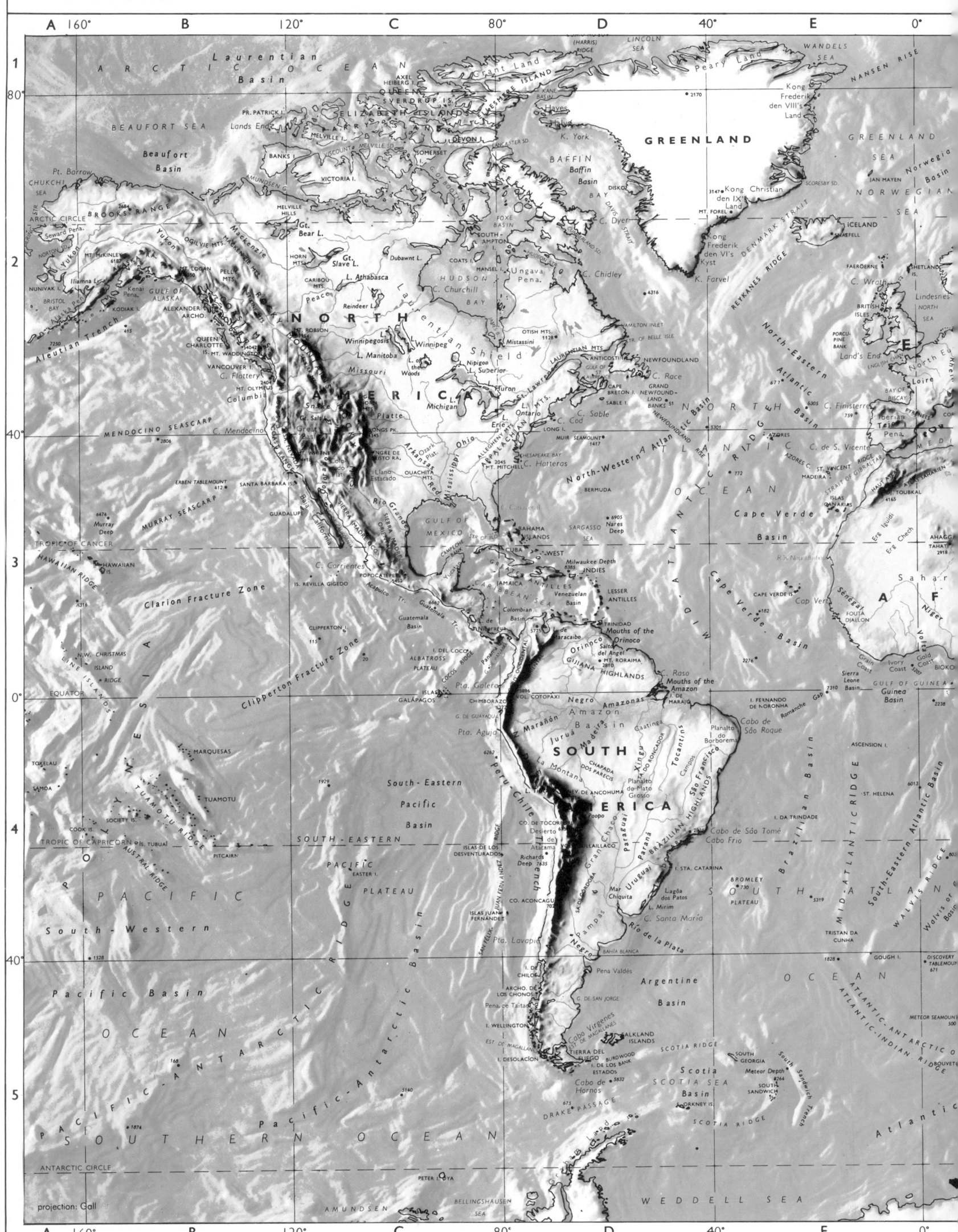

projection: Gall

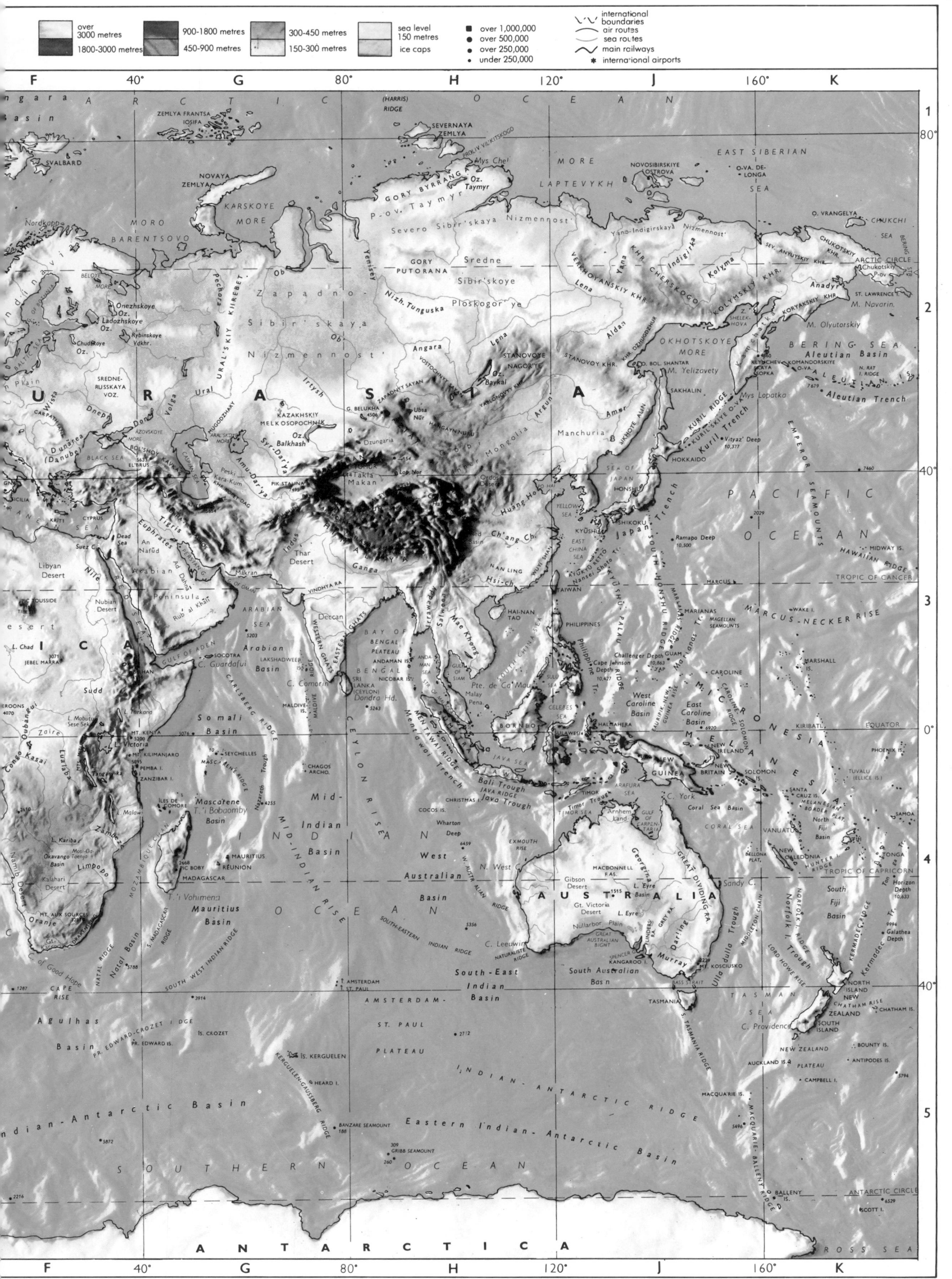

North America: introduction

North America is the third largest continent. The northern part of North America – Greenland, Canada and the United States – make up just over 88 percent of the land area. About 85 percent of Greenland, the world's largest island, is buried by ice, which is more than 11,000 feet (3,353 m) thick in the centre. The snow melts on some coastlands in summer to reveal tundra vegetation. But even the ice-free areas show all the characteristics of a glaciated landscape, with deep fiords and U-shaped valleys. There are some some small ice-caps on the islands of northern Canada, but most of northern Canada is tundra, which bursts into life during the short summer.

Northern North America contains four main land regions. First, the northeastern Canadian shield is composed of ancient rocks, mainly granites and metamorphosed gneisses and schists. This region represents all that is left of an old mountain region which has been planed down to generally low relief. A depression at the heart of the Canadian shield contains Hudson Bay, an inlet of the sea.

The landscape of the Canadian shield was recently buried by ice sheets, and polished rock surfaces and ice-deepened hollows containing lakes and marshes are evidence of ice action. In the south, the Great Lakes are the remains of a larger lake, called by geologists Lake Algonquin, which formed around the edge of the retreating ice-sheet. One of the Great Lakes, Lake Superior, is the world's largest freshwater lake. It covers 31,820 square miles (82,409 km²). Parts of another ancient lake, called Lake Agassiz, survive in lakes Manitoba, Winnipeg and Winnipegosis in Manitoba province. Areas of former lake floors are marked by mostly flat layers of silt and clay.

The second main land region is in the east, including the eastern coastlands and the eastern highlands. The coastlands, extending north from Florida, decrease in width from south to north. North of New York City, the coastal plain has been largely drowned by the sea, although it outcrops in islands and small areas, such as Cape Cod. Inland the coastal plain is bounded by the Fall Line, which is more of a zone than a line. Here the land rises and rapids and small waterfalls occur along the change of gradient. Farther inland are the eastern highlands, the Appalachians, which run from Newfoundland to the northeast corner of Alabama. This region of ridges, plateaus and valleys lacks high peaks, but it was an obstacle to early European settlers who wanted to move inland from the east.

Beyond the eastern highlands is the third region, the central plains, which extend from the Arctic Ocean and the Mackenzie River lowlands, through Saskatchewan and Manitoba, into the region drained by the Mississippi–Missouri river system and southwards to the plains around the Gulf of Mexico. The Mississippi–Missouri–Red River system is the world's third longest, after the Nile and Amazon. It is 3,800 miles (6,115 km) long. The northern part of these plains is glaciated, but the south lay beyond the Pleistocene ice-sheets. In the south, the low Ozark–Ouachita uplands rise above the plains in Arkansas and, to the west, the land rises to the Great Plains. The Great Plains are considerably higher than the central interior lowlands, rising from about 1,500 feet (457 m) in the east to 6,000 feet (1,829 m) in the west. Much of it is flat and featureless, but there are some rugged areas, such as Dakota's spectacular Badlands.

The fourth main region in northern North America, the western cordilleras, starts at the western edge of the Great Plains, extending in places to the Pacific Ocean. Here are high fold mountain chains, plateaus etched by canyons, block mountains and basins, many of which were sites of ancient lakes. The main ranges are the Rocky Mountains in the east, the Cascade Mountains and the Sierra Nevada, and the Coast Ranges along the Pacific in the west. The highest peak is Mount McKinley in the Alaska range, which is 20,320 feet (6,194 m) high.

Much of the western cordilleras was glaciated in the Ice Age and there is much glorious glaciated scenery, as in the Yosemite National Park in the Sierra Nevada. Here North America's highest waterfalls plunge over the near vertical sides of a deep, ice-worn U-shaped valley. Ribbon Falls is 1,612 feet (491 m) high. The south-western part of this region contains, in the downfaulted Death Valley, the lowest point on land in North America. A spot near a salt pond called Badwater is 282 feet (86 m) below sea-level.

The Pacific coastal mountains extend southward as the mountains of Baja California and the Sierra Nevada Occidental in Mexico. Between the Sierra Nevada Occidental and the Sierra Nevada Oriental is the broad central plateau of Mexico, which tapers to the south where there is a chain of volcanoes that continue through Central America. Volcanic eruptions and earthquakes are common events in this geologically unstable region. The Pacific coastal plains of Mexico and Central America are mostly narrow, but the Caribbean coastlands, including the Yucatan peninsula, are much more extensive.

The Caribbean Sea is that part of the West Atlantic enclosed by Central America, northern South America and the Greater and Lesser Antilles island groups in the West Indies. The West Indian islands have mostly rugged scenery and are volcanic in origin.

Geographically, the West Indies are divided into three main groups: the Bahamas, the Greater Antilles, and the Lesser Antilles. The Greater Antilles include Cuba, the largest West Indian island, Hispaniola (which is divided into two countries, French-speaking Haiti and the Spanish-speaking Dominican Republic), Puerto Rico and Jamaica. The Lesser Antilles are further divided into the Leeward Islands (including Antigua, St Christopher-Nevis, Anguilla, the US Virgin Islands, and Guadeloupe), the Windward Islands (including Dominica, Martinique, St Lucia, St Vincent, and Grenada), Barbados, Trinidad and Tobago, and the Netherlands Antilles.

The far north of North America has a polar climate, while southern Mexico, Central America and the West Indies are in the tropics. Between these extremes is a wide range of climates. The northern part of North America, where the continent is at its widest, is influenced in winter by the development of a cold, high-pressure air mass, from which icy winds blow outwards. By contrast, in the south, tropical, maritime air masses bring moist, warm air to coastlands. The interaction of air from the north and south controls the climate of the central lowlands of the United States.

The coastlands of the west, south and southeastern United States have mild weather in winter, although they are often cooler than places in the interior with a severe continental climate – cold winters and hot summers. In the United States, the rainfall decreases from east to west, and the semiarid prairies occur in the centre. The southwestern United States is arid, with deserts that extend into northern Mexico. But to the south, the climate is mostly tropical rainy, although the altitude modifies temperatures. In summer, the Caribbean and Gulf of Mexico regions are liable to be hit by hurricanes, some of which batter the Atlantic coast of the southeastern United States.

Vegetation is determined by climate. The tundra of northern Canada merges to the south into open parkland and then coniferous forest dominated by spruce and balsam fir.

Above The Grand Canyon, Arizona, was described by the American explorer and geologist John Wesley Powell as 'the most sublime spectacle on the earth'. The exposed rock strata, laying bare a long segment of Earth history, change colour according to the time of day. The Canyon has been etched into the slowly rising Colorado Plateau by the Colorado River. It is up to 18 miles (29 km) wide, around 1 mile (1.6 km) deep, and 277 miles (466 km) long.

Crater Lake in the Cascade Range of southern Oregon is the deepest lake in the United States.

In the east, the coniferous forest merges into mixed forest and then deciduous forest in temperate latitudes. But little deciduous forest survives in its original form, except in such protected areas as Tennessee's Great Smoky Mountains National Park.

The central plains contain huge tracts of grassland, although large areas have been converted into farmland. West of the Great Plains are mountain forests of various kinds. There are also forests on the Pacific ranges, and some of these contain the coast redwood (*Sequoia sempervirens*), the tallest known tree. The southwestern coastlands of California have a Mediterranean climate, but cacti are the characteristic plants of the inland deserts. Huge tropical forests cover the coastal lowlands of Central America and the West Indies.

North America's wildlife has been reduced in the last few centuries. But an international agreement of 1973 will probably ensure the survival of polar bears in the Arctic. Other northern animals include Arctic foxes, caribou, musk oxen and walruses. The western mountains are the home of Rocky Mountain goats, Bighorn sheep, elks, grizzly bears, moose and eagles.

The grasslands once supported huge herds of American bison (or buffalo). In 1820, the Plains bison probably numbered 60 million, but there were only a few hundred left by 1890 after remorseless hunting. There are now protected herds in Alberta's Wood Buffalo National Park. Other prairie animals which have been greatly reduced in numbers are the pronghorn antelope, coyote and mustang (wild descendants of horses introduced by Spaniards), but Canada and the United States are now as conscious of wildlife preservation as any other nation. The central and eastern parts of northern North America also have a varied wildlife, including black bears and musquash, but animal populations have been depleted by human settlement.

Northern North America belongs to the Nearctic realm, and its wildlife is similar to that of the Palearctic realm in Eurasia. But south of the Tropic of Cancer is the markedly different Neotropical realm. Here the abundant wildlife includes anteaters, alligators, armadillos, many species of colourful birds, jaguars and monkeys.

Above These American bison, or buffalo, are in Custer State Park, South Dakota. By 1890, overhunting of these powerful animals had almost caused their extinction. But from the few hundred survivors, several herds have been bred. Various other parks and reserves, including Wyoming's Yellowstone National Park and Canada's Wood Buffalo National Park, now contain herds. The only other ungulate native to the North American prairie, the graceful pronghorn antelope, also nearly disappeared. In 1922, there were no more than 30,000 left, but conservationist policies have ensured their survival.

Right The continental United States include 48 states. The 49th and 50th states are Alaska, which replaced Texas as the largest, and Hawaii. These latecomers both achieved statehood in 1959. The smallest state, Rhode Island, was one of the original 13 British colonies which revolted against Britain and founded the new republic. The continental United States are also often divided into seven regions: New England (six states); the Middle Atlantic States (three); the Southern States (14); the Midwestern States (12); the Rocky Mountain States (six); the Southwestern States (four); and the Pacific Coast States (three).

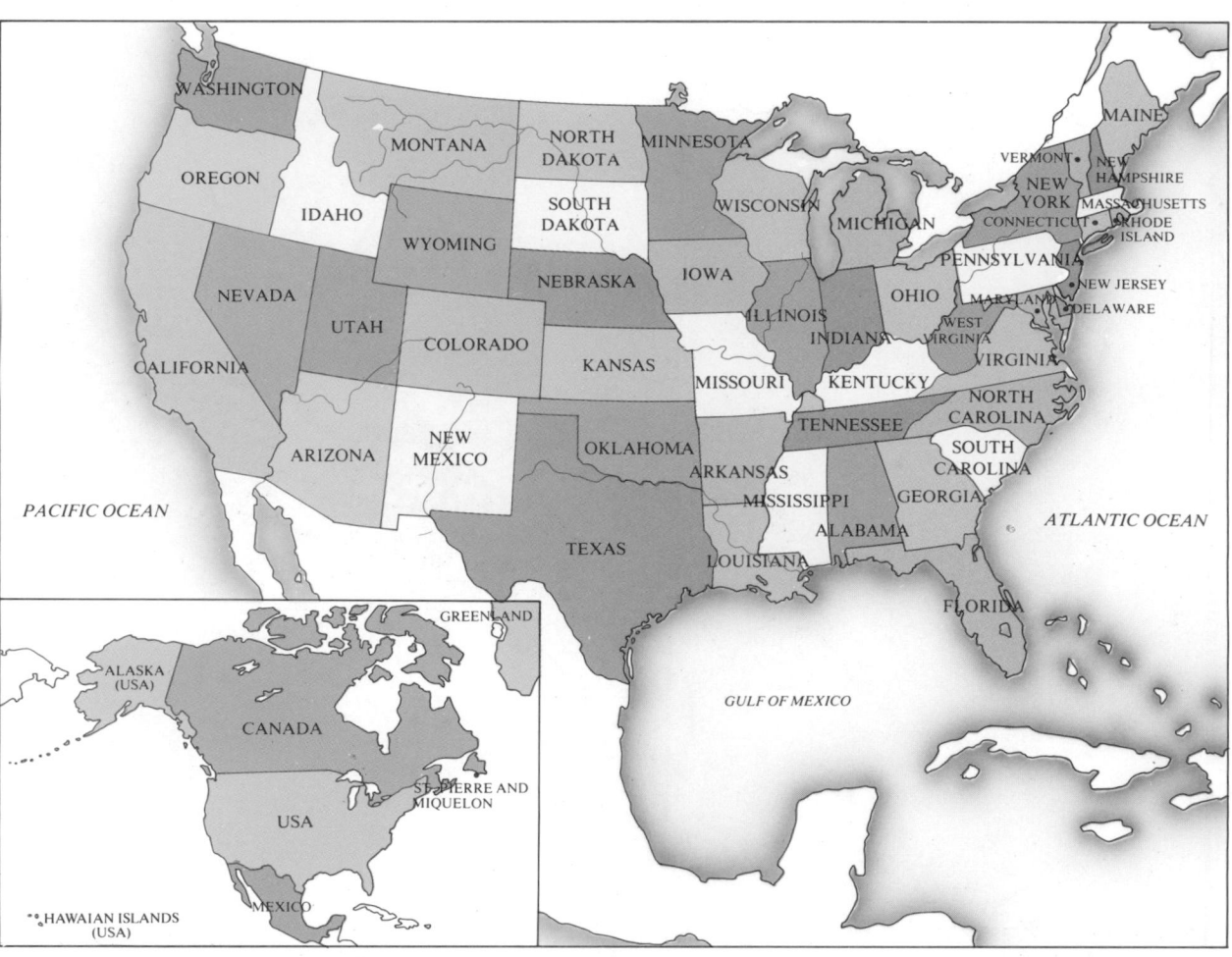

North America

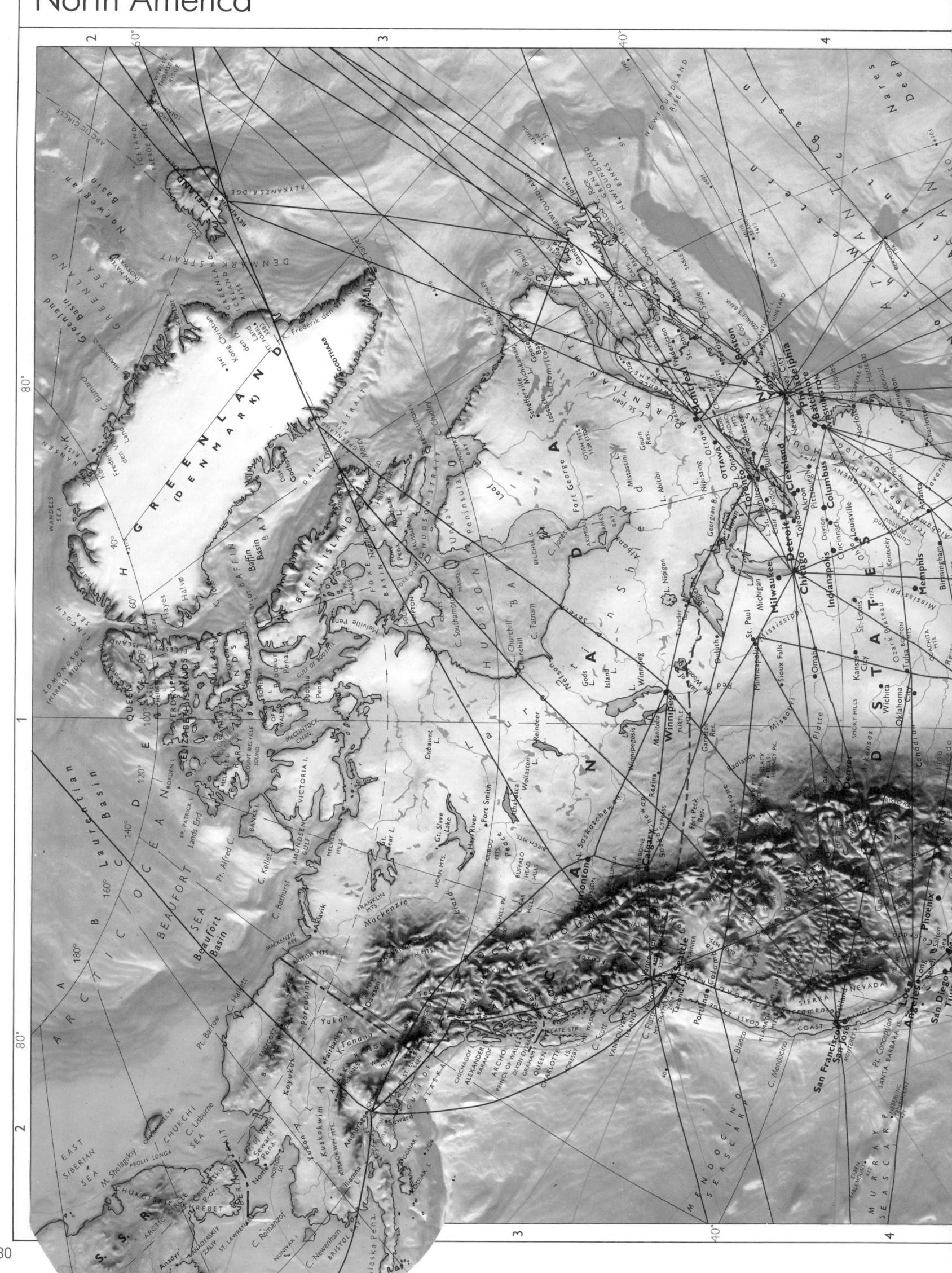

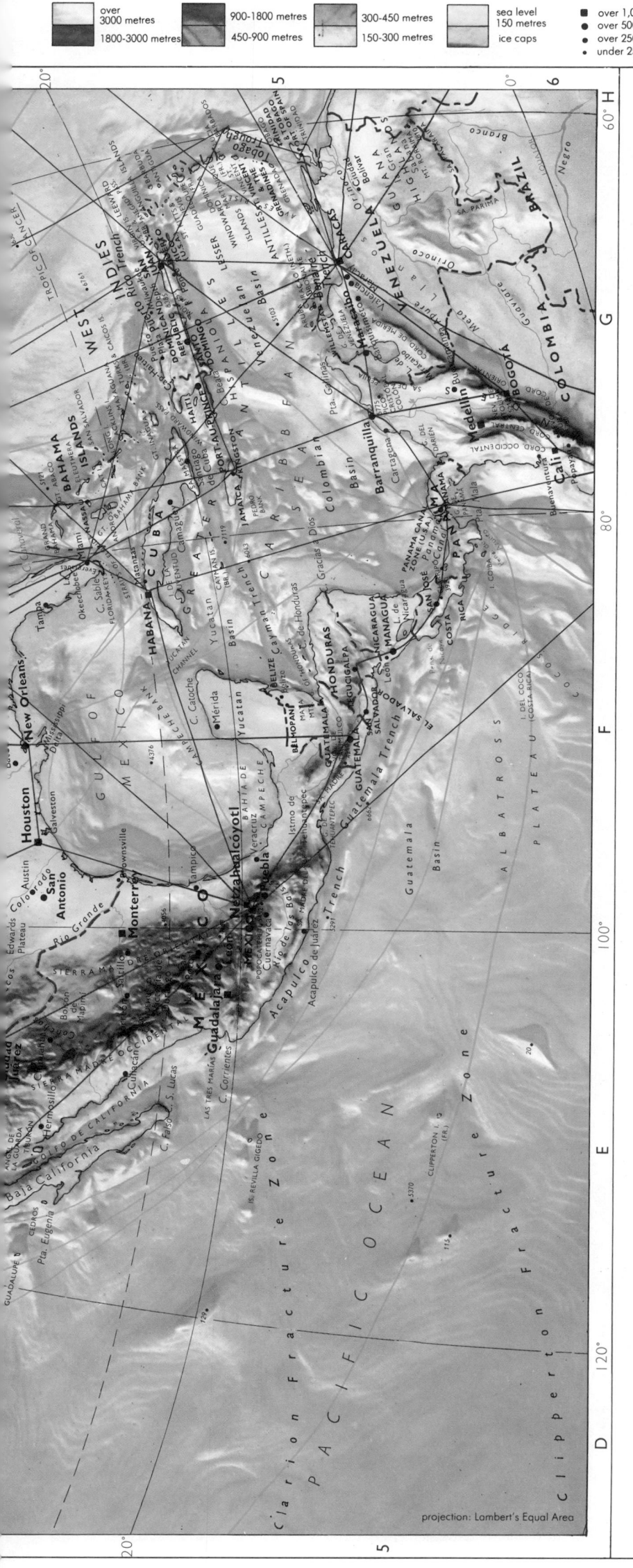

projection: Lambert's Equal Area

North America is sometimes defined as Canada, Greenland and the United States. But another, wider definition takes in Mexico, which straddles the Tropic of Cancer, and the tropical nations of Central America and the West Indies in the Caribbean Sea. Under this second definition, North America has an area of about 9,362,408 sq miles (24,248,528 km²)m or 16.3 percent of the world's land area.

The population density generally increases from the Arctic north to the tropical south. The average population densities of Canada and the United States are, respectively, 6 per sq mile (2 per km²) and 63 per sq mile (24 per km²). Mexico and Central America have an overall population density of 107 per sq mile (41 per km²), but the greatest population densities are in the West Indies. These island nations have an average population density of 329 per sq mile (127 per km²).

The North American plate is mostly an ancient landmass, which was once joined to western Europe. In fact, the northern Appalachians in the eastern United States and Canada are part of the same mountain system that includes the mountains of eastern Greenland, Scotland and Norway. But around 100 million years ago the North Atlantic began to open up, and North America and Europe drifted apart by 0.5 to 4 inches (1-10cm) a year.

To the west, the North American plate collided with the Pacific plate, the edge of which was pushed beneath the North American plate along a subduction zone. Friction caused by the descending plate created heat, which melted overlying rocks and thus created pockets of magma. The magma rose through volcanoes in the overlying North American plate. At one stage, the North American plate was moving quickly and it overrode the Pacific plate. Friction between the two plates buckled overlying rocks in the west-central part of the North American plate, pushing them up into the Rocky Mountain range, thus reducing the width of the plate.

The Rockies no longer represent a plate edge. After their formation, the North American plate began to move more slowly. The subduction zone then retreated west. As this happened, parts of the crust in the North American plate sagged, forming the Great Basin of Nevada and Utah. In places, lava welled to the surface, piling up to great thicknesses in the Columbia plateau, north of the Great Basin.

The Pacific plate is still being pushed under the North American plate in the northwestern United States. The explosive eruption of Mount St Helens, Washington, in 1980, in which 65 people died, is a reminder of this continuing plate movement. Other subduction zones with active volcanoes alongside them are off the Aleutians and the south Alaskan coast in the north; off the Pacific coast of southern Mexico and Central America; and to the east of the volcanic island chain in the Lesser Antilles in the West Indies.

But in northwestern Mexico and the southwestern United States, there is another type of plate movement along transform faults. This began around 15 million years ago, when the Pacific plate started to slide northwards alongside the North American plate. This movement is now occurring along the famous San Andreas Fault, in California. The movements are not smooth, because the rough edges of the plates become jammed together. But mounting pressure finally breaks the jams and the plates lurch forward, triggering off earthquakes, some being extremely intense, like the San Francisco earthquake of 1906.

The dragging movements of the plates have twisted and fractured rocks in the southwestern United States, creating many long fault lines. Some blocks of land between pairs of faults have sunk to create rift valleys, while other blocks have been raised to form block mountains, such as the Sierra Nevada, which is still rising.

In the last million years, during the Pleistocene Ice Age, ice-sheets and glaciers have played their part in shaping the scenery of northern North America. Because so much of the world's water supply was converted into ice, the sea-level fell and a land bridge between Asia and North America was formed in what is now the Bering Strait. Perhaps 40,000 years ago, people walked across this land bridge. They were the first human beings in North America — the ancestors of the Amerindians.

Scientists differ about exactly when the first people entered North America and there were probably several waves. A prehistoric settlement in the Yukon has been dated at about 25,000 BC, and the first wave of immigrants may have crossed a land bridge at what is now the Bering Strait as early as 40,000 years ago. The early people, who belonged to the Mongoloid subgroup of the human race, spread south and colonized the whole of North and South America. Because of an accident of history, they are often called Indians, but to avoid confusion, the term Amerindian is preferred. The ancestors of the Eskimos also came from Asia, but at a much later date than the Amerindians.

The colonization of the Americas by the Amerindians led to the development of several contrasting cultures: some were hunters and gatherers, some were farmers and some founded major civilizations. There were nine main groups of Amerindians in northern North America. The Subarctic Amerindians, including people who spoke languages belonging to the Algonquian and Athapascan families, were hunters and fishermen. The Northeast Woodland Amerindians, who spoke Algonquian, Iroquoian and Siouan languages, had a mixed economy, combining farming and hunting. A similar lifestyle was shared by the Southeast Amerindians, including Cherokees, Choctaws, Creeks and Seminoles. These people built towns of thatched, wooden houses.

The Plains Amerindians, including the ubiquitous Apaches, Cheyennes, Comanches, Crows and Pawnees, were hunters who became skilled horsemen after the introduction of horses by early Spanish explorers. The Great Basin Amerindians, such as the Shoshonis and the Plateau Amerindians, were essentially hunters and gatherers, while the Californian Amerindians also fished. The Northwest Coast Amerindians were hunters, fishers and seed-gatherers, who became known for their superb wood-carving. The Southwest Amerindians of Arizona and New Mexico included the Hopi, Mojave, Navaho and Pueblo. The Pueblo, whose name means 'village' in Spanish, built huge, terraced adobe houses. They had a farming economy.

Northern Mexico was a transitional area between the northern Amerindians and those of Middle America (Mexico and Guatemala), who included the Maya. The Maya developed a major civilization between the fourth and ninth centuries AD, and the Toltecs founded another civilization between about 900 and 1200. The Toltecs in turn influenced a second Mayan civilization which grew up in the Yucatan peninsula between about 1200 and 1450.

Another group, the Aztecs, occupied the Mexican plateau and, from about AD 1200, built up a powerful civilization, despite their lack of large draught animals and the wheel. The Aztecs were finally defeated by a Spanish force under Hernando Cortés in 1521. The Spanish also subjugated many small Amerindian groups who lived in the rest of Central America and the West Indies.

The first European contact with North America was probably made around AD 1000 when Leif Ericson, a Norseman from a settlement in Greenland, may have reached Cape Cod, Massachusetts. But Ericson's voyage was forgotten. In 1492 the continent was rediscovered by Christopher Columbus, an Italian sailing on behalf of Spain, who sighted San Salvador in the Bahamas on October 12. He went on to Cuba and Hispaniola before returning to Spain in triumph.

It was Columbus who called the people *los Indos* (Indians), because he believed until his death in 1506 that he had reached Asia. Some years passed before such people as Amerigo Vespucci, after whom the Americas are named, realized that Columbus had found a New World.

Central America was soon overrun by Spanish soldiers and settlers. The native Amerindians had no way of resisting European weaponry and European diseases, to which they succumbed in their thousands. In the years that followed, most of Central America and the West Indies became part of a new cultural entity, Latin America, whose ethnic mix was further complicated when large numbers of Black slaves were introduced from Africa. Soon, alongside Amerindian, European and Black communities, there were also groups of *mestizos* (people of mixed Amerindian and European origin) and *mulattos* (people of mixed African and European origin).

Spaniards also explored parts of what is now the southern United States, but their failure to find treasure or marvels

These Tigua Indians are baking apple turnovers at Tigua Reservation, El Paso, in western Texas. El Paso, which faces the Mexican Ciudad Juárez across the Rio Grande, became American only after the Mexican War of 1846–48. Now a thriving industrial city, the fifth largest in Texas, El Paso still reveals an extraordinary cultural mix. Amerindian, Spanish, Mexican and frontier American influences are still evident to visitors who use El Paso as a base for exploring the scenic country in southern Texas and its neighbour, New Mexico.

Opposite above The Cherokee reservation in North Carolina, adjoining the Great Smoky Mountains National Park, is one of the largest areas occupied by Indians in the eastern United States. These Cherokees are the descendants of Indians left behind in the late 1830s, when most of the Cherokee nation was forced to go west on the 'Trail of Tears'. The Cherokees, along with Creeks, Chickasaws, Choctaws and Seminoles, suffered terrible hardships and many deaths before they were settled on what was then thought to be useless territory in Oklahoma. The story of this tragic chapter in American history is told at the Cherokee Heritage Center at Tsa-La-Gi, Oklahoma, in a musical drama.

Opposite below A reflection of a street of old houses in Washington DC, capital of the United States. The focus of this great city, with its impressive government buildings, world-famous museums and unforgettable monuments and memorials, was originally planned by the French engineer, Pierre Charles de L'Enfant, who was commissioned in 1791 by George Washington himself. Washington DC was the first modern city to be planned from the outset to be the seat of national government. But there are other attractions, not least the pleasant riverport quarter of Georgetown, which was a prosperous port on the Potomac River in colonial times. Georgetown is now a desirable residential district.

such as springs giving eternal life led to a rapid loss of interest. Instead, Britain and France took the main initiative in exploring the north. They searched at first for a North-west Passage to Asia. But later they founded settlements which grew into colonies. In this way, the United States acquired its Anglo-American culture, while Canada had English and French cultures.

Black slaves were also taken to the English colonies of North America. However, by 1790, the population of the United States was only about four million. Between 1800 and 1900, the population increased by more than 70 millions, as wave upon wave of immigrants arrived from Europe. They were rapidly integrated into the Anglo-American culture, and second-generation immigrants, with no language problem, were soon making their mark. The integration of the Blacks and, later, the Puerto Ricans and Mexicans proved rather more difficult to achieve.

The United States had proclaimed its independence from Britain in 1776, and most of Central America broke with Spain in 1821. The Dominion of Canada was established in 1867 and Cuba became independent in 1898. But the small British West Indian colonies had problems in creating viable economies. As a result, independence was delayed until the last few decades. By 1984 there were ten independent West Indian members of the British Commonwealth, but Britain still controlled Bermuda, the Cayman Islands, the Turks and Caicos Islands, the British Virgin Islands, Anguilla, and Montserrat. France controls Guadeloupe and Martinique as French departments, and the Netherlands Antilles are ruled as part of the Netherlands. Puerto Rico is a self-governing Commonwealth in association with the United States.

In economic terms, Canada and the United States dominate the continent, with a combined gross domestic product which is more than 14 times as great as that of the rest of North America combined. The per capita GNP of Canada and the United States stood at $11,460 in 1980, which is more than six and a half times the per capita GNP of the rest of the continent (excluding Cuba for which comparable figures are not available), which stood at $1,740.

These stark contrasts are reflected in many aspects of life. For example, while the rate of population increase in Canada and the United States is 1 percent per year, the comparable rate in the West Indies is 1.8 percent. And in Mexico and Central America, the population is increasing at the extremely high annual rate of 3 percent. Should this rate continue, the population of Central America will double in only 24 years.

Canada and the United States are the most urbanized countries, with 76 and 77 percent of their populations, respectively, living in cities and towns. But the continent's largest city is Mexico City, and the proportion of people in Mexican cities and towns is increasing rapidly. It stood at 51 percent in 1960 and 67 percent in 1981. Cuba, where 66 percent of the people live in cities and towns, is the most urbanized country in the West Indies. And Havana, Cuba, is the only West Indian city with a population of more than a million.

But in most Caribbean and Central American countries, the proportion of urban inhabitants is less than 50 percent, and their economies are based essentially on agriculture. The proportions of the workforce engaged in farming in Canada and the United States are 5 percent and 2 percent respectively, although farms are so highly mechanized and efficient that both countries produce food surpluses. In Haiti, Honduras, Guatemala and El Salvador, the percentages of people working on farms are 74 percent, 63 percent, 55 percent and 50 percent respectively. And many of the Central American and West Indian countries are net food importers.

The United States is also the world's leading industrial nation, and Canada is in the top league of industrial powers. Because of the high levels of technology and production, Canada and the United States also have the highest percentages of people employed in service industries. Despite their many natural resources, however, the countries in the rest of North America belong to the developing world.

Increasing health standards and services have pushed up the average life expectancies at birth in Canada and the United States to 75 years, the highest in North America. There are some countries where the average life expectancies now exceed 70 years, including Costa Rica, Cuba, Jamaica, Panama, and Trinidad and Tobago. But the life expectancy in Mexico in 1981 was 66 years, in El Salvador it was 63 years, and in Haiti it was only 54 years.

Educational standards are also much lower in tropical North America than they are in Canada and the United States, where the adult literacy rates are effectively 100 percent. But the rates in Mexico, El Salvador and Haiti, for example, were only 83, 62 and 23 percent, respectively, in 1981. It is such differences in the rate of economic and social development that underlie the differences in political attitudes in North America, and the emergence of military dictators and left-wing revolutionaries in Central America and the West Indies.

Canada

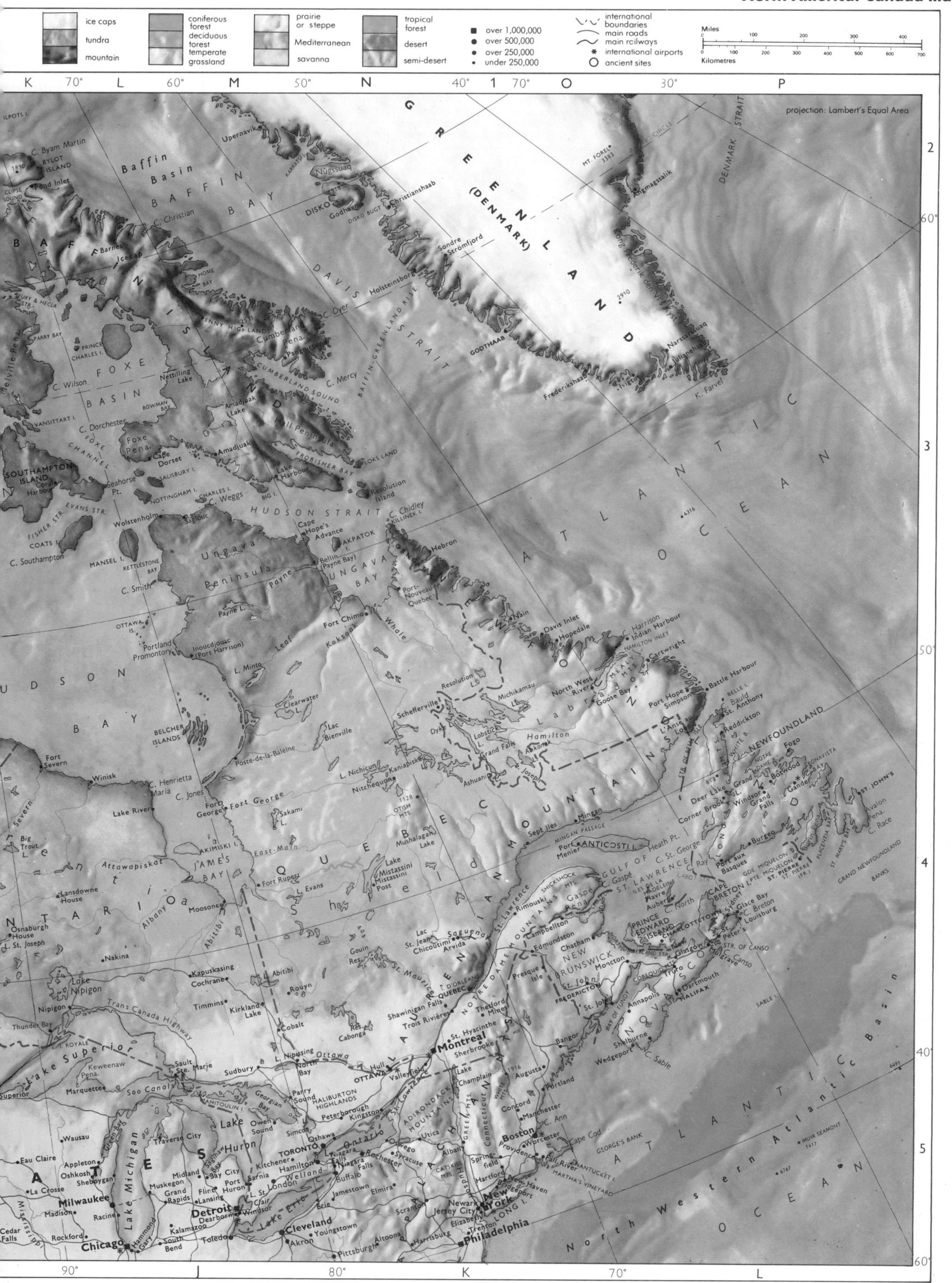

CANADA

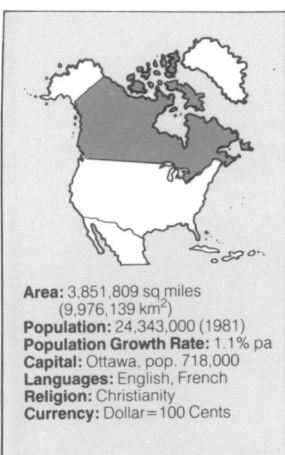

Area: 3,851,809 sq miles (9,976,139 km²)
Population: 24,343,000 (1981)
Population Growth Rate: 1.1% pa
Capital: Ottawa, pop. 718,000
Languages: English, French
Religion: Christianity
Currency: Dollar = 100 Cents

CANADA, which contains ten provinces and two territories, is the world's second largest country after the USSR. But it is thinly populated, with an average population density of only 6 per square mile (2 per km²). Newfoundland apart, more than 90 percent of Canadians live within 300 miles (483 km) of the US border.

Culture and People The first Canadians were Amerindians, whose ancestors came from Asia. Major Amerindian language groups include the Iroquois of the eastern woodlands, a group containing the Cayugas, Mohawks, Oneidas, Onondagas, and Senecas, and the Algonquian groups in the east and centre, including such Plains peoples as the Blackfoot and Cree. The Athapascans, including the Chipewyans, are found in the west and northwest, while the far west contains such groups as the Haidas, Salish, Tlingits and Tsimshians.

When the first Europeans began to settle in Canada, there were an estimated 220,000 Amerindians and Eskimos (called Inuit in Canada). They declined considerably in the face of European weapons and diseases to which they lacked resistance.

However, by 1981, there were about 368,000 Canadian Amerindians and 25,000 Inuit. About one-third of the Amerindians now live on one of the 2,000 or so reserves and settlements, which have a total area of more than 6 million acres (2.43 million ha). Most Inuit live in scattered settlements or camps. Few now follow their traditional semi-nomadic lifestyles, hunting and fishing in the Arctic wastes.

Norse explorers from Greenland probably visited the Canadian coast about 1,000 years ago. But the first voyage to Canada during the Age of Exploration was made in 1497 by an Italian, John Cabot, leading an English expedition. He reached Cape Breton Island and Nova Scotia and gave Newfoundland its name.

Cabot's son, Sebastian, returned in 1509 and explored Hudson Strait. Portuguese explorers sought vainly for a Northwest Passage to Asia, but of much more lasting significance were the journeys of the Frenchman Jacques Cartier in 1534–35 and in 1541. He discovered the Gulf of St Lawrence and sailed up the St Lawrence River, proving that it was not the Northwest Passage. He named the area he explored New France.

French interest was revived in the early 17th century, when Samuel de Champlain explored eastern Canada and, in 1608, founded Canada's first permanent settlement, Quebec. Montreal was founded in 1642 and, in 1663, Louis IV proclaimed Quebec a French province. This encouraged the immigration of more trappers and other settlers.

The English Hudson's Bay Company was established in Hudson Bay in 1670. Anglo-French rivalry, often the result of conflict in Europe, became a feature of Canadian history.

Matters came to a head with the Seven Years' War (1756–63), during which General James Wolfe's army defeated the French under the Marquis de Montcalm, and took Quebec in 1759.

France gave up Quebec to Britain under the Treaty of Paris (1763). But the Quebec Act (1774) guaranteed freedom of religion for Roman Catholics and recognized French civil law in British courts.

During the American War of Independence, Canadian colonists stayed loyal to Britain, although Montreal fell to the Americans in 1775. In 1776, at the end of the war, about 40,000 United Empire Loyalists from south of the newly fixed border went north and settled in Canada, mainly in Nova Scotia, New Brunswick and Ontario.

Fighting again occurred during the Napoleonic Wars, but Canada began to make peaceful progress after 1814.

The country was gradually being opened up. A Scottish fur trader, Alexander Mackenzie, explored the Mackenzie River in 1789, reaching its outlet in the Arctic Ocean. In 1792, he crossed the Rocky Mountains and reached the Pacific. His was the first overland journey across North America.

In the second half of the 19th century, the population increased through immigration from Britain and other European countries. But the French Canadians retained their identity, and rivalry with English-speaking Canadians, who were in the majority, continued.

Constitutional Development In 1867, the Dominion of Canada, containing four provinces – Quebec, Ontario, Nova Scotia and New Brunswick – was established by the British North America Act, which combined features of the governments of the United States and Britain.

Other provinces joined later: Manitoba (1870), British Columbia (1871), Prince Edward Island (1873), Alberta and Saskatchewan (1905) and Newfoundland and Labrador (1949). The Northwest Territories were annexed in 1870 and the Yukon Territory, formerly part of the Northwest Territories, was made a separate territory in 1898.

The completion of the transcontinental Canadian Pacific Railway in 1885 was an important step in unifying this vast country. And the Klondike Gold Rush in 1897 helped to open up the Yukon Territory and gave some indication of Canada's enormous potential in mineral resources.

More than 600,000 Canadian troops fought in World War I. In 1931, the Statute of Westminster made Canada a sovereign nation within the Commonwealth. In 1982, the British parliament passed further legislation whereby Canada's Constitution can be amended only in Canada. This Canada Act replaced the British North American Act.

Politics Canadians fought alongside Britain in World War II, after which it continued to develop its own identity, distinct from that of Britain or the United States. Canada has also played a major role in world affairs under Liberal or Progressive Conservative governments.

Canada has bicameral system of government, with a 104-member Senate and a 282-member House of Commons.

Totem poles, before a family home, show rank and lineage.

Exposure to civilization has reduced the numbers of the Inuit, or Eskimos, to around 22,000. They originally came from Asia, and belong to the Mongoloid sub-group.

Canada is a monarchy. The Head of State is the monarch of the United Kingdom, who is represented in Canada by a Governor-General. The federal government is led by the prime minister, who is the leader of the party which has won a parliamentary election.

Each of the ten provinces has its own legislature and government, and there are councils in the Northwest Territories and the Yukon.

Despite great economic progress in recent years, Canada has encountered a variety of problems, including resentment over US influence on Canadian industry, recession and unemployment. Anglo-French rivalry again came into the open in 1976, when the people of Quebec elected a premier who favoured separatism. But in 1980, a majority of Quebec's people rejected separatism in a referendum.

National Origins In 1901, Canadians of British and French origin combined made up 88 percent of the population. But because of immigration from other countries, mainly in Europe, the proportion of people of British and French origin declined to 73 percent in 1971, although the proportion of people of French origin remained fairly constant.

In 1971, 44.6 percent of the people were of British origin and 28.7 percent of French origin. People of German origin made up another 6.1 percent, people of Ukrainian origin 2.7 percent, people of Dutch origin 2 percent, and people from other European nations 7.9 percent.

In the 1981 census, however, people were asked to give their mother tongue. Some 61.3 percent gave English and 25.7 percent French. The percentage claiming English included immigrants of non-British origin who had adopted English as their first language.

Religion Just as the French Canadians are concentrated in Quebec province, so Roman Catholicism is the religion of nearly 90 percent of Quebec's citizens.

In Canada as a whole, 46.2 percent were Roman Catholics, 17.5 percent belonged to the United Church (Methodist, Presbyterian and Congregational), 11.8 percent were members of the Anglican Church of Canada, and 4 percent were Presbyterians not in the United Church.

Other denominations include Lutherans, Baptists, Greek Orthodox, Jews, Ukrainian Catholic, Pentecostal and Mennonite, and also members of the Muslim faith.

Population and Distribution In 1871, some 80 percent of Canada's population was rural. This percentage had declined to 46 percent in 1941, 30 percent in 1961, and 24 percent in 1981.

The chief areas of high population density are the St Lawrence Valley and the Great Lakes Peninsula, between lakes Ontario, Erie and Huron. The other centres are in and around the widely spaced cities of central and western Canada.

In 1981, 62 percent of the urban population lived in cities with more than 500,000

people. The largest city proper in 1976 was Montreal, with 980,000 people, but the Census Metropolitan Area (CMA) population was 2,828,000 as compared with 2,999,000 in Toronto CMA. (Toronto city proper had 559,000 people.)

Other large cities, with their CMA populations, are Vancouver (1,268,000), Ottawa-Hull (718,000), Edmonton (657,000), Calgary (593,000), Winnipeg (585,000), Quebec (576,000), and Hamilton (542,000).

Population Growth Canada is a thinly populated nation, although its population has increased by ten times since 1851, when it was 2,436,000. The rate of population increase has sometimes reached high levels, as in the 1950s when it was 2.7 percent per year. These high levels were the result of both high fertility and immigration. The annual rate has since declined, reaching 1.1 percent in 1975–81.

Death rates have steadily declined and this fact is reflected in the average life expectancies at birth. For example, the life expectancy in 1941 for men was 63 years and for women 66 years. By 1960, the average for both sexes was 71 years. By 1981 the average life expectancy at birth had reached 75 years.

Social Services The provincial governments are responsible for most health and welfare services. There is a federal Medical Care Act and a number of social security and social assistance schemes, together with monthly pensions for everyone over 65.

Provincial governments also control education, the cost being met by local taxation and provincial grants, although the federal government takes care of education for Amerindian and Inuit children, whose enrolment in 1981–82 was nearly 36,000.

Apart from Quebec, where there are private Roman Catholic schools, and Newfoundland, which has private Protestant schools, most children attend public schools, which are coeducational and free.

In 1982–83, there were 68 universities with the power to grant degrees. Adult literacy in 1981 was 99 percent.

The Land There are seven main land regions. The Canadian shield is the ancient heart of North America. It covers about 48 percent of Canada. Much of it is under 1,000 feet (305 m), but the Laurentian plateau of Quebec rises in the

east. The region is dotted with lakes, occupying hollows formed in the Ice Age. Rivers flowing from these lakes have been utilized for hydroelectric projects.

The Canadian shield almost encloses the Hudson Bay lowlands, where recent rocks overlie the ancient rocks of the shield. A third region consists of the bleak Arctic islands to the north of the Canadian shield.

In the southeast, the Appalachian region contains an extension of the Appalachian Mountains of the United States. This scenic region includes New Brunswick, part of Quebec southeast of the St Lawrence River (Canada's most important river), Nova Scotia, Prince Edward Island and Newfoundland.

The St Lawrence lowland and the Lower Great Lakes lowland form a fifth land region. The soils are generally fertile and farming is important. This is also the most industrialized and most densely populated region in Canada. Except for Lake Michigan, which is entirely within the United States, the Great Lakes are shared by Canada and its neighbour.

The western interior plains include most of southern Manitoba, most of Saskatchewan and Alberta, and the northeast corner of British Columbia. They then extend north through the western part of the Northwest Territories, including the Mackenzie River lowlands. The Mackenzie, Canada's longest river, is about 2,500 miles (4,023 km) long. Among its sources are the Great Bear and Great Slave lakes, the country's largest lakes apart from the Great Lakes. The Great Bear Lake has an area of 12,200 sq miles (31,596 km²). The Great Slave Lake covers 11,170 sq miles (28,929 km²).

The last main land region is the western cordilleras, which contain Canada's highest point, Mount Logan in Yukon Territory, which is 19,850 feet (6,050 m) above sea-level. There are many other high mountains, including Mount Robson, the highest peak in the Canadian Rockies at 12,972 feet (3,954 m).

The Canadian Rockies overlook the interior plains. To the west are a series of other ranges, alternating with fertile river valleys and basins, such as the Okanagan valley, and the Coastal Ranges which

border the narrow Pacific coastlands and various islands, including the mineral-rich Vancouver Island and the Queen Charlotte Islands.

Climate More than two-thirds of Canada has harsh winters. In the far north, some of the islands have average temperatures in January of −40°F (−40°C), while Winnipeg in the far south has an average January temperature of −0.4°F (−18°C).

The western cordilleras also have severe winters, but the ocean moderates the climate of the Pacific coast. For example, Victoria in southwestern British Columbia has an average January temperature of 39°F (4°C). But in the far east, the icy Labrador Current lowers coastal temperatures. The average temperature in January at St John's, Newfoundland, is 24°F (−4°C).

Most of Canada is warm in summer. Coppermine on the Coronation Gulf, an inlet of the Arctic Ocean, has an average July temperature of 49°F (9°C), as compared with 60°F (16°C) in Victoria, British Columbia, and 59°F (15°C) in St John's.

The interior has a continental climate, with hotter

PROVINCES AND TERRITORIES OF CANADA				
	total area			
province or territory	square miles	square kilometres	population	capital
Alberta	255,285	661,185	2,237,724	Edmonton
British Columbia	366,255	948,596	2,744,467*	Victoria
Manitoba	251,000	650,087	1,026,241	Winnipeg
New Brunswick	28,354	73,436	696,403	Fredericton
Newfoundland	156,185	404,517	567,681	St John's
Northwest Territories	1,304,903	3,379,683	45,471	Yellowknife
Nova Scotia	21,425	55,490	847,442	Halifax
Ontario	412,582	1,068,582	8,264,465	Toronto
Prince Edward Island	2,184	5,656	122,506	Charlottetown
Quebec	594,860	1,540,680	6,438,403	Quebec
Saskatchewan	251,700	651,900	968,313	Regina
Yukon Territory	207,076	536,324	22,135	Whitehorse

*1981 Census

The Rocky Mountains provides a backdrop to the Trans-Canada Highway in British Columbia.

summers than the coast. Winnipeg has an average July temperature of 67°F (19°C). Chinook winds sometimes blow down the eastern slopes of the Rockies. As they descend, they become warmer. In spring, they can melt all the snow and rapidly raise the temperatures on the plains.

The rainfall is heavy in the Appalachian and St Lawrence lowland regions, where between 30 and 40 inches (762–1,016 mm) falls every year. Much of this, however, falls in winter as snow. Parts of the interior plains are arid, with 10 to 14 inches (254–355 mm) a year, but places on Vancouver Island have an average annual rainfall of more than 200 inches (5,080 mm). By contrast with the wet Pacific coastlands, the Arctic has only about 10 inches (254 mm) of precipitation (snow, that is) per year.

Vegetation In the northern tundra, mosses, lichens and some flowering plants provide grazing for migrant animals in the short summer, but the subsoil remains frozen.

To the south, scattered trees grow on south-facing slopes, and this open parkland eventually merges into the northern coniferous, or boreal, forest zone. This forest of fir, larch, pine and spruce stretches from Newfoundland to the Alaskan border and is one of the world's largest.

In the southeast, the boreal forest merges into a mixed forest. Deciduous woodland is the natural vegetation of the St Lawrence lowlands and Great Lakes peninsula, although the original forest has been largely cut down.

Vast grasslands cover those parts of the interior lowlands not under cultivation. Forests cover much of the western cordilleras. These forests are complex, with species changing with the altitude. Dense forests, containing some valuable hardwoods, swathe the rain-drenched Pacific slopes.

Wildlife The wildlife regions correspond to the climatic regions. Polar bears, seals, musk oxen, caribou, lemming and Arctic foxes are among the animals of the Arctic.

The boreal forest contains black bears, beaver, moose and Canadian lynx. Deer live throughout Canada. The white-tailed deer is a familiar sight in the south.

The prairies have their own typical species, such as gophers and jackrabbits. Several sure-footed species, such as Rocky Mountain sheep and mountain goats, inhabit the western cordilleras.

Economy The Canadian economy has grown quickly since World War II and with a per capita GNP of $11,400 in 1981, Canada was one of the world's richest nations. Its economy is still expanding – it grew steadily in real terms by 2.6 percent per year in 1970–80 – and Canadians now enjoy one of the world's highest standards of living.

Manufacturing is the main sector of the economy, contributing 19 percent of the GDP in 1980. Industry as a whole contributed 32 percent, by comparison with agriculture which accounted for 4 percent, and service industries 64 percent. But underlying Canada's post-war development are its great mineral resources.

Mining Canada's chief industry at present is petroleum extraction. Alberta has rich oilfields and pipelines transport oil from Edmonton to both Vancouver and Montreal. At the end of 1980, 22,160 miles (35,662 km) of pipelines were in use.

The chief minerals, in order of the value of their production in 1981, were petroleum and natural gas, copper, nickel, iron ore, zinc, potash and coal. Canada is also among the world's top ten producers of antimony, asbestos, gold, lead, silver, tungsten and uranium.

Alberta, mainly because of its oil and natural gas production, produced 53 percent of the total value of Canada's mineral output in 1981. Other major producers were Ontario (13 percent), British Columbia (9 percent) and Saskatchewan and Quebec (7 percent each).

Farming Agriculture now employs only 5 percent of the workforce, but it contributes about 11.5 percent of Canada's exports.

Especially important are cereals, and Canada ranks among the top ten producers of barley, oats, rye and wheat. Canada has a short growing season, but the use of a fast-ripening wheat has made Canada a major wheat exporter and a granary for the world.

Only 7 percent of Canada is farmland and only half of this is under cultivation. About three-fifths of the cultivated land is in the prairie provinces of Saskatchewan and Manitoba. The other prairie province, Alberta, is drier and better suited to rearing beef cattle.

The leading dairy farming provinces are Quebec and Ontario, which together account for about 70 percent of the total dairy production.

Ontario is also the leading province for sheep and pig farming.

Forestry and Fishing Forests cover about 37 percent of Canada, which is the world's third largest producer of softwoods. It is also the second largest producer of wood pulp and the leading producer of newsprint – it produced about 35 percent of the world's output in 1980.

Fishing, Canada's oldest industry, is also important, especially in the Grand Banks off Newfoundland and Nova Scotia, off British Columbia and in inland waters. Major products by value are salmon, cod, lobster and herring.

The old fur trade also continues. Beaver is the most important of the wild animals still hunted, as also are muskrat, fox and lynx. Mink are reared on farms.

Manufacturing and Trade The chief industrial region is the St Lawrence valley and the Lower Great Lakes area, and Ontario is the most industrialized of Canada's ten provinces.

Canada is the world's fourth largest producer of electrical energy and the tenth producer of steel. Of the electrical energy, 68 percent comes from hydroelectric stations and 9 percent is produced by nuclear power stations.

Manufactured goods, including motor vehicles and parts, lead the exports. (Canada is the world's ninth largest producer of cars.) Other manufactures, petroleum and natural gas, and food and animals are also exported.

Canada's chief trading partner is the United States, which took 70 percent of Canada's exports and supplied 67 percent of its imports in 1981. Other major trading partners are Japan, Britain, Venezuela and West Germany.

Communications In such a vast country, communications are important. In 1976, Canada had 549,462 miles (884,275 km) of roads, of which 81 percent were surfaced. In 1980, 41,675 miles (67,069 km) of main rail track were in use. There are two main rail systems. The Canadian National Railway is government-owned. The Canadian Pacific Railway is a joint-stock company.

One of the most important arteries of trade is the St Lawrence Seaway, which is 189 miles (304 km) long. Officially opened in 1959, it enables ocean-going ships to enter the Great Lakes. But it is closed for 3½ months in winter, although ice-breakers keep the St Lawrence estuary open.

Tourism Tourism is a growing industry. In 1981, nearly 42 million tourists visited Canada.

ST. PIERRE & MIQUELON IS

Area: 93 sq miles (242 km²)
Population: 6,000
Population Growth Rate: na
Capital: St Pierre, pop. 5,000
Language: French
Religion: Christianity
Currency: Franc = 100 Centimes

THE SAINT-PIERRE AND MIQUELON ISLANDS form an Overseas Department of France. The islands lie off the south coast of Newfoundland.

Culture and People French immigrants settled on the islands in the early 17th century. Although the islands changed hands several times between France and Britain, they became permanently French in 1816.

The islands became an Overseas Department of France in 1976. They send one deputy and one senator to the French parliament. Local government is in the hands of a Commissioner and an elected General Council.

The Land There are eight islands in two groups. The Saint-Pierre group covers 10 square miles (26 km²) and the Miquelon-Langlade group 83 square miles (216 km²). The climate is mild and moist, but the islands consist mainly of bare rock.

Economy Fishing is the main industry, especially for cod. France makes sizeable grants in order to maintain the islands.

GREENLAND

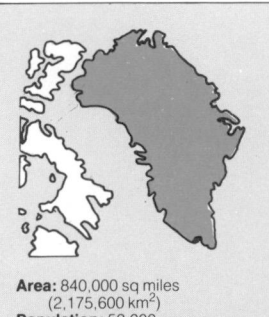

Area: 840,000 sq miles (2,175,600 km²)
Population: 52,000
Population Growth Rate: 0.5% pa
Capital: Godthaab, pop. 9,700
Languages: Greenlandic, Danish
Religion: Christianity
Currency: Krone = 100 Ore

GREENLAND is the world's largest island. It became part of Denmark in 1953.

In 1979 Greenlanders elected their own parliament and, in the early 1980s, they decided to withdraw from the European Economic Community, although Denmark remains a member. Greenland is important strategically. It contains US bases which are part of the NATO system.

Culture and People Norsemen founded a colony on Greenland in about AD 960. It was from this colony that Leif Ericson probably sailed to North America. This colony lasted about 500 years. It disappeared possibly because the weather changed for the worse, or because of attacks by Eskimos and pirates.

Greenland was recolonized by Denmark in 1721. Modern Greenlanders are of mixed Eskimo and European origin.

The Land Nearly 85 percent of Greenland, which lies mostly within the Arctic Circle, lies under a vast ice sheet, which has an average height of 4,500 feet (1,372 m) above sea-level. The people live in coastal areas where the snow melts in the spring.

Economy Fishing has replaced the hunting of sea mammals as the chief activity. Fish processing, construction and trade are also important. Greenland contains various minerals, but mining is difficult in this frozen land.

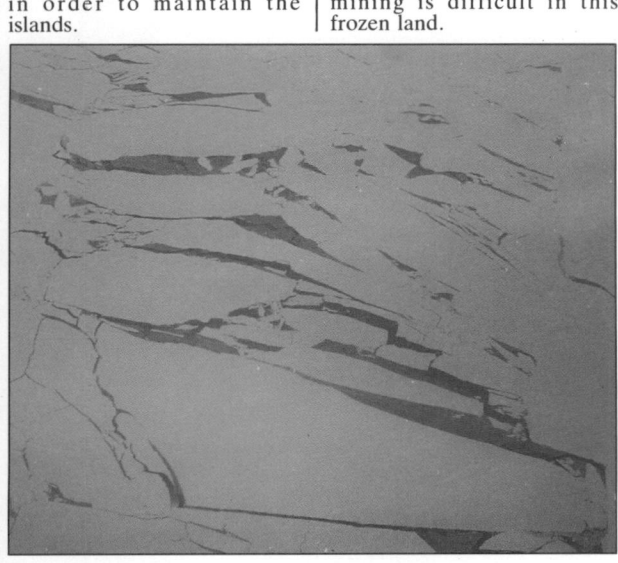

Polar ice starts to break up off the coast of Greenland.

United States of America

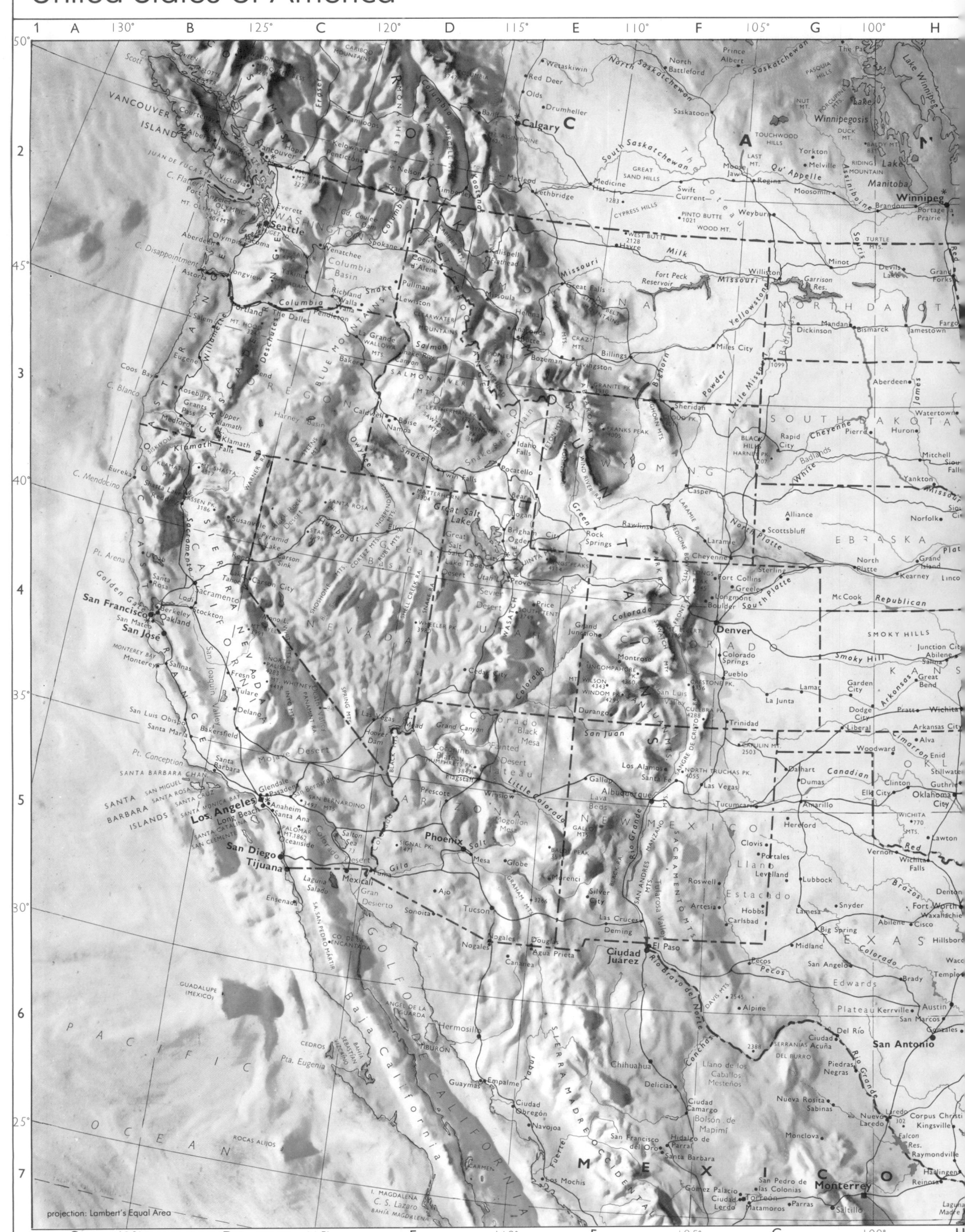

projection: Lambert's Equal Area

Western United States of America

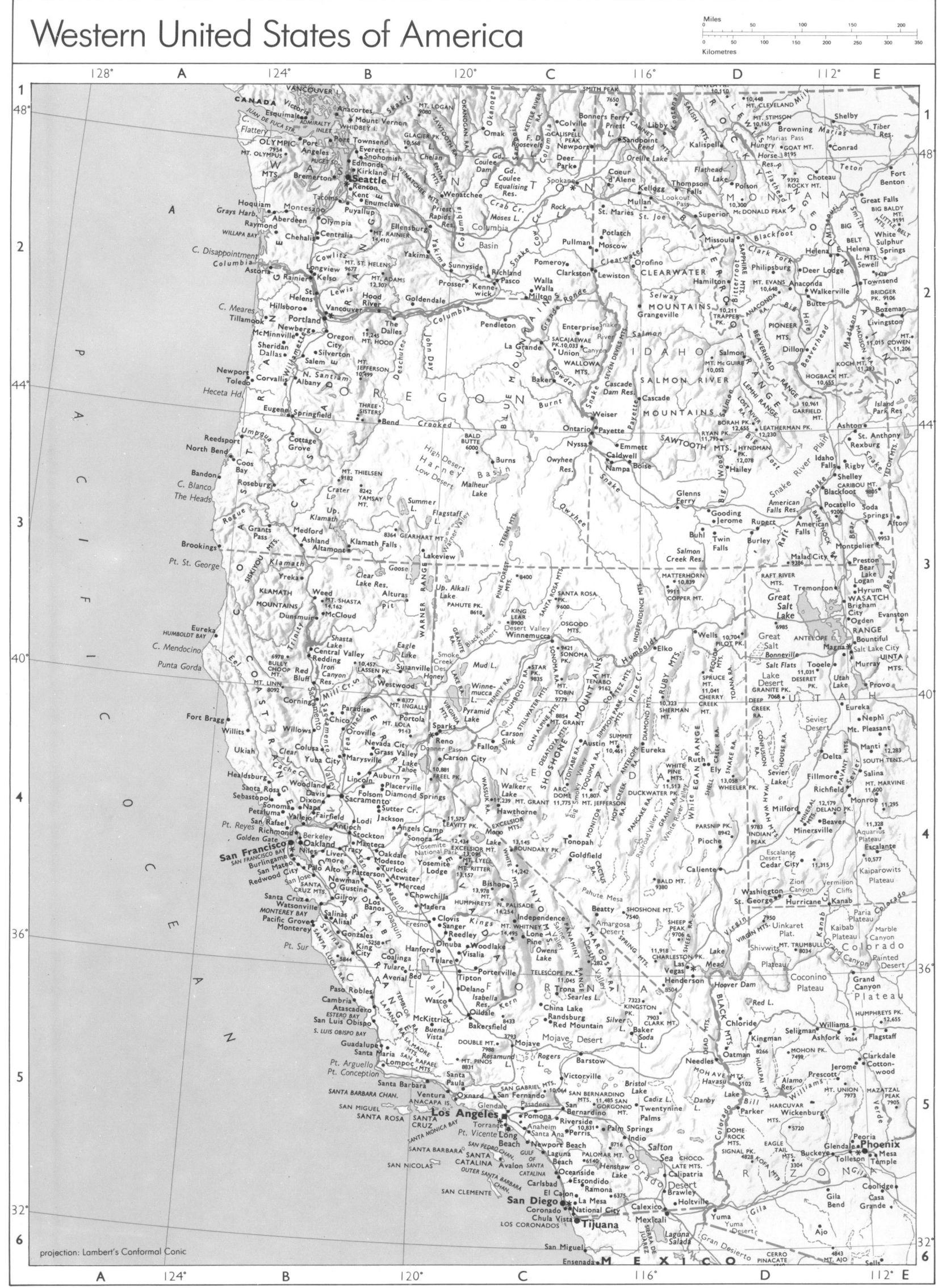

projection: Lambert's Conformal Conic

U.S.A.

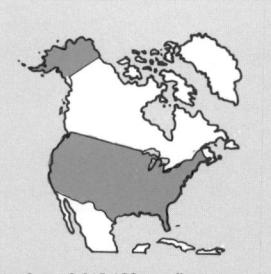

Area: 3,615,122 sq miles (9,363,123 km²)
Population: 226,546,000 (1980)
Population Growth Rate: 1% pa
Capital: Washington DC, pop. 638,000
Language: English
Religion: Christianity (95% of church members)
Currency: Dollar = 100 Cents

The United States has a diverse population, with Amerindians and people whose ancestors came from Europe, Africa and Asia.

THE UNITED STATES OF AMERICA is the world's fourth largest nation, both by its area and population. It consists of 50 states and the Federal District of Columbia, which contains the capital city of Washington.

The area between Canada and Mexico, called the conterminous or continental United States, consists of 48 states. Alaska, the 49th and largest state, is in the northwestern corner of North America, while Hawaii, the 50th state, is about 2,400 miles (3,862 km) off the west coast, in the central Pacific Ocean.

Culture and people The first inhabitants of the conterminous United States were the Amerindians, who probably numbered about two million before the European conquest of the West. Contact with Europeans undermined their cultures. On the one hand European diseases, to which the Amerindians lacked resistance, killed many people; on the other the use of firearms led to the obliteration of the wild animals on which these hunting communities depended.

Wars also took a heavy toll and, by 1890, the year of the last battle which took place at Wounded Knee, the Amerindian population had fallen to 248,000. But by 1980, it had risen again to 1,418,000, although this represented only 0.6 percent of the total population.

Following the voyages of discovery by Christopher Columbus (1492) and John Cabot (1497), the first Europeans who were actively involved in exploring the United States were Spaniards in the south and southwest, and the French who sent the Italian Giovanni da Verrazano to explore the eastern seaboard in 1524. He probably discovered the mouth of the Hudson River during his voyage from North Carolina to Newfoundland, although like other navigators, he failed to find the main prize, the Northwest Passage to Asia.

The Spaniards founded the oldest continuously inhabited settlement in the United States at St Augustine, Florida, in 1565.

In 1584, Sir Walter Raleigh organized the establishing of an English base in North Carolina. He named the eastern seaboard Virginia after the Virgin Queen, Elizabeth I. But his attempts in 1584 and 1587 to found a settlement on Roanoke Island in Pamlico Sound were unsuccessful.

However, in 1607, the English Virginia Company sponsored a settlement at Jamestown, Virginia. At first the settlers suffered greatly, but after receiving assistance and advice from local Amerindians, the colony survived.

In 1620, the Pilgrim Fathers, fleeing from persecution, landed in Massachusetts and founded Plymouth. Gradually, English influence spread down the eastern coast. In 1664, the English took over the island of Manhattan, New York, from the Dutch, who had bought it from the Amerindians in 1626 for goods worth $24.

The French, who had been active in exploring eastern Canada, explored the Mississippi region. After Robert Cavelier, Sieur de La Salle, had claimed the Mississippi valley for France in 1682, the French colony of Louisiana was founded in 1699.

Following the Seven Years' War (1756–63), British control extended westwards to the Mississippi, but the colony of Louisiana still covered a large area.

At this time, there were 13 British colonies: New Hampshire, Massachusetts, Rhode Island, Connecticut, New Jersey, New York, Pennsylvania, Delaware, Maryland, Virginia, North Carolina, South Carolina and Georgia. The colonies had a population of about 1.5 million, most of whom were of British origin, although there were also some Germans, French and a considerable number of Black slaves.

The American Revolution The War of Independence (1775–81) was heralded by the Boston Tea Party (1773), which symbolized the settlers' resentment of British 'taxation without representation'.

On July 2, 1776, the Continental Congress, which had been founded to oppose British laws called the Intolerable Acts, voted for

The Supreme Court, in Washington DC, is the highest court in the United States. It is built of white marble.

independence. On July 4, the Congress adopted the Declaration of Independence. Under the brilliant leadership of General George Washington, the colonists, who thought of themselves as Americans rather than Britons, won the war when British forces surrendered at Yorktown. In 1783, Britain recognized the independence of the new republic.

The US Constitution was written in 1787. This Constitution forms the basis of the present form of government, which is composed of three branches: the executive, the legislature and the judiciary.

Executive power is vested in the President, and legislative power is vested in Congress, which now consists of a Senate of 100 members (two from each state), and a 435-member House of Representatives. The highest court in the judiciary is the Supreme Court. Under the federal system of government, each state is self-governing in local matters, with its own executive (the Governor), legislature and judiciary.

George Washington became the first president in 1787 and, in 1800, the federal government moved to its new capital of Washington DC.

The first half of the 19th century saw a rapid expansion of the new nation. In 1803, the third President, Thomas Jefferson, purchased from France for US $15 million the Louisiana territory, which covered more than 828,000 square miles (2,144,393 km²). With this new land, which spread far beyond the present-day Lousiana, the United States was doubled in size.

The United States also purchased Florida from Spain in 1819 and Alaska from Russia in 1867. Other territory was gained by conquest. The American-Mexican War of 1846–48 led to the acquisition of Texas, New Mexico and most of the southwest, including California.

The first overland crossing of the United States by Meriwether Lewis and William Clark in 1804–06 provided a stimulus for expansion to the west. But while Lewis and Clark met many friendly Amerindians, early pioneers faced fierce opposition from Amerindian tribes who fought to save their territories.

Fur seals at Arena Point, north of San Francisco, California.

Civil War and After In the mid-19th century, the United States was facing a new danger in the east. By 1860, the United States contained 4,441,830 Blacks, who represented 14 percent of the total population.

A few Blacks lived in the states north of Maryland and Delaware, where slavery had been abolished since 1804. But the vast majority lived as slaves on the cotton plantations of the South.

Resentment to mounting abolitionist demands led seven Southern states to secede from the Union in 1861. They formed the Confederate States of America and elected Jefferson Davis as their president.

Civil War broke out when President Abraham Lincoln declared secession illegal. Virginia, Arkansas, North Carolina and Tennessee then joined up with the founders of the Confederacy: Alabama, Florida, Georgia, Louisiana, Mississippi, South Carolina, and Texas.

In January 1863, Lincoln issued a proclamation freeing the slaves in the South. But this could not be enforced until 1865 when the South, in the person of General Robert

E. Lee, surrendered at Appomattox, Virginia.

The South, where most of the war had been fought, was in ruins. Despite a period of reconstruction, bitterness between the North and South continued for many years.

In the North, the war had stimulated the growth of industry and the chance of a new life in a land of apparently unlimited resources attracted a flood of immigrants. Between 1860 and 1910, immigrants arrived in their thousands and the population almost tripled from 31.4 million to almost 92 million.

The construction of the first transcontinental railway began from the east and west in 1862 and, on April 9, 1869, the two sections met. By the end of the century, improved communications led to an enormous expansion of the populations of the western states.

Between 1860 and 1900, the number of farms in the United States increased from two million to six million. The first wave of European farmers who settled on the prairies were mostly ranchers. But after the invention of barbed wire in 1873, the ranchers had to compete with home-steaders, who effectively ended open-range farming by the 1890s.

A World Power In 1898, the Spanish-American War, in which the United States fought to free Cuba from Spanish rule,

Far left Monument Valley, Arizona, is familiar to many people who have never visited the United States, because the director John Ford made nine of his finest Western movies there, including *Stagecoach* (1939).

Left At sunset, the Grand Canyon, Arizona, is a spectacular sight, justifying its status as one of the natural wonders of the world.

Opposite (left to right): Mansions and luxury hotels now line Florida's Gold Coast, most of which was swamp only 50 years ago; Pueblo Indian basket dancers in New Mexico; and an apartment block in Chinatown, on the island of Manhattan, in New York City.

led to the acquisition of the nation's first colonies: Guam, the Philippines and Puerto Rico. In the same year she annexed Hawaii.

American influence in the Pacific increased after the opening of the Panama Canal in 1914. Until 1979, the United States governed a strip of land along the Canal, but this Panama Canal Zone has been returned to Panama. The United States retains control over the Canal itself until 1999.

THE FIFTY STATES

state (and abbreviation)	total area square miles	total area square kilometres	population (1980 census)	capital	year joined Union
Alabama (Al)	50,767	131,486	3,893,888	Montgomery	1819 (22)
Alaska (Ak)	570,833	1,478,450	401,851	Juneau	1959 (49)
Arizona (Ariz)	113,508	293,984	2,718,215	Phoenix	1912 (48)
Arkansas (Ark)	52,078	134,881	2,286,435	Little Rock	1836 (25)
California (Cal)	156,299	404,813	23,667,902	Sacramento	1850 (31)
Colorado (Colo)	103,595	268,310	2,889,964	Denver	1876 (38)
Connecticut (Conn)	4,872	12,618	3,107,576	Hartford	1788 (5)
Delaware (Del)	1,932	5,004	594,338	Dover	1787 (1)
Florida (Fla)	54,153	140,204	9,746,324	Tallahassee	1845 (27)
Georgia (Ga)	58,056	150,364	5,463,105	Atlanta	1788 (4)
Hawaii (Hi)	6,425	16,640	964,691	Honolulu	1959 (50)
Idaho (Id)	82,412	213,446	943,935	Boise	1890 (43)
Illinois (Ill)	55,645	144,120	11,426,518	Springfield	1818 (21)
Indiana (Ind)	35,932	93,063	5,490,224	Indianapolis	1816 (19)
Iowa (Ia)	55,695	144,949	2,913,808	Des Moines	1846 (29)
Kansas (Kan)	81,778	211,804	2,363,679	Topeka	1861 (34)
Kentucky (Ky)	39,669	102,742	3,660,777	Frankfort	1792 (15)
Louisiana (La)	44,521	115,309	4,205,900	Baton Rouge	1812 (18)
Maine (Me)	30,995	80,277	1,124,660	Augusta	1820 (23)
Maryland (Md)	9,837	25,478	4,216,975	Annapolis	1788 (7)
Massachusetts (Mass)	7,824	20,264	5,737,037	Boston	1788 (6)
Michigan (Mich)	56,954	147,510	9,262,078	Lansing	1837 (26)
Minnesota (Minn)	79,548	206,028	4,075,970	St Paul	1858 (32)
Mississippi (Miss)	47,233	122,333	2,520,638	Jackson	1817 (20)
Missouri (Mo)	68,945	178,567	4,916,686	Jefferson City	1821 (24)
Montana (Mont)	145,388	376,553	786,690	Helena	1889 (41)
Nebraska (Nebr)	76,644	198,507	1,569,825	Lincoln	1867 (37)
Nevada (Nev)	109,894	284,624	800,493	Carson City	1864 (36)
New Hampshire (NH)	8,993	23,292	920,610	Concord	1788 (9)
New Jersey (NJ)	7,468	19,342	7,364,823	Trenton	1878 (3)
New Mexico (N Mex)	121,335	314,256	1,302,894	Santa Fe	1912 (47)
New York (NY)	47,377	122,706	17,558,072	Albany	1788 (11)
North Carolina (NC)	48,843	126,503	5,881,766	Raleigh	1789 (12)
North Dakota (N Dak)	69,300	179,486	652,717	Bismarck	1889 (39)
Ohio (Oh)	41,004	106,200	10,797,630	Columbus	1803 (17)
Oklahoma (Okla)	68,655	177,816	3,025,290	Oklahoma City	1907 (46)
Oregon (Oreg)	96,184	249,115	2,633,105	Salem	1859 (33)
Pennsylvania (Pa)	44,888	116,259	11,863,895	Harrisburg	1787 (2)
Rhode Island (RI)	1,055	2,732	947,154	Providence	1790 (13)
South Carolina (SC)	30,203	78,225	3,121,820	Columbia	1789 (8)
South Dakota (S Dak)	75,952	196,715	690,768	Pierre	1889 (40)
Tennessee (Tenn)	41,155	106,591	4,591,120	Nashville	1796 (16)
Texas (Tex)	262,017	678,621	14,229,191	Austin	1845 (28)
Utah (Ut)	82,073	212,568	1,461,037	Salt Lake City	1896 (45)
Vermont (Vt)	9,273	24,016	511,456	Montpelier	1796 (14)
Virginia (Va)	39,704	102,833	5,346,818	Richmond	1788 (10)
Washington (Wash)	66,511	172,263	4,132,156	Olympia	1889 (42)
West Virginia (W Va)	24,119	62,468	1,949,644	Charleston	1863 (35)
Wisconsin (Wis)	5,426	140,963	4,705,769	Madison	1848 (30)
Wyoming (Wyo)	96,989	251,200	469,557	Cheyenne	1890 (44)

(District of Columbia: 63 sq mi [163 km²], pop 638,333)

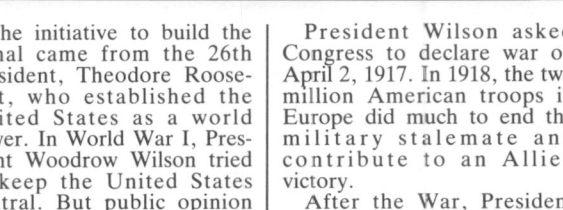

The initiative to build the Canal came from the 26th President, Theodore Roosevelt, who established the United States as a world power. In World War I, President Woodrow Wilson tried to keep the United States neutral. But public opinion increasingly supported the Allied cause, and after Germany had proclaimed unlimited submarine warfare in January 1917, the move to war became irresistible.

President Wilson asked Congress to declare war on April 2, 1917. In 1918, the two million American troops in Europe did much to end the military stalemate and contribute to an Allied victory.

After the War, President Wilson strongly favoured the establishment of the League of Nations. But Congress voted against joining the League, and the United States reverted to a policy of isolationism.

The country prospered in the 1920s, but a business crash in 1929 led to massive unemployment. In 1933, Franklin D. Roosevelt became the 32nd president and he revitalized the country with his 'New Deal' policies.

Roosevelt was the longest-serving president, remaining in office until he died in 1945. (A constitutional amendment in 1951 now limits a President to two four-year terms, plus two years for a Vice-President who has succeeded to the office of President.)

On December 7, 1942, Japan attacked the American naval base at Pearl Harbor, Hawaii. Congress declared war on Japan and, three days later, on Germany and Italy. American forces fought not only in the Pacific, but also in Europe.

Harry S. Truman became president in April 1945, just before Germany's unconditional surrender on May 7, 1945. He ordered the dropping of atomic bombs on Hiroshima and Nagasaki, in Japan, which led to Japan's surrender in September.

After World War II, the United States and the USSR emerged as the two superpowers, although they were divided by ideology. Periods of détente alternated with spells of 'Cold War'. But successive Democratic and Republican party presidents, namely Truman, Dwight D. Eisenhower, John F. Kennedy, Lyndon Johnson, Richard M. Nixon, Gerald Ford, James Earl Carter and Ronald Reagan have all firmly opposed Communist expansion.

The United States has been involved in the defence of Europe through the North Atlantic Treaty Organization and Americans have fought in wars against Communist forces in Korea (1950–53) and Vietnam (1961–73). The United States has also supported anti-Communist groups in the Americas. A setback to that policy occurred in 1959, when Communist forces led by Fidel Castro, took power in Cuba. But in 1962, President Kennedy forced the USSR to withdraw its missiles from the island.

Another example of US intervention in the region occurred when US troops occupied the West Indian island of Grenada in 1983 in order to overthrow a Marxist regime.

But the United States has also served as a mediator in world affairs. For example, it helped to achieve a peace treaty between Egypt and Israel in 1979.

At home, the United States has made much material progress in raising the living standards of most people, though not without some damage to the environment, particularly through industrial pollution.

However, poverty still exists. About 25 million Americans were classed as living below the poverty line in 1970. Two-thirds of these people were poor whites, many of whom lived in the Appalachians and the South. In 1973, the income of the average Black family was about 60 percent of that of whites.

Other problems which have concerned people in the United States in recent years are urban decay, increasing crime, the use of narcotic drugs, and the alienation of many young people. But in the last 25 years, much progress has been made in the field of civil rights. And the American genius for technological invention continues, as exemplified by the US Moon landing in 1969.

Population Growth In 1790, the United States had a population of nearly 3,930,000. Some 3,172,000 people were whites, 89 percent of whom were Anglo-Scottish. The rest were Black slaves.

The population increased rapidly in the 19th century, partly through natural increase, and partly because of immigration, which has played a great part in American history. Between 1820 and 1979, the number of immigrants totalled more than 49 million.

At first, most immigrants came from the British Isles. As late as 1860, the population was fairly homogenous. Apart from 4.4 million Blacks, 44,000 Amerindians and 35,000 Chinese, the rest of the population, numbering 26.9 million, or 85.6 percent of the total, were white, mostly Anglo-Saxon Protestants.

After the Civil War, immigrants from other parts of Europe, including the Balkans, Germany, Italy, Poland and Russia, arrived in greater and greater numbers, reaching a peak in 1900–10.

Although second generation immigrants who adopted English as their first language were soon assimilated, new cultures and religions were introduced. Of all the religious affiliations, the majority (54.5 percent) are still Protestants. But 37.4 percent are Roman Catholics, and they form the largest single denomination. Jews (4.4 percent) and Eastern Churches (2.8 percent) make up most of the rest.

In the 1980 census, 83.5 percent of the population was classed as white, 11.7 percent was Black, while 4.8 percent belonged to other racial groups. These minorities included Amerindians; Oriental Americans, including Japanese, Chinese and Filipinos; and Spanish Americans from Mexico, Puerto Rico and Cuba.

Golden Gate Bridge links the city of San Francisco with Marin County and northern California.

Eastern United States of America

Projection: Lambert's Conformal Conic

The annual rate of population increase in 1975–81 was 1 percent, which is considerably lower than the world average of 1.7 percent. But immigration continues. In 1970–79, an average of nearly 430,000 immigrants entered the United States every year.

The average life expectancy at birth in 1900 was 48 years for men and 51 years for women. Large falls in the death-rate were recorded in the first half of the 20th century. Between 1900 and 1954, the death-rate was almost halved from 17.2 per 1,000 to 9.2 per 1,000. And infant mortality rates dropped from 95.7 per 1,000 live births in 1915–19 to 13.1 per 1,000 in 1979. As a result, average life expectancies rose to an average for both sexes of 70 years in 1960, and 75 years in 1981.

The average figures conceal some wide variations. It is estimated that the average age of death among Blacks is 7 years less than the rest of the population. Among Amerindians it can be 20 years less. However, differences are decreasing.

Urbanization The United States is now a highly urbanized society, although in 1790 only 5 percent lived in urban areas. Indeed, only 100 years ago, three-quarters of the population lived in rural areas. In 1960, however, urban areas contain 70 percent of the population and, by 1981, this had risen to 77 percent.

1980 census were:
New York City (7,071,030)
Chicago (3,005,072)
Los Angeles (2,966,763)
Philadelphia (1,688,210)
Houston (1,594,086)

Gateway Arch, St Louis, Mo.

areas, there have been other movements of population. In 1910, 89 percent of Blacks lived in the South, but this percentage had fallen to 53 percent in 1970.

Blacks were in a majority in Washington DC; Newark, New Jersey; Gary, Indiana; and Atlanta, Georgia. Large Black communities also live in New York City, Chicago, Detroit and Philadelphia. Social problems have arisen, however, because the Blacks tend to be concentrated in the poorer sectors of the cities.

Other movements have also taken place, the most significant being a move to the west. In 1900, the Northeast contained 28 percent of the population; the North-central region, 35 percent; the South 32 percent; and the West 5 percent. By 1970, the Northeast contained 24 percent of the population; the North-central region, 28 percent; the South, 31 percent; and the West, 17 percent.

Social Services The states

In 1954, the Supreme Court ruled that segregation in public schools was illegal. The percentage of children completing high school has steadily increased. Enrolment in colleges and universities in 1981 was the equivalent of 42 percent of people between 18 and 24 years of age.

In 1930, 4.8 percent of persons over 14 years of age were illiterate. This per-

Below Florida Keys. **Above** A street party in New York City.

and Chesapeake bays. Farther south are spits and bars, enclosing the Pamlico Sound. Similar features border the coast of Florida. At the southern tip of Florida are a chain of coral islands, the Florida Keys.

The Appalachians is a complex region comprising the Piedmont, the Blue Ridge Mountains (known in the south as the Great Smoky

Saguaro cacti in Arizona.

20,320 feet (6,194 m).

Southern Alaska contains volcanoes, as does Hawaii, which is a chain of volcanic islands in the central Pacific. The active volcanoes, including Mauna Loa and Kilauea, are on the largest island, which is also called Hawaii. Here the dormant Mauna Kea, at 13,796 feet (4,205 m), can claim to be the world's highest mountain if measured from its base. This is because 19,680 feet (5,998 m) of its height is hidden under the ocean.

Climate Arctic conditions occur in Alaska while, by contrast, the largest islands of Hawaii (Hawaii itself, Maui, Oahu and Kauai) are in the tropics.

The continental part of the United States lies in temperate latitudes, but conditions vary greatly from one region to another in this vast country.

The interior plains are subject to icy north winds blowing from the high-pressure air system that forms over northern North America in winter.

The south-central lowlands are hit by tornadoes, which appear to form when warm air from the Gulf of Mexico flows northwards, while cold, dry air flows southwards above it. And regions around the Gulf of Mexico and on the eastern seaboard are also subject to hurricanes which form in the Atlantic.

The California coast has mild weather. For example, the average temperature range at San Francisco is 49°F (9°C) in January and 57°F (14°C) in July. On the Atlantic coast, Washington has an average temperature range of 34°F (1°C) to 77°F (25°C). The northeast is much colder and, due to the chilling effect of the Labrador Current, it has some of the nation's heaviest snowfall. But Florida is much warmer. Miami has an average January temperature of 66°F (19°C).

The interior, far from the moderating influence of the sea, has a more extreme climate. For example, Des Moines, Iowa, has an average temperature range of 19°F (−7°C) in January to 73°F (23°C) in July.

Detroit (1,203,339)
Dallas (904,078)
San Diego (875,504)
Phoenix (789,704)
Baltimore (786,775).
But the populations of metropolitan areas give a rather different picture. In 1983, the ten most populous metropolitan areas were:
New York City (9,120,346)
Los Angeles–Long Beach (7,477,503)
Chicago (7,103,624)
Philadelphia (4,716,818)
Detroit (4,353,413)
San Francisco–Oakland (3,250,630)
Washington DC (3,060,922)
Dallas–Ft. Worth (2,974,805)
Houston (2,905,353)
Boston (2,763,357).

Population Movements In addition to a shift of population from rural to urban

provide social assistance to the poor and they handled most welfare services until the passing of the Social Security Act (1935). More federal legislation followed in the 1960s. By 1970, about 90 percent of workers were covered by the federal social security programme, which entitles the elderly to pensions. In addition, nearly 30 million people belonged to private pension schemes.

Medical services have increased greatly, but most health insurance is on a private basis and many people are not covered by health insurance.

Education is traditionally the responsibility of the states, who provide a system of free schools covering 12 years of education, plus kindergarten.

centage had fallen to 0.6 percent by 1979.

The Land The eastern seaboard, where the early settlers first became established, contains the glaciated New England in the northeast. This rugged region with few lowlands rises to Mount Washington, on whose slopes the fastest known surface wind speed – 231 mph (372 km/h) – was recorded. The New England mountains are part of the Appalachian system.

South of New York, the coastal plain becomes broader, reaching its greatest width in Georgia. The plain extends inland to the Fall Line, along the hard, crystalline rocks of the Piedmont.

The coast contains such deep inlets as the Hudson River estuary and Delaware

Range), the Ridge and Valley region, and the Appalachian plateau. This is a rugged zone of great scenic beauty.

West of the Appalachians the land descends to the central plains drained by the Mississippi and its tributaries. To the north are the Great lakes and the Lake Superior upland. In the south, the Ozark–Ouachita uplands rise above the plain. South again is the Gulf Coast plain, containing the lower Mississippi valley. To the west, the lowlands rise to the Great Plains, drained by the Arkansas, Missouri and Red rivers.

Beyond the Great Plains are the western cordilleras, including the Rocky Mountains in the east and the Sierra Nevada, the Cascade Mountains and the Pacific coast ranges in the west.

Between these mountains are high plateaus and basins. In the north, some of the flat areas are covered by hardened lava. In the south, the Colorado River has worn the Grand Canyon in the Colorado plateau. West of the Sierra Nevada and Cascade ranges are broad, fertile valleys, but the Pacific coastal plains are mostly narrow or non-existent.

The highest peak in the continental United States is Mount Whitney in the southern part of the Sierra Nevada. It is 14,495 feet (4,418 m) above sea-level. The western cordilleras extend northward through Canada into Alaska, where the highest mountain in the United States, Mount McKinley, reaches

Kings Canyon, California, is a blaze of colour in autumn.

Cattle are auctioned at the stockyards at Fort Worth, Texas.

The Central Valley of California is a long and extremely fertile agricultural region.

The northwestern and northeastern coasts are wet. Seattle has an average annual rainfall of 38 inches (965 mm) and New York City has 40 inches (1,016 mm). But the interior is largely drier. Denver has 16 inches (406 mm) a year. The driest area is in the southwest. For example, Yuma, Arizona, has less than 4 inches (102 mm) a year.

Vegetation Alaska contains boreal forest and tundra regions which are extensions of the vegetation zones of Canada. But the southeastern coast of Alaska is milder, and coastal slopes are swathed in forests, including many western hemlock and Sitka spruce.

Farther south, in Washington and Oregon, the Douglas fir becomes dominant in the coastal forests. South again, between southwest Oregon and San Francisco, are forests containing Douglas fir and the giant redwood. But south of San Francisco, the vegetation becomes Mediterranean.

The vegetation of the western cordilleras is extremely varied, with mountain forests, including ponderosa pine and occasional giant sequoias, subalpine forest of white fir and white spruce, and, above the treeline, alpine flora, much like that in Alaska.

But the southwestern basins and plateaus are mostly barren. Saline areas are sometimes without vegetation. Other areas support sagebrush and, in the Sonora Desert, there are varieties of cacti and the ubiquitous creosote bush.

The grasslands of the Great Plains become more luxuriant to the east, where there is more rain. The eastern forests are mixed between the Great Lakes and the New England coast. Hardwood forests once covered most of the central and southern parts of the eastern United States, but they have been largely cut down.

In the far southeast are other mixed forests and southern pine forests, with swamps on the coast.

Wildlife The United States lies in the Nearctic realm and it contains a wide range of wildlife in its varying habitats.

The fossil record reveals that there was a far wider range of animals in the fairly recent past, including camels, horses, mammoths, and sabretoothed tigers. For reasons not entirely understood, many species became extinct in the late Pleistocene epoch.

Other extinctions, like that of the passenger pigeon, which numbered thousands of millions in 1810, but which died out in 1914, were definitely caused by human activity – in this case, hunting for pleasure.

Other animals, such as the buffalo (*Bison bison*) and pronghorn antelope, narrowly escaped extinction. Hunting is not the only way in which native species have been threatened. There has also been the massive desctruction of natural habitats, the introduction of foreign species, such as the European house sparrow, which occupied the niches of native birds, and the use of poisonous pesticides.

However, many fascinating species have survived, including the remarkable Monarch butterfly which migrates in huge swarms between Canada and the southern United States to spend the winter, the now rare California condor and the bald eagle, symbol of the United States, the opossum, North America's only marsupial, bears, like the huge Kodiak bear of Alaska, and so on. Today, with around 40 national parks and other reserves, the United States is doing much to preserve its wonderful natural heritage.

Economy The United States is the world's richest country. It has enormous resources, but its prosperity is also the result of the energy and inventiveness of its people.

In 1981, its gross national product totalled $2,946,020 million. No other country had a comparable GNP. Although the United States contains only 37 percent of the people of North and South America, its GNP is nearly three times greater than the combined

California is one of the top oil-producing states in the USA. This refinery is in Los Angeles.

GNP of all the other countries throughout the two continents.

The GNP of the United States is also greater than the combined GNP of the ten member nations of the European Economic Community. And in 1981, the per capita GNP of the United States was $12,820, as compared with $10,230 for the EEC.

In 1981, agriculture accounted for 3 percent of the GDP, manufacturing, 23 percent, other industry (principally mining), 11 percent, and services, 63 percent. And in 1980, agriculture employed 2 percent of the workforce, industry, 32 percent, and services, 66 percent.

Such figures contrast greatly with the situation existing only 100 years ago, when farming dominated the American economy.

Agriculture From colonial times until the 1920s, the United States seemed to have unlimited resources. Every decade, national farm production rose as increasing areas of forest and grassland were turned over to farming.

In the 1920s and 1930s, the number of farms reached its peak at around 6.5 million. But serious problems had arisen. By clearing the natural vegetation, by over-intensive farming and by over-grazing, farmers had exposed the soil to the wind and rain. By the 1930s, about 60 percent of the country had been affected by soil erosion.

After the 1930s, agricultural production continued to rise, but it was no longer due to an increase in the farm area. There was instead an emphasis on conservation, mechanization (which resulted in a reduction in the workforce), the use of fertilizers, plant hybrids, improved breeds of animals, and more effective control of pests and diseases.

Increasing mechanization made large farms more efficient than small ones. As a result, between 1940 and 1980, the size of farms has doubled, while the number of farms has decreased from 6.35 million to 2.43 million.

Farmland now covers about 44 percent of the country. The nature of farming varies from

place to place. For example, the cool, moist northeast, where hay and dairy products are the chief (but not the only) products, is called the dairy belt. It is well placed for markets in the many large cities, as is the truck-farming region in the Middle Atlantic coastal plains.

The dry interior in North Dakota, South Dakota and Montana is the spring-wheat belt, while the winter-wheat belt is in the south.

East of the wheat belts is the corn (maize) belt of Nebraska, Iowa, Illinois and Indiana. South of this belt is a mixed corn- and winter-wheat belt.

Texas, Louisiana and Mississippi are major cotton producers, which once belonged to a larger pre-Civil War cotton belt in the South. But cotton yields on irrigated land in Arizona and California are now almost twice those in traditional areas. Around the Gulf of Mexico is a humid subtropical crops region.

The western cordilleras are used for grazing, but irrigated land in the inter-montane

Skyscrapers tower above Battery Park, at the southern tip of Manhattan, New York City. They face the Statue on Liberty National Monument of Liberty Island.

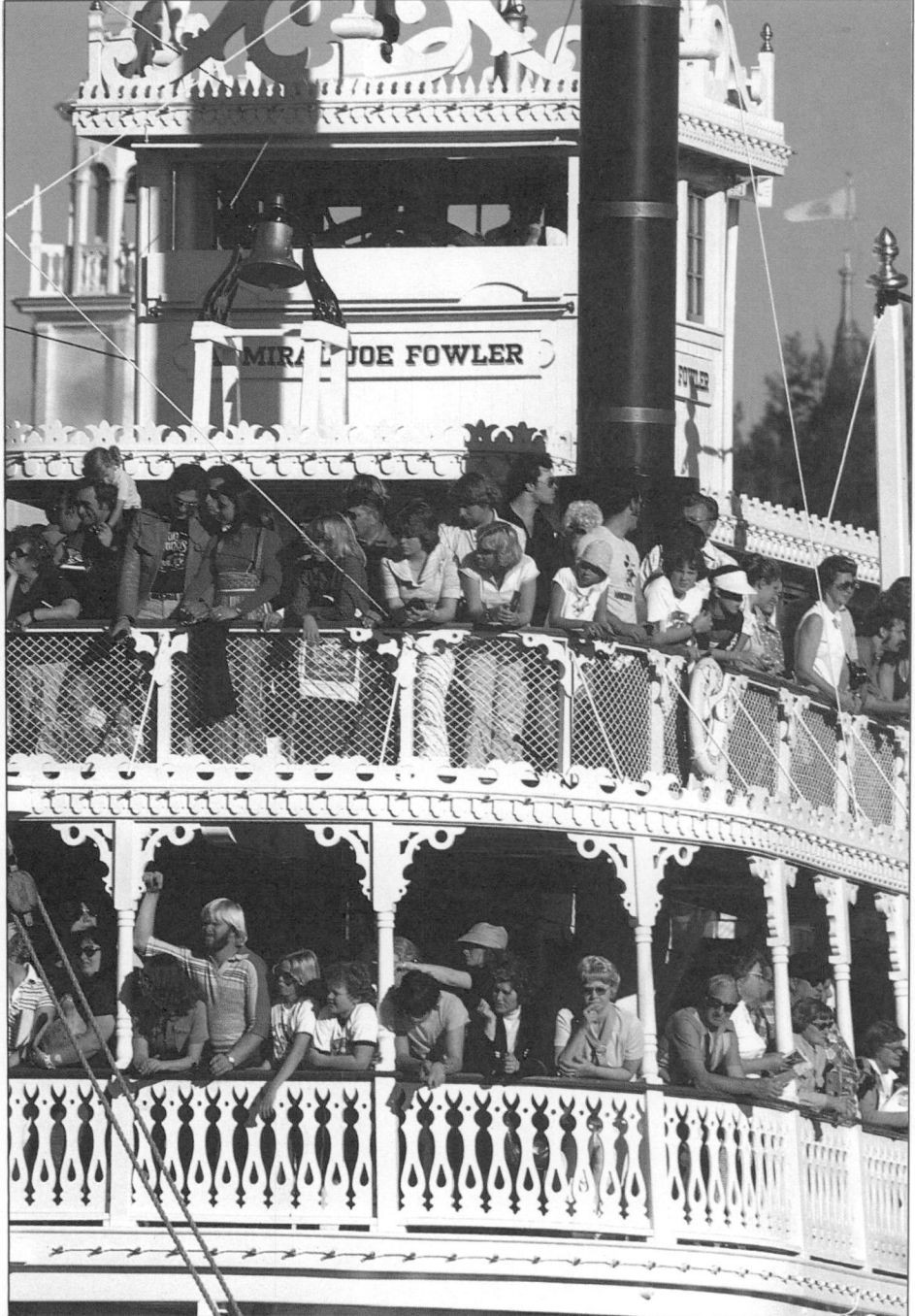

In central Florida, near Orlando, is Walt Disney World, the world's biggest amusement park. Tens of thousands of tourists arrive every week. Some stay for a week or two in the fine hotels.

basins is highly productive. The Californian valleys produce Mediterranean crops, such as citrus fruits, melons and grapes.

The United States ranks high in agricultural production. In 1981, it accounted for 46 percent of the world's corn, 31 percent of its sorghum, 22 percent of its cotton lint, 17 percent of its wheat, 56 percent of its grapefruits, 24 percent of its oranges, and 18 percent of its tobacco.

Of the leading animal products, it produced 23 percent of the world's beef and veal, 24 percent of its poultry meat, 14 percent of its hens' eggs, 19 percent of its cheese, and 8 percent of its butter.

Forestry and Fishing Forests cover about 21 percent of the country. The United States is the world's second largest producer of coniferous wood and newsprint, and it leads in producing wood pulp and paper and paperboard.

The United States produces the world's fourth largest fish catch. Major products include salmon (Alaska and Washington), anchovy, tuna and sole (California), turtles and sponges (Florida), and halibut (Washington).

Mining The United States is second only to the USSR in producing petroleum and coal, accounting for 17 and 25 percent, respectively, of the world production of these fuels. The United States also leads in natural gas production, accounting for 30 percent of the world output.

The main oil and gas fields are in the central lowlands (Texas and Lousiana) and in the Gulf of Mexico. The main coalfields are in Appalachian valleys (in Pennsylvania, West Virginia and Kentucky).

In order of value, the most important metals are iron ore (9 percent of world production), copper (18 percent), molybdenum (63 percent), gold (2.4 percent), silver (11 percent), lead (13 percent), and zinc (6 percent). The United States is also the world's leading producer of phosphate rock, salt, sulphur and uranium.

Manufacturing and Trade The United States leads the world in electrical energy generation. Hydroelectricity accounts for 11 percent and nuclear power stations for 10 percent of the total output.

Many industries process farm products. The United States also leads the world in manufacturing many metals and fuels and oils. It is second only to the USSR in steel production, and it is a major producer of chemicals, consumer goods, machinery and textiles. It ranks second in the world in producing cars and commercial vehicles and television sets.

Because of the size of its economy, the United States is important in world trade and investment. Machinery, transport equipment and other manufactures are leading exports, but food and live animals accounted for 13.4 percent of the exports in 1981. Mineral fuels and lubricants are the largest single group of imports.

Major trading partners are Canada, Japan, Mexico, the United Kingdom and West Germany.

Communications In 1980, public roads totalled 3,852,697 miles (6,200,315 km), of which 88 percent is surfaced. Railways have declined in recent years, but the United States still has 29 percent of the world's rail track. The chief waterway is the St Lawrence Seaway, which has spurred economic development in the Great Lakes region since it was opened in 1959.

The United States has also pioneered the development of the mass media, including radio and television, film-making and advertising.

Tourism In 1981, 23.1 million tourists visited the United States. About 47 percent were from Canada, 16 percent from Mexico, 15 percent from Europe, and 9 percent from Asia.

With their plentiful sunshine, California and Florida have become popular resort areas. Other major attractions are the national parks, many of which offer spectacular scenery.

Mexico and Central America

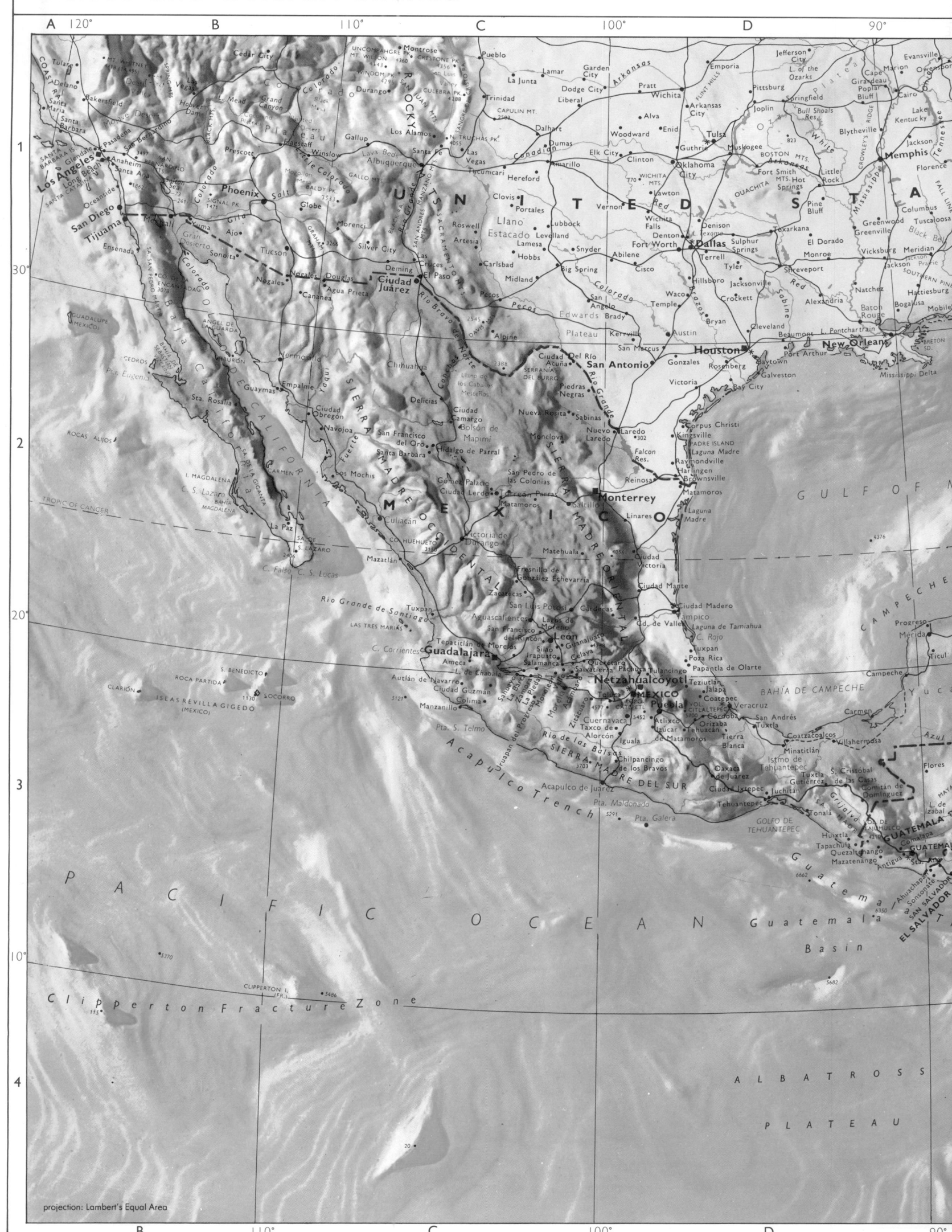

projection: Lambert's Equal Area

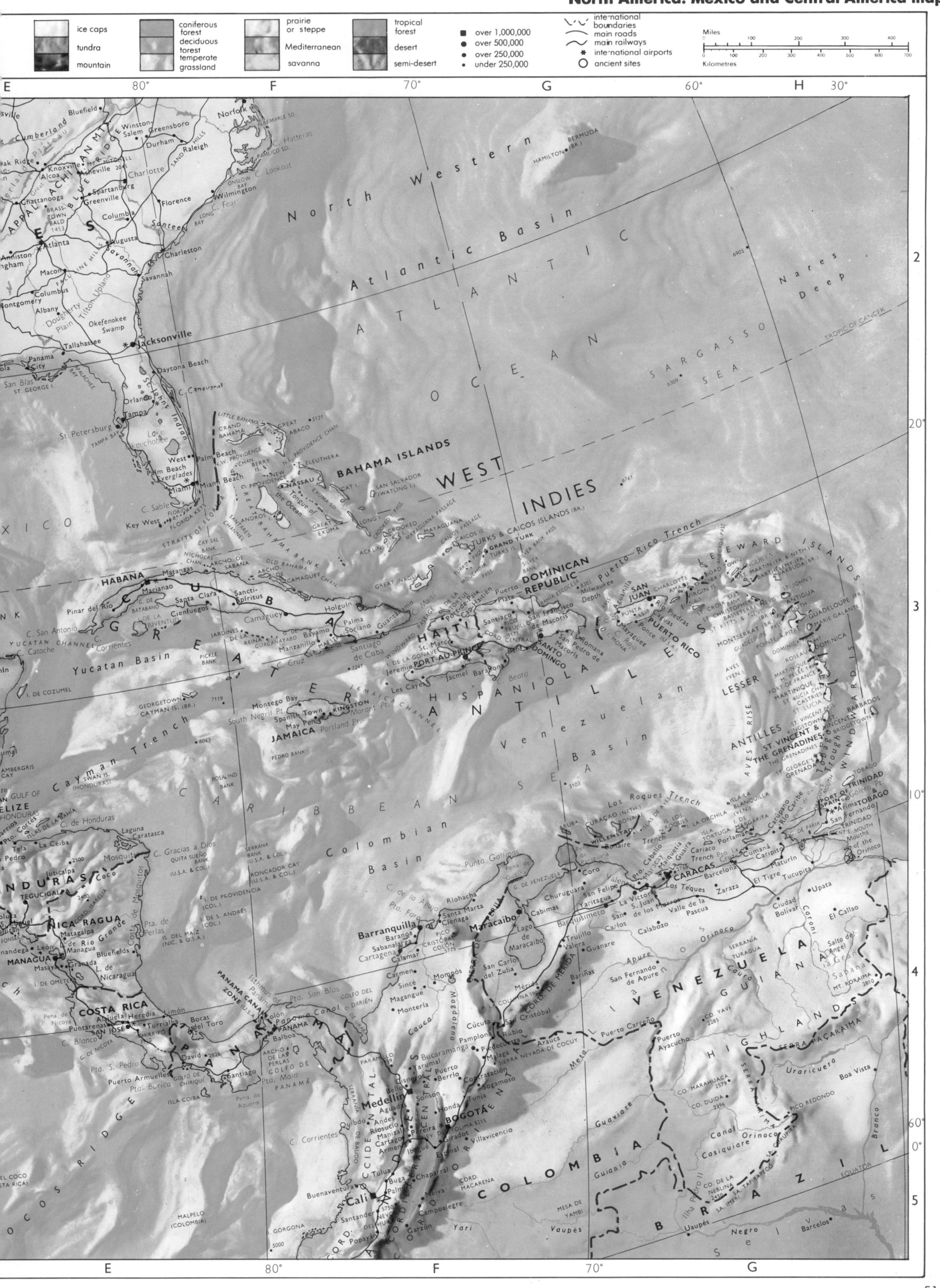

MEXICO

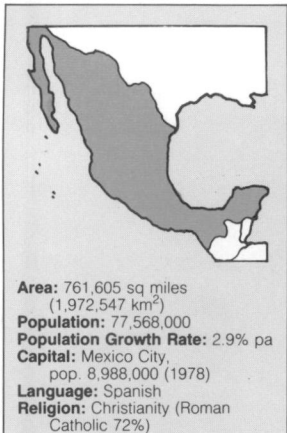

Area: 761,605 sq miles
(1,972,547 km²)
Population: 77,568,000
Population Growth Rate: 2.9% pa
Capital: Mexico City,
pop. 8,988,000 (1978)
Language: Spanish
Religion: Christianity (Roman
Catholic 72%)
Currency: Peso=100 Centavos

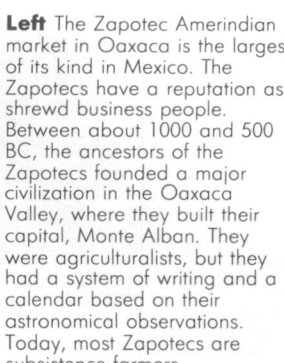

Left The Zapotec Amerindian market in Oaxaca is the largest of its kind in Mexico. The Zapotecs have a reputation as shrewd business people. Between about 1000 and 500 BC, the ancestors of the Zapotecs founded a major civilization in the Oaxaca Valley, where they built their capital, Monte Alban. They were agriculturalists, but they had a system of writing and a calendar based on their astronomical observations. Today, most Zapotecs are subsistence farmers.

Below This photograph shows the Grand Plaza at Monte Alban, which was probably the first city in the Americas. To build it, the Zapotecs levelled a hill overlooking Oaxaca and constructed their pyramidal buildings. Art objects have been excavated from tombs found here. The Olmec and Zapotec cultures were eventually absorbed by the Mayan civilization.

THE UNITED STATES OF MEXICO lies between the United States of America and the republics of Central America. It is the northernmost of the Latin-American countries.

People and Culture The great Amerindian civilizations of the Maya, the Toltecs, and the Aztecs flourished in Mexico from about AD 300 to the arrival of the Spaniards in 1519. Spain ruled the country until 1821, when Mexico became independent after an 11-year struggle.

Mexico originally extended very much farther north. But Texas seceded in 1845, and as a result of war with the United States (1846–48) Mexico lost to the United States California, Nevada, Utah, most of Arizona and New Mexico, and part of Colorado and Wyoming. Revolutions and dictatorships held Mexico back until 1917. Since then a new constitution has led to economic and social progress.

Mestizos form 55 percent of the population, while 29 percent are Amerindians and 15 percent are of European origin. Around 60 percent live in urban areas. Life expectancy had risen to 66 years by 1981, and adult literacy is around 83 percent. Mexico's high population growth rate was showing signs of slowing down in the early 1980s.

The Land Two mountain ranges, the Sierra Madre Occidental and the Sierra Madre Oriental, enclose a large, high central plateau, where most of the people live. To the south of the plateau are a series of lofty volcanic peaks. The vulcanism provides much rich soil, and this region is that of the greatest population density. The mountains contain many lakes and fast-flowing rivers.

In the northwest Baja (Lower) California is a long peninsula almost cut off from the rest of the country by the Gulf of California. Much of it is desert. The coastal plain on the Gulf of Mexico contains thick forests and some very fertile farmland. The Yucatán Peninsula in the southeast is partly dry bush and partly tropical rain forest.

The northern part of Mexico is mostly dry, with deserts. The south is wet and tropical, while in the high valleys and plateaux the climate is temperate.

Economy About 36 per cent of the workforce is engaged in agriculture, but it produces only 13 percent of the GDP. Maize is the main food crop, but for export cotton, sugar, bananas, and coffee are important. There is a great deal of livestock.

Industry grew rapidly in the four years up to 1982, and Mexico has become the world's fourth biggest oil producer. Mines produce coal, copper, gold, iron ore, lead, manganese, mercury, silver, and zinc. Power generation and manufacturing, particularly of automobiles, increased. But in mid-1982 falling oil prices caused a sudden economic crisis, with a 70 percent devaluation. The per capita GNP stood at $2,250 in 1981.

GUATEMALA

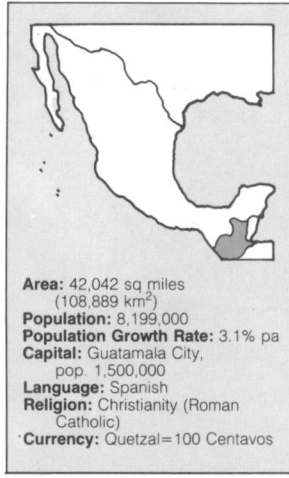

Area: 42,042 sq miles
(108,889 km²)
Population: 8,199,000
Population Growth Rate: 3.1% pa
Capital: Guatamala City,
pop. 1,500,000
Language: Spanish
Religion: Christianity (Roman
Catholic)
Currency: Quetzal=100 Centavos

THE REPUBLIC OF GUATEMALA is the westernmost of the Central American countries.

People and Culture Guatemala was the home of the Maya from about AD 250. It came under Spanish rule from 1523 to 1821, when the Guatemalans broke away. After a spell as part of Mexico,

Guatemala joined the United Provinces of Central America, and became fully independent in 1839. Dictators ruled until 1944, when a constitutional government took office. Since then there have been two military coups.

About 45 percent of the people are Amerindians. The rest are *Ladinos*, people who follow Spanish-American ways of life. They are mostly *mestizos*. Nearly 40 percent of the people, mostly *Ladinos*, live in urban areas. Adult literacy was only about 60 percent in the late 1970s, and life expectancy is only 59 years.

The Land The northern part of the country is a plain, mostly covered by tropical rain forests. The central highland region contains 27 volcanoes and is subject to earthquakes, but most of the people live in this area. Coastal lowlands border the Pacific, and form the main farming area. The climate is tropical, but is relatively mild in the highlands. Rainfall varies from 30 inches to 150 inches (762–3,810 mm).

Economy Agriculture employs 55 percent of the workforce, with coffee the main crop. Bananas, cotton, and chicle gum are also important. Oil exports began in 1980, and minerals include zinc, lead, and antimony. The per capita GNP stood at $1,140 in 1981.

Amerindian market in Antigua, ancient capital of Guatemala.

BELIZE

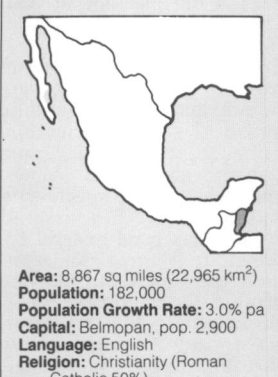

Area: 8,867 sq miles (22,965 km²)
Population: 182,000
Population Growth Rate: 3.0% pa
Capital: Belmopan, pop. 2,900
Language: English
Religion: Christianity (Roman Catholic 50%)
Currency: Belize dollar=100 Cents

BELIZE lies in northeast Central America on the Caribbean.
People and Culture Belize was formerly the British colony of British Honduras. It was renamed Belize in 1973 and became independent in 1981. About 50 percent of the people are of Black African orgin, 20 percent Amerindians and 20 percent *mestizos*. Guatemala claims Belize.
The Land Belize is hot and humid, with uplands in the south and flatter land in the north. The coastlands are swampy. Rainfall varies from 50 to 150 inches (127–380 mm).
Economy Agriculture is the backbone of the economy, employing 42 percent of the workforce. Sugar, citrus fruits and bananas are the main cash crops. Timber is exported from the extensive forests. In 1981 the per capita GNP was $1,080.

Lake Atitlán lies west of Guatemala City. It may occupy a caldera of an extinct volcano. Dormant volcanoes are to the south.

HONDURAS

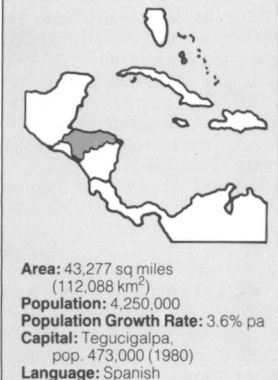

Area: 43,277 sq miles (112,088 km²)
Population: 4,250,000
Population Growth Rate: 3.6% pa
Capital: Tegucigalpa, pop. 473,000 (1980)
Language: Spanish
Religion: Christianity (Roman Catholic)
Currency: Lempira=100 Centavos

THE REPUBLIC OF HONDURAS is a V-shaped country with a very long Caribbean coast and a small Pacific outlet.
People and Culture Maya Amerindians lived in Honduras before the Spaniards arrived in the early sixteenth century. With other Central American countries, Honduras broke free from Spain in 1821, and became independent in 1838. Civil wars, revolutions, and disputes with neighbouring countries have marked Honduras' history ever since.

Nearly 90 percent of the people are *mestizos*. There are a few pure-blooded Amerindians, and some Blacks on the Caribbean coast. Urban dwellers total 36 percent of the population, and life expectancy is low at 59 years. Adult literacy is about 60 percent.
The Land More than 60 percent of the land is mountainous, and forests cover 45 percent, especially in the northeast. There is fertile land on the northern and southern coasts, where the climate is tropical. Many Hondurans live in the valleys and plateaux of the mountain region, where the climate is pleasantly warm.
Economy Agriculture is the mainstay of the economy, and employs 63 percent of the workforce. Bananas and coffee are the principal cash crops. Honduras also exports meat. Industry is on a small scale, and there is only a little mining. In the 1980s Honduras faced a severe economic crisis, compounded by threats from Nicaragua. Almost 60 percent of the people were either jobless or under-employed in 1982. The per capita GNP was only $600 in 1981.

EL SALVADOR

Area: 8,123 sq miles (21,041 km²)
Population: 5,491,000
Population Growth Rate: 3.6% pa
Capital: San Salvador, pop. 1,903,000
Language: Spanish
Religion: Christianity (Roman Catholic 80%)
Currency: Colón=100 Centavos

THE REPUBLIC OF EL SALVADOR is the smallest country in Central America. It lies on the Pacific Ocean.
People and Culture El Salvador formed part of the Spanish empire from 1524 until 1821. From 1823 to 1841 El Salvador was part of the United Provinces of Central America.

Since independence El Salvador has had a politically violent history. The present democratic constitution was adopted in 1962. Since 1972 left-wing guerrillas have fought against the right-wing government, despite that government's efforts to institute land reform. By 1980 violence had escalated into civil war.

About 92 percent of the people are *mestizos*. The rest are white or Amerindian. As elsewhere in Latin America, there is a big gulf between the very rich (about 3 percent of the population) and the very poor. Average life expectancy is only 63 years, and adult literacy is low at 62 percent. Only 41 percent of the people live in urban areas.
The Land El Salvador is mountainous, with a narrow coastal plain. There are several active volcanoes, notably Izalco, known as 'the lighthouse of the Pacific'. The tropical climate becomes temperate in the mountain plateaux.
Economy Half the workforce is engaged in agriculture, and coffee is the main cash crop. Cotton, maize, rubber, and balsam gum are also produced. Industry, developing slowly, accounts for 20 percent of the GDP. In 1981 the per capita GNP stood at only $650.

NICARAGUA

Area: 50,193 sq miles (130,000 km²)
Population: 3,232,000
Population Growth Rate: 4.6% pa
Capital: Manuaga, pop. 553,000 (1978)
Language: Spanish
Religion: Christianity (Roman Catholic)
Currency: Córdoba=100 Centavos

THE REPUBLIC OF NICARAGUA is the largest of the Central American countries.
People and Culture Nicaragua was ruled by Spain from 1534 to 1821. It was part of the United Provinces of Central America until it attained complete independence in 1838.

The history of Nicaragua is

one of dictators and revolts until the period 1912–33, when US Marines kept order.

Members of the Somoza family ruled Nicaragua from 1937 to 1979, when President Anastasio Somoza fled. A Marxist group, the Sandanista National Liberation Front, seized power.

Around 80 percent of the people are *mestizos*. The rest are Blacks, Amerindians, or of European stock. Some 54 percent live in urban areas, and adult literacy stands at 90 percent. But life expectancy is only 57 years.

The Land Highlands, mostly forested, dominate the centre of Nicaragua. Between them and the Caribbean lies the Mosquito Coast, a hot, humid region covered by tropical rain forests. Most of the people live in the Pacific lowlands, or around two large lakes, Managua and Nicaragua, that lie in the west. This area has 60 inches (1,524 mm) of rain a year.

Economy Less than 15 percent of the land is cultivated, but agriculture employs 43 percent of the workforce. Nicaragua exports cotton, coffee, and sugar, with some beef and rice. However, industry represents about one-third of the GDP. The per capita GNP stood at $860 in 1981.

COSTA RICA

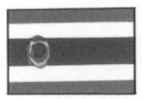

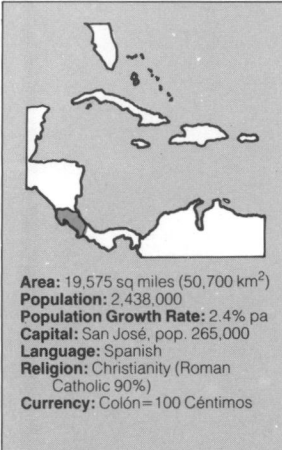

Area: 19,575 sq miles (50,700 km²)
Population: 2,438,000
Population Growth Rate: 2.4% pa
Capital: San José, pop. 265,000
Language: Spanish
Religion: Christianity (Roman Catholic 90%)
Currency: Colón = 100 Céntimos

THE REPUBLIC OF COSTA RICA is one of the more settled and prosperous countries of Central America.

People and Culture Costa Rica was part of the Spanish empire from 1564 to 1821. It was part of the United Provinces of Central America until 1838. After a number of dictatorships and revolutions, democratic government was established in 1919. More than 97 percent of the people are either *mestizos* or of pure European stock. Adult literacy is 90 percent, and life expectancy has risen to 73 years.

The Land Volcanic peaks, many of them active, dominate Costa Rica. Between the mountains lie fertile plateaux. Most of the people live on these plateaux, where the climate is mild and pleasant. Low-lying, swampy tropical forests border the Caribbean; the country's Pacific coast is drier, with some savanna.

Economy Industry accounts for 28 percent of the GDP, though only 44 percent of the people live in urban areas. Almost one-third of the people are engaged in agriculture. Coffee, the main cash crop, produces about half the country's overseas earnings. Bananas and sugar are other major crops. In the early 1980s falling demand for coffee and high oil prices led to an economic crisis, but the per capita GNP in 1981 was stable at $1,430.

PANAMA

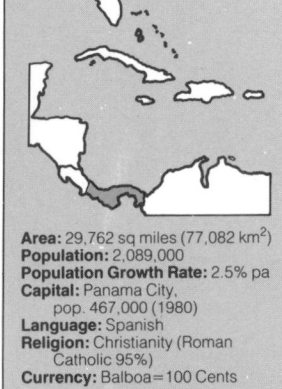

Area: 29,762 sq miles (77,082 km²)
Population: 2,089,000
Population Growth Rate: 2.5% pa
Capital: Panama City, pop. 467,000 (1980)
Language: Spanish
Religion: Christianity (Roman Catholic 95%)
Currency: Balboa = 100 Cents

THE REPUBLIC OF PANAMA is a narrow country linking North and South America.

People and Culture Panama was under Spanish rule from 1519 to 1821. It was then part of Colombia, but tried to break away many times. It finally declared independence, with United States' help, in 1903 in order to permit the construction of the Panama Canal.

Most of the people are of mixed European, Amerindian, and Black African ancestry. More than half live in urban areas, and the life expectancy is now 71 years. Adult literacy is about 85 percent.

The Land Panama is S-shaped with the Caribbean to the north and the Pacific to the south. Hills and mountains cover most of the country. Most Panamanians live in the west. The east is thick tropical forest, the 'Darien Gap' which breaks the Pan-American Highway.

Economy The Panama Canal, for which Panama receives an annual payment, is under US control until 1999, when it will revert to Panama. About 7 percent of the workforce is directly involved with the Canal. Some 27 percent is engaged in agriculture, but though bananas and sugar are grown for export and rice for consumption, Panama imports much of its food. The per capita GNP in 1981 was $1,910.

BAHAMAS

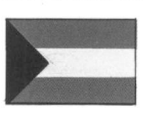

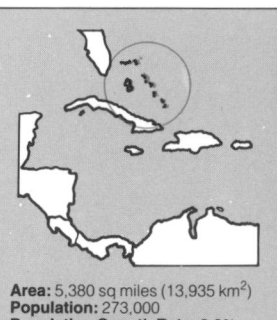

Area: 5,380 sq miles (13,935 km²)
Population: 273,000
Population Growth Rate: 3.3% pa
Capital: Nassau, pop. 130,000 (1977)
Language: English
Religion: Christianity
Currency: Bahamian Dollar = 100 Cents

THE COMMONWEALTH OF THE BAHAMAS is an archipelago country southeast of Florida.

People and Culture British settlers went to the Bahamas in the seventeenth century and the islands became a colony in 1717. They achieved independence from the British in 1973. About 85 per cent of the people are of Black African origin.

The Land The Bahamas consists of 14 large and about 700 small coral islands, plus 2,400 *cays* (islets). There are many pine forests, and the climate is mild and pleasant. About 65 percent of the people live on one of the smaller islands, New Providence. Adult literacy is estimated at about 90 percent.

Economy Tourism is the main activity, with 1,700,000 visitors in 1981. There is little agriculture. The per capita GNP was $3,620 in 1981.

Fumaroles emit columns of steam and various gases in the crater of Volcán Poas in Costa Rica.

CUBA

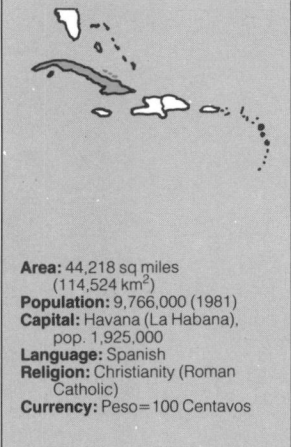

Area: 44,218 sq miles (114,524 km²)
Population: 9,766,000 (1981)
Capital: Havana (La Habana), pop. 1,925,000
Language: Spanish
Religion: Christianity (Roman Catholic)
Currency: Peso = 100 Centavos

THE REPUBLIC OF CUBA is the largest country and island in the West Indies.

People and Culture Cuba was discovered by Columbus in 1492, and Spain started colonizing it in 1511. It remained under Spanish rule until 1898, when a revolt which also sparked off war between Spain and the United States won independence for the Cubans. But they came under US rule until 1902, and again from 1906 to 1909. US influence remained strong until Communists led by Fidel Castro seized power in 1959.

About 75 percent of Cubans are of Spanish descent. Most of the rest are of Black African origin or mixed blood. Life expectancy is 73 years and adult literacy stands at 95 per cent.

The Land Most of Cuba is a gently rolling plain of fertile land. There are three mountain ranges. The climate is tropical but pleasant all year. The average annual rainfall is 54 inches (1,372 mm).

Economy Government farms cover 65 percent of the agricultural land. Cuba ranks third in world sugar production. Tobacco, coffee, rice, and fruit are also grown. Almost one-fourth of the workforce is on the land.

Cuba has good mineral deposits. It is the sixth largest producer of nickel, and also produces iron ore, copper, chromium, gold, and silver. Most trade is with eastern Europe, but Cuba imports more than it exports. The per capita GNP in 1979 stood at $1,410.

JAMAICA

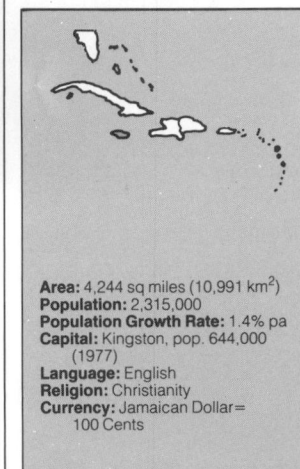

Area: 4,244 sq miles (10,991 km²)
Population: 2,315,000
Population Growth Rate: 1.4% pa
Capital: Kingston, pop. 644,000 (1977)
Language: English
Religion: Christianity
Currency: Jamaican Dollar = 100 Cents

JAMAICA is the fourth largest country in the West Indies.

People and Culture Britain took Jamaica from Spain in 1655 and ruled it until independence in 1962. More than 90 percent of the people are either of Black African ancestry or mixed Black and European origin. Over 40 percent live in urban areas, and adult literacy stands at 90 percent. Life expectancy, at 71 years, has increased by seven years since 1960.

The Land About 85 percent of the island is mountainous. Blue Mountain Peak, the highest point, is 7,402 ft (2,256 m). The tropical climate is tempered by sea breezes. Rainfall varies from 30 inches (762 mm) on the coast to 200 inches (5,080 mm) in the mountains.

Economy Jamaica is the world's third largest producer of bauxite, and manufacturing is increasing. Sugar is the most important agricultural crop, along with bananas and other fruit. Jamaica is also a major producer of rum and coffee – both of which are highly regarded around the world. Tourism is rapidly expanding, and in 1982 the island played host to more than 530,000 visitors. The per capita GNP in 1981 was $1,180.

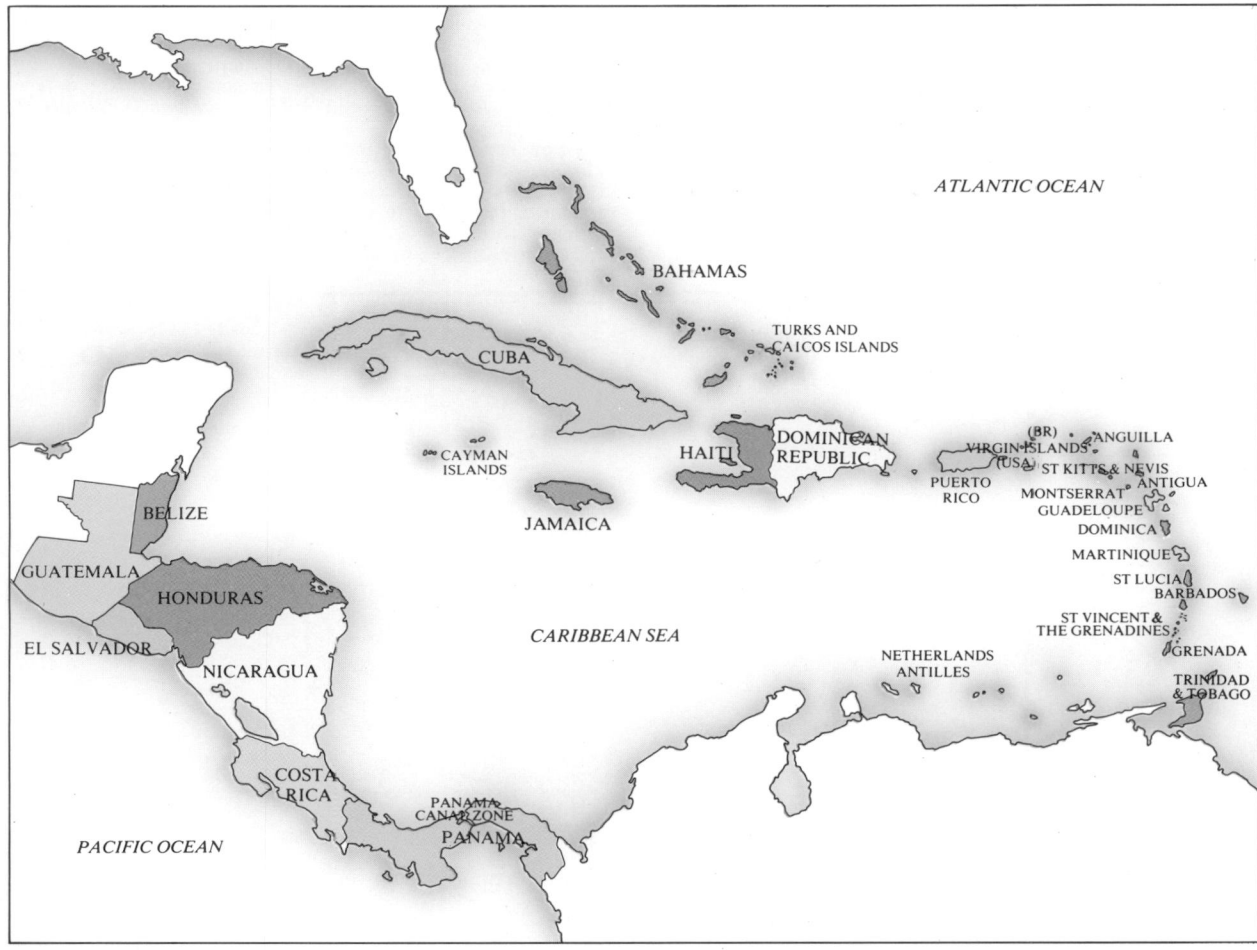

ATLANTIC OCEAN

BAHAMAS

TURKS AND
CAICOS ISLANDS

CUBA

CAYMAN
ISLANDS

HAITI

DOMINICAN
REPUBLIC

(BR)
VIRGIN ISLANDS
(USA)

ANGUILLA

ST KITTS & NEVIS

PUERTO
RICO

MONTSERRAT

ANTIGUA

GUADELOUPE

DOMINICA

BELIZE

JAMAICA

MARTINIQUE

GUATEMALA

HONDURAS

ST LUCIA

BARBADOS

EL SALVADOR

CARIBBEAN SEA

ST VINCENT &
THE GRENADINES

NICARAGUA

NETHERLANDS
ANTILLES

GRENADA

TRINIDAD
& TOBAGO

COSTA
RICA

PANAMA
CANAL ZONE

PACIFIC OCEAN

PANAMA

Central America and the Caribbean belong largely to the cultural region known as Latin America, which includes most of South America. Spanish is the official language of Central America, apart from Belize, and also of the two largest Caribbean nations, Cuba and the Dominican Republic. However, elsewhere in the Caribbean, English, French and Dutch are also spoken – a reflection of its colonial history. The population on the mainland and the islands is Amerindian, European, Black, mestizo and mulatto elements.

HAITI

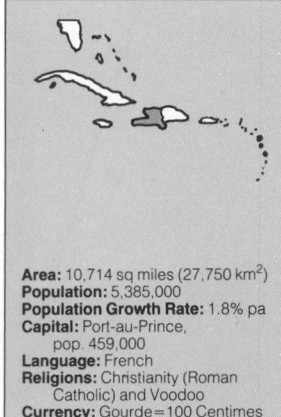

Area: 10,714 sq miles (27,750 km²)
Population: 5,385,000
Population Growth Rate: 1.8% pa
Capital: Port-au-Prince,
pop. 459,000
Language: French
Religions: Christianity (Roman Catholic) and Voodoo
Currency: Gourde=100 Centimes

THE REPUBLIC OF HAITI is the western third of the island of Hispaniola.
People and Culture About 95 percent of the people are descended from Black African slaves. The rest are mulattos, who form a French-speaking educated minority. A Creole dialect is spoken by the rest. Haiti was a French colony which won independence in 1804 in a bloody revolution. Dictators have ruled since 1957. Adult literacy is 23 percent.
The Land Forested mountains cover 80 percent of the country. The climate is tropical but mild in the mountains.

Economy Haiti is the poorest West Indian country, with the per capita GNP only $300 in 1981. Coffee and sugar are grown as cash crops, but most farming is at subsistence level. Bauxite and copper are mined for export.

DOMINICAN REP

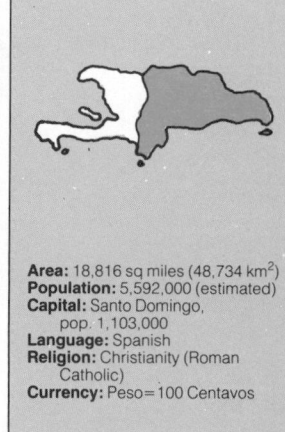

Area: 18,816 sq miles (48,734 km²)
Population: 5,592,000 (estimated)
Capital: Santo Domingo,
pop. 1,103,000
Language: Spanish
Religion: Christianity (Roman Catholic)
Currency: Peso=100 Centavos

THE DOMINICAN REPUBLIC occupies the eastern two-thirds of the island of Hispaniola.
People and Culture Spain controlled the eastern part of the island until 1801, when the people of neighbouring Haiti conquered it. It became independent in 1844, but was under United States' control

from 1916 to 1924. Stable government was established by the dictator Raphael Trujillo from 1930 to 1961.
About 65 percent of the people are mulattos, 20 percent Black, and the rest of European descent. Just over half live in urban areas and adult literacy is only 67 percent.
The Land The terrain is mountainous, and 75 percent of the land is forested. There are fertile valleys and lowlands. The country has a tropical climate.
Economy Almost half the workforce is employed in agriculture. Sugar, coffee, and cocoa beans are the main cash crops. Bauxite, copper, gold, and silver are mined. The per capita GNP was $1,260 in 1981.

A Banana grower brings in his crop in Montserrat.

ST CHRISTOPHER NEVIS

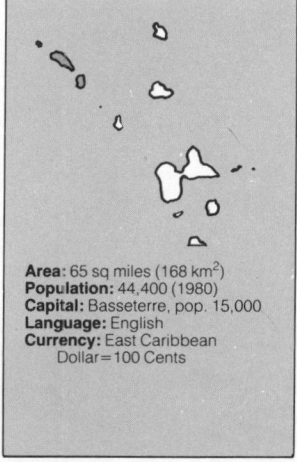

Area: 65 sq miles (168 km²)
Population: 44,400 (1980)
Capital: Basseterre, pop. 15,000
Language: English
Currency: East Caribbean
Dollar=100 Cents

ST CHRISTOPHER-NEVIS is an eastern Caribbean country in the northern Leeward Islands.
People and Culture Most of the people are of Black African descent. Britain owned the islands from 1783. With Anguilla, they became an associated state of Britain in 1967, and independent in 1983. Anguilla chose to stay separate.
The Land The islands of St Christopher (usually called St Kitts) and Nevis are 2 miles (3.2 km) apart. They are mountainous volcanic islands with a high rainfall.
Economy Sugar is the main crop on St Christopher, and

the main export. Cotton is grown on the poorer soils of Nevis, where fewer than 10,000 people live. In 1981 the per capita GNP was $1,040.

ANTIGUA AND BARBUDAS

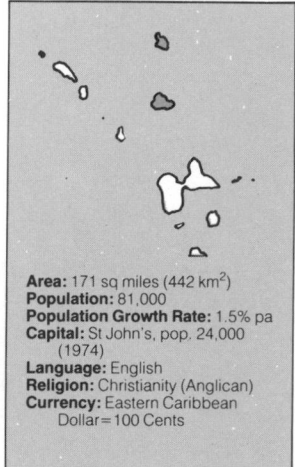

Area: 171 sq miles (442 km²)
Population: 81,000
Population Growth Rate: 1.5% pa
Capital: St John's, pop. 24,000 (1974)
Language: English
Religion: Christianity (Anglican)
Currency: Eastern Caribbean
Dollar=100 Cents

ANTIGUA AND BARBUDA is an independent country in the Leeward Islands.
People and Culture Nearly all the people are descended from Black Africans. The country was a British colony from 1632 until independence in 1981.
The Land The islands of Antigua and Barbuda are the flat tops of old volcanoes. They are 25 miles (40 km) apart. The average temperature is 80°F (27°C).
Economy Tourism is the main activity, and employs most of the people. Farms produce sugar and cotton. The per capita GNP was $1,550 in 1981.

DOMINICA

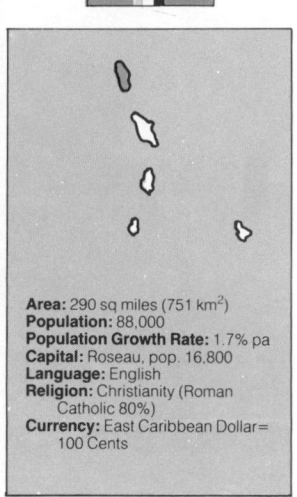

Area: 290 sq miles (751 km²)
Population: 88,000
Population Growth Rate: 1.7% pa
Capital: Roseau, pop. 16,800
Language: English
Religion: Christianity (Roman Catholic 80%)
Currency: East Caribbean Dollar= 100 Cents

THE COMMONWEALTH OF DOMINICA is a country in the Windward Islands.
People and Culture Dominica was a British colony from 1805 to 1978, when it became independent. Most of the people are of Black African origin. Outside the towns they speak a French *patois*.
The Land Dominica is a

mountainous, volcanic island, heavily wooded. It has a wet, tropical climate.
Economy More than 60 percent of the people work in agriculture, and about 33 percent of the land is cultivated. Bananas, fruit, and coconuts are the main exports. Tourism attracted 10,000 visitors to Dominica in 1982. In 1981 the per capita GNP was $750.

of Black African origin. Some speak a French dialect. Less than 20 percent live in urban areas.
The Land St Lucia is mountainous, and covered with tropical forests.
Economy Bananas, cocoabeans, copra, and coconut oil are exported, and more than 100,000 tourists visit the island each year. The per capita GNP was $970 in 1981.

The Land St Vincent itself is volcanic, and has a tropical climate with heavy rainfall. The Grenadines are a chain of small islands stretching towards Grenada, a few miles to the south.
Economy Agriculture is the most important industry. The country is a producer of arrowroot, and also exports bananas, coconuts and spices. The 1981 per capita GNP was $630.

97 percent, and population density is very high.
The Land Barbados is a pear-shaped island, the most easterly of the West Indies. It is mostly flat, with a rich soil and a tropical climate.
Economy Tourism is the main industry, with 353,000 visitors in 1981. About 65 percent of the land is farmed, with sugar the main crop. In 1981 the per capita GNP was $3,500.

cent of the population. A Marxist government took over in 1979 but was overthrown by US marines in 1983.
The Land The island is of volcanic origin. It has rich soil and a mild climate.
Economy Agriculture and tourism are the mainstays of Grenada's economy. Cocoabeans, nutmegs, and bananas are the main exports. In 1981 the per capita GNP was $850.

ST LUCIA

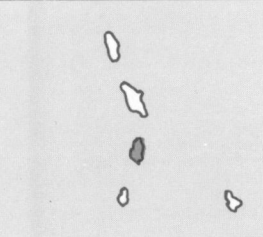

Area: 238 sq miles (616 km²)
Population: 128,000
Population Growth Rate: 1.6% pa
Capital: Castries, pop. 45,000
Language: English
Religion: Christianity (Roman Catholic 90%)
Currency: East Caribbean Dollar = 100 Cents

ST LUCIA is a country in the Windward Islands.
People and Culture France and Britain disputed possession of St Lucia until 1814, when it became a British colony. It was declared independent in 1979. About 10 percent of the people are of British and French descent. The rest are

ST VINCENT AND THE GRENADINES

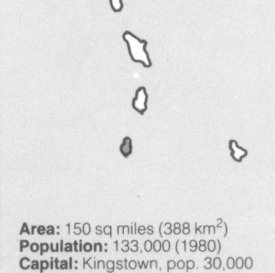

Area: 150 sq miles (388 km²)
Population: 133,000 (1980)
Capital: Kingstown, pop. 30,000
Language: English
Currency: East Caribbean Dollar = 100 Cents

ST VINCENT AND THE GRENADINES is a nation in the Windward Islands.
People and Culture St Vincent was ruled by Britain from 1783 until it became independent in 1979. Most of the people are of Black African origin. Fewer than 25 percent live in urban areas.

BARBADOS

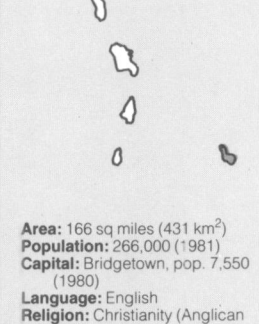

Area: 166 sq miles (431 km²)
Population: 266,000 (1981)
Capital: Bridgetown, pop. 7,550 (1980)
Language: English
Religion: Christianity (Anglican 70%)
Currency: Barbados Dollar = 100 Cents

BARBADOS is an island country in the West Indies.
People and Culture Barbados was a British colony from 1628 to 1966 when it became independent. About 80 percent of the people are of Black African descent, and most of the rest are of mixed African and British origin. Adult literacy is

GRENADA

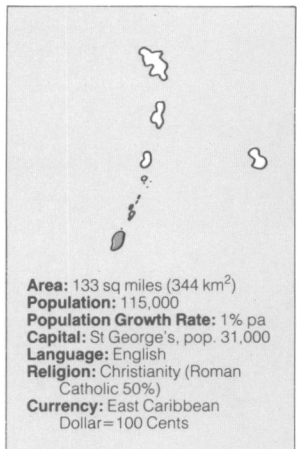

Area: 133 sq miles (344 km²)
Population: 115,000
Population Growth Rate: 1% pa
Capital: St George's, pop. 31,000
Language: English
Religion: Christianity (Roman Catholic 50%)
Currency: East Caribbean Dollar = 100 Cents

GRENADA is the southernmost country in the Windward Islands.
People and Culture Grenada was a British colony from 1873, and gained independence in 1974. Descendants of Black African slaves and people of mixed Black and European origin form 95 per-

TRINIDAD AND TOBAGO

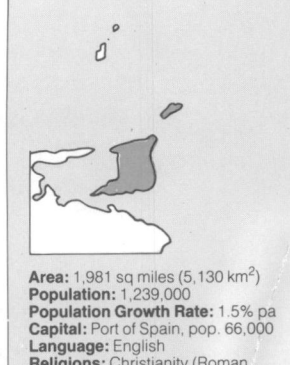

Area: 1,981 sq miles (5,130 km²)
Population: 1,239,000
Population Growth Rate: 1.5% pa
Capital: Port of Spain, pop. 66,000
Language: English
Religions: Christianity (Roman Catholic 36%, Anglican 18%), Hinduism 25%
Currency: Trinidad and Tobago Dollar = 100 Cents

TRINIDAD AND TOBAGO is the nearest West Indian country to South America.
People and Culture Columbus discovered the islands in 1498. Spain colonized Trinidad but ceded it to Britain in 1802. Tobago, formerly Dutch, became British in 1814. Blacks form 45 percent of the people,

Colombia owns the San Andrés and Providencia islands, together with some small keys, in the southwestern Caribbean Sea to the east of Nicaragua.

East Indians 35 percent, and people of mixed origin 17 percent. The rest are European or Chinese. Adult literacy is about 80 percent. Calypso and limbo-dancing originated in Trinidad.

The Land Trinidad, which is 19 times bigger than Tobago, has some hills but is largely flat. Tobago, to the northeast, has a mountain ridge in the centre. The climate is tropical.

Economy Petroleum is the main product, and accounts for 80 percent of exports. Pitch Lake, on Trinidad, is the world's largest source of asphalt. Sugar is the main crop, but agriculture accounts for only 2 percent of the GDP. Nearly 200,000 tourists visit the country annually. In 1981 the per capita GNP was $5,670.

PUERTO RICO

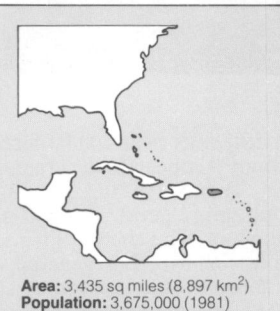

Area: 3,435 sq miles (8,897 km²)
Population: 3,675,000 (1981)
Capital: San Juan, pop. 1,083,664
Languages: English and Spanish
Religion: Christianity (Roman Catholic 80%)
Currency: US Dollar = 100 Cents

THE COMMONWEALTH OF PUERTO RICO is a semi-independent country in the West Indies.

People and Culture Puerto Rico was governed by Spain until 1898 when it was ceded to the United States. It became a self-governing commonwealth within the United States in 1952. Most people are of Spanish descent.

The Land Puerto Rico has a long central mountain chain, with coastal valleys and lowlands. It has a warm, pleasant climate, with between 37 and 200 inches (940–5,080 mm) annual rainfall.

Economy Manufactured goods represent more than 75 percent of the GDP, particularly chemicals and food products. Agriculture accounts for 19 percent, and sugar and coffee are the main crops. The per capita GNP was $3,350 in 1981.

DEPENDENCIES

BERMUDA is a British colony in the western Atlantic. It consists of about 300 small islands with an area of 20 sq miles (53 km²), and a population of about 61,000. The capital is Hamilton, on the largest island, Bermuda. Britain ruled the islands from 1684, and gave them internal self-government in 1968.

Curaçao is the largest island in the Netherlands Antilles. The population is mixed, with European, Black and Asian elements.

Curaçao's buildings and the old cannon reveal Dutch influence.

About 60 percent of the people are Blacks. Tourism represents 41 percent of the GDP. The per capita GNP was $12,910 in 1981.

THE CAYMAN ISLANDS are a British dependency in the Caribbean Sea. They have an area of 100 sq miles (259 km²), and a population of about 20,000. The capital is George Town, on Grand Cayman, the largest island. The other islands are Little Cayman and Cayman Brac.

Black, 17 percent white, and the rest mixed. The capital is Charlotte Amalie, on the second-biggest island, St Thomas. The other main islands are St Croix and St John. Tourism is the main industry.

THE BRITISH VIRGIN ISLANDS lie to the north of the US Virgin Islands. They are a dependent territory of Great Britain. They have an area of 59 sq miles (153 km²), and a population of 13,000. Tortola, the largest inhabited island, contains the capital, Road Town. Tourism is the main industry.

ANGUILLA, the most northerly of the Leeward Islands, is a British dependent territory. It has an area of 35 sq miles (90 km²) and a population of 6,500. The main industries are fishing and tourism. Anguilla was formerly part of the colony of St Christopher-Nevis.

THE TURKS AND CAICOS ISLANDS are a British colony. They have an area of 166 sq miles (430 km²) and a population of 7,440 in 1980. The main exports are shellfish.

THE VIRGIN ISLANDS OF THE UNITED STATES rank as an unincorporated US territory. They were bought from Denmark in 1917. They have an area of 133 sq miles (344 km²), and a population of 127,000. The people are 64 percent

MONTSERRAT is a British Crown Colony just southwest of Antigua. It has an area of 38 sq miles (98 km²) and a population of 12,000. The chief town is Plymouth. The island is volcanic and earthquakes are common. Many of the people are of Irish descent. Agriculture (cotton and tomatoes) is important. The per capita GNP was $1,640 in 1981.

GUADELOUPE is an overseas Department of France. It is a group of seven islands in the

Lesser Antilles, with an area of 687 sq miles (1,779 km²), and a population of 332,000. The capital is Basse-Terre on Basse-Terre Island. The other major island is Grande-Terre. Most of the people are of mixed Black, Asian, and French origin. Agriculture (bananas and sugar) is the main industry. The per capita GNP in 1981 was $4,340.

MARTINIQUE, in the Lesser Antilles, is an overseas Department of France. It has an area of 425 sq miles (1,102 km²) and a population of 300,000. The capital is Fort-de-France. The people are of Black, Asian, and French origin. The island is dominated by Mont Pelée, a volcano which erupted and wiped out the city of St Pierre in 1902. Agriculture (bananas, sugar, and rum) is the main industry. The per capita GNP in 1981 was $4,820.

THE NETHERLANDS ANTILLES are two groups of West Indian islands which form an integral part of the Kingdom of the Netherlands. Three islands, St Maarten, St Eustatius and Saba, lie east of Puerto Rico. Three others, Curaçao, Aruba, and Bonaire, lie just north of Venezuela. The total area is 371 sq miles (961 km²), and the population is 272,000. The capital, Willemstad, is on Curaçao, the largest island. Oil refining is the main industry. The per capita GNP in 1981 was $4,540.

South America: introduction

Although it is linked to North America by the Isthmus of Panama, South America is an independent continent, and geologically it has more in common with Africa and Australia than with North America. About 180 million years ago it was joined to Africa as part of the ancient supercontinent of Gondwanaland. From around 140 million years ago the plates bearing Africa and South America have moved apart to form the South Atlantic Ocean, which is increasing in width at the rate of about 1.6 inches (40 mm) a year.

The massive Brazilian shield which underlies the eastern bulge of South America has its counterpart in the plateau which forms the heart of Africa. The western edge of South America is a destructive plate margin, where the Nazca Plate of the Pacific is being driven under the South American plate. This movement has forced up the high mountain chain of the Andes, and the many volcanoes and frequent earthquakes of this region are some indication of the gigantic forces at work in the Earth's crust.

Land and Climate

Six major land areas form the topography of South America. The western coastlands form a narrow strip along the Pacific edge of the continent, ranging in width from 5 to 50 miles (8–80 km). The Andes are the world's longest

Many species of grass grow in the Andes.

mountain chain, with more than 50 peaks over 20,000 feet (6,100 m) high. The tallest is Mount Aconcagua in Argentina, 23,035 feet (7,021 m) high. The Andes rise steeply from the Pacific coastlands, but fall more gently through a series of steep-walled valleys to the east. The chain contains many high plateaux where people can live, but generally forms a formidable barrier to east–west communications.

About 60 percent of South America is covered by the central plains, and nearly 50 percent is occupied by the basins of three great river systems: the Orinoco in the north, the Amazon in the north central part, and the Río de la Plata further south. Three other highland regions lie to the north and east. The Guiana Highlands are north of the Amazon Basin; the Brazilian Highlands are southeast of the Amazon; and the Patagonian Plateau forms the southeastern part of the continent.

The Amazon, about 3,900 miles (6,280 km) long, is the world's second longest river. With its tributaries it drains an area of about 2,722,000 sq miles (7,050,000 km²). The Orinoco, 1,281 miles (2,062 km) long, drains the lowlands between the Andes and the Guiana Highlands. The Río de la Plata system comprises the Paraná and Uruguay rivers and their tributaries, which form an important waterway for communications. The Eastern Brazilian Highlands are drained by the São Francisco River, 1,988 miles (3,199 km) long. South America contains many waterfalls, including the world's highest, Angel Falls in Venezuela, 3,212 feet (979 m) high.

The widest part of South America lies in the tropics. Most of the continent is hot in summer and hot or warm in winter. The Andes are cool or cold all year, and the high peaks are covered with snow and glaciers. The areas of heaviest rainfall are in the Amazon Basin, the Guiana coastlands, and the coasts of Colombia, Ecuador and southern Chile. The Amazon Basin has heavy rainfall, totalling over 80 inches (2,032 mm) a year. By contrast, there are deserts in western Argentina and the Pacific coastlands of Peru and northern Chile.

Flora and Fauna

Most of the Amazon Basin is covered by *selvas*, or tropical rain forests. They contain more than 2,500 species of trees. Deciduous and evergreen forests are found in parts of the continent with lower rainfall. Areas of grassland are found in the Orinoco Basin, where they are known as *llanos*; in southeastern Brazil they are known as the *campos*, and in Argentina and Uruguay as *pampas*.

South America is rich in animal life, but it has no very large animals. The biggest is the pony-sized tapir. The earliest mammals were marsupials, the pouched mammals, related to the marsupials of Australia. Fossil forms were similar to today's opossums, of which there are many species. Opossums survived in South America because it was isolated until about 15 million years ago, when the Isthmus of Panama formed to link it to North America. The

Sheep grazing on the foothills of the Andes mountain chain.

The political boundaries of South America are today reasonably stable, although the internal politics of the individual countries are less so. Many countries suffer from civil unrest as the forces of Left and Right clash in the fight for power.

mix varies from country to country. Uruguay and Argentina are predominantly white, while the Indian element is strongest in the Andean countries. The descendants of Black Africans are found in Brazil and the Guianas.

The Spanish colonies rose in revolt from 1809 onwards, and they had all achieved independence by 1825. Brazil broke free from Portugal in 1822. Since independence the history of South America has been one of dictatorships and rebellions, and a number of boundary disputes have led to war between several of the countries. Unrest was fuelled by the system of *latifundos*, large estates, a relic of colonial days which left most of the land and wealth in the hands of a small elite. Many countries are now making a strong effort to redistribute land more fairly.

Economic and Demographic Trends
Like its politics, the economy of South America is both varied and unstable. In the early 1980s all countries faced crisis; many were burdened with huge overseas debts and suffering from galloping inflation. The average per capita GNP was $2,070 in 1980, with only Central America, Africa and Asia (excluding the Middle East and Japan) having lower figures. In 1981 the oil-rich Venezuela had the highest per capita GNP, $4,220, and Bolivia the lowest, $600.

Agriculture remains important but in most countries the proportion of the workforce engaged in it is falling steadily. Brazil leads the world in the production of bananas, cassava, coffee, oranges and sugar-cane; Argentina ranks first in linseed.

South America is rich in minerals, except for coal. Brazil is a leading producer of iron ore and manganese, Chile of molybdenum and copper, Bolivia of antimony – in which it ranks first – tin, and tungsten, Peru of lead and silver. Venezuela is the world's sixth largest oil producer. Argentina has few minerals except oil. Manufacturing is largely confined to consumer goods for home use and to food processing.

The rate of population increase, while still high at 2.3 percent per annum, has slowed down from the 2.9 percent of the mid 1970s. Life expectancy, however, is rising throughout the continent.

more successful placental mammals then entered the continent, while one species of marsupial, the Virginia opossum, spread to Central and North America.

South America has four members of the camel family, of which one, the llama, was until the European conquest the only beast of burden. There are many species of New World monkeys, most of them with prehensile tails. The biggest representative of the cat family is the jaguar, while among the rodents the capybara is the world's largest.

History and Culture
The earliest human inhabitants of South America were the Amerindians, who reached the continent via North America about 20,000 years ago. By 11,000 years ago they had reached the southernmost tip of the continent, and by the time Christopher Columbus arrived in the New World in 1492 there were perhaps 10 million Amerindians in South America. The Inca of Peru had established a major civilization and an empire of some 6 million people. Other tribes lived in the tropical forests of Amazonia and the grasslands of the south. They had a primitive way of life, which a few tribes in the rain forests still follow.

After the discovery of the Americas, Pope Alexander VI was persuaded to divide the world into Spanish and Portuguese spheres of influence. The line he drew, confirmed by the Treaty of Tordesillas in 1494, gave Spain a free hand west of a north–south line which cut through the bulge of Brazil, and Portugal a free hand to the east. The main European conquest of South America began in 1534, when the Spanish *conquistador* Francisco Pizarro with just 184 well-armed men overthrew the Inca empire. By 1560 the Spaniards controlled much of the continent, while the Portuguese set up an empire in Brazil. Dutch, British and French settlers occupied the Guianas in the seventeenth century.

Because the early settlers were unable to take women with them, they interbred with the Amerindians. This has given rise to large numbers of *mestizos*, people of mixed Amerindian and European blood. The present-day racial

Lush green valleys are a feature of the Andes.

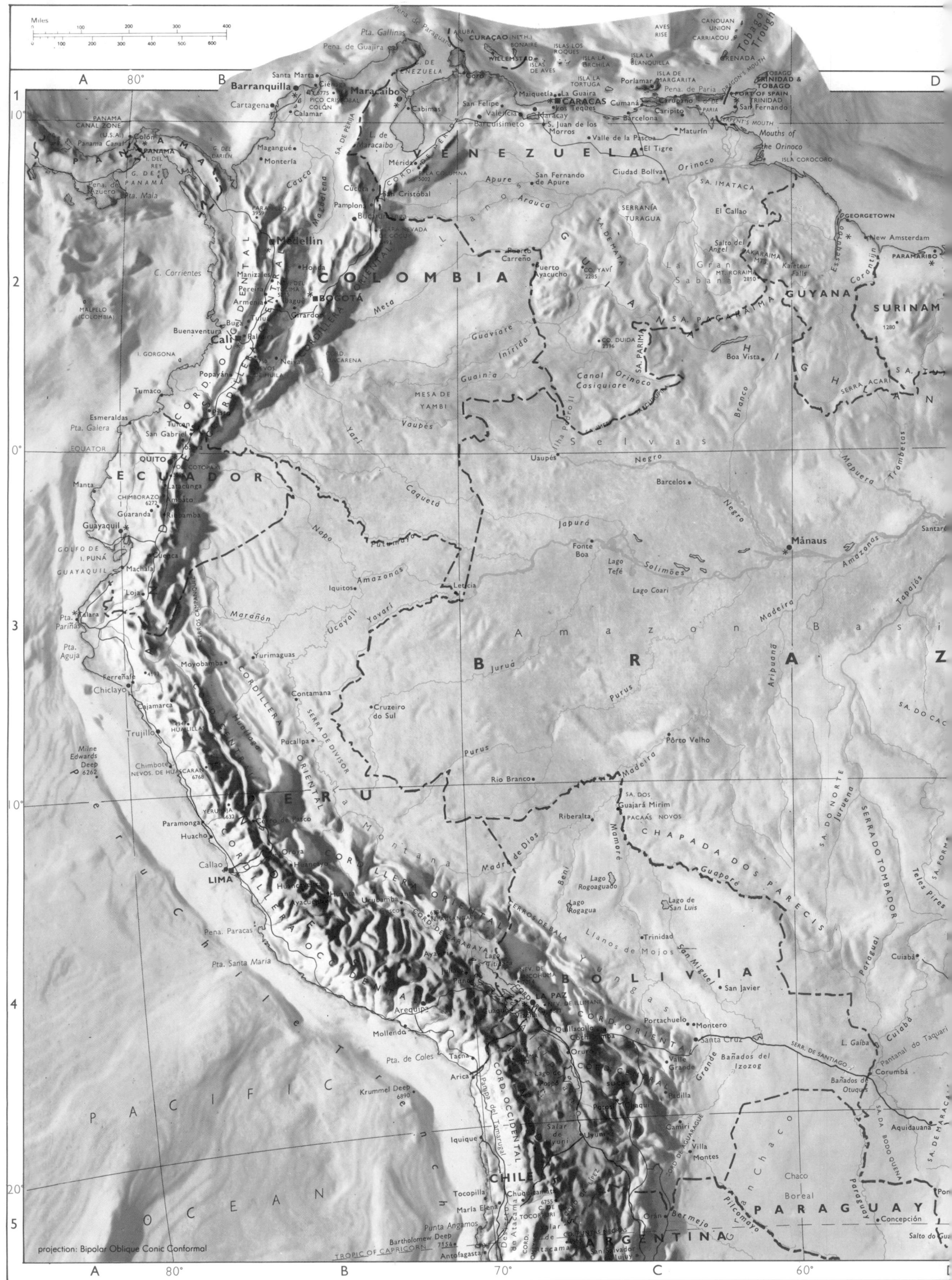

Miles

projection: Bipolar Oblique Conic Conformal

Northern South America

Key

ice caps
tundra
mountain
coniferous forest
deciduous forest
temperate grassland
prairie or steppe
Mediterranean
savanna
tropical forest
desert
semi-desert

■ over 1,000,000
● over 500,000
● over 250,000
• under 250,000

international boundaries
main roads
main railways
✱ international airports
○ ancient sites

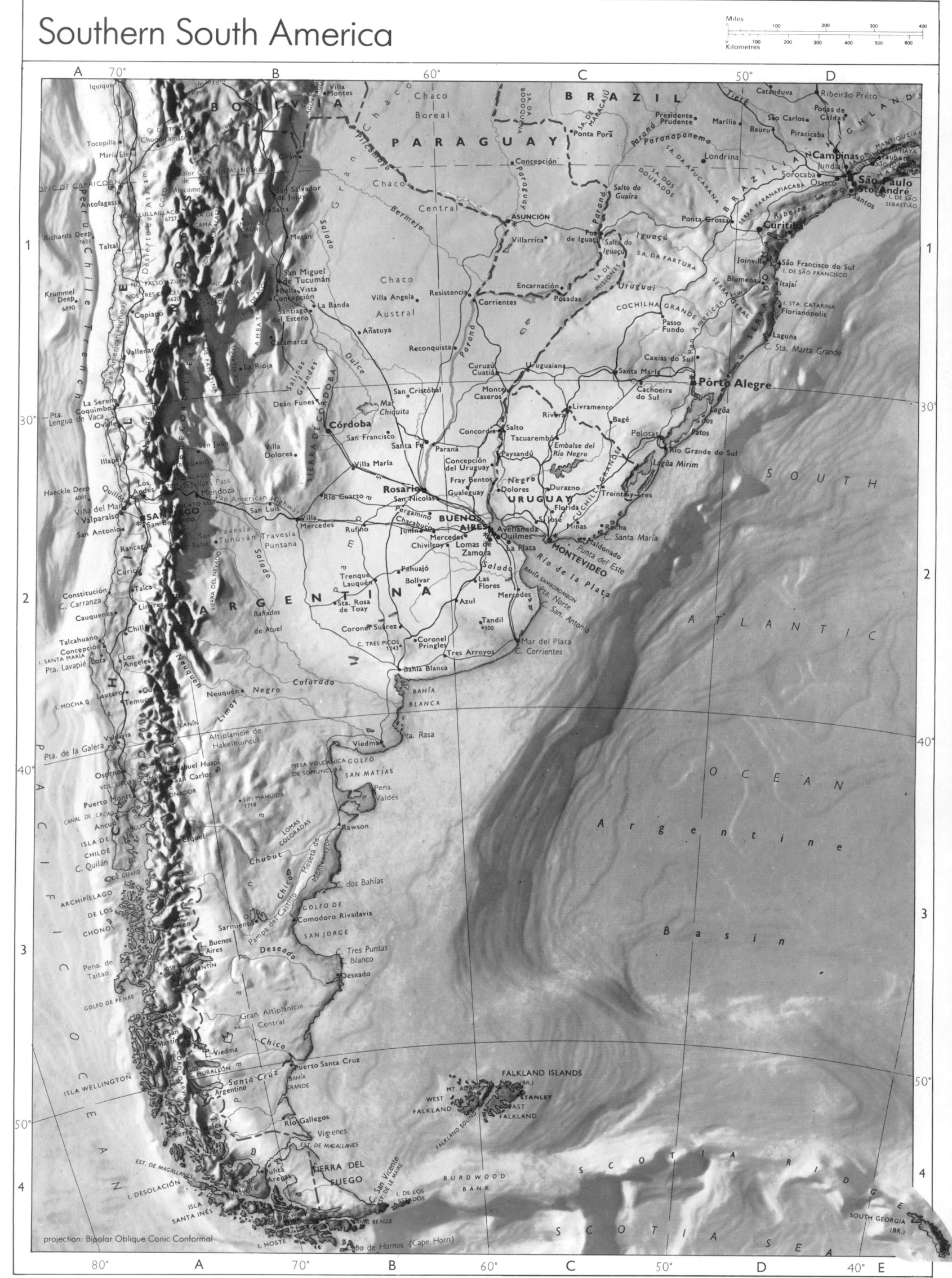

Southern South America

projection: Bipolar Oblique Conic Conformal

COLOMBIA

Area: 439,737 sq miles
(1,138,914 km²)
Population: 28,776,000 (1981)
Population Growth Rate: 1.9% pa
Capital: Bogotá, pop. 2,855,000
Language: Spanish
Religion: Christianity (Roman
Catholic)
Currency: Peso = 100 Centavos

THE REPUBLIC OF COLOMBIA is the only South American country with coastlines on both the Pacific Ocean and the Caribbean Sea.

People and Culture Chibcha Indians lived in Colombia before the Spaniards conquered it in the sixteenth century, and their descendants form 7 percent of today's population. About 20 percent of the people are of European origin, 5 percent Black, and the rest *mestizo* or mulatto.

As part of the Spanish viceroyalty of New Granada, Colombia gained independence in 1819. Venezuela and Ecuador broke away in 1830, and New Granada was renamed Colombia in 1863.

About 64 percent of the people live in urban areas, an increase from 48 percent in 1960. In the same period life expectancy has gone up by 10 years to 63. Adult literacy is 81 percent.

The Land In the northwest the Andes split into three ranges known as the Western, Central and Eastern Cordilleras. The latter is the most important because it consists of a series of vast tablelands. Most people live in the high fertile valleys of the Andes, where temperatures and rainfall are moderate. The eastern 60 percent of Colombia is a low-lying plain, partly grassland (the *llanos*) and partly tropical forest. Few people live there. The Pacific coastal lowlands are hot and wet, partly swampy.

Economy Agriculture accounts for about 27 percent of the GDP, although only about 25 percent of the land is in use – and most of that is pasture. About 26 percent of the people work on the land, half the proportion in 1960. Industry takes 21 percent of the workforce and accounts for 31 percent of the GDP. Manufactures include textiles, leather goods, chemicals, pharmaceutical products and steel. Proportionally, service industries have increased very little in the past 20 years, but the proportion of workers in them has risen from 29 to 53 percent. The GNP per capita at $1,380 is low. In the early 1980s inflation was running at 22 percent, with 20 percent unemployment.

Heavy clothes are needed in Colombia's highlands.

Farming remains important in Venezuela, despite oil resources.

VENEZUELA

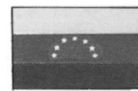

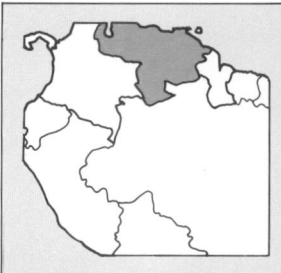

Area: 352,145 sq miles
(912,050 km²)
Population: 15,640,000
Population Growth Rate: 3% pa
Capital: Caracas, pop. 1,036,000
Language: Spanish
Religion: Christianity (Roman
Catholic 90%)
Currency: Bolivar

THE REPUBLIC OF VENEZUELA got its name – which means 'Little Venice' – because the original Amerindian inhabitants built their homes on stilts on Lake Maracaibo.

People and Culture Several Indian tribes lived in Venezuela before the Spaniards arrived. The first European to sight it was Christopher Columbus in 1498. Spain ruled Venezuela until 1811, when it became the first Spanish colony to declare independence. It was part of Great Colombia until 1830.

The Venezuelan flag is waved enthusiastically at a May Day parade in the capital, Caracas.

Over the years Venezuela has had 24 constitutions, many dictators, and constant border squabbles with its neighbours. Since 1958 democratic governments have held power.

There are now only a handful of pure-blooded Amerindians in Venezuela, but 70 percent of the people are *mestizos*. Of the rest, 20 percent are of European origin, and 10 percent are Blacks. Some 84 percent of the people live in urban areas. Life expectancy is 68 years and has increased very little in the past 20 years. The adult literacy rate is 82 percent.

The Land The Orinoco River divides the country in half. The southeastern half, on the right bank of the river, is part of the Guiana Highlands, a region of rounded hills, cut into by rivers, and covered with thick woodland and savanna.

The Orinoco ends in a broad delta covered with thick swamp forest. To the north and west of the river are the Orinoco Plains, a vast area of savanna.

The plains end at the Northern Highlands, much of which enjoys a spring-like climate all year. About 70 percent of the people live in this region. In the northwest lie the hot, humid lowlands surrounding Lake Maracaibo, a freshwater lake with an outlet to the sea. It is South America's largest lake. These lowlands contain good farmland and extensive petroleum reserves. The temperature seldom drops below 82°F (28°C). Like the rest of Venezuela, the Maracaibo Lowlands have a rainy season and a dry one.

Economy Venezuela ranks sixth among the world's oil-producing countries, and 27 percent of its workers are in industry. Mineral deposits are rich: Venezuela has the world's largest natural asphalt lake and iron-ore reserves, and natural gas, gold and diamonds. Manganese, sulphur, copper and asbestos are also exploited.

The GDP breakdown is: industry 45 percent, agriculture 6 percent and services 49 percent. Agriculture and services employ 18 and 55 percent of the workforce respectively. The per capita GNP, at $4,220, is the highest in South America, but falling demand for oil in the 1980s hit the economy hard.

GUYANA

Area: 83,000 sq miles
(214,969 km²)
Population: 903,000 (1981)
Population Growth Rate: 1.1% pa
Capital: Georgetown, pop. 187,000
Language: English
Religions: Christianity (50%),
Hinduism (33%), Islam (10%)
Currency: Guyana Dollar=
100 Cents

THE COOPERATIVE REPUBLIC OF
GUYANA is in the northeast of
South America.

People and Culture Carib,
Arawak, and Warrau Indians
were the first inhabitants, and
their descendants form about
5 percent of the present population. The Dutch were the
first European settlers, but in
1814 ceded the country to
Britain. It gained independence in 1966. There are few
Europeans. About 33 percent
of the people are descendants
of African slaves, and 51 percent are of Asian Indian origin. Political life is dominated
by rivalry between the African
and Asian communities.

The Land There are three
geographical regions. A narrow, marshy coastal strip
borders the Caribbean, and 90
percent of the people live
there. Behind it is a rolling
plateau, with some savanna
grasslands, and behind that, to
the east and south, the deeply
dissected Guiana Highlands.
Almost 85 percent of the land
is tropical forest. The coastal
plain is hot and humid, with
average annual temperatures
of 80°F (27°C), and about 90
inches (2,286 mm) of rain a
year.

Economy Guyana has valuable
mineral deposits, including
gold and diamonds – it was the
reputed site of the legendary

city of El Dorado. Bauxite is
today's most important mineral, but falling demand
because of the world economic
crisis seriously reduced
Guyana's output in 1981. The
country also produces manganese. Sugar, grown on large
plantations, is the main export, followed by rice, which
is also the main food crop.
The per capita GNP at $720 is
the second lowest in South
America.

SURINAM

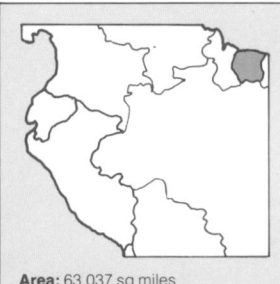

Area: 63,037 sq miles
(163,265 km²)
Population: 415,000
Population Growth Rate: 1.5% pa
Capital: Paramaribo, pop. 152,000
Languages: Dutch and English
Religions: Christianity (Roman
Catholic 18%, other Christians
14%), Hinduism (29%),
Islam (19%)
Currency: Guilder=100 Cents

THE REPUBLIC OF SURINAM
was formerly the colony of
Dutch Guiana. It is the second
largest of the three Guianas.

People and Culture English
settlers were the first Europeans to colonize Surinam. In
1667 the Dutch exchanged it
with Britain for the settlement
of New Netherland (now New
York). The Dutch brought in
foreign labour to work on
their sugar and cotton plantations – first Black slaves, and
after slavery was abolished,
free workers from India and
Indonesia.

As a result one-third of the
people are Asian Indians, one-
third Creoles (mixed European and African blood), and
the rest Indonesians, Blacks,
Amerindians, Chinese and
Europeans. Elementary education is free and compulsory,
and adult literacy is about 70

percent. Surinam gained its
independence in 1975.

The Land There is a narrow
coastal strip of marshland,
which has been drained and is
under cultivation. Inland is a
region of grassy plain, giving
way to mountains covered with
rain forests. The climate is
warm and humid, with annual
temperatures of 81°F (27°C).

Economy The backbone of
Surinam's economy is bauxite,
of which it is the world's sixth
largest producer. Industry
accounts for 29 percent of the
GDP and agriculture 11 percent. Rice, the principal cash
and food crop, covers about
75 percent of the farmland.
Services account for 60 percent of the GDP. The per
capita GNP at $3,030 is the
third highest in South
America. Transportation is a
major problem. Surinam relies
mainly on its rivers, having
poor road and rail links.

ECUADOR

Area: 109,484 sq miles
(283,561 km²)
Population: 9,556,000
Population Growth Rate: 3.4% pa
Capital: Quito, pop. 560,000
Language: Spanish
Religion: Christianity (Roman
Catholic)
Currency: Sucre=100 Centavos

THE REPUBLIC OF ECUADOR
is the fourth smallest and
fourth poorest country in
South America.

People and Culture The country came under the rule of the
Inca in the fifteenth century,
and was conquered by the
Spaniards in 1534. It won
freedom from Spain in 1822
and formed a confederation
with Colombia and Vene-
zuela. In 1830 it won complete
independence. It has had an
unsettled political history.

About 10 percent of the
people are of European
descent, and they have most
power and wealth. Blacks –
descendants of slaves – form
another 10 percent. The rest
are equally divided between
Amerindians and *mestizos*.
Only 45 percent of the people
live in urban areas, and life
expectancy is only 61 years.
Adult literacy was 81 percent
in 1981.

The Land Ecuador is an equatorial state. The Andes Mountains divide the country in two
from north to south. More
than half the people live in the
high valleys and plateaus of
this region, where the climate
is springlike. Forty percent of
the people live in the lowlands
between the Andes and the
Pacific. Few live in the
Oriente, the lowlands east of
the Andes which are mostly
tropical rain forests.

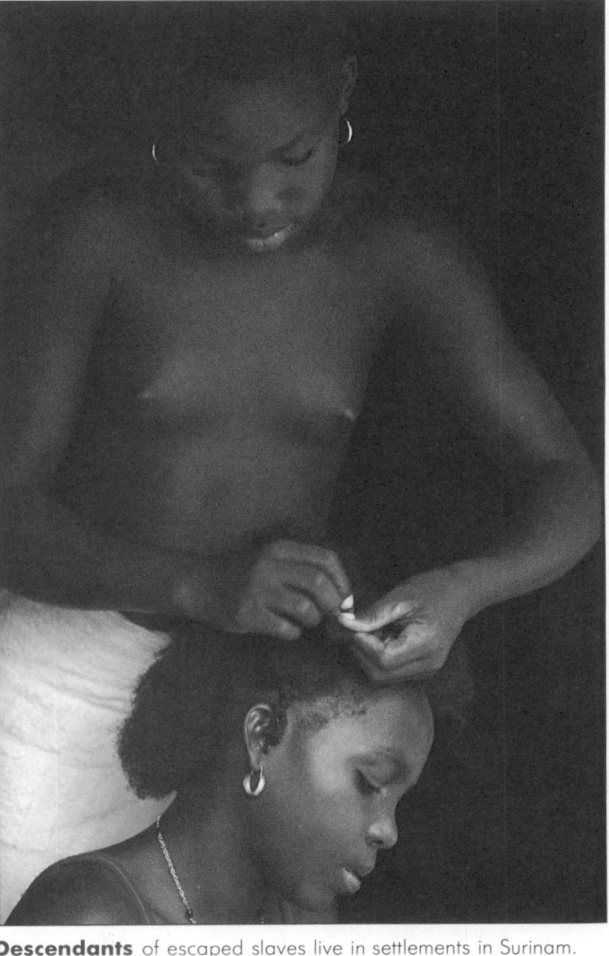

Descendants of escaped slaves live in settlements in Surinam.

About 600 miles (970 km)
to the west are the Galápagos
Islands, a volcanic group.

Economy Agriculture contributes only 12 percent of the
GDP, but employs 52 percent
of the labour force. Bananas,
cacao and coffee are the main
export crops. Industry produces 38 percent of the GDP,
with petroleum the leading
product, but the world oil glut
of the early 1980s sent Ecuador's oil exports plummeting.
Services account for 50 percent of the GDP and 31 percent of labour. The per capita
GNP is low at $1,180.

PERU

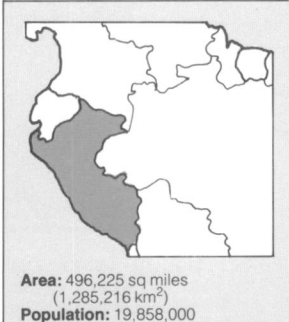

Area: 496,225 sq miles
(1,285,216 km²)
Population: 19,858,000
Population Growth Rate: 2.8% pa
Capital: Lima, pop. 4,279,000
Languages: Spanish and Quechua
Religion: Christianity (Roman
Catholic 95%)
Currency: Sol=100 Centavos

THE REPUBLIC OF PERU is
South America's third largest
country. It lies on the Pacific
coast, just south of the
Equator.

People and Culture Amerindians lived in Peru as much
as 12,000 years ago. From
about 900 BC they established
a series of civilizations. The
last was that of the Incas, who
built a great empire between
AD 1200 and 1500.

The Spaniards conquered
the Inca in 1532–33, but today
about 46 percent of Peruvians
are descendants of the Incas,
while about 43 percent are
mestizos. Most of the rest are
of Spanish descent. Only 66
percent live in urban areas.
Adult literacy is 80 percent,
about the same as the number
of Spanish speakers. The rest
speak Quechua or some other
Indian langue.

Peru declared its independence from Spain in 1821. For
long periods it has been ruled
by military dictators, but an
elected democratic government took office in 1980.

The Land Peru is a land of
sharp contrasts. The coastal
strip is a desert with little
rainfall, but the many rivers
that cross it supply water for
towns and farms, and this is
the most populous area. Behind it lie the Andes Mountains, the highest parts of
which are permanently snow-
covered and glaciated. Temperatures and rainfall both
vary greatly in this region. To
the east of the Andes lies the
selvas, an area of forests where
the temperatures average
nearly 80°F (27°C). Titicaca,
the world's highest major
lake, straddles the border
between Peru and Bolivia.
Earthquakes frequently shake
Peru.

Economy Agriculture employs
39 percent of the labour force
but produces only 9 percent of
the GDP. Industry accounts
for 41 percent of the GDP and
services for 50 percent. Fishing is a major industry, and
Peru ranks sixth among the

Amerindians make up 40 percent of Ecuador's population.

Left Cuzco is an ancient city with Inca remains. It stands in a fertile valley in Peru, about 11,440 feet (3,487 m) above sea-level.

Below This Amerindian woman lives in Huáncayo, Peru, a market and manufacturing city, which is often cold at night because of the altitude.

world's fishing nations. Petroleum and minerals – especially copper, iron ore, lead, silver and zinc – are major exports.

The GNP per capita is $1,170, but many of the people are very poor and there is high unemployment and under-employment.

BRAZIL

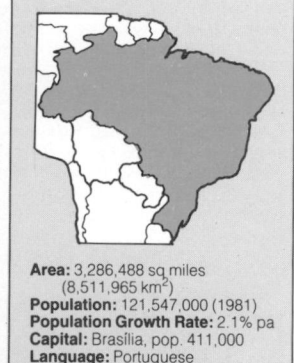

Area: 3,286,488 sq miles (8,511,965 km²)
Population: 121,547,000 (1981)
Population Growth Rate: 2.1% pa
Capital: Brasília, pop. 411,000
Language: Portuguese
Religion: Christianity (Roman Catholic 94%)
Currency: Cruzeiro = 100 Centavos

THE FEDERAL REPUBLIC OF BRAZIL covers more land than almost all the other countries of South America put together. It is the world's fifth largest country.
People and Culture Before Europeans reached America about a million Amerindian tribespeople were scattered over the vast area that is now Brazil. Today less than 0.2 percent of the population is Amerindian.

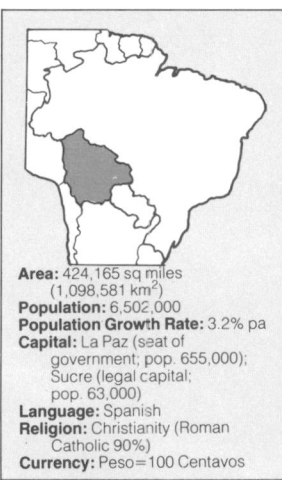

Sugar Loaf Mountain overlooks Guanabara Bay in Rio de Janeiro, the former capital of Brazil. Rio occupies one of the world's most glorious city sites.

The Portuguese began colonizing the land around 1500, and ruled it until 1822, when it became independent under Emperor Pedro I, son of the king of Portugal. Brazil became a republic in 1889. About 75 percent of the people are of European origin, but those of Portuguese descent rank second in numbers to those of Italian origin. There are also large numbers of people of Spanish, German, Japanese and Lebanese origin, and there are many Blacks, descended from slaves. A great many people are of mixed ancestry. The population is growing rapidly – 2.1 percent a year between 1970 and 1980.

Brazil has alternated between democratically elected governments and military régimes. Despite this political turmoil the overall lot of the people has improved in the past 20 years. Life expectancy at birth has risen from 55 years in 1960 to 64 years in 1981.

Free elementary education has been available since 1930, but there are not enough schools. As a result the adult literacy rate is still only 74 percent.

The Land The northern part of Brazil is dominated by the Amazon, the world's largest river and second longest. In its basin grow the world's largest remaining tropical rain forests, the *selvas*. They are gradually being exploited for their timber.

South and east of the *selvas* lie the *campos*, a vast plateau of tropical grassland. This is still a largely undeveloped area, though in 1960 the Brazilians built a new capital city in its midst, Brasilia, in an effort to open it up.

Brazil's heartland is the southern part of the country, a plateau land of rich soil and mineral deposits where more than 50 percent of the people live.

The highest point is the Pico da Neblina, at 8,038 feet (2,450 m), in the northwest near the Venezuelan border. The Iguaçu Falls, near the junction of the Iguaçu and Paraná rivers between Brazil and Argentina, are more than 2 miles (3 km) wide.

Brazil's climate is mostly hot, and a large part of the country has a heavy rainfall. The eastern and southern plateaux are cooler and drier.

Economy Up to the 1940s agriculture provided the mainstay of Brazil's economy, and it still employs 30 percent of the workforce. However, it produces only 13 percent of the GDP. Brazil leads the world in producing bananas, cassava, cane sugar, coffee and oranges, and is a leading producer of cacao, beef and pork. It has important mineral deposits, and is a leading exporter of manganese and iron ore. Industry accounts for 34 percent of the GDP and employs 24 percent of the workforce. But more than half the people are engaged in services. The per capita GNP stood at $2,220 in 1981.

Between 1960 and 1981 the number of people living in urban areas increased from 46 to 68 percent.

In the 1980s Brazil had a continuing balance of trade problem, with inflation running at 100 percent (1982). It was taking active steps to open up undeveloped parts of the country and to develop nuclear power and so reduce its dependence on imports of petroleum.

BOLIVIA

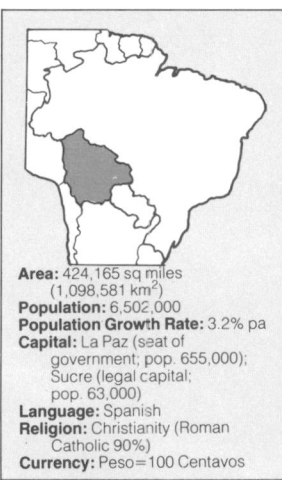

Area: 424,165 sq miles (1,098,581 km²)
Population: 6,502,000
Population Growth Rate: 3.2% pa
Capital: La Paz (seat of government; pop. 655,000); Sucre (legal capital; pop. 63,000)
Language: Spanish
Religion: Christianity (Roman Catholic 90%)
Currency: Peso = 100 Centavos

THE REPUBLIC OF BOLIVIA is named after its liberator Simon Bolivar (1783–1830). It is a land-locked country, much of which is covered by hot rain forests and grassy plains. Most Bolivians live on a cool plateau, the Altiplano, high in the Andes. The world's highest large lake, Titicaca, lies on the border with Peru.

People and Culture Over 60 percent of the people are Amerindians, descendants of the people who first settled there in the fourth century AD. Nearly 20 percent are of European origin, and 30 percent are of mixed blood. Bolivia was under Spanish rule from 1532 to 1825, when it became independent. It lost territory as a result of wars with Peru and Paraguay. Its history is one of frequent revolutions.

Although Bolivia remains South America's poorest country, the quality of life there is slowly rising, as shown by an increase in the expectancy of life at birth from 43 years in 1960 to 51 in the 1980s. Though primary education is free and compulsory, adult literacy remains low at 63 percent. Since 1960 the proportion of the population living in towns has almost doubled, to 45 percent.

The Land The eastern two-thirds of Bolivia is a vast, undeveloped lowland, with tropical forests in the north and grassy plains in the south. High valleys and deep gorges lead up to the Altiplano in the west, bounded by Andean peaks.

The Altiplano has a cool climate and moderate rainfall. The hot and humid lowlands have an average rainfall of 70 inches (1,778 mm), most of it between November and March.

Economy Fifty percent of the people work in agriculture, but only about 2 percent of the land is under cultivation. Almost a quarter of the labour force is employed in industry, of which mining is the most important element. The Bolivian Andes are rich in minerals. The country produces 13 percent of the world's tin, and 28 percent of the antimony, of which it is the leading producer. Other important minerals include copper, gold, lead, silver and zinc. Bolivia exports oil and natural gas, and has its own processing plant for uranium. Manufacturing represents only about 14 percent of GDP. The per capita GNP at $600 (1981) is the lowest in South America.

PARAGUAY

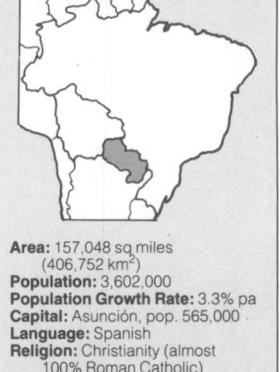

Area: 157,048 sq miles (406,752 km²)
Population: 3,602,000
Population Growth Rate: 3.3% pa
Capital: Asunción, pop. 565,000
Language: Spanish
Religion: Christianity (almost 100% Roman Catholic)
Currency: Guarani = 100 Céntimos

THE REPUBLIC OF PARAGUAY is a land-locked subtropical country.

People and Culture The first inhabitants were Guarani Indians, and about 3 percent of the population is now of pure Amerindian blood. Colonization was largely by Jesuit missionaries. The land came under direct Spanish rule from 1767, and won independence in 1811. A disastrous war against Uruguay, Argentina, and Brazil from 1865 to 1870 killed all but 221,000 of the people, of whom only 10 percent were males. Paraguay has still not recovered from this.

Today about 75 percent of the people are *mestizos*, and

Volcanic peaks rise near the Chile-Peru border. Volcanic activity occurs widely in the Andes, which overlies a subduction zone where a plate edge is being destroyed.

21 percent of European blood. Life expectancy is 65 years, and adult literacy stands at 84 percent. Most of the rulers have been dictators. General Alfredo Stroessner, who won power in 1954, was re-elected in 1983 for the sixth time.

The Land The Paraguay River divides the country in two. To the west lies the Chaco, a flat region often flooded in the rainy season, where fewer than 40 percent of the people live. To the east lie a fertile plain and hills. This region has hot summers and warm winters, with about 60 inches (1,524 mm) of rain a year. The west is drier.

Economy Poor communications are a handicap to Paraguay. The Paraná River, into which the Paraguay flows, provides a vital link with the sea. Agriculture employs 44 percent of the workforce and provides 28 percent of the GDP. Industry provides 26 percent of GDP. The per capita GNP is only $1,630.

Two large hydroelectric projects on the Paraná River will, it is hoped, provide much-needed power for the development of industry.

CHILE

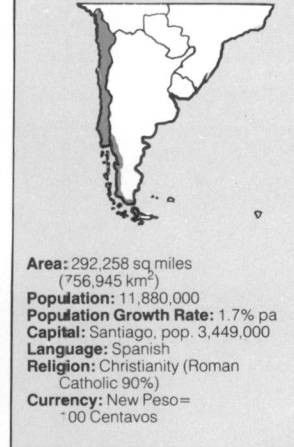

Area: 292,258 sq miles (756,945 km²)
Population: 11,880,000
Population Growth Rate: 1.7% pa
Capital: Santiago, pop. 3,449,000
Language: Spanish
Religion: Christianity (Roman Catholic 90%)
Currency: New Peso= 100 Centavos

THE REPUBLIC OF CHILE is a long, narrow country that extends from tropical desert in the north to Cape Horn, the southernmost point of South America.

People and Culture Araucanian Indians lived in Chile before the arrival of the Europeans in the sixteenth century. They resisted both the Inca and the Spaniards, and their descendants – around 2 percent of the population – still preserve their own culture. About 30 percent of Chileans are European in ancestry, and the rest are of mixed Amerindian and European stock.

Chile became independent of Spain in 1818. It wrested its northern territories from Peru and Bolivia in the War of the Pacific (1879–83).

The Land Chile is nowhere more than 217 miles (350 km) wide from east to west. Its long frontier with Argentina is formed by the rugged, volcanic Andes mountains. To the west lies the Cordillera de la Costa, a parallel chain of mountains leaving very little coastal lowland. Between the two ranges are lowland valleys and basins. In the north is the arid, almost rainless Atacama Desert, which has large mineral deposits. The south is cool with rainfall up to 200 inches (5,080 mm) a year, and heavily forested. The mountains break up into a chain of islands separated by fiords.

Central Chile has warm summers, mild winters, and a moderate rainfall. Most of the people live in this region. More than 80 percent are urban dwellers. Life expectancy is 68 years, and the adult literacy rate is 88 percent.

Economy Chile is rich in minerals. It is the chief mining country of South America, with copper, iron ore, nitrate and manganese as its chief minerals. Copper represents, by value, almost half the total exports. Industry employs 19 percent of the workforce, producing 35 percent of the GDP, two-thirds of that being manufactured goods. Agriculture employs the same number, but produces only 7 percent of the GDP. Services account for around 60 percent both of workers and the GDP. The per capita GNP stood at $2,560 in 1981, but in the early 1980s Chile was fighting a continuous balance-of-payments problem and unemployment running at 20 percent.

Lake Villarica is Chile's Lake District. A volcano, also called Villarica, is on the horizon.

Brick-making is a common rural industry. Argentina is changing rapidly. Its rural population fell from 26 percent in 1960 to 17 percent in 1981.

Argentinian fishermen bringing in the day's catch.

ARGENTINA

Area: 1,068,302 sq miles
(2,766,889 km²)
Population: 28,085,000 (1981)
Capital: Buenos Aires,
pop. 2,908,000
Language: Spanish
Religion: Christianity (Roman
Catholic 84%)
Currency: Peso = 100 Centavos

THE REPUBLIC OF ARGENTINA is the second largest country in South America, and also the second most important and powerful.

People and Culture Very few Amerindians lived in Argentina before the Spaniards arrived in the sixteenth century. For 286 years Argentina formed part of the viceroyalty of Peru, until independence in 1816. But Argentina's real development did not begin until the adoption of a constitution, modelled on that of the United States, in 1853.

About 90 percent of the people are descended from European settlers, mostly Italians, Spaniards, Germans and Slavs. Only 2 percent of the people are Amerindians, and the rest are *mestizos*. In 1981 urban dwellers accounted for 83 percent of the population, and 50 percent were found in Buenos Aires and the provinces around it.

Education is free and, up to the age of 14, compulsory. As a result Argentina has almost the highest literacy rate in South America. Good housing and medical care have increased life expectancy from 65 years at birth in 1960 to 71 years in 1981.

However, political and social unrest have dogged the country since 1930. A series of military dictatorships ruled Argentina until 1958, when free elections were held. There were more military dictatorships from 1966 to 1972, and from 1976 to 1983. In 1982 a disastrous attempt to capture the Falkland Islands (called Islas Malvinas by Argentina) threw the country into further turmoil.

The Land Argentina is a long, wedge-shaped country, running for 2,300 miles (3,700 km) from the Tropic of Capricorn in the north to within 800 miles (1,300 km) of the Antarctic Circle.

There are four main regions. The north is forested and tropical, partly swampy. The west is a semiarid region of high plateaux and valleys, rising to the Andes Mountains which form the frontier with Chile. The southern part of the country, Patagonia, is a dry, windswept plateau, where fewer than 2 people per square mile (under 1 per km) live. The central quarter of Argentina is the Pampas, flat or gently-rolling plains with fertile soil. This region has a mild climate with moderate rainfall. The north is tropical, with up to 60 inches (1,524 mm) of rain a year, while Patagonia is cool, with a light rainfall.

The main rivers are the Paraná, Paraguay and Uruguay rivers in the north, forming the Río de la Plata river system. Argentina has the Americas' tallest mountain, Mount Aconcagua, 23,035 feet (7,021 m) high.

Economy 11 percent of this great farming country is under cultivation and a further 41 percent is under pasture. Beef, wool and wheat are major products. Although agriculture represented only 9 percent of the GDP in 1980, 13 percent of the labour force was engaged in it.

The contribution of industry to the GDP has remained constant over the past 20 years at 38 percent (25 percent comes from manufacturing). Services, employing almost 60 percent of the people, account for over half the GDP.

The world economic crisis of the 1970s and 1980s hit Argentina hard. In 1982 inflation was running at 137 percent, and the peso had become almost worthless. The per capita GNP stood at $2,560 in 1981, a slight fall on the previous year, with high unemployment. From having been South America's richest country in the 1920s, Argentina, with a continuous and growing balance of trade deficit, had to call for massive international financial aid.

URUGUAY

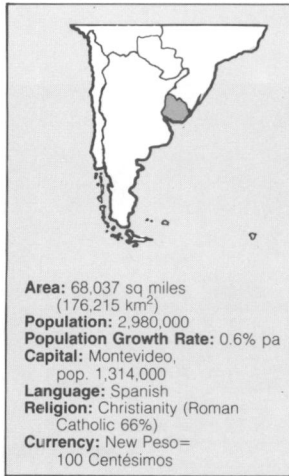

Area: 68,037 sq miles (176,215 km²)
Population: 2,980,000
Population Growth Rate: 0.6% pa
Capital: Montevideo, pop. 1,314,000
Language: Spanish
Religion: Christianity (Roman Catholic 66%)
Currency: New Peso= 100 Centésimos

THE EASTERN REPUBLIC OF URUGUAY is one of the smallest countries of South America. It faces the Atlantic Ocean.
People and Culture A fierce Amerindian nomad tribe, the Charrúas, lived in Uruguay before the Spaniards came. They were gradually eliminated by the new settlers. Portugal and Spain fought for possession of the land in the eighteenth century. Uruguay won its independence in 1828.

About 90 percent of the people are of Spanish or Italian descent. The rest are mostly *mestizos* living in rural areas. Some 84 percent of Uruguayans live in urban areas, and 45 percent are in Montevideo. Life exectancy is 71 years. Elementary education is free and compulsory, and adult literacy is 94 percent.
The Land Uruguay has a long coastline on the Atlantic and Río de la Plata, with the Uruguay River forming its western frontier. About 80 percent of the country is covered by the *cuchillas*, low rolling hills separated by wide valleys through which slow rivers run. The hills are more rugged towards the Brazilian border, but the highest point, Mirador Nacional, is only 1,644 feet (501 m). The main river, the Rio Negro, is dammed to provide half the electric power for the country.
Economy Agriculture produces 8 percent of the GDP and employs 11 percent of the workforce. Nearly 90 percent of the land is farmed, mostly for pasturing cattle and sheep. Meat, wool, and other livestock products are the principal exports. Industry produces 33 percent of the GDP, with 32 percent of the workers. Much of it is based on processing farm products. Services account for 59 percent of the GDP and absorb 57 percent of the workforce. Living standards are high, and the per capita GNP is $2,820.

DEPENDENCIES

FRENCH GUIANA is an overseas Department of France. It was a colony until 1946.

About 90 percent of the people are Black, or of mixed Black and European ancestry. There are about 4,500 Amerindians, descended from the original inhabitants. The land, the smallest of the three Guianas, has been under French rule since the seventeenth century.

The land is mostly low lying, with a tropical climate. Temperatures average 80°F (27°C), and the annual rainfall is 130 inches (3,302 mm). Nearly 90 percent of the land is covered by dense tropical forests. The economy is underdeveloped, and is largely based on shrimp fishing, but the per capita GNP is high at $3,430. Bauxite and other minerals have been discovered. France has a space research centre in the Department.

THE FALKLAND ISLANDS are a British Crown Colony in the South Atlantic, about 298 miles (480 km) east of the Magellan Strait. All but two of the 200 islands are tiny. They are bleak and windswept. After French, British, and Spanish claims to the islands, Britain resumed occupation for the protection of seal-fisheries, and colonized the Falklands in 1833. They were the most southerly organized colony of the British Empire. Argentina, which claims the islands under the name Islas Malvinas, seized them in 1982, but Britain promptly recaptured them, and set up a large garrison there. Up to 1982 the main occupation was sheep farming. South Georgia and the South Shetlands are administered as part of the colony.

Buenos Aires, the capital of Argentina.

A rural scene in Uruguay.

Tierra del Fuego, an archipelago at the foot of South America, is shared between Chile and Argentina. Sheep farming is a major industry in this wind-swept region.

Europe: introduction

Europe is the part of Eurasia between the Atlantic and the Ural Mountains. From north to south, it extends between latitudes 72° North and 35° North. Its coastline is deeply indented and branches of the Atlantic extend eastwards in the Baltic Sea in the north and the Mediterranean and Black seas in the south.

Land and Climate

The northwest highlands, including the mountains of Norway, Sweden, Scotland and Ireland, belong to the ancient Caledonian system, formed by a plate collision around 420 million years ago. The highest peaks in this glaciated region are in southern Norway. On the other hand, Iceland, which is included in northern Europe, is of volcanic origin. This island straddles the mid-Atlantic ridge – the boundary between the Eurasian and North American plates – and it is becoming wider as these plates move apart.

The central lowlands of Europe extend from southeastern England through northern France, Belgium, the Netherlands, Denmark, the southern tip of Sweden, northern Germany and Poland to the USSR, where they end in the foothills of the Ural Mountains. Mostly below 500 feet (152 m), this plain has provided an easy route for human migrations and advancing armies. North of the central lowlands is the Baltic shield, which is a low plateau slightly higher than the central lowlands.

Central Europe contains a group of disconnected highlands belonging to the Hercynian system (formed between about 300 and 225 million years ago as the African plate moved against Europe). These highlands include the Iberian *meseta* (plateau), the Massif Central of France, Brittany (Bretagne in French), the Vosges, the Ardennes, Sardinia, Corsica and, in the British Isles, the Pennines and southwestern England. Some of these highlands are blocks raised up between fractures created by plate movements. Similarly, there are rift valleys, such as the Rhine valley between Basel and Mainz, where blocks sank downwards between fractures.

A third highland region, the Alpine system, consists of young fold mountains. It includes a chain of mountains extending from the Cordillera Cantabrica in northwestern Spain through the Pyrenees to the Alps themselves and then on to the Carpathians, the Balkan Mountains and the Caucasus Mountains. The Caucasus Mountains include Europe's highest peak, El'brus, an extinct volcano, which is 18,481 feet (5,633 m) above sea-level. The highest mountain of western Europe is Mont Blanc, in the Alps, which is 15,771 feet (4,807 m) high. The Alpine system also contains many of Europe's highest waterfalls, including the Gavarnie in the Pyrenees, which is 1,385 feet (422 m) high, and the Staubbach, Switzerland, which is 980 feet (299 m) high.

Other mountains in the Alpine system include the Sierra Nevada in southern Spain, the mountains of southeastern Europe (Yugoslavia, Albania and Greece), and the Appennini (or Apennine) range, which forms the backbone of Italy. Southern Italy contains evidence on its surface of continuing plate movements. This is a chain of active volcanoes extending from Vesuvio (Vesuvius), near Napoli, through the Lipari Islands (which include Stromboli and Vulcano) to Mount Etna in Sicily. The magma which comes from these volcanoes is formed as one plate is pushed beneath another along a subduction zone under southern Italy. Vesuvius is an intermediate volcano, which sometimes erupts explosively. Etna in the south is a quiet volcano. When Etna erupts, there are no great explosions, but rivers of lava flow long distances downhill. Other signs of crustal instability in the Mediterranean region are earthquakes, which are fairly common. And in about 1470 BC, a volcano exploded on the Greek island of Thira (once called Santorini). This is the greatest known volcanic explosion.

In addition to its structure, European scenery was further shaped by the action of ice in the Pleistocene Ice Age. In northern Europe and in mountain regions throughout Europe, ice sheets and glaciers scoured out U-shaped valleys and rock basins. For example, Finland contains thousands of lakes which occupy ice-worn basins. Other lakes, including many in Sweden and Scotland, have formed behind dams of moraine (glacier-born rock debris). The central lowlands are also largely masked by moraine deposits. Such areas are generally poorly drained and marshy.

Above The central Plaza de España in Madrid, Spain's capital.

The largest freshwater lake in Europe is Lake Ladoga (Ladozhskoye Ozero), which covers 7,000 square miles (18,129 km^2) north of Leningrad. The largest lake in western Europe is Vänern, in southern Sweden.

Europe's longest river is the Volga, which flows about 2,300 miles (3,701 km) into the Caspian Sea. Western Europe's longest river is the Danube, which is also called the Donau (in German), Duna (in Hungarian), Dunav (in Serbo-Croat), and Dunărea (in Romanian). The Danube flows 1,725 miles (2,776 km) from the Schwarzwald (Black Forest) in West Germany to the Black Sea. Other major European rivers include the Dnepr and Don in the USSR, the Elbe, Rhein (Rhine) and Oder in Germany, the Ebro in Iberia, the Po in Italy, the Wisla (Vistula) in Poland, and the Shannon, Severn and Thames in the British Isles.

The western coastlands of Europe are warmed by the Gulf Stream and its northward extension, the North Atlantic Drift. As a result, the Norwegian port of Narvik, well to the north of the Arctic Circle, is ice-free throughout the year. The moderating effect of the ocean gives the northwest, including the British Isles, western France and the Low Countries, mild winters with average temperatures of 35°F to 45°F (2°C–7°C). Summers are warm, with average temperatures of 50°F to 60°F (10°C–16°C). The rainfall is heavy on western coasts, reaching more than 100 inches (2,540 mm) in places. It decreases inland and the rainfall of

The Colosseum in Rome.

Europe, excluding the USSR and the European part of Turkey, contains 32 independent nations, ranging in size from France to Vatican City, an enclave in Rome and the smallest independent nation in the world. Europe has had a tremendous influence on the rest of the world. English, French, German, Portuguese and Spanish are international business languages. Only Chinese, Russian and Arabic are languages of comparable importance. Europe also led the way in the Industrial Revolution, and its technology has spread throughout the former European colonial empires. Europe seeks to retain its influence on the superpowers through regional groupings, notably the 11-member European Economic Community (EEC) and the looser, six-member European Free Trade Association (EFTA). Six of the Communist countries of Eastern Europe are linked with the USSR through the Council for Mutual Economic Assistance (COMECON).

The dome of St Paul's Cathedral, London, withstood the air raids of World War II.

this region is generally 30 to 60 inches (762–1,524 mm), with the maximum in winter.

To the east and northeast, away from the influence of the Atlantic the climate becomes increasingly severe. For example, Glasgow has an average January temperature of 38°F (3°C), while in Moskva (Moscow), in roughly the same latitude, the average January temperature is 15°F (−9°C). To the east, summers are also hotter and the rainfall diminishes. Vienna has an average annual rainfall of 26 inches (660 mm) and Moscow 25 inches (635 mm), although the highlands are wetter. More rain falls in summer in central Europe than in winter.

Southern or Mediterranean Europe has hot, dry summers and mild winters, when depressions from the Atlantic bring moderate rainfall. For example, Nice in southeastern France has an average annual rainfall of 32 inches (813 mm), while Athens (Athinai) has 16 inches (406 mm). Summer temperatures increase to the east.

Flora and Fauna

Tundra covers northern Sweden, Finland and the USSR. Mosses, lichens, some flowering plants and occasional 1.5-foot (0.5-m) high Arctic willows grow during the short summer, when the snow melts. Similar conditions occur on the highlands of Norway and Sweden to the south and around the peaks of high mountains in southern Europe.

Boreal, or coniferous, forest covers a broad zone south of the tundra. Species of pine and spruce predominate. In the south, the forest thickens and merges into the deciduous forest region, which extends from the British Isles across the central lowlands and into the USSR. Typical trees are ash, beech, elm, horse-chestnut, oak and sycamore, but these forests have largely vanished and have been replaced by farmland. But if the land was abandoned and left for 200 to 300 years, the original deciduous forest would re-establish itself.

In the European USSR, the deciduous forest occupies a much narrower belt of land, because it gives way in the south to the steppes – vast grasslands which extend southeastwards to the Caspian Sea and southwestwards to the Black Sea. In southeastern Europe, the steppes extend into Romania and Hungary.

The Mediterranean region once supported evergreen forests, but these, too, have been largely cleared, causing soil erosion in many areas. The plants of the Mediterranean lands are adapted to survive the hot, arid, summers. They include the olive tree, cork oak and various aromatic herbs. Mediterranean scrub is called *maquis*.

Europe, together with most of Asia, belongs to the Palearctic faunal realm. But Europe's wildlife has been greatly depleted by human activity. Many species, such as aurochs (wild cattle) and tarpans (wild horses), have become extinct. Others, such as the wisent (European bison), are now extremely rare.

In summer, the tundra is alive with insects and birds, while reindeer migrate to the tundra from the boreal forests. These forests are the home of fur-bearing animals, such as ermine, lynx and marten. Wolves and wild boars are also found, with bears and elks in eastern Europe.

The mountains contain some specialized animals, such as the chamois and ibex in the Alps. A form of wild goat, related to the ibex, lives on Crete (Kriti), and Corsica and Sardinia contain wild sheep, called mouflon. These have now been introduced into the French Alps and also into Czechoslovakia and Hungary.

Western Europe has a wide variety of animals, but many of them, including foxes, hares, otters and rabbits, are still killed as pests. Europe's only primate is the Barbary ape in Gibraltar. It was probably introduced by the Moors when they invaded Spain. Iberia also contains some other African species, including the Egyptian mongoose, the Algerian hedgehog, and the genet, whose range extends into western France.

Pelicans live in the Danube delta on the Black Sea and birdlife is generally abundant, because Europe lies on many bird migration routes between the tundra and Africa.

Europe

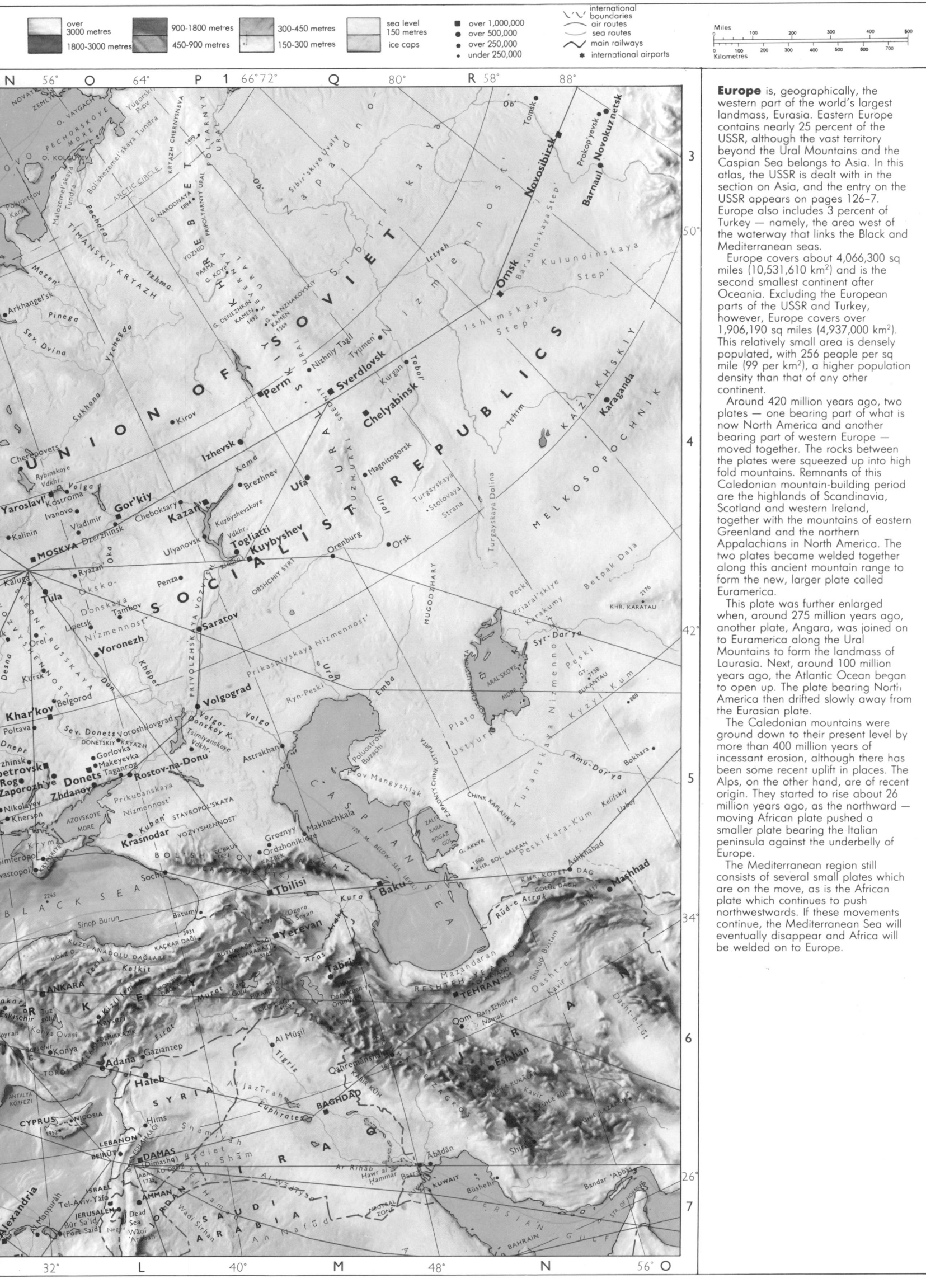

over 3000 metres	900-1800 metres	300-450 metres	sea level 150 metres	■ over 1,000,000	
1800-3000 metres	450-900 metres	150-300 metres	ice caps	● over 500,000	
				● over 250,000	
				● under 250,000	

international boundaries
air routes
sea routes
main railways
✴ international airports

Miles   100   200   300   400   500
Kilometres   0   100   200   300   400   500   600   700

Europe is, geographically, the western part of the world's largest landmass, Eurasia. Eastern Europe contains nearly 25 percent of the USSR, although the vast territory beyond the Ural Mountains and the Caspian Sea belongs to Asia. In this atlas, the USSR is dealt with in the section on Asia, and the entry on the USSR appears on pages 126–7. Europe also includes 3 percent of Turkey — namely, the area west of the waterway that links the Black and Mediterranean seas.

Europe covers about 4,066,300 sq miles (10,531,610 km²) and is the second smallest continent after Oceania. Excluding the European parts of the USSR and Turkey, however, Europe covers over 1,906,190 sq miles (4,937,000 km²). This relatively small area is densely populated, with 256 people per sq mile (99 per km²), a higher population density than that of any other continent.

Around 420 million years ago, two plates — one bearing part of what is now North America and another bearing part of western Europe — moved together. The rocks between the plates were squeezed up into high fold mountains. Remnants of this Caledonian mountain-building period are the highlands of Scandinavia, Scotland and western Ireland, together with the mountains of eastern Greenland and the northern Appalachians in North America. The two plates became welded together along this ancient mountain range to form the new, larger plate called Euramerica.

This plate was further enlarged when, around 275 million years ago, another plate, Angara, was joined on to Euramerica along the Ural Mountains to form the landmass of Laurasia. Next, around 100 million years ago, the Atlantic Ocean began to open up. The plate bearing North America then drifted slowly away from the Eurasian plate.

The Caledonian mountains were ground down to their present level by more than 400 million years of incessant erosion, although there has been some recent uplift in places. The Alps, on the other hand, are of recent origin. They started to rise about 26 million years ago, as the northward — moving African plate pushed a smaller plate bearing the Italian peninsula against the underbelly of Europe.

The Mediterranean region still consists of several small plates which are on the move, as is the African plate which continues to push northwestwards. If these movements continue, the Mediterranean Sea will eventually disappear and Africa will be welded on to Europe.

Northern Europe

ice caps
tundra
mountain

coniferous forest
deciduous forest
temperate grassland

prairie or steppe
Mediterranean
savanna

tropical forest
desert
semi-desert

■ over 1,000,000
▪ over 500,000
• over 250,000
· under 250,000

international boundaries
main roads
main railways
✳ international airports
○ ancient sites

Miles
0   50   100   150   200   250   300   350
Kilometres
0 50 100 150 200 250 300 350 400 450 500 550 600

projection: Azimuthal Equidistant

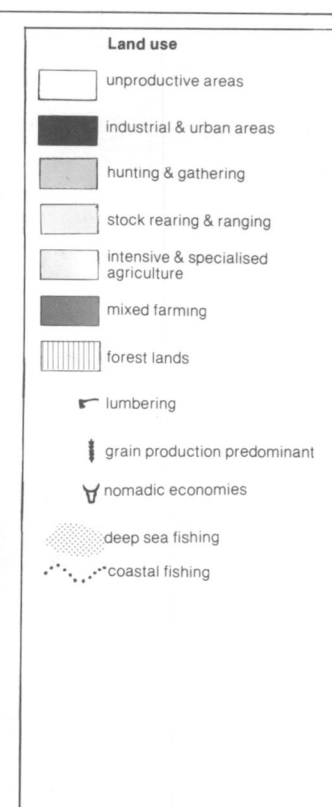

Excluding the European parts of the USSR and Turkey, Europe contains 32 independent nations. It covers only 3.3 percent of the world's land area, but with 10.8 percent of the population, it is the most densely populated region on Earth.

Of the larger countries, the most thickly populated are in the west, including the Netherlands with a population density of 922 per sq mile (356 per km²), Belgium with 840 per sq mile (324 per km²), West Germany with 642 per sq mile (248 per km²), and the United Kingdom with 591 per sq mile (228 per km²). England itself, with 919 per sq mile (355 per km²), is nearly as densely populated as the Netherlands.

The most thinly populated countries are in the north, namely Iceland with a population density of 6 per sq mile (2 per km²), Norway with 34 per sq mile (13 per km²), Finland with 37 per sq mile (14 per km²), and Sweden with 49 per sq mile (19 per km²). Apart from the USSR, France is the biggest country in Europe. The Vatican City, which covers 108.7 acres (44 ha) on the west bank of the Tiber River in Rome, is the smallest independent nation in the world.

The People of Europe and their Languages

Most Europeans belong to the Caucasoid subgroup of the human race, although in recent years some Negroids and Mongoloids have settled in Europe. Among the Caucasoids, there are several recognizable types. These are the Nordics of Scandinavia, who are tall, fair and blue-eyed; the Alpine peoples of central Europe, who are stocky and often brown-eyed; the Mediterranean peoples with dark hair and complexions; the round-headed Dinaric peoples of southeastern Europe; and the East Baltic people, who are fair-haired and broad-headed. However, these distinctions have been blurred in many areas because of intermarriage.

Most Europeans speak languages which belong to the Indo-European group, although there are some exceptions, such as the extremely ancient Basque language, which is unrelated to any other, and the Finnish, Hungarian and Lapp languages, which belong to the Uralic and Altaic family. The Indo-European group includes such Celtic langages as Breton, Irish, Scottish Gaelic and Welsh; Balto-Slavic languages, including Bulgarian, Czech, Polish, Russian, Serbo-Croat and Slovak; Germanic languages, including Danish, Dutch, English, German, Icelandic, Norwegian and Swedish; and Romance languages (derived from Latin), including French, Italian, Portuguese, Romanian and Spanish. Albanian and Greek are usually classed in subgroups of their own.

Above Bergen is a major seaport and Norway's second largest city. It stands in a fiord sheltered from Atlantic gales. Its mild climate and ice-free port are a consequence of the warm North Atlantic Drift, which flows north along the coast. This is an extension of the Gulf Stream, an ocean current which originates in the tropical Caribbean Sea.

Below The Lord Mayor's Show in the City of London is one of the many colourful events celebrating British traditions which are held in this great capital city. In addition to pageant, London is steeped in history and its famous museums and live theatre attract many visitors.

The Religions

Western Europe is a Christian continent, although there is a sizeable Jewish population and other religions, such as Islam, have recently been introduced by immigrants. But more than half of the people of Europe belong to the Roman Catholic Church. In eastern and southeastern Europe, many belong to the Eastern Orthodox Church, while Protestants live mainly in northern Europe, including Britain.

The Communist leadership in eastern Europe has actively discouraged religion and Albania officially became an atheist nation in 1967. But Communist policy has met with failure in some places. For example, in Poland in 1978, 93 percent of the people had been baptized into the Roman Catholic Church, and 74 percent of them were regular church-goers, which is a higher proportion than in many western countries.

Economic and Demographic Trends

Excluding the USSR, the rate of population increase in Europe was the lowest in the world between 1975 and 1980 at 0.4 percent per year. In some countries the population is static with zero growth, and in East Germany it has actually been declining. But in Albania, the least developed of European countries, the population growth rate is 2.4 percent a year. Generally, however, both birth and death rates have been falling and, as a result, the average life expectancies at birth have been rising. The highest average life expectancy in 1981 was 77 years in Sweden. In western Europe as a whole, the life expectancy is around 75 years, an increase of about 4 years since 1960. In eastern Europe, the average life expectancy in 1981 was around 72 years, as compared with about 69 in 1960.

There are other differences between the West and the East. The West has higher population densities and a much higher degree of urbanization. For example, in 1981, 91 percent of the population of the United Kingdom lived in cities and towns. In Sweden, the percentage was 88 percent, and in both Denmark and West Germany it was 85 percent. In the East, the percentages of the population in urban areas in Albania, Yugoslavia and Romania were 37, 43 and 50 percent respectively. Europe's two largest cities, Paris and London, are both in the West.

Further, only 2 percent of Britons work in agriculture, with 3 percent in Belgium and 4 percent in West Germany. But 61 percent of Albanians are farm workers. In Bulgaria, the percentage is 37 percent and in Poland it is 31 percent. In western Europe, service industries are the largest employers in most countries. But in eastern Europe, the continuing industrialization makes industry the largest employer. For example, 50 percent of the workforce is employed in industry in East Germany and 48 percent in Czechoslovakia.

Land use

☐ unproductive areas

■ industrial & urban areas

☐ hunting & gathering

☐ stock rearing & ranging

☐ intensive & specialised agriculture

☐ mixed farming

▥ forest lands

⌐ lumbering

⌁ grain production predominant

⋔ nomadic economies

⋰ deep sea fishing

⋯ coastal fishing

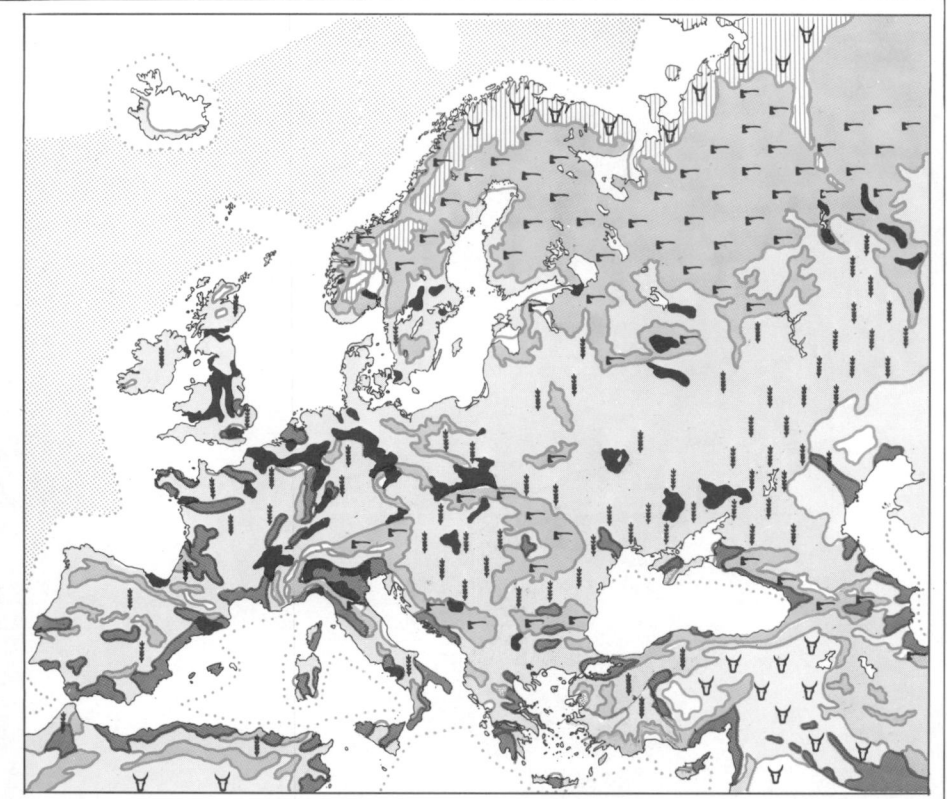

Most of Europe is industrialized. Its per capita GNP in 1980 (excluding the USSR) was about $7,540, as compared with $9.020 in Japan and $11,460 in Canada and the United States. But there are wide variations between individual nations. In 1980, Switzerland and Luxembourg had per capita GNPs of $15,980 and $15,100, respectively. But Albania had a per capita GNP in 1979 of only $840, and Hungary's per capita GNP in 1980 was $1,930. This was less than the lowest in western Europe – $2,300 in Portugal.

History and Culture
Western civilization first flowered in Ancient Greece, which reached its greatest heights in art, architecture, literature, philosophy, government and science, between 500 and 300 BC. The Romans, who achieved their greatest power in the second century AD, borrowed much from Greece, but theirs was essentially a practical culture. Christianity became the official religion of the Roman empire in the late fourth century. It survived the fall of Rome and invasions of nomads from the east, of Vikings and of Muslims.

Between about 1350 and 1550, the Renaissance restored much of classical learning, which had been lost in Europe, although it had been preserved in the Muslim Arab world. From the fifteenth century, the Age of Exploration extended European influence to most parts of the world. The sixteenth century was also the time of the Reformation, when Protestantism spread through northern Europe.

European colonization, begun in the early sixteenth century, continued. After the Industrial Revolution started in Europe in the late eighteenth century, western civilization became dominant throughout the world. With its new technology, the West was in the ascendant.

However, after the sapping of its vitality by two World Wars and the gradual loss of its colonies, Europe suffered a relative decline in power on the international scene. Great nations such as Britain, France and Germany had to give way to two new superpowers – the United States and the USSR.

East and West – opposing Alliances
Differences between eastern and western Europe developed after World War II, when the USSR made eastern Europe a Communist bloc, although two of the Communist countries, Albania and Yugoslavia, subsequently pursued independent policies. The division between East and West has been responsible for much tension. The continent is now divided into two military alliances.

The East, namely Albania, Bulgaria, Czechoslovakia, East Germany, Hungary, Poland, Romania and the USSR, united in the Warsaw Pact of 1955, although Albania's friendship with China led to its virtual expulsion in 1962. In 1981, Warsaw Pact forces were estimated at 4,820,000, of whom 77 percent were Soviet citizens. There were 20 Soviet divisions in East Germany, five in Czechoslovakia, four in Hungary and two in Poland. The presence of Soviet troops has enabled the Communist regimes of eastern Europe to survive, despite much opposition in East Germany (1953), Hungary (1956), Czechoslovakia (1968) and Poland, in 1956, 1970, 1976 and again in the early 1980s.

The North Atlantic Treaty Organization (NATO) was founded in 1949 by Belgium, Canada, Denmark, France, Iceland, Italy, Luxembourg, the Netherlands, Norway, Portugal, the United Kingdom and the United States. Greece and Turkey joined in 1952, West Germany in 1955, and Spain in 1982. In 1981, NATO forces numbered about 4,990,000.

Several economic organizations have been established. The European Economic Community (EEC), founded in 1957, consists of Belgium, Denmark, France, West Germany, Greece, Ireland, Italy, Luxembourg, the Netherlands and the United Kingdom. Applications from Portugal and Spain are pending. A looser organization, the European Free Trade Association (EFTA) was founded in 1960. In 1984, its members were Austria, Iceland, Norway, Portugal, Sweden and Switzerland, with Finland as an associate member. In the East, the Council for Mutual Economic Assistance (CMEA or COMECON) was founded in 1949. In 1984, its members were Bulgaria, Cuba, Czechoslovakia, East Germany, Hungary, Mongolia, Poland, Rumania, the USSR and Vietnam. These economic alliances have brought undoubted benefits, but the world recession from the late 1970s has proved a major setback.

A priest in a street in Athens. Some 97 percent of Greeks belong to the Eastern Orthodox Church.

Southern Europe

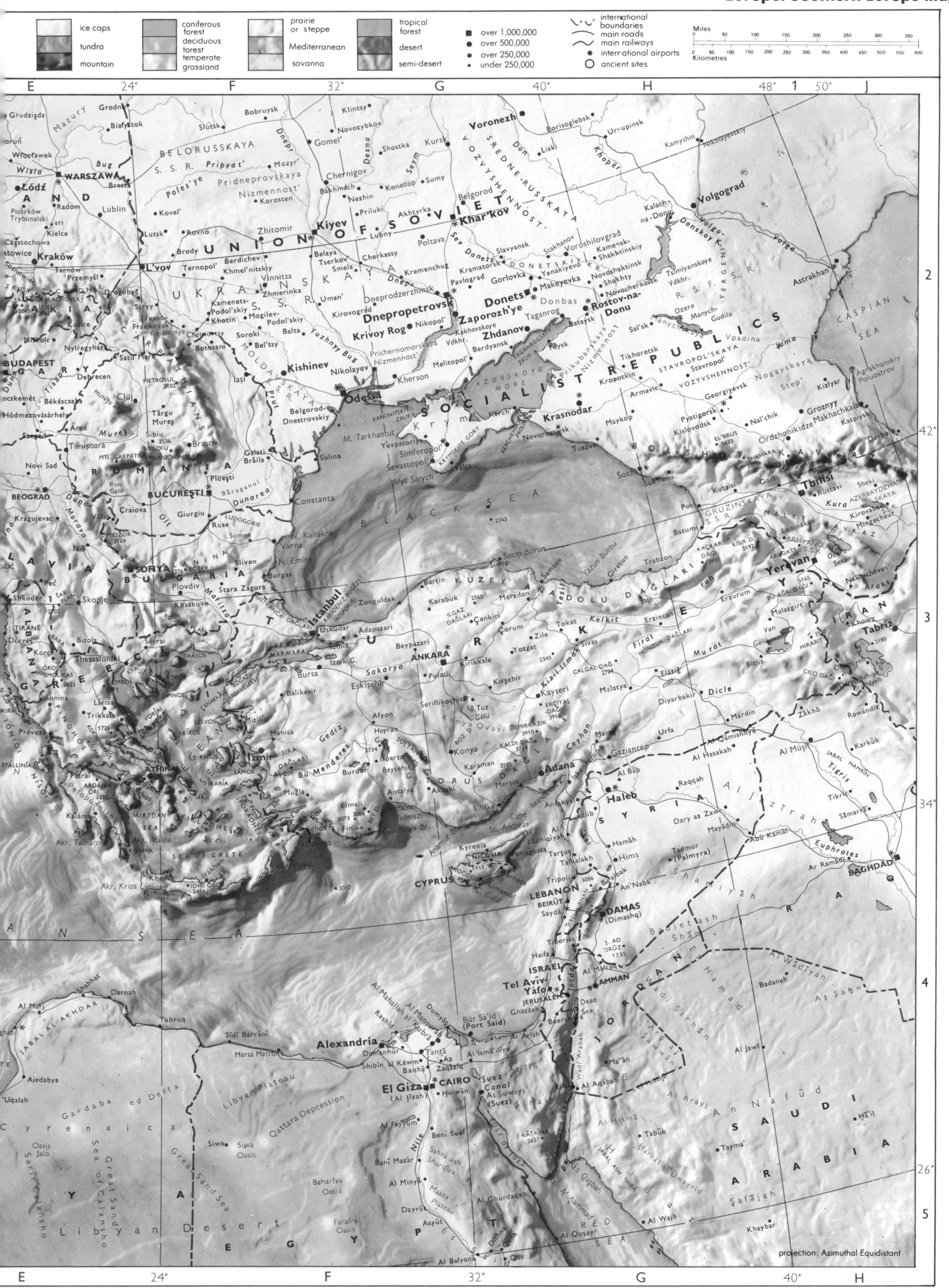

ice caps
tundra
mountain

coniferous forest
deciduous forest
temperate grassland

prairie or steppe
Mediterranean
savanna

tropical forest
desert
semi-desert

■ over 1,000,000
■ over 500,000
● over 250,000
• under 250,000

international boundaries
main roads
main railways
✱ international airports
○ ancient sites

Miles
Kilometres

projection: Azimuthal Equidistant

UNITED KINGDOM

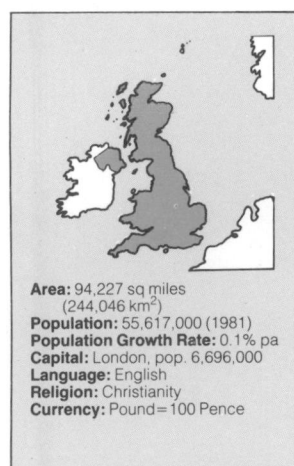

Area: 94,227 sq miles
(244,046 km²)
Population: 55,617,000 (1981)
Population Growth Rate: 0.1% pa
Capital: London, pop. 6,696,000
Language: English
Religion: Christianity
Currency: Pound = 100 Pence

THE UNITED KINGDOM OF GREAT BRITAIN AND NORTHERN IRELAND is made up of England, Scotland, Wales and Northern Ireland.

The Isle of Man and the Channel Islands are largely self-governing dependencies of the UK.

People and Culture Early Stone Age peoples probably settled in Britain about 25,000 years ago. Until about 7,500 years ago, people were able to cross a land-bridge between Britain and continental Europe. But water from the melting ice sheets of the Pleistocene Ice Age raised the sea-level and cut off Britain from the mainland.

But a narrow sea did not deter continuing waves of immigrants. Between about 5,000 and 4,500 years ago, Neolithic people from Iberia arrived. The Celts, who are now represented by the Irish, the Manx, the Highland Scots, the Welsh and the Cornish, reached the islands after the fifth century BC.

These accomplished metalworkers were well established when Julius Caesar arrived from Gaul in 55 BC. But the Romans did not settle until AD 43. They stayed until the early fifth century, when the Roman legions had to return to Rome to defend it against the Germanic Goths.

Without Roman soldiers to defend it, Britain was again invaded by waves of Angles, Jutes, Saxons and, from the eighth century, Vikings.

In 878, one of England's most famous kings, Alfred the Great, united the Christian Anglo-Saxon kingdoms against the pagan Danish Vikings in the north and east. Alfred's victories enabled his grandson, Edgar, to become king of all England in 973. But Danish raids continued and, in 1016, Canute, King of Denmark and Norway, became king of England.

Saxon rule, under Edward the Confessor, was restored in 1042. On Edward's death, William, Duke of Normandy, in France, claimed England's throne as also did Edward's brother-in-law, Harold. The Normans defeated Harold at the Battle of Hastings (1066). They ruled the country sternly under the feudal system.

In 1215, the feudal barons made King John accept the Magna Carta, an important step in the evolution of the Constitution. And a barons' revolt under Simon de Montfort in 1264 led to the growth of a parliament.

Wales was conquered in 1282 and Edward I made his son, later Edward II, the first Prince of Wales. But the Scots held out and Edward II was defeated by Robert Bruce at Bannockburn in 1314.

Between 1337 and 1453, English kings tried to regain French territory lost in the early thirteenth century, but they were finally defeated. At home, the Black Death of 1348 reduced the population of England by a third and undermined the status of the barons and the feudal system. This was gradually replaced by a system of tenant farmers and hired labourers.

In 1399, Henry Bolingbroke, Duke of Lancaster, seized the throne from Richard II and was crowned Henry IV. His son, Henry V, later won brilliant but ultimately pointless victories in France.

From 1455 to 1485, the rival houses of Lancaster and York fought the Wars of the Roses. Henry Tudor finally defeated Richard III of York, and became Henry VII. Under his son, Henry VIII, Wales was formally united with England in 1536.

Henry VIII broke away from the Church of Rome and set up the Church of England. Despite the brief restoration of Papal authority under his successor Queen Mary, Elizabeth I, who became queen in 1558, also became head of a Protestant church.

The Elizabethan period was a great age of literature, architecture and increasing naval power. The Spanish threat to England was ended with the defeat of the Spanish Armada in 1588.

The Stuarts, the kings of Scotland, took over from the Tudors when James VI of Scotland became James I of England in 1603. But clashes between the Stuarts and Parliament led to the Civil War in 1642. Charles I was beheaded in 1649 and Oliver Cromwell headed a republican government.

The monarchy was restored in 1660 under Charles II. But in 1688, James II, a Roman Catholic, was forced to give up the throne to his Protestant daughter Mary and her husband, William of Orange. In 1690, William defeated Irish supporters of James II at the Battle of the Boyne.

In 1707, England and Wales were united with Scotland to form Great Britain. Scottish attempts to restore the Stuarts to the throne continued until the clans were finally crushed at Culloden in 1746.

Empire and After From the seventeenth century, Britain became a colonial power, defeating the French in India and Canada between 1756 and 1763. But it received a major setback when the 13 American colonies declared themselves independent in 1776.

In the late eighteenth century, the Industrial Revolution began in Britain and this consolidated its power. It rapidly changed from an agricultural society into an industrial one, though not without much hardship and unrest, which led to a series of reforms, such as the legalization of trade unions in 1871.

Under Queen Victoria, who reigned from 1837 to 1901, the empire was enlarged. But in the early twentieth century, Britain had other rivals, notably Germany and the United States.

World War I sapped the UK's strength and, in 1919–21, the Irish fought for independence. Ireland was finally partitioned into the Irish Free State in the south and the mainly Protestant Northern Ireland, which remained part of the United Kingdom.

World War II practically bankrupted Britain, and it was no longer able to remain a top world power. The British colonies gradually gained their independence, and the empire was transformed into a loose alliance of equal nations, called the Commonwealth.

But Britain played an important part in the western defence alliance, NATO. It also joined the European Economic Community in 1973, which disappointed some of its traditional trading partners in the Commonwealth. But progress within the EEC was slow, because of the world economic recession.

In the 1980s, the UK faced many problems, including inflation, mounting unemployment, the rising cost of welfare services, and the decay of the inner cities, many of which housed large immigrant communities from the New Commonwealth (mainly Asia, the West Indies and Africa) and Pakistan.

Another problem was the violence in Northern Ireland instigated by the Irish Republican Army, who wanted the reunification of Ireland.

Population Distribution England, one of the world's most densely populated places, contains 83 percent of the UK's population.

Nearly 39 percent of England's population lives in seven metropolitan counties:

Greater London
(pop. 6,696,000)
West Midlands
including Birmingham
(2,645,000)
Greater Manchester
(2,559,000)
West Yorkshire
including Leeds
(2,038,000)
Merseyside including
Liverpool (1,513,000)
South Yorkshire
including Sheffield
(1,302,000)
Tyne and Wear including
Newcastle upon Tyne
(1,143,000).

The main centre of population in Wales is the south-east, where Gwent, Mid-Glamorgan, South Glamorgan and

Mousehole is a beautiful fishing village in Cornwall, southwestern England. Britain is an island nation and nowhere is far from the sea.

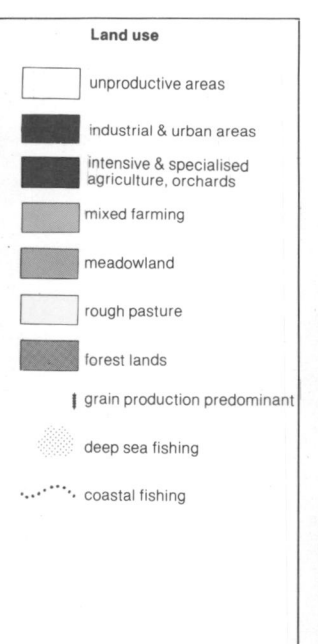

Land use

☐	unproductive areas
■	industrial & urban areas
■	intensive & specialised agriculture, orchards
▨	mixed farming
▨	meadowland
☐	rough pasture
▨	forest lands
❙	grain production predominant
⁙	deep sea fishing
⁖⁖	coastal fishing

West Glamorgan cover only 17.5 percent of Wales, but contain 62 percent of the population. This area contains the Welsh capital Cardiff (pop. 274,000).

In Scotland, the Central Lowlands contain about 80 percent of the population, including the large cities of Glasgow (pop. 762,000), Edinburgh (419,000) and Dundee (175,000). Aberdeen (190,000), in the northeast, is the service centre for the North Sea oil and gas industry.

Belfast (298,000) is the only large city in Northern Ireland.

Britain is one of the world's most urbanized countries. In 1981, 91 percent lived in cities and towns.

While English is the official language, more than 500,000 people in Wales speak Welsh and about 90,000 Scots speak Scottish Gaelic. The ancient Celtic language of Cornwall died out early in this century.

Regional nationalist movements, which resent England's dominant role in the UK, have attracted support recently.

Population Growth In recent years, the population has been increasing by only 0.1 percent per year. The average life expectancy at birth in 1981 was 74, compared with 71 in 1960.

In the last 100 years, emigration has usually exceeded immigration. But there were periods, such as 1931–46, when the trend was reversed. During that period, the main source of immigrants was mainland Europe.

The same situation occurred in 1956–61, when immigration, mainly from the New Commonwealth and Pakistan, exceeded emigration. Today, both emigration and immigration have declined.

Religion The established Church of England is Protestant Episcopal, while the established Church of Scotland is Presbyterian.

In 1982, Roman Catholics numbered 5,093,000 in Great Britain. In Northern Ireland, in 1981, Roman Catholics made up 28 percent of the population; Presbyterians, 23 percent; and the Church of Ireland, 19 percent.

Social Services Britain has a system of free education starting at the age of 5 and continuing until 16. Further education is voluntary. British

Churches are to be seen in great numbers throughout Britain and much of the character of rural life is associated with them.

British Isles

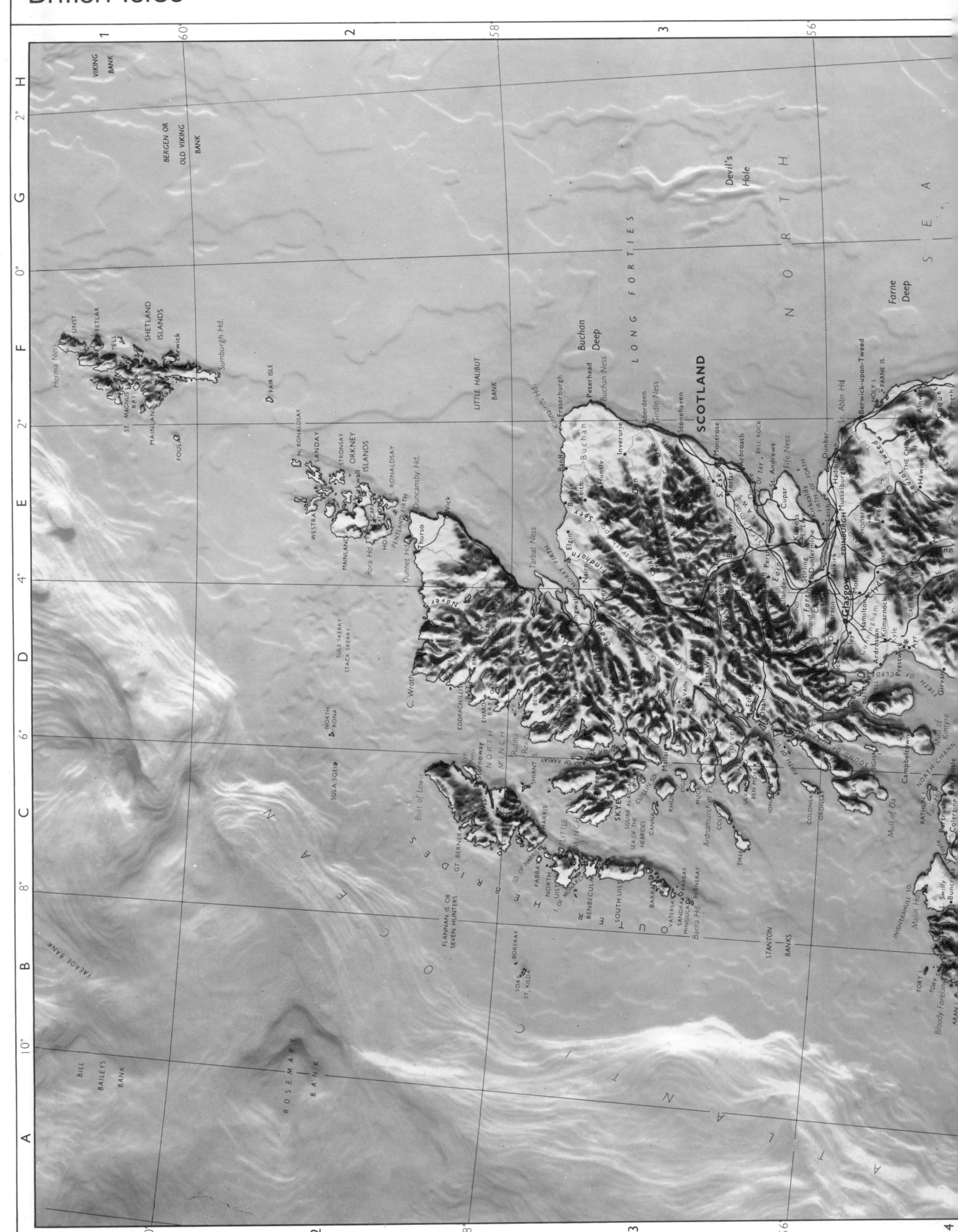

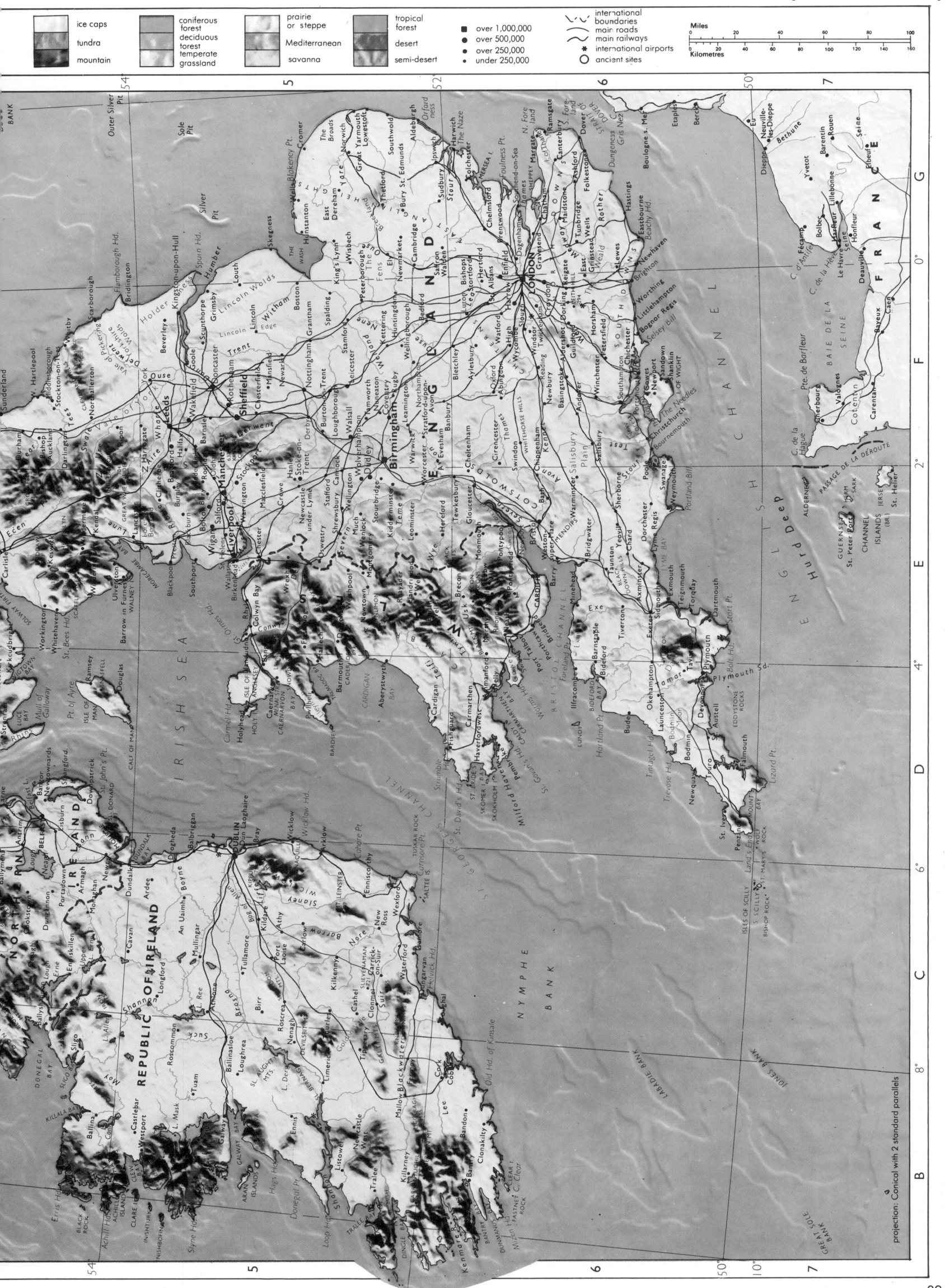

education and its ancient universities have served as models for others throughout the world.

After World War II, Britain set up an elaborate welfare system, including a National Health Service, which is a charge on the national income. But private practice goes on. There are also sickness and unemployment benefits, family allowances, maternity and widow's benefits, and retirement pensions.

The Land Great Britain has two main land regions. Lowland Britain lies mostly east of a line joining the mouth of the Tees in Cleveland to the mouth of the Exe in Devonshire. To the west and north of this line is Highland Britain.

Lowland Britain contains few places above 1,000 feet (305 m). Most of the rocks are young and were formed within the last 200 million years. They are mainly sedimentary in type.

The strata have been tilted or gently folded. The more resistant layers of sandstone, limestone and chalk form ranges of hills, often with a steep escarpment on one side and a gentle dip-slope on the other, as in the Jurassic-limestone Cotswold Hills, and the Cretaceous-chalk Chiltern Hills and the Yorkshire Wolds.

Southeastern England is rather different. It consists of an anticline in which the chalk forms the North and South Downs. But in the centre of the anticline, the chalk has been worn away in an area called the Weald.

Between the ranges of hills, there are several fertile clay vales and basins, such as the London Basin. The flattest area is East Anglia, parts of which (the Fens) have been reclaimed from the sea.

Highland Britain contains generally harder and older rocks, many of which are igneous or metamorphic in type. The main highlands in England are the south-west, including Dartmoor and Exmoor; the Pennine chain, the backbone of northern England; and the Lake District in Cumbria, which contains England's highest peak, Scafell Pike, which is 3,210 feet (978 m) above sea-level.

Wales is mostly mountainous, with its highest peak, Snowdon, reaching 3,560 feet (1,085 m).

Scotland has three main land regions: the Southern Uplands; the Central Lowlands; and the Highlands, where large areas are over 3,000 feet (914 m). Ben Nevis, the highest peak in the British Isles at 4,406 feet (1,343 m), overlooks the Great Glen, a long rift valley which divides the Highlands into two parts.

Highland Britain was glaciated during the Ice Age and lakes abound in the over-deepened valleys, some of which are dammed by moraine.

Loch Lomond, northwest of Glasgow, is the largest lake in Great Britain. But the largest lake in the British Isles is Lough Neagh in Northern Ireland. It covers 153 square miles (396 km²).

Northern Ireland has three main uplands: the Antrim plateau, where large areas are covered by hardened lava; the Sperrin Mountains; and the Mountains of Mourne.

Hops for making beer are dried in oast houses in Kent.

The longest rivers in the UK are the Severn, which flows about 220 miles (354 km) from its source near Plynlimon, Wales, to the Bristol Channel, and the Thames, which rises in the Cotswold Hills and flows to London on its way to the North Sea.

Climate The UK has a moist, temperate climate, which is moderated by the warm North Atlantic Drift. It lies in the path of Atlantic depressions which bring rainy, unsettled weather from west to east.

In January, temperatures in the southwest average 45°F (7°C), although it is colder to the north and east. The average January reading in Glasgow and on much of England's east coast is 38°F (3°C).

In summer, the effect of the ocean is to lower temperatures. In the far south, July temperatures average 63°F (17°C), as compared with 55°F (13°C) in northern Scotland.

The rainfall is heavy in the western uplands, particularly the western Highlands of Scot-

land, the Welsh mountains and the Lake District, where the average annual rainfall is between about 40 and 200 inches (1,016–5,080 mm). Sprinkling Tarn, Cumbria, holds the record rainfall for one year – 257 inches (6,528 mm) in 1954.

The rainfall diminishes to the east, where the average annual rainfall is usually less than 30 inches (762 mm).

Vegetation About 12,000 years ago, Britain was in the grip of the Ice Age. As the climate improved, plants colonized the land and, by 2,500 years ago, about two-thirds of the country was covered by mixed forests. Since Roman times, the forests have been largely cleared to make way for farms.

Today there are large tracts of heath and moorland in deforested areas, and in the uplands. But some of these regions have been reforested with economically valuable trees, such as fir, pine and spruce.

In Northern Ireland, the uplands are mostly poor pasture, while parts of the lowlands are marshy.

Wildlife Britain's coasts attract a wide variety of birds, many of which are protected in sanctuaries and other reserves.

Generally, the native mammals and reptiles have been greatly reduced in numbers, and large species, such as bears, wild boars and wolves, have vanished.

But some animals, such as foxes, which have become city scavengers, have shown remarkable adaptation to the changing environment. Others, such as martens, polecats and wild cats, have survived, but in small numbers. The UK also has introduced species, including the North American grey squirrel, the mink and several exotic birds.

Today there is a growing emphasis on conservation, through such organizations as the Countryside Commission and the National Trust. England and Wales have ten National Parks and 33 Areas of Outstanding Natural Beauty.

Economy The UK is an industrial nation. In 1981, 33 percent of its GDP came from industry (with manufacturing contributing 20 percent), as compared with 2 percent from agriculture and 65 percent from services. Similarly, the workforce broke down into agriculture 2 percent, industry 42 percent and services 56 percent.

The UK was the world's first nation to industrialize, but it has since been overhauled by other countries. For example, of the ten members of the EEC, the UK had the third largest gross national product (after West Germany and France) in 1981. But it ranked seventh in terms of its per capita GNP, which stood at $9,110. The only EEC

nations with lower per capita GNPs were Italy, Ireland and Greece.

Farming Although its farms are highly efficient and among the world's most productive, the UK is a net food importer.

Some 78 percent of the land is agricultural, with arable land making up 29 percent. Barley, wheat, oats, potatoes and sugar-beet are the leading crops.

Arable farming, market gardening and dairy farming are the most important types of farming in the east. In the wetter and more rugged west, livestock farming for meat and dairy products is more important. In 1981, the UK had 13.1 million cattle, 32.1 million sheep, 7.8 million pigs and 132 million poultry.

England contains the most productive farms. Wales consists largely of rough grazing, with an important arable area in the south. Scotland's chief farming region is the fertile Central Lowlands. In Northern Ireland, 86 percent of the land is pasture of varying quality. The main crop farms are around Lough Neagh.

Forestry and Fishing Productive woodland in 1981 covered nearly 8 percent of the UK. About half was managed by the Forestry Commission and half by private concerns.

The fishing industry produces about four-fifths of the country's needs.

Mining Abundant reserves of coal and iron ore enabled the UK to lead in the Industrial Revolution. But rising costs and overseas competition have caused a fall in production.

The chief coalfields are located around the Pennines, in South Wales, the English Midlands and the Central Lowlands of Scotland.

In the last decade, natural gas and petroleum from the North Sea have become im-

The Scottish Highlands are characterized by rounded mountains and lochs, which fill valleys formed by glaciers in the Ice Age.

portant. In 1981, the UK was the world's fifth largest producer of these fuels.

Some metals and other minerals has caused some manufacturing indus-imported.

Manufacturing and Trade Competition from some overseas countries has caused some manufacturing industries, such as textiles and shipbuilding, to decline by comparison with the past. And, while the UK led the world in steel production in the nineteenth century, it now ranks 16th and accounts for only 1.4 percent of world production (1981).

Major industries include metal manufacturing, mechanical, chemical and marine engineering, vehicle and transport equipment, many processing industries, and textile manufacturing.

The main industrial regions are on the coalfields and around large ports like London and Liverpool. Northern Ireland's main industrial region is in and around Belfast.

In 1981, machinery and transport equipment made up 33 percent of the UK's exports, mineral fuels and lubricants 20 percent, manufactured goods 24 percent and chemicals 11 percent. Imports included machinery and transport equipment (29 percent) manufactures (29 percent), mineral fuels and lubricants (13 percent) and food and live animals (11 percent).

The main trading partners are the EEC countries (47.6 percent of the total trade in 1982), the United States (12.5 percent), the Commonwealth (11.2 percent), EFTA coun-tries (11 percent) and Japan (3 percent).

Communications The UK is well endowed with surfaced roads, which totalled nearly 342,000 miles (550,380 km) in 1981. Railways have declined relatively, but 10,706 route-miles (17,229 km) were in operation in 1982, of which 22 percent were electrified. In 1982, the UK merchant fleet made up 5 percent of the world fleet.

Tourism About 11.5 million tourists visited the UK in 1981. They were a useful source of foreign currency, as are other invisible industries, such as banking and insurance.

DEPENDENCIES

THE CHANNEL ISLANDS off the northwest coast of France are Britain's only remaining possession from the Duchy of Normandy. But they are largely self-governing. The official languages are English and French. The largest island is Jersey, with an area of 45 square miles (117 km²) and a population of 76,100. Guernsey covers 24 square miles (62 km²) and has 53,300 people. Dependencies of Guernsey are Alderney, Brechou, Great Sark, Little Sark, Herm, Jethou and Lihou, which have a combined area of 6 square miles (15 km²).

Jersey and Guernsey have their own Lieutenant-Governor who is appointed by the British Crown. Jersey, Guernsey, Alderney and Sark have elected assemblies. Tourism and farming are the chief activities. The islands are known for their low taxation.

THE ISLE OF MAN is a dependency of the United Kingdom, which is largely self-governing. It is administered by the Court of Tynwald, consisting of a Governor appointed by the British Crown, a Legislative Council, and the elected House of Keys. Like the Channel Islands, the Isle of Man has its own taxation system. Tourism and farming are the chief industries.

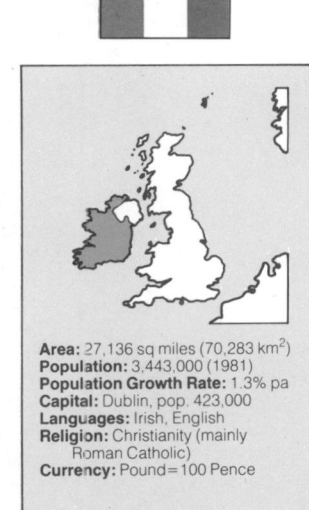

IRELAND

Area: 27,136 sq miles (70,283 km²)
Population: 3,443,000 (1981)
Population Growth Rate: 1.3% pa
Capital: Dublin, pop. 423,000
Languages: Irish, English
Religion: Christianity (mainly Roman Catholic)
Currency: Pound = 100 Pence

THE REPUBLIC OF IRELAND covers 83 percent of Ireland. It contains four provinces – Connacht, Leinster, Munster and Ulster – which are divided into 26 counties.

Of Ulster's nine counties, three of them – Cavan, Donegal and Monahan – are in the Republic. The others form Northern Ireland, which is part of the United Kingdom.

People and Culture The Celts, whose descendants make up much of the modern population, settled in Ireland after the fifth century BC.

In AD 432, St Patrick introduced Christianity. But the monasteries were pillaged by the Vikings, who settled in about 795. In the twelfth century, the Irish under Brian Boru defeated the Vikings.

In the 1160s, the Normans invaded eastern Ireland, although the Irish had won back much of their land by the late Middle Ages.

From the sixteenth century, Tudor and Stuart monarchs encouraged English settlement in Ireland and tried to convert the Irish to Protestantism. A series of unsuccessful rebellions culminated in the defeat of the Irish supporters of the deposed James II at the Battle of the Boyne (1690). The Act of Union (1801) established the United Kingdom of Great Britain and Ireland.

In 1845–46, potato blight caused famine. By 1851, a million people were dead and over a million had emigrated. In 1841, the 26 counties had a population of 6,529,000. This was halved by 1901. Continuing emigration made the population decline further, reaching a low of 2,884,000 in 1966.

In 1916, the British crushed an uprising in Dublin. But the armed struggle broke out again in 1919. In 1922, Ireland was partitioned into the Irish Free State and the mainly Protestant Northern Ireland. In 1937, the Free State was renamed Eire and in 1949 it became the Republic of Ireland.

Reunification remains a major political issue, although the Irish government opposes the activities of the illegal Irish Republican Army in Northern Ireland.

Irish, the first official language, is spoken by about 20 percent of the people. English is the second official language. In 1971, 94 percent of the people were Roman Catholics and 3.3 percent belonged to the Church of Ireland.

The average life expectancy in 1981 was 73 years. Urbanization is increasing. In 1981, 58 percent lived in urban areas.

The Land Much of the central plain is covered by glacial deposits, and bogs cover nearly one-third of the land. Various mountains surround the plain. The highest mountain is Carrantuohill in the southwest, where the sea has invaded river valleys to form bays, such as Dingle Bay. The River Shannon, the longest in the British Isles, is 240 miles (386 km) long.

The climate is mild and moist. The average annual temperature is 45°F–61°F (7°C–16°C) in the southwest, and 43°F–57°F (6°C–14°C) in the northeast.

Parts of the west have 60 inches (1,524 mm) of rain a year. Dublin has 30 inches (762 mm). Moorland and bog cover large areas.

Economy The per capita GNP was $5,230 in 1981, the second lowest in the EEC, which Ireland joined in 1973.

Agriculture is a major industry. It accounted for 17 percent of the GDP and 18 percent of the workforce in 1980.

Arable land and pasture cover nearly 70 percent of Ireland. The main crops are barley, wheat, potatoes, oats, hay and sugar-beet. In 1980, cattle numbered 6.7 million and sheep 3.5 million. Fishing is important and Irish horses are world-famous.

The processing of farm products forms much of the industrial sector, which employed 37 percent of the workforce in 1980. Large-scale manufacturing in Dublin and the second city, Cork (pop. 136,000), depends largely on imported fuels and minerals, although peat is still used as a domestic fuel. The UK accounted for 46 percent of the Republic's trade in 1981, and other EEC countries for 25 percent.

The number of tourists, including cross-border movements, in 1981 was 9,423,000.

Bath, in southwestern England, contains famous Roman Baths.

A Guardsman on sentry.

Loch Lomond, not far from industrial Glasgow, is the largest of Scotland's many lakes.

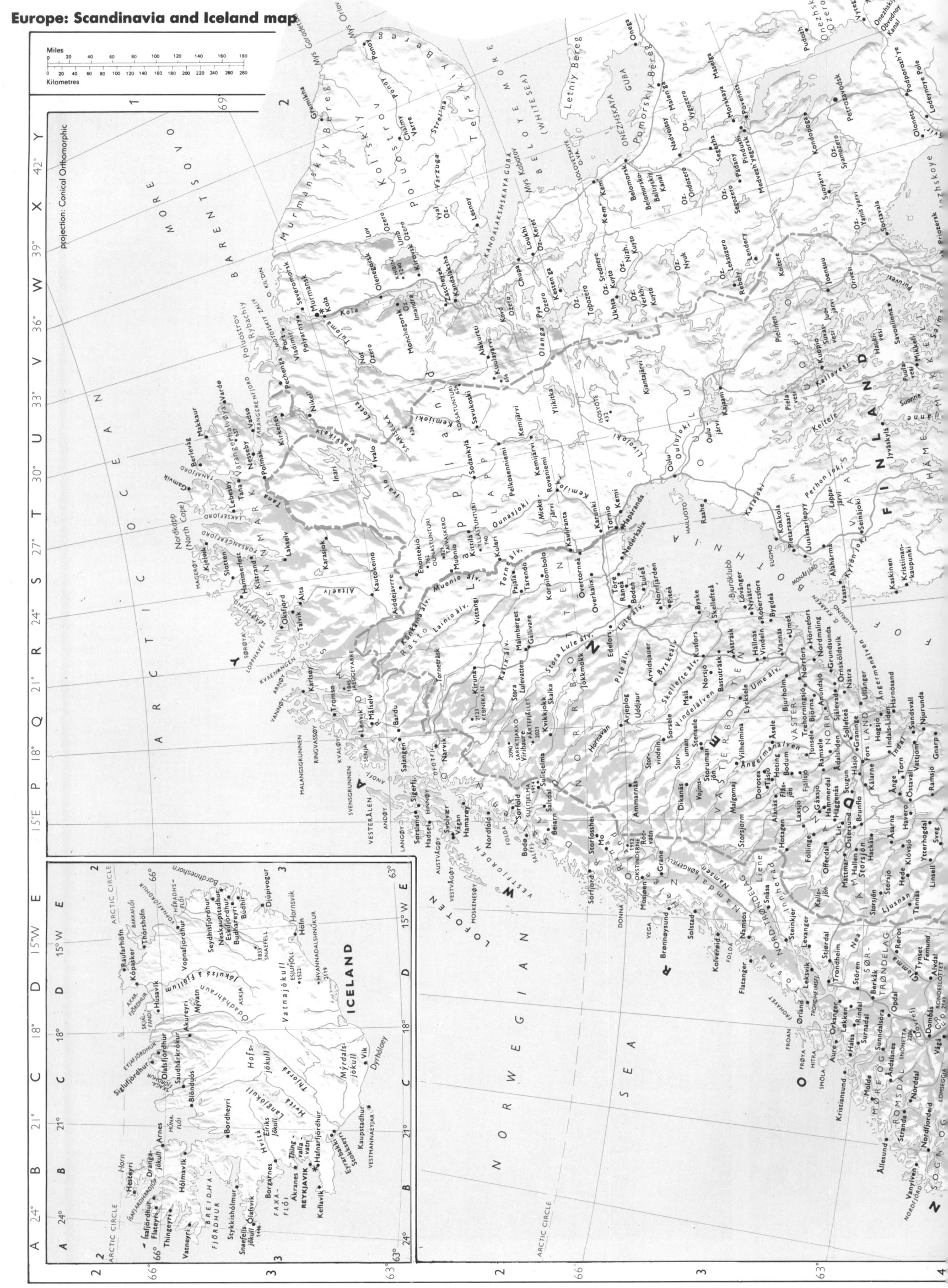

Scandinavia and Iceland

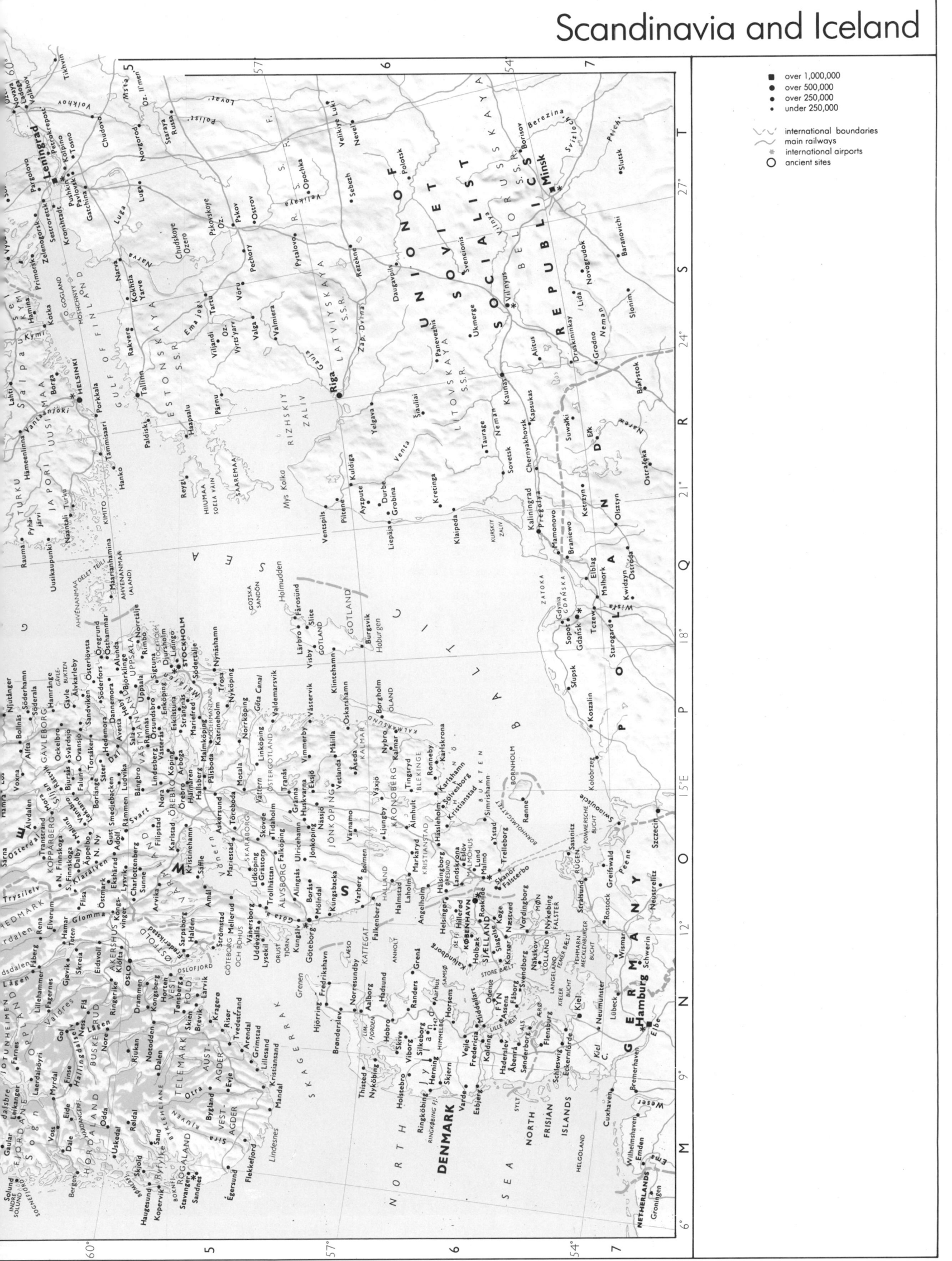

■ over 1,000,000
● over 500,000
● over 250,000
• under 250,000

〜 international boundaries
〜 main railways
✳ international airports
○ ancient sites

DENMARK

Area: 16,629 sq miles (43,069 km²)
Population: 5,153,000
Population Growth Rate: 0.2% pa
Capital: København (Copenhagen) pop. 491,000
Language: Danish
Religion: Christianity (Lutheran)
Currency: Krone = 100 Ore

THE KINGDOM OF DENMARK has two largely self-governing territories: Greenland (see page 39); and the Faeroe Islands (see below).

People and Culture Denmark became a nation in about AD 950 and soon afterwards was united with Norway. A later ruler, Canute, also became king of England in 1016. But after 1035, Denmark lost its overseas territories.

In the twelfth and thirteenth centuries, Denmark built up an empire around the Baltic Sea and, in 1380, it took Iceland, which remained Danish until 1944.

Denmark, Norway and Sweden were united under Danish rule by 1397. Sweden broke away in 1523, but Norway remained united with Denmark until 1814.

Denmark became a constitutional monarchy in 1849. It was neutral in World War I, but Germany occupied it in World War II.

Denmark has an elaborate welfare system and the average life expectancy at birth (1981) was 75 years.

Protestantism was adopted in 1536 and most Danes now belong to the Lutheran Church. About 85 percent of the people live in urban areas. København (Copenhagen), the largest conurbation, has a population of 1,337,000, including its suburbs. The second city is Aarhus (pop. 247,000).

The Land Denmark includes the low-lying Jylland (Jutland) peninsula and about 480 islands, 382 being uninhabited. The capital is on the largest island, Sjælland. Glacial deposits mask the underlying rocks in most places.

The climate is mild and moist. The average annual temperature range is 32°F–61°F (0°C–16°C). The average rainfall is between 20 and 30 inches (508–762 mm) a year. Sand dunes and heath are in the west. Low hills run through central Jylland, but the east and many of the islands are fertile.

Economy Farmland covers more than 70 percent of Denmark, though farming employs only 7 percent of the workforce, compared with 35 percent in industry.

Animal products, including bacon, butter, cheese and eggs, are produced, as are cereals, potatoes and sugar-beet. Fishing is important, but industry accounted for 32 percent of the GDP in 1981 (compared with 4 percent from agriculture).

Electrical machinery, transport equipment and various manufactures made up nearly half of the exports in 1981. Denmark is a member of the EEC, but trade with Scandinavia remains important. Denmark's per capita GNP (1981) was $13,120.

THE FAEROE ISLANDS are nominally part of Denmark. They are located in the North Atlantic between Scotland and Iceland. They have an area of 540 square miles (1,399 km²) and a population of 45,000. Most of the Faeroe Islanders live by fishing.

NORWAY

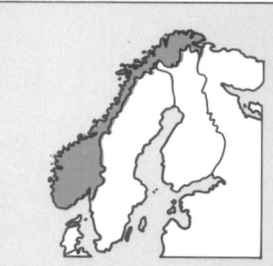

Area: 125,182 sq miles (324,219 km²)
Population: 4,148,000
Population Growth Rate: 0.4% pa
Capital: Oslo, pop. 450,000
Language: Norwegian
Religion: Christianity (Evangelical Lutheran)
Currency: Krone = 100 Ore

THE KINGDOM OF NORWAY occupies the western part of the Scandinavian peninsula.

People and Culture Norway became a united kingdom in AD 872. It was united with Sweden in 1219 and, in 1397, the union came under Danish rule. Although Sweden broke away in 1523, Danish rule of Norway continued until 1814. Norway was then united with Sweden.

In 1905, Norway dissolved the union and became a constitutional monarchy. Neutral in World War I, Norway was conquered by Germany in World War II. After the war, the Social Democratic party regained power and established a comprehensive welfare system. In 1981 a Conservative government was formed, the first since 1928.

In 1981, the average life expectancy was 76 years. About 53 percent of Norwegians live in urban areas. The main cities are Oslo (449,000), Bergen (207,000) and Trondheim (135,000).

The Land Most of Norway is over 1,000 feet (305 m); the highest point is Galdhøpiggen at 8,100 feet (2,469m).

The climate is mild in the south and west because of the warm North Atlantic Drift. The rainfall decreases from west to east in the south.

Ice-caps and snowfields cover 1 percent of the land, coniferous forests 27 percent and farmland 3 percent. The rest is mostly barren.

Economy The per capita GNP in 1981 was $14,060. In 1980, farming employed 7 percent of the workforce, industry 37 percent, and services 57 percent.

Norway is western Europe's second largest producer of petroleum and natural gas. Metals include copper, iron ore, lead and zinc. Petroleum dominates the exports, but machinery and transport equipment and various manufactures are also important. Nearly all the electrical energy comes from hydroelectric stations.

The UK, West Germany and Sweden are major trading partners. Norway also earns foreign exchange from its large merchant fleet.

Fishing and forestry are also important. The chief farm areas are around Oslo, Trondheim and Kristiansund.

TERRITORIES

SVALBARD is a Norwegian archipelago of nine main islands in the Arctic Ocean. The largest island, Spitsbergen, contains Norwegian and Soviet coal mines. Svalbard covers 24,000 square miles (62,160 km²). The population is 4,000.

JAN MAYEN ISLAND, north of Iceland, is a Norwegian territory. It is volcanic and covers 143 square miles (372 km²). The island has no permanent population.

SWEDEN

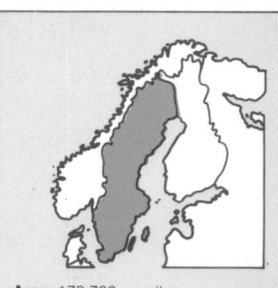

Area: 173,732 sq miles (449,964 km²)
Population: 8,399,000
Population Growth Rate: 0.3% pa
Capital: Stockholm, pop. 647,000
Language: Swedish
Religion: Christianity (Evangelical Lutheran)
Currency: Krona = 100 Ore

THE KINGDOM OF SWEDEN is western Europe's third largest nation. Most people live in the south.

People and Culture Between 800 and 1050, Swedish Vikings spread over large areas. A Swedish nation was formed in the eleventh century, and Christianity became established. From 1323, Sweden controlled Finland.

In 1397, Sweden was united with Denmark and Norway. The Swedes became independent in 1523 under King Gustavus I, who made Sweden a constitutional monarchy and introduced Protestantism.

Gustavus gained land around the Baltic, but by 1718, defeat by Russia ended Sweden's imperial power. The Swedes were later defeated by

Hälsingborg is a Swedish seaport and industrial city on the Øresund, a narrow strait which separates Sweden from Denmark.

Bergen, Norway, stands at the head of Byfjord. The indented coast of Norway, with its long fjords eroded by glaciers, affords protection for fishing fleets.

Napoleon and, in 1809, they lost Finland to Russia.

Between 1814 and 1905, Sweden and Norway were a united kingdom. Sweden was neutral in World War I.

From the 1920s, successive Labour governments set up an elaborate welfare system. The average life expectancy in 1981 was 77 years. Urbanization is also high at 88 percent.
The Land Mountains form the border with Norway. The highest peak at 6,965 feet (2,123 m) is Kebnekaise.

Most of northern Sweden is a plateau called Norrland. South of Norrland is the Central Lakes region. South again, there are infertile uplands, but Sweden's southern tip is a fertile plain.

Winters are long and cold, and northern Sweden (Lappland) is above the Arctic Circle. Summers are short, warm and sunny.

Moorland lies above the tree-line, which is between 2,600 and 2,900 feet (792–884 m). The north has vast coniferous forests. Mixed forests grow in the south.
Economy Sweden had the high per capita GNP of $14,870 in 1981. It has an industrial economy. In 1980, farming employed 5 percent of the workforce and industry 34 percent.

There is little coal, but hydroelectric and nuclear power stations produce 87 percent of the electrical energy. Sweden has large reserves of iron ore and steel is a major product.

Forests cover 57 percent of the land and Sweden is a major wood, and paper producer. Farmland covers 8 percent of the land. Cereals, potatoes, sugar-beet and dairy products are important. West Germany and the UK are major trading partners.

FINLAND

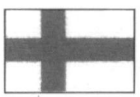

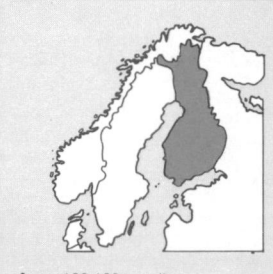

Area: 130,129 sq miles (337,032 km²)
Population: 4,844,000
Population Growth Rate: 0.3% pa
Capital: Helsinki, pop. 910,000
Languages: Finnish, Swedish
Religion: Christianity (Lutheran National Church 90%)
Currency: Markka = 100 Penniä

THE REPUBLIC OF FINLAND is also called Suomi.
People and Culture Early settlers were Finno-Ugrian tribes from the east, who arrived around AD 100. In 1157, Sweden introduced Christianity into Finland. From 1323, Sweden controlled all of Finland, but in 1809 Russia annexed the country.

Finland declared itself independent in 1917. A civil war occurred in 1918 and the victorious 'White' forces attempted to introduce a monarchy. But after a new parliament had been elected Finland in 1919 adopted a republican Constitution.

In 1939, the USSR declared war on Finland, which as a result lost one-third of its territory. In 1941, Finland allied itself with Germany, but it surrendered to the USSR in 1944. It lost more land in a peace treaty (1947). Since then, it has signed a series of friendship treaties with the USSR while preserving its independence.

In 1981, the average life expectancy was 75 years, and 63 percent of Finns lived in urban areas, especially in the southwest.
The Land During the Pleistocene Ice Age, ice eroded many hollows in the rocks. These are now filled by 55,000 or more lakes. Water covers 9 percent of Finland.

Winters are cold, with average January temperatures ranging from 25°F (−4°C) in the south to 10°F (−12°C) in the north. Most rain falls in summer or autumn.

Coniferous forests cover more than four-fifths of the land, and farmland 9 percent.
Economy In 1980, agriculture (especially dairy farming) employed 11 percent of the workforce and industry 35 percent. Forestry is a major industry. Finland ranks sixth among world coniferous-wood producers. It also produces many things that are made from timber.

ICELAND

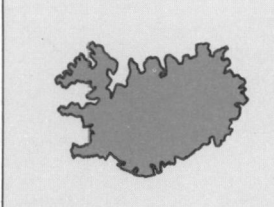

Area: 39,769 sq miles (103,000 km²)
Population: 238,000
Population Growth Rate: 1.0% pa
Capital: Reykjavik, pop. 86,000
Language: Icelandic
Religion: Christianity (Evangelical Lutheran)
Currency: Króna = 100 Aurar

THE REPUBLIC OF ICELAND is Europe's westernmost country.

People and Culture Norwegian Vikings colonized Iceland in AD 874. Other Vikings followed and, in 930, they founded the Althing, the world's oldest surviving parliament.

Christianity was introduced around 1000. In 1262, Iceland united with Norway and, in the late fourteenth century, it came under Danish rule along with Norway.

Iceland became independent in 1918, but Denmark's king remained its monarch. It became a fully independent republic in 1944. Various fishing disputes, mainly with the United Kingdom, occurred between 1958 and 1976.

Social welfare is highly developed and Icelanders enjoy a high standard of living.
The Land Iceland is a volcanic island. It acquired new territory in 1963 when an offshore island, Surtsey, appeared off its coast. The land is highly glaciated.

Iceland has cold winters and cool summers. The North Atlantic Drift moderates temperatures in the south.
Economy Iceland has large hydro-electric and geothermal resources. Fishing is a major industry. Meat and dairy farming are also important. In 1980, farming and fishing employed 23 percent of the workforce and industry, including textiles, fertilizers and cement, 24 percent. The main exports are fish, fishoil, skins and aluminium. The main imports are fuel, vehicles, textiles, animal feeds and timber. The per capita GDP in 1981 was $12,860 – one of the highest in Europe.

Spain and Portugal

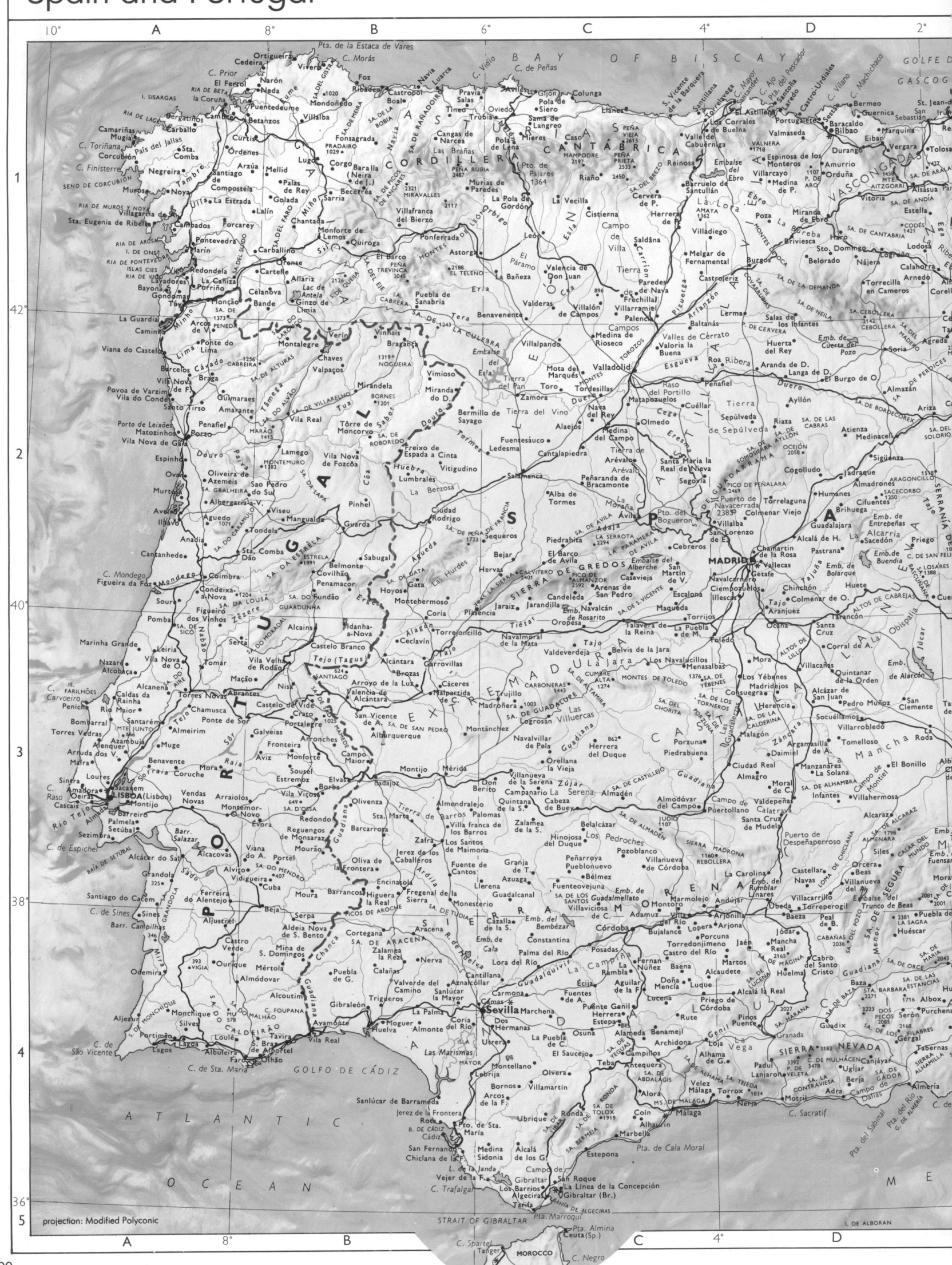

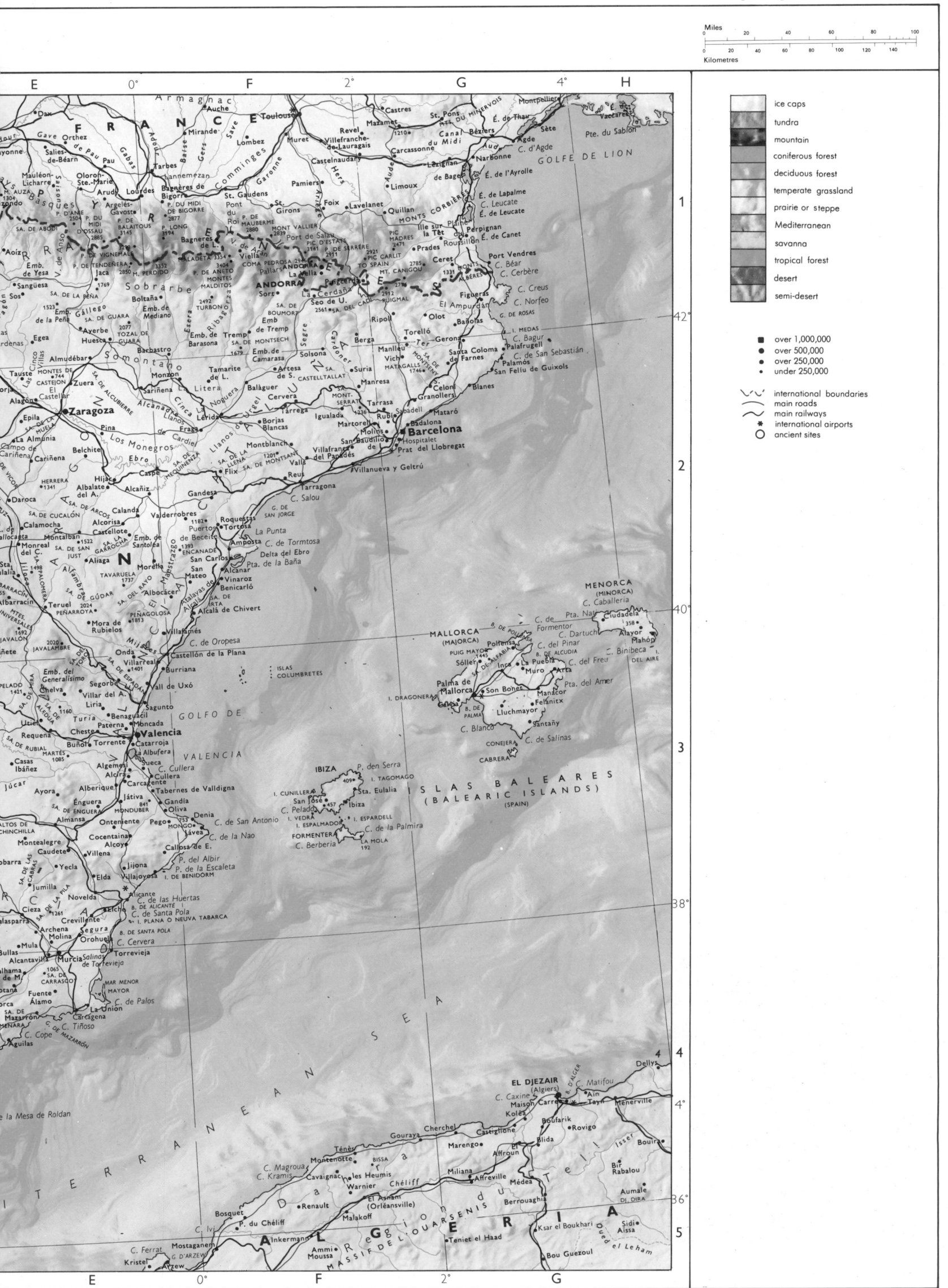

Miles
0   20   40   60   80   100
0 20 40 60 80 100 120 140
Kilometres

ice caps
tundra
mountain
coniferous forest
deciduous forest
temperate grassland
prairie or steppe
Mediterranean
savanna
tropical forest
desert
semi-desert

■ over 1,000,000
● over 500,000
● over 250,000
• under 250,000

international boundaries
main roads
main railways
✳ international airports
○ ancient sites

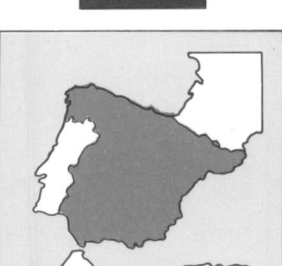

SPAIN

Area: 194,897 sq miles (504,782 km²)
Population: 38,680,000
Population Growth Rate: 0.9% pa
Capital: Madrid, pop. 3,188,000
Language: Castilian Spanish (official)
Religion: Christianity (Roman Catholic)
Currency: Peseta=100 Céntimos

ESPAÑA, or Spain, western Europe's second largest country, occupies 84 percent of the Iberian peninsula. It also includes the Balearic Islands in the Mediterranean and the Canary Islands off northwest Africa.

People and Culture Many peoples have colonized Spain. The cave paintings at Altamira, near Santander, in northern Spain, are between 10,000 and 20,000 years old.

Iberians from North Africa entered Spain in about 3000 BC, meeting Celtic tribes migrating from the north. From 1100 BC, Phoenicians, Greeks and, in 480 BC, Carthaginians colonized much of Spain. In 218–201 BC, the Romans made Spain a province called Hispania.

Germanic tribes invaded Spain around AD 400. Central-southern Spain became a Vandal kingdom called Vandalusia (now Andalucia). But Visigoths, who had entered Spain in 414, drove out the Vandals by 573.

In 711, Muslim Arabs and Berbers, called Moors, invaded Spain and established a major civilization. Christian armies eventually pushed the Muslims back. By 1276, only the southern state of Granada remained under Muslim rule.

On 1469, the marriage of Ferdinand of Aragon and Isabella of Castile led to the unification of two of Spain's most powerful Christian kingdoms. It also marked the start of a period of Spanish power. In 1492, the last Muslims were driven from Spain. In the same year, Columbus discovered the New World, and Spain soon became a great imperial power.

The period 1520–1680 is known as Spain's Golden Age. But under Philip II (reigned 1556–98), Spain began to decline. The Netherlands declared its independence from Spain in 1568, and in 1588 the Spanish Armada was destroyed. At the end of the War of the Spanish Succession (1701–14), Spain lost its Italian possessions and Gibraltar.

During the Napoleonic Wars, the French and Spanish fleet was defeated at the Battle of Trafalgar (1805), and Spanish sea power was ended. In the early nineteenth century, most Spanish-American colonies broke away. In 1898, war with the United States led to the loss of Cuba, the Philippines and Puerto Rico. By the twentieth century, Spain was a poor agricultural country.

Spain was neutral in World War I. In 1923, the military took power. With the approval of King Alfonso XIII, Primo de Rivera became dictator.

In 1931, following elections, Spain became a republic. In 1936, General Francisco Franco, with Spanish forces from Morocco, invaded Spain. At the end of the Civil War (1936–39), Franco became head of state, establishing one-party rule.

Spain was again neutral in World War II. In 1975, when Franco died, Don Juan Carlos I de Borbón y Borbón, grandson of Alfonso XIII, became head of state. He restored parliamentary government and held elections in 1977. Spain has a bicameral parliament (the Cortes), with a Senate and Chamber of Deputies. There was an unsuccessful army rising in 1981.

The Spanish language is Castilian. Other languages include Galician in the northwest, Basque in the provinces bordering the Bay of Biscay near the French border, and Catalan in the northeast.

Many Basques, Catalans and Galicians favour regional autonomy, and regional governments with limited powers were established for Basques and Catalans in 1980 and for Galicians in 1981.

Rapid economic and social change led to an increase in the urban population from 57 percent in 1960 to 75 percent in 1981. The proportion of the workforce engaged in farming fell from 42 to 14 percent, while the proportions in industry and services rose from 31 and 27 percent, respectively, to 40 and 45 percent. The average life expectancy at birth also rose from 69 years in 1960 to 74 in 1981.

The Land About five-sixths of Spain is a plateau, called the *Meseta*. It is largely between 2,000 and 3,000 feet (610–914 m) above sea-level, but high ridges (*sierras*) rise above the general level. The chief rivers, the Duero, Tajo, Guadiana and Guadalquivir, flow from east to west, following the tilt of the land.

Mountain ranges include the Cordillera Cantabrica in the northwest, which reaches heights of more than 8,500 feet (2,591 m). The Pyrenees are higher, reaching 11,168 feet (3,404 m) in the Pico de Aneto. Spain's highest peak, Mulhácen, is 11,410 feet (3,478 m) high in the south-eastern Sierra Nevada.

Lowlands include the Plain of Aragon, drained by the Ebro River, the Mediterranean coastal plains, and the Plains of Andalucia.

The Mediterranean coastlands have hot, dry summers, and mild, moist winters. Inland, temperatures are moderated by the altitude. Madrid has an average annual temperature range of 41°F–77°F (5°C–25°C), as compared with 51°F–85°F (11°C–29°C) at Sevilla in the south, and 51°F–66°F (11°C–19°C) at la Coruña in the northwest.

The northwest has a mild and rather wet climate. La Coruña has an average annual rainfall of 32 inches (813 mm), Madrid 17 inches (432 mm), Sevilla 19.5 inches (495 mm).

Deciduous forests grow in the north. Drought-resistant cork oak, pines and olive trees grow in the south. Scrub covers about one-sixth of Spain.

Many animal species have become extinct in the last few centuries. But some, such as deer, ibex, Spanish lynx and wild boar, are now protected in some areas.

Economy In 1981 agriculture accounted for 7 percent of the GDP, industry 36 percent and services 57 percent.

Important resources include coal and lignite, copper, iron ore, lead, mercury and zinc. The chief manufacturing centres are the largest cities: Madrid and Barcelona (pop. 1,755,000). Manufactures, machinery and transport equipment make up two-thirds of the exports; farm products, 15 percent.

Irrigation is widely practised. The main crops are barley, citrus fruits, grapes, olives, potatoes, wheat and vegetables. Spain is the world's third largest wine producer.

Cattle are important in the wetter north, with sheep and goats in scrub areas. Cod, sardines and tuna fish form the bulk of the fishing catch.

In 1981, 40,129,000 tourists visited Spain. Tourism is now a major source of foreign revenue. In 1981, the per capita GNP was $5,640.

The Arab-built Alhambra in Granada, Spain.

Mallorca, a Spanish Mediterranean island.

PORTUGAL

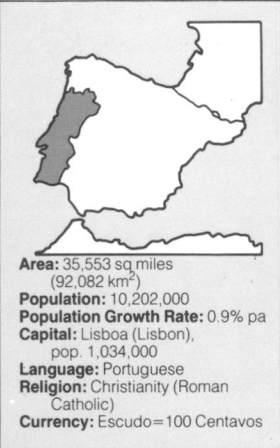

Area: 35,553 sq miles (92,082 km²)
Population: 10,202,000
Population Growth Rate: 0.9% pa
Capital: Lisboa (Lisbon), pop. 1,034,000
Language: Portuguese
Religion: Christianity (Roman Catholic)
Currency: Escudo = 100 Centavos

THE PORTUGUESE REPUBLIC borders the Atlantic Ocean in the Iberian peninsula.

People and Culture Portugal's modern frontiers were established in the thirteenth century. In the fifteenth century, Portugal took the lead in the European Age of Exploration and, by 1550, it had colonies in Africa, Asia and Brazil.

Philip II of Spain seized the Portuguese crown in 1580, but Portugal regained its independence in 1640. France occupied Portugal from 1807 to 1811 and in 1822 Portugal lost Brazil.

The nineteenth century was a time of instability. In 1910 Portugal became a republic and in World War I it fought on the side of the Allies.

From 1932 to 1960, Dr Antonio Salazar ruled as a dictator, keeping Portugal neutral in World War II.

In 1974, a coup led to the return of democracy and independence for Portugal's African possessions, where costly wars had been sapping Portugal's economy. General elections were held in 1979 and 1983, when a Socialist–Social Democrat coalition government was formed.

Only 31 percent of the population lived in urban areas in 1981. About one-fifth of adults are illiterate. The average life expectancy at birth in 1980 was 71 years.

The Land The interior contains plateaux and mountain ranges which are extensions of features in Spain. There are broad coastal lowlands in the west.

The climate is mild and moist. Lisboa (Lisbon) has an average annual temperature range of 52°F–72°F (11°C–22°C) and 27 inches (686 mm) of rain per year. Forests cover one-third of the land.

Economy The per capita GNP (1981) was low at $2,520. In 1981, agriculture accounted for 12 percent of the GDP and industry for 44 percent, but 29 percent of the workforce was engaged in farming, compared with 36 percent in industry.

Cereals, grapes and olives are major products. Fishing for cod and sardines is important.

Some coal, copper and other minerals are mined and manufacturing is increasing. Products include chemicals, steel and textiles.

The tourist industry is expanding. In 1981, 7,277,000 tourists visited Portugal.

Portugal's fine National Theatre is in Rossi square, Lisbon.

ANDORRA

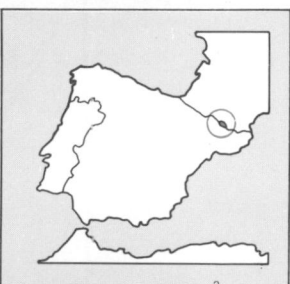

Area: 175 sq miles (453 km²)
Population: 35,000
Population Growth Rate: 3.2% pa
Capital: Andorra la Vella, pop. 16,000
Language: Catalan
Religion: Christianity (Roman Catholic)
Currency: French Franc; Spanish Peseta

THE PRINCIPALITY OF ANDORRA is an isolated nation between Spain and France.

People and Culture According to tradition, Andorra was granted independence by Charlemagne (742–814) for its services against the Moorish invaders of Spain.

The present suzerainty dates from 1278, when the country came under the joint control of the French Comte de Foix and the Spanish Bishop of Urgel. Later, the presidents of France took over from the House of Foix.

The Bishop of Urgel and the French President, the 'co-princes', receive nominal payments. They are represented in Andorra la Vella by two resident 'Viguiers'. Since 1868, the 28-member, elected General Council of the Valleys has effectively governed Andorra.

The Land Andorra contains six deep valleys separated by high peaks in the Pyrenees. Winters are cold and snowy, but summers are pleasant.

Economy Tourism is the main industry. There is some farming (tobacco, potatoes, cereals) and forestry.

GIBRALTAR

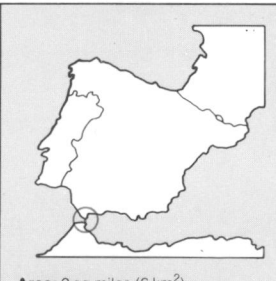

Area: 2 sq miles (6 km²)
Population: 30,000
Population Growth Rate: 0.3% pa
Capital: Gibraltar
Language: English, Spanish
Religion: Christianity
Currency: Pound = 100 Pence

GIBRALTAR is a British colony in the south of the Iberian peninsula.

People and Culture Gibraltar became a British colony in 1713 under the Treaty of Utrecht. It is important strategically because it provides facilities for ships passing into and out of the Mediterranean.

Spain claims Gibraltar and, in 1968, the United Nations asked Britain to withdraw. But in 1967, 12,138 out of an electorate of 12,762 voted to retain the British links. Spain closed the border in 1969, but it was reopened for pedestrians in 1982.

Executive authority is vested in the Governor. The House of Assembly is the legislature.

There are people of British, Genoese, Maltese, Portuguese and Spanish descent.

The Land Gibraltar is a rocky peninsula connected to the mainland by a sandy isthmus. The climate is typically Mediterranean.

Economy Most people work in the port, the ship repair yard and the NATO bases. Tourism is another important source of income.

Granada, in southern Spain, was once the capital of the large Moorish kingdom of Granada.

France

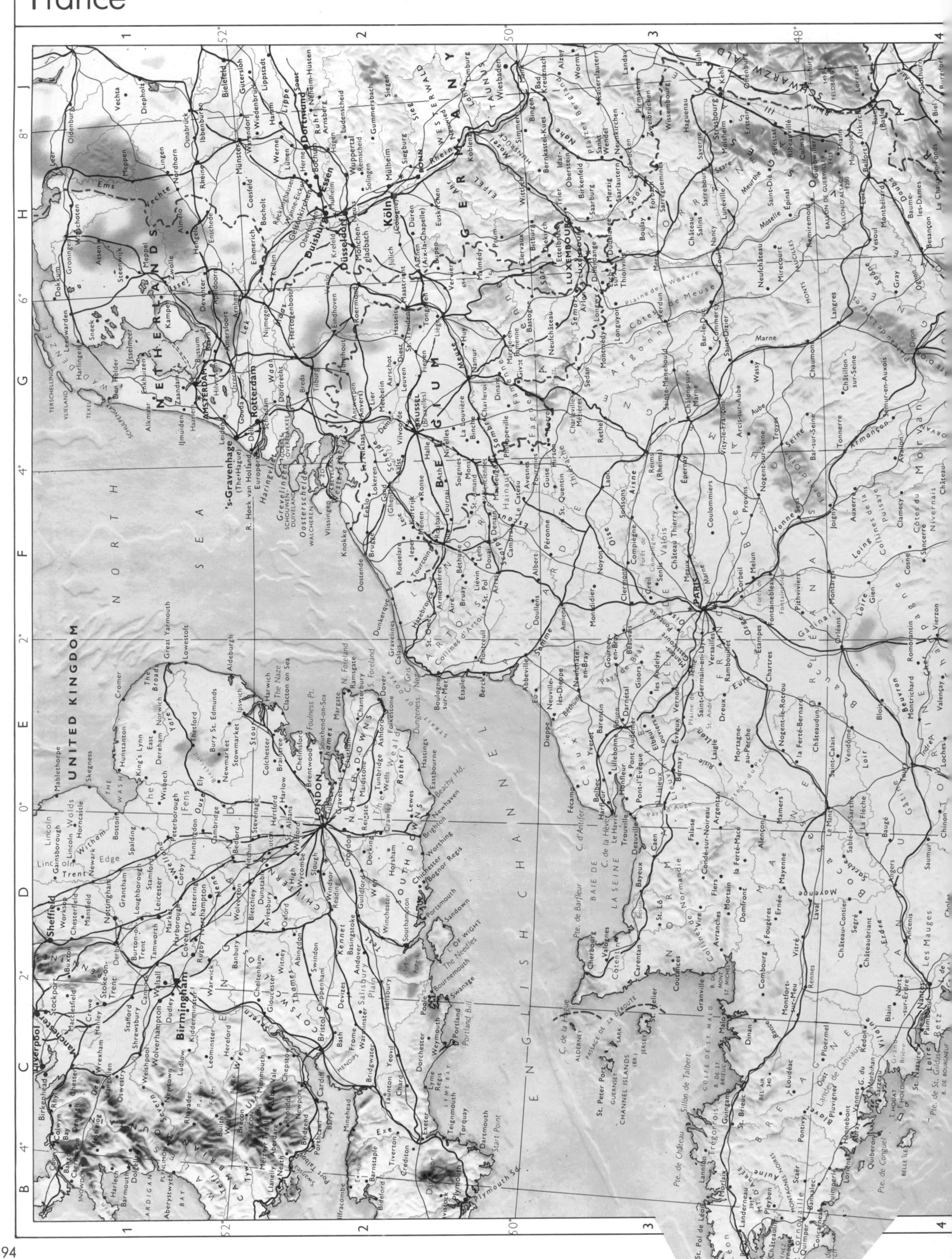

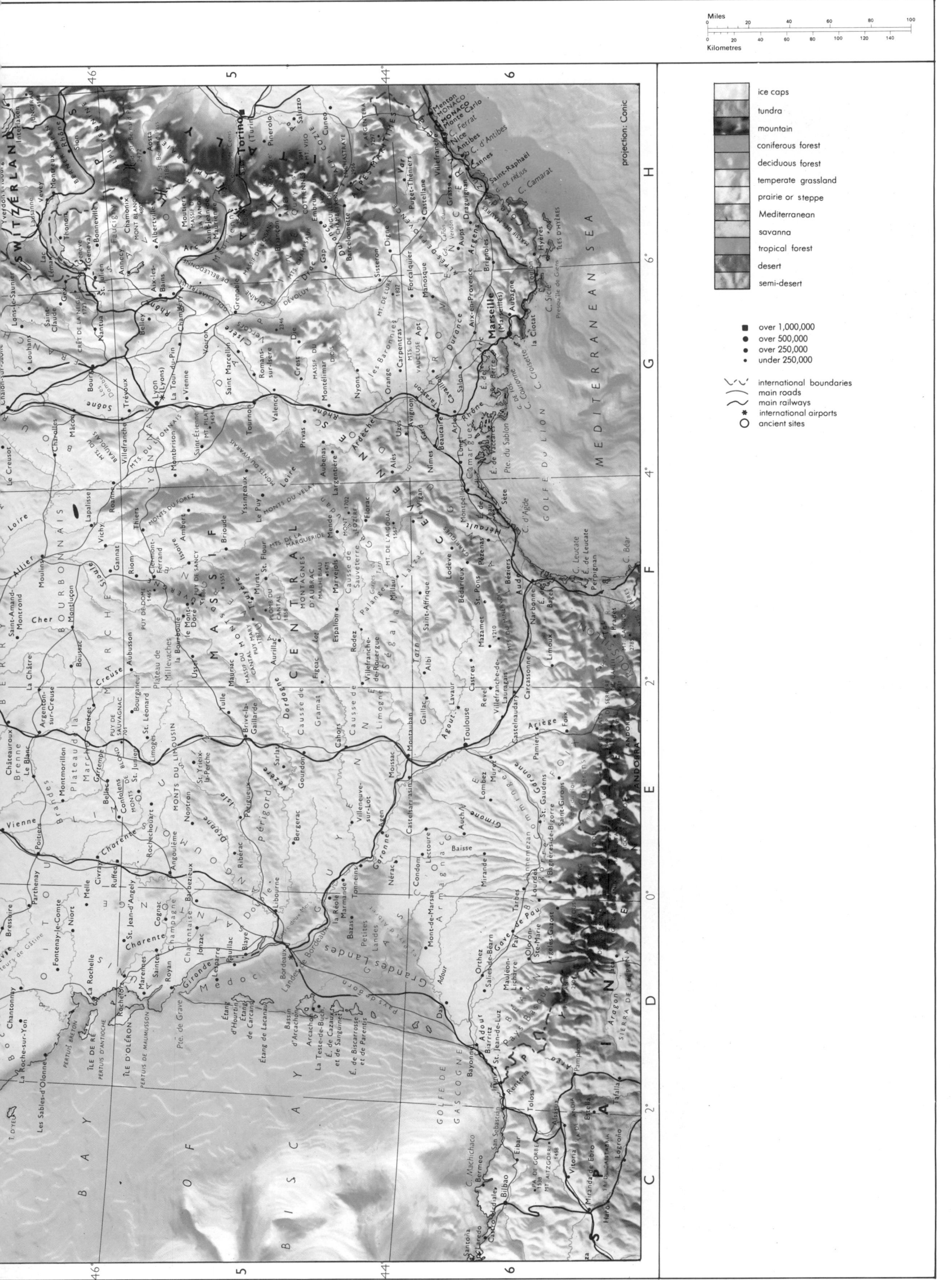

Miles
Kilometres

ice caps
tundra
mountain
coniferous forest
deciduous forest
temperate grassland
prairie or steppe
Mediterranean
savanna
tropical forest
desert
semi-desert

■ over 1,000,000
● over 500,000
● over 250,000
• under 250,000

⌐⌐ international boundaries
⌐⌐ main roads
⌐⌐ main railways
✳ international airports
○ ancient sites

projection: Conic

A fire-eater at work in front of the new Pompidou Centre, Paris.

FRANCE

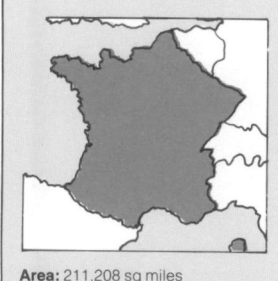

Area: 211,208 sq miles
(547,026 km²)
Population: 54,613,000
Population Growth Rate: 0.4% pa
Capital: Paris, pop. 8,550,000
Language: French
Religion: Christianity (Roman
Catholic Protestant), Islam
Currency: Franc = 100 Centimes

THE FRENCH REPUBLIC is the largest country in western Europe. It is a great cultural centre. French art and architecture, literature and music are widely admired and French institutions, fashions and even its cooking have been copied in many parts of the world.

People and Culture Farming was introduced into France around 7,000 years ago and, some 2,000 years later, large stone monuments (megaliths) were erected.

The Celts began to colonize France around 1500 BC. They were well established in 58–51 BC, when Roman armies, under Julius Caesar, conquered France, which they called Gaul.

In the fifth century AD, the prosperous, stable period of Roman rule was ended, when Germanic invaders swept into the country.

In AD 486, the Frankish realm (as France was called) was unified under a Christian king Clovis. In 800, Frankish power was extended when Charles the Great, King of all the Franks, was crowned Charlemagne, emperor of the Holy Roman Empire.

After Charlemagne's death, the empire broke up. In 843, the territory of the West Franks, consisting essentially of France, came under Charles the Bold. The territory of the East Franks consisted mainly of Germany. A third buffer territory between them, called Lotharingia, stretched from what is now Belgium through Switzerland into northern Italy.

In the tenth and eleventh centuries, France's kings exerted power over a diminishing area. In the tenth century, Norsemen occupied Normandy and, in 987, when Hugh Capet became king, founding the Capetian dynasty, he controlled only a small area around Paris and Orléans.

In 1066, William, Duke of Normandy, which had become a powerful feudal state, conquered England. As a result, large parts of northern France passed to the English crown and remained so until the end of the Hundred Years War (1337–1453).

In the seventeenth and eighteenth centuries, France became a great power and French art and literature thrived especially during the reign of Louis XIV 1643–1715). However, in the Seven Years War (1756–63), France lost its Canadian and Indian possessions to England.

In 1789, the French Revolution overthrew Louis XVI and, in 1792, the First Republic was established. Napoleon Bonaparte took power in 1799 and set up the First Empire in 1804. His brilliant military career which took him to Moskva (Moscow) finally ended at the Battle of Waterloo (1815).

The Bourbon monarchy was restored, but it was overthrown in a revolution in 1848, when the short-lived Second Republic was founded. But Napoleon I's nephew, Louis Napoleon, who had been President of the Republic, declared himself emperor in 1852.

The Second Empire came to an end with the Franco-Prussian War (1870–71). The Third Republic, which formally dates from the adoption of the Constitution in 1875, continued until 1940.

In the two World Wars, France became a battlefield and the deaths of more than two million young soldiers sapped France's strength. It also created an unbalanced sex ratio, with far fewer men than women. France was occupied by the Germans from 1940 to 1945.

The Fourth Republic, set up in 1946, was a time of reconstruction, but progress was slowed down by costly colonial wars and political instability at home.

In 1958, Charles de Gaulle, the wartime leader, was elected president. He introduced a new Constitution, establishing the Fifth Republic, under which the president had considerably increased powers over the legislature which consists of two houses: the directly elected National Assembly and the indirectly elected Senate. For example, the president now appoints the prime minister and presides over the Council of Ministers. He also acts as a check on both the government and the legislature.

With his new powers, de Gaulle acted quickly to dismantle most of France's colonial empire, although cultural and economic links were maintained through the French Community.

From 1958, France, with its major agricultural industry, benefited from its membership of the EEC. It also enjoyed stability achieved under a series of right-wing governments.

But in the late 1970s, economic progress slowed down because of the world recession and the stringent measures taken in France to protect the economy and the currency.

In 1981, François Mitterrand was elected president, heading a socialist administration with some Communist representatives. But expansionist policies to promote economic growth and create jobs had an inflationary effect and the government curbed expansion in order to avoid financial difficulties.

Besides French, the official language, Basque is spoken in the southwest, and Catalan near the Spanish border at the other end of the Pyrenees. Breton, a Celtic language, is used in Bretagne (Brittany), where some people favour regional autonomy, and Provençal is spoken in the southeast. In the northeast there are some people who speak German.

About 86 per cent of the population are members of the Roman Catholic Church, and there are also about two million Muslims and 750,000 Protestants. Foreign communities made up about 6.5 percent of the population in 1975. The largest groups were Portuguese, Algerians, Spaniards and Italians. Together, these four nationalities made up a total of 2.43 million.

Urbanization has been increasing rapidly in recent years. In 1960, 62 percent of the population lived in cities and towns. By 1981, the percentage had risen to 78. Apart from Paris, major cities include:

Lyon (pop. with suburbs, 1,171,000)
Marseille (1,071,000)
Lille (936,000)
Bordeaux (612,000)
Toulouse (510,000)
Nantes (453,000)
Nice (438,000).

France has a highly organized educational system, with free and compulsory education between the ages of 6 and 16. There is also an elaborate welfare system and rising health standards have pushed up the average life expectancy at birth from 70 years in 1960 to 76 in 1981.

Chartres, southeast of Paris, has a great twelfth/thirteenth-century cathedral. In 1974, France had 45.3 million Roman Catholics.

The Land France is a pleasant country with much beautiful and varied scenery.

The chief young fold mountains are along the borders, with the Pyrenees in the southwest, and the Jura and Alps in the east. The highest peak, Mont Blanc, reaches 15,771 feet (4,807 m) on the Italian border.

There are three other, older uplands. The northwest peninsula of Bretagne is the remains of an ancient range, in which the granitic cores of the mountains have been exposed by erosion. The Vosges in the northeast are an uplifted block between the Moselle and Rhein (Rhine) rivers.

The largest of these uplands is the Massif Central in south-central France. It contains old volcanic cones in the northwest and spectacular limestone scenery in the west and southeast.

There are four main lowlands. The Paris basin, drained by the Seine, Somme and middle Loire rivers, is a region of escarpments and fertile vales. Aquitaine, in the southwest, also has much rich farmland, although the coast is lined by sand dunes and lagoons. The Rhône–Saône basin is the third lowland region. It ends in the south in the marshy Camargues, which is part of the fourth main lowland, the Mediterranean coastlands.

Corsica (Corse in French) is a mountainous French island in the Mediterranean. Its mountains are part of the ancient Hercynian system, and so they are much more eroded than the youthful Alps to the north.

The climate changes from west to east and from north to south. The average January temperature in Bordeaux is 41°F (5°C) and the average rainfall is 31 inches (787 mm). By comparison, Paris has an average January temperature of 37°F (3°C) and an annual rainfall of 23 inches (584 mm).

Eastern France has an increasingly continental climate, although the altitude brings more rainfall to the highlands.

Temperatures increase to the south. The southern coast has a typical Mediterranean climate, with hot, dry summers and mild, moist winters.

As in much of western Europe, the vegetation has been modified by human activities. Only a few remnants of the northern and western deciduous forests survive. There are coniferous forests on mountain slopes, but the drought-resistant forests of the Mediterranean have been largely cleared, giving way to scrub, or *maquis*.

Most large animal species have disappeared, as they have also done in the rest of western Europe.

Economy In 1960, agriculture accounted for 10 percent of the GDP, industry for 39 percent and services for 51 percent. By 1981, a considerable change had occurred with agriculture accounting for 4 percent, industry 35 percent and services 61 percent.

Similarly, in 1960, agriculture employed 22 percent of the workforce, industry 39 percent and services 39 percent, while in 1981 the respective percentages were 8, 39 and 53. Despite this trend away from farming, however, only Greece, Ireland and Italy among EEC countries have a higher proportion of farm-workers.

About 31.5 percent of France is cultivated, 2 percent is under vines, 23.5 percent is pasture and 26 percent is forest.

Many French farms are small and often split into several plots. Yields tend to be low by EEC standards, because of lack of capital and mechanization. But France is a net food exporter.

The leading farm regions are the Paris basin, the Loire valley, the Aquitaine basin and the Rhône–Saône valley. Crops include barley, flax, fruits, maize, oats, potatoes and wheat. France is the world's leading producer of quality wines, although Italy produces a greater volume.

In 1981, there were 23.5 million cattle, 13 million sheep and 11.6 million pigs. Dairy farming is particularly important, and French cheeses are known internationally. The fishing industry employed 22,000 people in 1980.

France produces some petroleum, natural gas and coal, although coal is also imported from West Germany. The main mineral is iron ore, mostly from Lorraine, and France ranked seventh among world steel producers in 1981. Bauxite and potash are also mined.

Although the chemical and textile industries are widely scattered, many industries are concentrated in certain areas. Heavy industry is mainly in the northeast; and the lower Loire, Marseille and Dunkerque are shipbuilding centres.

France has many consumer industries. Paris is the centre of luxury-goods industries and the chief car-producing area. The country is among the world's top ten producers of cars, commercial vehicles, radios and television sets.

Machinery and transport equipment and various manufactured goods made up more than three-fifths of the exports in 1981. France's chief trading partners are the member countries of the EEC.

Tourism is a major source of foreign exchange. In 1981, the per capita GNP was $12,190, placing France fourth among the ten nations of the EEC.

MONACO

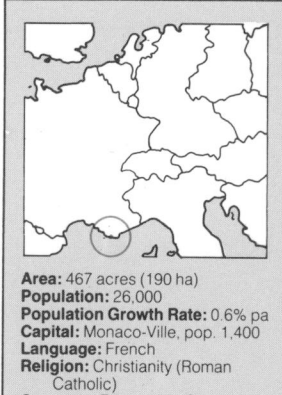

Area: 467 acres (190 ha)
Population: 26,000
Population Growth Rate: 0.6% pa
Capital: Monaco-Ville, pop. 1,400
Language: French
Religion: Christianity (Roman Catholic)
Currency: Franc = 100 Centimes

THE PRINCIPALITY OF MONACO is a small territory on the southeastern coast of France, between Nice and the Italian border.

People and Culture The Phoenicians founded a trading settlement at Monaco and the Genoese built a castle there in 1215. Monaco passed to the Genoese Grimaldi family in 1297.

It later came under the protection, at various times, of France, Sardinia and Spain, but full independence was achieved in 1861. It joined a customs union with France in 1865.

Monaco is a constitutional monarchy. Prince Rainier III became head of state in 1949. He governs with an elected, 18-member National Council.

The Land Monaco is divided into four districts, Monaco-ville is the capital. La Condamine is a residential resort area, with some light industry. Monte-Carlo is a resort with a famous casino. Fontvieille contains a new area reclaimed from the sea for office and residential development.

Economy The economy is based mainly on tourism, casino profits, taxes on gambling and postage stamps. There is no farmland.

The Arc de Triomphe, a Parisian landmark, shelters the tomb of France's Unknown Soldier.

Monte Carlo is a district in the small Principality of Monaco.

Belgium and the Netherlands

BELGIUM

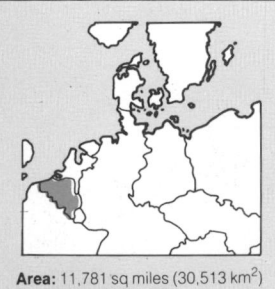

Area: 11,781 sq miles (30,513 km²)
Population: 9,891,000
Population Growth Rate: 0.1% pa
Capital: Brussel (Brussels),
pop. 995,000
Languages: Dutch, French,
German
Religion: Christianity (mainly
Roman Catholic)
Currency: Franc = 100 Centimes

THE KINGDOM OF BELGIUM is one of the world's most densely populated nations.

People and Culture Because of its position on the North European plain, Belgium has often been a battlefield. But its position has also given it a diverse culture.

Northern Belgium (north of an east–west line drawn just south of the capital), the people are Flemings, who speak a form of Dutch. The Flemings are descendants of the Franks. The French-speaking Walloons in the south are of Romano-Celtic origin. In the east, some Belgians speak German.

In 1981, 57.1 percent of the population was in the Flemish north, with 32.1 percent in the south, 0.7 percent in German-speaking areas, and 10.1 per-cent in bilingual Brussel. Communal conflict resulted from this language division.

The early Celtic people of Belgium were conquered by Rome in 50 BC and by the Franks in the fourth century AD. In the early ninth century, Belgium was part of Charlemagne's Holy Roman Empire, but it later split into semi-independent kingdoms. The country was united in the late fourteenth century, but for much of its history it was under foreign rule: mainly Austria, Spain, France and the Netherlands.

Belgium became an independent monarchy in 1831. It was occupied by Germany in both World Wars, but it recovered quickly through economic cooperation with the Netherlands and Luxembourg (Benelux) and from 1957 through the EEC.

The people now enjoy a high standard of living and the urban population was 73 percent in 1981, when the average life expectancy was 73 years.

The Land Belgium is mostly flat, with the dissected Ardennes plateau in the southeast. The plains are drained by the Schelde River and its tributaries.

The climate is mild and moist. Brussel has an average annual temperature range of 37°F–63°F (3°C–17°C). The rainfall is greatest in the southeast. Forests cover 20 percent of the land.

Economy In 1980, agriculture accounted for 2 percent of the GDP and 3 percent of the workforce, although many farmers have full-time jobs in industry. Cereals, flax, potatoes and sugar-beet are produced. In 1981, there were 2,859,000 cattle and 5,076,000 pigs. Market gardening and fishing are also important.

Industry accounted for 37 percent of the GDP and 41 percent of the workforce in 1980. Major industrial areas include the Kempenland coalfield in the northeast, Antwerpen (Anvers) with industries based on imported petroleum, and Brussel (luxury goods). The old industrial area in the Sambre–Meuse valley has declined as coal extraction became increasingly expensive. Flanders (Vlaanderen) produces textiles.

Industrial products dominate the exports. The per capita GNP (1981) was $11,920.

NETHERLANDS

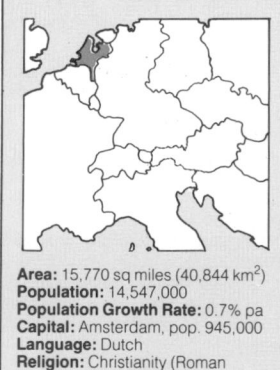

Area: 15,770 sq miles (40,844 km²)
Population: 14,547,000
Population Growth Rate: 0.7% pa
Capital: Amsterdam, pop. 945,000
Language: Dutch
Religion: Christianity (Roman Catholic, Protestant)
Currency: Guilder = 100 Cents

THE KINGDOM OF THE NETHERLANDS is a densely populated country.

People and Culture Early inhabitants included the Belgae, the Batavii and the Frisians, whom the Romans helped to reclaim land from the sea.

Wooden clogs are part of the national dress in the Netherlands.

Frankish (Germanic) peoples introduced Christianity in the eighth century. From 1369 to 1543, the area came under the rule of the Dukes of Burgundy and then the Hapsburgs.

Spain's attempt to suppress Protestantism led to a revolt in 1568 and, in 1579, the Dutch provinces joined in a confederation. Spain finally recognized the country's independence in 1648. In the seventeenth century, the country became a major naval and trading power.

France occupied the country in 1795. But the Netherlands, including Belgium and Luxembourg, became an independent monarchy in 1815. Belgium broke away in 1830, taking most of Luxembourg with it.

The Netherlands declared itself neutral in both World Wars, but Germany invaded it in 1940. After the war, the Netherlands developed rapidly. From 1957, it has been a member of the EEC.

In 1981, 76 percent of the people lived in urban areas. The average life expectancy at birth was 76 years.

The Land Large areas have been reclaimed from the sea and about 40 percent of the country is below sea-level at high tide. Reclamation has been achieved by building dykes (sea walls) around areas to be reclaimed (polders). Mild winters and cool summers characterize the climate.

Economy Agriculture is important, although it accounted for only 4 percent of the GDP in 1980.

Farmland covers 70 percent of the country and farm yields are high. The country is famous for its flowers and bulbs, and potatoes, sugar-beet and wheat are extremely important. Livestock farming is a major activity. In 1982, there were 5,240,000 cattle, 10,254,000 pigs, and 87,100,000 poultry.

In 1981, the Netherlands was the world's fourth largest natural gas producer and ranked fifth in western Europe in petroleum production. Industry dominates the economy, accounting for 33 percent of the GDP and 45 percent of the workforce in 1980. The per capita GNP (1981) was $11,790.

Europoort, Rotterdam's new port and industrial complex, is the world's busiest port, with the largest artificial harbour.

LUXEMBOURG

Area: 999 sq miles (2,586 km²)
Population: 367,000
Population Growth Rate: 0.3% pa
Capital: Luxembourg,
  pop. 79,000
Languages: French, German,
  Letzeburgisch
Religion: Christianity (mainly
  Roman Catholic)
Currency: Franc = 100 Centimes

THE GRAND DUCHY OF LUXEM-BOURG is bounded by Germany, Belgium and France, and covers an area of 999 square miles (2,857 km²).

People and Culture Luxembourg became a feudal state in AD 963 and a Grand Duchy in 1354. It later passed to the Dukes of Burgundy, the Spanish Hapsburgs and the Austrian Hapsburgs.

France occupied it in 1795 and in 1815 it became part of the Netherlands. Part of Luxembourg went to Belgium when Belgium broke with the Netherlands in 1830. The rest of Luxembourg gained autonomy in 1839, though Dutch kings governed it until 1890.

Germany occupied Luxembourg in both World Wars. Since 1945, Luxembourg has prospered through the Benelux customs union and the EEC. It is a constitutional monarchy with an elected Chamber of Deputies.

The Land The south is a lowland. The north is part of the Ardennes plateau. The climate is mild and moist.

Economy In 1980, agriculture accounted for 3 percent of the GDP and industry for 33 percent. Farmland covers half the land. Barley, oats, potatoes, sugar-beet and wheat are grown. Iron ore is mined and Luxembourg has the world's highest per capita steel production. In 1981, the per capita GNP was the highest in the EEC, at $15,910.

SWITZERLAND

Area: 15,942 sq miles
  (41,288 km²)
Population: 6,512,000
Population Growth Rate: 0.2% pa
Capital: Bern, pop. 287,000
Languages: German, French,
  Italian
Religion: Christianity (Roman
  Catholic, Protestant)
Currency: Franc = 100 Centimes

DIE SCHWEIZ, LA SUISSE, and LA SVIZZERA are the names in each of the three official languages, German, French and Italian, respectively, of Switzerland, a republic in south-central Europe.

People and Culture Julius Caesar conquered the area in 58 BC, but Germanic tribes invaded in AD 401.

In the ninth century, the area came under the Holy Roman Empire. But in the late 13th century, the cantons of Uri, Schwyz and Unterwalden formed an alliance to free themselves from Hapsburg domination. They defeated an Austrian army in 1315. By 1353, the league had eight members and more Austrian attacks were repulsed in 1386 and 1388. The Swiss cantons expanded and won complete independence in 1499.

France invaded in 1798, but Switzerland was again independent in 1815. The modern Constitution dates from 1874. It guarantees Switzerland's neutrality, which was maintained in World Wars I and II, after which Switzerland refused to join the UN.

Switzerland now has 23 cantons, each with its own government. The bicameral federal parliament contains a Council of States and a National Council.

About 74.5 percent of Swiss citizens speak German, 20 percent French, 4 percent Italian, and 1 percent Romansch (a language related to Latin).

Living standards are high and the average life expectancy in 1981 was 76 years. About 59 percent of the people live in urban areas.

The Land The Jura Mountains are in the west and the Alps in the south form three-fifths of the country. Most people live in the central plateau, the Mittelland, between Lac Léman (Lake Geneva) and the Bodensee (Lake Constance).

The average annual temperature range is 32°F–66°F (0°C–19°C) and rainfall is around 33 inches (838 mm) a year. The mountains are colder and wetter.

Economy In 1980, agriculture accounted for 6 percent of the GDP and 5 percent of the workforce, while industry accounted for 40 percent of the GDP and 46 percent of the workforce.

Dairy farming is important and crops include cereals, fruits, sugar-beet and grapes for wine. But Switzerland is a net food importer.

Lacking minerals, Switzerland has concentrated on high standards of workmanship and its precision instruments, clocks, machinery and processed foods became world-famous.

Tourism is a major source of foreign exchange. In 1981, Switzerland had Europe's highest per capita GNP, $17,430.

Cattle are grazed on summer mountain pastures in Switzerland.

LIECHTENSTEIN

Area: 61 sq miles (157 km²)
Population: 27,000
Population Growth Rate: 1.4% pa
Capital: Vaduz, pop. 5,000
Language: German
Religion: Christianity (mainly
  Roman Catholic)
Currency: Swiss Franc =
  100 Centimes

THE PRINCIPALITY OF LIECH-TENSTEIN is a small, land-locked country between Austria and Switzerland.

People and Culture Liechtenstein, a union of the countships of Vaduz and Schellenburg, became a principality in 1719.

It was part of the Holy Roman Empire until 1806 and in 1815–66 it was part of the German Confederation. It has been independent since 1866 and neutral since 1868. It is a constitutional monarchy with an elected Diet (parliament). Since 1918 it has been united with Switzerland in a customs union and it uses Swiss currency.

The Land There are mountains in the south, with a fertile plain drained by the Rhein and Ill in the north. The average annual temperature range is 32°F–68°F (0°C–20°C).

Economy Cattle-rearing and the growing of cereals, vines and fruits were once the main activities. By 1981, farming employed only 3 percent of the people and light industry, producing such things as textiles, pharmaceutical, precision instruments and processed foods, now dominates the economy. Tourism and postage stamp sales are also important.

Vaduz Castle stands on a mountain above Vaduz, the capital of the Principality of Liechtenstein, which is not far from the Rhine.

Switzerland

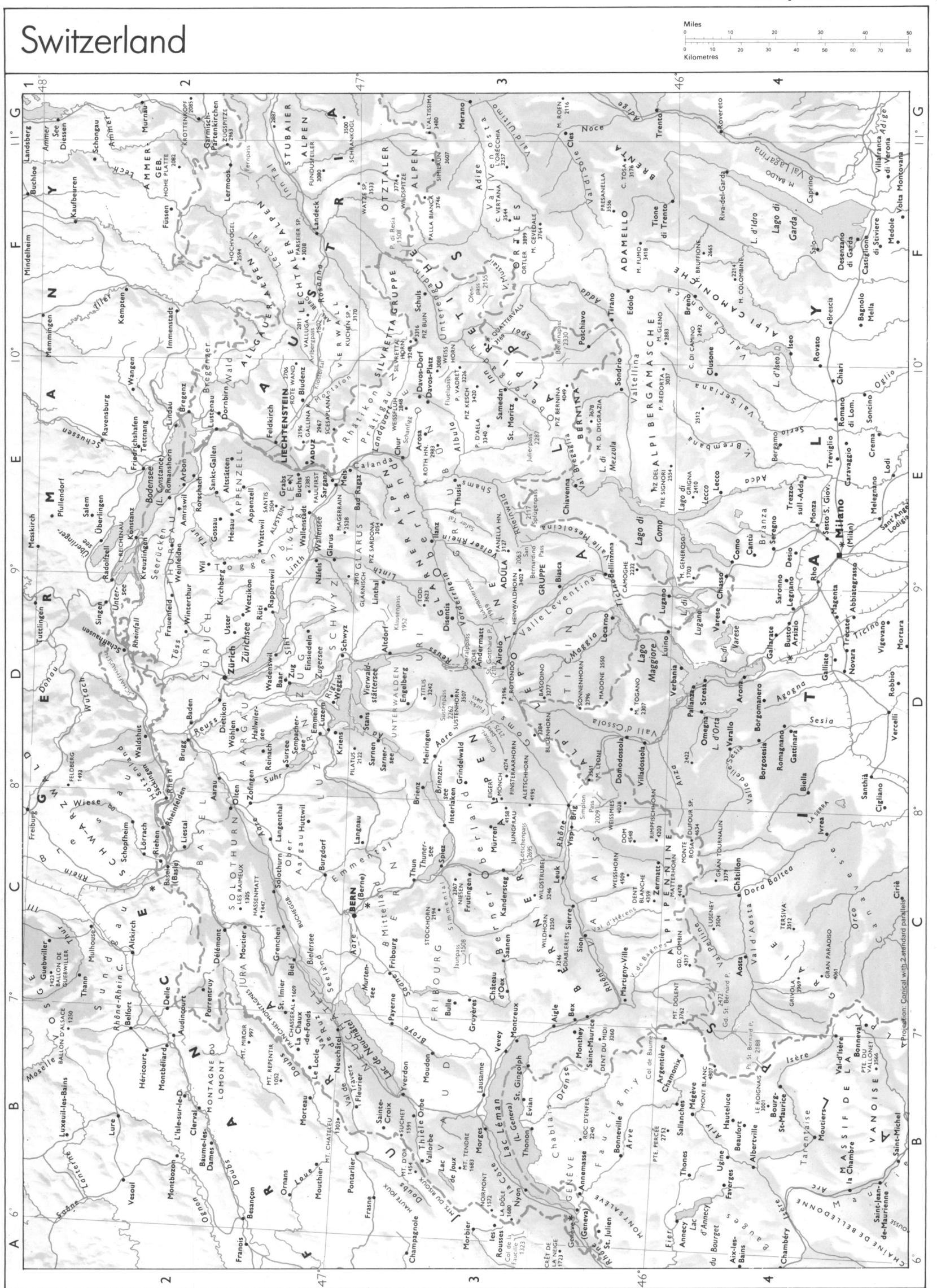

Austria and Germany

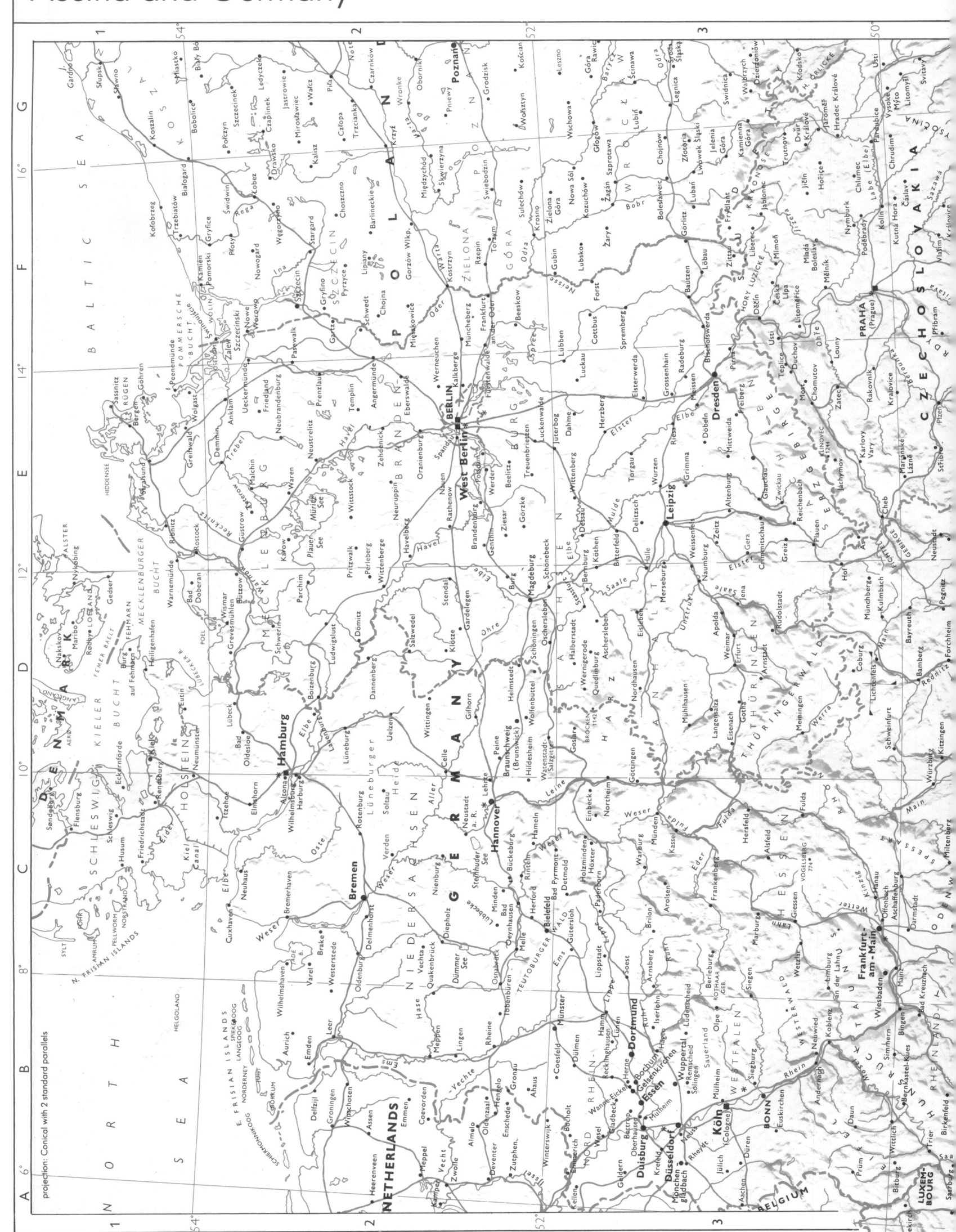

projection: Conical with 2 standard parallels

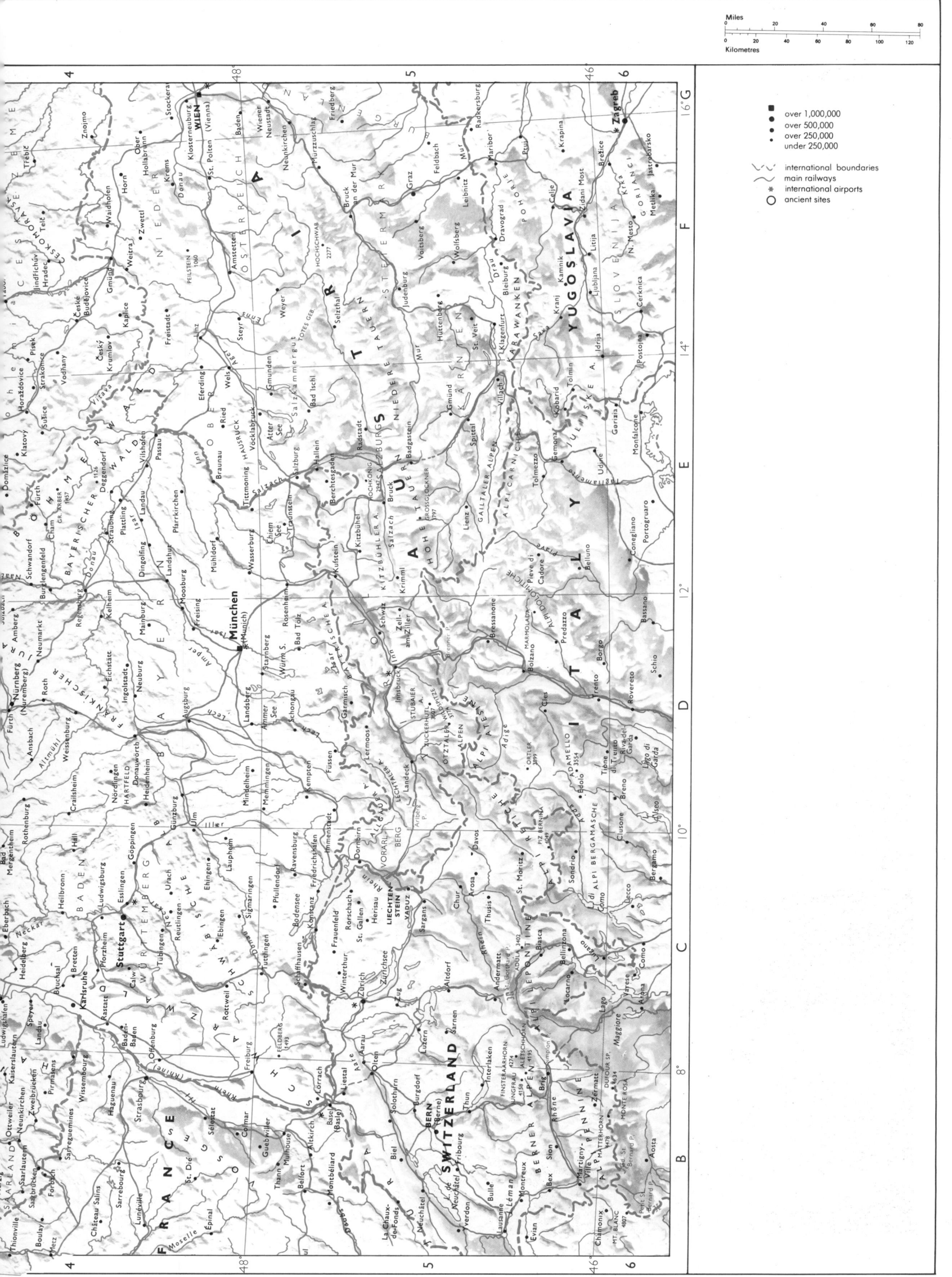

GERMANY

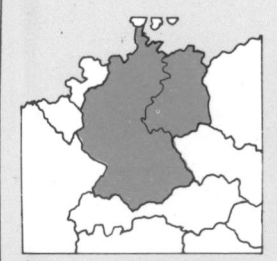

Area: 137,745 sq miles
(356,758 km²)
Population: 79,082,000
Population Growth Rate: −0.1 pa
Capital: Berlin, pop. 3,388,000
Language: German
Religion: Christianity (Protestant
43%, Roman Catholic 35%)
Currency: Deutsche Mark =
100 Pfennig

THE FEDERAL REPUBLIC OF GERMANY was created after the end of World War II when defeated Germany was divided into zones by the Allied powers. These zones later became the Federal Republic of Germany (or West Germany) and the German Democratic Republic (or East Germany). East Germany ceased to exist on October 3, 1990, when its territory became part of the Federal Republic of Germany.

People and Culture Most of what is now Germany lay outside the Roman empire. It was populated by many tribes, including the Alemanni, Franks, Goths, Lombards and Vandals.

In the fourth century AD, Germanic tribes began to move against the declining Roman empire. Eventually, a Frankish kingdom was established in France. This kingdom reached its peak in 800 when its king was crowned Charlemagne, Emperor of the Holy Roman Empire. He founded the First Reich (empire) from Germany's loose federation of principalities.

After Charlemagne's death, the empire broke up. In the tenth century, Germany came under attack from the east. But the Saxon Otto I, who became Holy Roman Emperor in 962, began to annex Slav territory. In the twelfth century, Germany also incorporated Prussia, although it split up again soon afterwards into small states.

In 1517, Martin Luther launched the Reformation, dividing Germany into Roman Catholic and Protestant states. Religious conflict was the cause of the Thirty Years War (1618–48). In the later stages of this war, Brandenburg and Prussia were welded into a strong Protestant state by Frederick William, the Great Elector, who made Berlin his capital.

His son, Frederick I, was named Frederick I of Prussia, and his grandson, Frederick II (the Great) made Prussia a leading European power.

In 1806, Napoleon defeated Prussia, though Prussian troops played a major part in Napoleon's defeat at Waterloo (1815).

The loose German Confederation was ended by a Prussian nobleman, Otto von Bismarck, chief minister of William I, who in 1867, set up the North German Confederation, with the Prussian king at its head as Kaiser (emperor). The Franco-Prussian War (1870–71) led to the annexation of Alsace-Lorraine from France. The Second Reich unified the Germans and rapid industrialization consolidated its power.

World War I, however, was a great setback. The Treaty of Versailles (1919) stripped Germany (now a republic) of its colonies and made it pay huge reparations. Economic collapse helped Adolf Hitler's National Socialist Party come to power in 1933, founding the Third Reich.

At the end of World War II, Germany occupied only 65 percent of its area in 1871. The Allies divided Germany into four zones. In 1948, the British, French and US zones in the west were amalgamated. But the Russian zone remained separate.

In 1949, the amalgamated zones became the Federal Republic of Germany, but East Germany remained under a Communist government. Berlin was similarly divided into east and west zones. Power in East Germany was effectively vested in the Politburo of the Socialist Unity (Communist) party. East Germany also had a 500-member People's Chamber, which elected the Council of State, the chairman of which represented the country in international law.

Germany and Berlin in particular became a focus of the Cold War. From 1945 to 1961, nearly three million people crossed from East to West Germany. In 1961, the East Germans built a wall to stem this movement.

In 1972, East and West Germany signed a treaty which reduced tension. It also paved the way to their admission to the United Nations in 1973.

West Germany was a federal republic, with a parliament consisting of two houses, the Bundestag (Federal Diet) and the Bundesrat (Federal Council), containing representatives from its 10 Länder (states) which have their own local governments.

The former states of East Germany had been abolished in 1952 and they were replaced by 14 districts. However, following the reunification of Germany in 1990, the former Länder (states) of East Germany were restored, giving the enlarged Federal Republic of Germany a total of 16 states, including Berlin, which was made the national capital.

In 1991, it replaced Bonn as the political capital.

World War II reduced the population by more than seven million, but Germany's population is now about 1.3 times as large as it was in 1940. The population of the West Germany increased disproportionately owing to immigration from East Germany and other parts of eastern Europe. Another factor was the arrival of *Gastarbeiter* ('guest workers') from Turkey, Yugoslavia, Italy and other countries.

In 1988, 84 percent of the population lived in urban areas. The largest cities in 1989 included:

Berlin (pop 3,317,000)
Hamburg (1,603,000)
München or Munich
(1,212,000)
Köln or Cologne
(937,000)
Frankfurt am Main
(625,000)
Essen (621,000)
Dortmund (587,000)

With the exception of Berlin (now re-united), all the above cities are in the former territory of West Germany. Before 1945, East Germany was mainly rural. But by 1988, 77 percent of the population lived in urban areas. The largest cities, apart from East Berlin which now forms part of the national capital, are Leipzig (545,000), Dresden (518,000), and Chemnitz (312,000), formerly called Karl-Marx-Stadt, before reunification.

The average life expectancy at birth (1989) was 75 years in West Germany and 74 years in East Germany.

The Land The North European plain in the north is largely covered by glacial deposits and is ill-drained and infertile. The main rivers, including the Elbe and Weser, follow courses formed by water from the melting ice sheets.

Central Germany includes Westphalia (Westfalen) and the Ruhr coalfield and several block mountains, including the Eifel, Westerwald, Hunsrück and Taunus, which are separated by the Rhein and its tributaries.

Southwest Germany includes the rift valley which is occupied by the Rhein between Basel and Mainz. To the east are the Schwarzwald (Black Forest) and the Odenwald. Southwest Germany is the country's leading farm region.

The southeast includes the Alpine foreland and the upper Donau (Danube) basin, including its tributaries, which rise in the Alps. Plateaus and block mountains rise in the southern part of what was once East Germany. The highest peaks are in the Erzgebirge in the southeast.

The northern plains have a maritime climate, with an average temperature range of 32°F–64°F (0°C–18°C). The rainfall – 20 to 40 inches (508–1,016 mm) a year – is well distributed through the year. Sheltered valleys in the south have warmer summers, but the highlands are cooler. The average annual temperature range at München is 28°F–64°F (−2°C–18°C).

Moorland and heath cover much of the north, but the centre and south have some large forests.

Economy Both East and West Germany made rapid economic progress after World War II.

With help from the Allies, West Germany's recovery was so rapid that it was called an economic 'miracle'. The country's total GNP in 1989 of $1,272,959 million was the largest in western Europe, giving it the high per capita GNP of $20,750. However, the per capita GNP for the re-united Germany was only about $18,200.

In West Germany in 1989, agriculture accounted for only 2 percent of the GDP and 4 percent of the workforce, while industry accounted for 51 percent of the GDP and manufacturing and construction 33 percent of the workforce.

Arable land covered 23.3 percent of the country, orchards and vineyards, 0.9 percent, pasture, 19.3 percent, and forest, 29 percent. The north produced such crops as potatoes and rye. The warmer centre and south produce fruits, hops, sugar-beet, tobacco and wheat. The south-east is mainly pastoral. In 1988, there were 15,023,000 cattle, 1,895,000 sheep, 23,755,000 pigs and 72,035,000 poultry.

West Germany's early industrial growth was based on coal mined in the Ruhr valley, Saarland and around Aachen. The country also produces iron ore and some other minerals.

Some petroleum is produced and more is imported. The use of petroleum has made it possible for new industrial areas to be established aways from the coalfields, as in München and Nürnberg. Other industrial centres include the ports of Bremen and Hamburg, and West Berlin.

Steel and chemicals, together with electrical engineering, machinery, textiles and vehicles are the leading industries. Industrial products dominate the exports. The EEC accounts for nearly half of West Germany's trade.

The area occupied by East Germany had been mainly agricultural prior to World War II. But, with financial and technical assistance from the USSR, East Germany developed large manufacturing industries. By 1989, it had a per capita GNP of $9,720. Agriculture accounted for 10 percent of the net material product and for 11 percent of the workforce. Mining and manufacturing accounted for 65 percent of the net material product and 40 percent of the

The Olympic Park in München (Munich), West Germany, was built for the 1972 Olympic Games.

workforce.

The industries were all government owned. They produced engineering products, chemicals, plastics, textiles, optical and precision instruments and consumer goods.

Lignite and potash are mined and used in the chemical industries. East Germany has some other minerals, but many materials, including iron ore and petroleum, and imported, Berlin and the southern cities were the chief industrial centres.

Farmland covers 44 percent of East Germany, pasture 11 percent, and forests 27 percent. The most fertile land is in the south. Barley, oats, potatoes, rye, sugar-beet and wheat are grown and livestock-farming is important. There were 5,710,000 cattle, 2,634,000 sheep, 12,464,000 pigs and 49,430,000 poultry in 1988.

Following re-unification, many problems arose in integrating the economies of West and East Germany. Unemployment in the East increased as many factories were forced to close because they could not compete with the more efficient industries in the West.

AUSTRIA

Area: 32,375 sq miles (83,849 km^2)
Population: 7,510,000
Population Growth Rate: 0.0% pa
Capital: Wien (Vienna),
    pop. 1,516,000
Language: German
Religion: Christianity (Roman
    Catholic 88%, Protestant 6%)
Currency: Schilling = 100 Groschen

THE REPUBLIC OF AUSTRIA is divided into nine Federal States, representatives of which form the Bundesrat (Federal Council). The Bundesrat and the directly elected Nationalrat (National Council) together form the National Assembly.

People and Culture Austria became part of the Roman Empire between 15 BC and AD 10. Germanic tribes invaded in the late fourth century.

In the ninth century, Austria was part of Charlemagne's Holy Roman Empire. The Babenberg dynasty ruled from 976 until the Hapsburgs took over in 1246. The Hapsburgs supplied all but one of the Holy Roman emperors between 1438 and 1806, when the title was abolished.

From 1806, the Hapsburg rulers were the Emperors of Austria. In 1867, Austria and Hungary became a dual monarchy, but this collapsed at the end of World War I.

Germany annexed Austria in 1938, but Austria was liberated at the end of World War II in 1945. In 1955, it became a federal republic. It agreed to occupy a neutral status between East and West.

About 55 percent of Austrians live in urban areas. Wien (Vienna) is the only conurbation. The average life expectancy at birth (1981) was 73 years.

The Land About three-fourths of Austria consists of Alpine ranges, the highest peak being Grossglockner 12,460 feet (3,834 m), near the Italian border. The northeast is divided into the undulating Alpine foreland and the Wien lowlands, drained by the Donau (Danube) River.

The climate is continental. Cold, snowy winters make Austria a winter sports centre. Above about 9,500 feet (2,896 m) is permanent snow and ice. Below are Alpine meadows, coniferous forests and deciduous forests on the lower slopes.

Economy The per capita GNP in 1981 was $10,210. In 1980, agriculture accounted for 4 percent of the GDP and 9 percent of the workforce. Farmland constitutes 37 percent of the country with the chief farming region in the Wien lowlands. The mountains provide summer pasture for livestock. Forestry is also important.

Industry accounted for 39 percent of the GDP and 37 percent of the workforce in 1980. Iron ore and lignite are mined and Austria produces about one-fourth of its petroleum needs. Steel, chemicals and textiles are leading products. Wien is the major industrial centre.

The Rhine Valley is a major farming region in West Germany, known for its vineyards and wines.

The Binnenalster is one of two lakes in Hamburg formed by the Alster River. Hamburg is West Germany's largest city after Berlin.

Italy

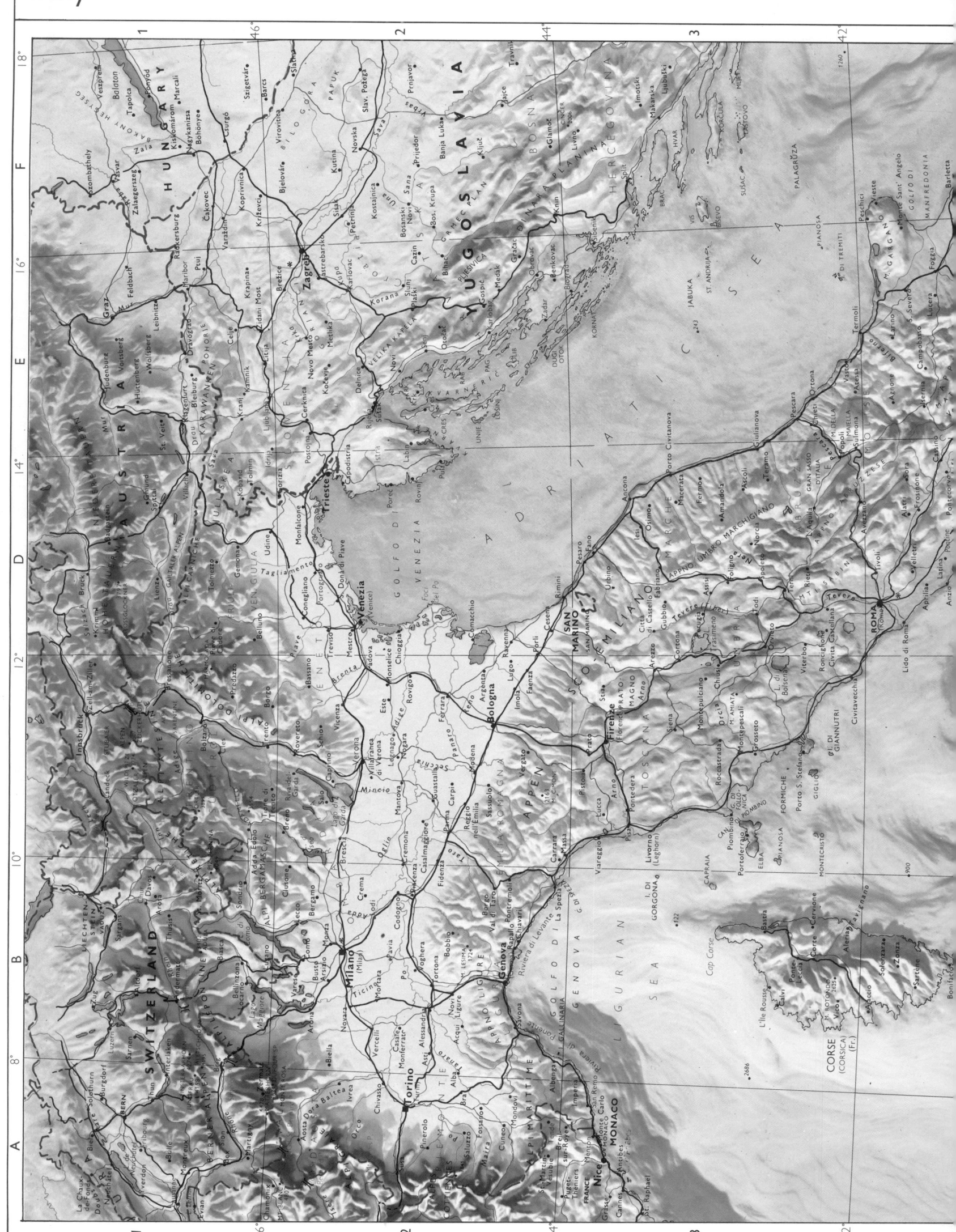

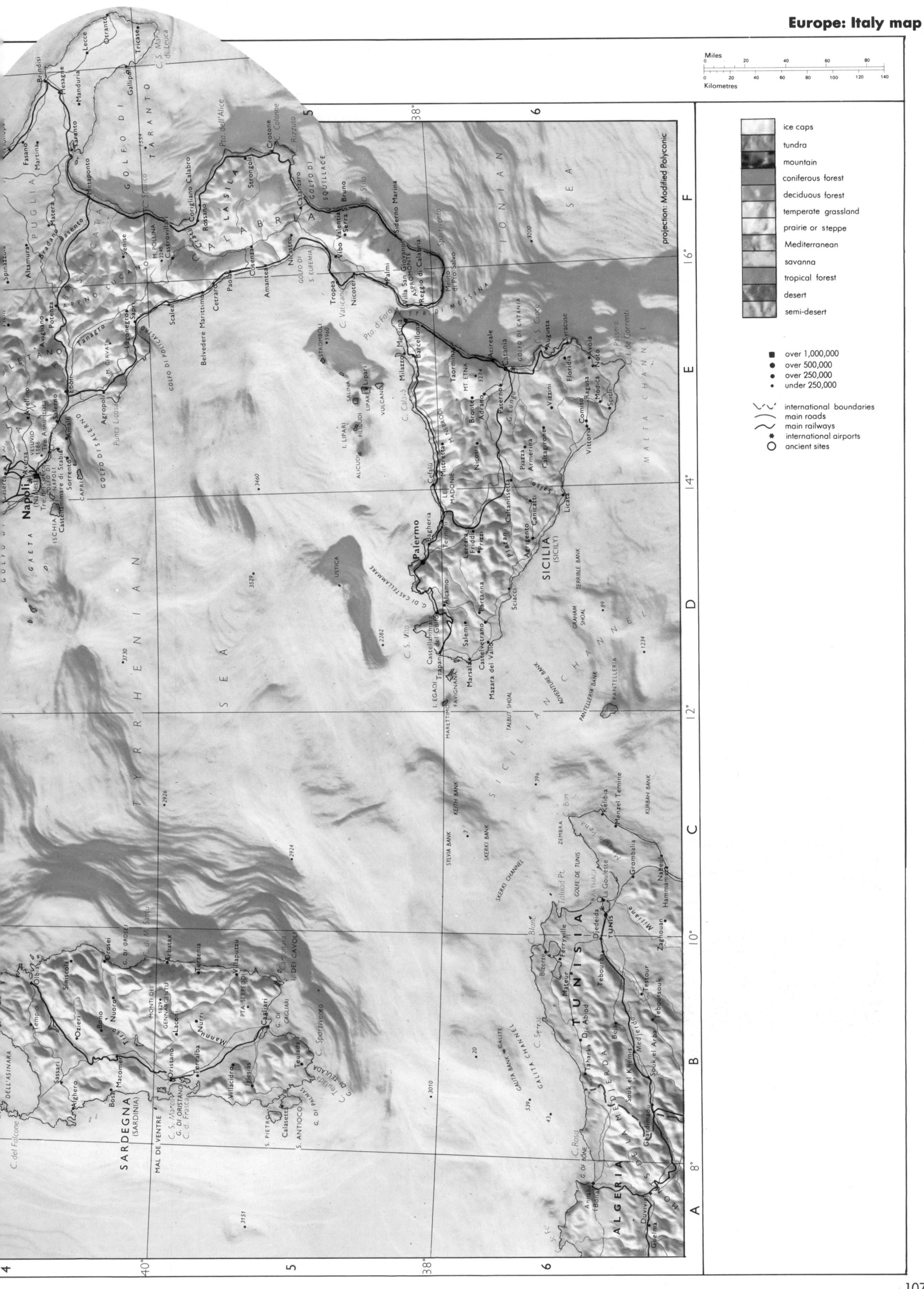

Miles
0 20 40 60 80

0 20 40 60 80 100 120 140
Kilometres

projection: Modified Polyconic

ice caps
tundra
mountain
coniferous forest
deciduous forest
temperate grassland
prairie or steppe
Mediterranean
savanna
tropical forest
desert
semi-desert

■ over 1,000,000
● over 500,000
● over 250,000
• under 250,000

international boundaries
main roads
main railways
✳ international airports
○ ancient sites

107

ITALY

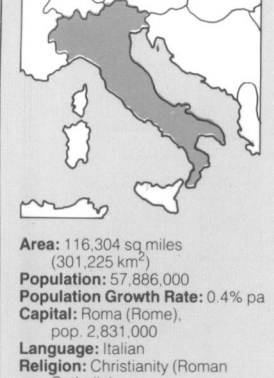

Area: 116,304 sq miles
(301,225 km²)
Population: 57,886,000
Population Growth Rate: 0.4% pa
Capital: Roma (Rome),
pop. 2,831,000
Language: Italian
Religion: Christianity (Roman
Catholic)
Currency: Lira=100 Centesimi

THE REPUBLIC OF ITALY has made a considerable contribution to western civilization.
People and Culture The development of Italian culture is evident in its abundant archaeological sites, its beautiful cities, its art galleries and its opera houses.

Some of Italy's earliest buildings date back to the eighth to fourth centuries BC, when the Greeks founded colonies in Italy. At the same time, the Etruscans in northern Italy were establishing an important civilization.

In 509 BC, the people of Rome expelled their Etruscan

Vandals. Later, the eastern Roman empire recovered much of Italy, but the Lombards invaded the north in the sixth century.

In the south, Arab Saracens took Sicily in 917. Their culture was later absorbed into a Norman kingdom which included part of southern Italy. Through this culture, classical texts known to Arab scholars but unknown in mediaeval Europe were revived and began to be circulated.

Northern and central Italy were nominally protected by the Holy Roman Empire. However, the region was divided into rival city states, some of which played a major part in the Renaissance.

The Italian Renaissance began in thirteenth-century Florence (Firenze), birthplace of the poet Dante (1265–1321). Later, other cities, such as Genoa (Genova), Milan (Milano), Pisa and Venice (Venezia) also became centres of learning and the arts.

The fifteenth and sixteenth centuries saw an extraordinary flowering of architecture, literature, painting and sculpture. But this was also a time when the people were divided between those who supported the popes (the Guelphs) and those who supported the emperors (the Ghibellines). Conflict between these groups hindered attempts to unify Italy.

In the eighteenth century, the Austrian Hapsburgs controlled northern Italy and the Spanish Bourbons the south. Napoleon invaded in 1796, but after his defeat in 1815, Italy was again disunited.

Revolts in 1848 and 1849 against the Austrians heralded

Germany and Japan. Italy entered World War II in 1940, but it lost Ethiopia in 1941 and surrendered in 1943.

After the war, a series of weak, mostly coalition governments failed to provide stability. From 1957, however, Italy developed rapidly within the EEC.

But major problems still exist, including the great economic differences between the rich industrial north and the impoverished rural south. High inflation, strikes and terrorist violence have also created instability.

Italy's bicameral parliament contains a 630-member Chamber of Deputies and a 315-member Senate. The largest parties are the Christian Democrats, the Communists, and the Socialists.

Overall, the rate of population increase in Italy is low at 0.4 percent per year, but one reason for this is that many people have emigrated to find work.

There is also internal migration from the under-populated south to the northern cities. In 1981, 70 percent of the population lived in urban areas, as compared with 59 in 1960.

Apart from Rome, the leading cities are:

Milan or Milano
(1,635,000)
Naples or Napoli
(1,211,000)
Turin or Torino
(1,104,000)
Genoa or Genova
(760,000)
Palermo (700,000)
Bologna (456,000)
Florence or Firenze
(453,000).

The Roman Forum was the centre of life in ancient Rome.

The Ponte Vecchio, the oldest bridge in Firenze (Florence), spans the Arno River, connecting two art galleries, the Uffizi and the Pitti.

king and founded a republic. By 220 BC, the Romans controlled most of peninsular Italy. From this base, they built up a huge empire, civilizing many areas. Sections of their roads, bridges, aqueducts and the ruins of once splendid buildings can still be seen throughout Europe, North Africa and the Middle East.

Visigoths took Rome in AD 410 and, in 455, it fell to the

a long struggle for independence. Italy finally became a united kingdom in 1861 under Victor Emmanuel II. But the Papal States did not become part of Italy until 1870.

Italy fought alongside the Allies in World War I. In 1922, Benito Mussolini's Fascist party took power. In 1935–36 Italy conquered Ethiopia and, in 1939, Mussolini signed a pact allying Italy with

The average life expectancy at birth in 1981 was 74 years, as compared with 69 in 1960. This reflects rises in living standards and health services.
The Land The highest mountains, including Italy's highest peak, Monte Rosa at 15,203 feet (4,634 m), are the Alps in the north. This scenic region contains some beautiful lakes and many rivers, which drain into the North Italian plain.

Many of these rivers are tributaries of the Po, Italy's longest river which flows about 400 miles (644 km). The North Italian plain is farming country, with livestock on the wetter pastures and arable farming in drier areas. The Po enters the Adriatic Sea through a complex delta.

The backbone of peninsular Italy is the Appennino range, whose highest peak is Monte

Corno, northeast of Rome (Roma), which reaches 9,560 feet (2,914 m). Within the range are many fertile basins and valleys, such as the Arno valley in Tuscany (Toscana). The rivers of peninsular Italy are mostly short.

The coastal plains vary in width and fertility. Fertile plains include the Campagna and Campania plains between the Tiber (Tevere) River and Naples. Apulia (Puglia) in the 'heel' of Italy is another fertile lowland.

Near Naples is Vesuvius (Vesuvio), the first of a chain of active volcanoes which extends south through the Lipari Islands to Mount Etna in Sicily. Southern Italy is also an earthquake zone and earthquakes are sometimes highly destructive of property and life.

The toe of Italy, Calabria, is underdeveloped, as is Sicily (Sicilia), which covers 9,926 sq miles (25,708 km²). Sicily is mainly mountainous, with lowlands in the far west and a plateau in the southeast. Mountains cover about nine-tenths of Italy's other large island, Sardinia (Sardegna), which covers 9,301 sq miles (24,090 km²).

Southern Italy has a typical Mediterranean climate, with most of the rain falling in winter. The North Italian plain has hot summers, but winters are much colder. The Alps have mild summers and cold, snowy winters.

The Alps contain various bands of vegetation below the permanent snow and ice, including Alpine meadows, coniferous forest and deciduous forest. The trees of peninsular Italy, such as cork oak, cypress and pine, are adapted to the summer drought. Scrub grows in deforested areas, with *macchia* (the equivalent of French *maquis*) in arid areas. Large animals have survived only in remote areas. They include the ibex in the Alps and wild boars and mouflon sheep in Sardinia.

Economy In 1980, farming accounted for 6 percent of the GDP and 11 percent of the workforce. Farmland, including pasture and land under permanent crops, covers about two-thirds of Italy, and forests about one-fifth.

Barley, various fruits, maize, olives, sugar-beet, tobacco, vegetables and wheat are grown. Grapes are used mainly for wine, of which Italy is the world's leading producer.

In 1981, cattle numbered 8,903,000, sheep and goats 10,620,000, and pigs 9,015,000. Dairy products are important and Italy is the world's sixth largest producer of cheese.

Industry accounted for 42 percent of the GDP and 45 percent of the workforce in 1980. Italy produces some petroleum, but it is generally short of minerals and fuels, which it imports.

However, Italy has many important industries, producing textiles, engineering goods, including vehicles, chemicals and steel. Italy ranks sixth in the world in producing cars and ninth in commercial vehicles. Leading trading partners are West Germany, France, the United States and the UK.

Tourism is important and 47,700,000 foreigners visited Italy in 1980. In 1981, the per capita GNP was $6,960, which placed Italy eighth among the ten nations of the EEC.

SAN MARINO

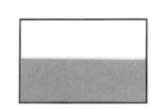

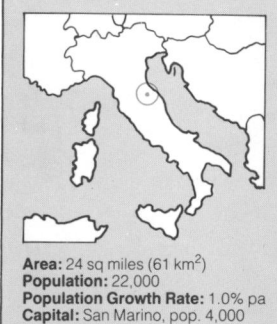

Area: 24 sq miles (61 km²)
Population: 22,000
Population Growth Rate: 1.0% pa
Capital: San Marino, pop. 4,000
Language: Italian
Religion: Christianity (Roman Catholic)
Currency: Italian Lira; San Marino also issues its own coins

THE REPUBLIC OF SAN MARINO is a small, landlocked nation near Rimini in central Italy.

According to tradition, it originated in a Christian community established in the mountains in about AD 300. It was recognized as independent by the Pope in 1631.

In 1862, it entered into a customs union with Italy. San Marino is governed by the elected Great and General Council.

The republic lies on the slopes of Monte Titano. Olives, vines and wheat are grown and livestock are raised. There are also some industries, but tourism is the chief source of income. San Marino was host to about 3.5 million tourists in 1980.

VATICAN CITY

Area: 108.7 acres (44 ha)
Population: 1,000
Currency: Italian Lira; Vatican City also issues its own coins

THE VATICAN CITY STATE, or the Holy See, is the world's smallest independent nation.

It is in northwest Rome and it contains the government of the Roman Catholic Church, which is headed by the Pope. Saint Peter's Basilica and the Sistine Chapel, with its famous frescoes by Michelangelo, attract millions of visitors.

The Vatican City has been the Pope's residence since the fifth century AD. It was formerly the centre of the large Papal States, which Victor Emmanuel II incorporated into Italy in 1870. The Pope did not accept this act until the Lateran Treaty (1929) recognized the See's independence.

MALTA

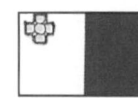

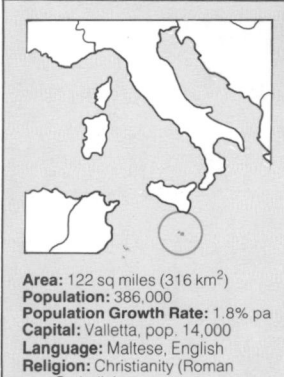

Area: 122 sq miles (316 km²)
Population: 386,000
Population Growth Rate: 1.8% pa
Capital: Valletta, pop. 14,000
Language: Maltese, English
Religion: Christianity (Roman Catholic)
Currency: Pound = 100 Cents

THE REPUBLIC OF MALTA is an island nation located south of Sicily in the Mediterranean. For its location, see the map of South Europe on pages 78–79.

San Marino is a small independent republic enclosed by Italy.

People and Culture Because of its strategic position, Malta has had many rulers. After the Phoenicians colonized the islands before 1000 BC, Malta came under Greek, Carthaginian, Roman, Byzantine, Arab and Norman rule. From 1530, it was governed by the Knights of St John.

Napoleon took the islands in 1798, but the French were driven out in 1800 with British help. From 1814 until 1964, Malta was a British colony. It became a republic in 1974, but remained within the Commonwealth.

The Land Malta contains three islands: Malta itself which covers 94.9 square miles (246 km²); Gozo, 25.9 square miles (67 km²); and Comino, 1.1 square miles (3 km²). There are two uninhabited islets.

Limestone covers most of the land and there is little surface water. Soils are mostly thin and scrub (*maquis*) is the natural vegetation.

The climate is Mediterranean, with hot dry summers and mild, moist winters.

Economy In 1981, agriculture and fishing employed 5 percent of the workforce. About 39 percent of Malta is farmed, and about half of the farmland is under wheat. Manufacturing, construction and quarrying employed 32 percent of the workforce. Tourism is important and Malta had nearly 706,000 visitors in 1981, when the per capita GNP was $3,600.

Gozo is the second largest island in Malta. Farming is important because Gozo is more fertile than the larger island of Malta.

The Balkans

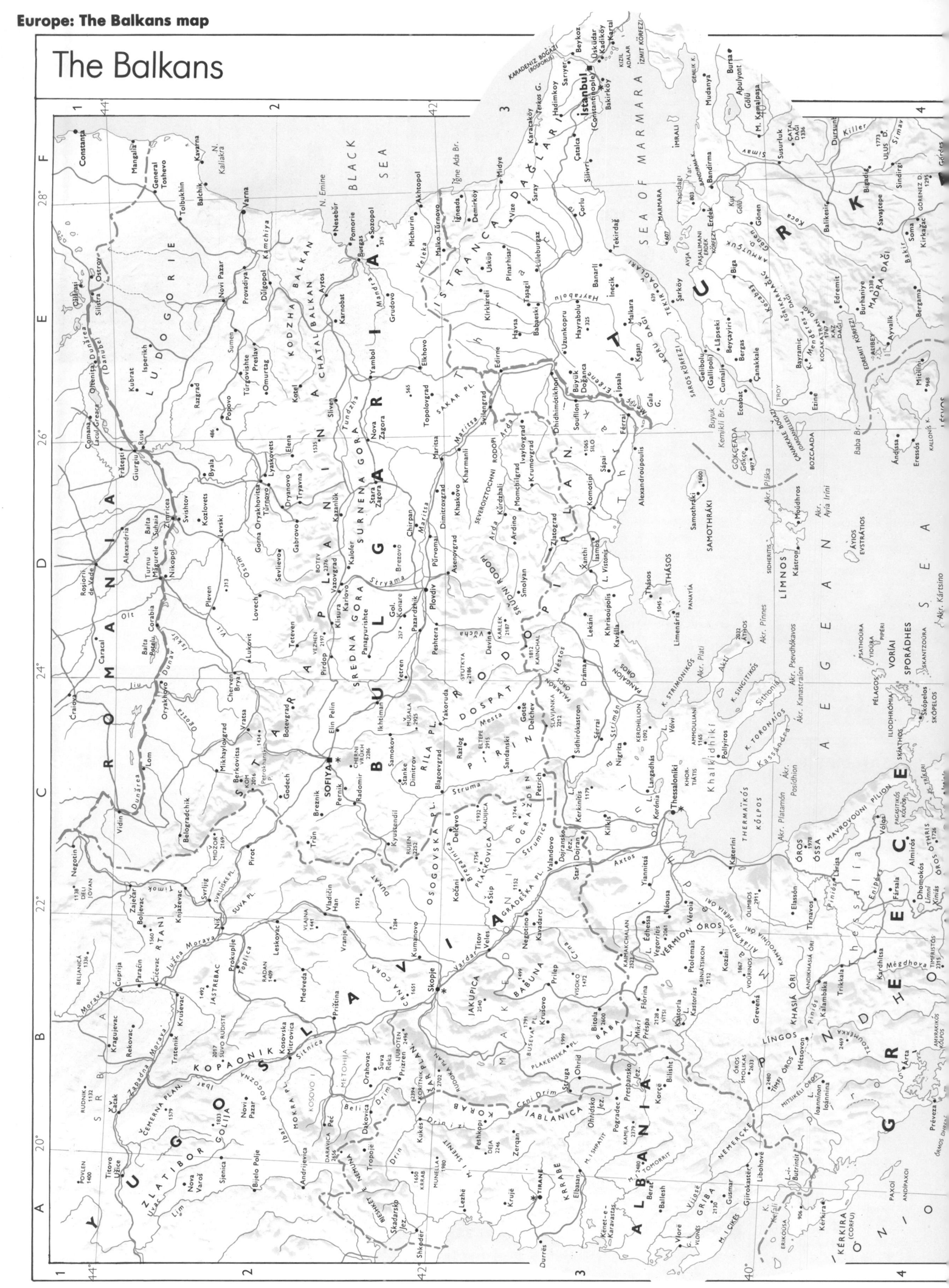

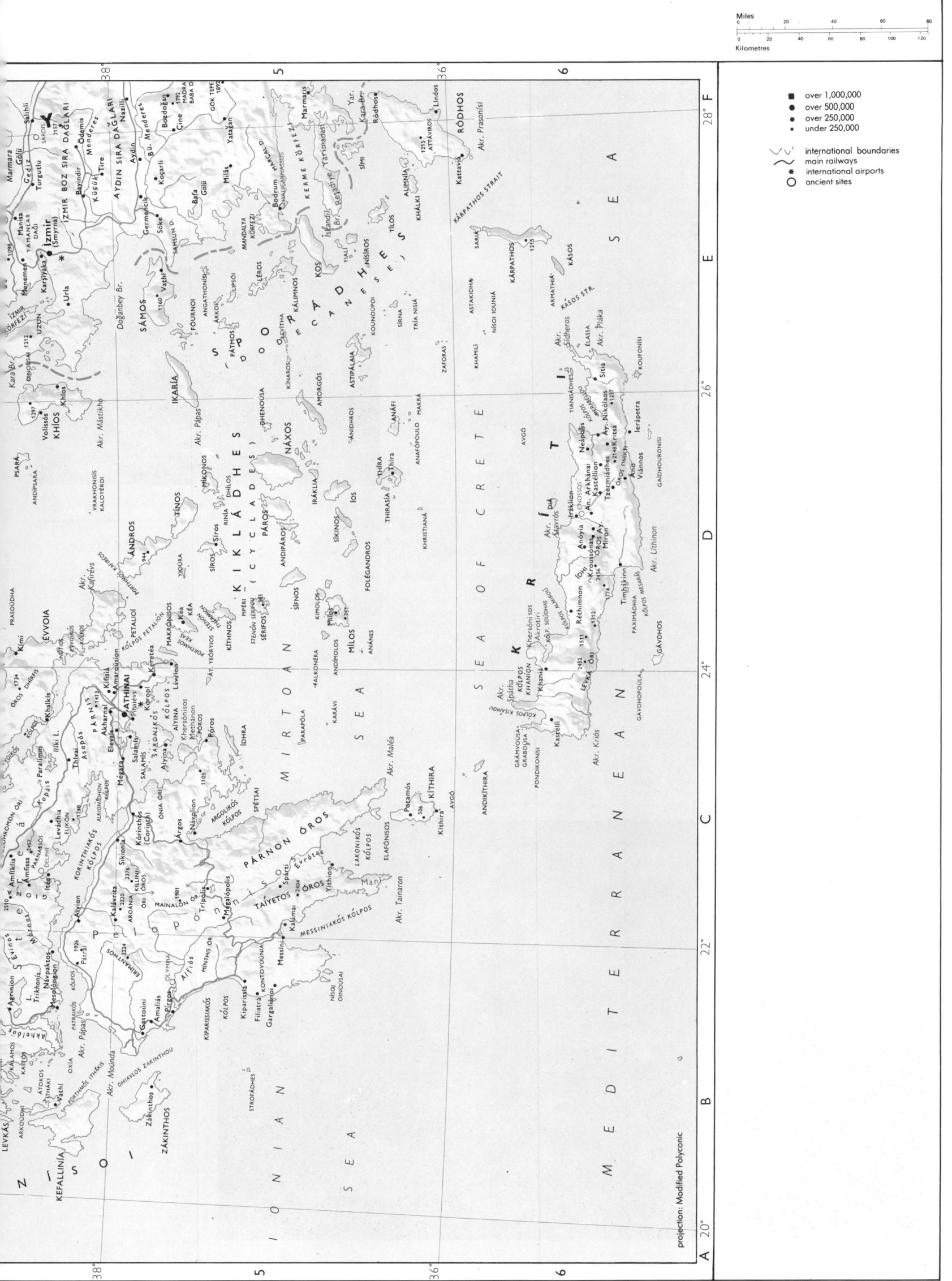

■ over 1,000,000
● over 500,000
● over 250,000
• under 250,000

ᴠᴠ international boundaries
∿ main railways
✳ international airports
○ ancient sites

projection: Modified Polyconic

YUGOSLAVIA

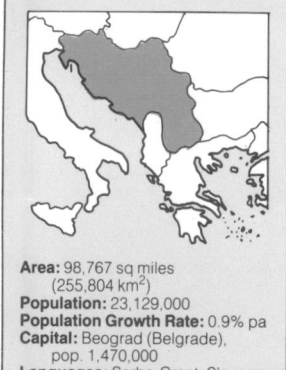

Area: 98,767 sq miles (255,804 km²)
Population: 23,129,000
Population Growth Rate: 0.9% pa
Capital: Beograd (Belgrade), pop. 1,470,000
Languages: Serbo-Croat, Slovene, Macedonian
Religions: Christianity, Islam
Currency: Dinar=100 Paras

THE SOCIALIST FEDERAL RE-PUBLIC OF YUGOSLAVIA contains six republics: Bosnia and Hercegovina (Bosna-i-Hercegovina); Croatia (Hrvatska); Macedonia (Makedonija); Montenegro (Crna Gora); Serbia (Srbija); and Slovenia (Slovenija). Serbia also contains two autonomous provinces.

People and Culture Yugoslavia did not become a nation until 1918 and, in the past, the various regions had separate cultures. The north was once part of the Holy Roman Empire and Roman Catholicism is the chief religion today. Serbia has Byzantine traditions and many Serbs now belong to the Eastern Orthodox Church. The south was once part of the Turkish Ottoman Empire. Islam is now the religion of 12 percent of Yugoslavs, Orthodox Christianity of 41 percent, and Roman Catholicism 32 percent.

The Slavs occupied the area in the seventh century AD. They founded the powerful kingdom of Serbia in the 12th century. In 1389, the Turks took southern Serbia, but Slovenia and Croatia remained under Hapsburg rule.

The independence of Serbia and Montenegro was recognized by the Congress of Berlin in 1878. After the Balkan Wars (1912–13), Macedonia was divided between Serbia, Bulgaria and Greece.

The assassination in 1914 of Archduke Franz Ferdinand in Bosnia-Hercegovina, then under Austro-Hungarian rule, led Austria-Hungary to declare war on Serbia and so start World War I.

In 1918, the South Slavs were united in the Kingdom of the Serbs, Croats and Slovenes, which was renamed Yugoslavia in 1929.

Germany invaded in 1941, but partisans led by Tito (Josip Broz) fought back. After the war, Tito established a socialist republic. In 1948, Yugoslavia broke with the USSR and pursued an independent course. Tito died in 1980. There is now a collective presidency.

In 1981, 43 percent of Yugoslavs lived in urban areas. Apart from Beograd, the largest cities are Zagreb (769,000), Niš (643,000) and Skopje (507,000). The average life expectancy at birth in 1981 was 71 years.

The Land Behind the indented coastline is a mountain zone. Narrow in the northwest, the mountains broaden to cover most of the south. The eastern lowlands are drained by the Drava, Sava, Dunav (Danube) and other rivers.

The climate varies from Mediterranean on the coast to continental in the interior.

Economy Agriculture accounted for 12 percent of the GDP and 29 percent of the workforce in 1980, while industry accounted for 43 percent of the GDP and 35 percent of the workforce.

Crops include cereals, cotton, fruits, olives, sugar-beet, sunflower seeds and tobacco. In 1981, there were 5,500,000 cattle, 7,400,000 sheep and 7,900,000 pigs. Forests cover 36 percent of the land.

Yugoslavia has sizeable mineral reserves and manufacturing has increased steadily in recent years. In 1981, 6,616,000 tourists visited the country. The per capita GNP (1981) was $2,790.

BULGARIA

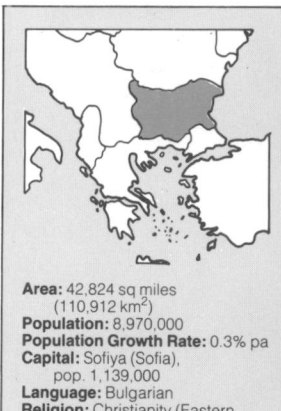

Area: 42,824 sq miles (110,912 km²)
Population: 8,970,000
Population Growth Rate: 0.3% pa
Capital: Sofiya (Sofia), pop. 1,139,000
Language: Bulgarian
Religion: Christianity (Eastern Orthodox)
Currency: Lev=100 Stotinki

THE PEOPLE'S REPUBLIC OF BULGARIA is one of the more prosperous countries in eastern Europe.

People and Culture About 4,500 years ago, Thracian tribes occupied the area, which later came under the Roman Empire. Slavic tribes moved in from AD 500 and Asiatic Bulgars invaded in the seventh century. A Slav-Bulgarian nation was founded in 681.

The Byzantine Empire ruled between 1018 and 1186 and in 1396 Bulgaria was absorbed into the Turkish Ottoman Empire.

Northern Bulgaria gained independence in 1878. The south was added in 1885. The Balkan Wars of 1912–13 fixed most of Bulgaria's frontiers. In World Wars I and II, Bulgaria was allied with Germany.

In 1944, a Communist government was established. Since then, the USSR has helped Bulgaria to develop its economy.

Bulgarian-speaking people make up 88 percent of the population and Turks 8.6 percent. There are also gypsies, Jews, Romanians and Armenians.

In 1981, 65 percent of Bulgarians lived in urban areas, as compared with 39 percent in 1960, and the average life expectancy at birth was 73 years.

The Land Lowlands border the Danube River in the north, but the most fertile region is the central lowlands bordering the Black Sea. The Balkan Mountains are in the north and the Rodopi Mountains in the southwest. Here is Bulgaria's highest peak, Mŭsala at 9,596 feet (2,925 m).

The climate is transitional between Mediterranean and continental types. The annual rainfall varies from 47 inches (1,194 mm) in the Rodopi Mountains to 18 inches (457 mm) in the northeast.

Economy Agriculture accounted for 19 percent of the GDP and 37 percent of the workforce in 1980. Mulberry leaves (to feed silkworms) and rose petals (for making attar of roses) are among Bulgaria's products. Others include fruits, sugar-beet, tobacco, wheat and wine. In 1981, Bulgaria had 1,796,000 cattle, 10,433,000 sheep and 3,808,000 pigs.

Industry accounted for 55 percent of the GDP and 39 percent of the workforce in 1980. Bulgaria produces copper, iron ore, manganese and some oil. The government-owned manufacturing industries are varied. In 1980, the per capita GNP was $4,150.

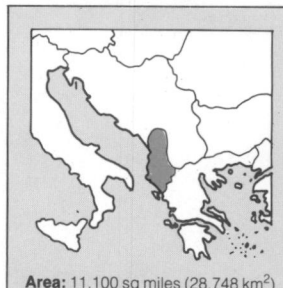

In Bulgaria, farming accounts for nearly one-fifth of the GDP.

ALBANIA

Area: 11,100 sq miles (28,748 km²)
Population: 3,001,000
Population Growth Rate: 2.4% pa
Capital: Tiranë, pop. 198,000
Language: Albanian
Religion: officially atheism
Currency: Lek=100 Qindarka

THE SOCIALIST PEOPLE'S RE-PUBLIC OF ALBANIA is one of Europe's least developed countries.

People and Culture Most Albanians are descendants of Illyrian tribes. The Romans conquered Illyria and the area later came under the Goths, Byzantines and Slavs.

Turkey ruled from the late fifteenth century until 1912, when Albania became independent. Albania became a republic in 1925, but its President, Ahmed Beg Zog, proclaimed himself king in 1928.

Italian and then German troops occupied Albania in World War II. In 1946, the country became a people's republic allied to the USSR. It broke with the USSR in 1961 and allied itself with China. This relationship ended in 1977, since when Albania has pursued an independent course.

The coast of Yugoslavia has subsided and the sea has flooded valleys parallel to the coast, producing long, narrow islands.

In 1981, only 37 percent of Albanians live in urban areas. The average life expectancy at birth was 70 years. Albania is, officially, an atheist country. All mosques and churches were closed in 1967.

The Land Communications are difficult in the mountainous interior. The coastal plain, with its Mediterranean climate, is a farming region. In summer, livestock are grazed on the cooler, wetter uplands.

Forests of oak, elm, pine and birch cover 47 percent of Albania.

Economy In 1980, farming employed 61 percent of the workforce. Farmland covers 17 percent of Albania and pasture 25 percent. Farming is collectivized. Barley, maize, potatoes, sugar-beet and wheat are major crops, but livestock-rearing is the chief activity. In 1979, there were 474,000 cattle and 1,828,000 sheep and goats.

Industry employed 25 percent of the workforce in 1980. Oil is produced and Albania's other mineral resources are now being exploited. Oil, bitumen, copper and nickel are exported, as are fruits, tobacco and vegetables. All manufacturing is government-owned, but the output is low. The per capita GNP in 1979 was $840.

GREECE

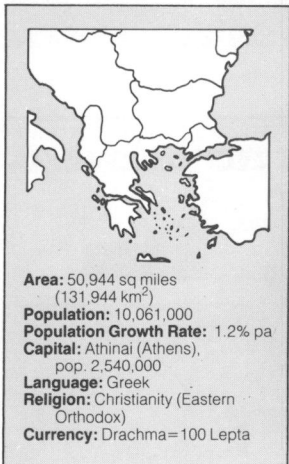

Area: 50,944 sq miles (131,944 km²)
Population: 10,061,000
Population Growth Rate: 1.2% pa
Capital: Athinai (Athens), pop. 2,540,000
Language: Greek
Religion: Christianity (Eastern Orthodox)
Currency: Drachma=100 Lepta

THE HELLENIC REPUBLIC, or Greece, can claim to be the birthplace of western civilization.

People and Culture The Minoan civilization flourished between about 3000 and 1400 BC in the eastern Mediterranean, with its centre on Crete (Kriti). On the mainland, the Mycenaean civilization developed between 1580 and 1100 BC, but Mycenae and other kingdoms were conquered by Dorian Greeks who came from the north in about 1100 BC.

From 750 BC, Greece began to found colonies through the Mediterranean and Black seas. Trade brought prosperity, making possible the great Classical Age in the fifth century BC, when Greek architecture, art, literature, philosophy, science, sculpture and social innovations, such as democratic government, reached their height.

But this was not a peaceful age. The Greeks had to fight off Persian invaders and in the Peloponnesian Wars (431–404 BC) Sparta (Sparti) defeated Athens (Athinai).

By 338 BC, Macedonia controlled most of Greece. Alexander (356–323 BC), ruler of Macedonia and Greece, reasserted Greek power by conquering an empire which stretched from North Africa into Asia as far as India.

Rome took Macedonia in 168 and Greece in 146 BC. In AD 365, Greece became part of the East Roman (Byzantine) Empire. In the eleventh century, the Church based on Constantinople (now Istanbul) became the Eastern Orthodox Church, the church to which 97 percent of Greeks today belong.

The Byzantine Empire disintegrated after 1453, when the Ottoman Turks took Constantinople.

The Greeks rebelled against the Turks in 1821, finally becoming an independent kingdom in 1830. In 1917–18, Greece fought alongside the Allies but, in 1919–23, Turkey defeated Greece in a struggle for Izmir (Smyrna) on the Turkish mainland.

After World War II, when Germany had occupied Greece, Monarchist and Communist forces fought a civil war, which ended in 1949.

A coup in 1967 brought a military government to power. This finally collapsed in 1974 after the government had failed to prevent Turkey from occupying northern Cyprus. The people then voted to make Greece a republic.

. In 1981, 63 percent of the population lived in urban areas, as compared with 43 percent in 1960. Living standards are rising and the average life expectancy at birth in 1981 was 74 years, as com-

pared with 69 percent in 1960.

The Land Greece includes the mountainous southern Balkan peninsula, whose highest peak is Olympus (Olimbos). In the south, Peloponnisos (the Peloponnese) is almost cut off from northern Greece by the Gulf of Corinth (Korinthiakós Kólpos).

Northern Greece includes Macedonia (Makedhonia) and Thrace (Thraki), a region of rolling plains rising to the north.

The country's islands are divided into six main groups: the Thracian islands in the northern Aegean Sea; the North Sporades (Voríai Sporádhes); the East Aegean Islands, including Lesbos (Lésvos); the Cyclades (Kikládhes); and the Dodecanese (Sporádhes). The largest island, Crete (Kriti), is in the south.

The climate of Greece is Mediterranean, with particu-

larly hot summers. Winters are severe in the mountains.

Economy In 1980, farming accounted for 17 percent of the GDP and 37 percent of the workforce. One-third of Greece is cultivated. Major crops include citrus fruits, grapes (for wine), olives, tobacco and wheat. In 1981, there were 899,000 cattle, 7,920,000 sheep, 4,700,000 goats and 1,000,000 pigs. Fishing is important and Greece has one of the world's largest merchant navies.

Industry accounted for 31 percent of the GDP and 28 percent of the workforce in 1980. Some minerals are produced. There are many processing industries and manufacturing industries are increasing.

Tourism is important: Greece received 5,094,000 tourists in 1981. It joined the EEC in 1981, when its per capita GNP was $4,420.

An aerial view of the Acropolis capped by famous ruins shows how this steep-sided hill dominates the city of Athens, Greece.

POLAND

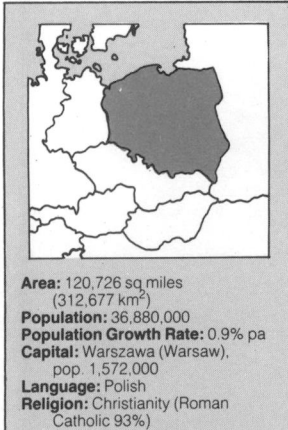

Area: 120,726 sq miles (312,677 km²)
Population: 36,880,000
Population Growth Rate: 0.9% pa
Capital: Warszawa (Warsaw), pop. 1,572,000
Language: Polish
Religion: Christianity (Roman Catholic 93%)
Currency: Zloty = 100 Groszy

THE POLISH PEOPLE'S REPUB-LIC is Eastern Europe's largest nation apart from the USSR.

People and Culture The Polians, a West Slav people, united with other tribes in the tenth century and, in 1025, Poland became an independent Christian kingdom. But it was later split into rival principalities.

Teutonic Knights, invited to subdue the heathen Prussians, eventually founded their own kingdom in Prussia. The Poles were reunited in the late thirteenth century and, in the fourteenth, they formed the Polish-Lithuanian Commonwealth. This union defeated the Teutonic Knights, but allowed them to keep Prussia.

From the sixteenth century, Poland was divided and weakened by wars. In the eighteenth century, Russia, Prussia and Austria partitioned Poland which, in 1795, disappeared altogether.

Napoleon restored independence to a territory called the Grand Duchy of Warsaw, but Poland was again absorbed by its neighbours by 1831.

In 1918, an independent Polish republic was established. In 1939, Poland was divided between Germany and the USSR. About six million Poles were killed during World War II. After the war, Poland lost territory to the USSR, but gained land from Germany. Most Germans departed.

A Communist government, established in 1945, pursued Russian policies, such as collectivizing agriculture and discouraging religion. But today, 75 percent of farmland is privately owned and the majority of Poles remain Roman Catholics.

Anti-Soviet feeling was manifested in riots in 1956. Further unrest occurred in the 1960s and 1970s. In 1980 workers led by Lech Wałęsa demanded the right to form free trade unions. A national confederation of trade unions, Solidarity, was formed, but it was outlawed in 1981.

In 1978, Poland's population was only 200,000 more than it was in 1939, a consequence of the slaughter in World War II and emigration. In 1982, 57 percent of Poles lived in urban areas. Apart from Warszawa (Warsaw), major cities included:

Lódź (832,000)
Kraków (705,000)
Wroclaw (608,000)
Poznan (544,000).

In 1980, the average life expectancy at birth was 66 years for men and 74 for women.

The Land The northern plains are largely covered by moraine. The central lowlands, containing Warszawa, are more fertile. Most of the south is a plateau, rising to the Sudety mountains in the southwest and the Carpathians in the southeast. The climate becomes more continental from north to south and from west to east.

Economy In 1980, industry accounted for 53 percent of the GDP and 39 percent of the workforce. Poland is the world's fourth largest coal producer. It also has reserves of lignite, lead, nickel and zinc. Poland has a great variety of light and heavy industry. The country is currently ranked as one of the world's top 15 industrial nations.

Farming accounted for 16 percent of the GDP and 31 percent of the workforce in 1980. Farmland covers 60 percent of Poland and forests 27 percent. Collectivization has been abandoned and there were 2,900,000 private farms in 1981. Government farms occupy 20 percent of the farmland and cooperatives 4 percent.

Cereals, potatoes and sugarbeet are major crops and, in 1981, there were 11,800,000 cattle, 18,500,000 pigs and 3,900,000 sheep.

The per capita GNP in 1980 was $3,900.

The round tower of the Fisherman's Bastion, Hungary, contains a popular restaurant.

Praha (Prague), capital of Czechoslovakia, is a city of great charm, best explored on foot.

CZECHOSLOVAKIA

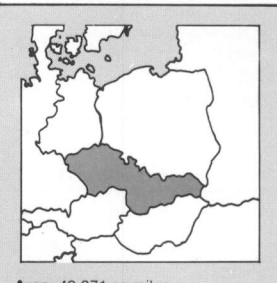

Area: 49,371 sq miles (127,869 km²)
Population: 15,591,000
Population Growth Rate: 0.6% pa
Capital: Praha (Prague), pop. 1,182,000
Languages: Czech, Slovak
Religions: Christianity (Roman Catholic, Protestant)
Currency: Koruna = 100 Haléru

THE CZECHOSLOVAK SOCIALIST REPUBLIC is a federation of the Czech Socialist Republic and the Slovak Socialist Republic.

People and Culture Most people are Slavs, descendants of people who settled in the area from the fifth century AD. From the eleventh century until 1918, Slovakia was occupied by Hungary. The west (Bohemia and Moravia) became a kingdom and later part of the Holy Roman and Austrian empires.

Czechoslovakia became an independent republic in 1918. In 1938, Germany seized areas with more than 50 percent German-speaking peoples, and Poland and Hungary annexed other areas. In 1939, Germany annexed the rest of Bohemia and Moravia, making Slovakia a puppet state.

The USSR took Ruthenia in the east after Czechoslovakia was liberated in 1945. Mass expulsions of Germans occurred in 1945–46. In 1939, Germans had formed 23 percent of the population, but only 62,000 were left by 1981. In 1948, a Communist government was established. In the 1960s, the government introduced liberal measures, but it was suppressed after Soviet troops occupied the country.

In 1981, 64.3 percent of the people were Czechs and 30.5 percent were Slovaks. Minorities included gypsies, Hungarians, Poles, Germans, Ukrainians and Russians. About 64 percent lived in urban areas. Besides Prague (Praha), other cities include Bratislava (381,000), Brno (371,000) and Ostrava (322,000). Two-thirds of the people are Roman Catholics. The average life expectancy in 1981 was 72 years.

The Land A basin-shaped plateau in the west, which is drained by the Labe (Elbe) River, is surrounded by low, forested mountains. Central Czechoslovakia (Moravia) is a mostly lowland region. Slovakia is a highland, apart from the Danube basin in the south.

Praha has an average annual temperature range of 28°F–68°F (−2°C–20°C) and 19 inches (483 mm) of rain per year. The climate becomes more continental to the east. Forests cover nearly 36 percent of Czechoslovakia.

Economy In 1980, industry accounted for 64 percent of the GDP and 48 percent of the workforce. Coal, lignite and some metals are mined, but many industrial materials are imported. All industries are government-owned.

Farming accounted for 7 percent of the GDP and 11 percent of the workforce. Farmland covers 55 percent of the land and barley, hops, rye, sugar-beet and wheat are grown. In 1979, there were 4,920,000 cattle and 7,600,000 pigs.

In 1980, the per capita GNP was $5,280, the highest in eastern Europe, excepting the USSR.

HUNGARY

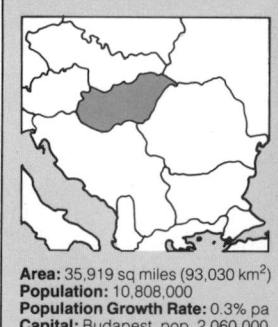

Area: 35,919 sq miles (93,030 km²)
Population: 10,808,000
Population Growth Rate: 0.3% pa
Capital: Budapest, pop. 2,060,000
Language: Magyar (Hungarian)
Religion: Christianity (Roman Catholic, Protestant)
Currency: Forint = 100 Fillér

THE HUNGARIAN PEOPLE'S REPUBLIC, unlike most East European countries, is populated by Magyars, not Slavs.
People and Culture Magyars from the Russian steppes settled in Hungary in the ninth century AD. Their language is related to Finnish.

Hungary came under foreign rule in the fourteenth century. The Ottoman Turks took central and southern Hungary in 1526, but they were driven out by 1699, when most of Hungary came under Austrian rule.

In 1867, in response to Hungarian nationalism, the dual monarchy of Austria-Hungary was established. After its collapse in 1918, Hungary became a monarchy, although it was ruled from 1920 not by a king but by a regent, Admiral Horthy.

In World War II, Hungary was allied with Germany. Soviet troops invaded in 1944–45 and a republic was proclaimed. By 1948, Hungary was a Communist country. An anti-Stalinist uprising in 1956 was put down and anti-Soviet sentiment has been suppressed.

In 1981, 54 percent of the population lived in urban areas, with about 37 percent in Budapest. In 1976, about 80 percent of Hungarians professed a religious faith. Roman Catholics made up 49 percent of the population and Calvinists 19 percent. The average life expectancy at birth in 1981 was 71 years.
The Land The main uplands are the Bakony Forest, a limestone ridge in the west, and the low mountains northeast of Budapest.

The northwest and southwest are undulating regions. The Duna (Danube) River flows through the western part of the Great Hungarian Plain. This Plain covers 56 percent of Hungary. It extends to the Romanian border.

The climate is continental. The average annual rainfall varies from 22–28 inches (559–711 mm) on the plains to 31 inches (787 mm) in the mountains.
Economy In 1980, farming accounted for 18 percent of the GDP and 21 percent of the workforce. Farmland, including pasture, covers 71 percent of Hungary. Barley, maize, potatoes, sugar-beet and wheat are major crops. In 1981, there were 1,918,000 cattle, 8,330,000 pigs and 3,090,000 sheep.

Coal and bauxite are the chief minerals and some oil is produced. All manufacturing industries are government-owned. The main industrial centre is Budapest. In 1981, the per capita GNP, according to World Bank estimates, was $2,100.

ROMANIA

Area: 91,700 sq miles (237,500 km²)
Population: 23,069,000
Population Growth Rate: 0.9% pa
Capital: Bucuresti (Bucharest), pop. 2,090,000
Language: Romanian
Religion: Christianity (Eastern Orthodox)
Currency: Leu = 100 Bani

THE SOCIALIST REPUBLIC OF ROMANIA is so called because its culture is substantially Latin in origin. The Romanian language has Latin roots, although it contains many Slav and some Hungarian and Turkish words.
People and Culture Many Romanians are descendants of the Dacians who settled the area in the fourth century BC. The Romans arrived in the second century AD, but left in 271, after which Romania was conquered by various barbarians. But the Romanized Dacians maintained their identity.

In the 13th century, the principalities of Moldavia (in northeast Romania) and Walachia (in the south) had emerged. These principalities later came under Turkish rule, while Transylvania came under the Hapsburgs.

In 1861, Moldavia and Walachia united to form Romania, which officially became a kingdom under King Carol I in 1881. Romania gained territory after both the Second Balkan War (1913) and World War I, taking, for example, Transylvania and Banat from Hungary in 1918. After World War II, Romania lost Bessarabia to the USSR.

Romania became Communist after King Michael was forced to abdicate in 1947. But under Nicolae Ceauşescu, who became president in 1967, Romania has pursued an increasingly independent course, while remaining in the Warsaw Pact alliance.

In 1981, 50 percent of the people lived in urban areas. The average life expectancy at birth in 1981 was 71 years.
The Land The western lowlands are part of the Hungarian plain. Transylvania consists of a central plateau surrounded by mountains, including the Carpathians in the east and the Carpatii Mountains in the south. Plains cover the northeast and south, which is within the Dunărea (Danube) River Basin. A low limestone plateau (Dobruja) borders the Black Sea. The climate is continental.
Economy In 1980, farming accounted for 13 percent of the GDP and 29 percent of the workforce. Farmland including pasture, occupies 63 percent of the land.

Barley, maize, potatoes, rye, sunflower seeds, sugar-beet and wheat are grown. In 1981, there were 6,500,000 cattle, 15,900,000 sheep and 11,500,000 pigs.

Industry accounted for 60 percent of the GDP and 36 percent of the workforce in 1980. Romania produces oil and natural gas, coal and lignite and a variety of metallic ores. The government-owned manufacturing sector has expanded greatly since the 1960s. The per capita GNP in 1981 was $2,540.

The Chain Bridge over the Danube River in Budapest is the city's oldest bridge, having been completed in 1849. It was rebuilt and reopened 100 years later.

Eastern Europe

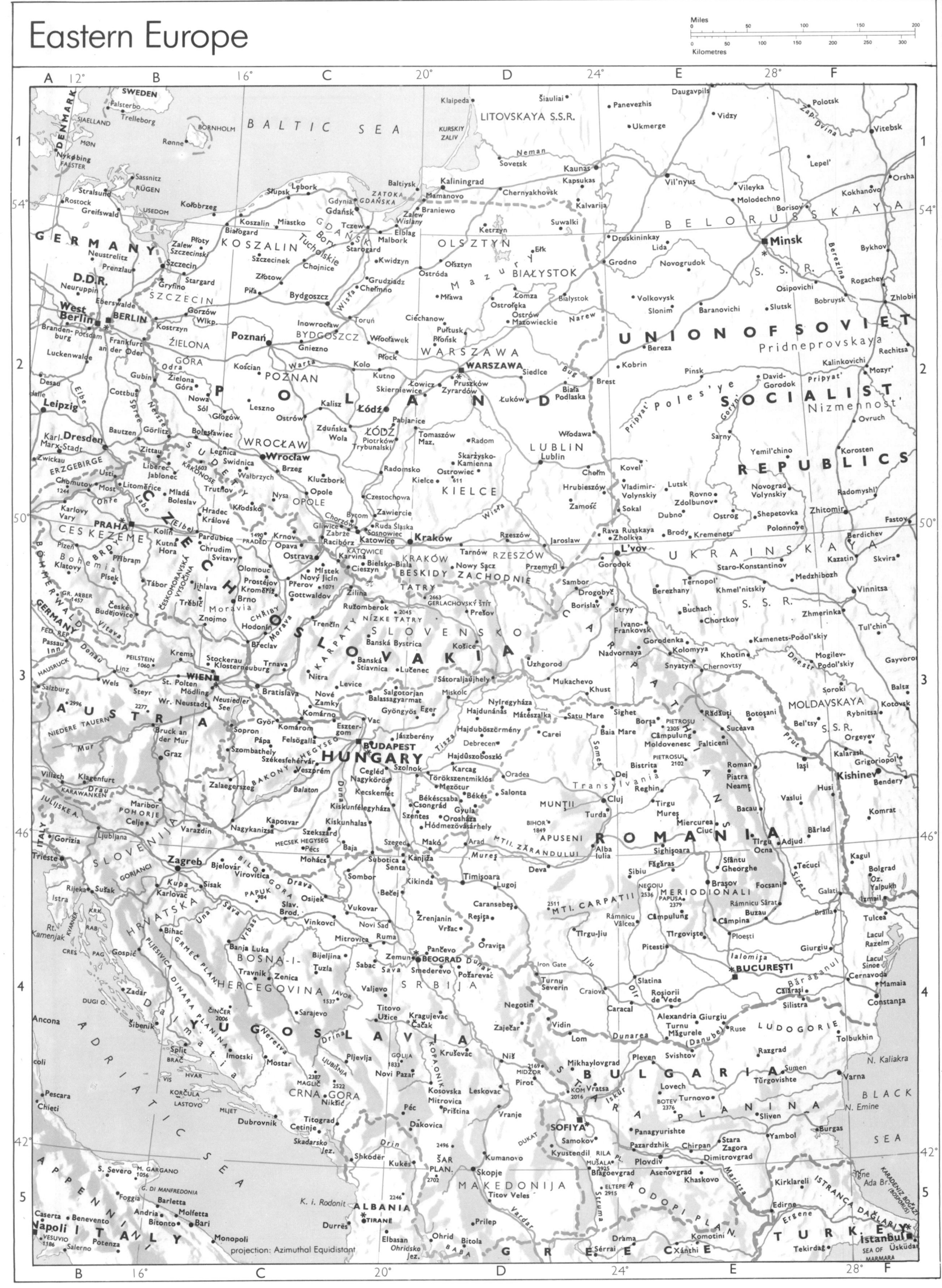

projection: Azimuthal Equidistant

Eurasia: introduction

Europe and Asia form a single landmass, which is often called Eurasia. The boundary between the two continents runs from the Arctic Ocean along the Ural mountains to the Caspian Sea. This boundary divides the USSR, the world's largest nation, into two parts, with nearly 25 percent in Europe and 75 percent in Asia. For information on the USSR, see pages 126–127.

The Land and its Structure
The Ural mountains may seem to be an arbitrary boundary, but they have special significance in Earth history. Around 300 million years ago, there were only three landmasses: *Euramerica*, consisting of much of present-day North America and western Europe; *Angara*, which was composed of most of Asia, east of the Urals; and *Gondwanaland*, comprising South America, Africa, India, Antarctica and Australia. About 275 million years ago, these three landmasses moved together to form the single landmass of *Pangaea*. The collision of Euramerica and Angara forced up the Ural mountains and, eventually, the two landmasses became locked together along the Ural range. After plate movements had ceased, the forces of erosion planed the mountains down to their present subdued relief.

From 180 million years ago, Pangaea began to break up. A plate bearing the Indian peninsula eventually broke away from the southern part of Pangaea–Gondwanaland – and drifted slowly towards the Eurasian plate. Around 50 million years ago, the Indian and Eurasian plates were pushing against each other. Sediments on the floor of the intervening Tethys Sea were folded upwards to form the

Above Varanasi (Benares) is visited by Hindu pilgrims who bathe in the sacred Ganga (Ganges). All the world's major religions originated in Asia.

Below Beyond the terraced foothills of Nepal are the majestic Himalayas.

lofty Himalayan range. The sea disappeared and the Indian plate was locked on to the Eurasian plate, roughly along the line now represented by the Hindu Kush, the Pamirs, and the Karakoram and Himalayan ranges. This mountainous zone is still marked by considerable earthquake activity, which suggests that the Indian plate is still pushing against Eurasia, and that the Himalayan range is still rising. However, this is difficult to prove because, even as mountains rise, so the forces of erosion whittle them down.

Other active plate boundaries run through southwestern Asia – one running from Afghanistan, through northern Iran into central Turkey, and another through southwestern Iran, Iraq and Syria. These boundaries are zones of great earthquake activity. And in the Red Sea, ocean-spreading is widening the gap between Africa and Arabia, pushing the Arabian peninsula towards Iran. This will, in perhaps 50 million years' time, close up the Persian Gulf. In its place will be a new, high fold mountain range.

East of the Himalayas, a plate boundary runs southwards to Sumatra and then it loops around the islands of Indonesia. It then turns northwards through the Moluccas, along the Philippine and Ryukyu trenches and onwards to the Japan trench, the Kuril trench and the Kamchatka peninsula. This north–south boundary forms part of the edge of the Pacific plate. Alongside this plate edge, part of the famous Pacific 'ring of fire', there is much volcanic and earthquake activity.

Mountains, Lakes and Rivers
Asia contains the world's highest peak, Everest, which reaches 29,028 feet (8,848 m) on the China–Nepal border. The second highest peak, K2 (or Mount Godwin Austen), is 28,250 feet (8,611 m) high in the Karakoram range. In fact, of the world's 109 mountains which exceed 24,000 feet (7,315 m) in height, 96 are in the Himalayan–Karakoram ranges. These are fold mountains, like most of Asia's other interior ranges. Volcanic mountains are special features of regions near the plate edges at the ocean trenches, especially in Japan, the Philippines and Indonesia. Indonesia contains more volcanoes than any other country. Out of a total of 167, 77 have been active in historic times.

Asia, the world's largest continent, also contains the world's biggest enclosed area of water, the Caspian Sea, whose area is about 170,000 square miles (440,298 km²). The Aral'skoye More (Aral Sea), at 26,000 square miles (67,340 km²), and Lake Baykal, at 12,150 square miles (31,468 km²), are also among the world's ten largest lakes. The shoreline of the Dead Sea, between Israel and Jordan, is the world's lowest point on land. It is 1,291 feet (393 m) below the mean sea-level of the Mediterranean. The Dead Sea is in a northern extension of the African Rift Valley.

Of the world's ten longest rivers, six are in Asia. The longest is China's Chang Chiang (Yangtse), which is about 3,400 miles (5,472 km) long. The Ob'-Irtysh system in the USSR is 3,200 miles (5,150 km) long, while the Huang Ho in northern China is 2,900 miles (4,667 km) long. Other major Asian rivers include the Amur and Lena in the USSR and the Mae Khong (Mekong) in southeastern Asia.

Eurasia

projection: Lambert's Azimuthal Equal Area

Eurasia is the world's largest landmass. It has an area of about 21,202,800 sq miles (54,915,000 km²), or 38 percent of the world's land area. Eurasia contains two continents. Europe, the smallest continent apart from Oceania, makes up 19 percent of Eurasia, while Asia covers 81 percent.

The geographical boundary between Europe and Asia follows the Ural mountains in the USSR, the Caspian Sea and the USSR's border with Iran and Turkey. Because of this boundary, the USSR is divided into two parts: 25 percent is in Europe and the rest is in Asia. Another part of the geographical boundary between Europe and Asia runs through the Bosphorus, the Sea of Marmara and the Dardanelles. The part of Turkey to the west of this major international waterway, connecting the Black and Mediterranean seas, belongs to Europe. It represents only 3 percent of Turkey, the other 97 percent being in Asia.

By world standards, Eurasia is densely populated. In 1984, Europe (excluding the USSR) had an average population density of 246 per sq mile (99 per km²), while Asia (also excluding the USSR) had 246 people per sq mile (95 per km²). The average population density in the USSR is much lower at 31 per sq mile (12 per km²). But the USSR's population is unevenly distributed. As the map shows, most of the largest cities are in the European part of the USSR. In fact, 75 percent of the population lives west of the Urals, while the Asian USSR is thinly populated.

Eurasia lies mainly in the northern hemisphere, although some Indonesian islands spill over the Equator. In the far west, Eurasia includes Iceland. Between Iceland and the Bering Strait, there are more than 210 degrees of longitude, so this huge landmass stretches more than half way around the world.

Most of northern and central Eurasia is an ancient and stable landmass. But the highest mountain ranges, the Himalayas and the Alps, have been thrown up in fairly recent geological time by plate collisions. Similarly, the volcanic activity in southern Italy and, on a much larger scale, in Indonesia, the Philippines, Japan and the northeastern USSR, are the result of one plate being pushed beneath another. Plate movements are also responsible for crustal instability and earthquakes in the Mediterranean region and in southwestern Asia.

Climate

Asia lies mainly in the northern hemisphere, although part of the island nation of Indonesia is south of the Equator. A continent of contrasts, Asia contains hot regions, such as the Rub' al Khālī (Empty Quarter) of Saudi Arabia, where daytime shade temperatures often soar to 122°F (50°C), while such places as Verkhoyansk, in northeastern Siberia, have average January temperatures of −59°F (−51°C).

Besides the hot deserts of the southwest, Asia also has cold deserts, such as the Gobi desert of China and Mongolia, and some of the wettest places on Earth. Cherrapunji, in India, holds the record for the world's highest annual rainfall – 1,041.78 inches (26,461 mm) in 1860–61.

The climate of much of Asia results from the seasonal development of air masses. In winter, intensely cold conditions occur in northern and central Asia. Cold, sinking air creates a vast continental high-pressure air mass, from which cold, dry winds blow outwards towards the sea. In summer, however, the northern hemisphere tilts towards the Sun, which is overhead at the Tropic of Cancer (which runs through northern India and southeastern China) on about June 21. Intense heating of the land over large areas makes air rise, and so a low pressure air mass is created. Moist winds are drawn into this air mass, causing a reversal of wind directions, or monsoon. Monsoon climates with hot, rainy summers, are most developed in India, southeastern Asia and southeastern China.

Flora and Fauna

Asia's main climatic regions include the Arctic and tundra regions of the northern USSR, together with similar climates on the high plateaux and mountains of central Asia. South of the tundra is a broad, cold, temperate zone, which contains coniferous forests, called the *taiga*. Further south, rainfall decreases and steppeland or deserts occur.

Beyond the mountains of south-central Asia are the hot deserts of the southwest, and the monsoon and equatorial regions in the southeast. The equatorial and the wetter parts of the monsoon lands are blanketed by dense forest. Drier monsoon regions contain more open forest or scrub. Some coastlands in southwestern Asia, have a Mediterranean climate and the characteristic *maquis* vegetation.

Asia is the home of a wide range of animals. The polar bear is the largest Arctic carnivore, while in summer, when insects are plentiful, the tundra is the breeding ground for a great number of birds. The *taiga* is the home of such animals as the elk, wolf and ermine. Antelopes roam the steppes, and the camel inhabits southwestern Asia.

Specially adapted species are found in the mountains. For example, the wild yak shows remarkable resistance to the cold, while the rare Giant Panda is now confined to a remote mountain area in western China. The Lesser Panda is found from Nepal to southwestern China.

Northern Asia belongs to what biologists called the Palearctic realm, which also includes Europe and most of southwestern Asia. But south-central and southeastern Asia form the very different Oriental realm. Here live some species of great apes, including the orang-utan of Borneo and Sumatra, and several species of Gibbons are found throughout southeastern Asia. Of the forest predators, leopards and tigers are well known, although all the subspecies of tigers are now threatened with extinction. The need for conservation, however, is increasingly recognized, but the destruction of habitats caused by the demand for land by the ever increasing population, together with overhunting and war, still take a heavy toll. But many national parks and wildlife sanctuaries have been set up. A small part of a third zoological realm, the Australasian, is found in eastern Indonesia, east of Borneo and Bali. The boundary between the Oriental and Australasian realms is called the Wallace line. The Australasian realm is distinguished by its marsupial mammals, which have been replaced in the Oriental realm by the more advanced placental mammals.

Asia is also the home of the ancestors of many domesticated animals, including goats, sheep and chickens. Other domesticated animals include elephants, reindeer, water buffalo and yaks.

History and Culture

Asia contains more than 30 percent of the world's land area and nearly 60 percent of its people, including representa-

tives of each of the three main subgroups of the human race. Mongoloids make up the most numerous group, with Caucasoids in southwestern Asia and parts of India, and a few Negroids in parts of southeastern Asia.

Vast areas of Asia are too cold, too arid or too mountainous for settlement, and 90 percent of Asia's population is crowded into less than one-third of its area. The main centres of population are fertile river valleys, deltas, and coastal plains.

Asia's fertile valleys gave birth to several major civilizations. In Mesopotamia, the region around the Tigris and Euphrates rivers, civilizations contemporary with that of Ancient Egypt developed. Between 2500 and 1500 BC, the Indus valley was the focus of another glittering culture, while sometime after 1500 BC a powerful civilization arose in northern China's Huang Ho valley. Besides its great civilizations, Asia was the birthplace of the world's leading religions: Judaism, Christianity and Islam in the southwest; Hinduism and Buddhism in India; and Confucianism, Shintoism and Taoism in eastern Asia.

From the early sixteenth century, European countries became established and colonizers in Asia, and European influence remains important until after World War II. India and Pakistan (which was further divided into Pakistan and Bangladesh in 1971) achieved independence in 1947 and, within a few years, many other countries followed. By 1984 only the tiny Portuguese Macau (or Macao) and the British dependency of Hong Kong remained under foreign control. But political freedom was not achieved without much conflict, including several wars prior to and after independence. Accompanying the conflicts, there have been several massive movements of population. For example, Hindus and Muslims were displaced by the 1947 partition of the Indian subcontinent, while the plight of Arab refugees has been a constant source of dispute between Israel and the Arab world. Many other people, especially in southeastern Asia, have migrated because of political changes.

Perhaps the most significant of these changes was the victory of the Communists over the Nationalists in China in 1949. The Nationalists fled to Taiwan, while the Communists made China a world power. China, the world's

Above: Mountains, plateaux and unproductive, hilly deserts cover about two-thirds of Pakistan. The main centres of population in this fairly arid country are in the valley of the Indus River and its tributaries, where irrigation and farming are possible. The chief farming region is the province of Punjab, a Sanskrit word meaning 'five waters', namely the five tributaries of the Indus, the Beas, Chenab, Jhelum, Ravi and Sutlej rivers.

Opposite: About 60 percent of the people of Karnataka, which was once called Mysore, speak a language called Kannada (or Kanarese). Other important languages include Telugu, Urdu, Marathi and Tamil. Karnataka, in southwestern India, is one of India's 22 states, each of which has its own legislature. The capital and largest city of Karnataka is Bangalore. Apart from the coastal plains, the state lies mostly in the Deccan plateau region, which has dense forests and much fertile farmland. Farming provides employment for three-quarters of the people. The state was named Karnataka in 1973.

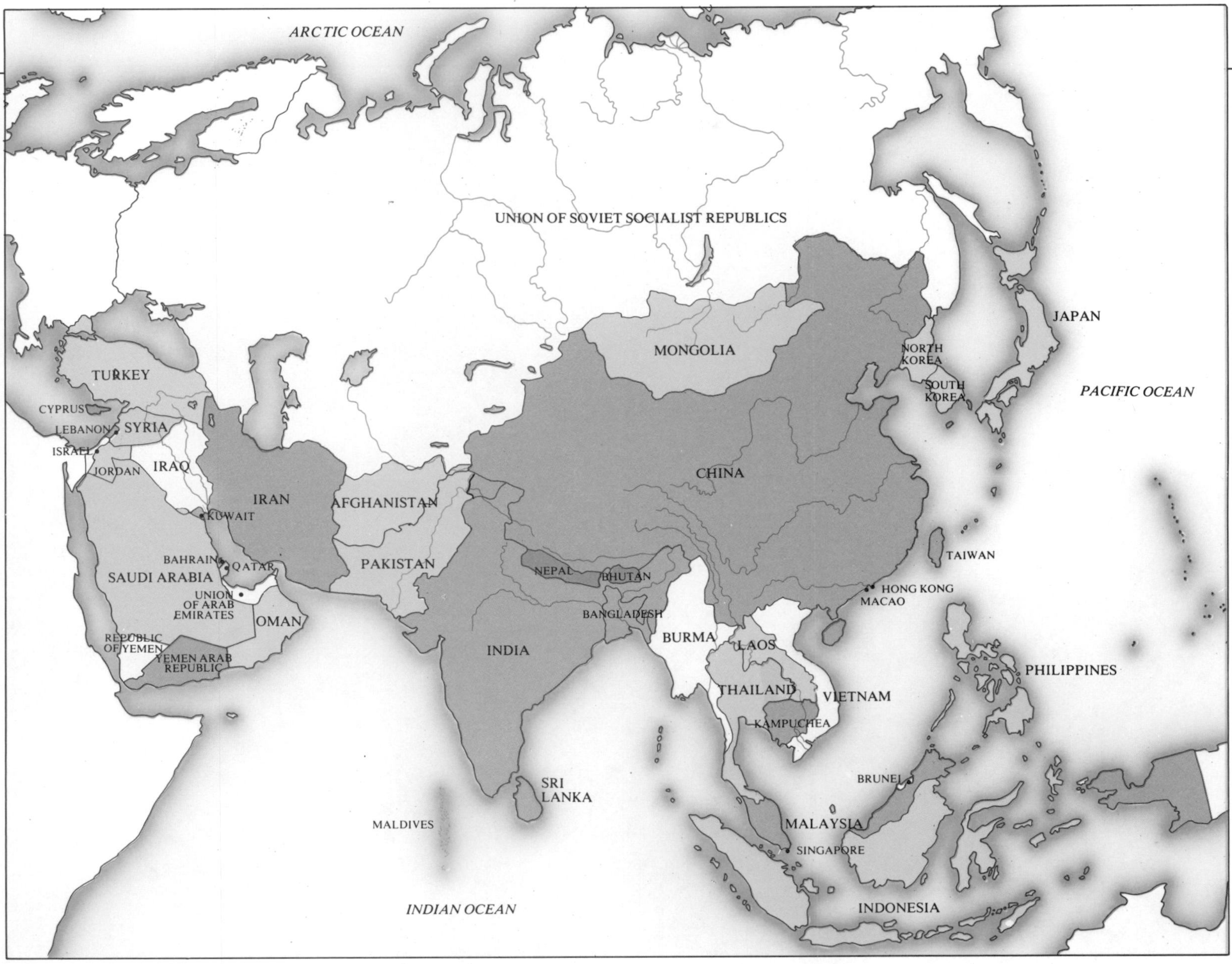

ARCTIC OCEAN

UNION OF SOVIET SOCIALIST REPUBLICS

JAPAN

MONGOLIA

NORTH KOREA

SOUTH KOREA

PACIFIC OCEAN

TURKEY

CYPRUS

LEBANON SYRIA

ISRAEL

JORDAN IRAQ

IRAN

AFGHANISTAN

CHINA

KUWAIT

TAIWAN

BAHRAIN QATAR

SAUDI ARABIA

PAKISTAN

HONG KONG

MACAO

UNION OF ARAB EMIRATES

OMAN

NEPAL BHUTAN

BANGLADESH

REPUBLIC OF YEMEN

YEMEN ARAB REPUBLIC

INDIA

BURMA

LAOS

PHILIPPINES

THAILAND VIETNAM

KAMPUCHEA

SRI LANKA

BRUNEI

MALDIVES

MALAYSIA

SINGAPORE

INDIAN OCEAN

INDONESIA

Asia is the largest and most populous of the continents. Geographically, it includes 75 percent of the USSR, the world's largest nation. Excluding the USSR, Asia contains 40 independent countries and two dependencies, Hong Kong (British) and Macau (Portuguese), which are tiny enclaves on the Chinese coast. Some 16 Asian countries are usually classified as belonging to the mostly arid southwestern Asia, which is also called the Middle East or, sometimes, the Near East; 18 constitute southern Asia; and eight, including the two dependencies, China, and Japan, are grouped together as northern Asia.

most populous nation, is still a developing country, but its potential as a world superpower is enormous.

Economic and Demographic Trends

Economically, Asia is a continent of contrasts. In 1980, Japan had a per capita GNP of $9,020. In the same period, formerly impoverished Arab countries in southwestern Asia have greatly benefited from the exploitation of oil reserves. But the rest of Asia, excluding these areas, had a per capita GNP of only $330 in 1980. In most of Asia, agriculture is the chief activity; for example, in 1980, farming employed 93 per cent of the workforce in Nepal, 74 percent in Bangladesh and 69 percent in both China and India.

Poverty and malnutrition are everyday realities for millions of Asians, and it is not surprising that Communism has found much support. Low living standards are reflected in some countries by low average lifespans. For example, the average life expectancies at birth in 1981 in Afghanistan and Bangladesh were 37 and 48 years respectively. But some countries, including China and Japan, have made great strides in improving health services and raising living standards. By 1981, the average life expectancies in China and Japan had reached 67 and 77 years respectively.

One of Asia's most critical problems is the fast rate of population increase. But there is a marked difference between eastern Asia, where China and Japan have taken many steps to control population growth, and southern Asia, where the annual rate of increase was over 2 percent. In 1975–81, the annual rate of population increase in China was 1.4 percent and in Japan 0.9 percent – a lower rate than in the United States. By contrast, the population of India increased during the same period by an estimated 2.2 percent per year. In human terms, this means that India has about 15 million more mouths to feed every year.

Northern Asia

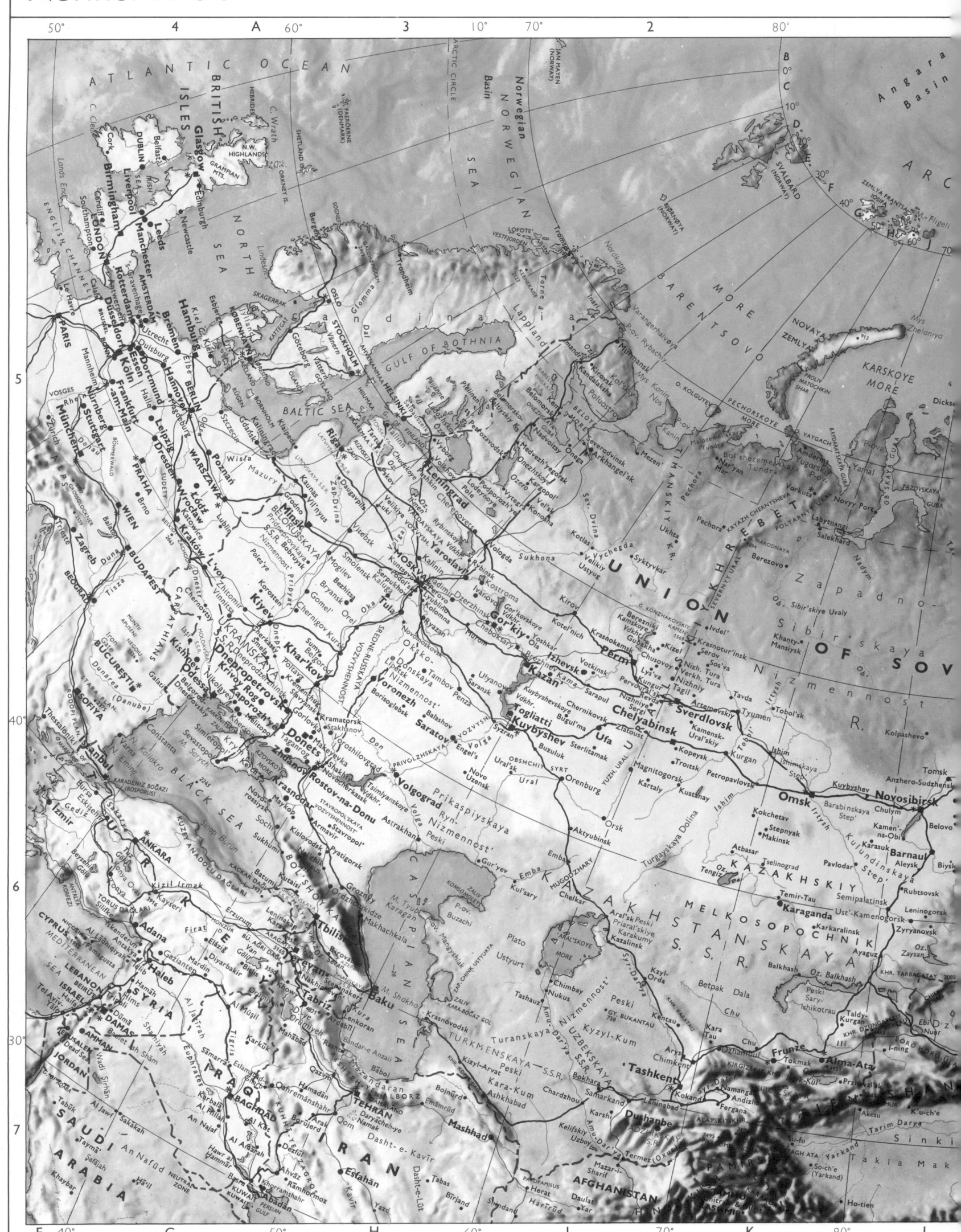

Northern Asia: introduction

This region includes the Asian part of the USSR, China, Mongolia, North and South Korea, Taiwan, Japan and the dependencies of Hong Kong and Macau on the south coast of China. Together these countries make up about 64 percent of Asia's land area, although they contain less than half of the continent's population, despite the fact that China and Japan are two of the world's ten most populous countries. The reason for the comparatively low population density in northern and eastern Asia is that most of the Asian part of the USSR, Mongolia and western China are extremely thinly populated.

Large parts of western China and Mongolia have an average annual rainfall of less than 1 inch (25 mm), while much of the northeastern USSR is in the permafrost zone, where the subsoil remains frozen throughout the year preventing the growth of large plants. Even to the south of the permafrost zone, where summers are warm, cold winds from the north bring bitterly cold conditions in winter. The main activity in this region is reindeer herding.

But other parts of this region are among the world's most densely populated. For example, while Mongolia has an average population density of less than 3 people per square mile (1 per sq km), Macau has about 47,400 people per square mile (18,300 sq km). The main centres of population are located on the generally narrow coastal plains, in the lower courses of river valleys, and on deltas.

Japan, the most industrialized nation, is also the most urbanized. In 1981, 79 percent of its population lived in cities and towns. The capital Tokyo, one of the world's largest cities, is one of ten in Japan with a population of more than 1,000,000. Another city which vies with Tokyo in

Right: Hong Kong's magnificent harbour lies between the island of Hong Kong and the mainland Kowloon peninsula, which can be seen in the background. Hong Kong was once largely an entrepôt for foreign trade. But a substantial part of its trade is now taken up with domestic exports and imports. This change has come about because of a vigorous and successful policy of industrialization within Hong Kong. The lease of the New Territories, which make up most of this British colony, excluding only Hong Kong Island, Stonecutter's Island and the Kowloon Peninsula, expires in 1997.

Below: Kowloon, Hong Kong, is a busy industrial and commercial area which is popular with tourists. Some 98 percent of the population of Hong Kong is Chinese and about 57 percent of the people were born in Hong Kong. But there are also many refugees from Communist China.

the world league of cities is Shanghai in China. China has many other huge cities, although only about one-fifth of the total population lives in urban areas, a consequence of Communist China's emphasis on rural development. South Korea also contains one of the world's largest cities in its capital Seoul.

Most people in northern and eastern Asia are Mongoloid in origin, although there are some minorities, including the Ainu, the original inhabitants of Japan. Eastern Asia has been the home of major advances in civilization, and its technology, art and philosophy have often been superior to those of the West. After the Industrial Revolution, however, Europe and the United States were able to assert their superiority. In 1853, the United States forced Japan to abandon its isolationist policy – an action, incidentally, which led Japan to emerge, in time, as a world military power. China was weak and divided and could not resist European and, later, Japanese pressure. It ceded Hong Kong to Britain, Port Arthur to Russia and Taiwan and Korea to Japan.

After World War II, Japan developed quickly to become the world's third industrial power after the United States and the USSR. The standards of living of the Japanese people rose swiftly, although industrial pollution has become a problem. But Japan was considered to be an advertisement for western laissez-faire economics in a region increasingly dominated by Communism. The USSR had, of course, had a Communist regime since 1917, and attempts had been made to develop parts of the vast Siberian wasteland. China became Communist in 1949 and Korea, which had been partitioned in 1949 into a Communist North and a non-Communist South, was the scene of a war from 1950 to 1953. The war ended with the boundary being fixed roughly along the 38th parallel.

Rivalry between Western and Communist ideologies has been a feature of the region in recent years and Chinese territorial claims, on Taiwan in particular, have threatened stability. Also significant in global terms has been the rivalry between China and the USSR. As China's relations with the USSR worsened, so its relations with the West improved and its isolation decreased.

In economic terms, Japan, South Korea, Hong Kong and Macau had per capita GNPs in 1981 of $10,080, $1,700, $5,100 and $2,630 respectively. Although comparable figures for the Asian USSR, Mongolia and North Korea are not available, the per capita GNP of China in 1981 was estimated to be only $300. But it would be a mistake to underestimate China's huge potential for rapid development in the future, especially since the death of Mao Tse-tung in 1976, which was followed by a shift in policy from rigid Communism to a more pragmatic, flexible approach, including the expansion of consumer industries, which will make life easier for the average Chinese family.

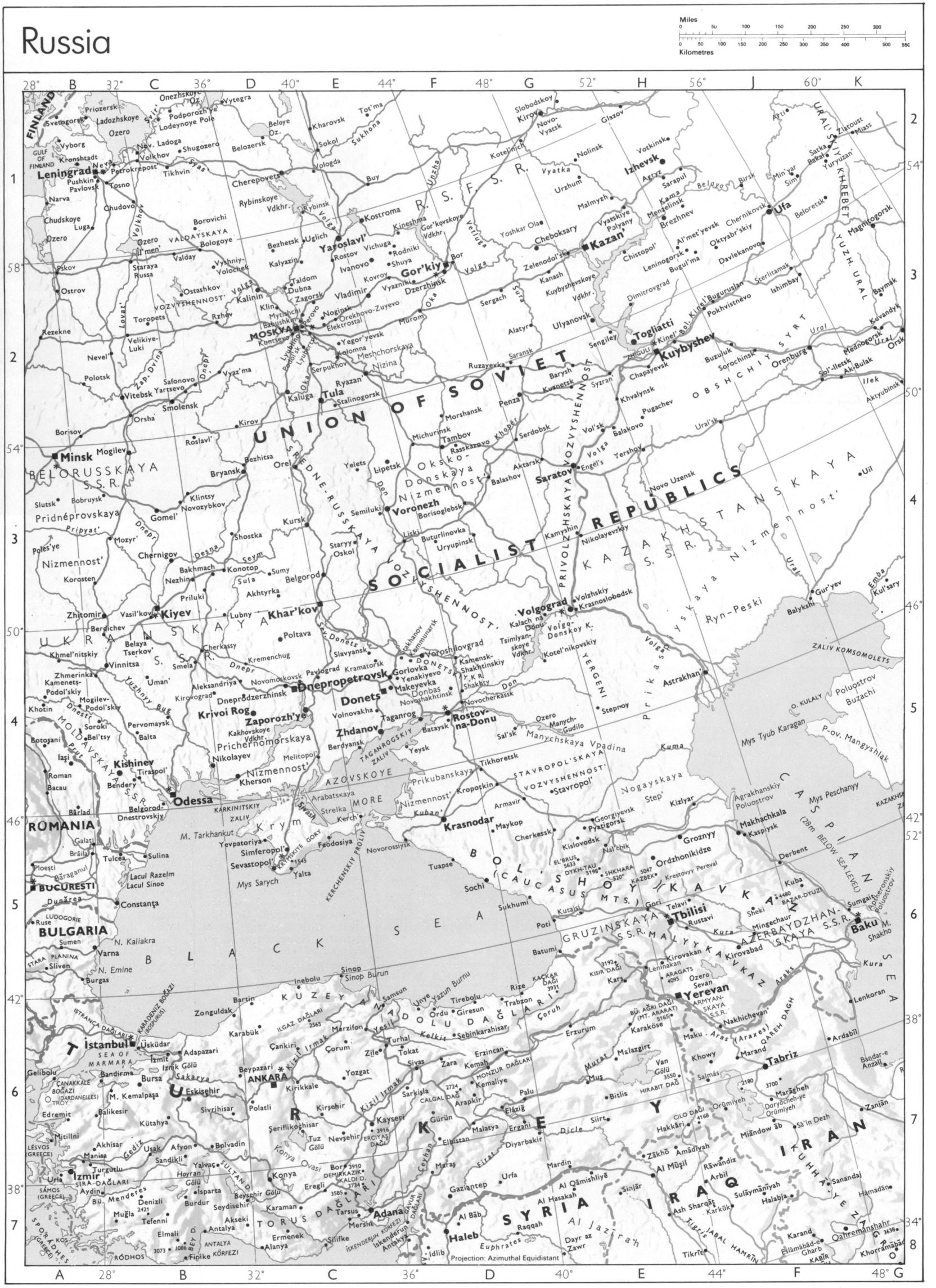

Russia

Miles

Kilometres

FINLAND

GULF OF FINLAND

Leningrad

R.S.F.S.R.

UNION OF SOVIET SOCIALIST REPUBLICS

MOSKVA

BELORUSSKAYA S.S.R.

Minsk

UKRAINSKAYA S.S.R.

Kiyev

Khar'kov

KAZAKHSTANSKAYA S.S.R.

ROMANIA

BUCUREŞTI

BULGARIA

Odessa

Krym

BLACK SEA

Rostov-na-Donu

Volgograd

Kuybyshev

Kazan'

Ufa

CASPIAN SEA

GRUZINSKAYA S.S.R.

Tbilisi

AZERBAYDZHAN-SKAYA S.S.R.

Baku

ARMYAN-SKAYA S.S.R.

Yerevan

CAUCASUS MTS.

Krasnodar

ISTANBUL

ANKARA

T U R K E Y

SYRIA

IRAQ

IRAN

Tabriz

SEA OF MARMARA

Haleb

Projection: Azimuthal Equidistant

125

USSR

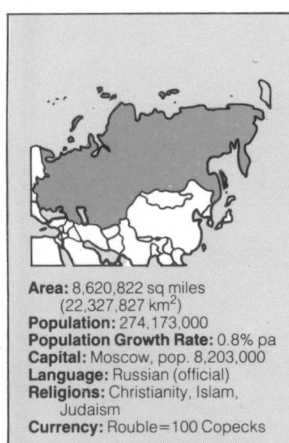

Area: 8,620,822 sq miles
(22,327,827 km²)
Population: 274,173,000
Population Growth Rate: 0.8% pa
Capital: Moscow, pop. 8,203,000
Language: Russian (official)
Religions: Christianity, Islam,
Judaism
Currency: Rouble = 100 Copecks

THE UNION OF SOVIET SOCIAL-IST REPUBLICS (USSR) is the world's largest nation. Its total area is substantially greater than that of Canada and the United States combined.

The USSR is divided into 15 Constituent Republics, some of which are further subdivided into Autonomous Republics and Regions. The largest Constituent Republic is the Russian Soviet Federal Socialist Republic (RSFSR), which covers about 76 percent of the country. The USSR is often called the Soviet Union or Russia, though the name Russia strictly applies only to the RSFSR.

People and Culture Within such a vast territory, straddling Europe and Asia, there are many peoples and cultures. About 60 languages are spoken.

The Slavs form the largest group. They include the Russians (52 percent of the total population of the USSR in 1979), Ukrainians (16 percent) and Belorussians (3.6 percent). Turkic peoples, including Uzbeks (4.8 percent), Kazakhs (2.8 percent) and Tartars (2.7 percent), form the second largest group. Other groups include Finno-Ugric peoples; the Caucasians, including the Georgians (1.6 percent) and Ossetians; the Armenians (1.8 percent); the Tadzhiks in central Asia (1.2 percent); and the Mongols of eastern Siberia.

The most important part of the USSR is in Europe, west of the Urals, for it is here that 75 percent of the people live. Early inhabitants in the southwest, north of the Black Sea, were Scythians and Sarmatians.

The Slavs first lived in the north, between the Wisla (Vistula) river in present-day Poland, and the Dnepr river. In the third century AD, they migrated south. By the ninth century, the eastern Slavs had founded the trading cities of Novgorod in the north and Kiyev in the south.

Kiyev developed into the first Russian state. Through Kiyev came European influences, including Orthodox Christianity from Byzantium (now Istanbul).

Kiyev began to break up in the twelfth century and, in the thirteenth century, Mongols invaded, reaching the Adriatic Sea. In the fifteenth century,

Moskva (Moscow) emerged as a powerful state. Successive leaders broke the hold of the Mongols by 1480. Moskva then consolidated its influence. But, after the death of Ivan the Terrible in 1548, there were internal disorders and foreign invasions.

In 1613, Michael Romanov became tsar (emperor), founding a dynasty that lasted for over 300 years. The seventeenth and eighteenth centuries saw a gradual extension of Russian influence into Siberia. Peter the Great became tsar in 1696 and tried to modernize his country. Westernization continued in the later eighteenth century under Catherine the Great. Napoleon invaded Russia in 1812, but was forced to retreat.

The late nineteenth century was marked by repressive government (serfdom was not abolished until 1861), much discontent, and a great flowering of literature and music. It was also a time of imperial expansion, when Asian territories were acquired.

Russia suffered defeat in a war against Japan in 1905. In World War I, it fought against Germany and Austria. After much suffering, a revolution occurred in 1917. The Romanovs were deposed and, in November 1917, Vladimir Ilyich Ulyanov, better known as Lenin, and his Bolshevik party seized power.

Civil war in 1918–20 disrupted the country, but the USSR was formally established in 1922.

Lenin died in 1924 and was succeeded by Joseph Stalin. Stalin eliminated all opposition to his socialist policies,

Samarkand is in Uzbekistan in the Asian part of the USSR.

whereby all private ownership was abolished. His aim was to make the USSR a great industrial and military power.

In World War II, German armies invaded and, at the end of 1941, they were at the gates of Moskva. But, despite enormous losses, the Red Army drove the Germans from the USSR and eastern Europe, meeting up with Allied forces in Berlin in 1945.

After the war, the USSR emerged as one of the world's two superpowers. It consolidated its influence in Europe through the Communist regimes in eastern Europe. Hostility between East and West led to a 'Cold War'.

Stalin died in 1953. Successive leaders since Stalin have included Nikita Khrushchev, Leonid Brezhnev, Yuri Andropov and Konstantin Chernenko. In the last 30 years, the USSR has demonstrated its spectacular progress in technology with its achievements in space research. But relations with the West have fluctuated between periods of détente and cold war.

The USSR has made much material progress, although its emphasis on heavy industry had led to a neglect of consumer industries and shortages of the consumer goods that make life comfortable.

But all health services are free, though private practice still exists, and the average life expectancy at birth had risen to 72 years by 1981 (it was 68 in 1960). Social policies include low rents, which averaged about 3 percent of the expenditure of an average worker's family in 1982. Social insurance and government pension schemes are in operation, as are holiday sanatoria.

Adult literacy is now 100 percent and there is free and compulsory education from 7 to 16 or 17 in coeducational schools. There are 65 university towns.

In 1917, the country had an agrarian economy, but the proportion of people in cities and towns had risen to 63 percent in 1981. Apart from Moskva, the largest cities are Leningrad (pop. 4,676,000) and Kiyev (2,248,000). There

Leningrad, the second largest city in the USSR, is an industrial and cultural centre.

CONSTITUENT REPUBLICS OF THE USSR

republic	total area		population*	capital
	square miles	square kilometres		
Armyanskaya SSR (Armenia)	11,306	29,282	3,222,000	Yerevan
Azerbaydzhanskaya SSR (Azerbaijan)	33,436	86,599	6,400,000	Baku
Belorusskaya SSR (Belorussia)	80,300	207,976	9,806,000	Minsk
Estonskaya SSR (Estonia)	17,413	45,100	1,507,000	Tallinn
Gruzinskaya SSR (Georgia)	26,911	69,700	5,137,000	Tbilisi
Kazakhstanskaya SSR (Kazakhstan)	1,064,980	2,758,286	15,470,000	Alma-Ata
Kirgizskiya SSR (Kirgizia)	76,642	198,502	3,803,000	Frunze
Latviyskaya SSR (Latvia)	24,695	63,960	2,568,000	Riga
Litovskaya SSR (Lithuania)	26,173	67,788	3,504,000	Vil'nyus (Vilnius)
Moldavskaya SSR (Moldavia)	13,912	36,032	4,053,000	Kishinev
Rossiiskaya SFSR (Russian SFSR)	6,593,391	17,076,804	140,952,000	Moskva (Moscow)
Tadzhikskaya SSR (Tadzhikistan)	54,019	139,909	4,236,000	Dushanbe
Turkmenskaya SSR (Turkmenistan)	188,417	487,998	3,045,000	Ashkhabad
Ukrainskaya SSR (Ukraine)	252,046	652,796	50,456,000	Kiyev (Kiev)
Uzbekskaya SSR (Uzbekistan)	157,181	407,097	17,044,000	Tashkent

*1983 estimate

were 18 other cities with more than a million people in 1981.

After the 1917 Revolution, Soviet leaders tried to discourage religious worship and the Russian Orthodox Church lost its dominance, as all religions were given equal footing. The Church is still separated from the state and religious instruction for children under 18 is forbidden. But about 50 million people still worship regularly at Russian Orthodox churches. There are also Armenian and Georgian Orthodox, Roman Catholic and Protestant churches, some 30 million Muslims, and some large Jewish communities, notably in Moskva and Kiyev.

The Land The European part of the USSR consists largely of flat plains, broken by occasional hills, such as the Valday Hills northwest of Moskva.

The chief rivers are the North Dvina which flows north to the Arctic, the West Dvina and Neman rivers which flow to the Baltic, the Dnepr which empties into the Black Sea, the Don which reaches the Sea of Azov, and the Volga which flows into the Caspian Sea, the world's largest lake.

The northern parts of these plains were under ice during the Ice Age and there are now large areas covered by glacial deposits. Much of this land is swampy. But the southern part of the western plains contains much fertile land.

Beyond the Urals, a mostly low fold mountain range, are the West Siberian plains, drained by the Ob'-Irtysh rivers. The Yenisey River marks the eastern boundary of these plains.

Another lowland area lies in the Asian USSR, east of the Caspian Sea. This consists of inland drainage basins, with rivers flowing into the Aral'skoye More (Aral Sea) and Lake Balkhash.

The Caucasus Mountains, between the Black and Caspian seas, contain Mount El'brus, Europe's highest peak at 18,481 feet (5,633 m) above sea-level. Higher mountains rise in Tadzhikistan and Kirgizia in ranges which are offshoots of the Pamirs. The USSR's highest peak is Mount Communism, at 24,590 feet (7,495 m).

East of the Yenisey River are ancient plateaux and mountain ranges which are part of the ancient Angara landmass. Kamchatka peninsula in the far east borders the Pacific plate. It contains many active volcanoes.

Climate Climates tend to be extreme, because most of the USSR is far from the moderating influence of the sea.

The Arctic and tundra regions have long, cold winters. The northwestern part of the European plain has a cool temperate climate, but the climate becomes more extreme to the east. Moskva has an average annual temperature range of 12°F (−11°C) to 64°F (18°C). At Verkhoyansk, in eastern Siberia, the annual temperature difference between the warmest and coldest months is even greater at 120°F (67°C).

The southwest has a warm temperate climate. This region, which extends eastwards from the Black Sea north of the Caspian Sea into Asia, is drier and the typical vegetation is that of the steppeland. But east of the Caspian Sea is a large semi-arid region extending to Lake Balkhash and beyond. Here the steppeland merges into scrub and scorching desert.

Economy In 1913, farming accounted for 58 percent of the gross social product. This had fallen to 14.6 percent by 1977, when the contribution of industry and transport had risen to 78.8 percent. The proportion of the workforce employed in farming fell from 75 percent in 1913 to 14 percent in 1980.

The USSR is rich in resources. It leads the world in producing asbestos, coal, iron ore, lead, manganese, mercury, petroleum and potash. The USSR claims to have 58 percent of the world's coal reserves, 41 percent of its iron ore, 89 percent of the manganese and 59 percent of the petroleum.

The main oilfield was formerly the Caucasian field, around Baku, but today the Tyumen field in West Siberia produces over half of the total output. Other oilfields are in the Ural–Volga region and in the Saratov area to the south.

The USSR leads the world in producing apples, barley, butter, cows' milk, flax, mutton and lamb, oats, potatoes, rye, softwoods, sugarbeet, wheat and wool yarn.

The entire economy is based on public ownership, with government-fixed production goals established in five- or seven-year plans.

Arable land covers 10 percent of the USSR and pasture another 17 percent. Forests cover about one-third of the land. Government-owned farms hold three-fourths of the farmland, with collectives owning most of the rest. Nearly 98 percent of the forests are owned and worked by the government, but some areas are left for use by the peasantry.

Manufacturing is the most important activity. Nearly 80 percent of the nation's energy comes from 57 large fuel-burning power stations. Hydroelectric plants account for 13 percent and nuclear power stations for 4 percent. Only the United States produces more electrical energy than the USSR, which is the world's leading steel producer.

The growth of industry since the Revolution has been phenomenal, but the development of agriculture has been much slower. Periodic crop failures force the USSR to import food from abroad. Nearly 60 percent of the USSR's trade is with other socialist countries. Oil is a major export.

Samarkand's beautiful mosques recall its glittering Islamic culture in earlier times.

China and Korea

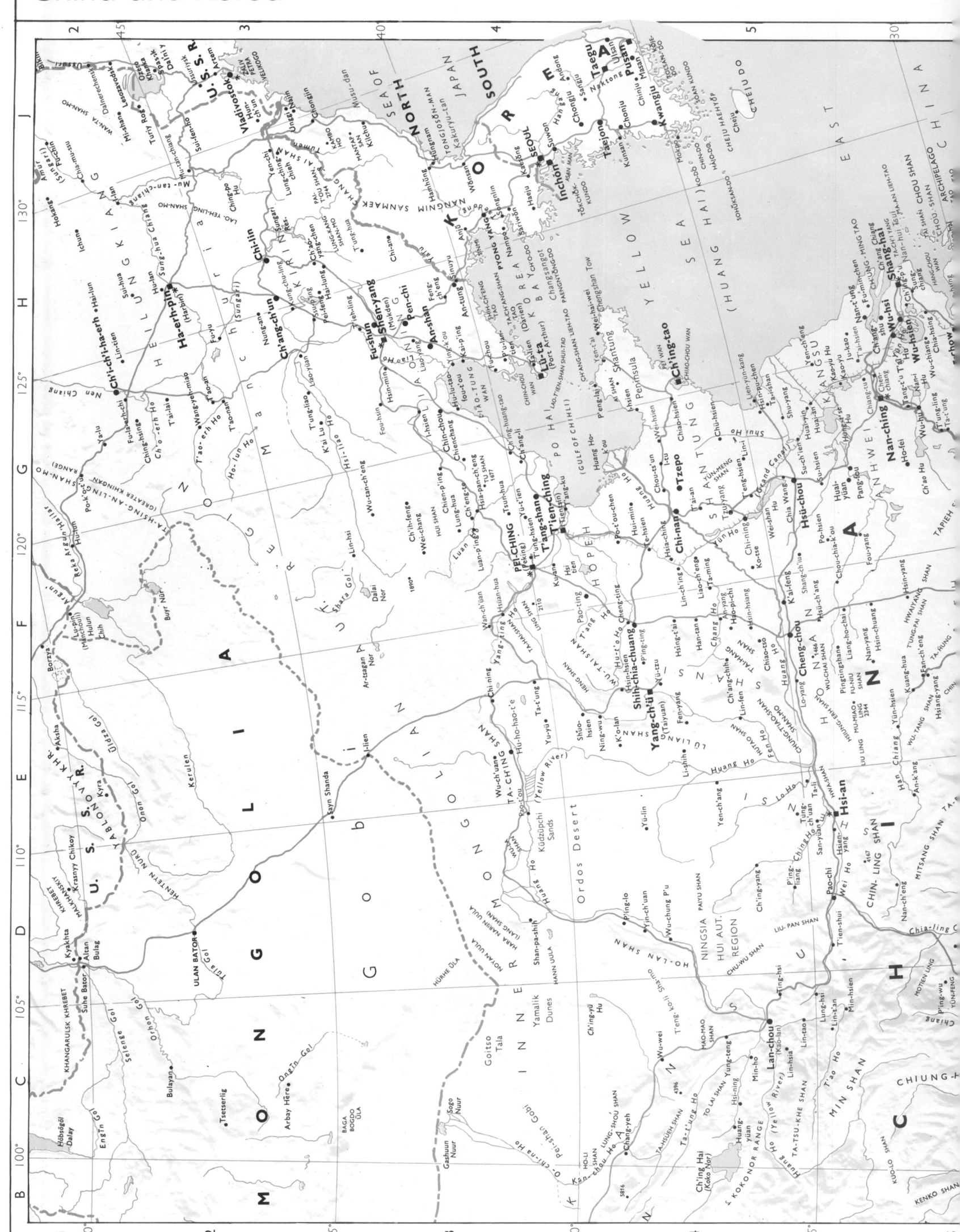

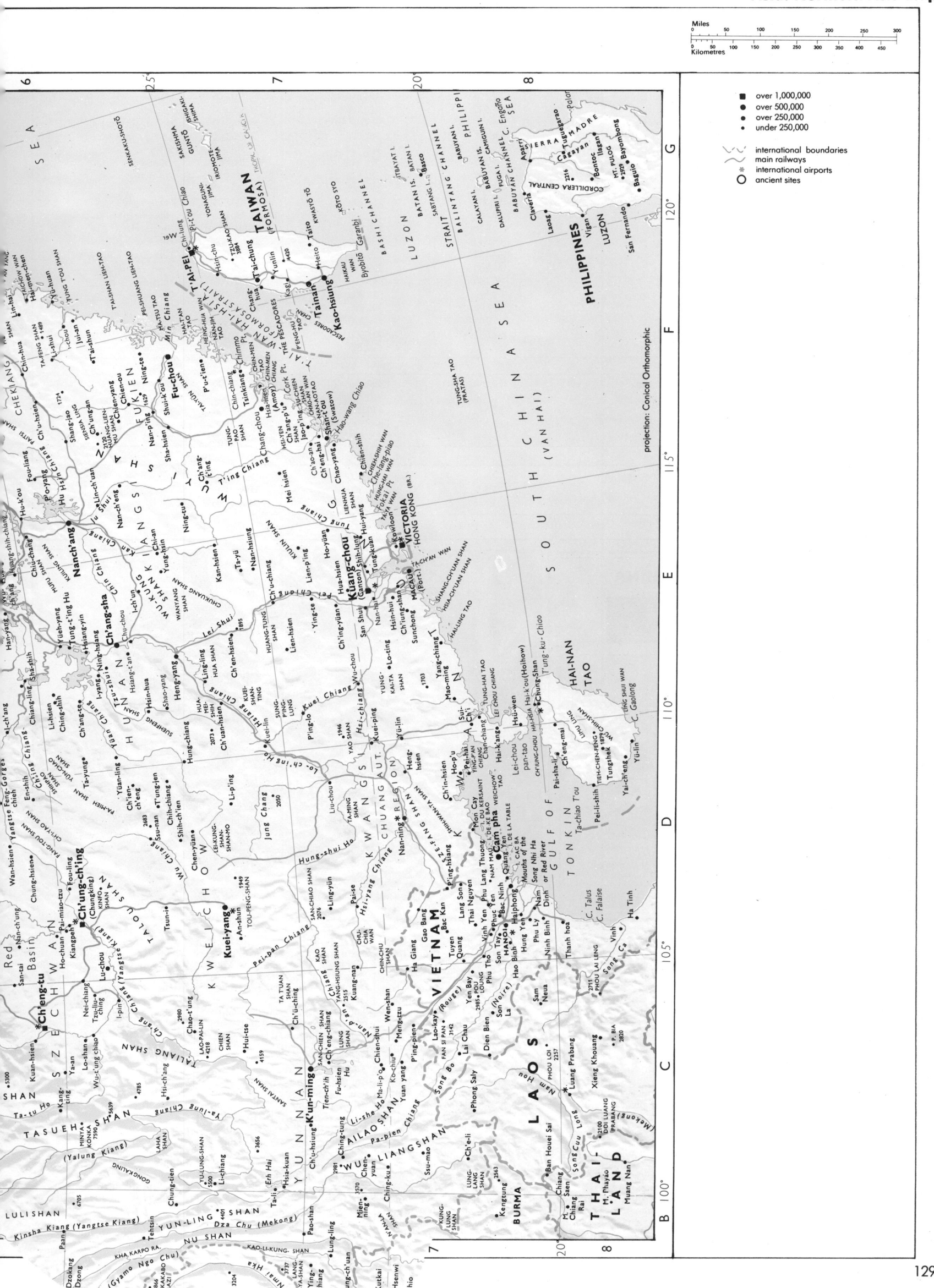

MONGOLIA

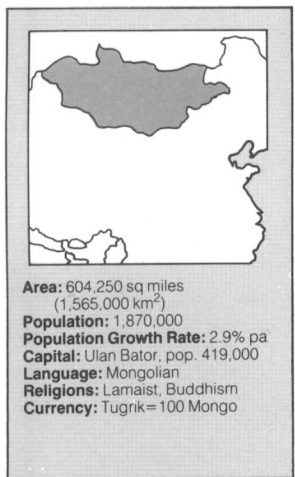

Area: 604,250 sq miles
(1,565,000 km²)
Population: 1,870,000
Population Growth Rate: 2.9% pa
Capital: Ulan Bator, pop. 419,000
Language: Mongolian
Religions: Lamaist, Buddhism
Currency: Tugrik=100 Mongo

THE MONGOLIAN PEOPLE'S REPUBLIC is a large landlocked country in east-central Asia.
People and Culture The Mongols were a group of scattered nomadic tribes until Genghis Khan united them in the thirteenth century. He and his grandson, Kublai Khan, created a vast empire that extended from China in the east to parts of eastern Europe in the west.

In the seventeenth century the Manchus from Manchuria gained control both of China and Mongolia. In 1911 the Mongols revolted and gained control of their own affairs, though they were actually under the supervision of Russia.

In 1924 Russian and Mongolian Communists seized power and set up the Mongolian People's Republic. Mongolia continues to maintain close contact with the Soviet Union.

More than 75 percent of the people are Mongolian, and 5 percent are Kazakhs. Some 51 percent live in urban areas, and they have a life expectancy of 64 years. The country has a state university and seven other colleges of higher education. The traditional religion is Buddhist lamaism, but the government discourages religious practices.
The Land Most of Mongolia is a high plateau, broken by the Altay mountains in the west and the Hangayn Nurū range in the centre. The mountains contain many lakes, and are forested. To the east are grassy plains and in the south the bleak Gobi Desert. Temperatures range from 59°F (15°C) in summer to −29°F (−34°C) in winter. Rainfall varies from 5 to 20 inches (130–500 mm).
Economy Agriculture employs 55 percent of the workforce, operating on state or collective farms. Herdsmen care for 14 million sheep, and more than 9 million cattle, horses, camels and goats. Wheat, rye and barley are the main crops.

Industry employs 22 percent of the labour force, and is being developed. Mongolia does 80 percent of its overseas trade with the Soviet Union. The most recent per capita GNP figures available were $940 for 1978.

PROVINCES OF CHINA

province	total area		population*	capital
	square miles	square kilometres		
Anhwei	54,020	139,910	48,030,000	Ho-fei
Chekiang	39,310	101,810	37,920,000	Hang-chow
Fukien	47,530	123,100	24,800,000	Fu-chou
Heilungkiang	274,130	709,995	31,690,000	Ha-erh-pin (Harbin)
Honan	64,480	167,000	71,890,000	Cheng-chou
Hopeh	78,270	202,720	51,040,000	Shih-chia-chuang
Hunan	81,280	210,515	52,230,000	Ch'ang-sha
Hupeh	72,400	187,515	46,320,000	Wu-ch'ang
Kansu	204,640	530,015	18,940,000	Lan-chou
Kiangsi	63,630	164,800	32,290,000	Nan-ch'ang
Kiangsu	39,460	102,200	58,930,000	Nan-ching (Nanking)
Kirin	111,970	290,000	21,850,000	Ch'ang-ch'un
Kwangtung	89,340	231,390	56,810,000	Kuang-chou (Canton)
Kweichow	67,180	173,995	27,310,000	Kuei-yang
Liaoning	88,800	229,990	34,430,000	Shen-yang (Mukden)
Shanshi	60,660	157,110	24,470,000	Yang-ch'ü
Shantung	59,190	153,300	72,310,000	Chi-nan
Shenshi	75,600	195,805	28,070,000	Hsi-an
Szechwan	219,700	569,020	97,740,000	Ch'eng-tu
Tsinghai	278,380	721,000	3,720,000	Hsi-ning
Yunnan	168,420	436,205	31,350,000	K'un-ming
autonomous regions				
Inner Mongolia	173,750	450,010	18,510,000	Hu-ho-hao-t'e
Kwangsi	85,100	220,410	34,700,000	Nan-ning
Ningsia Hui	65,640	170,005	3,640,000	Yin-ch'uan
Sinkiang	635,830	1,646,790	12,560,000	Ti-hua Shih
Tibet	471,660	1,221,595	1,830,000	Lhasa
municipalities				
Pei-ching (Peking)	6,873	17,800	9,231,000	
Shang-hai	2,239	5,800	11,860,000	
T'ien-ching	1,544	4,000	7,764,000	

* 1980 estimate

CHINA

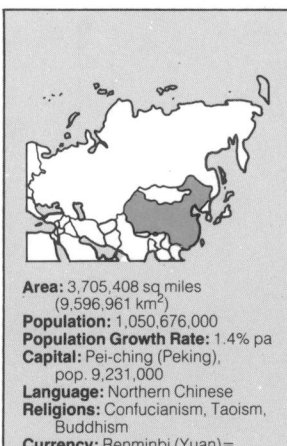

Area: 3,705,408 sq miles
(9,596,961 km²)
Population: 1,050,676,000
Population Growth Rate: 1.4% pa
Capital: Pei-ching (Peking),
pop. 9,231,000
Language: Northern Chinese
Religions: Confucianism, Taoism, Buddhism
Currency: Renminbi (Yuan)=
100 Jiao=100 Fen

A Chinese couple in the traditional costume of Kwangtung province, near the Hong Kong frontier.

THE PEOPLE'S REPUBLIC OF CHINA dominates eastern Asia. It has the world's largest population, and is the third largest in area.
People and Culture People have lived in China for at least 500,000 years. Peking Man, an early form of *Homo erectus*, the precursor of modern Man, lived there. More recently there were two Stone Age cultures: the Yang-shao, which reached its peak about 5,000 years ago, in the valley of the Huang Ho (the Yellow River); and the Lung-shan, which followed it.

For hundreds of years China was ruled by dynasties. The first of these was the Shang dynasty, which began in the eighteenth century BC, arising from the Lung-shan. The first really strong dynasty was the Ch'in, in the third century BC.

The name China comes from that family. Apart from a brief interlude from 1279 to 1368, when the Yuan dynasty from Mongolia ruled China, the land was governed by Chinese emperors until the twentieth century.

China had little contact with Europe until the nineteenth century, when Western traders began to exploit the country. In particular the merchants smuggled in opium, which the Chinese banned. This led to the Opium War between China and Britain from 1839 to 1842. The Treaty of Nanking which ended the war gave Britain trading rights in China, and also possession of the little island of Hong Kong.

China was torn by rebellion in the mid-nineteenth century. Many people were dissatisfied with the rule of the Manchu or

Ch'ing dynasty, which had been in power since 1644. Gradually the rule of the Manchus became more and more feeble. A war with Japan cost the country control over Taiwan and Korea, and European powers gained more and more trading rights.

In 1911 military leaders overthrew the Manchus and established a republic. It was unstable, and years of civil war followed, with rival warlords battling for power. In 1924 the Kuomintang, or Nationalist Party, became a new focus for stability, under the leadership of one of the 1911 revolutionaries, Sun Yat-sen. The newly-formed Communist Party was allied with the Nationalists.

By 1928 the Nationalists had occupied Peking and become the effective rulers of China.

They established a form of dictatorship under Chiang Kai-shek, who had succeeded Sun in 1925. But they had fallen out with the Communists, who set up a rival government.

In 1931 and 1932 Japan occupied Manchuria, which was renamed Manchukuo and set up as a puppet state. In the meantime Chiang's armies were campaigning against the Chinese Communists, who in 1934 had to set out on the so-called 'Long March' to safety in the remote northern province of Shensi. Only a few thousand of the 100,000 Communists who began the march completed it.

An undeclared war with Japan began in 1937, and continued until the end of World War II, into which it merged. The Communists under Mao

Tse-tung controlled the north, and waged their own war against the Japanese. A new civil war began in 1946, and after nearly three years of fighting the Communists won. Chiang and many of his supporters fled to Taiwan, where they set up a Nationalist state.

Government The law-making body in China is the National People's Congress, which meets once a year. In practice the Politburo of the Communist Party takes all decisions. The chairman of the congress serves as head of state, while the day-to-day affairs of the country are handled by a premier and a council of other ministers.

China's local government is on four levels. There are 29 major political divisions, consisting of 21 provinces, five autonomous regions, and three municipalities – Peiching (Peking), Shang-hai, and Tien-ching. Below these major regions come prefectures, counties, and towns and rural communities.

China has 21 cities of more than 1 million inhabitants and 7 over 2 million. Besides Peiching, the largest are:

Shang-hai (11,860,000)
T'ien-ching (7,764,000)
Shen-yang (2,800,000)
Wu-han (2,560,000)
Ch'ang-ch'un, or Canton (2,500,000)
Ch'ung-ch'ing (2,400,000).

But despite these huge cities, only 21 percent of the people live in urban areas.

Almost 94 percent of the people of China belong to the Han ethnic group, the true Chinese. They occupy about two-thirds of the country, while another 50 or so minority groups occupy the remaining third. They include Tibetans, Mongols, and Uighurs. Tibet was an independent country until it was annexed by China in the 1950s and 1960s.

Language Chinese is the language of the Han people, but there are a great many dialects, some of which may almost be called separate languages. The Communist government had made the Northern Chinese dialect, often called Mandarin, the country's official language.

However different the pronunciation, all Chinese dialects look the same and can be understood throughout China when written in the traditional Chinese script. This is an ideographic, not a phonetic, alphabetic system consisting of around 10,000 characters (5,000 form a reasonable working vocabulary). A simplified version of this writing system was introduced in the 1950s in the interests of literacy, but the ultimate aim of language reform is for the general use of the Roman alphabet.

The most popular system for transcribing Chinese names

into the Roman alphabet has been the Wade-Giles system, which two British scholars, Sir Thomas Wade and Herbert Giles, devised in the nineteenth century. In 1979 the Chinese government issued a new transcription system, Pinyin, which is claimed to be nearer the true pronunciation. Under this system Pei-ching (Peking) is Beijing, Tien-ching is Tianjin, and Ch'ang-ch'un is Guangzhou. China itself is Zhongguo. In this atlas the more familiar Wade-Giles transcription is retained.

Religion The traditional religions of China are Confucianism, Buddhism, and Taoism. For a time the Communists discouraged religious practices, but in 1979 this attitude was relaxed. Confucianism, more a philosophy than a religion, is probably still the main creed, but no accurate estimates of its adherents are possible. There are about 10 million Muslims and 2 million Roman Catholics.

Education Adult literacy in 1980 stood at 69 percent. After much radical reform the education system has settled down, and 75 percent of children attend school. There are 1 million primary schools, and 200,000 secondary schools, while by 1980 there were 675 universities and other colleges of higher education.

Health Life expectancy in 1981

was 67 years. Medical care is not free, but in many cases the patients' employers pay all or most of the cost. Western-style medicine and traditional Chinese methods, such as acupuncture, are in use. Rural districts rely on so-called 'barefoot doctors', who have limited training and skills.

The Land About 80 percent of China is mountains, plateaux or hills, the rest being formed by the North China Plain and the valley and delta of the Yangtse River. The whole country slopes in a series of terraces from west to east.

In the southwest is the Tibetan Plateau, a very high tableland bordered on three sides by mountains. To the south lie the Himalayas, to the west of the Karakoram range and the Pamirs, and to the north the Kunlun mountains. A great deal of Tibet is a rocky waste, with only limited grazing and even less arable land.

In the northwest is the Takla Maklan Desert, with the Dzungarian Basin to the north of it, and separated from it by the Tien Shan range of mountains. On the edge of the Takla Maklan Desert is the Turfan Depression, an oasis 505 feet (154 m) below sea-level, and the lowest point in China. The highest point is Mt Everest on the southern Tibetan border.

To the east of the Takla

Maklan Desert lie the Ordos Desert, and the Gobi Desert which extends into Mongolia.

A further range of rugged mountains gives way to the eastern lowlands, a plain that extends from Manchuria in the north southwards to the Yangtse valley. This area contains most of the best farmland, and the largest urban areas. In the middle of the region is the valley of the Huang Ho, or Yellow River, often called 'China's Sorrow' because of its frequent and disastrous floods.

Just to the south of the Huang Ho lies the Chin-ling Shan, a range that divides eastern China into two climatic zones. To the north the land is relatively dry and suitable for wheat. To the south lies the warm, humid area of the Szechwan Basin, where steep valleys are terraced to grow rice, wheat, and sweet potatoes.

Much of the southern part of China is hilly, with rich farmland in the valley of the Hsiang Chiang. This is the area of tea and rice.

Climate The climate of China is as diverse as its landscape. Eastern and southern China receive from 40 to 80 inches (1,000–2,000 mm) of rain a year. The desert areas have less than 4 inches (100 mm) of rain, while in the rest of the country rainfall varies from 4 to 40 inches (100–1,000 mm).

Lake Tien-ch'ih is in Yunnan province. It is 25 miles (40 km) long and 7 miles (11 km) wide, and drains into the Yangtse River. It is well-stocked with fish.

Temperature varies largely with altitude. Tibet and the north have very cold winters, with temperatures below 0°F (−18°C). Summer temperatures rarely rise above 45°F (7°C) in Tibet, but can be over 75°F (24°C) in the northern deserts, and in most of southeastern China.

Vegetation About 9 percent of the land is covered by forests. The northwest is dominated by deserts and dry grasslands, while the southeast is a region of woodland and grassland.

Wildlife China has a wide range of animal life, and a number of species not found elsewhere. Among the rarest animals is the giant panda, found in the hills near Tibet. The rivers and lakes are rich in carp, from which the world's goldfish are descended.

Economy The per capita GNP is low at $300 in 1981. Agriculture is the keystone of China's economy, employing 69 percent of the workforce and producing 35 percent of the GDP. Production in 1981 included 325 million tonnes of grain, 143 million tonnes of rice, and 340,000 tonnes of tea. Chinese farmers keep 310 million pigs, which provide both meat and fertilizer, and raise chickens, cattle, goats, sheep and horses.

Fishing China ranks third after Japan and the Soviet Union in the world's fishing industry. In 1980 the catch totalled 4,240,000 tonnes. The China Sea is one of the world's great fishing zones.

Industry employs 19 percent of the workforce, and produces 46 percent of the GDP. The government has concentrated on the development of heavy industries such as steel production. Important sectors include chemicals – including man-made fibres – textiles, cars and trucks, bicycles, and agricultural implements.

Mining China has good reserves of many minerals. It ranks fourth in world coal production, with 620 million tonnes in 1981; third in antimony ore; fifth in iron ore; fourth in phosphate rock; second in salt; and leads the world in the production of tungsten ore. It also produces sizeable quantities of aluminium, copper, lead, zinc, manganese, and asbestos.

Power About 60 percent of China's power is produced in coal-burning plants. Much of the rest is generated from oil and natural gas. There are at least 100 oilfields in production.

Communications China has 32,300 miles (52,000 km) of railways, and 557,400 miles (897,000 km) of roads. Only about 12.5 percent of roads have hard metalling. But a great deal of local transport is provided by human and animal labour. A network of rivers and canals provides transport over at least 25,000 miles (40,000 km).

NORTH KOREA

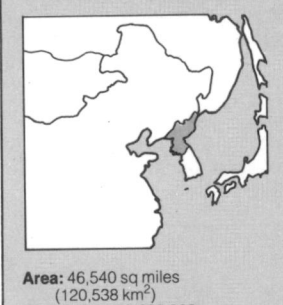

Area: 46,540 sq miles (120,538 km²)
Population: 19,668,000
Population Growth Rate: 2.4% pa
Capital: Pyong Yang, pop. 1,500,000
Language: Korean
Religion: Buddhism
Currency: Won = 100 Chon

THE DEMOCRATIC PEOPLE'S REPUBLIC OF KOREA occupies the northern half of the Korean Peninsula. It is generally called North Korea.

People and Culture Korea was one country until 1948. The Yi dynasty ruled it until 1910, though it was conquered by China in 1627 and paid tribute to China for many years. It was isolated for about 200 years until 1876, when the Japanese forced it to open some ports to international trade.

In 1910 the Japanese took control of Korea, and dominated it until the end of World War II in 1945. Russian troops then occupied the northern half of the peninsula, and American troops the southern half. In 1948 the country was partitioned.

In 1950 North Korea tried to reunite the country by force of arms. The Korean War lasted until 1953, and was inconclusive. Talks aimed at reunification were held in 1980 and 1982, but had no result.

Almost all the people are Korean in ancestry. Their life expectancy is 66 years, an increase of 12 years since 1960. Sixty percent live in urban areas. Education is free and compulsory to the age of 16, and there are three universities and 167 other colleges of higher education. The government officially discourages religion, and also early marriage.

Mist-shrouded Hong Kong looms behind a group of fishing boats at anchor.

Taiwanese collecting mussels on the rocky beach at Yehliu.

There is an elected national assembly, but power is exercised by the Politburo of the Korean Workers' (Communist) Party.

The Land Mountains cover most of North Korea; they are forested and contain mineral deposits. The west is a broad plain, where about half the people live and most of the farmland is located. There is a narrower coastal lowland to the east.

North Korea has warm summers and cold winters, though the east coast is warmer in winter than the rest of the country. Rainfall varies from 30 to 60 inches (762–1,524 mm), mostly falling in summer.

Economy Agriculture employs 49 percent of the workforce, though only 16 percent of the land is suitable for farming. Most of the land is farmed by co-operatives, and the government has sponsored major irrigation projects.

Industry employs 33 percent of the workforce. Government-owned factories produce chemicals, steel, machinery, textiles and processed food. The latest per capita GNP available is $730 for 1978.

SOUTH KOREA

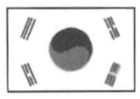

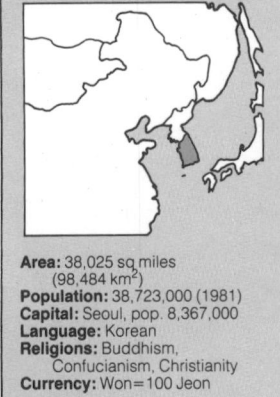

Area: 38,025 sq miles (98,484 km²)
Population: 38,723,000 (1981)
Capital: Seoul, pop. 8,367,000
Language: Korean
Religions: Buddhism, Confucianism, Christianity
Currency: Won = 100 Jeon

THE REPUBLIC OF KOREA, often called South Korea, occupies the southern half of the Korean Peninsula.

People and Culture The history of South Korea was identical with that of North Korea until partition in 1948. In the Korean War of 1950–53, South Korea received support from the United Nations.

A democratic system of government was set up in 1948, which was modified by a new Constitution in 1980. This provides for an elected president and a national assembly.

Life expectancy stands at 66 years, as compared with 54 years in 1960, and this is coupled with a percentage of 56 in urban areas, against 28 percent in 1960. The adult literacy rate is 93 percent. Elementary education is compulsory and partly free. There are 224 colleges of higher education, including universities.

The Land Most of the central and eastern part of the country is covered by forested mountains. Plains cover the western and southern coasts, and form the main agricultural region. About half the people live in the western plains. The climate is similar to that of North Korea, but the rainfall is lower, at 30–50 inches (762–1,270 mm) a year.

Economy Agriculture, first in importance at partition, has given way to industry, which now accounts for 39 percent of the GDP, and employs 29 percent of the workforce. Heavy and petrochemical industries are expanding rapidly, while there is a strong section making light consumer goods.

Agriculture accounts for 34 percent of the workforce and 17 percent of the GDP. Rice, barley and wheat are the main crops. The country's fishing fleet is expanding very fast. Recession hit the economy at the end of the 1970s, but in the early 1980s recovery was under way. South Korea's per capita GNP stood at $1,700 in 1981.

TAIWAN

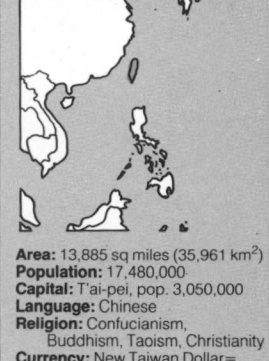

Area: 13,885 sq miles (35,961 km²)
Population: 17,480,000
Capital: T'ai-pei, pop. 3,050,000
Language: Chinese
Religion: Confucianism, Buddhism, Taoism, Christianity
Currency: New Taiwan Dollar = 100 Cents

TAIWAN is an island country in the South China Sea. It is sometimes called Formosa, and it uses the title Republic of China.
People and Culture The Chinese settled in Taiwan in the seventeenth century. It was ceded to Japan in 1895, but restored to China after World War II.

In 1949 the Nationalist government of China retreated to Taiwan after its defeat by the Communists. Until 1971 Taiwan retained China's seat in the United Nations.

All but 1 percent of the people are of Chinese origin. The remainder are tribesmen related to the Filipinos. Life expectancy is about 72 years, and adult literacy is 82 percent. Elementary education is free and compulsory, and there are 27 universities and other colleges of higher education.
The Land About 66 percent of the land is covered by mountains, but there are fertile plains in the west. Taiwan has hot, humid summers and cool winters. Rainfall averages more than 100 inches (2,540 mm) annually.
Economy Manufacturing is the basis of Taiwan's economy, and employs about 33 percent of the workforce. Textiles, machinery and electrical goods are among the chief exports. Mines produce coal, copper and gold, and Taiwan has reserves of oil and natural gas. About 25 percent of the land is under cultivation, with rice, tea and fruit the main crops. The per capita GNP was $1,869 in 1979.

DEPENDENCIES

HONG KONG is a British Crown colony on the south coast of China. It has an area of 403 sq miles (1,045 km²), and a population of 5,583,000. The population growth rate is 2.7 percent a year.

Hong Kong Island was ceded by China to Britain in 1842, and Kowloon Peninsula and Stonecutter's Island were ceded in 1860. The New Territories, consisting of a further stretch of mainland and about another 200 small islands, were leased to Britain in 1898 for a term of 99 years. This region comprises about 90 percent of Hong Kong's total area.

Negotiations about the future of Hong Kong began in the 1980s. In 1984 the British announced that Hong Kong would revert to China, with special status, when the lease expired in 1997.

All but about 2 percent of the people are of Chinese origin, and speak Chinese, though English is also widely spoken. Life expectancy is 75 years, and adult literacy is 90 percent. There is little farmland or countryside, and 90 percent of the people live in urban areas.

Hong Kong is very hilly and rocky, particularly the main island. The New Territories contain a flat plain, used for farming. The climate is subtropical.

Hong Kong's economy is based on manufacturing. In 1982 it had almost 48,000 factories, employing 57 percent of the workforce. The main products are textiles, electronic apparatus, plastics, cameras and footwear. Shipbuilding and aircraft engineering are also important. Hong Kong is a free port and does a flourishing *entrepôt* trade. The per capita GNP was $5,100 in 1981.

MACAU is a tiny Portuguese territory on the southeast coast of China. It has an area of 6 sq miles (16 km²) and a population of 312,000. The Portuguese first settled there in 1557.

The territory consists of the town of Macau, which is on a small peninsula, and two islands. More than 97 percent of the people are Chinese. Matches and fire-crackers are the main exports, and there is a large gambling industry. Macau is a centre for gold dealing. The per capita GNP was $2,630 in 1981.

A Macau girl punts ashore from a typical sampan home, where many people live.

Chinese children in colourful costumes take part in a parade in the Cheung Chau Bun Festival, a spectacular celebration.

Japan

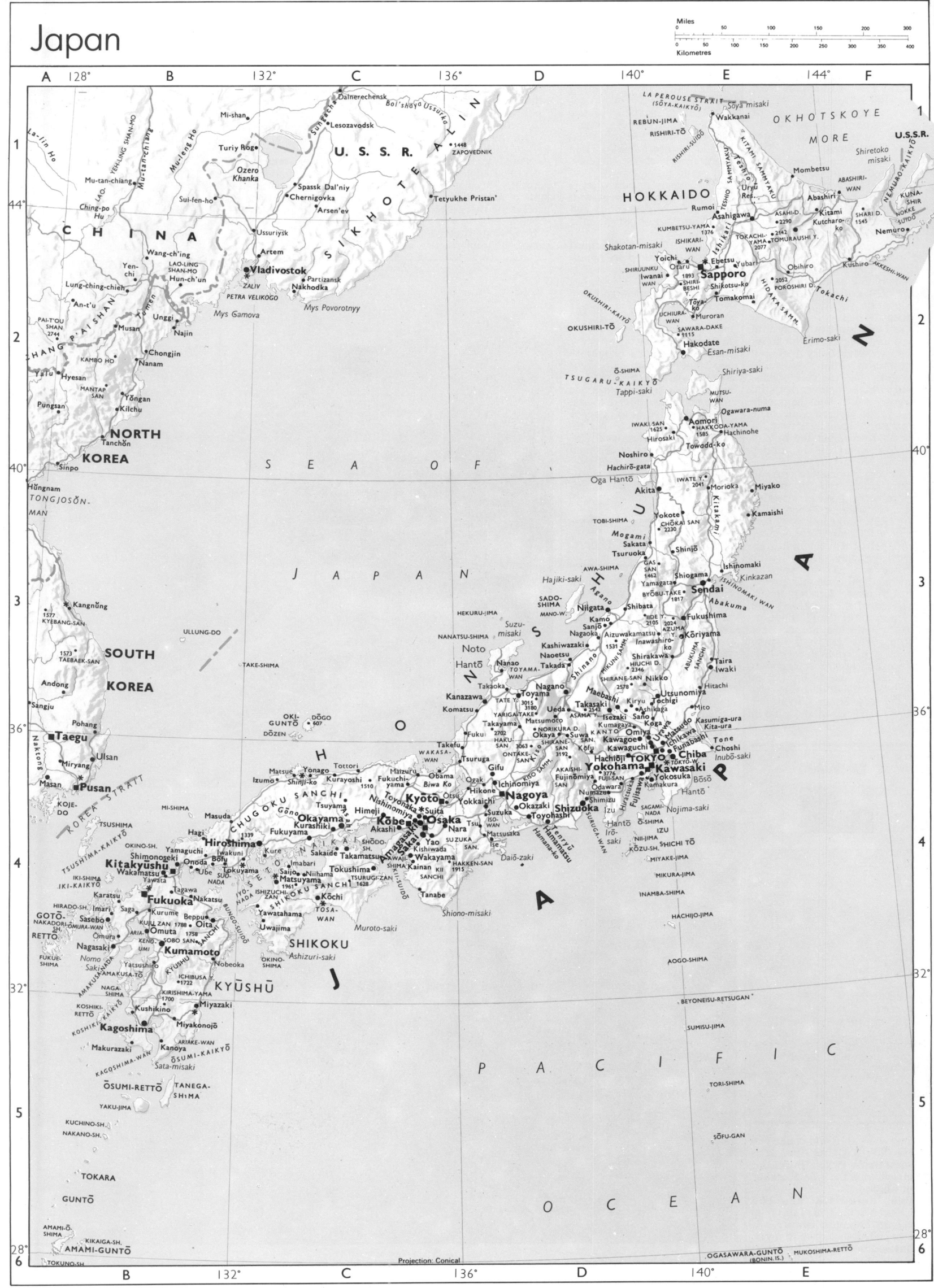

Miles
0 50 100 150 200 300

Kilometres
0 50 100 150 200 250 300 350 400

Projection: Conical

JAPAN

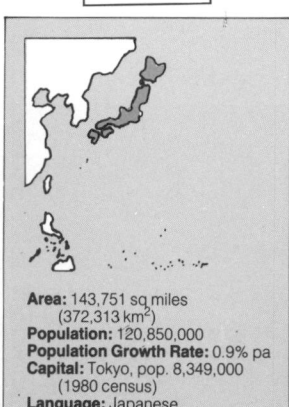

Area: 143,751 sq miles (372,313 km^2)
Population: 120,850,000
Population Growth Rate: 0.9% pa
Capital: Tokyo, pop. 8,349,000 (1980 census)
Language: Japanese
Religion: Shinto (81%)
Currency: Yen

A brooding menace: one of Japan's 150 major volcanoes. About 40 are active, but others could spring suddenly to life again.

NIPPON, or NIHON, known as Japan to Western nations, is an island country off the eastern coast of Asia. It consists of four large islands and thousands of smaller ones.

People and Culture People were living in Japan at least 6,500 years ago, and probably earlier. They are known as the Jomon (cord pattern) because of the way they decorated their pottery.

Present-day Japanese came into the country slightly over 2,200 years ago, probably from Korea. In Hokkaido, the northernmost of Japan's principal islands, live the Ainu, a very different race who have more affinities with the people of Europe or northern India than they do with the Japanese. They may be survivors of the aboriginal inhabitants.

According to legend, the first emperor of Japan was Jimmu Tenno, who reigned from 660 BC. Japan has been ruled by emperors ever since. From the third century AD powerful noble families controlled the government, and from 1192 to 1867 the country was under the rule of a series of *shoguns*, or military governors.

Japan remained isolated from the rest of the world until the mid-nineteenth century, when the ending of the shogunate and trade treaties negotiated more or less at gunpoint by the United States ended the country's insularity.

However, with modernization came a spirit of militarism, which led to the acquisition of Korea in 1905, the conquest of Manchuria in 1931, and from 1941 to 1945 an attempt to conquer all of eastern Asia. Japan was defeated in this during World War II.

An Allied (mostly US) occupation force introduced democratic systems of government and helped to rebuild Japan's war-shattered economy.

Life Today The Japanese themselves form about 92 percent of the population. The rest are mostly Koreans, with some Chinese and Ainu. Almost 80 percent live in urban areas, an increase from 62 percent in 1960. Life expectancy is 77 years, which has risen from 68 since 1960.

Education Schooling is free and compulsory for children from 6 to 15. Higher education is provided by high schools, and there are around 450 universities and more than 500 other senior colleges.

Religion Shinto used to be the state religion. It no longer holds that position, but more than 80 percent of the people follow it. About 75 percent are Buddhists, a large proportion following both religions. Christianity has less than 1 percent of adherents.

The Land The four main islands are Honshu, 87,805 sq miles (227,414 km^2); Hokkaido, 30,144 sq miles (78,073 km^2), the northernmost of the islands; Kyushu, 14,110 sq miles (36,544 km^2), the southernmost island; and Shikoku, 7,049 sq miles

The shrine where Iyemitsu, shogun from 1623 to 1651, is buried at Nikko, in central Honshu.

Shichi-go-san Ceremony, presenting children at the temple.

(18,256 km^2). Around 80 percent of the people live in Honshu. Japan has ten cities of more than 1 million people, and seven of them are in Honshu. Besides Tokyo, three are over 2 million – Yokohama, Osaka, and Nagoya.

Japan lies next to the chain of deep ocean trenches that mark the Pacific plate's subduction under the Eurasian plate. As a result the land is very unstable. There are 150 major volcanoes, 40 of them active, while around 1,500 minor earthquakes occur every year. Major earthquakes happen about every six years.

Mountains and forests cover about 70 percent of Japan. The tallest peak is Mt Fuji, 12,388 feet (3,776 m) high. Among the mountains are many small lakes, and a great many short, fast rivers, which can cause disastrous floods.

The climate varies from north to south. Summers are hot and humid, except in the north. Winters are cold in the north, with snow, but are mild in the south. Almost the whole country has abundant rainfall, only eastern Hokkaido receiving less than 40 inches (1,016 mm) a year, while many parts receive twice as much. Violent typhoons strike the country in late summer and early autumn.

Japan has a rich flora and fauna. There are more than 9,000 different species of plants, sub-tropical in the south and temperate in the north and at higher elevations. There are about 140 mammals, from bears and badgers to deer and wild pigs, 450 species of birds, and many snakes, tortoises and frogs.

Economy Japan's economic recovery, after its devastation in World War II, is one of the twentieth century's miracles. It is one of the world's richest countries, with a per capita GNP of $10,080.

Manufacturing is the basis of Japan's economy. It produces 30 percent of the GDP. Japan leads the world in the production of cars, television sets, and merchant ships, and is second in radio production. It is a leading producer of computers and cameras.

Other industries include metal refining. Japan is a leading producer of aluminium, copper, iron and steel, and zinc, and a major refiner of petroleum. Industry employs 39 percent of the workforce.

Japan has small mineral resources, though of a wide variety of minerals. It ranks sixth in the production of zinc ore, and tenth in silver, but imports most of its minerals.

Agriculture accounts for 4 percent of the GDP, and employs 12 percent of the workforce. Japan is a leading producer of rice, tea, eggs, tobacco, and raw silk. It has the world's largest fishing fleet, catching 10,410,000 tonnes annually.

Southern Asia: introduction

Southern Asia includes the 16 Asian countries usually classed as part of the Middle East; Afghanistan and the five countries of the Indian subcontinent; the Indian Ocean island countries of Sri Lanka and the Maldives; and the ten countries that make up Southeast Asia and the East Indies. It includes three of Asia's smallest countries in terms of area – the Maldive Islands, Singapore, and Bahrain; the world's second largest country in terms of population, India; and three other countries in the world's ten most populous, Indonesia, Pakistan and Bangladesh.

Climate
The temperatures of southern Asia cover all extremes. Part of the region lies in the tropics, and most of the rest is classed as subtropical. The islands of the East Indies have hot, wet weather all the year round. Most of southeast Asia and the Indian subcontinent have monsoon weather, with alternate wet and dry seasons. Most of the Middle East has either dry summers and mild winters with moderate rainfall, or else low rainfall at all times. The driest region is probably the Rub' al Khālī of the Arabian peninsula.

Subarctic and polar conditions are found in the Himalaya range because of its height above sea-level. The main part of the range lies at an average elevation of 20,000 feet (6,100 m) above sea-level. At this altitude, the temperature seldom rises above freezing point even at the height of summer. The lower part of the range has temperatures above freezing point from the end of May to the middle of October. The Himalayas are heavily glaciated.

Religion
Religion has played an important part in the cultural and political make-up of southern Asia. The oldest of these religions, and the world's most ancient, is Hinduism, the major religion of India. It has more than 515,000,000 adherents, more than 450,000,000 of them in India itself. It developed over thousands of years and its origins are lost in the prehistoric past.

Islam, which has more than 513,000,000 followers worldwide, is the dominant religion of the Middle East, and the chief rival to Hinduism in the Indian subcontinent. The clash between Islam and Hinduism was the principal reason for the partition of the old British India into the modern states of Hindu India and Muslim Pakistan and Bangladesh. Islam arose in Arabia as a result of the teachings of the Prophet Muhammad in the seventh century AD. It is split into several sects, of which the most important are the Sunnites, the great majority, and the Shiites. However, Shiites are the dominant Muslims in Iran and Iraq, though the fact that many Iraqui political leaders are Sunni Muslims has had a divisive effect.

Buddhism, founded on the teachings of Siddhartha Gautama, known as the Buddha, the Enlightened One, arose in India around 500 BC. It has about 224,000,000 followers, and in southern Asia their strongholds are the mainland part of southeast Asia, and Sri Lanka.

History and Culture
The Fertile Crescent of the Middle East was the cradle of possibly the world's earliest civilization, that of Sumeria, which came into being more than 5,500 years ago. It was followed by the Babylonian empire around 3,900 years ago, and that in turn was succeeded by the empire of the Assyrians.

Another of the great early civilizations arose in the valley of the Indus River, now in Pakistan. It lasted from about 2500 BC to 1500 BC. Exactly how and why it came to an end is not clear, but it is generally thought that it was extinguished by an invasion of Aryan peoples from the north. The Aryans came from the plains of central Asia, and another group of them migrated into Europe. Many modern languages of India and Europe have a common origin.

An early civilization existed in southeast Asia, but archaeologists have only recently begun to discover its traces. It seems likely that metal-working began there at about the same time as it did in the Middle East.

The Persian empire dominated western Asia from the sixth to the fourth century BC, when it was overthrown by the Macedonian conqueror Alexander the Great. Buddhist empires flourished in India and southeast Asia, notably the Maurya in India and the Khmer in Kampuchea.

The Bodnath stupa near Katmandu, Nepal, is an ancient place of pilgrimage for Buddhists.

The Islamic empire arose in the seventh century AD in Arabia and spread to cover the whole of the Middle East. The Muslim religion spread eastwards into the Indian subcontinent. Arab influence in the Middle East gave way to that of the Ottoman Turks, who came into southwestern Asia from central Asia. An offshoot of the Mongols who dominated northern Asia in the thirteenth century was the Mogul empire in India, which was founded by a Muslim descendant of the Mongol conquerors in the sixteenth century.

European influence in southern Asia began in 1498, when a Portuguese fleet commanded by Vasco da Gama reached India. European desire for spices from the East Indies and the wealth of southern Asia led to swift exploitation. The Portuguese had an early lead which they were unable to maintain, and the French were unable to hold any major position in India.

By the nineteenth century the British dominated the Indian subcontinent, Sri Lanka, and Malaya; the Dutch controlled most of the East Indies; the French had established their rule in much of the southeast Asian peninsula, then known as French Indo-China; and the Spaniards held the Philippines. British influence was strong over much of the Middle East, though the French controlled Syria and Lebanon.

The people of southern Asia had built up their culture and traditions over many centuries. Those of India, in particular, predated those of the European powers who were now colonizing the continent. The Industrial Revolution, which began in Europe in the mid-eighteenth century, was taken to Asia ready-made in the nineteenth century, and superimposed on ways of life that had been unchanged for hundreds of years. The European powers made considerable profits out of the lands they ruled, but they also brought benefits, too. Modern Western-style cities arose, Western ways of government were introduced, and some barbaric customs, such as, in India, *suttee*, the semi-compulsory suicide of widows on their husbands' funeral pyres, were discouraged. Probably one of the greatest assets of colonial times was the introduction of railways, which still serve southern Asia well.

But Western ideas of government also brought ideas of independence, and moves towards the break-up of the colonial empires were already well under way before the outbreak of World War II. The Japanese attempt, begun in 1941, to create a 'Greater East Asia Co-Prosperity Sphere', with Japan as its hub, merely accelerated the process.

Within four years of the ending of the war only the French possessions in Indo-China remained as major colonial territories, and a bitter five-year war brought independence to that area too.

One relic of colonial days is that most countries of the old British Empire are today members of the Commonwealth: Bangladesh, Brunei, India, Malaysia, the Maldive Islands, Singapore and Sri Lanka. Burma left the Commonwealth immediately on gaining independence, and Pakistan withdrew in 1972.

Economy

The economies of the countries of southern Asia vary enormously. The region is predominantly poor, with about two-thirds of the people making their living from agriculture, much of it subsistence farming. But the small oil-producing states of the Persian Gulf are mostly very rich indeed. Qatar heads the list with a per capita GNP of $27,720, followed by the United Arab Emirates with $24,660 and Kuwait with $20,900. At the other end of the scale comes the tiny Himalayan country of Bhutan, virtually isolated from the rest of the world until the 1950s and only recently beginning to develop, whose per capita GNP in 1981 stood at just $80. An equally poorly developed country is Laos, which also had a per capita GNP of $80. Laos is heavily dependent on foreign aid, mostly from Vietnam and the Soviet Union.

Political Alliances

In addition to the Commonwealth and the United Nations, several other associations of countries have importance in southern Asia. A dozen countries in the Middle East are members of the League of Arab States, which has eight other members in Africa. The Asian members are Bahrain, Iraq, Jordan, Kuwait, Lebanon, Oman, Qatar, Saudi Arabia, Syria, the United Arab Emirates and the two Yemens. In addition the Palestine Liberation Organization is a member. Iran, Iraq, Kuwait, Qatar, Saudi Arabia and the United Arab Emirates are members of the Organization of Petroleum Exporting Countries (OPEC).

Farther east, Indonesia, Malaysia, the Philippines, Singapore and Thailand are members of the Association of South East Asian Nations (ASEAN). The 26-member Colombo Plan, formed to help developing countries, has the following southern Asian members: Afghanistan, Bangladesh, Bhutan, Burma, Indonesia, Iran, Kampuchea, Laos, Malaysia, the Maldive Islands, Nepal, Pakistan, the Philippines, Singapore, Sri Lanka and Thailand.

Above left A street market in Singapore. In less than two centuries Singapore has grown from a tiny village to a bustling city with more than 11,000 people per square mile. Sir Stamford Raffles, of the British East India Company, founded the city in 1819 as a trading post which he forecast would become 'the emporium and pride of the East'. Today, with 2,400 factories, the biggest ship repair yard in South-East Asia, a huge seaport, and a per capita GNP of $5,240, Singapore bids fair to fulfil Raffles' prophecy.

Above Mount Everest is the world's highest mountain, a super-giant among giants. It is named after Sir George Everest, a British surveyor-general of India in the nineteenth century. But the Sherpas, Nepalese people famous as mountain climbers and porters, call it Chomolungma, 'Goddess Mother of the World'. The mountain was first climbed on May 29, 1953, by two men in a British-led expedition: the Sherpa Tenzing Norgay, and the New Zealander Edmund Hillary.

Southern Asia

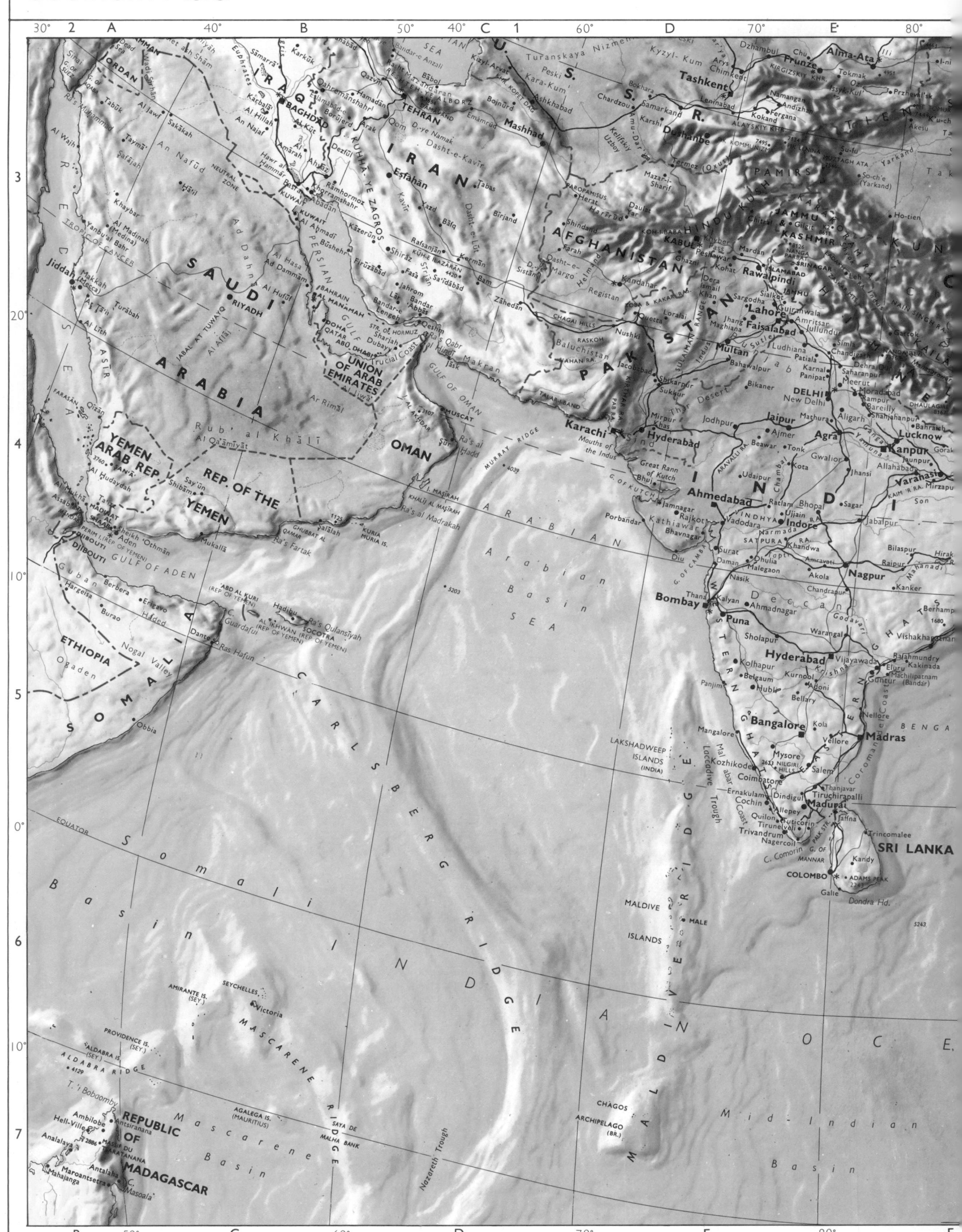

AFGHANISTAN

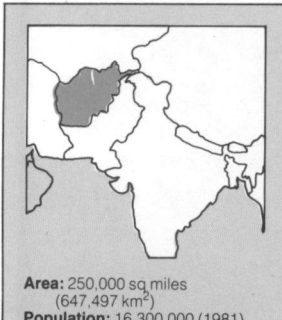

Area: 250,000 sq miles
(647,497 km²)
Population: 16,300,000 (1981)
Capital: Kabul, pop. 588,000
Languages: Pushtu; Dari (Persian)
Religion: Islam
Currency: Afghani = 100 Puls

THE DEMOCRATIC REPUBLIC OF AFGHANISTAN is a landlocked country in western Asia.

People and Culture Arabs conquered Afghanistan in the seventh century AD and introduced Islam. Ahmad Shah Durrani, an Afghan chief, created a united Afghanistan in 1747. In the nineteenth century Britain and Russia competed for control of Afghanistan. From 1880 to 1919 Britain took control of Afghanistan's external affairs.

Afghanistan was a monarchy until 1973, when a revolution led to a republic. In 1978 another revolution brought a pro-Russian government to power. Its Marxist and atheist views were opposed by Afghan tribesmen, and in 1979 Soviet troops invaded Afghanistan to support the régime. Guerilla warfare continued into the 1980s, and about one million Afghan refugees fled to Pakistan and Iran.

About 60 percent of the people are Pashtuns, and 30 percent are Tadzhiks. The major languages are Pushtu and Persian, but there are nearly 20 others in use. Adult literacy is 20 percent, and life expectancy is only 37 years, largely because there is little medical care. Only 16 percent of the people live in urban areas.

The Land Afghanistan is largely mountainous. Mountain plateaux and hills lie in the north, while in the centre and west are the lofty peaks of the Hindu Kush. Among these peaks are valleys where most Afghans live. Southern Afghanistan is largely lowland deserts.

Rainfall in the Hindu Kush area is about 15 inches (380 mm) a year and in the rest of the country is even less. In many parts farming is possible only with irrigation from the rivers.

Economy Only 12 percent of the land is under cultivation, but agriculture absorbs 79 percent of the workforce. Afghanistan was almost self-sufficient in food before the Soviet invasion but now imports food from the Russians. Wheat and fruit are the principal crops. Nomadic herdsmen tend more than 18 million sheep, plus goats, cattle, horses, donkeys and mules.

Natural gas is the main mineral exploited, 90 percent of which is sold to Russia. There are rich deposits of coal, iron ore, and other minerals, which are largely unexploited. Most industries are small. Before the invasion, in 1979, the per capita GNP stood at $170.

PAKISTAN

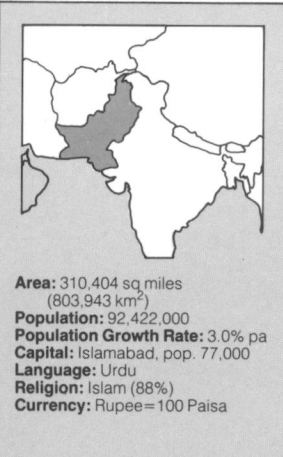

Area: 310,404 sq miles
(803,943 km²)
Population: 92,422,000
Population Growth Rate: 3.0% pa
Capital: Islamabad, pop. 77,000
Language: Urdu
Religion: Islam (88%)
Currency: Rupee = 100 Paisa

THE ISLAMIC REPUBLIC OF PAKISTAN is a country in central southern Asia.

People and Culture One of the world's early civilizations began in the Indus River valley of Pakistan about 4,500 years ago. The land later came under many rulers, including Greeks and Persians. Arabs took Islam there in the eighth century.

The land became part of British India in the early nineteenth century. Moves for independence began in the 1930s, and because of disagreements between Hindus and Muslims, it was agreed to partition India. The separate Muslim state of Pakistan came into being in 1947.

Pakistan fought India from 1948 to 1949 over Kashmir, a predominantly Muslim region that was occupied by India. In 1957 it became a republic. In 1971 eastern Pakistan seceded and became Bangladesh.

The people of Pakistan are largely Punjabis and Pathans, plus several smaller groups, and at least five major languages are spoken. Urdu is the official tongue. Islam is dominant, but 11 percent of the people follow Hinduism.

The government is in the process of setting up free compulsory education. Adult literacy at present stands at only 24 percent. Life expectancy is 50 years, as compared with 43 years in 1960. Urban dwellers total 29 percent.

The Land In the north lie the mountains of the Hindu Kush and Himalaya ranges. The Himalayas include the world's second highest mountain, K2 (Mt Godwin Austen). In the southwest is the Baluchistan plateau, dry and rocky with little vegetation; to the southeast is the sandy Thar Desert.

In the east and centre are the Punjab and Sind plains, in the valley of the Indus River and its tributaries.

Pakistan generally has hot summers and cool winters, but temperature varies with elevation. Rainfall varies from 20 inches (508 mm) in the eastern Punjab to less than 5 inches (127 mm) in Baluchistan.

Economy Agriculture accounts for 30 percent of the GDP, and employs 57 percent of the workforce. It also accounts for more than one-third of Pakistan's exports, by value. Irrigation allows wheat, cotton, maize, sugar-cane and rice to be grown. Sheep, goats and cattle are raised.

An armed Pathan watches over the North-West Frontier which lies between Pakistan and Afghanistan, the scene of many battles.

Women picking tea at Nuwara Eliya, near Kandy, in Sri Lanka.

Pathans in the bazaar at Peshawar, capital of the North-West Frontier Province, Pakistan.

cent of the people live in urban areas, life expectancy is 48 years, and adult literacy is 26 percent.

The Land The country occupies most of the vast delta area of the Ganges, Brahmaputra, and Meghna rivers; 75 percent of this region is less than 50 feet (15 m) above sea-level, and it is liable to disastrous floods when cyclones sweep in across the Bay of Bengal.

The climate is warm and humid. Rainfall varies between 65 and 250 inches (1,651–6,350 mm) a year. The heavy rainfall and fertile soil are ideal for growing rice.

The Chittagong Hills in southeastern Bangladesh have valuable teak forests.

Economy Bangladesh ranks as one of the world's poorest countries, with a per capita GNP in 1981 of $140.

Agriculture employs 74 percent of the workforce, and produces 54 percent of the GDP. About 80 percent of the farmland is devoted to rice, and Bangladesh ranks sixth in world rice production. Even so, outdated farming methods mean that it does not produce enough to keep its huge population adequately fed.

Jute is the next biggest crop, and processing it the main industry. Industry as a whole employs 11 percent of the workforce and contributes 14 percent of the GDP. There are few other large industries.

The main mineral resources are coal and natural gas, and oil has been discovered offshore in the Bay of Bengal.

The inland waterway network covers most of the country, with canals supplementing the many natural streams. It forms the main means of transport and is also a source of fish.

BANGLADESH

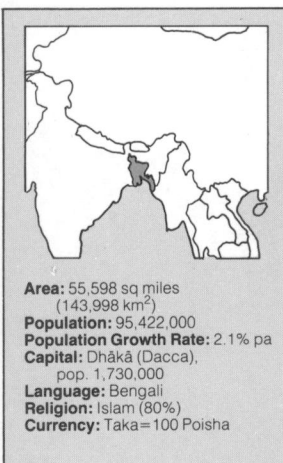

Area: 55,598 sq miles (143,998 km²)
Population: 95,422,000
Population Growth Rate: 2.1% pa
Capital: Dhākā (Dacca), pop. 1,730,000
Language: Bengali
Religion: Islam (80%)
Currency: Taka = 100 Poisha

THE PEOPLE'S REPUBLIC OF BANGLADESH is an Islamic country in southern Asia.
People and Culture Bangladesh is the eastern part of the former Indian province of Bengal. Its people were converted to Islam during the period of the Mogul empire (1576–1857). In 1947, it became part of the new nation of Pakistan, and was called East Pakistan.

In 1971 East Pakistan broke away and formed the independent nation of Bangladesh. More than 95 percent of the people are Bengalis. The country is poor: only 12 per-

percent are Tamils. The Tamils are Hindus and the Sinhalese are Buddhists. A further 7 percent are of Arab origin, and follow Islam. Racial tension between Tamils and Sinhalese led to riots in 1983 and 1984.

Life expectancy is 69 years, and adult literacy is 85 percent. Only 27 percent of the people live in urban areas.

The Land Mountains lie in the centre and south of the island, but more than 80 percent of Sri Lanka is a low-lying plain. The climate is tropical, but sea breezes temper the heat. Rainfall varies from 40 inches (1,016 mm) in the north to 200 inches (5,080 mm) in the mountains.

Economy Agriculture employs 54 percent of the workforce and produces 28 percent of the GDP. About 36 percent of the land is under cultivation. Tea is the leading cash crop and the biggest export item. Rubber ranks second, and coconuts and their products third. Rice is the staple food crop.

Sri Lanka is a leading source of gemstones, including sapphires, rubies, beryls, spinels, and garnets. Graphite is another important mineral, and plants for processing it are among the many industries. Industry as a whole produces 28 percent of the GDP and employs 14 percent of the workforce. The per capita GNP was $300 in 1981.

SRI LANKA

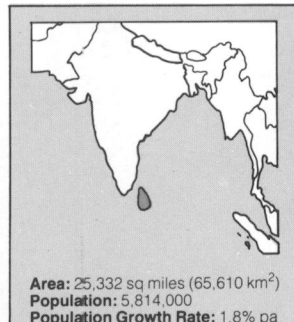

Area: 25,332 sq miles (65,610 km²)
Population: 5,814,000
Population Growth Rate: 1.8% pa
Capital: Colombo, pop. 1,412,000
Language: Sinhala
Religion: Buddhism (67%)
Currency: Rupee = 100 Cents

THE REPUBLIC OF SRI LANKA is an island country 20 miles (32 km) southeast of India. It was formerly called Ceylon.
People and Culture Sinhalese from India settled in Sri Lanka about 500 BC and Tamils invaded later. The Portuguese and Dutch in turn ruled the island, and it was a British colony from 1802 to 1948, when it became independent.

About 75 percent of the people are Sinhalese, and 13

MALDIVES

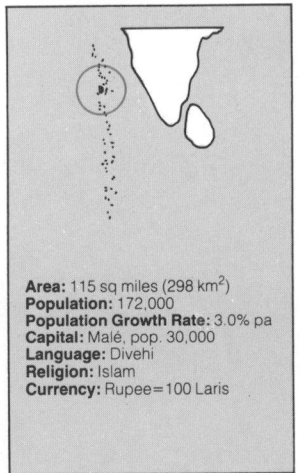

Area: 115 sq miles (298 km²)
Population: 172,000
Population Growth Rate: 3.0% pa
Capital: Malé, pop. 30,000
Language: Divehi
Religion: Islam
Currency: Rupee = 100 Laris

THE REPUBLIC OF MALDIVES is an island country in the Indian Ocean.
People and Culture Most of the people of the Maldive Islands are of Sinhalese origin. The Dutch ruled the islands from 1656 to 1796, and Britain controlled them from 1887 to 1965. They gained independence in 1965, and became a republic in 1968.
The Land The republic consists of a chain of 1,200 coral islands, of which 202 are inhabited. The climate is hot and humid, and rainfall is heavy.
Economy Fishing is the main occupation, and dried fish the principal export. Millet, fruit and coconuts are the leading crops. Sri Lanka and Japan are the Maldives' main trading partners. The per capita GNP in 1980 was $260.

Coal, iron ore, chromite and gypsum are among the main minerals, and copper and gold have also been found. The country has large natural gas reserves and several oil fields. Hydroelectric schemes produce power and water for irrigation.

Manufacturing produces 17 percent of the GDP, and employs about 13 percent of the workforce. Textiles, cement, and fertilizers are the major products. The per capita GNP in 1981 was $350.

141

India and Pakistan

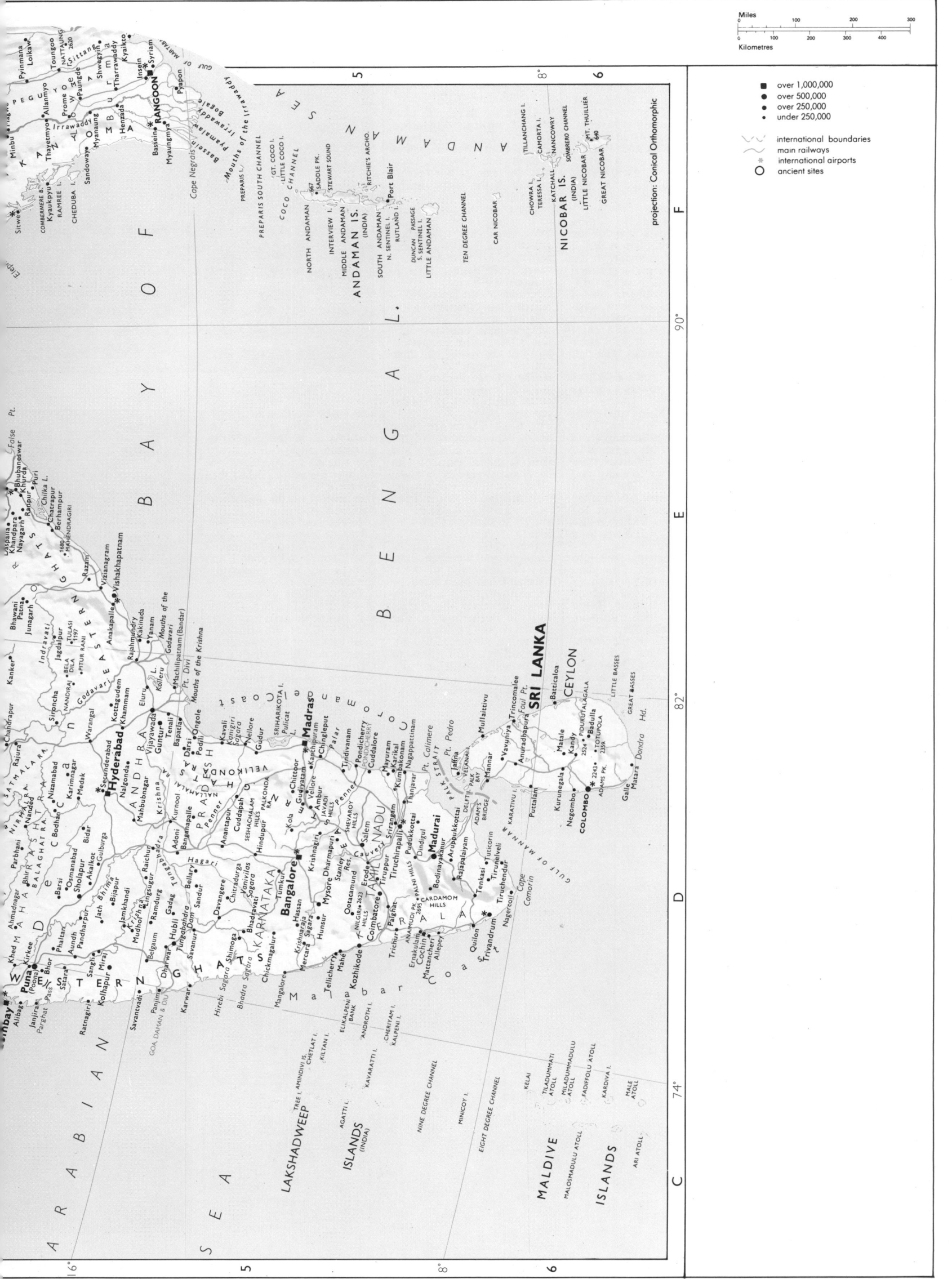

INDIA

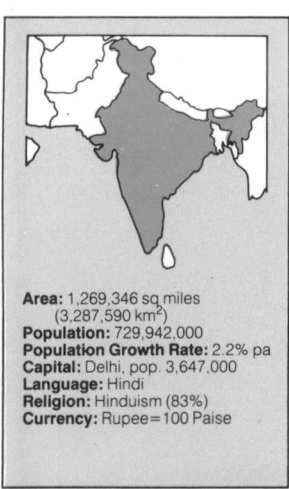

Area: 1,269,346 sq miles
(3,287,590 km²)
Population: 729,942,000
Population Growth Rate: 2.2% pa
Capital: Delhi, pop. 3,647,000
Language: Hindi
Religion: Hinduism (83%)
Currency: Rupee = 100 Paise

THE UNION OF INDIA (Bharat) is the world's second biggest country in terms of population, and the seventh largest in area. It is also one of the poorest.

People and Culture The original inhabitants of India were Dravidians, a dark-skinned people whose descendants live in southern India. Fair-skinned Aryans invaded from the north about 1500 BC.

A series of independent states grew up in India. From time to time they were united in empires, notably the Maurya empire (321–184 BC); the Gupta dynasty (AD 320–535); and the Mogul (Mongol) empire (1526–1857), established by Moslem invaders.

Europeans began trading in India in 1498. From 1757 to 1858 the British East India Company was the main power in India. From then until 1947 the British government ruled most of India as an empire.

Up to then, British India included the lands that are now Pakistan and Bangladesh. India is predominantly Hindu, the others mainly Muslim. When independence was planned Hindus and Muslims could not agree on a way to share power, and partition was the only solution. It was marked by mass migrations and massacres.

Government In 1947 India became a dominion within the Commonwealth, but in 1950 it was declared a republic. It has a two-chamber parliament and a cabinet system of government. The country is divided into 22 states and nine territories. The states have their own legislatures and chief ministers, and control their own internal affairs. The federal government administers the territories, and has considerable powers over the states.

Languages Many different peoples live in India. They speak 15 major languages and 857 other languages and dialects. These differences are a great barrier to unity and communication. The official language is Hindi, which is the mother tongue of about 162 million Indians. English is also used by many Indians as a common language.

Indian languages fall into two main groups. Dravidian languages are spoken in southern India and include Kannada, Malayalam, Tamil and Telugu. Indo-European languages are spoken by the Aryan peoples of the north, and include Hindi and Urdu, which are similar, Assamese, Bengali, Gujarati, Kashmiri, Marathi, Oriya, Punjabi and Rajasthani.

Ways of Life India has four cities with more than 4 million people:

Calcutta (9,166,000)
Bombay (8,227,000)
Delhi (5,714,000)
Madras (4,277,000).

There are three with more than 2 million: Bangalore, Hyderabad and Ahmedabad; and five with over 1 million: Kanpur, Pune, Nagpur, Lucknow and Jaipur. But only 24 percent of the people live in urban areas.

Life expectancy is 52 years, an increase of nine years since 1960. But the population growth rate has caused concern to the government, and there have been efforts to reduce the birth rate.

Education Adult literacy is 36 percent, more than double the rate when India gained its independence. Primary education is free, and is compulsory in 16 of the states, but there are not enough schools and teachers to go round. There are 108 universities and 19 other institutions of similar standing.

The Land There are three major land regions. In the north are the Himalayas and their foothills. Parallel with the Himalayas are the northern plains, which extend from west to east for about 1,560 miles (2,510 km). They are about 200 miles (322 km) wide.

These plains were originally a marine gulf between India and the mainland of Asia. This gulf has been filled by deposits brought down by rivers, especially the Ganges and the Brahmaputra. The alluvial deposits reach a depth of about 6,500 feet (1,980 m). The soil is fertile, easy to irrigate and cultivate, and as a result the greatest proportion of the people live here.

Most of southern India is formed by the Deccan, a vast plateau sloping toward the east. At its western edge is a mountain range with an average height of 3,000 feet (910 m) above sea-level, called the Western Ghats. This range falls steeply on the west to a narrow coastal plain.

In the east lie the Eastern Ghats, a lower range of hills with a broader coastal plain. The Vindhya and Ajanta Hills form the northern boundary of the Deccan.

India's tallest mountain is Nanda Devi, 25,643 ft (7,816 m), in the Himalayas. The Ganges is not only India's most important waterway, but is also sacred to all Hindus.

Climate India's climate depends on the monsoons, seasonal winds bringing contrasting weather. The north-

Fishermen on a beach in India hauling in their nets.

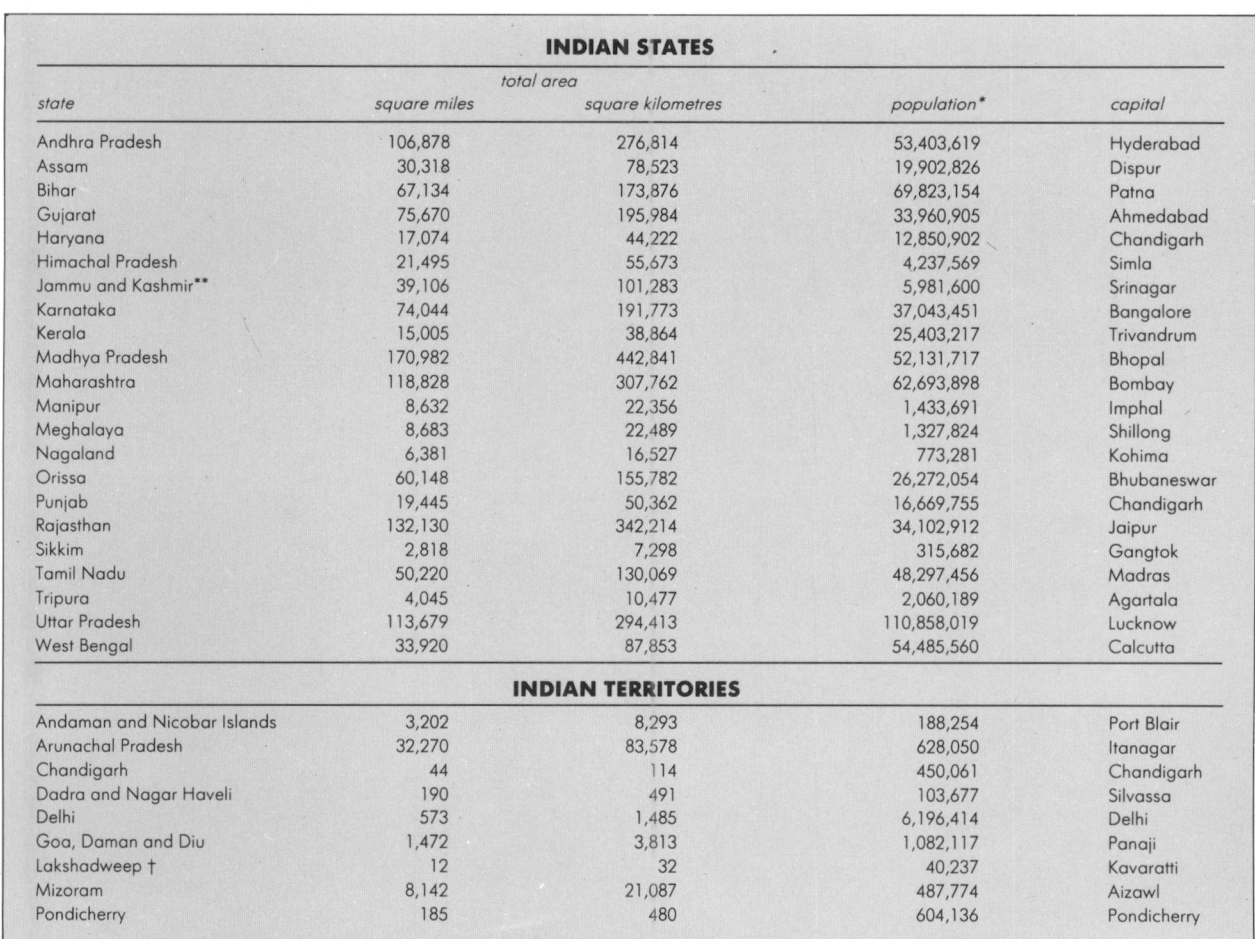

INDIAN STATES

state	total area square miles	square kilometres	population*	capital
Andhra Pradesh	106,878	276,814	53,403,619	Hyderabad
Assam	30,318	78,523	19,902,826	Dispur
Bihar	67,134	173,876	69,823,154	Patna
Gujarat	75,670	195,984	33,960,905	Ahmedabad
Haryana	17,074	44,222	12,850,902	Chandigarh
Himachal Pradesh	21,495	55,673	4,237,569	Simla
Jammu and Kashmir**	39,106	101,283	5,981,600	Srinagar
Karnataka	74,044	191,773	37,043,451	Bangalore
Kerala	15,005	38,864	25,403,217	Trivandrum
Madhya Pradesh	170,982	442,841	52,131,717	Bhopal
Maharashtra	118,828	307,762	62,693,898	Bombay
Manipur	8,632	22,356	1,433,691	Imphal
Meghalaya	8,683	22,489	1,327,824	Shillong
Nagaland	6,381	16,527	773,281	Kohima
Orissa	60,148	155,782	26,272,054	Bhubaneswar
Punjab	19,445	50,362	16,669,755	Chandigarh
Rajasthan	132,130	342,214	34,102,912	Jaipur
Sikkim	2,818	7,298	315,682	Gangtok
Tamil Nadu	50,220	130,069	48,297,456	Madras
Tripura	4,045	10,477	2,060,189	Agartala
Uttar Pradesh	113,679	294,413	110,858,019	Lucknow
West Bengal	33,920	87,853	54,485,560	Calcutta

INDIAN TERRITORIES

Andaman and Nicobar Islands	3,202	8,293	188,254	Port Blair
Arunachal Pradesh	32,270	83,578	628,050	Itanagar
Chandigarh	44	114	450,061	Chandigarh
Dadra and Nagar Haveli	190	491	103,677	Silvassa
Delhi	573	1,485	6,196,414	Delhi
Goa, Daman and Diu	1,472	3,813	1,082,117	Panaji
Lakshadweep †	12	32	40,237	Kavaratti
Mizoram	8,142	21,087	487,774	Aizawl
Pondicherry	185	480	604,136	Pondicherry

* 1981 census   **India and Pakistan dispute the ownership of Jammu and Kashmir   †Formerly the Laccadive, Minicoy, and Amindivi Islands

Washing in the street in Calcutta, India's largest city.

The buffalo is used as a domestic animal in India.

east monsoon brings dry weather from January to June; the southwest monsoon brings the wet season from June to September. Rainfall varies from less than 10 inches (254 mm) in the Thar Desert of the northwest to 450 inches (11,430 mm) in the northeast.
Vegetation Natural plant life has been greatly modified by centuries of human occupation. Teak and thorn forests, with bamboo, still exist in the Deccan, while deciduous and evergreen forests are found in the Ganges plain. Pine and deciduous forests clothe the Himalayas' lower slopes.
Wildlife The Asian lion, once common, now survives only in the Gir Wild Life Sanctuary in western India. Bengal tigers also survive in national parks. Panthers are more common, and there are wolves in the northwest. Other large animals include elephants, bears, rhinoceroses, jackals, dholes (wild dogs), deer and antelope.

There are more than 2,000 species of birds. Reptiles include three species of crocodiles and a large number of snakes and lizards.
Economy The per capita GNP is only $260, placing India among the bottom rank in the world wealth league.
Agriculture About 69 percent of the workforce is engaged in farming, and about half the land is used for agriculture. It provides 37 percent of the GDP. India leads the world in the production of millet, groundnuts, tea and jute; is second with rice, cane sugar, sorghum and hemp; third with tobacco and coconuts; fourth with wheat, rubber and cotton. But it must increase production by at least 2 percent a year to keep pace with its growing population, and even now many Indians do not have enough to eat.

India has 182 million cattle, more than any other country. But the Hindu religion forbids them to be killed for food, though milk and butter are produced. There are 71 million goats and 41 million sheep.
Minerals India has valuable mineral deposits, which are mostly underdeveloped. The major minerals mined are coal, iron ore, bauxite, chron-

ite, copper ore, manganese ore and gold. Some oil and natural gas are produced.
Manufacturing The proportion of the GDP produced by industry is 26 percent, employing 13 percent of the workforce. Manufacturing accounts for 18 percent of the GDP, and has increased considerably since independence. Heavy industries include the production of iron and steel, aluminium, petrochemicals and shipbuilding. Textile production employs the largest number of workers. Hydroelectric schemes provide 40 percent of electric power, and atomic power stations nearly 3 percent.
Communication India has about 37,900 miles (61,000 km) of railways, the world's fourth largest rail system. There are 994,000 miles (1,600,000 km) of roads, of which nearly 44 percent are metalled. Rivers and canals are also used for transport. There are four international airports and more than 80 other airfields.

NEPAL

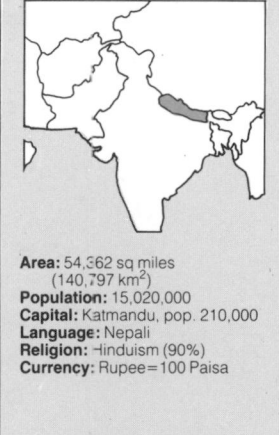

Area: 54,362 sq miles (140,797 km²)
Population: 15,020,000
Capital: Katmandu, pop. 210,000
Language: Nepali
Religion: Hinduism (90%)
Currency: Rupee = 100 Paisa

NEPAL is a constitutional monarchy in the Himalayas.
People and Culture Nepal became united as a kingdom

in 1768, under a prince from the town of Gurkha. It became an ally of Britain in 1816, and many Gurkha soldiers have since served in the British army. A new democratic constitution was introduced in 1962.

The people are of Indian or Tibetan origin. They include the mountain-climbing Sherpas. Only 6 percent live in urban areas. Their life expectancy is 45 years, and the adult literacy is 19 percent. The number of schools is increasing, and there is a university.
The Land Most of Nepal is covered by the Himalayas. Mt Everest, the world's highest mountain, stands on the Nepalese–Chinese border. In the foothills are valleys with cool, wet summers and dry, cold winters. Farther south is the Terai, a strip of tropical jungle and swamp, partly cleared for farming.
Economy Agriculture employs 93 percent of the workforce. Rice, maize, and wheat are the main crops, and people raise cattle, buffaloes, sheep and goats. The per capita GNP was $150 in 1981.

BHUTAN

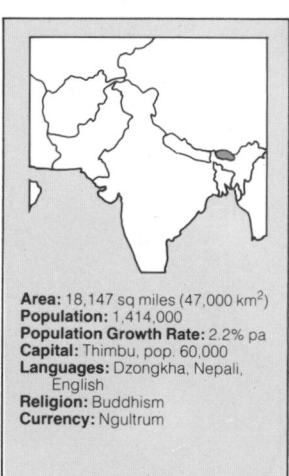

Area: 18,147 sq miles (47,000 km²)
Population: 1,414,000
Population Growth Rate: 2.2% pa
Capital: Thimbu, pop. 60,000
Languages: Dzongkha, Nepali, English
Religion: Buddhism
Currency: Ngultrum

BHUTAN is an independent monarchy in the Himalayas.
People and Culture About 66 percent of the people are descendants of Tibetans who settled in Bhutan in the ninth century AD, and 25 percent are of Nepalese origin. Britain controlled Bhutan's external affairs from 1865 to 1949, when India took over this role.

Only 4 percent of the people live in urban areas. They have a life expectancy of 43 years, and adult literacy is 44 percent.
The Land In the south are plains and river valleys with a hot humid climate. The rest is mountainous, partly forested, partly under permanent snow and ice cover.
Economy Bhutan receives an annual subsidy from India. About 11 percent of the land is cultivated, and 93 percent of the workforce is engaged in agriculture. There is little industry, but hydroelectric schemes have brought power to many villages. There are large undeveloped mineral resources. The per capita GNP was $80 in 1981.

South East Asia

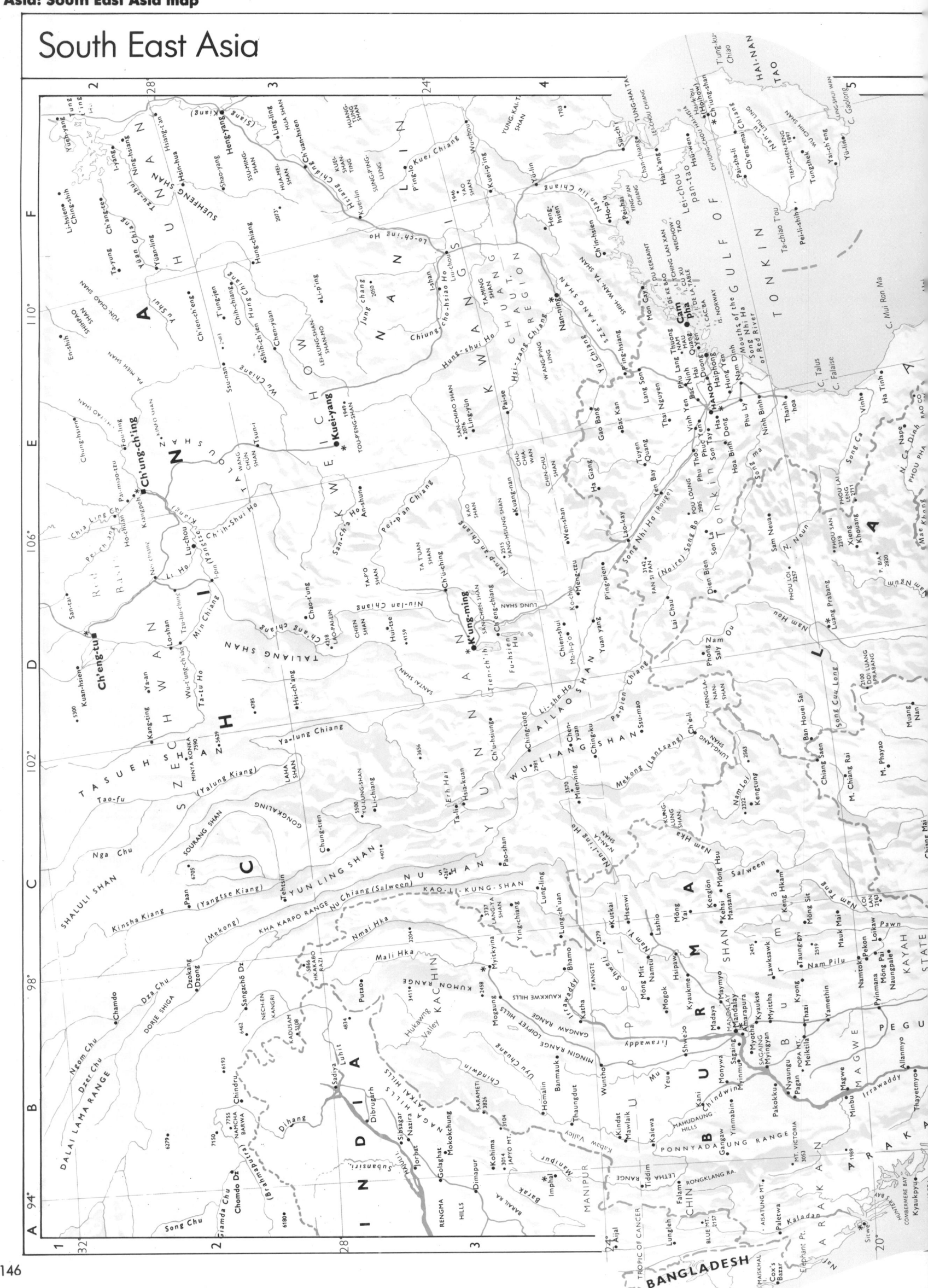

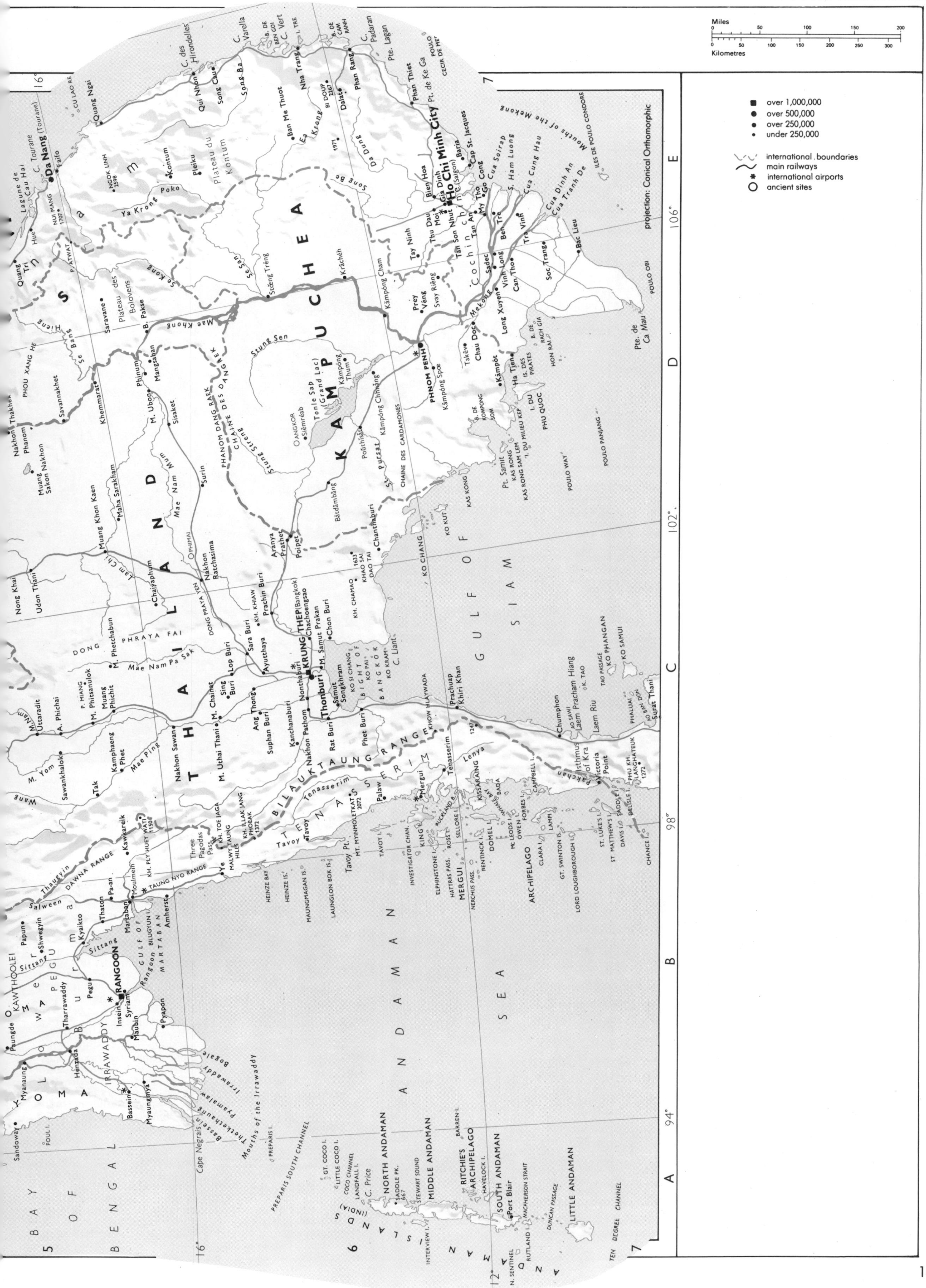

Miles
0   50   100   150   200

Kilometres
0   50   100   150   200   250   300

projection: Conical Orthomorphic

■ over 1,000,000
● over 500,000
● over 250,000
• under 250,000

〰 international boundaries
main railways
✳ international airports
○ ancient sites

BAY OF BENGAL

ANDAMAN SEA

GULF OF SIAM

GULF OF MARTABAN

THAILAND

KAMPUCHEA

BURMA

LAOS

NORTH ANDAMAN
MIDDLE ANDAMAN
SOUTH ANDAMAN
LITTLE ANDAMAN
ANDAMAN ISLANDS

Da Nang (Tourane)
Ho Chi Minh City (Saigon)
PHNOM PENH
KRUNG THEP (Bangkok)
Thonburi
RANGOON
Cochin China

Mouths of the Mekong
Mouths of the Irrawaddy
Tonle Sap (Grand Lac)

DAWNA RANGE
BILAUKTAUNG RANGE
TENASSERIM
MERGUI ARCHIPELAGO
Isthmus of Kra
Victoria Point

BURMA

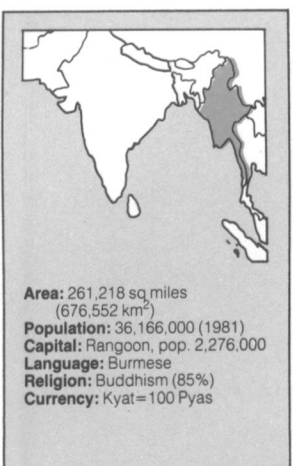

Area: 261,218 sq miles (676,552 km²)
Population: 36,166,000 (1981)
Capital: Rangoon, pop. 2,276,000
Language: Burmese
Religion: Buddhism (85%)
Currency: Kyat=100 Pyas

THE SOCIALIST REPUBLIC OF THE UNION OF BURMA is the most northerly country of southeast Asia.

People and Culture Burma was united by King Alaungpaya in 1755–57. The Burmese also conquered part of India, which brought them into conflict with the British. Britain took the Indian territories from Burma and between 1852 and 1886 captured the whole of Burma itself. Burma became a province of India.

In 1922 Burma received self-government, and in 1948 it became completely independent. In 1974 it adopted a new Constitution and became a one-party socialist country.

About 65 percent of the people are true Burmans, related to Chinese and Tibetans, and speaking Burmese. Large minority groups include the Karens, Shans, Mons, Arakanese, Chins and Kachins, and there are many isolated hill tribes. More than 100 languages are spoken in Burma. Only 28 percent of the people live in urban areas. The life expectancy is 54 years.

The Land The western part of Burma is occupied by the Chin Hills and the Arakan Yomas, mountain ranges which separate Burma from the Indian sub-continent. To the east lies the Shan Massif, a highland plateau. Between these two highland regions is the valley of the Irrawaddy, which ends in a huge delta. The Salween River flows through the eastern highland plateau.

Burma has a monsoon climate with distinct cool, hot, and rainy seasons. The coastal regions are always hot and humid, while in the mountains the temperature may drop to freezing point in winter. The average annual rainfall is 98 inches (2,489 mm).

Economy Burma is a farming country, with 67 percent of the people engaged in agriculture. It produces 47 percent of the GDP. Burma is the world's fifth largest producer of rice. Other major crops include sugar-cane and groundnuts. The forests yield teak.

Burma produces enough oil and natural gas for its own needs. Other important minerals include silver, zinc, copper, lead, nickel, antimony, coal, tin and iron ore.

Manufacturing is mostly on a small scale. Industry produces only 13 percent of the GDP. The per capita GNP was $190 in 1981.

LAOS

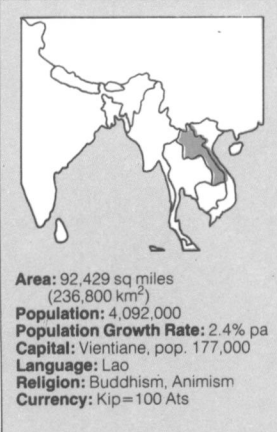

Area: 92,429 sq miles (236,800 km²)
Population: 4,092,000
Population Growth Rate: 2.4% pa
Capital: Vientiane, pop. 177,000
Language: Lao
Religion: Buddhism, Animism
Currency: Kip=100 Ats

THE LAO PEOPLE'S DEMOCRATIC REPUBLIC, commonly known as Laos, is the only landlocked country in southeast Asia.

People and Culture Laos was a group of small states until it was united in the fourteenth century. In the eighteenth century it split again into three kingdoms. In 1893 it came under French control. Japan conquered it in 1941 and ruled it until 1945. It became an independent monarchy in 1954.

Civil war ravaged Laos in the 1960s and 1970s. The Communist-led Pathet Lao movement won the war, and founded the People's Democratic Republic in 1975.

There are three ethnic groups of people. About 56 percent are Lao-Lum (Valley Lao); 34 percent are Lao Theung (mountain folk); and 9 percent are Lao-Sung (mountain people of the north). Only 14 percent live in urban areas. Life expectancy is only 43 years, and adult literacy is 44 percent.

The Land Laos lies between the Mekong River on the southeast and the Annamese Mountains to the northwest. Most of the people live in the fertile Mekong plains.

Laos has a tropical monsoon climate. It is cool and dry from November to February; hot and dry from March to May; and hot and wet from June to October. Rainfall ranges from 80 inches (2,032 mm) in the north to 120 inches (3,048 mm) in the south.

Economy Agriculture is the occupation of 75 percent of the people, with rice the chief product. Forests cover 50 percent of the country, and exploitation of their valuable timber is now under way. However, the rich mineral deposits are largely untouched and the country depends on aid from Vietnam and the Soviet Union. The per capita GNP stood at $80 in 1981.

Thailand townscapes show traditional and modern architecture.

The Burmese girls: the white marking on the face is powdered sandalwood, used as a protection against the sun.

VIETNAM

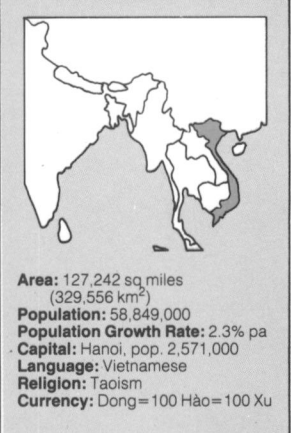

Area: 127,242 sq miles (329,556 km²)
Population: 58,849,000
Population Growth Rate: 2.3% pa
Capital: Hanoi, pop. 2,571,000
Language: Vietnamese
Religion: Taoism
Currency: Dong=100 Hào=100 Xu

THE SOCIALIST REPUBLIC OF VIETNAM lies on the eastern coast of southeast Asia.

People and Culture The French took control of Vietnam in 1883, and ruled it as part of the territory of French Indo-China, which included Laos and Kampuchea. The Japanese ruled Vietnam from 1940 to 1945.

After Japan's defeat in World War II, a Communist revolutionary group, the Vietminh, took control of northern Vietnam and set up a Democratic Republic there. A non-Communist government was set up in the south, with French support. In 1954 Vietnam was formally split into two countries, known as North and South Vietnam.

The Vietnam War began in 1957 when the Vietcong, a Communist guerrilla force, began to attack South Vietnam. American troops supported South Vietnam until 1973, when a ceasefire was signed. Two years later North Vietnam conquered the south and united the country under Communist rule.

The Vietnamese, also called Annamese, total about 84 percent of the people, and the rest are largely Thais and Khmers. Only 19 percent live in urban areas, about half of them in Hanoi and in Vietnam's largest city, Ho Chi Minh City (formerly Saigon,

THAILAND

Area: 198,457 sq miles
(514,000 km²)
Population: 51,523,000
Population Growth Rate: 2.3% pa
Capital: Bangkok, pop. 4,702,000
Language: Thai
Religion: Buddhism (94%)
Currency: Baht = 100 Stangs

MUANG THAI, or Thailand, the Land of the Free, is a constitutional monarchy in central southeast Asia.

People and Culture The Thai people moved into the area that is now Thailand more than 1,000 years ago. From 1782 to 1939 the country was called Siam. During World War II the country was occupied by the Japanese and became Japan's ally.

Though Thailand is a democracy, it has had two spells of military government since World War II.

About 85 percent of the people are Thais. Most of the rest are Chinese, and there are also many refugees from Vietnam, Laos and Kampuchea.

Life expectancy is 63 years. Adult literacy is 86 percent, and there is free and compulsory primary education. Only 15 percent of the people live in urban areas, but Thailand's cities are growing rapidly.

The Land The heart of Thailand is the plain of four major rivers, the Nan, Ping, Wang and Yom, which together form the Chao Phraya river system. There are thickly forested mountains in the northwest. Almost one-third of the country is occupied by the Khorat plateau in the northeast, where most of the people live. The south has rolling hills and thick jungles.

The climate is monsoonal, with three seasons: a mild winter, a hot dry spring, and a hot wet summer.

Economy Agriculture provides 24 percent of the GDP and employs 76 percent of the workforce. Rice is the main food and export crop. Sugarcane and maize are also important. Thailand ranks third in world rubber production. It is also third in the production of tin and tungsten ores. It is a major producer of teak and other timber. The per capita GNP in 1981 was $770.

KAMPUCHEA

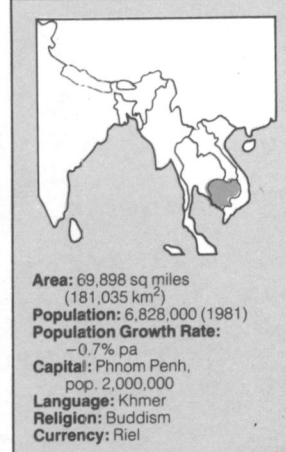

Area: 69,898 sq miles
(181,035 km²)
Population: 6,828,000 (1981)
Population Growth Rate:
−0.7% pa
Capital: Phnom Penh,
pop. 2,000,000
Language: Khmer
Religion: Buddism
Currency: Riel

DEMOCRATIC KAMPUCHEA is a republic formerly called the Khmer Republic, and before that Cambodia.

People and Culture The Khmer people had a great kingdom from the ninth to the fifteenth century, and part of it survived until 1863, when the French took over the area. After Japanese occupation during World War II, Cambodia, as it was then called, became independent in 1953.

It became involved in the Vietnamese War in 1969 when Communist fighters established bases there. From this a civil war developed between the Khmer Rouge Communists and non-Communist forces. By 1982 Vietnam controlled most of the country, opposed by a government formed by the Khmer Rouge and non-Communist groups.

The people of Kampuchea are 96 percent Khmers, with the rest Chinese. Life expectancy in 1981 was put at 43 years, but no accurate statistics for this war-torn country are available.

The Land Most of Kampuchea is a large, low-lying basin with the Tonle Sap (Great Lake) in its middle. The Tonle Sap River drains the lake into the great Mekong River, which flows through the country. At flood time the Tonle Sap river reverses its flow and fills the lake from the Mekong. Low mountains surround the basin, except along the coast. The climate is hot, and the average annual rainfall varies from 60 to 200 inches (1,524–5,080 mm).

Economy Agriculture is the mainstay of Kampuchea's economy, but the devastation of war has crippled it, and in the early 1980s the country relied on external food aid to survive. About half the country is covered by forests. There are valuable deposits of phosphates and iron ore.

pop. 3,500,000). Life expectancy is 63 years, and adult literacy is about 87 percent.

The Land Northern Vietnam is formed by the delta of the Red River, and southern Vietnam by the delta of the Mae Khong (Mekong) River. Between them is a narrow coastal strip backed by mountains, and there are mountains in the northwest.

Vietnam has a monsoon climate, with two main seasons, a wet, hot summer and a dry, cooler winter. The country has an average of more than 70 inches (1,778 mm) of rain a year.

Economy Agriculture occupies 71 percent of the workforce, and a series of five-year plans aims to make the country self-sufficient in food. Rice is the main crop.

Vietnam possesses deposits of coal, iron ore, bauxite, chromite, manganese and titanium, and some of the world's biggest reserves of phosphates.

Ten percent of the workforce is engaged in industry, 50 percent of which is smallscale. Food processing and textile manufacturing are the main large industries. The per capita GNP in 1978 was $170.

Collecting opium from poppies.

East Indies

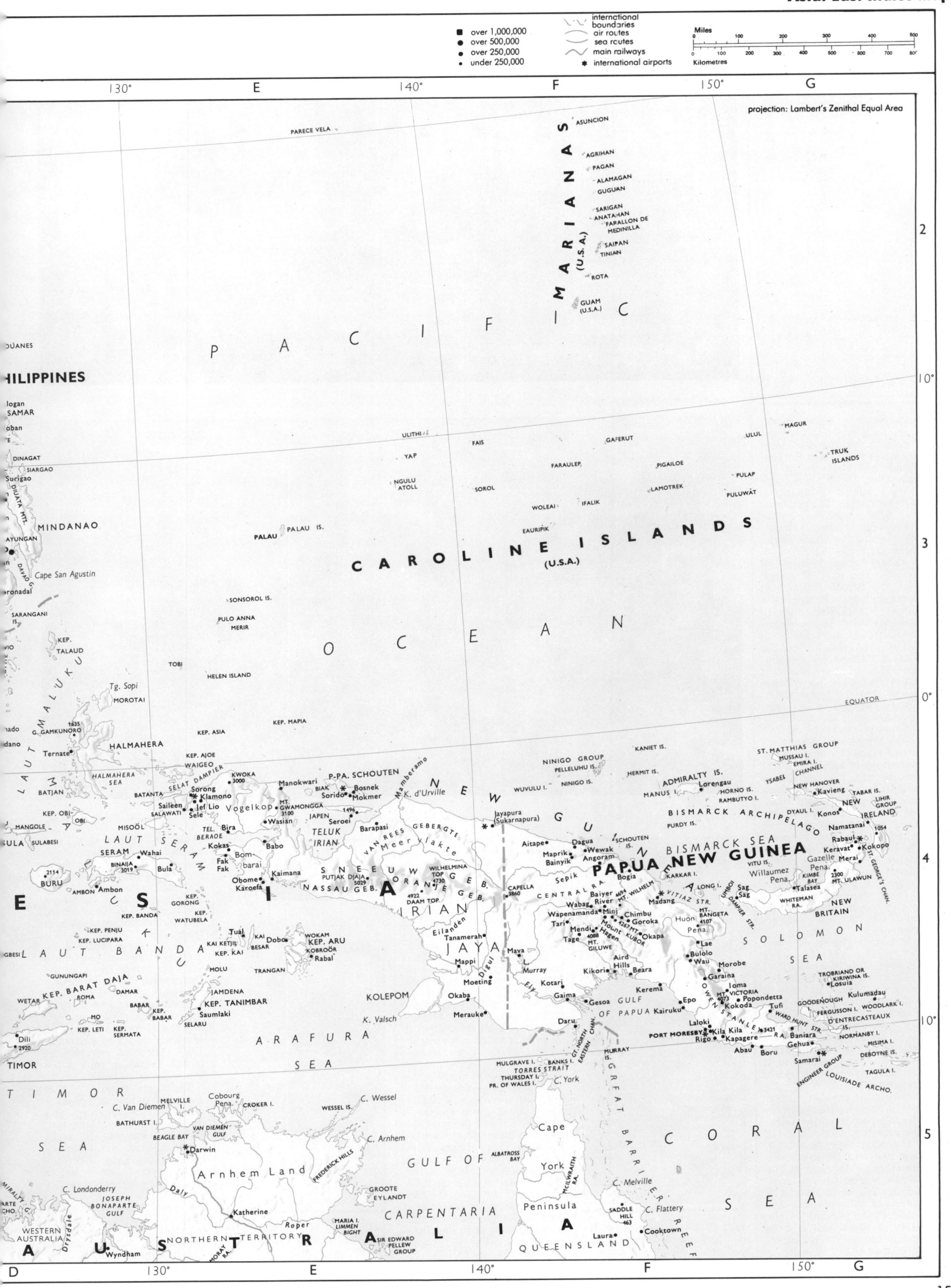

over 1,000,000
over 500,000
over 250,000
under 250,000

international
boundaries
air routes
sea routes
main railways
international airports

Miles
0   100   200   300   400   500

Kilometres
0 100 200 300 400 500 600 700 800

projection: Lambert's Zenithal Equal Area

130° E   140°   F   150°   G

2

PARECE VELA

M
A
R
I
A
N
A
S
(U.S.A.)

ASUNCION
AGRIHAN
PAGAN
ALAMAGAN
GUGUAN
SARIGAN
ANATA-HAN
FARALLON DE
MEDINILLA
SAIPAN
TINIAN
ROTA
GUAM
(U.S.A.)

P   A   C   I   F   I   C

PHILIPPINES   10°

logan
SAMAR
oban

DINAGAT
SIARGAO
Surigao
DIUATA MTS.

ULITHI
YAP
NGULU
ATOLL
SOROL
FAIS
FARAULEP
WOLEAI
EAURIPIK
IFALIK
GAFERUT
PIGAILOE
LAMOTREK
PULAP
PULUWAT
ULUL

MAGUR

TRUK
ISLANDS

MINDANAO
AYUNGAN
Cape San Agustin
DAVAO G
ronadal
SARANGANI
IS.

KEP.
TALAUD

PALAU
PALAU IS.

SONSOROL IS.

PULO ANNA
MERIR

C A R O L I N E   I S L A N D S
(U.S.A.)

3

O   C   E   A   N

TOBI
HELEN ISLAND

KEP.
TALAUD

LAUT MALUKU

Tg. Sopi
MOROTAI
nado
G. GAMKUNORO
1635
Ternate
HALMAHERA
HALMAHERA
SEA
BATJAN

KEP. ASIA

KEP. MAPIA

EQUATOR   0°

KEP. AJOE
WAIGEO
SELAT DAMPIER
KWOKA
3000
Sorong
Klamono
Saileen
SALAWATI
Jef Lio
Sele
MISOÖL

Manokwari
BIAK
Sorido
Mokmer
Bosnek
MT.
GWAMONGGA
3100
JAPEN
Seroei
Wasian
1496

P.-PA. SCHOUTEN

K. d'Urville

KANIET IS.
NINIGO GROUP
PELLELUHU IS.
WUVULU I.
HERMIT IS.
NINIGO IS.

ST. MATTHIAS GROUP
MUSSAU I.
EMIRA I.
YSABEL
CHANNEL

DYAUL I.
Konos

NEW
IRELAND
LIHIR
GROUP
Namatanai
1054

N   E   W

ADMIRALTY IS.
MANUS I.
Lorengau
HORNO IS.
RAMBUTYO I.
PURDY IS.

BISMARCK ARCHIPELAGO

Kavieng
NEW HANOVER
TABAR IS.

Rabaul

KEP. OBI
OBI
MANGOLE
SULA
SULABESI

Vogelkop
TEL.
BERAOE
Bira
Kokas
Fak
Fak
Bombarai
Babo

Jayapura
(Sukarnapura)

Aitape
Dagua
Maprik
Bainyik
Angoram
Sepik

Wewak

Bogia

KARKAR I.

Dampier

SCHOUTEN
IS.
VITU IS.
LONG I.

BISMARCK SEA

PAPUA NEW GUINEA

MUSSAU I.

Merai
St. GEORGE'S CHAN.

MT. ULAWUN
2300

4

LAUT SERAM
SERAM
Wahai
BINAIJA
3019
Bula
BURU
2114
AMBON
Ambon

VAN REES GEBERGTE
Meer Yakte
SNEEUW
PUTJAK DJAJA
5029
ORANJE GEB.
NASSAU GEB.
4922
WILHELMINA
TOP
4730
Meramo
Barapasi

TELUK
IRIAN

Kaimana
Obome
Karoefa

Wabag
Wapenamanda
Tari
Mendi
Tage
MT.
GILUWE

Bayer
Mini
Chimbu
Hagen
MOUNT
HAGEN
4068

CENTRAL R.A.
River
MT. WILHELM
4267

Madang
Goroka
Okapa

HUON
PENA.

MT.
BANGETA
4107

WILLAUMEZ
PENA.
KIMBE
BAY
Talasea

Keravat
Kokopo

WHITEMAN
RA.

NEW
BRITAIN

KEP. OBI
KEP. BANDA
KEP. GORONG
KEP. WATUBELA

I   R   I   A   N

N   E   W   G   U   I

Lae
Bulolo
Wau
Morobe
Garaina

SOLOMON

KEP. PENJU
KEP. LUCIPARA
gbesi
LAUT BANDA

Tual
KAI
DOBA
BESAR
KEI KETIL
KAI
WOKAM
KEP. ARU
KOBROOR
Rabal

Eilanden
Tanamerah
Maya
Murray

J   A   Y   A

Aird
Hills
Kikori
Beara

Ioma
Popondetta
Kokoda
Tufi

GOODENOUGH I.
Kulumadau

TROBRIAND OR
KIRIWINA IS.
Losuia

S   E   A

GUNUNGAPI
KEP. BARAT DAJA
WETAR
ROMA
DAMAR
BABAR
KEP.
BABAR
KEP. LETI
KEP.
SERMATA
MO
2920
Dili

MOLU
TRANGAN
JAMDENA
KEP. TANIMBAR
Saumlaki
SELARU

Mappi
Kotari
Gesoa

KOLEPOM

Okaba
Merauke

K. Valsch

Gaima
Daru

GULF
OF PAPUA

Kerema
Epo
Kairuku
Laloki
Rigo
PORT MORESBY
Kila Kila
Kapagere
Abau
Boru

MT.
VICTORIA
4073
OWEN
STANLEY
R.A.
3421

Gehua

FERGUSSON I.
D'ENTRECASTEAUX
NORMANBY I.

WOODLARK I.

MISIMA I.
DEBOYNE IS.
TAGULA I.

Samarai
ENGINEER GROUP
LOUISIADE ARCHO.

TIMOR

A   R   A   F   U   R   A

S   E   A

MULGRAVE I.
BANKS I.
TORRES STRAIT
THURSDAY I.
PR. OF WALES I.

GT. NORTH
EASTERN CHN.

C. York

MURRAY
IS.

G
R
E
A
T

B
A
R
R
I
E
R

R
E
E
F

C   O   R   A   L

TIMOR
SEA
MIRALTY G.
CHO.
C. Londonderry
JOSEPH
BONAPARTE
GULF
Darwin

MELVILLE
C. Van Diemen
Cobourg
Pena.
CROKER I.
BATHURST I.
VAN DIEMEN
GULF
BEAGLE BAY

C. Wessel
WESSEL IS.
C. Arnhem
FREDERICK HILLS

Arnhem Land

GROOTE
EYLANDT

Cape
York

ALBATROSS
BAY

GULF OF

Cape
York
Peninsula

C. Melville

SADDLE
HILL
463
C. Flattery

5

WESTERN
AUSTRALIA
Drysdale
Wyndham
Daly
Katherine
Roper

NORTHERN TERRITORY

MARIA I.
LIMMEN
BIGHT
SIR EDWARD
PELLEW
GROUP

MORAY R.A.

A   U   S   T   R   A   L   I   A

CARPENTARIA

McILWRAITH
RA.

Laura

QUEENSLAND
Cooktown

D   130°   E   140°   F   150°   G

151

MALAYSIA

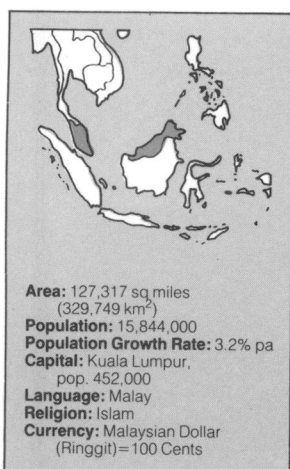

Area: 127,317 sq miles
(329,749 km²)
Population: 15,844,000
Population Growth Rate: 3.2% pa
Capital: Kuala Lumpur,
pop. 452,000
Language: Malay
Religion: Islam
Currency: Malaysian Dollar
(Ringgit) = 100 Cents

Tropical rain forests cover about 80 percent of Sabah, the Malaysian state in northern Borneo.

Skyscrapers dominate the skyline of Singapore, which is a densely populated country.

MALAYSIA is a constitutional monarchy consisting of the southern part of the Malay peninsula and part of Borneo. **People and Culture** The ancestors of the Malays came from southern China about 4,500 years ago. The peninsula was ruled successively by the Portuguese, Dutch and British, who formed the Straits Settlements colony in 1826.

Malaya became independent in 1957 and in 1963 joined with the British colonies of Sarawak, Sabah (British North Borneo) and Singapore to form Malaysia. Singapore left the federation in 1965.

The monarch, called the Yang di-Pertuan Agong (Supreme Head of State), is elected for a five-year term from among the nine Malay states' rulers. The four other states have appointed governors.

Some 47 percent of the people are Malays, 34 percent are of Chinese origin, and 9 percent come from the Indian subcontinent. Life expectancy is 65 years. Most children receive a primary education, but adult literacy is still only 60 percent. Only 30 percent of the people live in urban areas. **The Land** About 75 percent of peninsula Malaysia is mountainous and thickly forested. There are lowlands, often swampy, along the coasts and in the south. Sarawak and Sabah also have low, swampy coastlines.

Malaysia's climate is tropical, and rainfall varies between 100 inches (2,540 mm) in the peninsula to 150 inches (3,810 mm) in Sarawak and Sabah.
Economy Malaysia normally has a flourishing economy based on exports of rubber, palm oil and petroleum, but a world slackening of demand in the early 1980s hit at trade balances.

Agriculture employs 50 percent of the people and produces 23 percent of the GDP. The main food crop is rice.

The main minerals are tin, iron ore and titanium ore (ilmenite). Malaysia is the world's biggest tin producer. Industry as a whole absorbs 16 percent of the workforce and produces 36 percent of the GDP, of which half is from manufacturing. The per capita GNP stood at $1,840 in 1981.

SINGAPORE

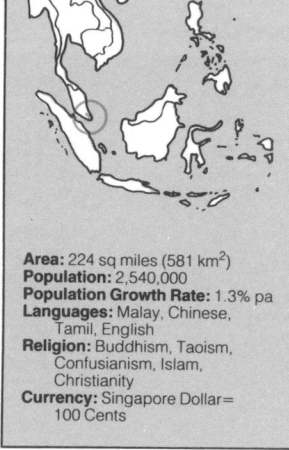

Area: 224 sq miles (581 km²)
Population: 2,540,000
Population Growth Rate: 1.3% pa
Languages: Malay, Chinese,
Tamil, English
Religion: Buddhism, Taoism,
Confusianism, Islam,
Christianity
Currency: Singapore Dollar =
100 Cents

THE REPUBLIC OF SINGAPORE is a tiny island country at the end of the Malay peninsula.

People and Culture Singapore, which means 'City of the Lions' was a tiny village in 1819 when the British founded a trading port there. It became part of the Straits Settlements, a colony which included Malaya. A major air and naval base, it was easily captured by the Japanese in World War II.

In 1963 Singapore became part of the Federation of Malaysia but left it in 1965.

About 75 percent of the people are of Chinese origin, and 15 percent are Malays. They have a life expectancy of 72 years, and the adult literacy rate is 83 percent. Because Singapore is a city-state, all the people live in urban areas. **The Land** Singapore Island is low, with some hills. The average annual temperature is 80°F (27°C), and the rainfall is about 95 inches (2,413 mm).
Economy There is little farmland, and agriculture produces only 1 percent of the GDP. The country has about 2,400 factories, the largest ship-repairing facilities in southeast Asia, and major oil refineries. It is a leading port and financial centre. The per capita GNP in 1981 was $5,240.

INDONESIA

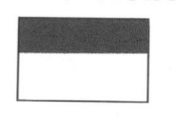

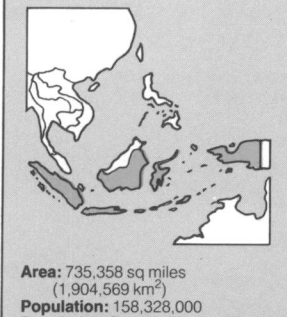

Area: 735,358 sq miles
(1,904,569 km²)
Population: 158,328,000
Population Growth Rate: 1.7% pa
Capital: Djakarta, pop. 4,576,000
Language: Bahasa Indonesian
Religion: Islam (80%)
Currency: Rupiah = 100 Sen

THE REPUBLIC OF INDONESIA has the world's fifth largest population.

People and Culture Most Indonesians are of Malay origin, and their ancestors arrived in the islands between 2500 and 500 BC, Hindu, Buddhist, and Islamic kingdoms succeeded one another over the centuries. The Dutch controlled the area from 1799.

The Japanese captured Indonesia in 1942 during World War II. After the war the Dutch were unable to reassert their authority, and Indonesia became independent in 1949. The country's first president, Sukarno, mismanaged the economy and was ousted in 1967. The new government ended tentative moves towards Communism.

There are 16 main ethnic groups in Indonesia, speaking more than 250 languages and dialects. The official language, Bahasa Indonesian, is taught in the schools. Adult literacy is 62 percent. Only 21 percent of the people live in urban areas. Their life expectancy is 54 years.
The Land Indonesia consists of more than 13,500 islands, but most of the people live on five of them – Java, Sumatra, Celebes, Indonesian Borneo

Rice is the major crop grown in the warm climate of the Philippines.

PHILIPPINES

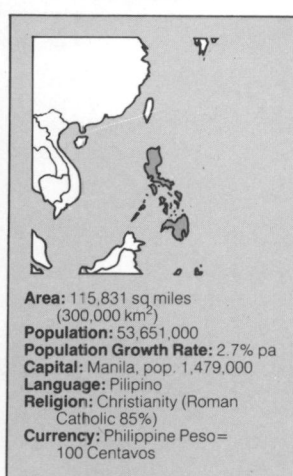

Area: 115,831 sq miles
(300,000 km²)
Population: 53,651,000
Population Growth Rate: 2.7% pa
Capital: Manila, pop. 1,479,000
Language: Pilipino
Religion: Christianity (Roman
Catholic 85%)
Currency: Philippine Peso=
100 Centavos

THE REPUBLIC OF THE PHILIP-PINES is the most northerly of the East Indies.

People and Culture The first Europeans to reach the Philippines were a Spanish expedition led by Ferdinand Magellan in 1521. The Spaniards ruled the islands until 1898, then lost them to the United States.

The Americans ruled the Philippines for more than 40 years, during which time the islands gradually gained self-government. They were captured by the Japanese in 1942, but freed in 1945. In 1946 the country gained independence.

In 1973, following rebellions by Communist guerrillas, the country was put under martial law but began a return to free elections in 1982.

The true Filipinos are of Malay origin and form most of the population. There are also people of Chinese and European origin, plus Negritos, pygmy people who were the first inhabitants, and a number of mountain tribes of Indonesian origin. Only 37 percent live in urban areas; they have a life expectancy of 63 years, and adult literacy is 75 percent. About 32 percent of the people speak English, and there are 77 other languages.

The Land The Philippines are a chain of about 7,000 islands, of which only 730 are inhabited. The largest and most important island is Luzon, where the capital is located. The other major islands are Mindanao, Samar, Negros, Palawan, Panay, Mindoro, Leyte, Cebu, Bohol and Masbate.

The islands are mountainous, and there are only a few lowlands. There are a great many volcanoes, some of which are active, and earth tremors are frequent. About 60 percent of the land is forested. The climate is warm and equable, and most of the country has two seasons, one wet and one dry. Rainfall averages between 50 and 180 inches (1,270–4,572 mm).

Economy Agriculture contributes 23 percent to the GDP, and employs 46 percent of the workforce. About 20 percent of the land is farmed. The main crops are rice, hemp, coconuts, cane sugar and maize.

Minerals exploited include gold and silver, plus copper, zinc, nickel and coal. Industry as a whole contributes 37 percent of the GDP, and 25 percent is represented by manufacturing. Factories are mostly small scale. The economy was badly hit by the recession in the early 1980s. The per capita GNP stood at $790 in 1981.

and Bali. Seven other islands have sizeable populations.

Java, Sumatra and Celebes are mountainous with volcanoes: 77 volcanoes have erupted in Indonesia in comparatively recent times. Large areas of the country are covered by tropical forests.

The climate is hot all the year, though cooler in the mountains. Monsoons bring two seasons: wet from December to March, and dry the rest of the year. Some islands have no dry season.

Economy Agriculture produces 24 percent of the GDP, and occupies 55 percent of the workforce. Indonesia ranks third in world production of rice and cassava and second in coconuts and rubber. Other important crops include maize, sweet potatoes and coffee.

There are large mineral resources, mostly undeveloped. Indonesia is the second biggest producer of tin. There is some natural gas, and the country is the biggest oil producer in Southeast Asia. Manufacturing includes shipbuilding, cement, chemicals and textiles. The per capita GNP was $530 in 1981.

BRUNEI

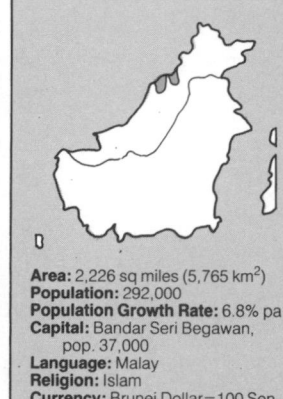

Area: 2,226 sq miles (5,765 km²)
Population: 292,000
Population Growth Rate: 6.8% pa
Capital: Bandar Seri Begawan,
pop. 37,000
Language: Malay
Religion: Islam
Currency: Brunei Dollar=100 Sen

THE SULTANATE OF BRUNEI is a small country in northwestern Borneo.

People and Culture A sultanate was established in Brunei in the fifteenth century and within a hundred years controlled almost all Borneo. By the nineteenth century the Sultan's power had declined and Brunei had become a pirates' haven. In 1888 it came under British protection which continued until it became independent in 1984. It is now ruled by a sultan and an elected legislative council. The people are 68 percent of Malay descent, and 25 percent of Chinese ancestry.

Malay is the official language, but English is also used. Education is free.

The Land Brunei is split in two by the Limbang River, whose banks are part of the Malaysia state of Sarawak. There is a narrow coastal plain, and the interior is rough and densely forested. The climate is hot and humid, with rainfall of between 100 and 200 inches (2,540–5,080 mm).

Economy Oil and natural gas are the basis of Brunei's economy. Rubber is the most important agricultural crop. The per capita GNP was $17,380 in 1981. This wealth pays for extensive social services.

An orang-utang sits on a feeding platform in a reserve in Sabah.

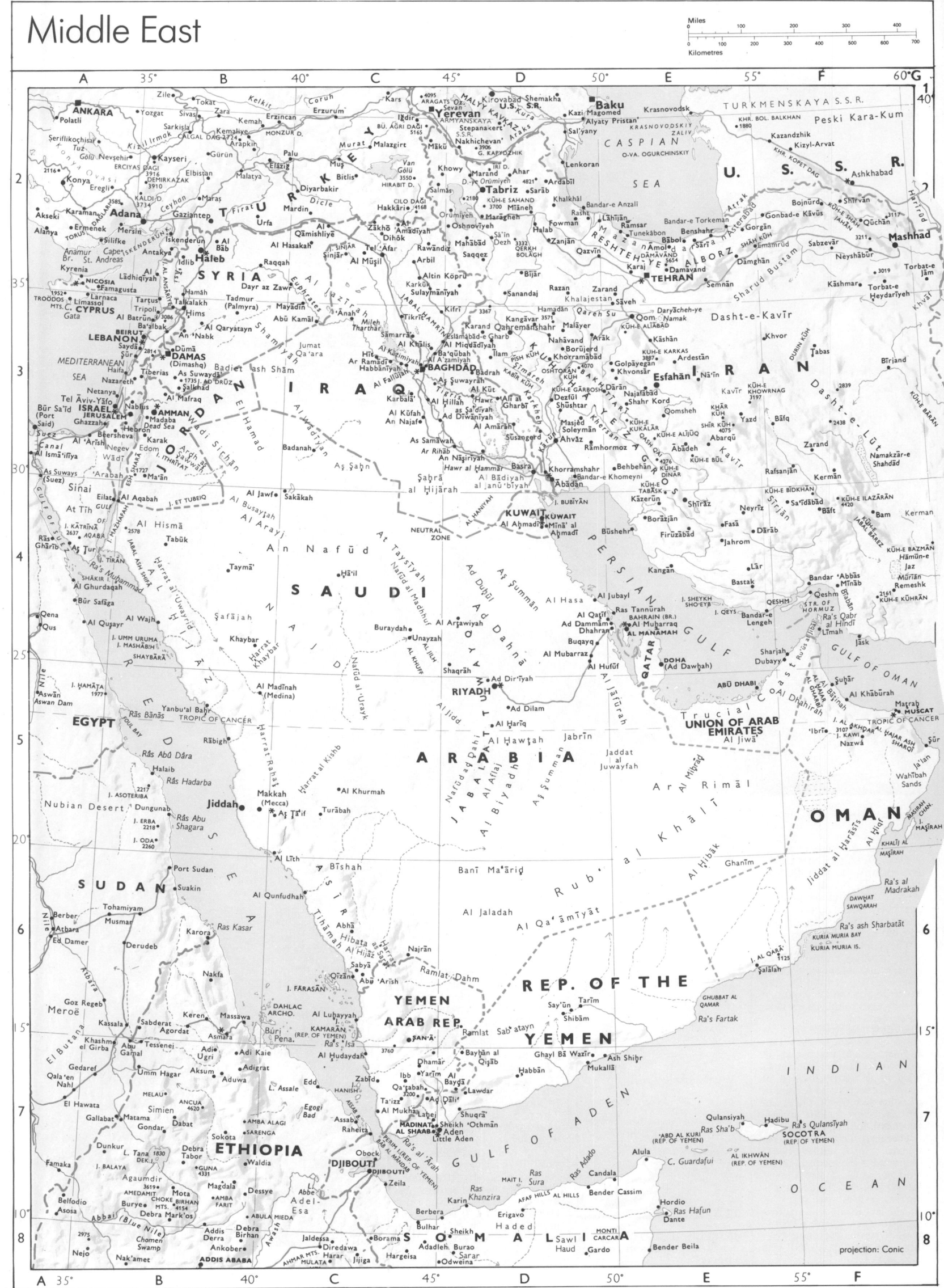

Middle East

Miles
0 100 200 300 400

Kilometres
0 100 200 300 400 500 600 700

projection: Conic

CYPRUS

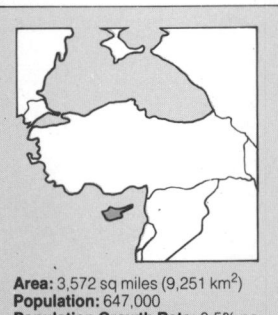

Area: 3,572 sq miles (9,251 km²)
Population: 647,000
Population Growth Rate: 0.5% pa
Capital: Nicosia, pop. 147,000
Languages: Greek; Turkish
Religion: Christianity (Greek Orthodox 80%), Islam
Currency: Cyprus Pound = 1,000 Mils

Cliff homes cut into sandstone at Göreme, in central Turkey.

TURKEY

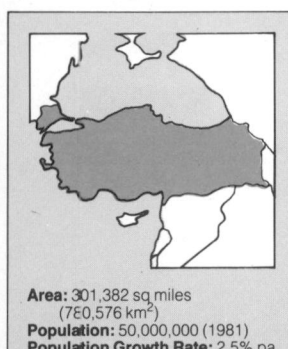

Area: 301,382 sq miles (780,576 km²)
Population: 50,000,000 (1981)
Population Growth Rate: 2.5% pa
Capital: Ankara, pop. 2,204,000
Language: Turkish
Religion: Islam (98%)
Currency: Turkish Lira = 100 Kurus

THE REPUBLIC OF CYPRUS is an island country in the eastern Mediterranean Sea.
People and Culture Greeks have lived in Cyprus since about 1200 BC. From 1571 to 1878 it was part of the Ottoman empire, and it then came under British rule.

From 1955 Greek Cypriots campaigned for *Enosis* (union with Greece), which was opposed by Turkish Cypriots. In 1960 Cyprus became independent. Clashes between Greek and Turks persisted, and in 1974 Turkey invaded Cyprus. The following year a Turkish Cypriot Federated State, covering about 40 per-cent of the island, was pro-claimed.

About 80 percent of the people are of Greek origin, and the rest of Turkish ances-try. The Greeks are Christians, the Turks Muslims. Each group forbids intermarriage with the other. Each group speaks its own language, but English is also widely used. Education is free and there is little adult illiteracy.

Each part of Cyprus is ad-ministered separately, but the United Nations regards the Turkish Cypriot government as illegal.
The Land Two mountain ranges dominate Cyprus, one parallel with the northern coast, the other in the south. Between them is a broad cen-tral plain, and coastal plains border the ranges. Cyprus has hot, dry summers, and cool, moist winters.
Economy Almost half the land is farmed, and about 21 percent of the workforce is engaged in agriculture. The principal cash crops include grapes, potatoes and citrus and other fruits. Wine is also exported. Asbes-tos, copper and iron ores are mined. Since partition it has been difficult to obtain reliable data on the economy, but in 1981 the per capita GNP was estimated at $3,740.

THE REPUBLIC OF TURKEY is the only Middle Eastern country that is partly in Europe. See the map on page 79.
People and Culture The Seljuk Turks came from central Asia to Anatolia (the Asian part of Turkey) in 1071. They founded an empire which by the six-teenth century included most of the Middle East, North Africa and southeastern Europe as far north as Hungary. This empire broke up after World War I, leaving Turkey with just the territory it has now. Turkey became a republic in 1922. It has a par-liamentary government.

All but 10 percent of the people are Turkish. The rest are Arabs, Armenians, Cauca-sians and Greeks. Adult liter-acy is 60 percent. The repub-lican government has done a lot to modernize the Turkish language and has changed from Arabic script to the Roman alphabet. Education is free and compulsory. Medical care is free, and life expect-ancy has risen from 61 years in 1960 to 62 years in 1981.
The Land Plains extend from European Turkey along the Black Sea coast. There are mountains to north and south, and a plateau region in central Anatolia. This plateau is more mountainous and barren in the east. The highest point is Ağri Daği (Mt Ararat) at 16,945 feet (5,165 m). The largest of several salty lakes is Lake Van with an area of 1,450 sq miles (3,755 km²).

Eastern Turkey has mild or hot summers and bitterly cold winters. The west and south have hot dry summers and mild wet winters.
Economy Agriculture employs 54 percent of the workforce, and the fertile soil usually produces enough food for some to be exported. Farming accounts for 23 percent of the GDP. Some 47 percent of the people live in urban areas, where 13 percent of the work-force is engaged in industry. Manufacturing accounts for some 23 percent of the GDP, and other industry a further 9 percent.

Mining is developing slowly, even though Turkey has rich mineral deposits. It is one of the world's leading producers of chromium. It produces about half its own oil needs. The per capita GNP was $1,540 in 1981.

A field of poppies growing in Turkey. The country used to be a major producer of opium from poppies, especially in the period immediately following World War II.

SYRIA

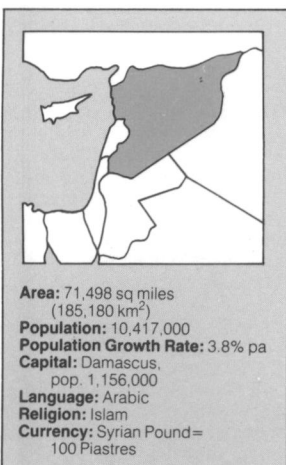

Area: 71,498 sq miles
(185,180 km²)
Population: 10,417,000
Population Growth Rate: 3.8% pa
Capital: Damascus,
pop. 1,156,000
Language: Arabic
Religion: Islam
Currency: Syrian Pound=
100 Piastres

THE SYRIAN ARAB REPUBLIC is a large country at the eastern end of the Mediterranean Sea.
People and Culture Syria has been fought over for many hundreds of years. Its coast was part of the old Phoenecian kingdom, and later part of the Greek and Roman empires. Arabs conquered it in the seventh century AD, and from 1516 to 1916 it was ruled by the Ottoman Turks. France ruled it until it became independent in 1941. In 1948, 1967, and 1973 it was involved in wars with Israel and from 1976 to 1958 it was in the Lebanese civil war.

Most Syrians are Arabs, and more than 85 percent follow the Muslim religion. Life expectancy is 65 years. Adult literacy is 58 percent, and primary education is compulsory.
The Land The narrow coastal plain and the mountains just behind it have a mild climate with up to 40 inches (1,000 mm) of rain. Inland is a broad plateau, much of it desert.
Economy One-third of the workforce is engaged in agriculture, which accounts for 19 percent of the GDP. Industry is developing steadily and now accounts for 31 percent of the GDP, employing 31 percent of the workforce. Mineral re-

sources include oil, natural gas and phosphates. Cotton and oil are among the chief exports. The per capita GNP was $1,570 in 1981.

IRAQ

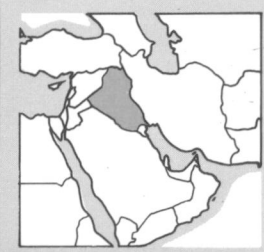

Area: 167,925 sq miles
(434,924 km²)
Population: 14,911,000
Population Growth Rate: 3.3% pa
Capital: Baghdad, pop. 2,969,000
Language: Arabic
Religion: Islam
Currency: Iraqui Dinar=1,000 Fils

THE REPUBLIC OF IRAQ lies at the head of the Persian Gulf.
People and Culture The land between Iraq's twin rivers, the Euphrates and the Tigris, saw some of the world's earliest civilizations. The land has been a centre of strife for thousands of years. It was conquered by the Arabs in AD 637, and by the Ottoman Turks in 1534. After World War I it became a British mandate until 1932. From 1921 to 1958 it was a monarchy. Then a military revolt made it a republic. After several years of revolutionary government a National Assembly was elected in 1980.

Arabic-speaking Arabs form 80 percent of the population, with Kurdish speakers forming 15 percent. In 1981 72 percent of the people lived in urban areas. Life expectancy is 57 years, an increase of 11 years since 1960.

Primary and secondary education is free, but adult literacy is low. Iraq has six universities.

The Land Between the Tigris and the Euphrates is a large alluvial plain. East of the Tigris is a highland zone in northern Iraq, with an annual rainfall of 16–24 inches (400–600 mm). The rest of the country is dry, and the south and west are desert. Agriculture is possible only with irrigation.
Economy Iraq's economy has been severely affected by the Gulf War, which began when Iraqi forces invaded Iran in 1980. At that time 42 percent of the workforce was engaged in agriculture and 26 percent in industry.

Agriculture has since suffered as men have been transferred to military service. When the war began Iraq produced most of the world's dates and exported wool and cotton.

Oil is the major export, but some oil installations were destroyed or damaged in the fighting.

IRAN

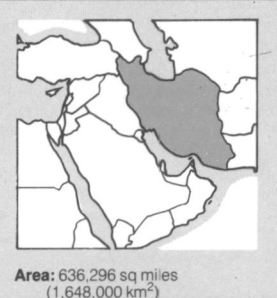

Area: 636,296 sq miles
(1,648,000 km²)
Population: 42,700,000
Population Growth Rate: 2.8% pa
Capital: Tehran, pop. 4,496,000
Language: Persian (Farsi)
Religion: Islam
Currency: Rial=100 Dinars

THE ISLAMIC REPUBLIC OF IRAN is the easternmost country of the Middle East.
People and Culture Persia, the old name for Iran, was the centre of a great empire in the sixth century BC. In the next

Carpet weavers in Iran learn their craft at an early age.

2,000 years the country was ruled by Parthians, Arabs, Seljuk Turks and Mongols. From the sixteenth century AD the country was a monarchy, ruled by a shah.

In 1979 the last shah was overthrown by a revolution headed by Ayatollah Ruhollah Khomeini, leader of the Shiite Muslims in Iran, and a republic was proclaimed. A new constitution gave the country a supreme religious leader (Khomeini for the rest of his life) above the elected president. The new regime's insistence on Islamic purity led to civil strife with minorities.

In 1980 a long-standing dispute with Iraq, which is ruled by Sunni Muslims, flared into the Gulf War, which proved costly to both sides.

Most of the people are Persian-speaking Iranians, but there are groups of Kurds, Lurs, Qashqai, and other non-Iranians. Life expectancy is 58 years, and adult literacy is 50 percent. Some 51 percent of the people live in urban areas.
The Land Iran has major mountain ranges in the west and north, covering about 25 percent of the land. The centre of the country is a high plateau, and includes two vast deserts. Lowlands border the Caspian Sea and the northern part of the Persian Gulf.

Iran has hot summers and very cold winters. Most of the land has about 12 inches (304 mm) of rain a year, with less in the deserts and more near the Caspian.
Economy Revolution and war have seriously disrupted Iran's economy. Industry, particularly oil, absorbs 34 percent of the workforce, but some major oil installations were destroyed in the early 1980s in the Gulf War. More than 39 percent of the workforce is engaged in agriculture, but only about 15 percent of the land can be cultivated, owing to lack of water. Wheat, rice and barley are the main crops. Many people raise sheep, goats, cattle, horses, camels and donkeys.

LEBANON

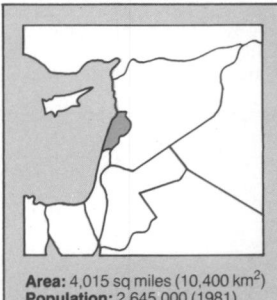

Area: 4,015 sq miles (10,400 km²)
Population: 2,645,000 (1981)
Population Growth Rate:
−0.5% pa
Capital: Beirut, pop. 700,000
Language: Arabic
Religion: Islam, Christianity
(Maronite)
Currency: Lebanese Pound=
100 Piastres

THE REPUBLIC OF LEBANON is at the eastern end of the Mediterranean Sea.
People and Culture Lebanon was the centre of the ancient Phoenician empire. Later it came under Roman rule, when Christianity was introduced, and was in turn dominated by the Arabs and the Turks. It was under temporary French rule from 1920 to 1946, when it became independent.

Some 90 percent of the people are Arabs, and there are minorities of many other peoples. About half the inhabitants are Muslims, and slightly less are Christians. Most of the Christians are Maronites, and the majority of the Muslims are in the Sunni sect.

Religious divisions are a fundamental part of Lebanese history and life. On independence, its political leaders agreed that the president should always be a Maronite Christian, the prime minister a Sunni Muslim, and the

The entrance to the 'Street Called Straight' in Damascus where the Apostle Paul lodged.

speaker of parliament a Shiite Muslim. Political power was to be divided among religious groups according to their numbers.

Civil war broke out in 1958 and again in 1975 when Muslims demanded more power. The situation was exacerbated when the Palestine Liberation Organization (PLO) made Lebanon its base for war against Israel. Syrian and Israeli forces both entered Lebanon to try to keep order. Since 1975 fighting among the rival factions – Christians, Muslims, Syrians, Israelis, Druses and others – has been almost continuous, broken only by sporadic truces. The PLO forces left in 1982.

Adult literacy is high, and life expectancy is 66 years. About 77 percent of the people live in urban areas. However, all statistics are unreliable because of the continued fighting.

The Land A narrow coastal plain lies along the Mediterranean. Two mountain ridges run from north to south, separated by a high plateau. The country has hot dry summers and mild moist winters. Forests cover some of the mountains.

Economy War has played havoc with Lebanon's economy. Beirut used to be the banking centre of the Middle East, but most financial operations have moved elsewhere. Industry and trade have both suffered. Agriculture is of major importance, and employs some 11 percent of the workforce.

ISRAEL

Area: 8,019 sq miles (20,770 km²)
Population: 4,233,000
Population Growth Rate: 2.3% pa
Capital: Jerusalem, pop. 398,000
Languages: Hebrew, Arabic
Religion: Judaism
Currency: Shekel = 100 New Agora

THE STATE OF ISRAEL, at the eastern end of the Mediterranean Sea, covers most of the historical area of Palestine.

People and Culture Palestine was the ancient homeland of the Jews until they were dispersed by the Romans in the first century AD. European Jews began to settle in Palestine in the nineteenth century, and the modern state of Israel was created in 1948 as a new Jewish homeland.

The new country was involved in four wars with its Arab neighbours. The first was in 1948, the second in 1956, the third in 1967, and the fourth in 1973. As a result of these wars Israel occupied

The Mosque at Qom, Iran, is a centre of pilgrimage for members of the Shiite sect of Islam.

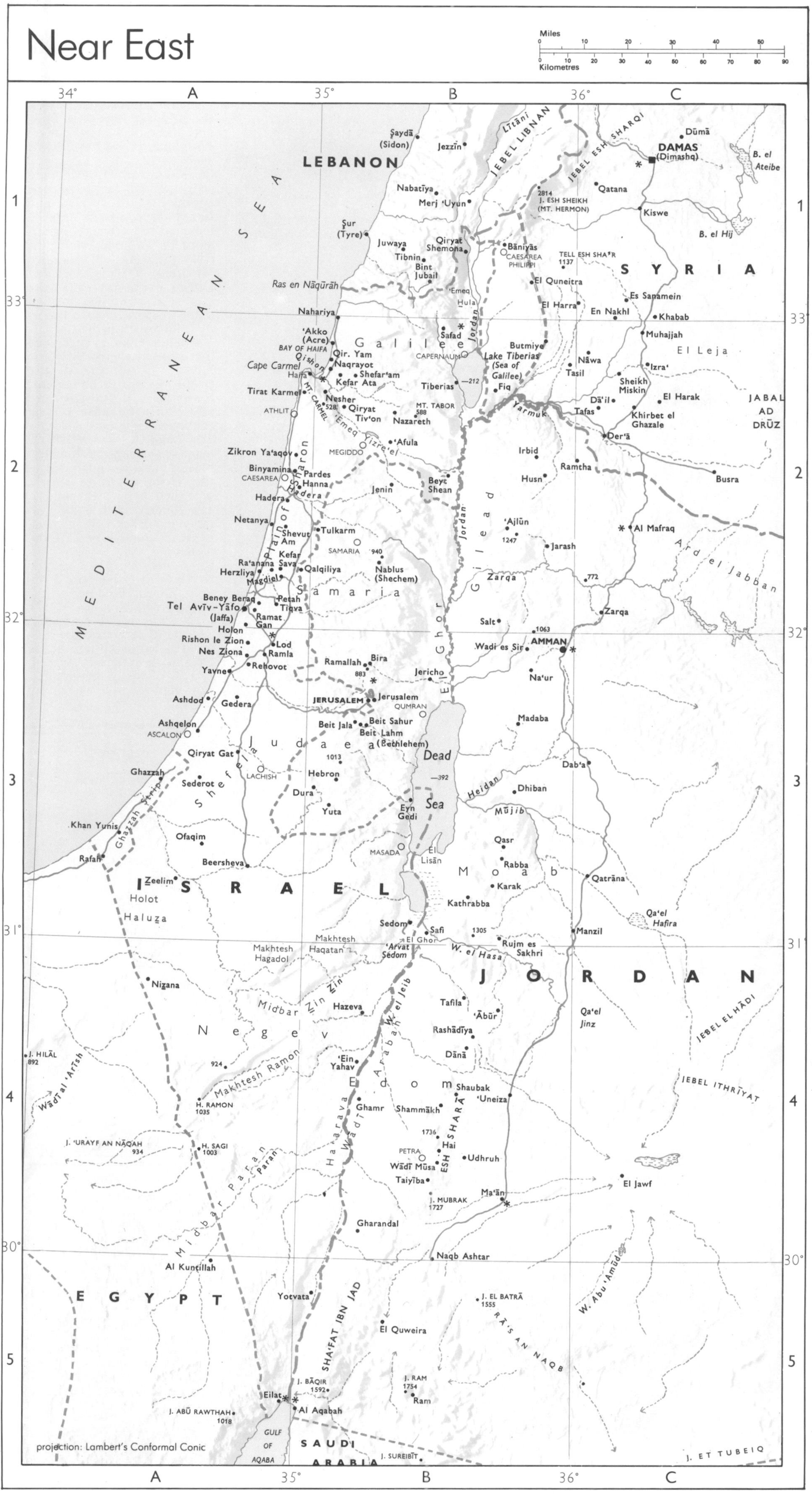

Near East

Miles
0 | 10 | 20 | 30 | 40 | 50
Kilometres
0 | 10 | 20 | 30 | 40 | 50 | 60 | 70 | 80 | 90

LEBANON

Şaydā (Sidon)
Jezzîn
Nabatîya
Merj 'Uyun
Şur (Tyre)
Juwaya
Tibnin
Qiryat Shemona
Bint Jubail

Lîtāni
JEBEL LIBNAN

Dūmā
DAMAS (Dimashq)
B. el Ateibe
Qatana

2814
J. ESH SHEIKH
(MT. HERMON)
JEBEL ESH SHARQI

Kiswe
B. el Hij

Ras en Nāqūrāh

Nahariya

SYRIA

'Emeq Hula
El Quneitra
El Harra
En Nakhl
Es Sanamein
Khabab

'Akko (Acre)
BAY OF HAIFA
Qir. Yam
Naqrayot
Shefar'am
Kefar Ata
Tiberias
Safad
CAPERNAUM
BāNIYĀS
CAESAREA PHILIPPI
1137
TELL ESH SHA'R

Galilee

Butmiye
Lake Tiberias
(Sea of Galilee)
Fiq
−212
Nāwa
Tasil
Muhajjah
Izra'
Sheikh Miskin
El Harak
El Leja
JABAL AD DRŪZ

Cape Carmel
Haifa
Nesher
528
Qiryat Tiv'on
Nazareth
ATHLIT
MT. CARMEL
Tirat Karmel
MT. TABOR
588

Dā'il
Tafas
Khirbet el Ghazale
Der'a

Zikron Ya'aqov
Binyamina
CAESAREA
Pardes Hanna
Hadera
MEGIDDO
Emeq Izre'el
'Afula
Jenin
Beyt Shean
Irbid
Husn
Ramtha
Busra

Netanya
Shevut Am
Kefar Sava
Ra'anana
Herzliya
Magdiel
Tulkarm
Qalqiliya
Nablus (Shechem)
940
Samaria
'Ajlūn
1247
Jarash
Al Mafraq
Ard el Jabban

Beney Beraq
Tel Avîv-Yāfo (Jaffa)
Ramat Gan
Petah Tiqva
Holon
Rishon le Zion
Nes Ziona
Ramla
Lod
Yavne
Rehovot
Zarqa
772
Zarqa
Salt
Wadi es Sir
AMMAN
Na'ur

Ashdod
Gedera
Ramallah
Bira
883
Jericho
JERUSALEM
Jerusalem
QUMRAN
Madaba

Ashqelon
ASCALON
Beit Jala
Beit Sahur
Beit Lahm (Bethlehem)
1013
Qiryat Gat
Shefela
LACHISH
Hebron
Dura
Yuta
Eyn Gedi
Dead Sea
−392
Dab'a
Dhiban
Heidan
Mūjib

Ghazzah
Sederot
Ofaqim
Khan Yunis
Rafah
Judaea
Qasr
Rabba
Qatrāna

Beersheva
Zeelim
Holot
Haluza
MASADA
El Lisān
Karak
Kathrabba
Qa'el Hafira

ISRAEL
Makhtesh Haqatan
Sedom
Safi
El Ghor
1305
Rujm es Sakhri
Manzil

Makhtesh Hagadol
'Arvat Sedom
W. el Hasa
Moab
Ghazzah Strip

Nizzana
Midbar Zin
Hazeva
Tafila
'Abūr
Qa'el Jinz
JORDAN

Negev
Rashādīya
Dāna
JEBEL EL HĀDI

924
Makhtesh Ramon
'Ein Yahav
'Arava
Edom
Shaubak
'Uneiza
JEBEL ITHRĪYAT

J. HILĀL 892
Wādī el Arîsh
H. RAMON 1035
Ghamr
Shammākh
1736
Hai
PETRA
Wādī Mūsa
Taiyîba
Udhruh
Ma'ān

J. 'URAYF AN NĀQAH 934
H. SAGI 1003
Midbar Paran
Paran
1727
J. MUBRAK

Gharandal
El Jawf

Naqb Ashtar

Al Kuntillah
Yotvata
J. EL BATRĀ 1555
W. Abu 'Amūd
RĀ'S AN NAQB

EGYPT
El Quweira
SHA'FAT IBN JAD

J. BĀQIR 1592
J. RAM 1754
Ram

Eilat
Al Aqabah
J. ABŪ RAWTHAH 1018
GULF OF AQABA
SAUDI ARABIA
J. SUREIBIT
J. ET TUBEIQ

projection: Lambert's Conformal Conic

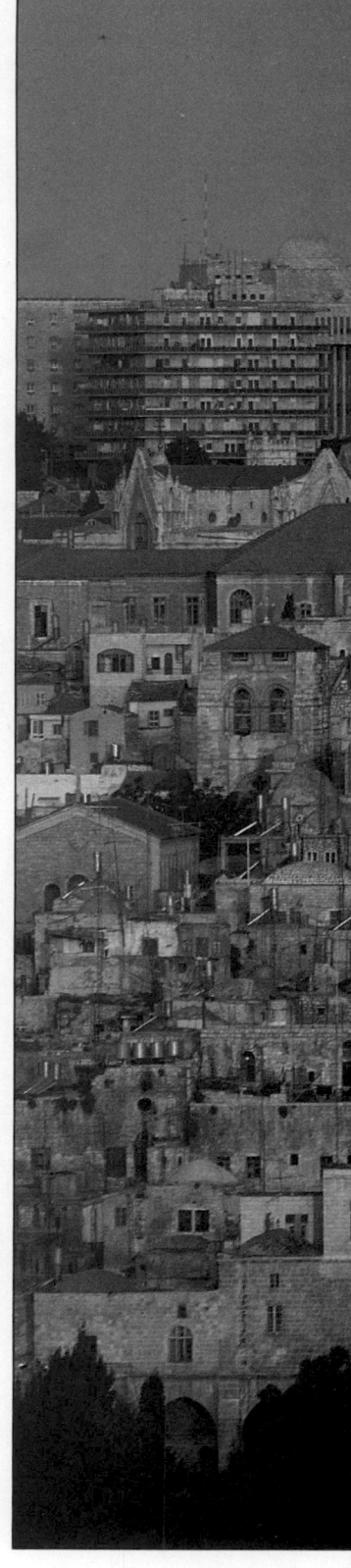

Jordanian land west of the River Jordan, the Gaza strip held by Egypt, and the Golan Heights which were Syrian. For 15 years it also held Sinai but handed it back to Egypt in 1982 under the terms of a peace treaty (1979).

About 85 percent of the people are Jews, half of whom were born in Israel. The other 15 percent are Arabs. For this reason, both Hebrew and Arabic are official languages. Although the Jewish religion is paramount, religious freedom is guaranteed under the Constitution.

Education is free until the age of 18, and compulsory until 16. Life expectancy is 73 years, and 89 percent of the people live in urban areas.

The Land Most of the people live in the coastal plain, where the second largest city, Tel-

Jerusalem's Old City is dominated by the Hilton Hotel.

An Israeli soldier pauses at the Wailing Wall in Jerusalem.

Avîv–Yāfo (Tel-Aviv–Jaffa), stands (pop. 334,900 in 1981). This area contains fertile soil. In the northeast are the highlands of Galilee and the disputed Golan Heights. Jerusalem and the disputed West Bank territory are hilly. To the south is the dry triangle of the Negev, partly desert.

To the east lies the valley of the River Jordan, which is part of the great Rift Valley which includes the Red Sea and the Rift Valley of eastern Africa. The Dead Sea lies in the valley, most of which is well below sea-level.

The climate is hot in summer and mild in winter. The north has more rain than the south, and sometimes snow.

Economy Israel's economy has grown rapidly in spite of poor natural resources, though the world financial crisis of the 1970s and 1980s, plus the costs of defence, plunged the country deeply into debt.

Agriculture provides a large part of the nation's food. Irrigation, using water from Lake Tiberias (Sea of Galilee), is opening up the Negev, and has tripled Israel's farmland since 1948.

Mineral resources are few, but salts from the Dead Sea include potash and bromine. Phosphates, copper, petroleum and natural gas are also produced. Israel's industry employs 36 percent of the workforce and produces 36 percent of the GDP. There is a wide range of manufacturing and processing, including diamond-cutting. Major exports include textiles, foodstuffs and chemicals. Military industries are highly advanced. The 1981 per capita GNP was \$5,160.

JORDAN

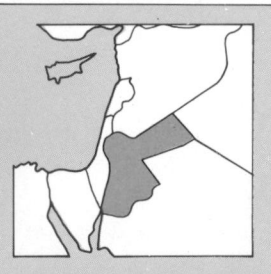

Area: 37,738 sq miles (97,740 km²)
Population: 3,751,000
Population Growth Rate: 3.7% pa
Capital: Amman, pop. 649,000
Language: Arabic
Religion: Islam
Currency: Jordanian Dinar = 1,000 Fils

THE HASHEMITE KINGDOM OF JORDAN lies northwest of the Arabian Peninsula.

People and Culture The land now called Jordan was successively under Greek, Roman, Arab and Turkish rule. After World War I, the Amirate of Transjordan was established east of the River Jordan under a British mandate, which also covered the area west of the river historically known as Palestine. The mandate ended after World War II and the Amirate, under its founder Abdullah, became the Hashe-

mite Kingdom of Jordan in 1946. Abdullah was assassinated in 1951 to be succeeded by his sons – first, briefly, by Talal, then in 1952 by Hussein, the present ruler.

In 1948 Palestine was split into Jewish and Arab states. War followed, after which Transjordan held land on the west bank of the Jordan, and half of Jerusalem. It changed its name to Jordan in 1950. In the Six-Day War of 1967, Israel captured the West Bank region and the rest of Jerusalem. Jordan fought Israel again in 1973.

About 90 percent of the people are Muslim Arabs, including some nomadic Bedouin. In 1981 57 percent lived in urban areas. Life expectancy stood at 62 years, a big increase from 47 years in 1960. Adult literacy is 70 percent. There are large numbers of Palestinian refugees in Jordan.

The Land The West Bank, now held by Israel, is a fertile upland. The Jordan River valley is a deep rift, largely below sea-level. To the east lies the Transjordan plateau, covered with forest or brush, and east of that is a wide desert. Jordan has an outlet to the Red Sea at Al Aqabah. The climate is hot. The western part of the country receives up to 30 inches (762 mm) of rain, but the east has less than 4 inches (102 mm).

Economy Agriculture is the most important part of the economy as far as exports are concerned, though it produces only 8 percent of the GDP and employs 20 percent of the

workforce. Mining and processing potash is the most important industry. The per capita GNP stood at \$1,620 in 1981.

SAUDI ARABIA

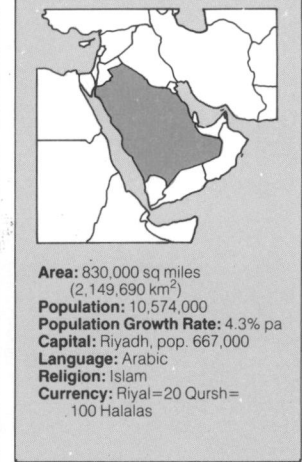

Area: 830,000 sq miles (2,149,690 km²)
Population: 10,574,000
Population Growth Rate: 4.3% pa
Capital: Riyadh, pop. 667,000
Language: Arabic
Religion: Islam
Currency: Riyal = 20 Qursh = 100 Halalas

THE KINGDOM OF SAUDI ARABIA occupies 80 percent of the Arabian Peninsula.

People and Culture Saudi Arabia is the home of Islam, and was the centre of the first Arab empire. It was under Turkish rule from 1517. The present country was founded by the desert warrior Abdul Aziz ibn Saud in 1902, and reached its present form and name in 1932. Most of the people are Muslim Arabs.

Wealth from oil has been used to improve the quality of life. Life expectancy rose from 43 years in 1960 to 55 years in 1981. Adult literacy is only 25 percent, but free education is being expanded to improve this condition. Today 68 percent of the people live in urban areas.

The Land Saudi Arabia has a narrow coastal plain on the Red Sea, rising quickly to a mountain range. The land then slopes down to the north and east. Much of the interior is desert, with large oases, one of which contains Riyadh. In the south is the Rub' al Khāli, the Empty Quarter, a vast sandy desert. In the eastern coastal plain there are tracts of sand and gravel, under which lie the world's largest known petroleum deposits.

Most of the country is hot and dry, except for the coastal plains which are hot and humid. The southwest receives 12–20 inches (305–533 mm) of rain a year, the rest of the country much less.

Economy Saudi Arabia is the world's leading exporter of oil. The oil industry employs less than half the industrial workers, who in turn represent only 14 percent of the total workforce. But it is responsible for most of the 78 percent of the GDP which industry produces.

By contrast agriculture employs 61 percent of the workforce and produces only 1 percent of the GDP. The country imports most of its food. New industries are being encouraged in a series of five-year plans. The per capita GNP stood at \$12,600 in 1981.

YEMEN ARAB REP

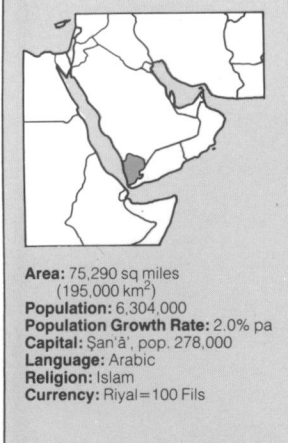

Area: 75,290 sq miles (195,000 km²)
Population: 6,304,000
Population Growth Rate: 2.0% pa
Capital: Şan'ā', pop. 278,000
Language: Arabic
Religion: Islam
Currency: Riyal=100 Fils

THE YEMEN ARAB REPUBLIC is located on the Red Sea in the southwestern Arabian Peninsula.

People and Culture The country was famous in ancient times as the kingdom of Sheba (950–115 BC). It was under nominal Ottoman control from 1517 to 1918, when it became an independent monarchy. The monarchy was overthrown in 1962 and a republic was proclaimed. After a war with the People's Democratic Republic of Yemen the two countries agreed to unite, but no date was set for unification.

Most of the people are Arab tribesmen, 89 percent of whom live in rural areas. Life expectancy is 43 years, and adult literacy is only 21 percent.

The Land A hot and humid plain, the Tihāmah, borders the Red Sea, but its rainfall is only 5 inches (130 mm). Inland is a highland region of fertile valleys and plateaux,

with up to 35 inches (900 mm) of rain a year.

Economy Agriculture employs 75 percent of the workforce and produces 28 percent of the GDP. Crops include the popular Mocha coffee and cotton, which are exported, cereals, and *qat*, a narcotic. There are no minerals except salt. The per capita GNP was $460 in 1981.

YEMEN PDR

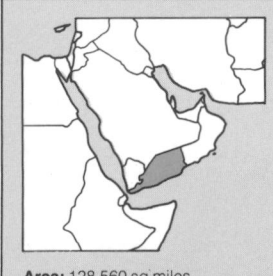

Area: 128,560 sq miles (332,968 km²)
Population: 2,225,000 (1981)
Population Growth Rate: 3.1% pa
Capital: Aden, pop. 270,000
Language: Arabic
Religion: Islam
Currency: Southern Yemen Dollar=1,000 Fils

THE PEOPLE'S DEMOCRATIC REPUBLIC OF YEMEN occupies the southwestern corner of the Arabian Peninsula.

People and Culture Aden was a British colony from 1839, and became a refuelling port for shipping using the Suez Canal. The rest of the land consisted of tribal sultanates. The country became independent in 1967 after a civil war between rival factions.

All but 10 percent of the people are Arabs. Only 37 percent of them live in urban areas, life expectancy is only 46 years, and adult literacy is 40 percent.

The Land Most of the land is mountainous, behind a narrow, sandy coastal plain. The Hadhramaut valley in the mountains is a major farming region. The northeast is mostly desert. The climate is hot, with rainfall of 30 inches (760 mm) in the Hadhramaut, 5 inches (130 mm) on the coast, and almost none elsewhere.

Economy Aden's oil refinery and transit port are the mainstay of the economy. Agriculture employs 45 percent of the workforce, but is mostly at subsistence level. There is little industry. The per capita GNP was $460 in 1981.

KUWAIT

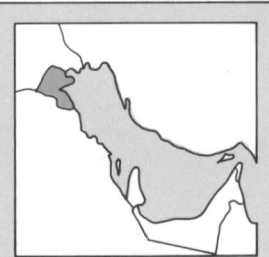

Area: 6,880 sq miles (17,818 km²)
Population: 1,763,000
Population Growth Rate: 6.4% pa
Capital: Kuwait, pop. 775,000
Language: Arabic
Religion: Islam
Currency: Kuwait Dollar=1,000 Fils

THE STATE OF KUWAIT is a small country in the northwestern corner of the Persian Gulf.

People and Culture Kuwait has been an important port for

Twin water-towers dominate the skyline in Kuwait City.

centuries. Since the 1750s it has been ruled by the al-Sabah family as emirs. From 1899 to 1961 a treaty made Britain responsible for Kuwait's external affairs.

The population stood at 75,000 in 1937. It has soared since World War II as a result of the discovery of oil. The increase is due to immigration, and almost 60 percent of the people are immigrants. Some 89 percent live in urban areas, and the life expectancy is 70 years. Adult literacy is about 60 percent.

The Land Kuwait is mostly flat, hot, and dry. A little rain falls in the winter. Most fresh water is imported or distilled from the sea. There is some grassland and desert scrub.

Economy Kuwait depends on its large production of oil and natural gas, which provides 67 percent of the GDP. Manufac-

turing provides another 4 percent, and industry as a whole employs 34 percent of the workforce. Agriculture is negligible. The per capita GNP is among the world's highest, at $20,900 in 1981. Money from oil sales finances an elaborate welfare system.

BAHRAIN

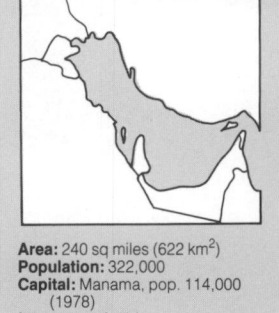

Area: 240 sq miles (622 km²)
Population: 322,000
Capital: Manama, pop. 114,000 (1978)
Language: Arabic
Religion: Islam
Currency: Dinar=1,000 Fils

THE STATE OF BAHRAIN is an island country in the Persian Gulf.

People and Culture More than 4,000 years ago Bahrain, then known as Dilmun, was an important entrepôt for trade between Ur and other Sumerian cities and lands further east and south. It came under Arab rule in the seventh century AD, and the Portuguese used it as a trading base from 1521 to 1602. Persia (Iran) ruled Bahrain from 1602, but was driven out by the Arab al-Khalifa dynasty in 1783. This dynasty still rules Bahrain as emirs.

Britain took Bahrain under its protection in 1861; the country became completely independent again in 1971.

The people are mostly Arabs, but about 20 percent

Rugged landscape near Manakhah, in the Yemen Arab Republic. Manakhah is noted for its fine coffee beans.

are of Iranian stock. The population grew at the rate of 7.2 percent a year from 1970 to 1979; the present growth rate is hard to estimate. Immigrants contributed to the population increase. Bahrain has free education and medical care.

The Land The country consists of 33 islands, the main island being also called Bahrain. The islands are low and sandy, and mostly desert, with oases. Rainfall is about 3 inches (76 mm) a year, but springs provide a good supply of fresh water. Summers are hot and winters are mild.

Economy Oil and natural gas are the basis of Bahrain's economy. A large refinery processes oil from Saudi Arabia as well as Bahrain's own oil. Other industries are being developed, including aluminium smelting and ship-building and repair. The government is also developing Bahrain's traditional rôle as an international trading port and banking centre. The per capita GNP was $8,960 in 1981.

QATAR

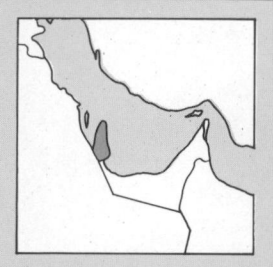

Area: 4,247 sq miles (11,000 km²)
Population: 298,000
Population Growth Rate: 6.3% pa
Capital: Doha, pop. 130,000
Language: Arabic
Religion: Islam
Currency: Qatar Riyal= 100 Dirhams

A **natural-gas flare** stands like a desert lighthouse above an oilfield in Abu Dhabi, in the United Arab Emirates.

Dubai has one of the Persian Gulf's main ports, where merchants import and export goods from 60 countries.

THE STATE OF QATAR is an Arab emirate in the Persian Gulf.

People and Culture From 1872 to 1916 Qatar was part of the Ottoman empire. It then passed under British protection until 1971 when it became independent. The country has been ruled by sheikhs of the al-Thani family since 1868; the head of state has the title of emir.

The people are mostly Muslim Arabs, though immigration of foreign workers has led to the high rate of population increase. Nearly 80 percent of the people live in Doha. Free medical services and education have been introduced since the 1950s.

The Land Qatar consists of the Qatar peninsula and some small islands. Most of the land is flat and stony, with salt marshes in the south. The only natural vegetation is in the low hills of the northwest. The climate is hot and arid, and annual rainfall is about 5 inches (130 mm).

Economy Oil exploitation began in 1949, since when Qatar has become rich. In 1981 the per capita GNP stood at $27,720, one of the highest in the world.

UNITED ARAB EMIRATES

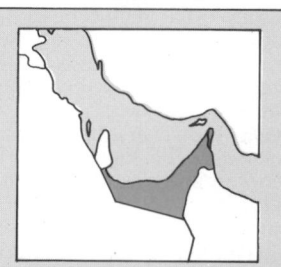

Area: 32,278 sq miles (83,600 km²)
Population: 933,000
Population Growth Rate: 7.0% pa
Capital: Abu Dhabi, pop. 449,000
Language: Arabic
Religion: Islam
Currency: Dirham = 100 Fils

THE UNITED ARAB EMIRATES are a federation of seven sheikdoms at the southern part of the Persian Gulf.

People and Culture Pirates dominated the area until 1820, when Britain signed a treaty with the sheikhs to eradicate it. This and other treaties gave Britain control of the external affairs of the sheikhdoms, which became known as the Trucial States.

The states became independent in 1971, but each of the seven – Abū Dhabi, Dubayy (Dubai), Sharjah, Ras al-Khaimah, Fujairah, Umm al-Quwain, and Ajman – controls its own internal affairs.

The people are mostly Arabs, but up to 85 percent of the population is immigrant, which accounts for the very high population growth rate in recent years. Some 73 percent live in urban areas. Their life expectancy is 63 years, and the adult literacy is 56 percent.

The Land The Persian Gulf coast is lined with swamps, while to the east there are mountains. The interior is mostly desert. The climate is hot with little rainfall.

Economy Oil is the mainstay of the economy. Before its development began in 1962 the country was one of the poorest. It is now one of the richest, with a per capita GNP in 1980 of $30,070. Oil produces about 75 percent of the GDP.

OMAN

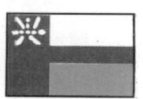

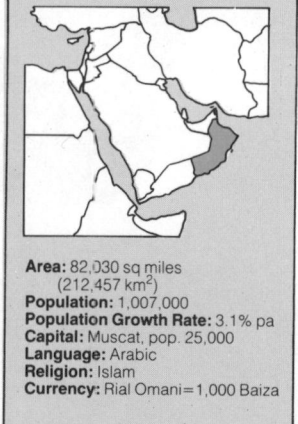

Area: 82,030 sq miles (212,457 km²)
Population: 1,007,000
Population Growth Rate: 3.1% pa
Capital: Muscat, pop. 25,000
Language: Arabic
Religion: Islam
Currency: Rial Omani = 1,000 Baiza

THE SULTANATE OF OMAN lies on the southeastern corner of the Arabian Peninsula.

People and Culture Oman was ruled by Portugal from 1508 to 1648, when Imam Nasir bin Murshid seized power. Oman has been independent ever since, though it was under British protection from 1891 to 1971. It is an absolute monarchy, ruled by a sultan.

About 90 percent of the people are Arabs, and the rest are Black Africans, Indians, Pakistanis and Iranians. Adult literacy is low. Education and health services have been greatly increased since 1970, when the reforming Sultan Qaboos bin Said deposed his reactionary father.

The Land In the north are rugged highlands with a fertile coastal plain. The coast in the south is also fertile. In between is a barren, dry plateau. Oman also holds the tip of the Musandam peninsula, controlling the Strait of Hormuz, which is separated from the rest of the country by United Arab Emirates territory. Much of the land is hot and arid, but the northern highlands have 10–20 inches (250–500 mm) of rain a year.

Economy Oil production, which began in 1967, has transformed Oman from a poor country to the seventh richest in the Arab world, with a per capita GNP of $5,920. Mining and other industries are being developed.

Africa: introduction

Africa, the second largest continent after Asia, is more than three times as large as the United States. It is an ancient landmass, which has existed since Precambrian times, although the older Precambrian rocks are largely masked by generally thin layers of late Precambrian or more recent rocks. Around 200 million years ago, Africa lay at the heart of the ancient supercontinent of Pangaea. Pangaea began to break up around 180 million years ago, and South America, India and Antarctica, which had been attached to Africa, slowly drifted to their present positions.

Land and Climate

Because of its ancient origin, much of Africa consists of level tablelands. About 60 percent of the continent is more than 1,200 feet (366 m) above sea-level, while more than half of Africa south of the Equator is above 3,000 feet (914 m). The interior tablelands are bordered by a pronounced rim, over which the rivers plunge in a series of rapids and waterfalls to a narrow coastal plain. This is most marked in southern Africa, especially along the Drakensberg range, the uptilted rim of the interior plateau.

The only strongly folded younger rocks are on Africa's northern and southern extremities – namely, the Atlas Mountains in the northwest and the Cape ranges of South Africa. The Atlas Mountains reach a maximum height of 13,665 feet (4,165 m). However, most of Africa's highlands, including the Ahaggar and Tibesti massifs of northern Africa, are volcanic in origin. The continent's highest peaks, Kilimanjaro in Tanzania, which is 19,341 feet (5,895 m) high, and Mount Kenya, which reaches 17,060 feet (5,200 m), are extinct volcanoes. They were formed during the massive earth movements which created the East African Rift Valley. The Ruwenzori range alongside the Rift Valley is not volcanic. It is a raised block of land.

The Rift Valley is the world's most extensive feature of its kind. It extends from Mozambique, through East Africa and the Red Sea, to the Jordan valley in Asia. It encompasses many lakes, including Africa's second largest, Lake Tanganyika, which covers 12,700 sq miles (32,891 km^2). The largest lake, Victoria, occupies a depression in the plateau between two arms of the Rift Valley and covers 26,828 sq miles (69,484 km^2). Lake Victoria is one of the sources of the world's longest river, the Nile, which flows north to the Mediterranean Sea. The Nile is 4,150 miles (6,679 km) long. Other major rivers include the Zaire (Congo), which is 2,900 miles (4,667 km) long, and the Niger, which is 2,600 miles (4,184 km) long.

The Atlas Mountains extend from Morocco, shown here, through Algeria into Tunisia. These mountains are one of the few areas of folded rocks in the ancient and mostly stable continent of Africa.

Africa straddles the Equator and reaches about 37° North and 35° South latitudes. Nearly two-thirds of its area lies in the tropics and temperate zones are confined to the northern and southern extremities, principally Africa's northern coastlands and the region around Cape Town in South Africa, both of which have Mediterranean climates, with hot, dry summers and mild, moist winters.

Because of Africa's location, there are similarities between the climatic and vegetation zones north and south of the Equator, although the pattern is upset by the far larger area north of the Equator. The equatorial region, extending from the coast of Tanzania, over most of the Zaire basin and along the West African coast as far as Liberia, has high temperatures of 80°–90°F (27°–32°C) with little variation from month to month and low air pressures caused by the intense heating of the surface. The rainfall is generally heavy – the slopes of Mount Cameroon being the wettest place with about 400 inches (10,160 mm) of rain per year. However, the altitude greatly modifies the equatorial climate. The high plateaux of equatorial Africa are much cooler and drier than the lower-lying Zaire basin and Guinea coast, while Mounts Kilimanjaro and Kenya are snow-capped throughout the year.

To the north and south of the equatorial region is a tropical zone with a dry winter. In the northern hemisphere, this region merges eventually into the desert zone. One-third of Africa has less than 10 inches (254 mm) of rain per year and the Sahara, the world's largest hot desert, covers about 3,250,000 sq miles (8,417,000 km^2). It is a region of high air pressure, because air is sinking downward. The eastern Sahara is the sunniest place on earth, and the world's highest shade temperature, 136.4°F (58°C), was recorded at Al 'Aziziyah, south of Tripoli, Libya, in 1922. The equivalent desert in the southern hemisphere covers a much smaller area. This is the Namib desert of southwest Africa, which merges into the semi-desert Kalahari region of Botswana.

Southeastern Africa is more humid than the southwest. Parts of the coast of Mozambique have an average annual rainfall of 39 inches (991 mm).

Nomadic Tuaregs (a Berber people) live in the Sahara, as here near the Niger-Algerian border.

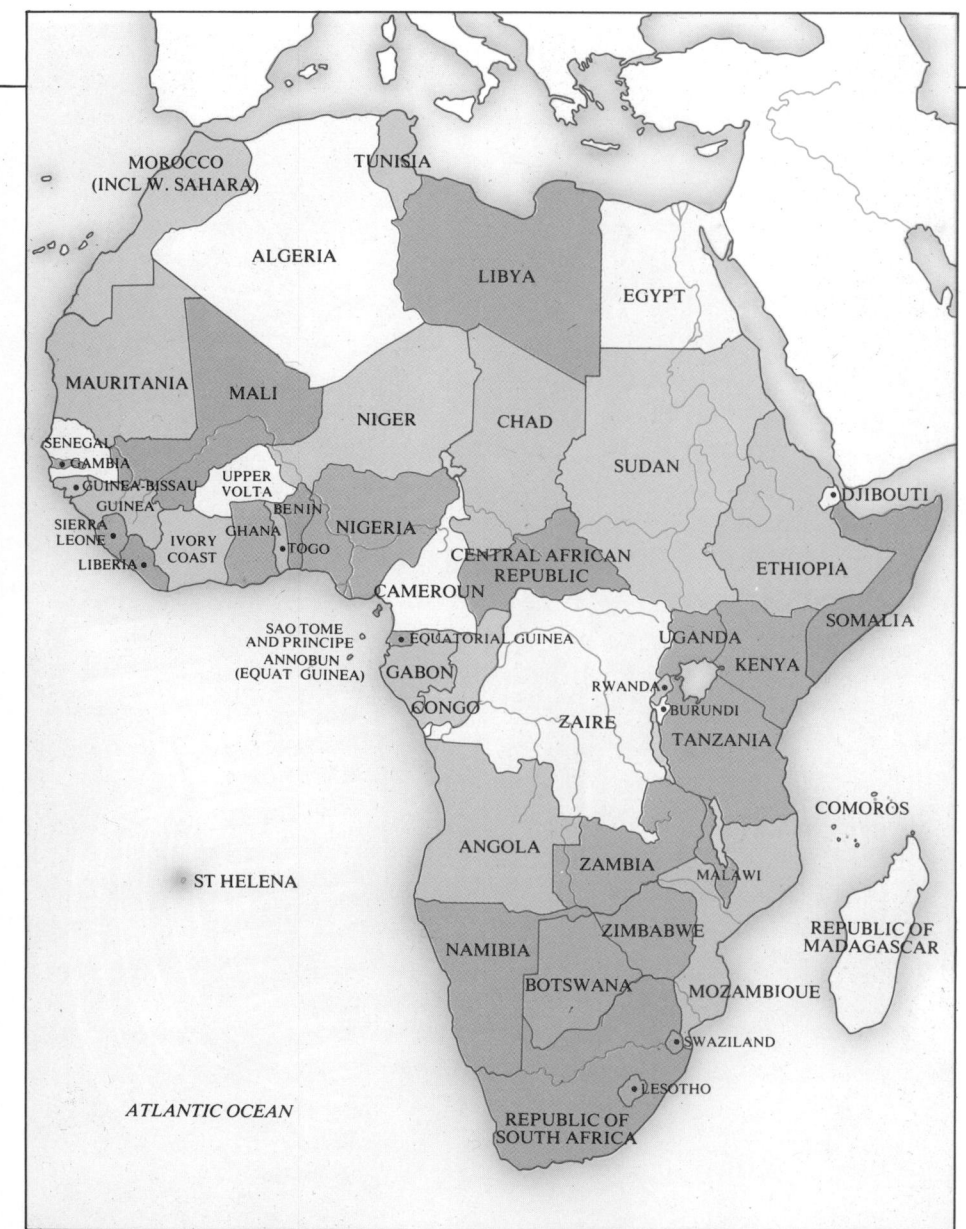

The map of Africa has changed greatly since World War II. In 1914, only two countries, Ethiopia and Liberia, were not European colonies. But today, only Namibia (or South West Africa) on the mainland has yet to achieve nationhood. With the end of colonialism has come a change in geographical names. Many countries have new names and many cities and geographical features have also been retitled. Change has resulted from a desire by Africans to turn back to their roots and remove the marks of colonialism from their maps. A recent example is Zimbabwe, which was formerly named Rhodesia after the British empire builder Cecil Rhodes.

Flora and Fauna

The natural vegetation of the equatorial zone is rain forest, which covers a vast area in the Zaire basin and along the Guinea coast. The rain forest covers about 10 percent of Africa. It merges into savanna (tropical grassland), the typical vegetation of the tropical, dry winter climate. Wooded savanna with high grasses occurs in wet areas, with tree-less grassland in drier places. The mountains, which rise above the forest, and the savanna contain varying belts of vegetation determined by the altitude. A trip up Mount Kilimanjaro takes one from savanna, through mountain rain forest, grassland, moorland and tundra to permanent snow and ice about 15,750 feet (4,801 m).

The savanna merges to the north and south into dry steppeland, where the rainfall becomes increasingly unreliable. In northern Africa, this region, called the Sahel, has recently suffered prolonged droughts and, in consequence, the Sahara has moved south. The deserts of Africa contain few plants, except around oases. The Mediterranean regions are characterized by drought-resistant plants which can survive the summer drought. South Africa also contains an arid grassland region, the high veld, while warm temperate forests grow in the humid southeast.

The hot and wet equatorial forests are rich in plant species, insects, birds and tree-living reptiles and mammals, including primates, such as chimpanzees, gorillas, many monkeys, bush-babies and, in Madagascar, lemurs. Only a few animals, such as the shy okapi, live on the dank forest floor, where sunlight cannot penetrate. But along rivers, several species, including the pygmy hippopotamus of West Africa, can be found. The only large forest predator is the leopard.

The savanna offers habitats for a wide range of animal species, such as buffalo, elephant, giraffe, hippopotamus and rhinoceros; such predators as the lion and cheetah (the world's fastest sprinter); antelopes, wildebeest and zebra; an enormous variety of birds; and such reptiles as crocodiles, lizards, tortoises and snakes. The mountains contain their own distinctive species, including the rare mountain gorilla, and the gelada baboon of Ethiopia. The deserts have few large animals, although wild camels (descendants of domestic camels) and some antelopes live in the Sahara. Most desert animals are specially adapted to the severe conditions. For example, the fennec, the smallest of the foxes, has huge ears which help to keep it cool; while a ground squirrel in the Namic desert uses its bushy tail as an umbrella to shade its body.

A frog rests on a frangipani leaf in the tropical rain forest of the Ivory Coast. African's rain forests contain a great variety of plant and animal species.

Several African countries have established national parks and reserves to protect wildlife, which has been greatly reduced through hunting and the destruction of habitats. The parks attract tourists and tourism has become a major source of income in several countries.

History and Culture

Large parts of Africa are too arid for agriculture and these regions are also very sparsely populated. However, some areas have attracted high population densities. About 10,000 years ago when the climate was changing, the Sahara, a former grassland, dried up and its people moved into the Nile valley, where there was abundant water and fertile soils formed from silt deposited by the annual floods. Agriculture was introduced into the Nile valley from western Asia, where it had begun in about 9000 BC. By about 3000 BC, one of the world's greatest early civilizations had been founded.

Until quite late in its history, Ancient Egypt was a Bronze Age civilization, but south of the Sahara bronze tools were not used and the people passed directly from the Stone to the Iron Age. Iron was introduced into the West African savanna in the sixth century BC and, in about 100 BC, a major, iron-using group developed in what is now Cameroun. This was the original Bantu-speaking group. Over the centuries, the Bantu-speakers spread east and south, displacing Stone Age peoples, such as pygmies, Bushmen and Hottentots. The southernmost group, the Xhosa, reached the Fish River, South Africa, by 1776.

Many Bantu languages evolved and they now form the largest language family in Africa, making up many of the 1,000 or more languages and dialects. The other main groups of people, south of the Sahara, include the West African Negroids, such as the Ashanti, Hausa and Yoruba; the Nilotes, of mixed Negroid and Hamitic origin, such as the Dinka; and the Nilo-Hamites, including the Masai of East Africa. The people of Madagascar are descendants of immigrants from Indonesia and mainland Africa.

Arab armies introduced Islam to North Africa in the seventh century AD and, with a common religion and language, Arabic, North Africa developed a cultural homogeneity unlike anything in the rest of Africa. In the Middle Ages, the West African savanna was the home of a series of civilizations, including ancient Ghana and Mali. These were unknown in Europe, but North African traders visited them regularly with their camel caravans. Islam was thus introduced into the savanna lands south of the Sahara, although Coptic Christianity survived in the remote highlands of Ethiopia.

Above The gold mask of Tutankhamun was placed on the head of this pharaoh of ancient Egypt. Tutankhamun reigned in the fourteenth century BC. He is best known, however, because his tomb, discovered in 1922 by the archaeologist Howard Carter in the Valley of the Kings, near Al Uqsur (Luxor), contained treasures that astonished the world. Ancient Egypt was one of the world's greatest early civilizations. It had much influence on other cultures.

Left People wash clothes or bathe in the Bandama River at Bouaflé, a town in central Ivory Coast. Since independence in 1960, this West African country has made considerable economic progress. It has attracted foreign investment because of its free enterprise policies.

In most of Black Africa, the people had their own traditional religions. Many were monotheistic, while others emphasized ancestor worship and the existence of spirits in nature. Many of these religions are still practised, and they are reflected in much Black African art.

European exploration of Africa south of the Sahara began in the fifteenth century and the Dutch founded a settlement at Cape Town in 1652 – the forerunner of modern South Africa. However, it was not until the late nineteenth century that the bulk of Africa was colonized by European powers, who introduced Christianity and a monetary economy. By 1914, only two African countries, Ethiopia and Liberia, were not under European rule.

Economic and Demographic Trends

After World War II, the map of Africa changed steadily as more and more African countries achieved independence. By 1984, only Namibia on the African mainland had not gained nationhood. Colonization, though resented by nationalists, brought benefits, as in the field of health where infant mortality was reduced and many indigenous diseases were eliminated or brought under control. The average life expectancy at birth has increased, although it remains low by world standards. For example, in 1981, Chad, Upper Volta and Ghana had average life expectancies of 43, 44 and 54 years respectively, as compared with 75 years in the United States. The Europeans of southern Africa have the longest life spans.

Improved health facilities and economic development have led to a population explosion. In 1975–80, Africa's population was increasing by an estimated 2.9 percent per year, the highest rate in the world. Should it continue, the population of Africa will double in the next 25 years.

The rapid increase in the population has strained the limited resources of many nations. In 1980, almost 45 percent of Africa's people were under 15 years of age, as compared with 23 percent in North America and 21 percent in western Europe. As a result, Africa has to fund expensive educational and health services for a non-productive section of the population. Although Africa's economy is still based on agriculture (nearly three-fourths of Africans are engaged in farming), the cities and towns are growing rapidly, but the newcomers are often unemployed and forced to live in unhealthy shanty settlements on the outskirts of the towns.

Most Africans are poor. The per capita gross national product (GNP) for Africa in 1980 was $760, or one-fifteenth of that of North America. Twenty-two of the world's 32 poorest nations (with per capita GNPs of under $360 in

Above A woman pounds plantains (a kind of banana) in a village near Man, in west-central Ivory Coast. Plantains, together with cassava, maize, millet, rice and yams, are a staple food. These villagers are Yakuba, a subgroup of the Dan, who make up about five percent of the population of the Ivory Coast. About 60 languages and dialects are spoken in the country. But no single African tongue is sufficiently widely spoken, so French has been retained as the official language. Ethnic and language divisions in African countries are a source of instability.

Left Since 1980, Liberia has been ruled by a military group. In many African countries, failures in economic policies have led to unrest and to the overthrow of governments by military regimes.

1980) are in Africa. The richest African countries, defined by their per capita GNPs, are Libya, Gabon, South Africa and Algeria, and all, except South Africa, derive their wealth from oil sales, although Gabon also exports other minerals. South Africa is the continent's only truly industrialized nation and also its leading economic and military power, but it faces one of Africa's main problems – ethnic diversity and conflict. South Africa's white community, only 18 percent of the population, dominates the government and the economy.

Many African countries are vulnerable to fluctuations in price and demand because they depend on one or two products for most of their foreign earnings. For example, Nigeria's oil sales brought great prosperity in the late 1960s and early 1970s, but the world recession from the late 1970s caused a massive fall in revenue and an economic crisis. Zambia, overdependent on copper, and Ghana, whose leading export is cocoa, face similar problems.

Economic problems, the multiplicity of languages and ethnic groups, high rates of adult illiteracy and periodic natural disasters, such as droughts, are among the factors which have caused instability in many African countries. Most of the democratic constitutions established by the ex-colonial powers have been overthrown in favour of one-party constitutions and autocratic rule, usually by military groups. But Africa contains many resources and, with aid from the outside world, economic development has raised living standards in many areas. To further development, regional organizations have been set up to coordinate economic policies, and Africa is now playing an increasingly important role in world affairs.

Northern Africa

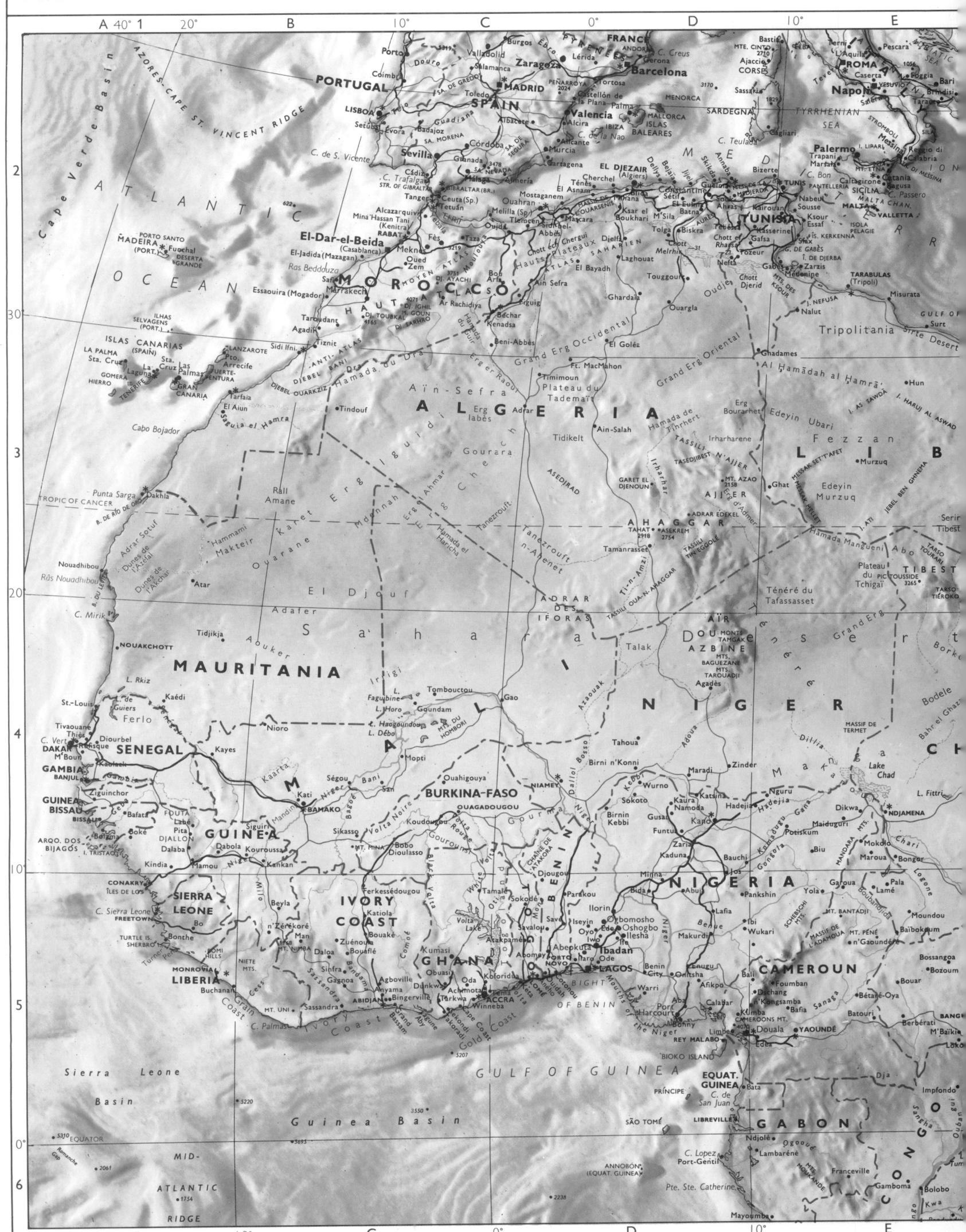

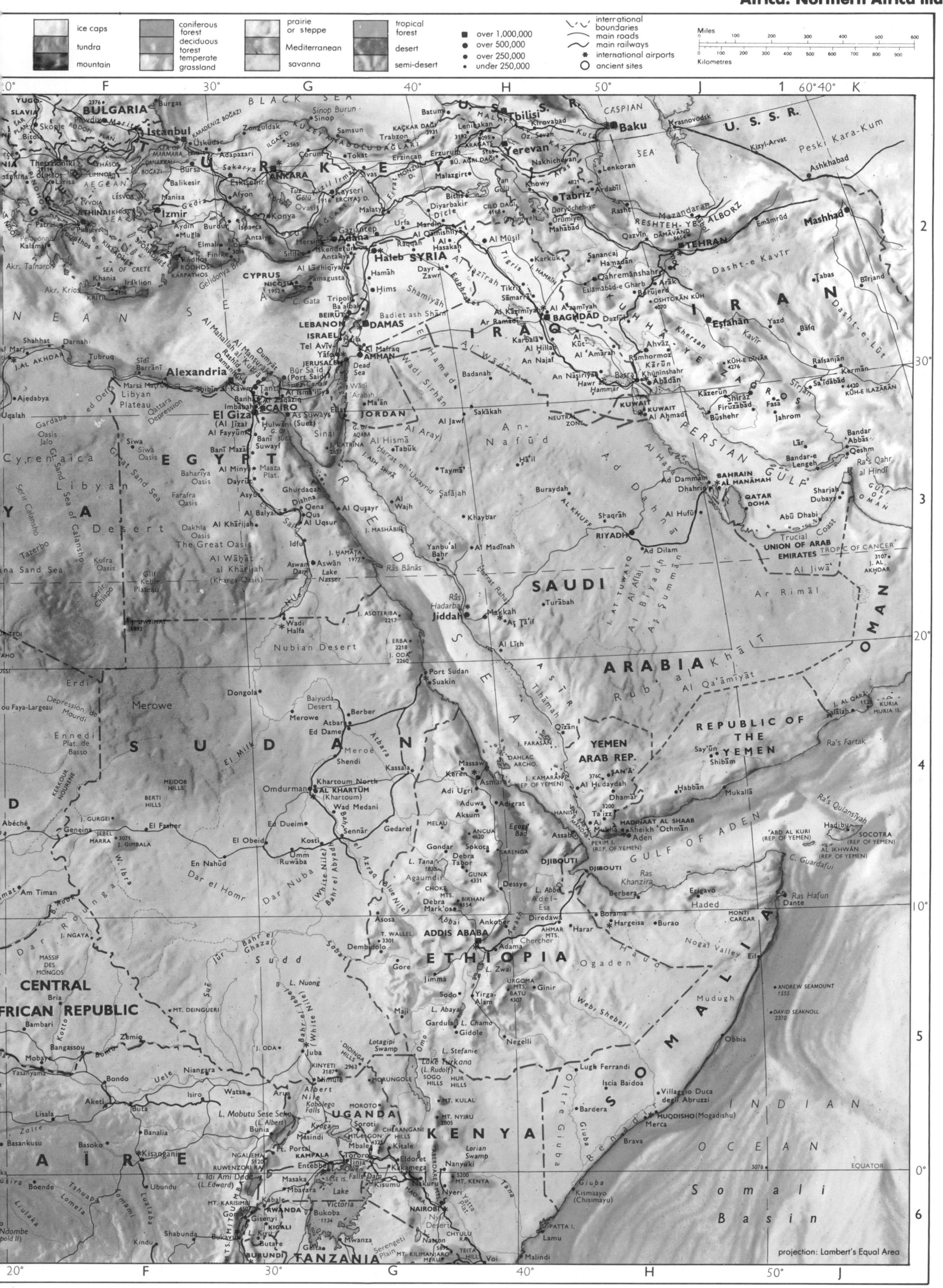

ice caps
tundra
mountain

coniferous forest
deciduous forest
temperate grassland

prairie or steppe
Mediterranean
savanna

tropical forest
desert
semi-desert

■ over 1,000,000
■ over 500,000
● over 250,000
• under 250,000

international boundaries
main roads
main railways
✱ international airports
○ ancient sites

Miles
Kilometres

projection: Lambert's Equal Area

167

MOROCCO

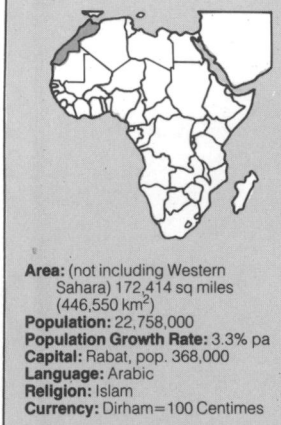

Area: (not including Western Sahara) 172,414 sq miles (446,550 km²)
Population: 22,758,000
Population Growth Rate: 3.3% pa
Capital: Rabat, pop. 368,000
Language: Arabic
Religion: Islam
Currency: Dirham=100 Centimes

THE KINGDOM OF MOROCCO (officially AL-MAMLAKA AL-MAGHREBIA) is in northeast Africa.

People and Culture The Arabic language and Islam were introduced in the early eighth century, but about 30 percent of Moroccans still speak the original Berber language.

France ruled most of Morocco from 1912, with Spain occupying parts of the north. Independence was achieved in 1956. The average life expectancy at birth in 1981 was 57 years.

In 1976, Morocco and Mauritania partitioned the intervening Western (formerly Spanish) Sahara. Local Saharans, with Algerian assistance, proclaimed their country the Sahrawi Arab Democratic Republic. A guerrilla war ensued, continuing into the 1980s after Mauritania had

withdrawn in 1979 and Morocco had occupied the entire territory. Western Sahara covers 102,703 sq miles (266,000 km²) and has a population of 150,000.

The Land The Atlas Mountains cover most of Morocco, with fertile lowlands in the north and the Sahara in the south and east. Western Sahara is hot desert.

Economy Agriculture employs half of the workforce. Barley, fruits and wheat are grown and livestock farming is important. Morocco's chief resource is phosphate, huge deposits of which also occur in Western Sahara. The per capita GNP of $860 (1981) is above the average for Africa.

ALGERIA

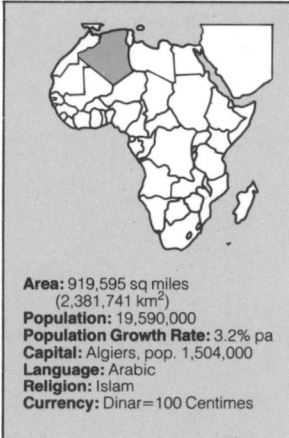

Area: 919,595 sq miles (2,381,741 km²)
Population: 19,590,000
Population Growth Rate: 3.2% pa
Capital: Algiers, pop. 1,504,000
Language: Arabic
Religion: Islam
Currency: Dinar=100 Centimes

THE DEMOCRATIC PEOPLE'S REPUBLIC OF ALGERIA is Africa's second largest country.

People and Culture Algeria's Islamic, Arab-speaking culture

was introduced in the seventh century AD. The original Berber language survived and is now spoken by nearly one-fifth of the population.

France ruled Algeria from 1848, but a guerrilla war waged by the FLN (*Front de Libération Nationale*) ended with Algeria becoming an independent republic in 1962. French is still widely spoken, but most French settlers have left. Military regimes ruled from 1965. Elections were restored in 1976 when Algeria became a one-party nation, the sole party being the FLN. In 1981 the average life expectancy at birth was 56 years, but adult illiteracy remains high at 35 percent.

The Land The Sahara covers 85 percent of Algeria. Most people live in the northern Atlas mountains, where the annual rainfall reaches 60 inches (1,524 mm) a year, and on the Mediterranean coast, which has about 27 inches (686 mm).

Economy Oil and natural gas, found in the Sahara in the 1950s, dominate the economy, providing about 44 percent of the GDP. Farming still employs 25 percent of the workforce, but manufacturing is increasing. The per capita GNP in 1981 was one of Africa's highest at $2,140.

TUNISIA

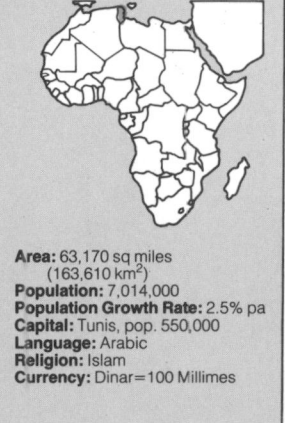

Area: 63,170 sq miles (163,610 km²)
Population: 7,014,000
Population Growth Rate: 2.5% pa
Capital: Tunis, pop. 550,000
Language: Arabic
Religion: Islam
Currency: Dinar=100 Millimes

THE REPUBLIC OF TUNISIA IS North Africa's smallest country.

People and Culture Islam was introduced in AD 647 and modern Tunisians are of Arab or Berber origin. Tunisia achieved independence from France in 1956 as a monarchy. A republic was established in 1957. The first President, Habib Bourguiba, was elected President for life in 1974.

The average life expectancy at birth in 1981 was 61 years.

The Land In the north are the Atlas mountains; in the south is the Sahara. Central Tunisia is semi-arid grassland.

Economy Oil and phosphates are the most valuable products. Farming employed 35 percent of the workforce in 1980. Manufacturing and tourism are growing in importance. With a per capita GNP of $1,420 in 1981, Tunisia is one of Africa's wealthier nations.

LIBYA

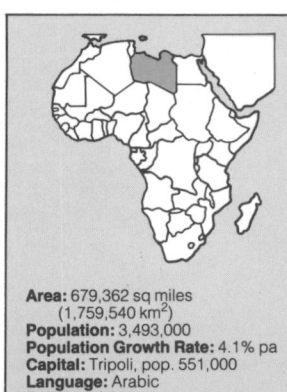

Area: 679,362 sq miles (1,759,540 km²)
Population: 3,493,000
Population Growth Rate: 4.1% pa
Capital: Tripoli, pop. 551,000
Language: Arabic
Religion: Islam
Currency: Dinar=100 Dirhams

SOCIALIST PEOPLE'S LIBYAN ARAB JAMAHIRIYAH has since 1977 been Libya's official name. *Jamahiriyah* means 'State of the Masses'.

People and Culture Arab armies introduced Libya's Arabic-speaking, Islamic culture in the AD 640s. After centuries of foreign rule, Libya became an independent monarchy in 1951. A military group under Colonel Muammar al-Gaddafi established a republic in 1969.

In 1951 Libya was one of Africa's poorest nations, but oil production, begun in 1961, has given Libya Africa's highest per capita GNP – $8,450 in 1981. With its new wealth, Libya has become increasingly active internationally.

The people are of Arab-Berber origin. In 1981 the average life expectancy at birth was 57 years and the urban population 54 percent.

The Land About 95 percent of Libya is hot desert. Most people live in the northwest and northeast coastlands, where the average rainfall reaches 24 inches (610 mm) and 13 inches (330 mm) respectively.

Economy Oil dominates the economy, but farming still employs 19 percent of the workforce. Cereals, dates, olives and vegetables are grown. Sheep and goats are raised.

EGYPT

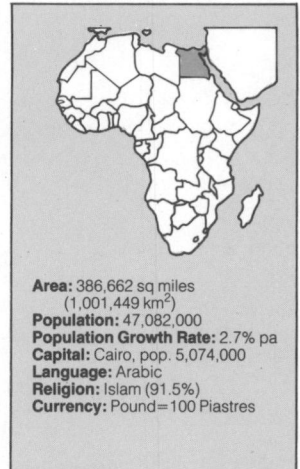

Area: 386,662 sq miles (1,001,449 km²)
Population: 47,082,000
Population Growth Rate: 2.7% pa
Capital: Cairo, pop. 5,074,000
Language: Arabic
Religion: Islam (91.5%)
Currency: Pound=100 Piastres

THE ARAB REPUBLIC OF EGYPT is largely desert. Only 4 percent of the land is farmed, mostly in the irrigated Nile valley.

People and Culture One of the greatest early civilizations, Ancient Egypt was ruled by 31 dynasties between 3100 and 332 BC. The Old Kingdom (2700–2200 BC), when the pyramids were built, the Middle Kingdom (2050–1800 BC) and the

In north Africa, including Morocco, water sellers are common.

Dead branches are removed from a date palm tree in Algeria.

New Kingdom (1570–1070 BC) were separated by periods of instability. In the late dynastic period, Egypt often had foreign rulers.

Christianity, introduced in AD 45, survived as a minority religion (the Coptic Orthodox Church) after Islam was imposed by Arab forces in 639–642. Foreign rulers continued to govern Egypt until recent times, culminating in British occupation in 1882. Egypt became independent in 1922, although British troops remained until the mid-1950s.

Since Egypt became a republic in 1953, successive governments have carried out much-needed reforms. Progress was hindered by the Arab–Israeli wars of 1948–49, 1957, 1967 and 1973. Under the 1979 peace treaty with Israel, Egypt regained the Sinai peninsula in 1982.

Rising living standards have caused an increase in the life expectancy at birth, which stood at 57 years in 1981. Illiteracy is common, but primary education is now compulsory, and there are 12 universities. In 1981, 44 percent of the population lived in urban areas.

The Land The western desert covers over three-fifths of Egypt. It includes some oases and depressions. The Qattara depression is 436 feet (133 m) below sea-level. The Nile valley contains the man-made Lake Nasser south of Aswan, and the triangular delta where the Nile empties through two main channels into the Mediterranean.

The eastern desert includes rocky plateaux and mountains bordering the Red Sea. Jebel Katrinah in the Sinai peninsula is at 8,652 (2,637 m) Egypt's highest peak. The northern coast has an average annual rainfall of 8 inches (203 mm). The south is hot and virtually rainless. Wildlife is sparse. There are no forests and little pasture.

Economy Half of the people work on farms, the main crops being cotton (the chief export), sugar-cane, cereals, rice, fruits and vegetables. Egypt is Africa's second most industrialized country. It produces most of the oil it needs and cheap electricity is generated at the Aswan High Dam. Manufactures include textiles, sugar, cement, chemicals, plastics and steel. The chief port is Alexandria. The leading trading partners are the EEC and the USA. Tourism and revenue from the Suez Canal are also important. The per capita GNP was $650 in 1981.

MAURITANIA

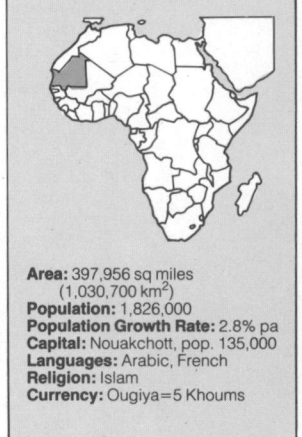

Area: 397,956 sq miles (1,030,700 km²)
Population: 1,826,000
Population Growth Rate: 2.8% pa
Capital: Nouakchott, pop. 135,000
Languages: Arabic, French
Religion: Islam
Currency: Ougiya=5 Khoums

THE ISLAMIC REPUBLIC ÖF MAURITANIA is in northwest Africa.

People and Culture France ruled Mauritania from 1903 until 1960 when independence was achieved. Mauritania occupied the southern third of Western Sahara in 1976. After an expensive war against Saharan guerrillas, a military group seized power in 1978 and withdrew from Western Sahara in 1979.

About 80 percent of Mauritanians are of Arab-Berber origin. Black Africans live in the south. The average life expectancy at birth is low at 44 years and 83 percent of adults are illiterate.

The Land The greater part of Mauritania consists of low desert plateaux. In the south, however, there are fertile plains through which the Senegal River flows. Here the average annual rainfall reaches 26 inches (660 mm), and savanna flourishes.

Economy Farming and fishing employ 69 percent of the workforce, but iron ore makes up four-fifths of the exports. The per capita GNP in 1981 was $460.

The Great Pyramid (in the distance) and the Pyramid of Khafre are at El Giza, near Cairo, Egypt.

Oases in the Sahara, such as Beni Isguen, Algeria, are fertile islands amid barren wasteland. Some support sizeable populations.

CAPE VERDE

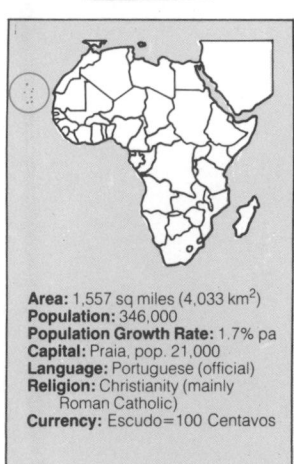

Area: 1,557 sq miles (4,033 km²)
Population: 346,000
Population Growth Rate: 1.7% pa
Capital: Praia, pop. 21,000
Language: Portuguese (official)
Religion: Christianity (mainly Roman Catholic)
Currency: Escudo=100 Centavos

THE REPUBLIC OF CAPE VERDE is an island nation west of Senegal.

People and Culture Portugal claimed these uninhabited islands in 1460. Independence was achieved in 1975.

Most people are of mixed African and Portuguese origin. The average life expectancy at birth is about 50 years.

The Land Cape Verde contains 10 islands and 5 islets. They are of volcanic origin. São Tiago, the largest island, contains the capital Praia. The climate is hot and arid.

Economy The economy is based on farming, but Cape Verde imports food. Many men emigrate. The per capita GNP in 1981 was $340.

GAMBIA

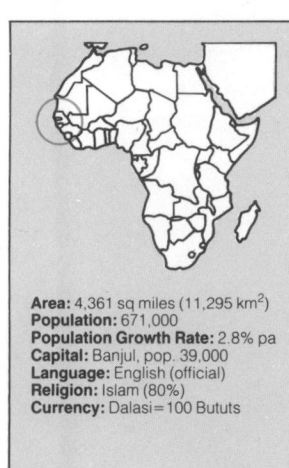

Area: 4,361 sq miles (11,295 km²)
Population: 671,000
Population Growth Rate: 2.8% pa
Capital: Banjul, pop. 39,000
Language: English (official)
Religion: Islam (80%)
Currency: Dalasi=100 Bututs

THE REPUBLIC OF THE GAMBIA is almost completely enclosed by Senegal.

People and Culture Gambia was British from 1888 until 1965. In 1981, Senegal helped to crush a revolt in Gambia. In 1982, the two nations established a confederation, Senegambia, but retained their sovereignty.

Most Gambians are Blacks, belonging to the same ethnic groups as in Senegal. But Gambia's English traditions separate it culturally from French-speaking Senegal.

The Land Wooded savanna covers much of this tropical nation. The rainfall averages 30–45 inches (762–1,143 mm).

Economy Farming employs 85 percent of the workforce. Groundnuts dominate the economy. The per capita GNP (1981) was $370.

SENEGAL

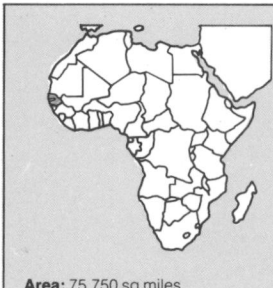

Area: 75,750 sq miles (196,192 km²)
Population: 6,276,000
Population Growth Rate: 2.6% pa
Capital: Dakar, pop. 979,000
Language: French (official)
Religion: Islam (90%)
Currency: Franc CFA= 100 Centimes

THE REPUBLIC OF SENEGAL is a mostly low-lying country.

People and Culture Senegal became a French colony in 1887 and independent in 1960. Senegal joined Gambia in 1982 in a confederation, Senegambia.

The average life expectancy in 1981 was 44 years.

The Land Broad plains lie in the west. The interior plateaux are hot. The rainfall increases from north to south and savanna covers much of Senegal.

Economy Farming employs 77 percent of the workforce. Groundnuts dominate the economy, but industry is important in Dakar. The per capita GNP in 1981 was $430.

MALI

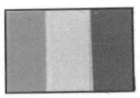

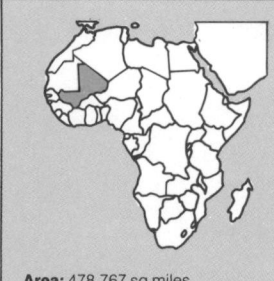

Area: 478,767 sq miles (1,240,000 km²)
Population: 7,778,000
Population Growth Rate: 2.8% pa
Capital: Bamako, pop. 404,000
Language: French (official)
Religion: Islam (65%)
Currency: Mali Franc= 100 Centimes

THE REPUBLIC OF MALI is one of Africa's poorest nations.

People and Culture Modern Mali was part of ancient Ghana and ancient Mali. France ruled Mali (then French Sudan) from 1880 until independence in 1960. After the army took power in 1968 Mali is now a one-party state. People of Arab-Berber origin live in the north, but over 80 percent of Malians are Black. The life expectancy at birth is 45 years and 90 percent of adults are illiterate.

The Land The north is desert. The Niger River drains the humid southern plains. The rainfall increases to the south, where many savanna animals can be seen.

Economy In 1980 farming and fishing employed 73 percent of the workforce. The chief crops are cotton, oilseeds and peanuts (groundnuts). Livestock-raising is important, but many animals have died during recent droughts. There is little industry. The per capita GNP in 1981 was $190.

NIGER

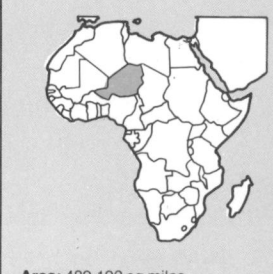

Area: 489,192 sq miles (1,267,000 km²)
Population: 5,987,000
Population Growth Rate: 3.0% pa
Capital: Niamey, pop. 225,000
Language: French (official)
Religion: Islam (85%)
Currency: Franc CFA= 100 Centimes

THE REPUBLIC OF NIGER is in north-central Africa.

People and Culture France occupied Niger in 1897–1900

Dakar, in Senegal, is a fishing port and manufacturing city.

Dakar's Great Mosque, a gift from Morocco, was inaugurated by Mohammed V of Morocco.

and ruled until independence in 1960. Niger has some Tuareg (Berber) nomads, but most people are Black Africans. The average life expectancy at birth is 45 years and 90 percent of adults are illiterate.
The Land The rugged Air massif rises above the Sahara in the north. Central Niger is dry scrubland, with savanna in the south. The Niger River drains the southwest.
Economy Farming employs about nine-tenths of the workforce. Niger has large uranium deposits, but few manufacturing industries. The per capita GNP in 1981 was $330.

Blacks who live in the south. Cultural divisions led to a military coup in 1975 and, from 1980, civil war involving Libyan, OAU and French troops.

The average life expectancy at birth is only 43 years and 85 percent of adults are illiterate.
The Land Sandy deserts and the volcanic Tibesti massif are in the north, with savanna in the south. The shallow Lake Chad occupies an inland drainage basin in the west.
Economy In 1980, farming employed 85 percent of the workforce. The chief crop is cotton. Livestock-farming is important in central Chad.

Muslims. The southern Nilotes and Blacks follow traditional religions or Christianity. With 115 languages, Sudan is culturally diverse. A North–South civil war occurred in 1964–72. Although regional autonomy was granted to the southern provinces, guerrillas revived anti-government activities in 1983.

Sudan is under-developed. The average life expectancy at birth is 47 years and nearly 70 percent of the people are illiterate.
The Land Sudan is mostly flat, with highlands in the west and south. Desert covers most of

this hot, arid land. In the southern White Nile region is the *Sudd*, a vast area of marshland where the flow of the river is impeded by the luxuriant growth of aquatic plants. The wet south is rich in wildlife. Most people live in the irrigated valleys of the White Nile, Blue Nile and Atbara rivers.
Economy Farming employed 72 percent of the workforce in 1980. Cotton dominates the exports. Livestock are raised and there is some industry in the cities. Port Sudan is the only seaport. In 1981, the per capita GNP was $380.

GUINEA

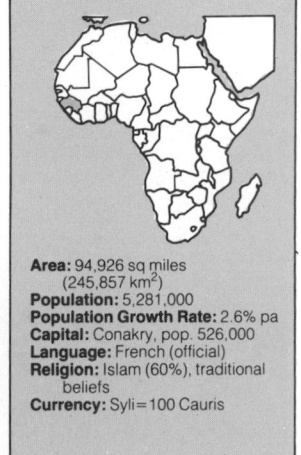

Area: 94,926 sq miles (245,857 km²)
Population: 5,281,000
Population Growth Rate: 2.6% pa
Capital: Conakry, pop. 526,000
Language: French (official)
Religion: Islam (60%), traditional beliefs
Currency: Syli=100 Cauris

CHAD

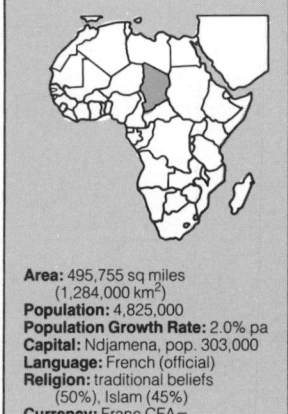

Area: 495,755 sq miles (1,284,000 km²)
Population: 4,825,000
Population Growth Rate: 2.0% pa
Capital: Ndjamena, pop. 303,000
Language: French (official)
Religion: traditional beliefs (50%), Islam (45%)
Currency: Franc CFA= 100 Centimes

SUDAN

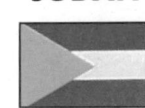

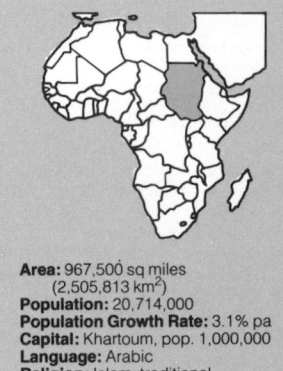

Area: 967,500 sq miles (2,505,813 km²)
Population: 20,714,000
Population Growth Rate: 3.1% pa
Capital: Khartoum, pop. 1,000,000
Language: Arabic
Religion: Islam, traditional beliefs, Christianity
Currency: Pound=100 Piastres

Abandoned cars are occasionally seen in Saharan Niger.

THE REPUBLIC OF CHAD is one of Africa's poorest nations, with a per capita GNP in 1981 of $110.
People and Culture France ruled Chad from 1900 until independence in 1960. French is the official language, because over 100 languages and dialects are spoken in Chad. Arabic-speaking Muslims of Arab-Berber origin live in the north, but most people are

THE DEMOCRATIC REPUBLIC OF THE SUDAN is Africa's largest country.
People and Culture From 2800 BC, Sudan was influenced by Ancient Egypt and from 750 to 666 BC a Sudanese dynasty ruled Egypt. Egypt and Britain jointly ruled Sudan from 1899, but Sudan became independent in 1956.

The northern Sudanese, including Arabs and Blacks, are

THE POPULAR AND REVOLUTIONARY REPUBLIC OF GUINEA is the world's second largest bauxite producer.
People and Culture France began to colonize Guinea in 1849. In 1958 Guineans voted for independence. A fast withdrawal of French personnel caused chaos. Guinea, aided by Ghana and the USSR, adopted socialist policies and a one-party Constitution. But relations with the West improved in the late 1970s.

Most people are Blacks. In 1981 the average life expectancy at birth was 43 years and adult literacy was 20 percent.
The Land Guinea contains a coastal plain, the Fouta Djallon plateau, the Upper Niger plains and mountains in the southeast. The climate is tropical with heavy rainfall. Savanna covers the interior and forests the coast.
Economy Farming employed 82 percent of the workforce in 1980. But industry, especially bauxite mining, made up 33 percent of the GDP. The per capita GNP (1981) was $300.

The Sahel, a zone of dry savanna (grass with scattered trees), passes through Niger. Droughts, deforestation and overgrazing are turning parts of the Sahel into desert.

Cattle in Burkina-Faso and many other African countries signify wealth and status.

LIBERIA

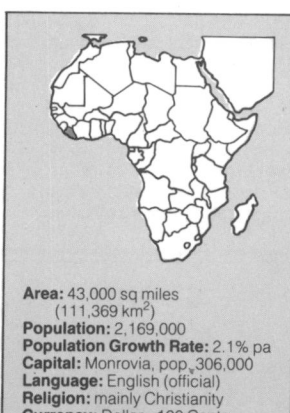

Area: 43,000 sq miles (111,369 km²)
Population: 2,169,000
Population Growth Rate: 2.1% pa
Capital: Monrovia, pop. 306,000
Language: English (official)
Religion: mainly Christianity
Currency: Dollar=100 Cents

THE REPUBLIC OF LIBERIA was founded by American abolitionists.

People and Culture The American Colonization Society founded Monrovia as a home for freed slaves in 1822. In 1847 Liberia became an independent republic. The elected government was overthrown in 1980 by a military group.

Liberia has 16 language groups and about 50,000 Americo-Liberians, the descendants of freed slaves, who have played an important part in Liberian society. The life expectancy at birth was 54 years in 1981, and adult literacy was only 25 percent.

The Land The high temperatures and heavy rainfall have encouraged the growth of forest and luxuriant savanna.

Economy Farming employs 70 percent of the workforce, but industry, especially iron-ore mining, makes up 27 percent of the GDP. Liberia's large merchant navy earns foreign currency. The GNP per capita in 1981 was $520.

IVORY COAST

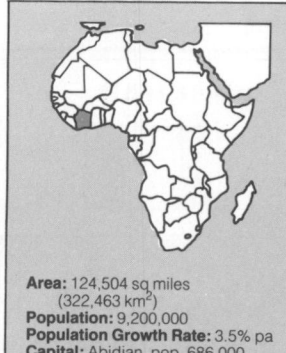

Area: 124,504 sq miles (322,463 km²)
Population: 9,200,000
Population Growth Rate: 3.5% pa
Capital: Abidjan, pop. 686,000
Language: French (official)
Religion: traditional beliefs (65%)
Currency: Franc CFA= 100 Centimes

THE REPUBLIC OF THE IVORY COAST is one of West Africa's wealthiest nations.

People and Culture The Ivory Coast was French from 1893 until independence in 1960. The Black population is divided into about 60 language groups. But the country has had stable government since 1960, with power focused in the *Parti Démocratique de la Côte d'Ivoire* (PDCI) and its leader President Félix Houphouët-Boigny. No opposition

Dirt roads in the Ivory Coast are often impassable when wet.

GUINEA-BISSAU

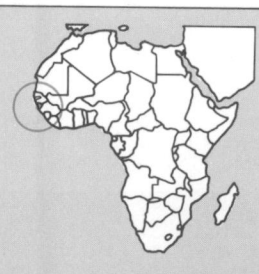

Area: 13,948 sq miles (36,125 km²)
Population: 810,000 (1981)
Population Growth Rate: not available
Capital: Bissau, pop. 109,000
Language: Portuguese (official)
Religion: Islam, traditional beliefs
Currency: Peso = 100 Centavos

THE REPUBLIC OF GUINEA-BISSAU was so-named to distinguish it from neighbouring Guinea.

People and Culture Portugal's links with Guinea-Bissau date back to 1446. Independence was achieved in 1974 following a long guerrilla war. Most people are Blacks.

The Land Guinea-Bissau is mostly flat, with a tropical climate and heavy rainfall. Forests grow on the coast, with savanna inland. Wildlife is abundant.

Economy Most people are poor subsistence farmers. The chief cash crop is groundnuts. In 1981, the per capita GNP was extremely low at $190.

BURKINA FASO

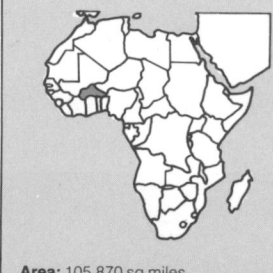

Area: 105,870 sq miles (274,200 km²)
Population: 7,662,000
Population Growth Rate: 2.6% pa
Capital: Ouagadougou, pop. 173,000
Language: French (official)
Religion: traditional beliefs (53%)
Currency: Franc CFA= 100 Centimes

BURKINA-FASO, formerly the Republic of Upper Volta, is land-locked and poor.

People and Culture France ruled the country from 1896 to 1960. Since independence, the country has experienced many military coups.

The average life expectancy at birth is 44 years.

The Land Low plateaux cover most of the land. The climate is tropical and the rainfall unreliable.

Economy Farming employs 82 percent of the workforce. Pastoralism is important in drier areas. Cotton is the chief cash crop. The per capita GNP (1981) was low at $240, and many young people seek work abroad.

SIERRA LEONE

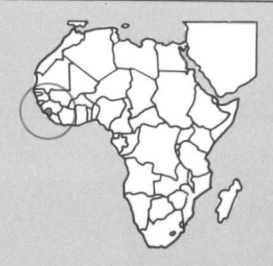

Area: 27,700 sq miles (71,740 km²)
Population: 3,868,000
Population Growth Rate: 2.7% pa
Capital: Freetown, pop. 274,000
Language: English (official)
Religion: mainly traditional beliefs
Currency: Leone = 100 Cents

THE REPUBLIC OF SIERRA LEONE is in West Africa.

People and Culture In 1787, Britain founded Freetown for freed slaves and, in 1808, began to colonize the area. In 1961 Sierra Leone became independent. It adopted a one-party Constitution in 1978. Most people are Blacks. There is a Creole minority. In 1981 the average life expectancy at birth was 47 years and the adult literacy rate was 15 percent.

The Land Behind the coastal plain are plateaux and mountains. The climate is tropical.

Economy Farming employs 65 percent of the workforce, but diamonds and bauxite are leading exports. The per capita GNP in 1981 was $320.

group has emerged. The PDCI favours free-enterprise policies.

In 1981 the average life expectancy at birth was 47 years. Adult literacy was 35 percent.

The Land Coastal plains, high inland plains and mountains in the northwest are the main features. The climate is tropical and savanna covers large areas, with forest in the south.

Economy Farming employed 79 percent of the workforce in 1981. Cocoa and coffee are major exports. Industry is important in Abidjan. The per capita GNP in 1981 was $1,200.

GHANA

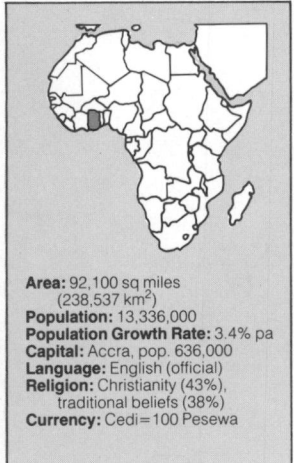

Area: 92,100 sq miles (238,537 km²)
Population: 13,336,000
Population Growth Rate: 3.4% pa
Capital: Accra, pop. 636,000
Language: English (official)
Religion: Christianity (43%), traditional beliefs (38%)
Currency: Cedi = 100 Pesewa

THE REPUBLIC OF GHANA was called Gold Coast before 1957.

People and Culture The coast became British in 1875 and the interior was colonized by 1901.

Independence was achieved in 1957 and Ghana became a republic in 1960. Ambitious development projects overstretched the economy and, from 1966, alternating military and civilian governments have tried to restore the economy and eliminate corruption.

Ghana's Black population speaks about 100 languages and dialects. The life expect-

ancy at birth in 1981 was high for West Africa at 54 years.

The Land Most of Ghana is low-lying. The man-made Lake Volta dominates central Ghana. Ghana has a hot equatorial climate, with heavy rainfall except in the drier southeast.

Economy Farming employs 53 percent of the workforce and accounts for 60 percent of the GDP. The main crop and export is cocoa. Industry is growing. The per capita GNP (1981) was $400.

TOGO

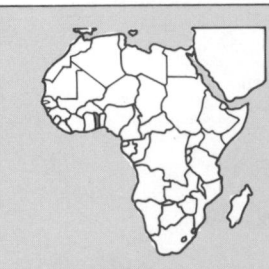

Area: 21,925 sq miles (56,785 km²)
Population: 2,705,000 (1981)
Population Growth Rate: 2.5% pa
Capital: Lomé, pop. 247,000
Language: French (official)
Religion: traditional beliefs (66%)
Currency: Franc CFA = 100 Centimes

THE TOGOLESE REPUBLIC is a small West African country.

People and Culture Togo was German from 1884. After World War I, it was partitioned between Britain and France. British Togoland is now part of Ghana. French Togo became independent in 1960. Military groups have ruled since 1967.

The Black population consists of about 30 language groups. The average life expectancy at birth is 48 years. Most adults are illiterate.

The Land Mountains in central Togo separate the southern plains from the low northern plateau. The climate is tropical and wet.

Fire can destroy vast areas of savanna in the dry season, as here in Benin (formerly Dahomey).

Economy Farming employs 67 percent of the workforce. Cocoa, coffee and phosphates are exported. The per capita GNP (1981) was $380.

BENIN

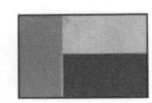

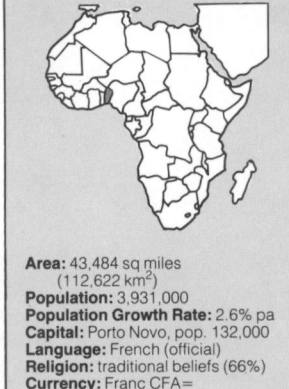

Area: 43,484 sq miles (112,622 km²)
Population: 3,931,000
Population Growth Rate: 2.6% pa
Capital: Porto Novo, pop. 132,000
Language: French (official)
Religion: traditional beliefs (66%)
Currency: Franc CFA = 100 Centimes

THE PEOPLE'S REPUBLIC OF BENIN was called Dahomey until 1975.

People and Culture France ruled Benin from the 1890s until independence in 1960. Six coups occurred between 1960 and 1972, when President Kerekou took power, proclaiming Benin a Marxist-Leninist state.

The Black population is divided into about 50 groups. The average life expectancy at birth is 50 years. The literacy rate is 28 percent.

The Land Low plateaux rising to the northwest cover much of Benin. The hot, wet south is forested. The savanna-covered north has dry winters.

Economy Farming employs 46 percent of the workforce. The chief exports are cotton and palm-oil. Petroleum exists offshore, but the per capita GNP (1981) was only $320.

NIGERIA

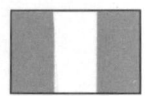

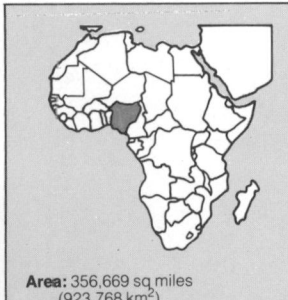

Area: 356,669 sq miles (923,768 km²)
Population: 87,831,000
Population Growth Rate: 3.3% pa
Capital: Lagos, pop. 1,061,000
Language: English (official)
Religion: Islam, Christianity, traditional beliefs
Currency: Naira = 100 Kobo

THE FEDERAL REPUBLIC OF NIGERIA has a larger population than any other African country.

People and Culture The history of central and southern Nigeria is marked by three cultures which produced superb sculptures: Nok (900 BC to AD 200); Ife (twelfth to fourteenth centuries AD); and Benin, which was flourishing when Portuguese explorers arrived in 1486.

Northern Nigeria was part of several sub-Saharan cultures. Trade with North Africa

led to the introduction of Islamic culture. Traditional beliefs survived in the south, even after the arrival of Christian missionaries in the nineteenth century. Britain annexed Lagos (then a slave depot) in 1861, and gradually colonized Nigeria, taking the north in 1901–03.

Independence was achieved in 1960. The Federal Constitution, giving powers to the Northern, Eastern and Western Regions, reflected Nigeria's cultural diversity. The Muslim Hausa and Fulani dominate the north, the Yoruba the southwest, and the Igbo the southeast. In fact, Nigeria has about 250 languages and dialects.

A civil war occurred from 1967 to 1970, when the Igbo tried to establish a breakaway nation, Biafra. Nigeria had military governments from 1966 to 1979 and the army again seized power at the end of 1983.

The average life expectancy at birth has risen from 39 years in 1960 to 49 in 1981. But the literacy rate is low at 34 percent.

The Land Behind the coastal plains and the swampy Niger River delta are uplands and plateaux which cover two-thirds of the land. The highest peaks are near the Cameroun border.

The south has an equatorial climate, with rain throughout the year. The north has a dry winter. Forests in the south merge into the northern savanna.

Economy Farming employs 54 percent of the workforce. Leading products are cocoa, groundnuts, palm-oil, rubber and timber. But industry, mainly oil production, accounted for 37 percent of the GDP in 1981, as compared with 23 percent from agriculture. Petroleum has recently dominated the economy, and Nigeria is Africa's largest producer. But the world recession led to a fall in demand and plunged Nigeria into economic crisis.

Nigeria is potentially one of Africa's greatest economic powers, although the per capita GNP in 1981 was only $870.

Manufacturing is developing, although the urban population is only 21 percent. A new capital at Abuja is due to be completed by the mid-1980s.

Chiefs in all their finery compete with each other in horsemanship at Kaduna, northern Nigeria.

Southern Africa

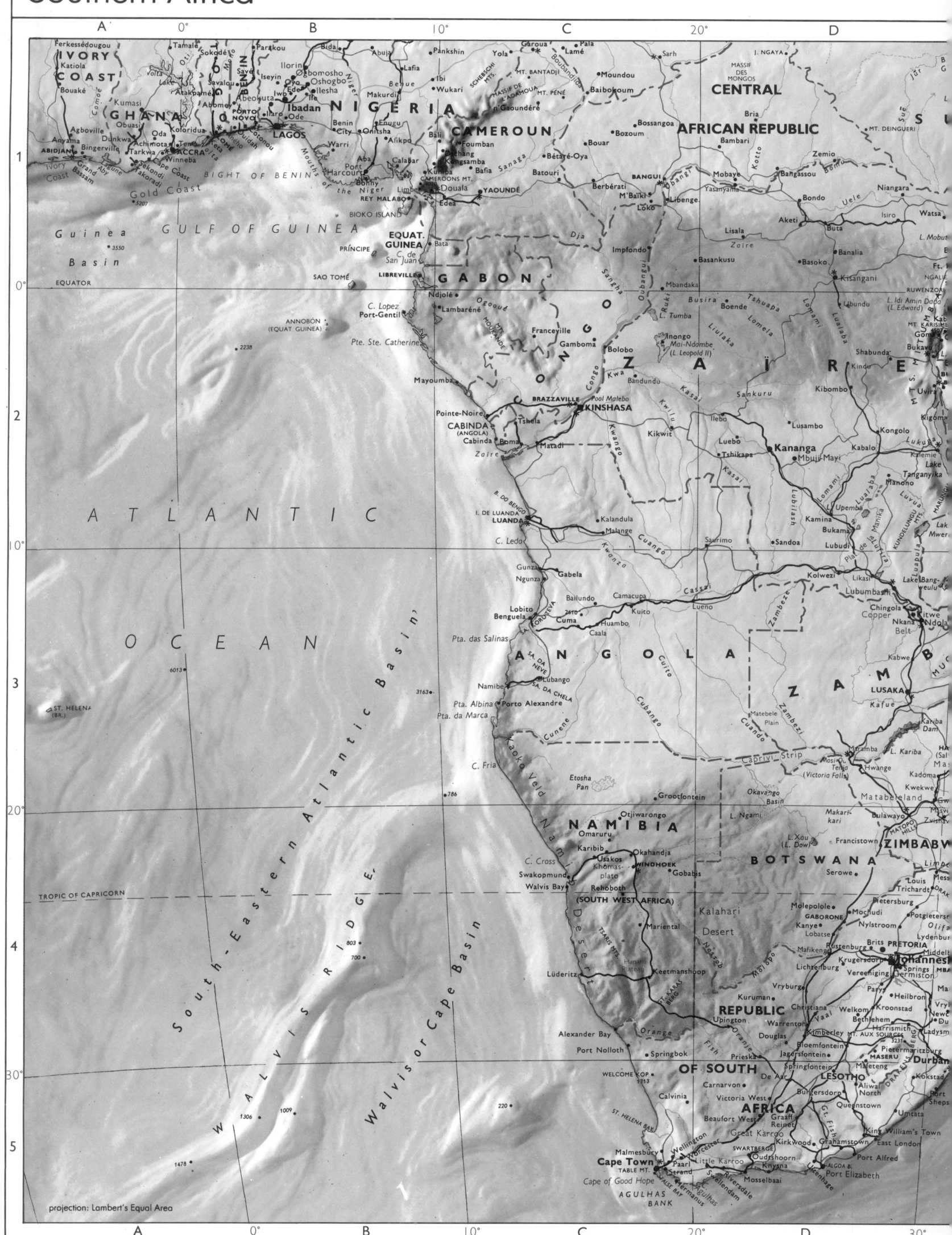

projection: Lambert's Equal Area

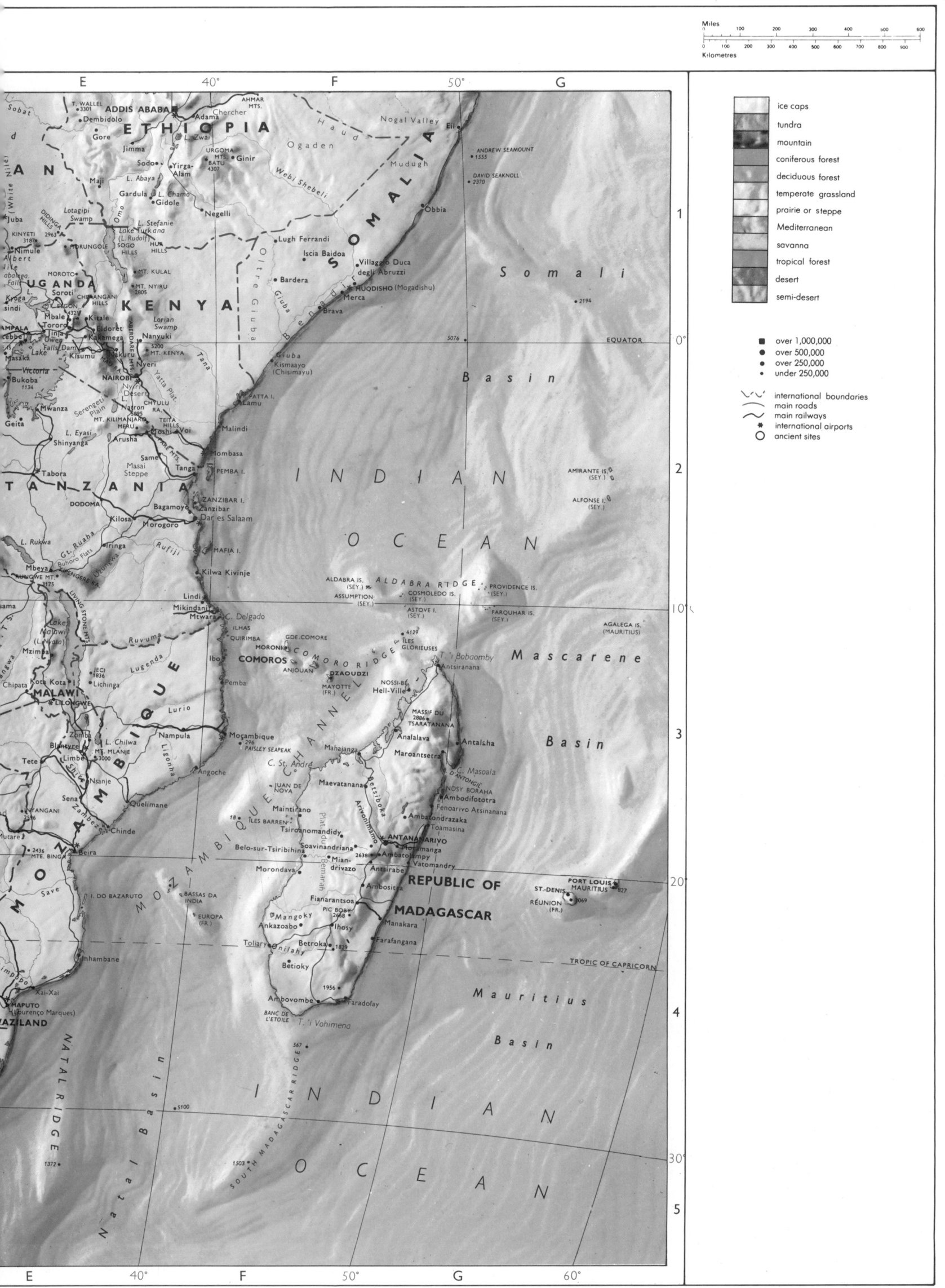

Miles
0   100   200   300   400   500   600
0   100 200 300 400 500 600 700 800 900
Kilometres

	ice caps
	tundra
	mountain
	coniferous forest
	deciduous forest
	temperate grassland
	prairie or steppe
	Mediterranean
	savanna
	tropical forest
	desert
	semi-desert

■ over 1,000,000
● over 500,000
● over 250,000
• under 250,000

international boundaries
main roads
main railways
✱ international airports
○ ancient sites

DJIBOUTI

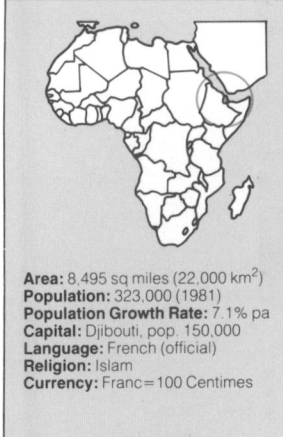

Area: 8,495 sq miles (22,000 km²)
Population: 323,000 (1981)
Population Growth Rate: 7.1% pa
Capital: Djibouti, pop. 150,000
Language: French (official)
Religion: Islam
Currency: Franc = 100 Centimes

THE REPUBLIC OF DJIBOUTI is a small country on the Red Sea.
People and Culture Djibouti was called French Somaliland from 1881 and, later, the Territory of the Afars and Issas. Independence was achieved in 1977. The people include Somali-speaking Issas and nomadic Afars (or Danakils).
The Land Djibouti is mostly desert, with average annual temperatures of 86°F (30°C).
Economy The chief activity is livestock-raising. Animals and hides and skins are exported. The capital is a major port, handling most of Ethiopia's seaborne trade. The per capita GNP (1981) was $480.

CENTRAL AFRICAN REPUBLIC

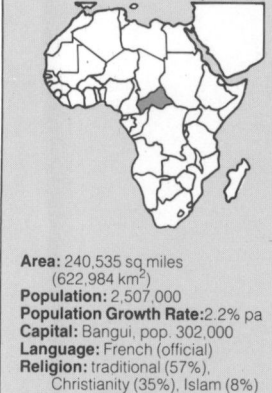

Area: 240,535 sq miles (622,984 km²)
Population: 2,507,000
Population Growth Rate: 2.2% pa
Capital: Bangui, pop. 302,000
Language: French (official)
Religion: traditional (57%), Christianity (35%), Islam (8%)
Currency: Franc CFA = 100 Centimes

THE CENTRAL AFRICAN REPUBLIC is a remote, land-locked country.
People and Culture France ruled from the 1880s until independence in 1960. From 1965 to 1979, a dictator Jean-Bédel Bokassa ruled the country.
Over 90 percent of the people speak Sudanic languages and 5 percent Bantu languages. There are some pygmies (Babinga). The average life expectancy at birth (1981) was 43 years.

The Land Plateaux cover most of the country. The wet south is forested, but the north is arid.
Economy Farming employs 88 percent of the workforce. Manufacturing is small-scale, but diamonds are mined. The per capita GNP (1981) was $320.

ETHIOPIA

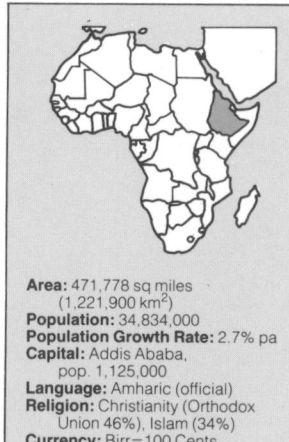

Area: 471,778 sq miles (1,221,900 km²)
Population: 34,834,000
Population Growth Rate: 2.7% pa
Capital: Addis Ababa, pop. 1,125,000
Language: Amharic (official)
Religion: Christianity (Orthodox Union 46%), Islam (34%)
Currency: Birr = 100 Cents

ETHIOPIA was an ancient monarchy until a military group took power in 1974.
People and Culture Christianity, introduced in the fourth century AD, survived in the mountains of Ethiopia among the ruling Amharas, although Islam later spread into the east and south.
Ethiopia was never colonized, although Italy occupied it in 1935–41. The monarchy was abolished in 1974 and a socialist military government, aided by Cuba and the USSR, fought to put down secessionist forces, especially in Eritrea in the east and in Somali-speaking Ogaden in the south.
About 100 languages are spoken. Amhara is a Semitic language. Cushitic languages include Somali and Galla, the language of the largest single ethnic group. Blacks in the west speak Sudanic languages.
The Land The Ethiopian highlands contain volcanic mountains and Lake Tana, source of the Blue Nile. An arm of the East African Rift Valley is in the south. The highlands are cool and generally moist, while the east and south are hot and arid.
Economy Farming employs 80 percent of the workforce. Coffee is the main export. Underdevelopment and the continuing conflict in the east and south have shattered the economy. In 1981 Ethiopia's per capita GNP was $140.

SOMALIA

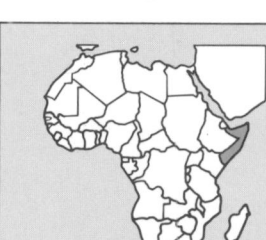

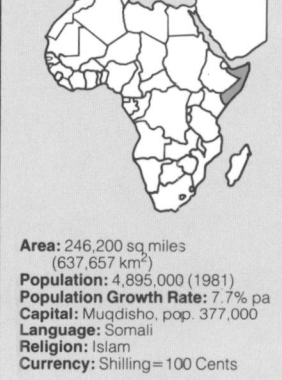

Area: 246,200 sq miles (637,657 km²)
Population: 4,895,000 (1981)
Population Growth Rate: 7.7% pa
Capital: Muqdisho, pop. 377,000
Language: Somali
Religion: Islam
Currency: Shilling = 100 Cents

THE SOMALI DEMOCRATIC REPUBLIC is also called Somalia.
People and Culture Formerly divided between Britain and Italy, Somalia was united on independence in 1960. The army ruled from 1969 but, under a new Constitution, elections were held in 1979, although there is only one legal party.
Somalis, who are united by their Cushitic language, also live in Djibouti, Ethiopia and Kenya. The wish to create Greater Somalia has led to border problems. And in 1977–78, Somalia supported Somali-speaking secessionists in Ethiopia.
Living standards are low and the life expectancy at birth is 39 years (1981). Adult literacy is 60 percent.
The Land Highlands dominate the north, with plateaus, plains and the only permanent rivers in the south. Somalia is hot and arid, but rainfall increases from north to south. Muqdisho (Mogadishu) has 16 inches (406 mm) a year.
Economy Farming employs 82 percent of the workforce. Most Somalis are nomadic pastoralists. Animals, meat and hides are the chief exports. The per capita GNP (1981) was only $280.

SEYCHELLES

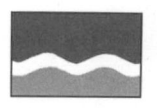

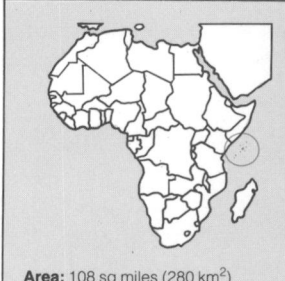

Area: 108 sq miles (280 km²)
Population: 70,000
Population Growth Rate: 1.8% pa
Capital: Victoria, pop. 25,000
Languages: Creole, English, French
Religion: mainly Christianity (Roman Catholics)
Currency: Rupee = 100 Cents

THE REPUBLIC OF SEYCHELLES is an island nation in the Indian Ocean.

People and Culture The islands were settled by France in the eighteenth century, but Britain ruled from 1810 until independence in 1976. A coup in 1977 brought a socialist regime to power. A mercenary-led invasion was defeated in 1981.
Most people are Creoles (of mixed African and French origin). There are some Chinese, Europeans and Indians.
The Land The Seychelles contain about 90 islands, the largest of which is Mahé. The climate is tropical.
Economy Farming and tourism are the main activities. The per capita GNP (1981) was $1,800.

CAMEROUN

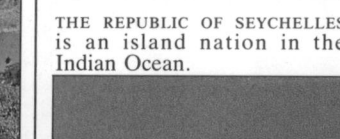

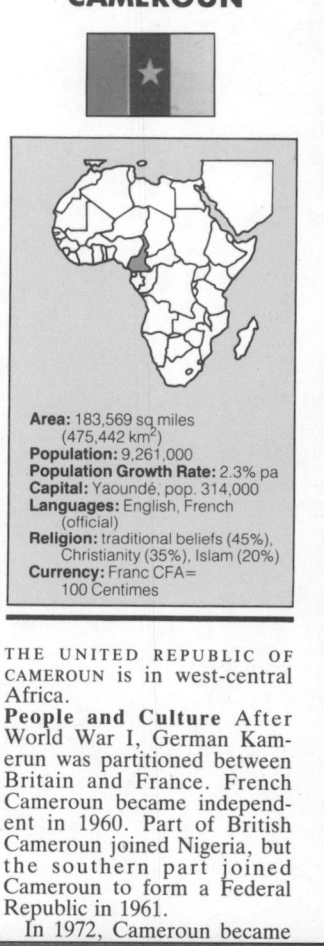

Area: 183,569 sq miles (475,442 km²)
Population: 9,261,000
Population Growth Rate: 2.3% pa
Capital: Yaoundé, pop. 314,000
Languages: English, French (official)
Religion: traditional beliefs (45%), Christianity (35%), Islam (20%)
Currency: Franc CFA = 100 Centimes

THE UNITED REPUBLIC OF CAMEROUN is in west-central Africa.
People and Culture After World War I, German Kamerun was partitioned between Britain and France. French Cameroun became independent in 1960. Part of British Cameroun joined Nigeria, but the southern part joined Cameroun to form a Federal Republic in 1961.
In 1972, Cameroun became

The Blue Nile rises in the rugged highlands of Ethiopia.

The Blue Nile's gorge is an obstacle to transportation.

a United Republic, although French and English remain official languages, alongside 200 Bantu and Sudanic languages. The average life expectancy at birth is 50 years.

The Land Inland plateaus rise to highlands along the Nigerian border. The Lake Chad basin is in the north. The highest peak is the volcanic Mt Cameroon.

The forested south has a wet equatorial climate. Central Cameroun is wooded savanna, with grassland in the drier north.

Economy Farming employs 83 percent of the workforce. Manufacturing is small-scale, but mining for bauxite and oil is becoming important. This politically stable country's per capita GNP was $880 in 1981.

SÃO TOMÉ AND PRÍNCIPE

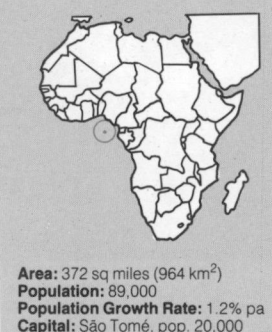

Area: 372 sq miles (964 km²)
Population: 89,000
Population Growth Rate: 1.2% pa
Capital: São Tomé, pop. 20,000
Language: Portuguese (official)
Religion: Christianity (Roman Catholic)
Currency: Dobra = 100 Centavos

THE DEMOCRATIC REPUBLIC OF SÃO TOMÉ AND PRÍNCIPE IS an island nation in the Gulf of Guinea.

People and Culture Portugal governed from 1522 until independence in 1975. The people are descendants of slaves brought from the mainland and European settlers.

The Land The country includes the volcanic island of São Tomé, where the capital is located, Príncipe to the north, and some smaller islands. The climate is equatorial, with forests on lower slopes, and grassland at higher levels.

Economy Farming is the main activity and cocoa the chief export. The per capita GNP (1981) was $370.

EQUATORIAL GUINEA

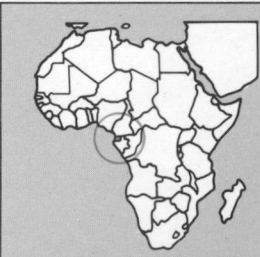

Area: 10,831 sq miles (28,051 km²)
Population: 399,000
Population Growth Rate: 2.4% pa
Capital: Malabo, pop. 9,000
Language: Spanish (official)
Religion: Christianity (Roman Catholic 88%)
Currency: Ekuele = 100 Céntimos

THE REPUBLIC OF EQUATORIAL GUINEA contains Río Muni on the mainland and the islands of Bioko (formerly Fernando Póo) and Annobón (Pagalu).

People and Culture Spain ruled from the 1840s until independence in 1968. From 1968 to 1979 President Francisco Macías Nguema ruled with great brutality.

The Bantu-speaking Fang form the majority of the population.

The Land Río Muni is mostly low-lying. The islands are volcanic. The climate is equatorial, with forests on the lowlands and savanna on higher ground.

Economy Most people are farmers. Coffee is the main crop. The per capita GNP in 1981 was very low at $180.

Agriculture is Ethiopia's main industry; periodic droughts can cause starvation.

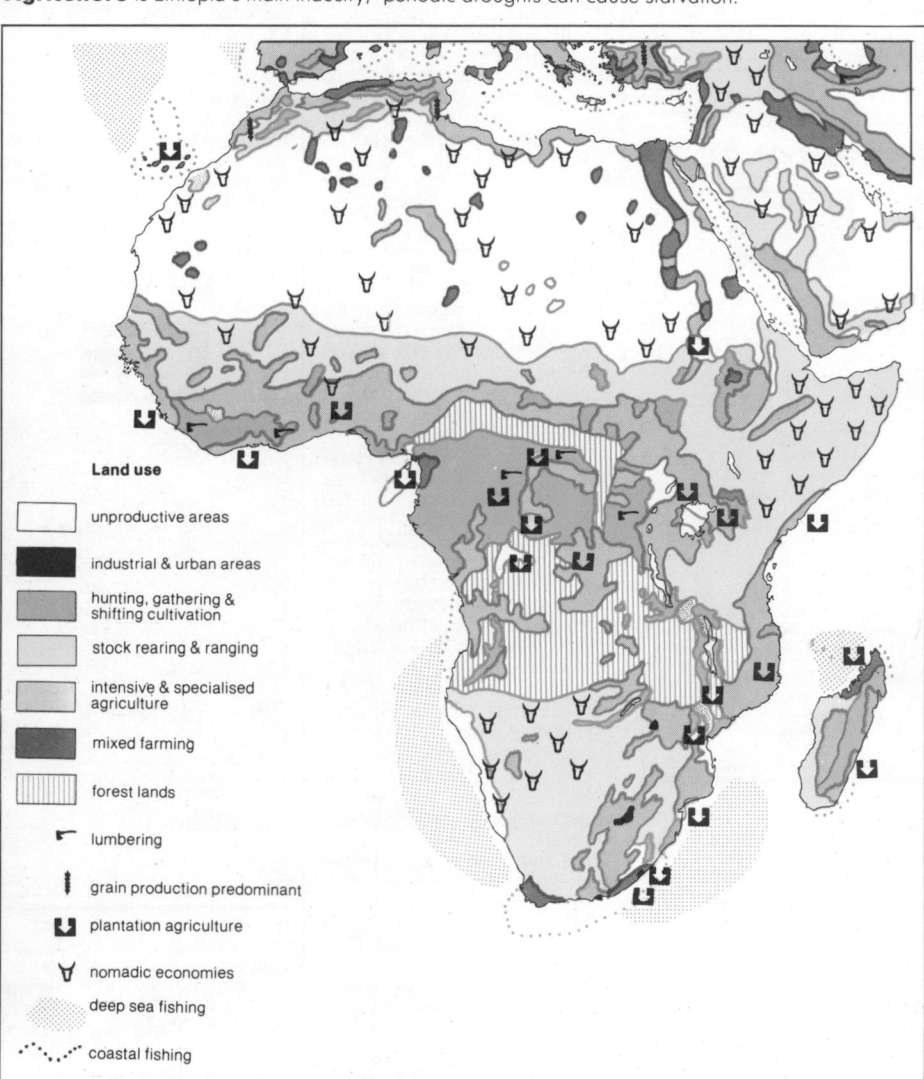

Land use

- unproductive areas
- industrial & urban areas
- hunting, gathering & shifting cultivation
- stock rearing & ranging
- intensive & specialised agriculture
- mixed farming
- forest lands
- lumbering
- grain production predominant
- plantation agriculture
- nomadic economies
- deep sea fishing
- coastal fishing

GABON

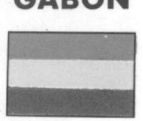

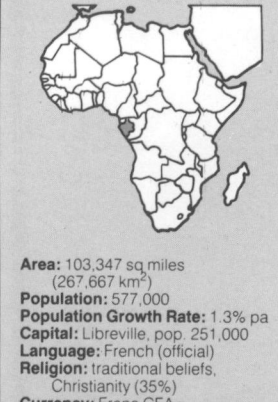

Area: 103,347 sq miles
(267,667 km²)
Population: 577,000
Population Growth Rate: 1.3% pa
Capital: Libreville, pop. 251,000
Language: French (official)
Religion: traditional beliefs,
Christianity (35%)
Currency: Franc CFA=
100 Centimes

THE GABONESE REPUBLIC is in west-central Africa.
People and Culture France founded Libreville in 1849 for freed slaves. Gabon was a French colony from the 1880s until independence in 1960. Gabon became a one-party country in 1968. About 40 languages are spoken; the Bantu-speaking Fang form the largest group.
The Land Plateaux and mountains lie inland. The climate is equatorial and forests cover three-quarters of the land.
Economy Farming employs 70 percent of the workforce. But petroleum production, together with manganese and uranium resources, have given Gabon the second highest per capita GNP in mainland Africa of $3,810.

THE CONGO

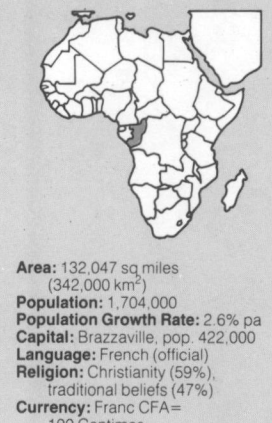

Area: 132,047 sq miles
(342,000 km²)
Population: 1,704,000
Population Growth Rate: 2.6% pa
Capital: Brazzaville, pop. 422,000
Language: French (official)
Religion: Christianity (59%),
traditional beliefs (47%)
Currency: Franc CFA=
100 Centimes

THE PEOPLE'S REPUBLIC OF THE CONGO was once called Congo (Brazzaville).
People and Culture France ruled from the 1880s until independence in 1960. Military regimes have governed since 1968, pursuing socialist policies. But Congo maintains close ties with the West.
Most people are Bantu-speakers, with a few pygmies (Binga). The average life ex-

pectancy at birth (1981) was 60 years.
The Land Uplands border the coastal plain. Northern Congo is swampy, drained by the Congo (Zaire) River. The climate is equatorial. Forest and wooded savanna cover most of Congo.
Economy One-third of the population works on farms, but in 1980 industry accounted for 53 percent of the GDP. Oil is especially important. The per capita GNP in 1981 was $1,100.

ZAIRE

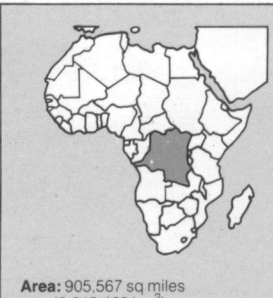

Area: 905,567 sq miles
(2,345,409 km²)
Population: 29,777,000 (1981)
Population Growth Rate: 3.0% pa
Capital: Kinshasa, pop. 2,444,000
Language: French (official)
Religion: traditional beliefs (59%),
Christianity (40%)
Currency: Zaire=100 Makuta

THE REPUBLIC OF ZAIRE IS Africa's second largest nation. It was formerly called Congo (Kinshasa).
People and Culture Iron-using Bantu-speaking people settled in Zaire between about 100 BC and AD 800, displacing the original pygmies, of whom only a few survive in remote areas.
Portuguese explorers reached the area in 1482, but powerful Bantu kingdoms blocked inland penetration. In 1874–77, Henry Morton Stanley explored the Congo (now Zaire) River. He interested King Léopold II of Belgium in his discoveries. Léopold made Zaire his personal property in 1884. Ill-treatment of local people by *concessionaires* led the Belgian government to take over in 1908.
The country became independent in 1960, but chaos and civil war ensued, with the UN providing a peace-keeping force. In 1965 General Mobutu Sese Seko became president. His government has maintained stability, despite further uprisings in the mineral-rich Shaba (formerly Katanga) province.
About two-thirds of the people now speak Bantu. Hamitic, Nilotic, Sudanic and Pygmy languages are also spoken, making a total of about 200. The average life expectancy at birth (1981) was 50 years.
The Land Most of Zaire lies in the Zaire River basin, with plateaux and highlands in the south and east, where Zaire's border passes along the East African Rift Valley.
The climate is equatorial. Vast rain forests cover central Zaire, with savanna in the north and south and mountain vegetation in the highlands.

Tanzania's wonderful wildlife is protected in such national parks as Serengeti in the north.

Wildlife is varied and abundant. Tourism is increasing.
Economy Farming employs 75 percent of the workforce. Coffee, cotton, palm products and rubber are important, but minerals, including copper, cobalt and diamonds, are the most valuable exports. Manufacturing is increasing in Kinshasa and Lubumbashi. The per capita GNP in 1981, however, was low at $210.

UGANDA

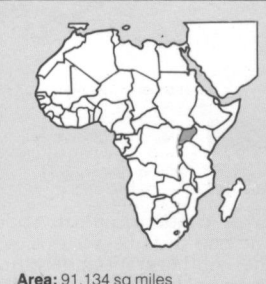

Area: 91,134 sq miles
(236,036 km²)
Population: 13,620,000 (1981)
Population Growth Rate: 2.6% pa
(tentative)
Capital: Kampala, pop. 332,000
Language: English (official)
Religion: Christianity (63%)
Currency: Shilling=100 Cents

THE REPUBLIC OF UGANDA is a land-locked equatorial country.
People and Culture Britain took over Uganda between 1894 and World War I. Independence was achieved in 1964 and Uganda became a

republic in 1967. General Idi Amin's dictatorial rule lasted from 1971 until 1979, when Ugandan forces, aided by Tanzanian troops, invaded Uganda. Since 1980, President Milton Obote's government has sought to restore the shattered economy, although internal disorder has marred progress.
Uganda has about 40 language groups. The largest is the Bantu-speaking Baganda. Most of Uganda's Asians were expelled in 1972. In 1981, the average life expectancy at birth was only 48 years, and the adult literacy rate was 52 percent.
The Land Uganda consists mainly of plateaux. Lake Victoria occupies a shallow depression. Other lakes are in the deep Rift Valley.
Temperatures are around

A pride of lions relaxes in Ngorongoro Crater, Tanzania.

70°–75°F (21°–24°C) throughout the year. The rainfall is generally abundant.
Economy Farming employs 83 percent of the workforce. Coffee, cotton and tea are major exports. Copper is mined, but manufacturing is small-scale. The per capita GNP declined by about 4 percent a year in 1970–80, reaching $220 in 1981.

KENYA

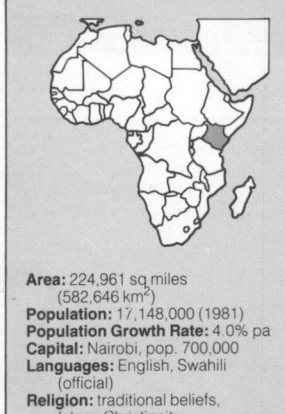

Area: 224,961 sq miles (582,646 km²)
Population: 17,148,000 (1981)
Population Growth Rate: 4.0% pa
Capital: Nairobi, pop. 700,000
Languages: English, Swahili (official)
Religion: traditional beliefs, Islam, Christianity
Currency: Shilling = 100 Cents

THE REPUBLIC OF KENYA, with its spectacular scenery, pleasant climate and varied wildlife, has developed an important tourist industry.
People and Culture Kenya was settled by Bantu-speaking peoples from about AD 100. The population now includes 40 language groups, the largest being the Bantu-speaking Kikuyu (21 percent), the Nilotic Luo, the Bantu-speaking Luhya and Kamba, and the Nilo-Hamitic Kalenjin. There are Asian, Arab and European minorities.

Mombasa, Kenya's chief port, was founded nearly 1,000 years ago as an Islamic city state.

Britain made the Kenya coast a protectorate in 1895. British settlers opened up the interior and Kenya became a British colony in 1920.

African opposition to European land ownership led to the Mau Mau rebellion (1952–60). Independence was achieved in 1963. Kenya became a republic in 1964. Kenya has enjoyed stable one-party rule since 1969, broadly following free enterprise policies.
The Land Behind the hot, humid coastal plain are savanna-covered plateaux, rising to Mt Kenya, the highest peak. Several lakes are in the East African Rift Valley and part of Lake Victoria is in the southeast. Temperatures on the plateaux are moderated by the altitude. But only 15 percent of Kenya has a reliable annual rainfall of 30 inches (762 mm).

Kenya has much superb wildlife, protected in such places as Amboseli, Nairobi and Tsavo national parks.
Economy Farming employed 78 percent of the workforce in 1981. The chief cash crops are coffee and tea. Mining is small-scale, but manufacturing is increasing, especially in Nairobi and Mombassa (pop. 342,000). The per capita GNP (1981) was $420.

RWANDA

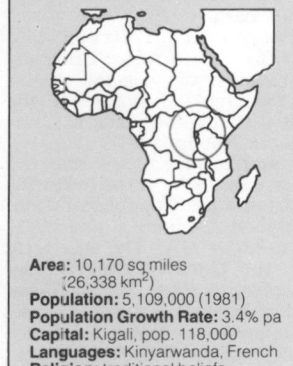

Area: 10,170 sq miles (26,338 km²)
Population: 5,109,000 (1981)
Population Growth Rate: 3.4% pa
Capital: Kigali, pop. 118,000
Languages: Kinyarwanda, French
Religion: traditional beliefs, Christianity
Currency: Franc = 100 Centimes

THE REPUBLIC OF RWANDA was once part of Ruanda-Urundi.
People and Culture Ruanda-Urundi was German before 1916 and Belgian until independence in 1962. Rwanda was once a monarchy, whose

mwami (king) belonged to the minority Nilo-Hamitic Tutsi group. In 1959, Bantu speaking Hutu peasants (who form 90 percent of the population) revolted. Rwanda became an independent republic in 1962 under Hutu leaders, but communal conflict has continued.

The average life expectancy at birth (1981) was 46 years.
The Land Rwanda contains part of the Rift Valley and mountains in the west, with plateaux in the east. The climate is moderated by the altitude.
Economy Farming employs 91 percent of the workforce. Coffee is the main export and industry is small-scale. The per capita GNP (1981) was $250.

TANZANIA

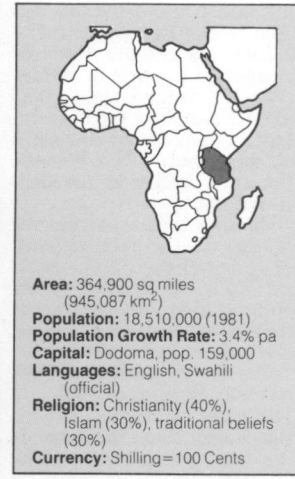

Area: 364,900 sq miles (945,087 km²)
Population: 18,510,000 (1981)
Population Growth Rate: 3.4% pa
Capital: Dodoma, pop. 159,000
Languages: English, Swahili (official)
Religion: Christianity (40%), Islam (30%), traditional beliefs (30%)
Currency: Shilling = 100 Cents

THE UNITED REPUBLIC OF TANZANIA consists of mainland Tanganyika and the former island nation of Zanzibar.
People and Culture Germany ruled Tanganyika from 1890 until World War I, while Britain ruled Zanzibar. After World War I, Britain also governed Tanganyika until independence in 1961.

Zanzibar achieved independence in 1963 and, in 1964, united with Tanganyika.

Most people speak Bantu languages. There are about 120 languages. Tanzania is a one-party nation. It has pursued socialist policies, emphasizing rural development. The average life expectancy (1981) was 52 years, while adult literacy stood at 79 percent.
The Land Most of the mainland is formed by plateaux, rising to Mt Kilimanjaro in the north. Two arms of the Rift Valley run north–south through Tanzania. The climate is moderated by the altitude, except on the coast and on the low coral islands of Zanzibar and Pemba.

Savanna is the commonest type of vegetation. The wildlife, which is still abundant, particularly the large mammals, is now protected in huge parks. The Serengeti National Park, 6,000 sq miles in area, is the largest of these.
Economy Farming employs 83 percent of the workforce. Coffee and cotton are important and diamonds are mined. The per capita GNP (1981) was $280.

BURUNDI

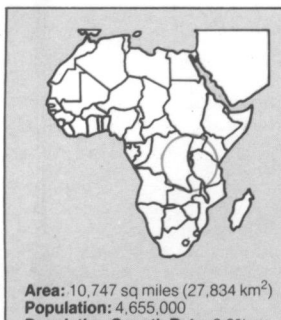

Area: 10,747 sq miles (27,834 km²)
Population: 4,655,000
Population Growth Rate: 2.3% pa
Capital: Bujumbura, pop. 157,000
Languages: French, Kirundi
Religion: Christianity (67%)
Currency: Franc = 100 Centimes

THE REPUBLIC OF BURUNDI was once part of Ruanda-Urundi.
People and Culture Ruanda-Urundi was German before 1916 and Belgian until 1962 when Burundi became an independent monarchy controlled by the minority Nilo-Hamitic Tutsi (13 percent of the population).

Burundi became a republic in 1966 but the Tutsi retained control over the Bantu-speaking Hutu (85 percent of the population), but communal conflict has continued to cause much bloodshed.

The life expectancy at birth was only 45 years in 1981.
The Land Mountains and the Rift Valley lie in the west. In the east are plateaux. The altitude moderates temperatures. The rainfall is abundant.
Economy Farming employs 84 percent of the workforce. Coffee is the main export. The per capita GNP (1981) was $230.

ANGOLA

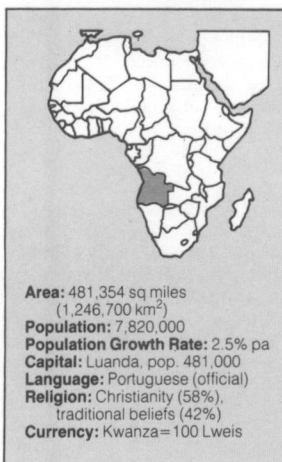

Area: 481,354 sq miles (1,246,700 km²)
Population: 7,820,000
Population Growth Rate: 2.5% pa
Capital: Luanda, pop. 481,000
Language: Portuguese (official)
Religion: Christianity (58%), traditional beliefs (42%)
Currency: Kwanza = 100 Lweis

THE PEOPLE'S REPUBLIC OF ANGOLA includes the small enclave of Cabinda.
People and Culture The Portuguese explored the Angolan coast in the 1480s and gradually became established there. After a guerrilla war, begun in 1961, Angola achieved independence in 1975.

Most Angolans are Blacks. Bantu languages, including Kongo, Mbundu, Ovimbundu and Lunda-Chokwe, are spoken.

At independence the socialist *Movimento Popular de Libertação de Angola* (MPLA), with Mbundu and mestizo support, took command, establishing one-party rule. With Cubanese aid, it put down a Kongo rebellion in the north, but could not defeat UNITA, an Ovimbundu movement in the south, controlling large areas with South African support. In the 1980s, South African forces entered southern Angola to attack Namibian guerrillas. In 1984 Angola and South Africa began to negotiate a truce plan.
The Land Plateaux cover most of this tropical country. Savanna covers large areas, with forests in the south and northeast.
Economy Agriculture employs 59 percent of the workforce, but mining is becoming more important, including oil extraction in Cabinda. But the continuing warfare has damaged the economy. The per capita GNP (1980) was $470.

ZAMBIA

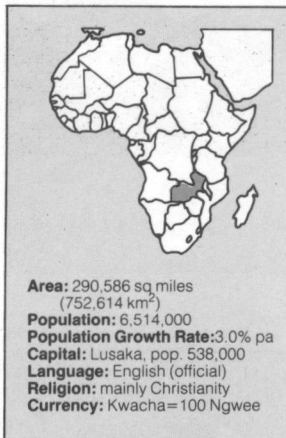

Area: 290,586 sq miles (752,614 km²)
Population: 6,514,000
Population Growth Rate: 3.0% pa
Capital: Lusaka, pop. 538,000
Language: English (official)
Religion: mainly Christianity
Currency: Kwacha = 100 Ngwee

THE REPUBLIC OF ZAMBIA was once known as Northern Rhodesia.
People and Culture The British South Africa Company started to develop the area in 1889. In 1911 it became the British protectorate of Northern Rhodesia.

Independence was achieved in 1964 when the country became the Republic of Zambia. It became a one-party nation in 1972. The sole party is the United National Independence Party led by President Kenneth Kaunda, a strong supporter of Black nationalist movements in southern Africa.

Most Zambians speak one of the six major Bantu languages or one of the 66 dialects. The average life expectancy at birth in 1981 was 51 years and the adult literacy rate was 44 percent.
The Land Most of Zambia is a high, savanna-covered plateau. The Zambezi/Luangwa trough in the south contains Lake Kariba and the Victoria Falls. The altitude moderates the tropical climate. The Kafue and Luangwa national parks are rich in wildlife.
Economy Farming employs 67 percent of the workforce, but industry, especially copper mining, usually dominates the economy. Manufacturing, using electricity from the Kariba Dam, is increasing. Recent falls in the world demand for copper have caused some economic problems. The per capita GNP (1981) was $600.

MALAWI

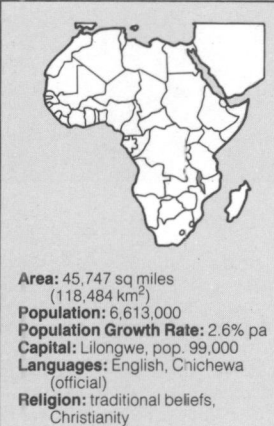

Area: 45,747 sq miles (118,484 km²)
Population: 6,613,000
Population Growth Rate: 2.6% pa
Capital: Lilongwe, pop. 99,000
Languages: English, Chichewa (official)
Religion: traditional beliefs, Christianity
Currency: Kwacha = 100 Tambala

THE REPUBLIC OF MALAWI was once called Nyasaland.
People and Culture Malawi was ruled by Britain from 1891 until independence in 1964. It became a republic in 1966. A one-party nation, it has enjoyed stability under its President-for-life, Hastings Kamuzu Banda.

Most people speak Bantu languages. There are Asian and European minorities. The average life expectancy at birth (1981) was 44 years, and the adult literacy rate was 25 percent.
The Land Malawi includes part of Lake Malawi (Nyasa), with highlands in the west and south. The lowlands are hot but the uplands have a pleasant climate.
Economy Farming employs 86 percent of the workforce. The main exports are tobacco and tea. The per capita GNP (1981) was $200.

The Cuanza River flows across the Angolan plateau. It is utilized for hydroelectric power.

The Victoria Falls straddle the Zimbabwe border.

COMOROS

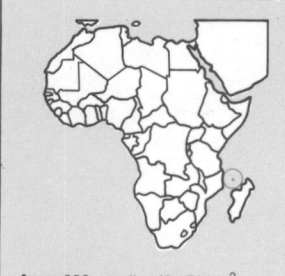

Area: 838 sq miles (2,171 km²)
Population: 407,000
Population Growth Rate: 3.3% pa
Capital: Moroni, pop. 16,000
Languages: Arabic, French
Religion: mainly Islam
Currency: Franc CFA = 100 Centimes

THE FEDERAL ISLAMIC REPUBLIC OF THE COMOROS consists of three islands: Njazidja (formerly Grande Comore), Nzwani (Anjuan) and Mwali (Mohéli).

Geographically, there is a fourth, Mahoré (Mayotte), but this island is French.
People and Culture France ruled the islands from the 1880s until independence in 1976 following a vote in the Chamber of Deputies in 1975. But a majority on Mayotte voted to stay French.

The population is mixed, with African, Asian and European elements.
The Land The islands are volcanic and the climate is tropical.
Economy Most people are subsistence farmers. The per capita GNP (1981) was $320.

NAMIBIA

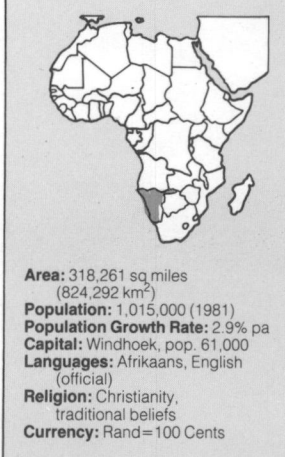

Area: 318,261 sq miles (824,292 km²)
Population: 1,015,000 (1981)
Population Growth Rate: 2.9% pa
Capital: Windhoek, pop. 61,000
Languages: Afrikaans, English (official)
Religion: Christianity, traditional beliefs
Currency: Rand = 100 Cents

NAMIBIA was known as South-West Africa until the United Nations renamed it in 1968.
People and Culture South-West Africa became a Ger-

man protectorate in 1884. South African troops occupied the territory in 1915 and in 1920, the League of Nations gave South Africa a mandate to rule it. In 1946, the UN asked South Africa to accept trusteeship status to replace the old mandate, but South Africa refused.

International criticism of South African rule increased and African nationalist groups, including the South-West African People's Organization (SWAPO), demanded independence. In 1971, the International Court of Justice ruled that South Africa's presence there was illegal.

A guerrilla war, begun in 1966, continued into the 1980s. Fighting spread in 1983 when South African forces entered southern Angola to attack SWAPO bases.

The people of Namibia include Europeans (12 percent), Hottentots (Nama) and Bushmen (16 percent), and Bantu-speaking peoples (72 percent). The Ovambo are the largest of the Bantu-speaking groups.

The Land The main regions are: the coastal Namib desert; the central plateau; and the Kalahari.

The north is tropical and the south subtropical. It is arid everywhere. The Namib has virtually no rain. Windhoek, on the central plateau, has 8–10 inches (203–254 mm) a year, but rainfall increases to the north. The Kalahari has 4–10 inches (102–254 mm) of rain a year.

The wetter north contains one of Africa's most varied wildlife reserves, the Etosha National Park.

Economy There is sheep farming on the southern plateau, while crops are grown and cattle raised on the northern plateau. Fishing is important, but minerals dominate the economy. Diamonds, lead, tin, uranium and zinc are all exported. The per capita GNP (1981) was $1,960.

BOTSWANA

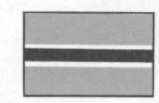

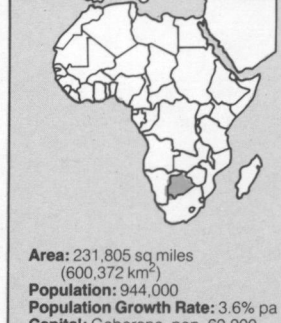

Area: 231,805 sq miles (600,372 km²)
Population: 944,000
Population Growth Rate: 3.6% pa
Capital: Gaborone, pop. 60,000
Languages: English (official), Setswana
Religion: Christianity, traditional beliefs
Currency: Pula = 100 Thebe

THE REPUBLIC OF BOTSWANA was formerly Bechuanaland.
People and Culture Britain ruled Bechuanaland from 1885 until independence in 1966.

Most people belong to the Bantu-speaking Tswana group and live in the east, near the Cape Town–Bulawayo railway. There are also some Bushmen and Eurafrican and European minorities.

The Land Botswana is a large plateau. The Kalahari, a semi-desert, covers 84 percent of the land. The wetter north has dry wooded savanna, while the rainfall in the east averages 15–20 inches (381–508 mm) a year.

The only surface water is in the inland Okavango delta in the north, an area rich in wildlife.

Economy Until the late 1960s, livestock farming was the basis of the economy. But recently diamond, copper and nickel mining have raised the per capita GNP to $1,010 in 1981.

ZIMBABWE

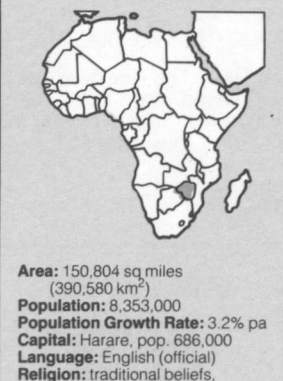

Area: 150,804 sq miles (390,580 km²)
Population: 8,353,000
Population Growth Rate: 3.2% pa
Capital: Harare, pop. 686,000
Language: English (official)
Religion: traditional beliefs, Christianity
Currency: Dollar = 100 Cents

THE REPUBLIC OF ZIMBABWE was formerly called Southern Rhodesia.

People and Culture Iron Age settlements in Zimbabwe date back to AD 300. There are also impressive stone ruins built by a civilization in the eleventh to fifteenth centuries.

A British High Commissioner ruled Southern Rhodesia between 1898 and 1923, when the country became a self-governing British colony.

About 270,000 whites once lived in the country, but even then 96 percent of the population were Black Africans, who spoke Bantu languages, including Ndebele in the south and Shona in the north.

The whites, who controlled the government and economy, asked Britain for independence in 1963. Britain refused, because the whites would not give up their dominance. In 1965 Rhodesia made a unilateral declaration of independence.

A guerrilla war against the illegal white government began in the early 1970s. Finally, independence with Black majority rule was achieved in 1980.

Robert Mugabe's mainly Shona Zimbabwe African National Union (ZANU) won an electoral victory over Joshua Nkomo's mainly Ndebele Zimbabwe African People's Union (ZAPU).

Mugabe pursued a policy of Africanization. Many whites emigrated. In early 1984, they numbered around 100,000. The average life expectancy at birth (1981) was 50 years. The adult literacy rate was 69 percent.

The Land The main regions are the hot, arid southern veld, drained by the Limpopo River; the cooler, wetter high veld, covered by wooded savanna; and the wet, forested eastern highlands. The Zambezi River occupies a trough in the north, containing Lake Kariba and the Victoria Falls.

Economy Farming employs 60 percent of the workforce, but industry is more important to the economy. Tobacco, sugar, tea and fruits are exported. Asbestos, chrome, coal and gold are mined. Manufacturing, which is important in the cities, contributed 27 percent of the GDP in 1980, as compared with 18 percent from agriculture. In 1981, the per capita GNP was $870.

MOZAMBIQUE

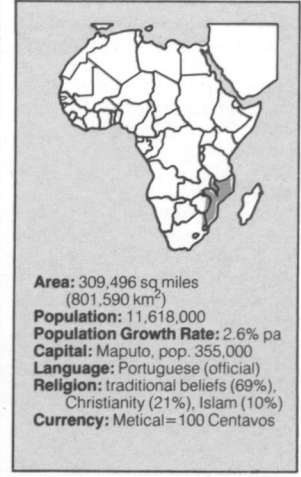

Area: 309,496 sq miles (801,590 km²)
Population: 11,618,000
Population Growth Rate: 2.6% pa
Capital: Maputo, pop. 355,000
Language: Portuguese (official)
Religion: traditional beliefs (69%), Christianity (21%), Islam (10%)
Currency: Metical = 100 Centavos

THE PEOPLE'S REPUBLIC OF MOZAMBIQUE is in southeast Africa.

The Kung of Botswana belong to the San (Bushmen) group of people in southern Africa. Many Bushmen are still nomadic hunters and gatherers.

People and Culture Portuguese explorers reached Mozambique in 1498 and colonization began in 1505.

A guerrilla war (1964–74) preceded independence in 1975, when most Portuguese left the country. The Mozambique Liberation Front (FRELIMO) government pursued socialist policies. In the early 1980s, anti-government guerrilla activity disrupted the country and South African troops raided South African exile bases in Maputo. In 1984 Mozambique and South Africa signed a non-aggression pact.

Most people are Black Africans, divided into 12 major and 30 minor Bantu-speaking groups. The average life expectancy at birth (1980) was 47 years and the adult literacy rate was 33 percent.

The Land Broad coastal lowlands, drained by such rivers as the Limpopo, Rovuma and Zambezi, cover 44 percent of the country. Plateaux, hills and uplands cover the rest. Northern Mozambique has a tropical climate, with rains from October to April. The subtropical south is drier. Droughts in the early 1980s caused much suffering.

Forests grow along the rivers, but savanna is the commonest vegetation. Some areas have abundant wildlife.

Economy Farming employs 66 percent of the workforce. Cashew nuts, cotton and tea are exported. Some coal is mined and manufacturing is increasing. In 1980, the per capita GNP was $270, but the early 1980s were marked by internal disorder, droughts and economic decline.

Dhows sail down the East African coast off Mozambique.

The Land Two-thirds of the country is a savanna-covered plateau, interrupted by occasional volcanic peaks. Here the altitude moderates the climate. The narrow eastern coastlands are hot, humid and forested. The northwest is wet, but the southwest coast is arid.

Madagascar is the home of a group of primitive primates called lemurs.

Economy Farming employs 87 percent of the workforce. Coffee, cloves and vanilla are produced. There is little mining and manufacturing is small-scale. The per capita GNP (1981) was $330.

the east. The climate is warm and humid.

Economy Sugar forms the basis of the economy, and tourism is increasing. The per capita GNP in 1981 was $1,270.

SWAZILAND

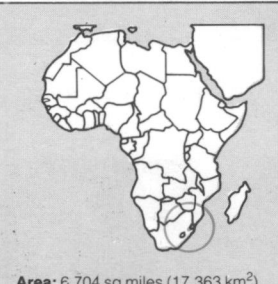

Area: 6,704 sq miles (17,363 km²)
Population: 606,000
Population Growth Rate: 2.3% pa
Capital: Mbabane, pop. 22,000
Language: English (official)
Religion: Christianity (60%), traditional beliefs
Currency: Lilangeni=100 Cents

THE KINGDOM OF SWAZILAND is a small, land-locked country.
People and Culture The Swazis settled in the 1820s. In 1894, the Transvaal Republic made Swaziland a protectorate, but Britain took over in 1902 and ruled until independence in 1968.

The Ngwenyama (king) Sobhuza II took supreme power in 1973 and retained many powers after a National Assembly was elected in 1978. A power struggle in the royal clan followed Sobhuza's death in 1982. Queen Ntombi, mother of the schoolboy Crown Prince, became head of state.
The Land This subtropical country contains four main regions: the western Highveld; the Middle Veld; the Lowveld; and the eastern Lebombo mountains. Most of Swaziland is adequately watered, although irrigation is practised in Lowveld.
Economy Over 80 percent of the people work in farming. The per capita GNP (1981) was $760.

The Fish River has cut an impressive canyon in Namibia.

MADAGASCAR

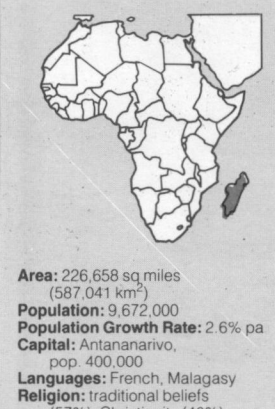

Area: 226,658 sq miles (587,041 km²)
Population: 9,672,000
Population Growth Rate: 2.6% pa
Capital: Antananarivo, pop. 400,000
Languages: French, Malagasy
Religion: traditional beliefs (57%), Christianity (40%)
Currency: Franc Malgache= 100 Centimes

MAURITIUS

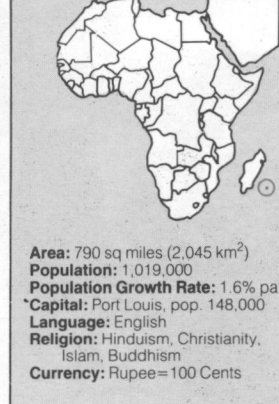

Area: 790 sq miles (2,045 km²)
Population: 1,019,000
Population Growth Rate: 1.6% pa
Capital: Port Louis, pop. 148,000
Language: English
Religion: Hinduism, Christianity, Islam, Buddhism
Currency: Rupee= 100 Cents

LESOTHO

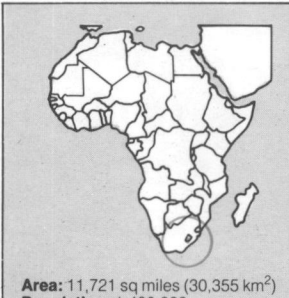

Area: 11,721 sq miles (30,355 km²)
Population: 1,480,000
Population Growth Rate: 2.5% pa
Capital: Maseru, pop. 45,000
Languages: English, Sesotho
Religion: Christianity (80%)
Currency: Loti=100 Lisente

The Land Lesotho is mostly mountainous. But most people live in the western lowlands or in the southern Orange River valley. Warm, wet summers contrast with cold, dry winters.
Economy Farming employs one-third of the workforce. Wool, mohair and diamonds are the chief exports. The per capita GNP (1981) was $540.

SOUTH AFRICA

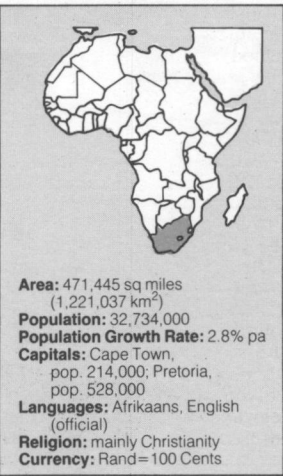

Area: 471,445 sq miles (1,221,037 km²)
Population: 32,734,000
Population Growth Rate: 2.8% pa
Capitals: Cape Town, pop. 214,000; Pretoria, pop. 528,000
Languages: Afrikaans, English (official)
Religion: mainly Christianity
Currency: Rand=100 Cents

THE DEMOCRATIC REPUBLIC OF MADAGASCAR was formerly the Malagasy Republic.
People and Culture Indonesians settled on Madagascar before AD 1000 and the present population is of mixed Indonesian, African and Arab origin. The largest of the 18 main groups is the Merina.

France ruled from 1885 to independence in 1960. The army has been involved in the government since 1972. Under a Constitution of 1975, there is only one political party. The average life expectancy in 1981 was 48 years. The adult literacy rate was 50 percent.

MAURITIUS became an independent member of the Commonwealth in 1968. The Head of State is the British monarch.
People and Culture Britain took Mauritius from France in 1810 and ruled until independence.

Asian Hindus make up 53 percent of the population, Asian Muslims 17 percent, and people of European, African and mixed origin another 28 percent.
The Land The country includes the volcanic islands of Mauritius and Rodrigues, about 350 miles (563 km) to

THE KINGDOM OF LESOTHO was formerly called Basutoland.
People and Culture The Basotho nation was created in the 1820s by King Moshoeshoe I from refugees escaping tribal wars. Britain ruled from 1884 until independence in 1966.

The Constitution was suspended in 1970, but parliamentary rule was restored in 1973. Lesotho remains heavily dependent on South Africa, which encircles it.

The average life expectancy at birth in 1981 was 52 years and the adult literacy rate was 52 percent.

THE REPUBLIC OF SOUTH AFRICA is Africa's most powerful nation. Its racial problems arise from its complex history.
People and Culture In 1652 the Dutch established a settlement

Cape Town has a scenic site near the tip of southern Africa.

The Cape region has a Mediterranean climate and *maquis* vegetation. Forests grow on parts of the south and east coasts.

The wildlife is protected in reserves, especially the Kalahari and Kruger national parks.

Economy In 1980, industry made up 53 percent of the GDP. Manufacturing is important in the southern Transvaal, especially in and around Johannesburg (pop. 1,536,000), and in the ports of Cape Town (214,000), Durban (506,000) and Port Elizabeth (492,000). South Africa produces many minerals, including asbestos, coal, diamonds, copper, gold, iron ore, manganese, tin, uranium and zinc.

Cattle and sheep farming are extremely important. Maize is the chief food crop and a great variety of cash crops are grown, although arable land covers only 5 percent of the country. The per capita GNP in 1981 was $2,770.

DEPENDENCIES

RÉUNION, a French Overseas Department, lies about 120 miles (193 km) southwest of Mauritius. It has an area of 969 square miles (2,510 km^2), and a population of 519,000. The capital is St Denis. Sugar is the main product and the per capita GNP (1981) was $3,840.

Also included in Africa is St Helena, an island territory in the South Atlantic which has been British since 1833. Including its two dependencies, Ascension and Tristan da Cunha, it has an area of 121 sq miles (314 km^2) and a population of 6,000. The chief town is Jamestown.

on the site of Cape Town to provision Dutch ships. Most early settlers were Dutch. Some moved inland eventually meeting up with Bantu-speaking peoples. The first European–Bantu conflict occurred in 1784. Such conflicts continued until 1869.

The Dutch settlers called themselves Boers (farmers) or Afrikaners (Africans). Their language (Cape Dutch) became known as Afrikaans. Between 1795 and 1803, Britain occupied the Cape, returning in 1806. The British introduced anti-slavery laws and other legislation which angered the Boers.

In 1835, many Boers moved north and east to escape British rule, a migration called the Great Trek. They established two territories: Transvaal and Orange Free State. Anglo-Boer rivalry finally led to wars in 1880–81 and 1899–1902.

Britain emerged victorious. In 1910 the Boer states were united with the British Cape Province and Natal to form the Union of South Africa.

In 1948, the mainly Afrikaner National Party won a general election. It introduced *apartheid*, under which each of the races was supposed to develop separately. This involved much discriminatory legislation. Under mounting international criticism of its racial laws, South Africa withdrew from the Commonwealth and became a republic in 1961.

South Africa has four main racial groups: Europeans (17.5 percent); Bantu-speaking Black Africans (70.2 percent); Coloureds of mixed race (9.4 percent); Asians (2.9 percent).

In 1975, 55 percent of the Europeans spoke Afrikaans as a first language and 38 percent English. The Europeans effectively control the government.

The chief Black groups are the Zulu, Xhosa, Tswana, Sepedi and Seshoeshoe. The government has set up 10 Homelands, or Bantustans for Black settlement. Four of them, Transkei, Bophuthatswana, Venda and Ciskei, have been given 'independence'. But no country outside South Africa recognizes their independence, partly because they depend almost entirely on white South Africa, and partly because over half of Black Africans work for whites outside the Homelands.

In 1983, the government offered Coloureds and Asians elected assemblies, within a tricameral parliament. The White, Coloured and Asian assemblies would be elected on separate rolls, and the White Assembly would keep overall power.

The average life expectancy at birth in 1981 was 63 years.

The Land A plateau drained by the Limpopo and Orange rivers covers the interior. Part of its uptilted rim forms the Drakensberg range. Beyond the rim, the land descends in steps to the sea.

Most of South Africa is subtropical, but the altitude modifies temperatures. Half of South Africa is arid or semiarid. The interior plateau contains the dry, grassy Highveld, the arid Bushveld in northwestern Transvaal, the wet Lesotho Highlands, and the arid scrub of the western plateau.

Blacks work in the great city of Johannesburg, South Africa, but their homes are outside the city.

Australasia: introduction

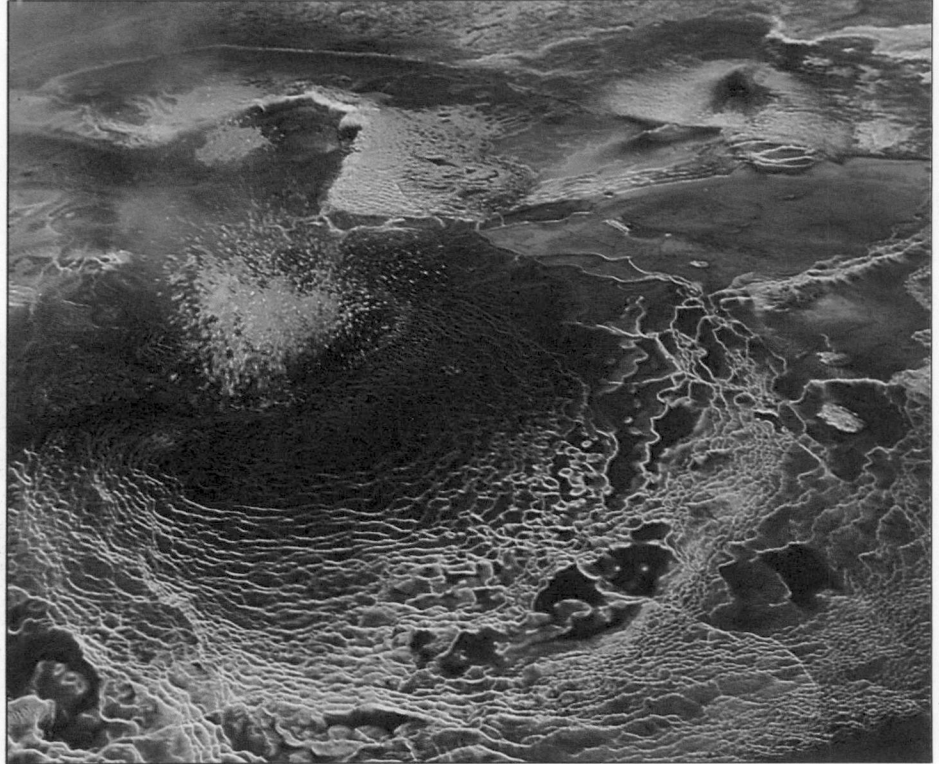

Australasia is a general term that is used to describe Australia, New Zealand, and the islands of the South Pacific Ocean, together with Papua New Guinea, which forms the eastern half of the island of New Guinea. The term Oceania is often preferred for the scattered islands, plus Papua New Guinea, which share a common culture, and whose languages, though there are many hundreds of them, belong to the same language family. The Maoris of New Zealand belong in the same culture, whereas the ancestors of the Australian Aborigines probably migrated from southeast Asia.

The Area and its Structure

Geologically, the various parts of Australasia vary considerably. Australia is a continent, the smallest in the world. The island of New Guinea, which is the world's second largest island after Greenland, lies on the same continental shelf as Australia. During the last Ice Age, 15,000 years ago, the sea-level had fallen so far that land bridges connected Australia with New Guinea and Tasmania.

Australia contains some of the oldest rocks in the world, the Yilgarn and Pilbara Shields which underlie large areas of Western Australia. New Zealand shows rather younger rocks, though there are traces of Pre-Cambrian deposits. New Zealand has its own continental shelf, and stands on a large submarine plateau system. It is on the same plate as Australia and is moving slowly northwards with it. It is close to a destructive plate margin: the Kermadec Trench, which extends northeastwards from it, is 35,700 feet (10,700 m) deep.

The smaller Pacific islands are almost always volcanic in origin. The larger ones are rocky and mountainous, and many contain active volcanoes. Most of the smaller and lower islands are coral reefs that have formed on the top of old volcanic cones, that have subsided or been eroded to below sea-level. Many are atolls, ring-shaped coral islands enclosing lagoons.

Flora and Fauna

The flora and fauna of Australasia are as varied as the

Top The Olgas, in Australia's Northern Territory, are in the geographical centre of the continent. They are a group of 30 huge, dome-shaped rocks, which glow in various shades of red.

Above One of the many hot springs that bubble to the surface in the North Island of New Zealand.

Right 'Here is the news . . .' A tribesman of Papua New Guinea shouts in a 'singout', a news broadcast. In the mountains, densely forested terrain, his role is similar to that of a town crier in medieval England, or the throbbing tribal drums of tropical Africa. The voice carries a surprising distance.

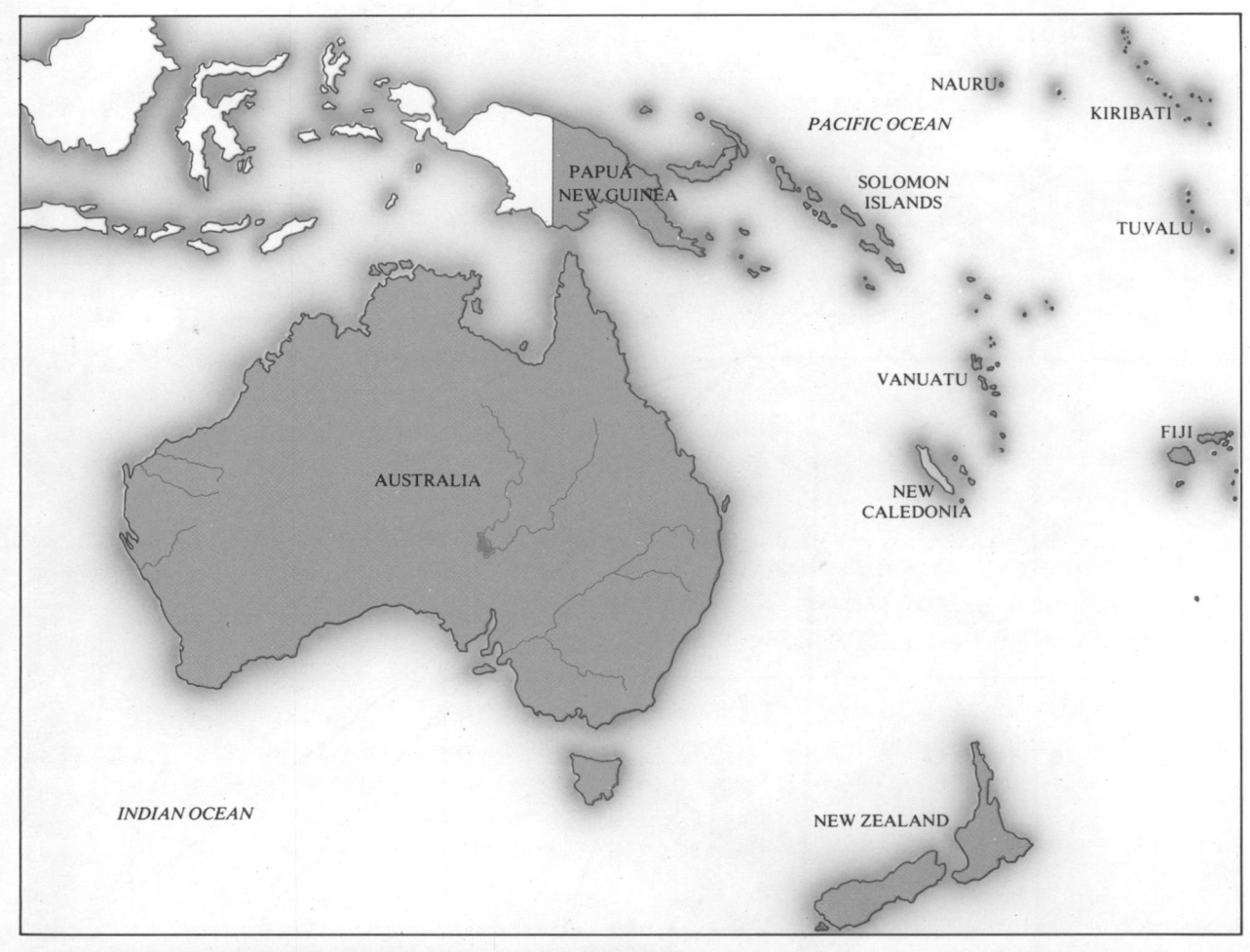

Australasia is a term that has been coined to cover lands scattered over a wide area of the South Pacific Ocean, most of which belong to no continent. Australia itself is a continent, and is very different in character from the rest of Australasia. New Guinea and New Zealand make up four-fifths of the remaining land area. However, the western half of New Guinea is part of Indonesia, so politically it is regarded as part of Asia rather than of Australasia. The easternmost island of Australasia is Easter Island, which lies more than 4,000 miles (6,400 km) east of New Zealand. The total number of islands in the South Pacific has never been calculated, but geographers estimate that there are between 20,000 and 30,000. Many are tiny rocks that are barely visible above the waves.

Australasia

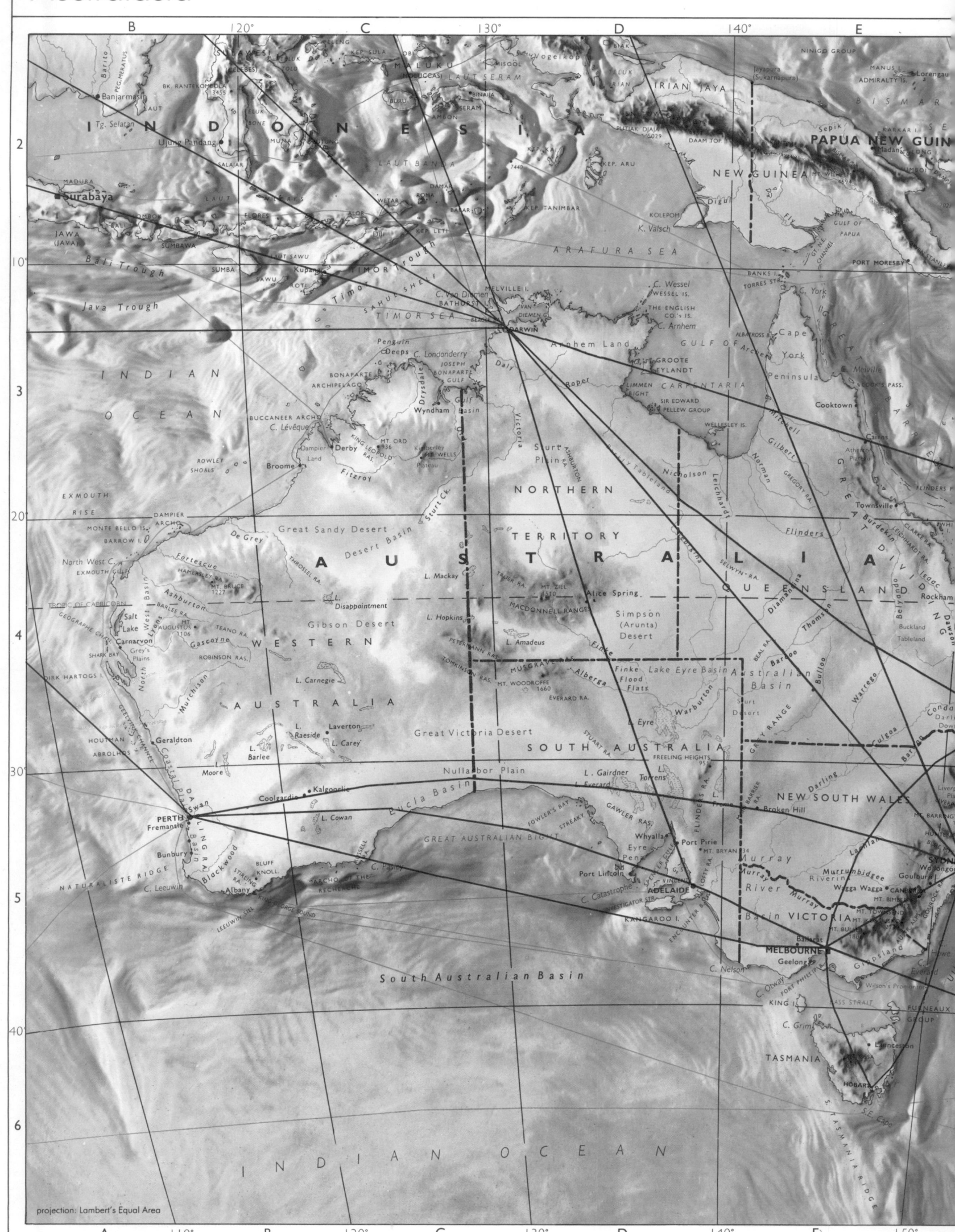

projection: Lambert's Equal Area

over
3000 metres

1800-3000 metres

900-1800 metres

450-900 metres

300-450 metres

150-300 metres

sea level
150 metres

ice caps

over 1,000,000

over 500,000

over 250,000

under 250,000

international
boundaries

air routes

sea routes

main railways

international airports

Miles

Kilometres

Australasia is a region of vast distances, which the early explorers conquered only with difficulty by ship and canoe. The three largest land regions are Australia, 2,967,909 sq miles (7,686,848 km²), which is a continent by itself; New Guinea, 311,796 sq miles (807,548 km²), which lies on the same continental shelf as Australia; and New Zealand, 103,736 sq miles (268,676 km²). The remaining islands together total about 300,000 sq miles (777,000 km²).

New Guinea is closest to Australia, the Torres Strait which separates them being 95 miles (153 km) at its narrowest point. New Zealand is about 1,200 miles (1,930 km) from Australia.

The highest point in New Guinea is Jaya Peak, 16,503 ft (5,030 m) high, but since it lies in Irian Jaya, which is politically part of Indonesia, it is not reckoned to form part of Australasia. The highest peak in Australasia is also in New Guinea — Mount Wilhelm, 14,793 ft (4,509 m), in Papua New Guinea. New Zealand's highest mountain is Mount Cook, 12,349 ft (3,764 m), while the highest peak in Australia is Mount Kosciusko, 7,310 ft (2,228 m). The lowest point in Australasia is Lake Eyre in South Australia which lies 52 ft (16 m) below sea-level.

The biggest river system in Australasia is the Murray–Darling system in Australia, which drains an area of 414,000 sq miles (1,072,000 km²). The Murray itself is 1,609 miles (2,589 km) long. The Darling, its principal tributary, is 1,702 miles (2,740 km) long, and the longest river in Australia. The Murrumbidgee, another major tributary, is 1,050 miles (1,690 km) long, and it has a very long tributary of its own, the Lachlan, which is 922 miles (1,484 km) long.

In New Zealand, the longest river is the Waikato in North Island, which is 220 miles (354 km) long. However, the Clutha River in South Island, which is 210 miles (338 km) long, discharges a greater volume of water.

The highest waterfall in Australasia, and the fifth highest in the world, is the Sutherland Falls in New Zealand's South Island, which descend 1,903 ft (580 m). Australia has two major falls. Wollomombi Falls on the Macleay River in New South Wales drop 1,580 ft (482 m), and the Wallaman Falls in Queensland, on Stony Creek, descend 1,150 ft (351 m).

geology. They also differ greatly from those of southern and southeastern Asia. Australasia lies to the southeast of Wallace's Line, an imaginary line drawn by the nineteenth-century naturalist Alfred Russel Wallace to indicate the divergence of animal, and especially mammalian, life on either side of it. New Zealand and the islands of Oceania had no mammals except bats until Man introduced them. Australia and New Guinea have two forms of primitive mammals that have survived because of the long isolation of these lands from the rest of the world. Monotremes, the egg-laying mammals, exist nowhere else, and no fossil traces have been found elsewhere. The marsupials, the pouched mammals, exist also in South America, with one species in North America, but they are most abundant and diverse in Australia and New Guinea.

Marsupial fossils have been discovered in other parts of the world, but not in Africa or Asia. Their survival in Australia and New Guinea was due to the lack of competition from the more successful and later placental mammals. The only placentals in either land before Man's advent were bats, which could fly there, and a few rodents, which it is thought may have reached the islands on floating logs, or across exposed land bridges during the last Ice Age.

Smaller forms of animal life, such as birds and insects, are well represented in Australasia. A number of birds, such as the bronze cuckoo of New Zealand and the Mongolian plover of Australia, are annual migrants from Asia, but in all parts of Australasia many unique species have developed, though they have relatives in other parts of the world. The same applies to invertebrates.

The plant life of Papua New Guinea is closely linked to that of Southeast Asia, but Australia has many plants not found elsewhere. Tropical rain forest dominates Papua New Guinea, and there are some rain forests in Australia and New Zealand. But the much drier climate of most of Australia and the temperate climate of New Zealand have produced a divergence of vegetation. Australia is the land of the eucalyptus, of which there are more than 400 species, and the acacias (wattles), which run to 600 species. In both Australia and New Zealand, possibly 75 percent of the flowering plants are native to those countries.

The plant life of the islands of Oceania was, before the advent of Man, confined to plants whose seeds were seaborne, such as the ubiquitous coconut palm, or could be carried by birds or the wind. As with the rest of Australasia, many of the plants now flourishing there were brought in by Man.

History and Culture

The historical pattern of settlement has determined the present political structure of Australasia. Following the colonization of the islands by peoples from Asia, over a period of many centuries, European exploration of the Pacific began in the seventeenth century. Settlement by Europeans began in the late eighteenth century and continued through the nineteenth century, pioneered in the smaller islands by missionaries.

By the end of the nineteenth century, Britain, France, Germany and the United States controlled most of Australasia. Australia and New Zealand were virtually self-governing parts of the British empire. Britain also held Fiji, the Gilbert and Ellice Islands, Papua, the Solomon Islands and Tonga, and shared control of the New Hebrides with France. France also ruled New Caledonia and French Polynesia, as it still does. Germany held Nauru, northeastern New Guinea, Western Samoa and most of the islands of Micronesia. The United States held Guam and the eastern part of Samoa, as it still does.

Germany lost its possessions in World War I: Australia took over Nauru and northeastern New Guinea, New Zealand administered Western Samoa, and Japan ruled the islands of Micronesia, which it lost as a result of World War II.

Today the following countries are independent members of the Commonwealth: Australia, New Zealand, Fiji, Kiribati (formerly the Gilbert Islands), Nauru, Papua New Guinea, Western Samoa, the Solomon Islands, Tonga, Tuvalu (formerly the Ellice Islands), and Vanuatu (formerly the New Hebrides). The United States administers the Micronesian islands as a trust territory for the United Nations. See the world map on pages 24–25 for the location of the Trust Territory, Guam, the Samoas, and French Polynesia.

Economic Survey

The economies of Australasia vary greatly. Australia, with a per capita GNP of $11,080, ranks among the 28 richest countries of the world, while Kiribati, Papua New Guinea, the Solomon Islands, Tonga, and Vanuatu come towards the bottom of the wealth table, with per capita GNPs between $360 and $829. But they are not among the poorest countries of the world, with per capita GNPs below $360.

Australia and New Zealand both have thriving agriculture and industry. Elsewhere there is little industry apart from mining. Nauru's tiny population derives its income from mining phosphate deposits, but when these are exhausted the Nauruans will either have to develop alternative sources of revenue or move elsewhere. Mineral deposits elsewhere are in the process of being developed, especially in Papua New Guinea, which has particularly good deposits of copper, and New Caledonia, which is rich in mineral deposits, especially nickel, chronium, and iron. Fiji had gold mines, but many of the best lodes have been dug up.

The basic industry throughout Oceania is agriculture. For most of the people it is subsistence farming, but they live in a climate where needs for housing and clothing are minimal. They are close to the sea, and many people earn a living by fishing. The coconut palm is the mainstay of most island economies, and the production of copra, the dried meat of the coconut, is a basic occupation. Copra is in worldwide demand as a source of coconut oil, used in soap and margarine. Bananas are exported by Fiji, Tonga and Western Samoa. Papua New Guinea has valuable sources of timber.

A growing industry throughout Australasia is tourism, which has expanded greatly with the development of fast jet airliner services. However, tourism is regarded in many island countries as a mixed blessing, since a major influx of visitors may have the effect of destroying the charm of the Pacific that lures the visitors in the first place.

Above Sydney Harbour Bridge was opened in 1932, and took nine years to build. Linking the north and south sides of the Harbour, it carries a double-track railway, an eight-lane highway, a cycle track and a path for pedestrians. The road is used by about 100,000 vehicles a day. The main span is 1,650 feet (503 m) long, and with its approach spans the bridge totals 3,770 feet (1,149 m).

Above right A herd of cattle mills around a water-hole in the dusty semi-desert of an Australian outback ranch. On such stations the livestock depend on artesian water, brought to the surface by wind-driven pumps. Around watering places the already sparse vegetation is further eroded by the trampling of cattle and sheep.

Above The coconut palm is the mainstay of the economy in most island countries of Australasia. Its lumber is used for building houses, which are thatched with its leaves. Strips of the leaves are woven into mats and baskets. The young flower stalks yield a sweet sap called toddy, which can be drunk fresh, fermented as an alcoholic drink, or distilled to a spirit. It can also be used to make sugar or vinegar.

Left A South Sea islander squeezes the flesh of a coconut to extract the oil. The refined oil is used in many countries as an ingredient of margarine, and as a cooking oil. The dried flesh, known as copra, is used as cattle feed. The whole flesh, shredded and dried, is the dessicated coconut used in candy.

The islands of Oceania are generally divided into three groups according to the pattern of settlement and the kinds of people who occupied the islands. This settlement had taken place within the past 30,000 years. Before that the islands were uninhabited. Much of the animal life and some of the plants were introduced by Man.

Geographers give the term Melanesia to a block of islands running southeast from New Guinea to Fiji. The term 'Melanesia' refers to the generally dark skins of the dominant race. Micronesia, meaning 'small islands', lies to the north of Melanesia, and contains mostly very tiny islands. Polynesia includes all the islands to the east in a triangle from Midway Island in the north to New Zealand in the south, and Easter Island in the east.

In addition to being darker-skinned than the other two groups, the Melanesians are shorter and have woolly hair. They include the pygmy race called Negritos, who are mostly less than 5 feet (1.5 m) tall. The Micronesians are taller than the Melanesians, with lighter skins, but they vary considerably, some showing distinct characteristics of Melanesian or Polynesian types. The Polynesians are the tallest of the groups and have the lightest skins. They include the Maoris of New Zealand.

Melanesia and Micronesia were settled first, by small bands of people who voyaged by canoe or raft from southeastern Asia. The settlement of Polynesia took longer, and was probably not completed until around AD 500 – some scholars think even later. Certain cultural affinities with South America suggest that some of the more easterly islands may have had some settlers from that continent. It has been proved that such a migration is possible, using prevailing winds and currents.

European exploration of the Pacific and its islands began with the epic voyage of Ferdinand Magellan in 1520–21. Abel Tasman discovered New Zealand and Fiji in the seventeenth century. The principal voyages of discovery were made in the eighteenth century, the outstanding explorer being James Cook. He found or visited the Society Islands, the Marqueses, Niue, Tonga, the New Hebrides, Hawaii and many smaller islands. During the ninteenth century many Christian missionaries went to the Pacific Islands so now most of the Pacific Islanders are Christians.

Geographers divide the Pacific Islands into two main groups: the high islands – those with mountains or hills – and the coral islands. The high islands include many active volcanoes and are subject to earthquakes. Most of the high islands are surrounded by coral islands or coral reefs.

Most of the islands of Oceania lie within the tropics, and enjoy a warm, equable climate all the year. The mean temperatures range from 70°F (21°C) and 85°F (29°C), while the daily flunctuation on any particular island is between 10°F and 20°F (5.5°–11°C). Rainfall varies greatly, and while some Melanesian islands have more than 150 inches (3,810 mm) a year, some of the lowest coral islands have very little rain. Rainfall is often accompanied by thunderstorms, and tropical hurricanes occur two or three times a year.

Outside the major islands (New Guinea, New Zealand) there are few large towns. The village is the typical focus of life. On the smaller and more remote islands people still follow ways of life that have not changed for generations, but the impact of western civilization is rapidly changing lifestyles in many parts of Oceania. Most communities now have schools, and more advanced students can attend the University of the South Pacific in Fiji, or universities in New Zealand, Australia, Guam and Hawaii.

Communications are still a problem for the scattered island communities. Many islanders still use their traditional canoes, though fitted with outboard motors for longer voyages. They have not lost their ancient navigational skills, which depend on the stars and ocean currents. Air services link the larger islands. Ships bring supplies and take away the cash crops, mostly copra, which the islands produce. Within the islands there are few major roads, except in or near the larger towns, such as Suva in Fiji. Radio also helps to keep the islands in touch with one another and with the rest of the world.

Outrigger canoes like this played a large part in the settlement of the islands of Oceania. Today, small canoes are used for coastal trips, or for family outings between neighbouring islands. For deepsea voyages the Pacific islanders use double-hulled canoes 60 feet (18 m) long, with tall triangular sails. Steering by the stars and following ocean currents, the early colonizers of the Pacific voyaged for thousands of miles, making accurate landfalls. Canoes for long voyages were in regular use when Captain James Cook first explored the Pacific in the eighteenth century, but their use died out under European influence after the development of steamships.

Oceania

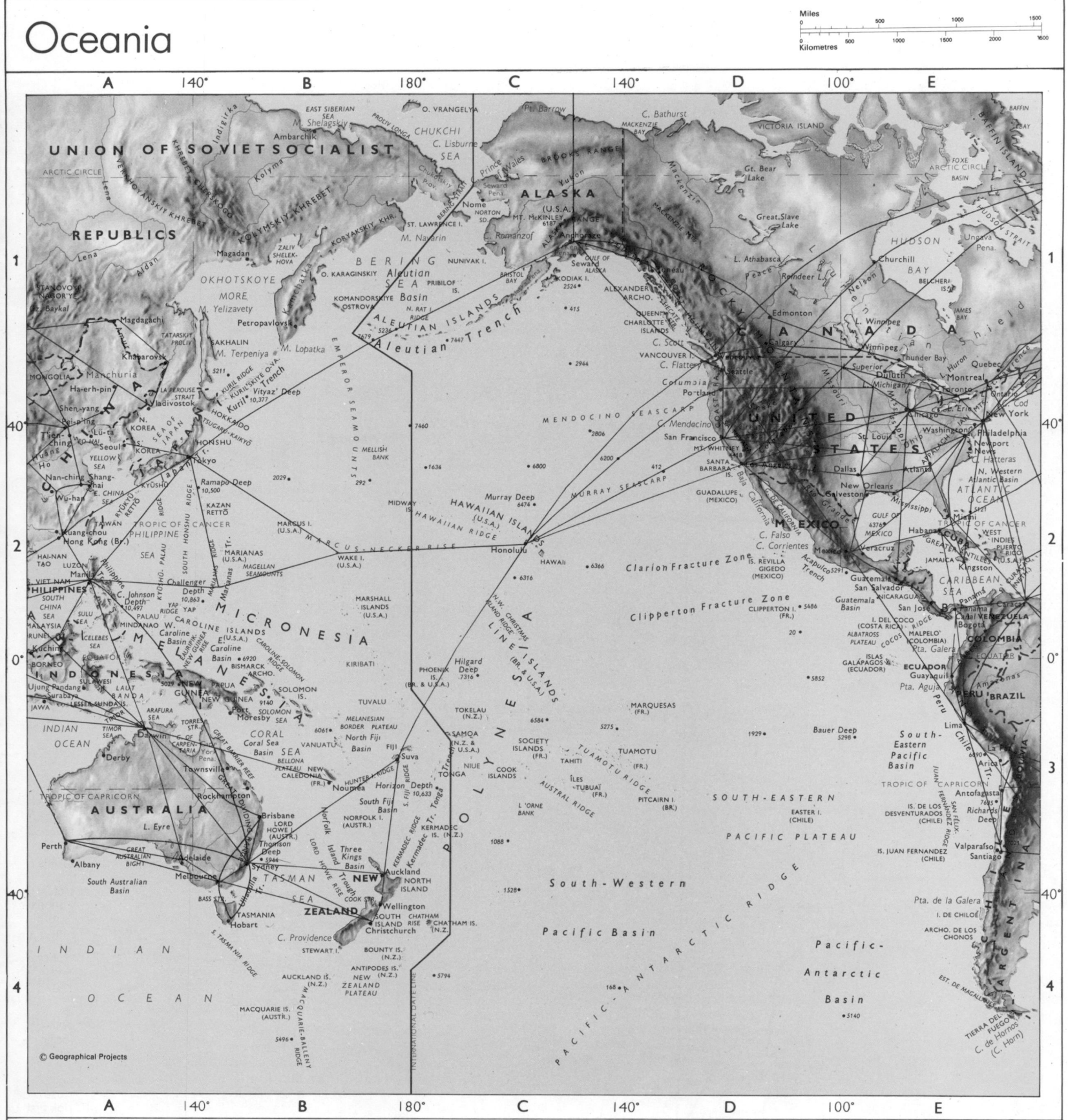

Miles
Kilometres

The islands of Oceania, which number more than 30,000, are scattered across the vast Pacific Ocean, which itself covers nearly a third of the Earth's surface. The colonization of these islands began during the Ice Age, although the far-flung islands of Polynesia were not peopled until much later.

The modern history of Oceania began with the arrival of Europeans in the Age of Exploration in the 16th century. Explorers and traders returning to Europe extolled the beauty, tranquillity and remoteness of the islands, likening them to the Garden of Eden. Such descriptions soon gave the islands a romantic image in Western minds. This image, which was misleading in many ways, was fostered by writers and artists, among them the Scottish novelist Robert Louis Stevenson, who died on Samoa, and the Frenchman Paul Gauguin, who made his island home of Tahiti world famous through a series of extraordinary paintings.

The strategic significance of the islands in both military and economic terms was not fully appreciated until World War II, when many territories were occupied by Japan. After the war, when colonial rule by Western powers was re-established, constitutional changes were gradually introduced to satisfy the aspirations of the local people. However, there were many islanders in Oceania who accepted Western rule and the benefits it bestowed, because their territories lacked the resources and populations sufficient to make them viable as independent nations. But many island nations did opt for independence and, as a result, the political geography of the region has been changing in recent years. Long-familiar place names, such as the former British Gilbert and Ellice Islands and the Anglo-French Condominium of the

New Hebrides have recently been erased from the map, being replaced by the unfamiliar names of Kiribati (pronounced Kiri-bass), Tuvalu and the Vanuatu Republic. These and other emergent nations in Oceania face many social, economic and political problems, arising from such factors as high annual rates of population increase, low per capita GNPs and inadequate health, educational and other welfare services. But the desire for self-determination, which has swept through other continents, has recently been proving itself to be equally irresistible in Oceania.

Australia

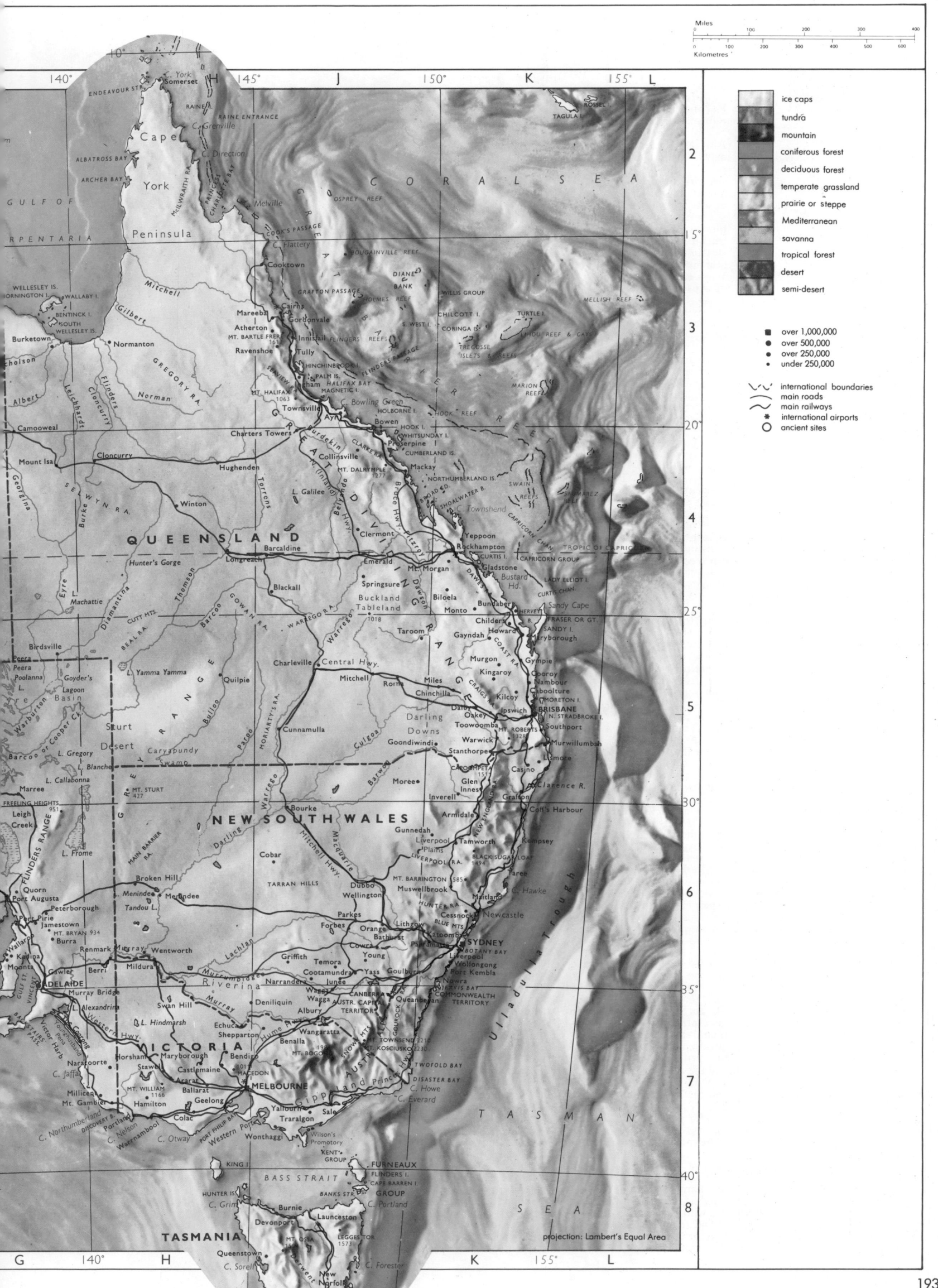

Miles
0   100   200   300   400

Kilometres
0   100   200   300   400   500   600

	ice caps
	tundra
	mountain
	coniferous forest
	deciduous forest
	temperate grassland
	prairie or steppe
	Mediterranean
	savanna
	tropical forest
	desert
	semi-desert

■ over 1,000,000
● over 500,000
● over 250,000
• under 250,000

＼＿＿＿＿ international boundaries
～～～ main roads
～～～ main railways
＊ international airports
○ ancient sites

projection: Lambert's Equal Area

AUSTRALIA

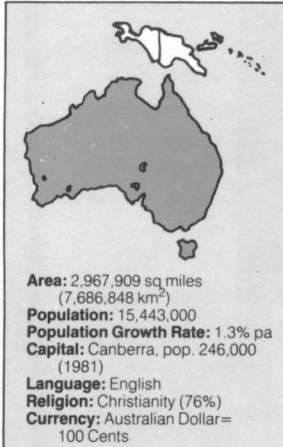

Area: 2,967,909 sq miles
(7,686,848 km²)
Population: 15,443,000
Population Growth Rate: 1.3% pa
Capital: Canberra, pop. 246,000
(1981)
Language: English
Religion: Christianity (76%)
Currency: Australian Dollar=
100 Cents

THE COMMONWEALTH OF AUS-TRALIA is the only country that is also regarded as a continent. Politically it is a federation of six states and two mainland territories and it also possesses seven overseas territories. It was formerly a British possession and it is a member of the Commonwealth of Nations.

People and Culture The first people to reach Australia were the Aborigines. They are a dark-skinned people, who probably came to Australia across the seas from south-eastern Asia at least 40,000 years ago. Before Europeans began settling in Australia there were about 300,000 Aborigines, who had a Stone-Age, hunter-gatherer culture. There are now around 136,000, including people of mixed Aborigine and European descent.

For hundreds of years, European geographers had assumed the existence of *Terra Australis incognita* – the unknown southern land – but nobody knew its shape or extent, or indeed whether it existed at all. In 1605, two Spanish navigators, Luis Vaez de Torres and Diego de Prado, sailed their ships through the strait that is now called after Torres. In the same year a Dutchman, Willem Jansz, penetrated into the Gulf of Carpentaria, though he did not realize that he had sighted Australia. He thought the land was part of New Guinea.

In 1642 another Dutchman, Abel Janszoon Tasman, found Tasmania, which he named Van Diemen's Land. As a result of these Dutch explorations the continent was at first known as New Holland.

In 1770, the English navigator James Cook landed at Botany Bay, on the south-eastern coast, and claimed the land for Britain. As a result of his reports, the British government decided to use Australia as a place to which they could transport convicts. They had previously sent convicts to the American colonies, which were now lost as a result of the American War of Independence.

The first penal colony was established at Sydney in 1788. The first free settlers arrived in 1793. Britain continued to send convicts to Australia until 1868.

Until after World War II, most settlers were from the British Isles. Between 1945 and 1970, more than 1 million people from Continental Europe, a quarter of them refugees, arrived in Australia.

The basic language of Australia is English, though many immigrants speak their native tongues. There were several hundred Aboriginal languages and dialects, many of which have been lost.

There is no official religion, but most Australians are Christians, with Anglicans and Roman Catholics as the largest groups.

Ways of Life Some 89 percent of Australians live in urban areas, and 50 percent are in the six State capitals.

Life expectancy at 74 years shows a three-year increase since 1960. The country has a well-developed system of social services. It provides old age pensions, sickness benefit, unemployment pay, and public health care.

Aborigines receive special attention, and reservations have been set aside for those who wish to follow their traditional way of life as nomadic hunters.

Education Adult literacy stands at 100 percent. Primary education is compulsory, and both primary and secondary education are free. Children in outlying areas – the Outback – can receive tuition by two-way radio through one of the ten Schools of the Air.

Australia has 19 universities, with a total of more than 165,000 students, plus 68 colleges of advanced education with about the same number of students.

Constitutional Development The first settlements, penal and free, were in New South Wales. Other colonies were set up in Van Diemen's Land (now Tasmania) in 1825, Western Australia (1829), South Australia (1836), Victoria (1851) and Queensland (1859).

At first the colonial governors had full powers, but law-making bodies known as legislative councils were set up from 1823 onwards. From 1851 the colonies had partial self-government, and within a few years full self-government applied as far as internal affairs were concerned.

Moves to unite the colonies began in 1885 with the setting up of a federal council. The Commonwealth of Australia was founded on January 1, 1901. Under its constitution, the federal parliament makes laws on matters that affect the country as a whole, such as foreign affairs and defence. The six State legislatures make laws affecting their own internal affairs. The federal government is responsible for the two mainland territories and the overseas territories.

Australia is a monarchy, and the nominal head of state is the British queen, Elizabeth II. Her powers and duties are exercised by a Governor-general for the whole of Australia, and by governors in each of the six States. Moves were afoot in the early 1980s to change the country to a republic and sever the direct ties with Britain.

The federal parliament has two houses. The House of Representatives is elected by popular vote and has about twice as many members as the upper house, the Senate. Senators are also elected by popular vote but are supposed to represent more directly the individual States.

All but one of the State parliaments also has two houses, a legislative council and a legislative assembly. Queensland has only a legislative assembly.

Politics There are three main political parties in Australia, but in effect the country has a two-party political system, because two of the parties, the Liberal Party and the National Country Party (NCP) have acted as a coalition since the 1950s. The third party is the Australian Labor Party (ALP) which is closely allied to the country's trade union movement.

Territories The two mainland territories are the Northern Territory and the Australian Capital Territory (ACT). The Northern Territory has had its own government since 1978, but remains under the general control of the federal government. It occupies nearly one-sixth of the total land area of Australia, but has less than 0.09 percent of the population. It is planned that the Northern Territory will become a full State as soon as its people are ready for it.

The Australian Capital Territory is an enclave in southeastern New South Wales. It was created in 1911 to provide a federal capital for the new Commonwealth that would be independent of the States.

Canberra, the capital, occupies only about one-sixth of the Territory, and the urban development is not expected to total more than double that

Above The Blue Mountains of New South Wales. **Below** Kangaroo paw, a unique flowering plant.

area. Government of the Territory is under the direct control of the federal government.

The Land Some 200 million years ago Australia formed part of the super-continent of Gondwanaland. It was joined to Antarctica, which in turn was joined to Africa.

Gondwanaland broke up about 180 million years ago, and Australia slowly moved to its present position. Its isolation from the rest of the world has had a significant effect on its development.

Pre-Cambrian rocks, some as much as 3,000 million years old, underlie the western two-thirds of the country. The mountains of the eastern part are the result of later folding, somewhere between 600 and 200 million years ago. Between the Pre-Cambrian Shield and the fold mountains of the east a depression formed, which for tens of millions of years was covered by sea. The present rock strata of this region are the result of massive sedimentary deposits.

As a result of this geological development Australia is predominantly low and flat, with its main mountains, the Great Dividing Range, in the east. The country consists of three main regions: the eastern highlands, the western plateau, and between them the central lowlands.

The eastern highlands are called the Great Dividing Range because they separate the well-watered east coast from the dry interior. The range runs from Cape York in the north for about 2,400 miles (3,860 km) into Victoria and across the Bass Strait to Southeast Cape in Tasmania. The average width of this range is 150 miles (240 km).

The mountains are nowhere very high – the tallest peak is Mount Kosciusko, 7,316 feet (2,230 m) – and considerably lower than the main ranges of any of the other continents. Most of the range consists of plateau land, with deep river-cut gorges on its margins.

A narrow coastal plain lies between the highlands and the Pacific Ocean. This area contains the country's richest soils and is where the majority of the people live.

The western plateau is similar in structure to the Deccan of India, the Brazilian plateau, and the ice-buried plateau lands of Antarctica, to all of which it was once linked. It covers Western Australia, South Australia, Northern Territory and parts of Queensland and New South Wales. Most of it is desert and it has been worn into a flat, monotonous landscape through millions of years of erosion. It

Aborigines are widely employed on sheep and cattle stations.

The main street and post office in the mining town of Broken Hill, New South Wales.

is broken in the middle by the Macdonnell and Musgrave ranges, which are split by deep gorges.

The central lowlands in fact lie well to the east, just west of the eastern highlands. They are divided into three portions by the Barkly Downs in the north, and the Grey and Flinders ranges in the south. The northern coastal lowland drains into the Gulf of Carpentaria. In the south the land drains to the southwest, while in between lies a large dry area. Most of the central lowlands are less than 500 feet (150 m) above sea-level.

The prevailing, rain-bearing winds reach Australia from the east. The Great Dividing Range is high enough to trap most of this rainfall and prevent it reaching the interior of the country. The east and north have moderate rainfall, heavy in places, and so does the extreme southwest. The

rest of the country has very little rain.

Many relatively short, fast rivers flow eastwards from the Eastern Highlands into the Pacific. Some, such as the Dawson, begin by flowing westward, then make a sharp turn and head east.

The main river system is that of the Murray and its many tributaries, especially the Darling, the Murrumbidgee and the Lachlan. Because of irregular rainfall, the Murray, which is regarded as one of the world's greatest rivers, has been known to dry up, but it now flows through the Hume Reservoir which holds enough water to keep it flowing for two years.

Of the many inland rivers, most flow only after a spell of rain, and are dry for long periods. They flow into a series of *playas*, shallow lakes which are often dry. The largest, Lake Eyre, is usually dry with a thick crust of salt. Lake George in New South Wales is sometimes as much as 20 feet (6 m) deep and covers an area of 60 sq miles (96 km²), but most of the time it is grassy plain used for grazing.

There are short rivers along the northern and southwestern coast, but many stretches of coastline, especially the Nullarbor Plain, have no rivers. A very large area of the interior is completely riverless. Western Australia contains a number of *playas*.

However, the dry regions are helped by the fact that artesian water lies under about 1,000,000 sq miles (2,600,000 km²) of the country. The largest artesian area is the Great Artesian Basin below the central lowlands and the eastern part of the western plateau.

The east coast of Australia is guarded by the Great Barrier Reef, the world's largest coral reef. It is about 1,200 miles (2,000 km) long. In places it is less than 10 miles (16 km) off the shore. The reef is about 45 miles (72 km) wide, and has only 10 openings for ships in it. It includes several hundred small islands.

Vegetation Because it has been isolated from the rest of the world for many millions of years, Australia has developed a distinct flora. The vegetation varies according to climate.

In the north, which lies within the tropics, there is a belt of tropical monsoon forest, while down the east coast there are temperate forests. In the drier regions is bush, an area of scattered, stunted trees, mostly close to rivers. In the dry season the ground is bare of herbage, whereas when the rains come there is abundant grass.

Where the ground is too salty for grass, the saltbush flourishes and provides grazing for animals.

Beyond the bush lies the scrub, and then comes the desert. In a few places no plants can grow, but most of the desert has some vegetation, mostly porcupine grass.

The dominant trees in Australia are the eucalypts, only one or two species of which are found native outside Australia. They include some of the world's tallest trees. The wattle or acacia is another native tree, and has been adopted as the national flower.

Wildlife The most remarkable feature of Australian wildlife is its distinctive mammals, survivals of primitive mammalian evolution.

The most primitive are the Monotremata, the egg-laying mammals, found nowhere outside Australasia. Two species live in Australia, the duck-billed platypus and the echidna, or short-beaked spiny anteater. Platypuses live in eastern Australia and Tasmania, burrowing in riverbanks. Excellent swimmers, they catch their food in the water. The echidnas roam open forests or sandy desert regions, feeding mainly on termites and ants. A related species, the giant echidna or long-beaked spiny anteater, lives in New Guinea, where the short-beaked species can also be found.

Around 200 species of marsupials live in Australia. These animals bear live young in an immature form, and the babies then complete their development in a pouch on the mother's abdomen. Developing in isolation from the rest of the world, the marsupials have evolved to fill similar ecological niches to those occupied by the placental mammals elsewhere. Wombats are burrowing animals, with a lifestyle similar to that of a badger. Kangaroos and wallabies are grazing animals. Numbats, bandicoots, and bilbies are insect-eaters. Marsupial moles and mice fulfil many of the same functions as their placental namesakes.

The Tasmanian wolf and Tasmanian devil are fierce carnivores. The Tasmanian wolf is all but extinct, and since the arrival of Europeans with their placental mammals many other species of marsupials have indeed become extinct.

The only placental mammals in Australia before the British began settling and

bringing in their own animals were bats, a few rodents and the dingo, a semi-wild dog which was introduced by the Aborigines. The most destructive of the introduced species is the rabbit.

Although migrant birds visit Australia, and some species are common to nearby lands, the country has many native species. The emu and the cassowary are both large flightless birds. Kookaburras (or Laughing Jackasses) are the world's largest kingfishers. The lyrebird is famous for the male's remarkable tail-feather display. Many families of birds have specialized representatives among the approximately 750 species in the country. There are also species introduced from Europe and elsewhere, such as the European house sparrow and blackbird, and the Indian mynah bird.

Australia has about 130 species of snakes, most of them venomous. The taipan of the north and east is the most deadly. The dangerous, sea-going, estuarine crocodile is found along the northern coast. The northern rivers also harbour the harmless freshwater crocodile. Australia has many species of lizards, tortoises, and frogs.

Insects parallel those found elsewhere, but there are many endemic species. Other invertebrates include the Gippsland giant earthworm, which can become over 10 feet (3 m) long when fully extended.

Economy Australia's prosperity was built on agriculture and mining, but these now represent only a small percentage of the GDP. However, they still form a very high proportion of the country's exports. The per capita GNP was $11,080 in 1981.

The Birdsville Track runs from Birdsville in Queensland to Marree, 300 miles (500 km).

Countryside near Pago Pago, capital of American Samoa.

Farming Australia is a major producer of wheat. It had 42,500 sq miles (110,000 km^2) under wheat in 1981–82, and more than 16 million tonnes of wheat a year are produced. Smaller quantities of oats and barley are also produced.

Crop-spraying is possible only in the southeast and southwest. A much larger area is available for stock-raising, using artesian water in the dry lands. Australia had more than 24 million head of cattle in 1981–82, and meat and dairy products ranked next to cereals in agricultural exports. These represent about 30 percent of Australia's annual exports by value.

Sheep-farming is very big business in Australia. The country has around 137 million sheep, producing more than 700 million tonnes of wool annually. Altogether, agriculture represents 5 percent of the GDP, and employs 6 percent of the workforce.

Mining Australia's development received a boost in the great gold rushes of the 1850s, which brought thousands of prospectors from all over the world. They were lured by stories of major finds, such as the world's largest pure nugget, found in 1869 at Moliagul, Victoria. Named 'The Welcome Stranger', it yielded 2,248 oz (69.92 kg) of pure gold.

Although gold has now declined in importance, Australia is still the world's seventh biggest producer, with about 35,300 lb (16,000 kg) of gold a year. However, by value the country has a higher production of coal, iron ore, lead, copper and zinc. There are major deposits of uranium, particularly in the Northern Territory.

Since the 1970s, Australia has been largely self-sufficient in oil and natural gas, though it has to import the heavier crude oils.

Hydroelectric Schemes Austra-

lia's economy is dependent on two scarce commodities: water and power. With rainfall low and variable, there is a shortage of water for domestic, agricultural, and industrial use, and only a limited amount for hydroelectric schemes. The biggest of these is the Snowy Mountains Scheme in New South Wales and Victoria. The headwaters of the Snowy River, which normally flows eastward where water is relatively plentiful, have been captured and used to augment the westward flow of the Murray River. In this way good irrigation has been provided for the Murray and Murrumbidgee river valleys, and a source of cheaper power for New South Wales, Victoria, and the Australian Capital Territory.

Plans to inaugurate a similar scheme in southwest Tasmania ran into stiff oposition from conservationists in the early 1980s.

Industry Between 1960 and 1980 the proportion of the labour force employed in industry declined from 40 percent to 33 percent. While industry as a whole represented about 30 percent of GDP in 1978–80, manufacturing contributed around 23 percent, and was about 18 percent of total exports.

Service industries absorbed 62 percent of the workforce in 1980, and were estimated to produce around 65 percent of the GDP at that time.

Communications Australia has for years been bedevilled by a variety of railway gauges. Standard gauge, 4 feet 8½ inches (1,435 mm), is the norm in New South Wales and on most of the Australian National Railways. Standard-gauge lines link Sydney with Brisbane, Melbourne and Perth, and now extend to Alice Springs in the Northern Territory. Most of Victoria's lines are broad gauge, 5 feet

3 inches (1,600 mm), while narrow-gauge lines, 3 feet 6 inches (1,067 mm), are general in Queensland, Western Australia, Tasmania and around Darwin.

Airlines provide a quick means of passenger transport and internal flights in 1981 totalled 84 million miles (136 million km), and carried 11,300,000 passengers. Because there are so many people in remote parts of the Outback, the Flying Doctor Service was inaugurated in 1928. Its doctors fly over 1,800,000 miles (3 million km) each year, operating from 12 bases.

The country has about 508,000 miles (817,000 km) of roads, of which 148,000 miles (238,000 km) have a hard, sealed surface, and 131,000 miles (211,000 km) are surfaced with crushed stone or gravel. The remainder of the roads are dirt tracks. Nearly 8 million vehicles use the road system.

External Territories By far the largest of Australia's external territories is the Australian Antarctic Territory, which covers the lion's share of that ice-bound continent. Several scientific research stations are maintained there, but there is no permanent population.

Christmas Island in the Indian Ocean is an important source of phosphates, which provide the island's only industry. It came under Australian rule in 1958. In 1957–58, it was used as a base for British hydrogen bomb tests. The Cocos or Keeling Islands, also in the Indian Ocean, are a group of 27 low-lying coral islands, densely covered with coconut palms. They produce copra. The islands also have a major airstrip which can be used as an emergency stop for aircraft on the Australia–South Africa service.

Australia is also responsible for several groups of small, uninhabited islands.

PAPUA NEW GUINEA

Area: 178,260 sq miles (461,691 km^2)
Population: 3,066,000 (1981)
Capital: Port Moresby, pop. 123,600 (1980)
Languages: Over 700
Religion: Christianity (50%), ancestor worship (50%)
Currency: Kina = 100 Toea

PAPUA NEW GUINEA is an independent country northeast of Australia.

People and Culture Nearly all the people are Melanesians, living in small tribes and settlements. Subsistence farming is their main occupation. The large number of languages makes communication difficult. The land came partly under British control and partly under German rule in 1894 and later passed to Australian supervision. The country became independent in 1975.

The Land The country consists of the eastern part of the island of New Guinea plus the islands of the Bismark Archipelago and some other islands nearby. Mainland New Guinea is mountainous, thickly forested, and has a tropical climate with rainfall between 80 and 100 inches (2,032–2,540 mm) annually.

Economy Agriculture employs 82 percent of the workforce. The country exports coconut products, cocoa beans, coffee, rubber and tea. The main export is copper, and gold and silver are also mined. The per capita GNP in 1981 was $840.

SOLOMON ISLANDS

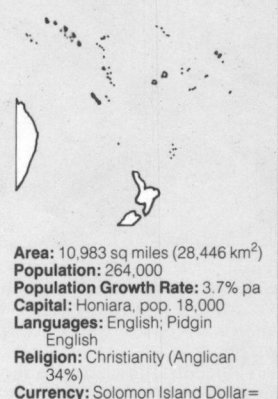

Area: 10,983 sq miles (28,446 km^2)
Population: 264,000
Population Growth Rate: 3.7% pa
Capital: Honiara, pop. 18,000
Languages: English; Pidgin English
Religion: Christianity (Anglican 34%)
Currency: Solomon Island Dollar = 100 Cents

THE SOLOMON ISLANDS are an island chain in the southwest Pacific Ocean, extending for 900 miles (1,400 km).

People and Culture Most of the Solomon Islanders are Melanesians. The islands were under British rule from 1893 until independence in 1978.

The Land The six main islands are rugged and mountainous, and volcanic in origin. There are thick forests. Many of the smaller islands are coral atolls. The climate is tropical.

Economy Fish, timber and copra are the main exports. The per capita GNP stood at $640 in 1981.

NAURU

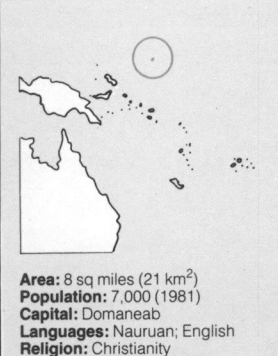

Area: 8 sq miles (21 km²)
Population: 7,000 (1981)
Capital: Domaneab
Languages: Nauruan; English
Religion: Christianity
Currency: Australian Dollar=
  100 Cents

NAURU, in the central Pacific, is the world's third smallest country.
People and Culture Almost half the people are of mixed Melanesian, Polynesian and Micronesian origin. The rest are workers from other Pacific islands and Hong Kong.
The Land Nauru is a coral island. About three-fifths is a central plateau of phosphate rocks.
Economy Valuable deposits of phosphate on the island are its main resource and only export. However, they are expected to run out in the 1990s.

KIRIBATI

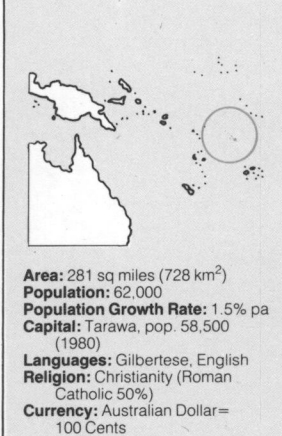

Area: 281 sq miles (728 km²)
Population: 62,000
Population Growth Rate: 1.5% pa
Capital: Tarawa, pop. 58,500 (1980)
Languages: Gilbertese, English
Religion: Christianity (Roman Catholic 50%)
Currency: Australian Dollar=
  100 Cents

KIRIBATI is a country in the southwest Pacific.
People and Culture Most of the people are Micronesians living in small villages. From 1916 to 1975 Kiribati formed part of the British colony of the Gilbert and Ellice Islands. It became independent in 1979.
The Land Kiribati consists of the Gilbert and Phoenix Islands, Ocean Island and also of some smaller islands.
Economy Copra is the main agricultural product and export. Some phosphates are mined. The per capita GNP was $420 in 1981.

TUVALU

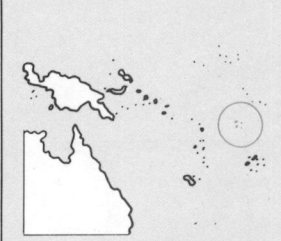

Area: 61 sq miles (158 km²)
Population: 9,000
Population Growth Rate: 4.9% pa
Capital: Funafati, pop. 900
Languages: Tuvaluan and English
Religion: Christianity (Protestant)
Currency: Australian Dollar=
  100 Cents

TUVALU is an island nation in the South Pacific.
People and Culture Most of the people are Polynesian in origin. Tuvalu was part of the British colony of Gilbert and Ellice Islands, and became independent in 1978.
The Land Tuvalu consists of nine islands, formerly called the Ellice Islands. They are the coral-topped peaks of submarine mountains. The climate is tropical.
Economy Coconuts are the main source of income. The per capita GNP was $680 in 1981.

VANUATU

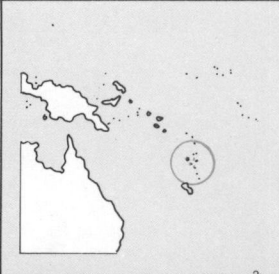

Area: 5,700 sq miles (14,763 km²)
Population: 135,000
Population Growth Rate: 4.2% pa
Capital: Vila, pop. 17,000
Languages: Bislama, English, French
Religion: Christianity (85%)
Currency: Vatu

THE REPUBLIC OF VANUATU is made up of 80 islands in the southwest Pacific.
People and Culture Over 90 percent of the people are Melanesians. The islands, formerly called the New Hebrides, were jointly governed by Britain and France until independence in 1980.
The Land The islands are volcanic. The climate is largely tropical.
Economy Agriculture is the most important feature. The main exports are copra, canned meat and frozen fish. The per capita GNP was $350 in 1981.

FIJI

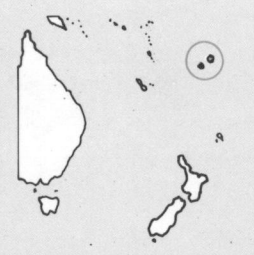

Area: 7,056 sq miles (18,274 km²)
Population: 680,000
Population Growth Rate: 2.0% pa
Capital: Suva, pop. 68,000 (1981)
Language: English, Fijian, Hindustani
Religion: Christianity (52%)
Currency: Fiji dollar=100 Cents

FIJI is an island country in the South Pacific.
People and Culture About 50 percent of the people are of Indian descent, 40 percent Melanesians, and the rest are of various origins. Fiji was a British colony until independence in 1970.
The Land More than 500 islands, 106 of them inhabited, make up Fiji. They are volcanic and surrounded by coral reefs.
Economy Agriculture is the main occupation, and sugarcane is the principal cash crop. Gold and silver are mined.

WESTERN SAMOA

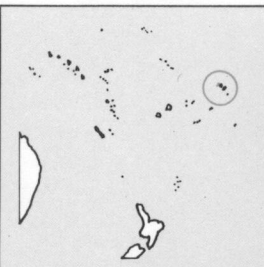

Area: 1,097 sq miles (2,842 km²)
Population: 160,000
Population Growth Rate: 0.7% pa
Capital: Apia, pop. 33,000 (1976)
Languages: Samoan, English
Religion: Christianity
Currency: Western Samoan Talà (Dollar)=100 Cents

WESTERN SAMOA is a Pacific Ocean country.
People and Culture About 90 percent of the people are of Polynesian descent. They live a simple life, but adult literacy is about 90 percent. The islands were under New Zealand protection until independence in 1962.
The Land Western Samoa consists of two large and two small islands, plus some uninhabited islets. The climate is mild with heavy rainfall.
Economy About 70 percent of the people work in agriculture. There is very little industry.

TONGA

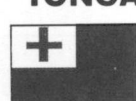

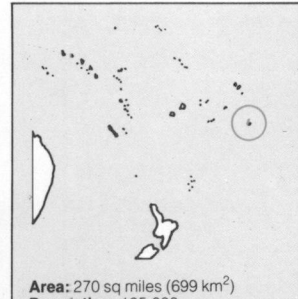

Area: 270 sq miles (699 km²)
Population: 105,000
Population Growth Rate: 2.0% pa
Capital: Nuku'alofa, pop. 18,300
Language: Tongan
Religion: Christianity (Wesleyan Methodist)
Currency: Pa'anga=100 Seniti

THE KINGDOM OF TONGA lies in the South Pacific.
People and Culture The Tongans are Polynesians. Most of them live on the largest island, Tongatapu. There are about 150 islands in the country. Tonga was under British protection from 1900 to 1970.
The Land Most of the islands are coral reefs, but some are active volcanoes. The soil is fertile and the climate is warm and pleasant.
Economy About 75 percent of the people work in agriculture, producing bananas and copra for export. The per capita GNP in 1981 was $530.

DEPENDENCIES

AMERICAN SAMOA is a United States territory in the South Pacific. It has an area of 76 sq miles (197 km²) and a population of 33,000. The seven islands of the territory are mostly mountainous. Nearly all the people are Polynesians. Fish and fish products are the main industry. The per capita GNP was $4,170 in 1981.

GUAM was probably discovered by Ferdinand Magellan in 1521. It was claimed by Spain in 1565 and ceded to the USA after the Spanish-American war in 1898. It is now a major American air and naval base. It has an area of 212 sq miles (549 km²) and the population was 104,000 in 1981.

THE TRUST TERRITORY OF THE PACIFIC ISLANDS is administered by the United States for the United Nations. It consists of 2,125 islands (84 of which are inhabited) with an area of 687 sq miles (1,779 km²) and a population of 153,000. The people are Micronesians.

PITCAIRN ISLAND is a British colony under New Zealand care. It has an area of 2 sq miles (5 km²) and a population of just over 50.

NEW CALEDONIA is an Overseas Territory of France. It has an area of 7,358 sq miles (19,058 km²) and a population of 148,000, half French and half Polynesian. There are rich mineral resources and it is the world's largest producer of nickel after Canada and the USSR.

FRENCH POLYNESIA, a French Overseas Territory, has an area of 1,545 sq miles (4,000 km²) and a population of 160,000. It consists of the Austral, Gambier, Marquesas, Society and Tuamoto island groups.

A head-dress of cockatoo and bird-of-paradise feathers.

New Zealand

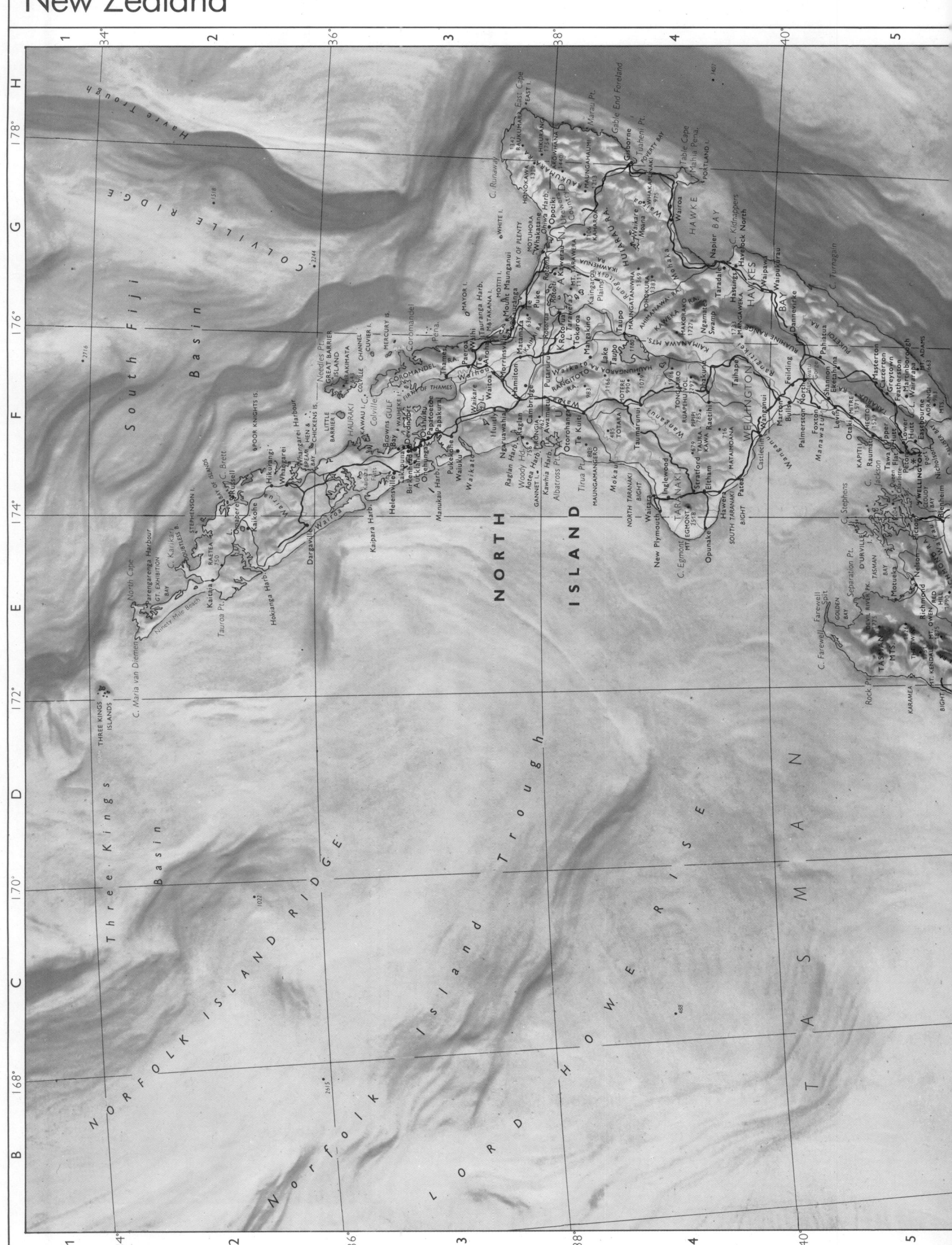

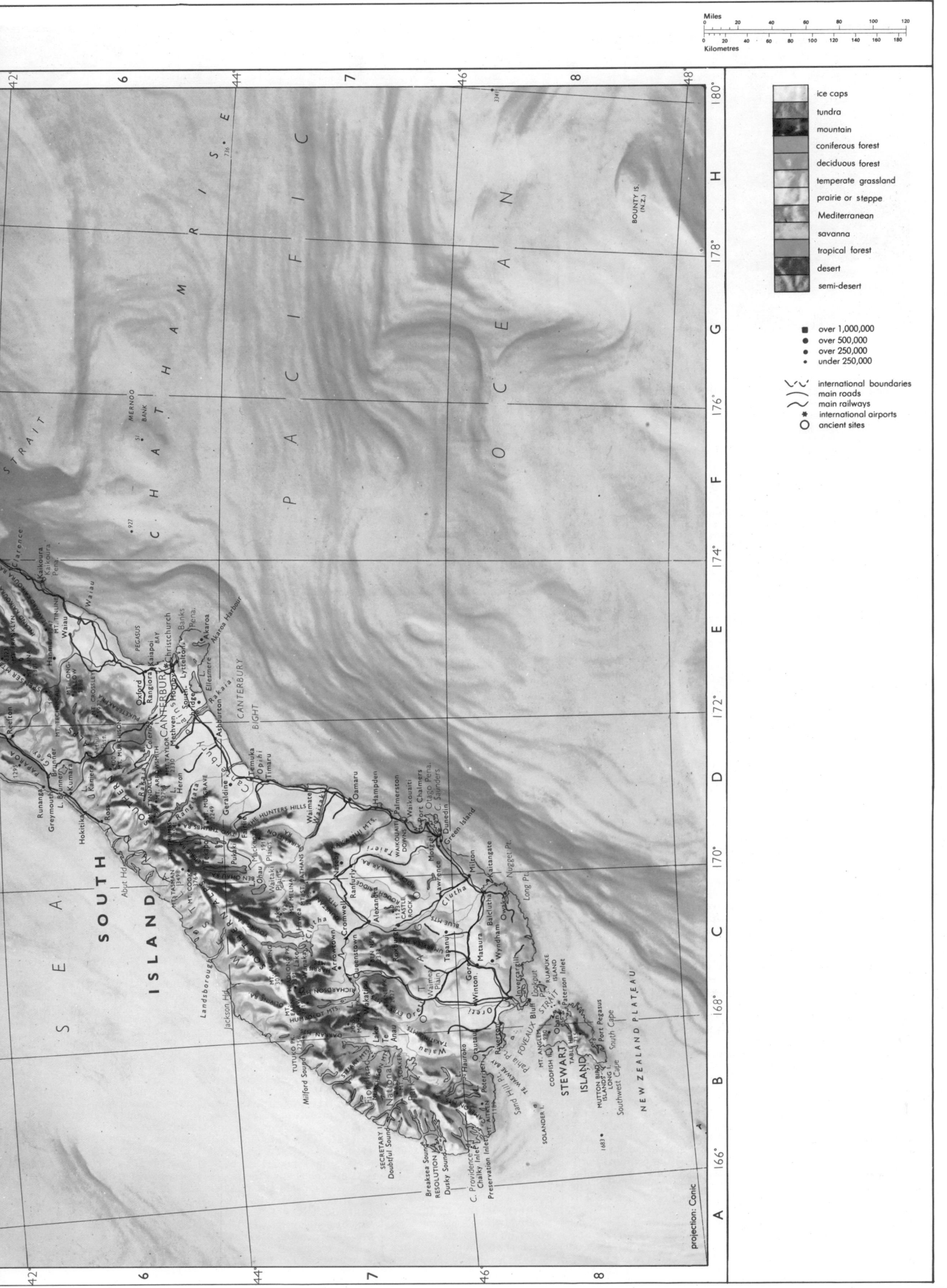

Miles
0   20   40   60   80   100   120
Kilometres
0 20 40 60 80 100 120 140 160 180

ice caps
tundra
mountain
coniferous forest
deciduous forest
temperate grassland
prairie or steppe
Mediterranean
savanna
tropical forest
desert
semi-desert

■ over 1,000,000
● over 500,000
● over 250,000
• under 250,000

〰 international boundaries
〰 main roads
〰 main railways
✳ international airports
○ ancient sites

projection: Conic

Sheep-farming is a major feature of New Zealand's economy.

NEW ZEALAND

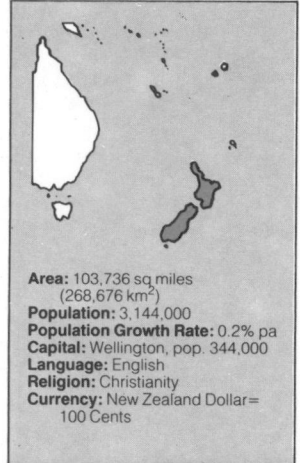

Area: 103,736 sq miles
(268,676 km²)
Population: 3,144,000
Population Growth Rate: 0.2% pa
Capital: Wellington, pop. 344,000
Language: English
Religion: Christianity
Currency: New Zealand Dollar=
100 Cents

NEW ZEALAND is the third largest country of Australasia, after Australia and Papua New Guinea. It was formerly a British colony, and is now an independent country in the Commonwealth of Nations. It consists of two main islands and many small ones.
People and Culture The first inhabitants of New Zealand were the Maoris, a Polynesian people. Their own traditions say they arrived about 650 years ago, but they may have reached New Zealand in the tenth century AD or earlier.

The Dutch navigator Abel Janszoon Tasman was the first European to sight New Zealand. The English seaman James Cook explored and mapped the coast in 1769, and his reports led others to New Zealand. Whalers and traders were the first. They supplied the Maoris with weapons, which encouraged tribal warfare. They were followed by missionaries, mostly from Britain. By the early 1830s there were hundreds of settlers, from Europe and Australia.

Britain signed the Treaty of Waitangi with Maori chiefs in 1840, and made New Zealand a colony.

The pattern of settlement in the early days is reflected in the religious pattern of present-day New Zealand.

Presbyterian Scots settled Southland and Otago, and built Dunedin (an old name for Edinburgh). Anglicans founded Christchurch. There are Methodists in North Auckland, and Roman Catholics and Baptists scattered throughout the islands.

From 1853 New Zealanders had self-government, at first through provincial governments, and from 1876 through a central government. A strong, progressive Liberal government from 1890 to 1912 gave the country old age pensions and also votes for women – the first country to do so.

In 1907 New Zealand became a selfgoverning Dominion within the British empire. It was effectively completely independent, but retained formal links with Britain until 1947.

A majority of New Zealanders are of British descent, but there have also been many settlers from other European countries, particularly the Netherlands, Yugoslavia, Austria and Switzerland. The Maoris numbered over 280,000 in 1981.

Life expectancy is high, at 74 years. New Zealanders have a high standard of living, and plenty of good food. Just over 73 percent live on North Island, the smaller of the two main islands, and 89 percent live in urban areas. This last proportion has risen from 81 percent in 1960.
Education Adult literacy stands at 99 percent. Education is compulsory up to the age of 15, and free up to the age of 19. The country has six universities.

Constitutional Development New Zealand is a monarchy, acknowledging the British sovereign, Queen Elizabeth II, as its head of state. She is represented by a Governor-general. There is a unicameral legislature, the General Assembly of New Zealand in Parliament Assembled, to give it its formal title. The only House is the House of Representatives.

There are two major political parties, the National Party and the Labour Party, plus some minor parties. There is thus a simple two-party political system.
The Land Most of New Zealand consists of two islands. North Island has an area of 44,281 sq miles (114,687 km²),

An 80-year-old Maori farmer at Rotorua, North Island.

while South Island has an area of 58,093 sq miles (150,460 km²). Smaller islands make up the rest of the country's land surface, the largest of them being Stewart Island, 672 sq miles (1,740 km²), which is separated from South Island by the Foveaux Strait.

Geologically New Zealand is a relatively young land. It stands at a destructive plate margin, where the Pacific plate is subducted under the Indian plate. As a result New Zealand is a land of earthquakes and vulcanism.

The visible surface of the North Island is largely built up of sedimentary deposits and volcanic debris. The northern peninsula and the north-western part of the island are largely low-lying, with rich soil, and the remains of once dense forests. The west coast has sandy beaches.

The eastern part of the island is partly mountainous, with rugged hills and more gentle slopes. Earthquakes are relatively frequent in this area.

In the west is a large plateau of volcanic rock, containing three active volcanoes. They are Mt Ruapehu, at 9,177 feet (2,797 m) the island's highest peak, Mt Tongariro and Mt Ngauruhoe. There are also many dormant and inactive volcanoes, notably Mt Tarawera which erupted in 1886 after a resting period of 800 years. In this area there are also geysers and hot springs, forming one of the world's major sources of geothermal power.

South Island is largely covered by the Southern Alps, which lie closer to the west coast than the east. They include Mt Cook, at 12,349

feet (3,764 m) the country's highest peak. Rain forests cover most of this region. In the east the Canterbury Plains form New Zealand's largest region of arable land.

New Zealand has many lakes, the largest being Lake Taupo on North Island, 234 sq miles (606 km²). The rivers are mostly short and fast-flowing, which makes them useless for navigation but ideal for hydroelectric schemes. There are hundreds of waterfalls.
Climate New Zealand has a mild climate, with winter temperatures rarely falling below 35°F (2°C), though frost and snow occur on higher ground, and some of the higher peaks have permanent ice-caps. The country is well-watered: the west coastal region has more than 100 inches (2,540 mm) of rain a year, with some parts receiving up to three times that amount. By contrast, parts of the east coast receive only 20 inches (508 mm) or less.
Vegetation The original plant life of New Zealand, before the arrival of the European settlers, was largely grassland and evergreen forests. The forests contained giant conifers and tree ferns, some of which still survive. The natural pines are slow-growing, so quick-growing pines from California have been planted.
Wildlife The only endemic mammals in New Zealand were some species of bats. There were about 250 species of birds, including a number of flightless birds. They include the kiwi, weka, takahe, and kapako. There are many penguin colonies.

Two species of cuckoos and several species of waders visit

New Zealand as annual migrants. A number of birds have colonized the country from Australia, and settlers have brought others from Europe.

New Zealand possesses one unique reptile, the tuatara, the last survivor of a group common in prehistoric times. Otherwise it has only lizards. There is a comparatively limited number of invertebrate species by the standards of other lands.
Economy New Zealand ranks among the second class in the world wealth table, with a per capita GNP of $7,700. The mainstay of the economy is agriculture, but it employs only 9 percent of the workforce – a quarter of that engaged in industry.
Agriculture New Zealand has 40,867 sq miles (105,844 km²) of land devoted to crop-growing and grazing. In 1980 its farms produced 305,800 tonnes of wheat, 228,300 tonnes of barley, and 156,500 tonnes of maize. Apples, pears, and oats are the other main cash crops.

Meat and dairy products are the mainstay of New Zealand's agriculture and of its exports. Australia, Britain, Japan, and the United States are its principal customers.

The country has more than 8 million cattle and 70 million sheep. It sells abroad large quantities of beef and lamb, and more than 380,000 tonnes of wool; it ranks third in the world in wool production, second in mutton and lamb, and eighth in butter. Agriculture accounts for 11 percent of the GDP.

Forestry is growing in importance, and is based largely

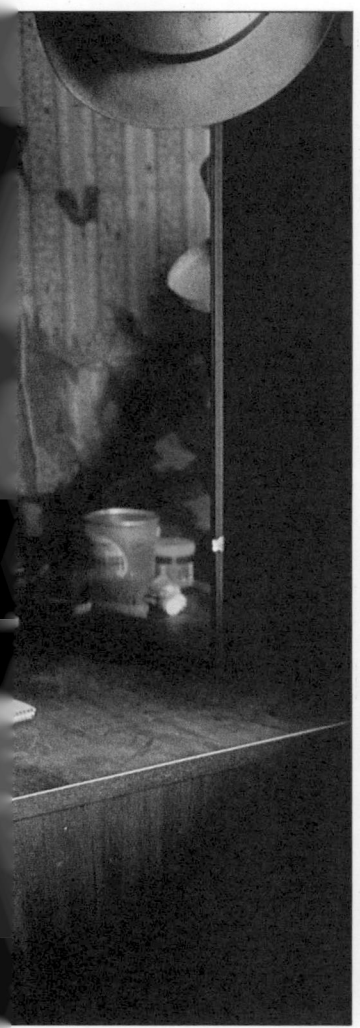

Croquet is popular in New Zealand. People place great value on quiet, settled ways of life.

Mount Egmont on North Island last erupted 300 years ago.

on plantations of non-endemic species.

Mining Gold was discovered in Otago in 1861, which brought in a flood of immigrants. Few made much money from gold, though for 30 years it was New Zealand's second most important export. Annual production today is about 440 lb (200 kg).

The country has few minerals, apart from coal and natural gas. Coal production runs at more than 2 million tonnes a year. Natural gas, discovered in 1959, now supplies many cities in the North Island. There is some petroleum and iron ore, and a little copper, silver, and tungsten.

Power Hydroelectric schemes provide more than 87 percent of New Zealand's power requirements, and some power is also derived from geothermal energy at Wairakei in the North Island. The rest comes from power stations fired by coal, gas or oil.

Industry New Zealand's industry has been slow to develop, largely because of a shortage of native raw materials. However, there is a flourishing iron and steel industry, an oil refinery and an aluminium smelter. Industry contributes 31 percent of the GDP, with manufacturing responsible for 23 percent. It employs 35 percent of the workforce, a slight drop since the early 1960s.

Communications Railways in New Zealand use narrow-gauge, 3 feet 6 inches (1,067 mm), lines because they are cheaper to build in the often rugged terrain. Rail lines link all the major cities in each of the two main islands, but passengers must change to ferries to cross the Cook Strait from one island to the other.

Altogether there are 2,745 miles (4,418 km) of line.

There are 60,000 miles (97,000 km) of roads, which includes the 6,800 miles (11,000 km) State Highway network. Vehicles using the roads totalled 2,220,990 in 1981. Domestic air services carried more than 2,300,000 passengers in 1981, while over 1,750,000 passengers travelled on international flights.

Overseas Territories New Zealand has four overseas territories. Two of them are self-governing. Cook Islands are a group of 15 small islands in the Pacific lying northeast of New Zealand. The people are Polynesians and closely related in language and customs to the mainland Maoris. They have New Zealand citizenship. The economy is based on citrus and other fruits, and copra. The islands have their own legislative assembly.

Niue, to the west of the Cook Islands, also has a Polynesian population, whose language is related to Samoan. The island has its own assembly and the people are New Zealand citizens. A fortnightly shipping service links Niue and Cook Islands with New Zealand. Niue's main exports are passion-fruit and copra. Both Niue and Cook Islands receive financial aid from New Zealand.

Tokelau, a group of three coral atolls to the north of Samoa, is governed as part of New Zealand. The Ross Dependency is a segment of Antarctica that lies nearest to New Zealand. It has no permanent inhabitants, but a scientific base on Ross Island is manned all year.

Aa-Alençon

Gazetteer

For list of geographical terms and their abbreviations see page 249.

Aa, *France, river* 98 A 4
Aa, *Switzerland, river* 101 D 3
Aachen 102 B 3
Aalborg 74 G 3
Aalst 98 C 4
Aalten 98 E 3
Aarau 101 D 2
Aare, *river* 101 C 2
Aargau, *canton* 101 D 2
Aarhus 74 G 3
Aarschot 98 C 4
Aba 166 D 5
Âbādān 118 D 4
Âbādeh 154 E 3
Abakan 123 M 4
Abakuma, *river* 134 E 3
Abarqū 154 E 3
Abashiri 134 F 1
Abashiri-wan,*bay* 134 F 2
Abau 151 F 5
Abaya L., *lake* 167 G 5
Abbai, *river* 167 G 4
Abbe L., *lake* 154 C 7
Abbeville 94 E 2
Abbiategrasso 101 D 4
Abdalagis, Sa. de, *mts.* 90 C 4
'Abd al Kuri 167 J 4
Abéché 167 F 4
Âbenrå 87 N 6
Abeokuta 166 D 5
Aberdare 94 C 2
Aberdare Mts., *mts.* 167 G 5
Aberdeen, *Scotland* 74 E 3
Aberdeen, *U.S.A., North Dakota* 40 H 2
Aberdeen, *U.S.A., Washington* 40 C 2
Aberdeen L.,*lake* 34 H 2
Aberystwyth 83 D 5
Abhā 154 C 6
Abidjan 166 C 5
Abilene, *U.S.A., Kansas* 40 H 4
Abilene, *U.S.A., Texas* 40 H 5
Abingdon 83 F 6
Abitibi, *river* 34 J 3
Abitibi, L., *lake* 30 F 3
Abo, *region* 166 E 3
Abodi, Sa. de, *mts.* 90 E 1
Abomey 166 D 5
Abrantes 90 A 3
Abrolhos, Arquipélago dos, *island group* 61 F 4
Abruzzese, Appenine, *mountains* 106 D 3
Abruzzi e Molise, *prov.* 106 D 3
Absaroka Ra., *mountains* 30 E 3
Abu 'Amūd, W., *wadi* 158 C 5
Abū 'Arīsh 154 C 6
Abū Dâra, Râs, *cape* 154 B 5
Abū Dhabi 78 C 3
Abu Gamal 154 B 7
Abuja 166 D 5
Abū Kamāl 79 H 3
Abukuma sanchi, *mts.* 134 E 3
Abula Mieda 154 B 7
'Âbūr 158 B 4
Abut Hd., *cape* 199 D 6
Abu Shagara, Râs, *cape* 154 B 5
Aby, Lagune, *lake* 166 C 5
Abyssinian Highlands 118 C 5
Acámbaro 50 C 2
Acapulco de Juárez 31 F 5
Acapulco Trench, *sea feature* 31 E 5
Acari, Serra, *mountains* 60 D 2
Accra 166 C 5
Achchik Köl, *lake* 142 E 2
Achill Hd., *cape* 83 A 5
Achill Island, *island* 83 A 5
Achimota 166 C 5
Acireale 107 E 6
Acklins I., *island* 31 G 4
Aconcagua, Co., *mt.* 67 A 2
Aconquija, Nev. de, *mts* 62 B 1
Acqui 106 B 2
Acre, *see 'Akko* 158 B 2
Adadleh 154 C 8
Adado, Ras, *cape* 154 D 7
Adafer, *region* 166 C 4
Adaja, *river* 90 C 2
Adak Habchuka, *mt.* 142 F 2
Adalsliden 86 P 3
Adama 167 G 5
Adamello, *mountain* 106 C 1
Adamoua, Massif de l', *mountains* 166 E 5
Adam, Mt., *mountain* 62 C 4
Adam's Bridge, *shoals* 143 D 5
Adams, Mt., *U.S.A., mt.* 40 C 2
Adams, Mt., *New Zealand, mountain* 198 F 5
Adams Peak, *mountain* 138 F 5
Adamuz 90 C 3
Adana 73 L 5
Adapazari 79 F 3
Adare, Cape, *cape* 15 L 2
Adda, *river* 106 B 1
Ad Dahnā, *region* 118 D 4
Aḑ Ḑāli' 154 C 7
Ad Dammām 138 C 3
Addan Tso, *lake* 142 E 3
Ad Dawhah, *see Doha* 154 E 4
Ad Dilam 154 D 5
Ad Dir'īyah 154 D 5
Addis Ababa 167 G 5
Addis Derra 154 B 7
Ad Dīwānīyah 154 C 3
Ad Duhūl, *region* 154 D 4
Adelaide 186 D 5
Adelaide I., *island* 15 R 2
Adelaide Pena., *peninsula* 34 H 2
Adel-Esa, *region* 167 H 4
Aden 118 D 5
Aden, Gulf of, *gulf* 118 D 4
Adige, *river* 75 D 2
Adigrat 167 G 4
Adi Kaie 154 B 7
Adirondack Mountains, *mountains* 41 M 3
Adi Ugri 167 G 4
Adjud 116 E 3
Admer, Erg d', *sand dunes* 166 D 3
Admiralty G., *gulf* 192 E 2
Admiralty Inlet, *Canada, inlet* 34 J 1
Admiralty Inlet, *U.S.A. inlet* 42 B 1
Admiralty I., *island* 30 D 3
Admiralty Is., *island group* 119 J 6
Admiralty Mts., *mts.* 15 L 2
Adoni 138 E 4
Adoua, *river* 166 D 4
Adour, *river* 95 D 6
Adra 90 D 4
Adrano 107 E 6
Adrar 166 C 3
Adrar des Iforas, *mts.* 166 D 3
Adrar Edekel, *mountain* 166 D 3
Adrar Sotuf, *region* 166 B 3
Adriatic Sea 72 H 4
Adula, *mountain* 103 C 5
Adula Gruppe, *mts.* 101 E 3
Aduwa 167 G 4
Adventure Bank, *sea feature* 107 D 6
Aegean Sea 72 K 5
Aela, P. d', *mountain* 101 E 3
Ærø, *island* 87 N 6
'Afaf Hills, *mountains* 154 D 7
Affreville 91 G 4
Afghanistan 118 E 4
Afikpo 166 D 5
Aflāj, Al, *region* 138 B 3
Afognak I., *island* 30 C 3
Afsluitdijk 98 D 2
Afton 42 E 3
'Afula 158 B 2
Afyon 79 F 3
Agadès 166 D 4
Agadir 166 C 2
Agalega Is., *island group* 118 D 6
Agano 134 D 3
Agartala 142 F 4
Agassiz, C., *cape* 15 R 2
Agatti I., *island* 143 C 5
Agaumdir, *region* 167 G 4
Agboville 166 C 5
Agde 91 G 1
Agde, C. d', *cape* 95 F 6
Agen 78 C 2
Ager, *river* 103 F 4
Agger, *river* 98 F 4
Agnone 106 E 4
Agnona, *river* 101 D 4
Agordat 154 B 6
Agout, *river* 95 E 6
Agra 118 E 4
Agrakhanskiy Poluostrov, *peninsula* 79 H 2
Agreda 90 E 2
Agrigento 107 D 6
Agrihan, *island* 151 F 2
Agrinion 110 B 4
Agropoli 107 E 4
Agryz 125 H 2
Aguadas 51 F 4
Aguadilla 51 G 3
Agua Prieta 50 C 1
Aguarague, Cord. de, *mountains* 60 C 5
Aguascalientes 50 C 2
Agueda 90 A 2
Agueda, *river* 90 B 2
Aguilar de la F. 90 C 4
Aguilas 91 E 4
Aguia, C. de la, *mts.* 51 F 3
Aguja, Pta., *cape* 60 A 3
Agulhas Bank, *sea bank* 174 C 5
Agulhas Basin, *sea basin* 26 F 5
Agulhas, C., *cape* 174 D 5
Agulhas Negras, *mt.* 61 E 5
Ahaggar, *mountains* 166 D 3
Ahar 154 D 2
Ahaus 102 B 2
Ahimanawa Ra., *mts.* 198 G 4
Ahmadnagar 138 E 4
Ahmar, Erg el, *sand dunes* 166 C 3
Ahmar Mts., *mountains* 166 H 5
Ahmedabad 118 E 4
Ahr, *river* 94 H 2
Ahrgeb, *mountains* 98 E 4
Ahuachapán 50 E 3
Ahvāz 118 D 4
Ahvenanmaa, *island group* 72 J 2
Ahvenanmaa, *province* 87 Q 4
Aiddejavrre 86 R 2
Aigle 101 B 3
Aigoual, Mt. de l', *mt.* 95 F 5
Aiguille de Chambeyron, *mountain* 95 H 5
Aijal 146 A 4
Ailao Shan, *mountains* 129 C 7
Ain Salah 166 D 3
Ain Sefra 166 C 2
Ain-Sefra, *region* 166 C 3
Ain Taya 91 G 4
Aird Hills, *mountains* 151 F 4
Aire 94 F 2
Aire, *England, river* 83 F 5
Aire, *France, river* 98 D 5
Aire, I. del, *island* 91 H 3
Aire, Sa. do, *mountains* 90 A 3
Airolo 101 D 3
Aïr ou Azbine, *mts.* 166 D 4
Aisatung Mt., *mountain* 146 A 4
Ai Shan, *mountain* 128 G 4
Aisne, *river* 94 F 3
Aitape 151 F 4
Aitken, Mt., *mountain* 199 B 8
Aitzgorri, Mt., *mt.* 95 C 6
Aix-en-Provence 78 C 2
Aix-la-Chapelle, *see Aachen* 94 H 2
Aix-les-Bains 95 G 5
Aíyina 111 C 5
Aíyina, *island* 111 C 5
Aíyion 111 C 4
Aizwakamatsu 134 D 3
Ajaccio 72 H 5
Ajedabya 167 F 2
Ajjer, *mountains* 166 D 3
'Ajlūn 158 B 2
Ajmer 118 E 4
Ajo 40 E 5
Ajo, Cabo, *cape* 90 D 1
Ajo, Mt., *mountain* 42 D 5
Ajoe, Kep., *island group* 151 E 3
Akaishi-san, *mountains* 134 D 4
Akalkot 143 D 4
Akaroa 199 E 6
Akaroa Harb., *harbour* 199 E 6
Akashi 134 C 4
Akato Tagh, *mountains* 142 E 2
Ak-Bulak 125 H 3
Akcha 142 C 2
Akchar, Dunes de l', *sand dunes* 166 B 3
Akershus, *county* 87 N 4
Akesu 118 F 3
Aketi 167 F 5
Akharnaí 110 C 4
Akhdar, J. al, *Libya, mountains* 167 F 2
Akhḑar, J. al, *Muscat & Oman, mountains* 118 D 4
Akhelóös 111 B 4
Akhisar 110 E 4
Akhtopol 110 E 2
Akhtyrka 75 K 3
Akimiski I., *island* 30 F 3
Akita 123 R 6
Ak Kar Chekyl Tagh, *mountains* 142 D 2
Akkeshi-wan, *bay* 134 F 2
'Akko 158 B 2
Akkyr, G., *mountains* 73 N 5
Aklavik 30 D 2
Akola 138 E 3
A-k'o-su 142 D 1
Akpatok I., *island* 35 L 2
Akranes 86 B 3
Akron 30 F 3
Akseki 79 F 3
Aksha 123 O 4
Aksum 167 G 4
Aktarsk 125 F 3
Aktí 110 D 3
Aktyubinsk 75 N 3
Akureyri 74 C 2
Alabama, *river* 30 F 4
Alabama, *state* 41 K 5
Alaejos 90 C 2
Alagón 91 E 2
Alagón, *river* 90 B 3
Alahärmä 86 R 3
Al Aḩmadī 138 B 3
Alajuela 51 E 4
Alakurtti 86 U 2
Al' Amādīyah 154 C 2
Alamagan, *island* 151 F 2
Al Amārah 138 B 2
Alameda 90 C 4
Alamo Res., *reservoir* 42 D 5
Alanäs 86 P 3
Aland, *see Ahvenanmaa* 87 Q 4
Alanya 125 C 7
Alapaha, *river* 46 D 4
Alapayevsk 75 N 3
Al Aqabah 79 G 4
Alarcón, Emb. de, *lake* 90 D 3
Al 'Arīsh 79 G 4
Al Arţawiyah 154 D 4
Alaska, *state* 30 C 2
Alaska, Gulf of, *gulf* 30 C 3
Alaska Highway 34 C 2
Alaska Pena., *peninsula* 30 C 3
Alaska Ra., *mountains* 26 B 2
Alas, Selat, *strait* 150 C 4
Alatri 106 D 4
Alatyr 75 L 3
Alayor 91 H 3
Alayskiy Khr., *mts.* 118 E 4
Al A'ẓamīyah 154 C 3
Alba 106 B 2
Al Bāb 154 B 2
Albacete 78 B 3
Alba de Tormes 90 C 2
Alba Iulia 116 D 3
Albalate del A. 91 E 2
Al Balyanā 167 G 3
Albania 72 J 5
Albany, *Australia* 186 B 5
Albany, *U.S.A., Georgia* 41 L 5
Albany, *U.S.A., New York* 41 N 3
Albany, *U.S.A., Oregon* 42 B 2
Albany, *river* 30 F 3
Albarracín 91 E 2
Albarracín, Sa. de, *mt.* 90 E 2
Albatross B., *bay* 186 E 3
Albatross Plateau, *sea feature* 11 E 2
Albatross Pt., *cape* 198 F 4
Al Batrūn 154 B 3
Al Bayḑā 154 D 7
Albemarle Sd., *sound* 41 M 4
Albenga 106 B 2
Alberche, Embalse del, *lake* 90 C 2
Albères, Mts., *mts.* 95 F 6
Alberga, *river* 186 D 4
Albergaria-a-V. 90 A 2
Alberique 91 E 3
Albert 94 F 2
Albert, *river* 193 G 3
Alberta, *province* 34 F 3
Albert, L., *see Mobutu Sese Seko, L.* 167 G 5
Albert Lea 41 J 3
Albert Nile, *river* 167 G 5
Albertville 95 H 5
Albi 78 C 2
Albina, Pta., *cape* 174 C 3
Albir, P. del, *region* 91 E 3
Albocácer 91 E 2
Alboran, I. de, *island* 90 D 5
Alborz, Reshteh-ye, *mts.* 118 D 4
Albox 90 D 4
Albret, Les Pays d', *region* 95 D 5
Albufeira 90 A 4
Albufera, La, *lake* 91 E 3
Albula, *river* 101 E 3
Albuquerque 40 F 4
Alburquerque 90 B 3
Albury 193 J 7
Alcácer do Sal 90 A 3
Alcains 90 B 3
Alcalá de Chivert 91 F 2
Alcalá de H. 90 D 2
Alcalá de los G. 90 C 4
Alcalá la Real 90 D 4
Alcamo 107 D 6
Alcanadre, *river* 91 E 2
Alcanar 91 F 2
Alcanena 90 A 3
Alcañiz 91 E 2
Alcántara 90 B 3
Alcantarilla 91 E 4
Alcaraz 90 D 3
Alcaraz, Sa. de, *mts.* 90 D 3
Alcarria, La, *region* 90 D 2
Alcasovas 90 A 3
Alcaudete 90 C 4
Alcázar de San Juan 90 D 3
Alcazarquivir 78 B 3
Alcira 78 B 3
Alcoa 41 L 4
Alcobaça 90 A 3
Alcorisa 91 E 2
Alcoutim 90 B 4
Alcoy 78 B 3
Alcubierre, Sa. de, *mts.* 91 E 2
Alcudia, B. de, *bay* 91 G 3
Aldabra Is., *island group* 175 F 2
Aldabra Ridge, *sea feature* 13 B 3
Aldan 123 P 4
Aldan, *river* 119 H 2
Aldanskoye Nagor'ye, *highlands* 119 H 3
Aldeburgh 83 G 5
Aldeia Nova de S. Bento 90 B 4
Alderney, *island* 83 E 7
Aldershot 83 F 6
Aledua, Sa. de., *mts.* 91 E 3
Aleksandriya 125 C 4
Aleksandrovsk-Sakhalinskiy 123 R 4
Alençon 94 E 3

Anjouan–At Tīh

Anjouan, *island* 174 F 3
Anjū 123 P 6
An-k'ang 119 G 4
Ankara 72 L 5
Ankazoabo 175 F 4
Anklam 102 E 2
Ankober 167 G 5
Anlier, Forêt d', *forest* 98 D 5
Ann, C., *cape* 35 K 4
Annaba 166 D 2
An'Nabk 79 G 4
An Nafūd, *region* 118 D 4
An Najaf 138 B 2
Annam, *region* 146 E 5
Annan 82 E 4
Annan, *river* 83 E 4
Annapolis, *Canada* 35 L 4
Annapolis, *U.S.A.* 41 M 4
Annapurna, *mountain* 147 E 3
Ann Arbor 41 L 3
An Nâşirīyah 154 D 3
Annecy 101 B 4
Annecy, Lac d', *lake* 101 B 4
Annemasse 101 B 3
Anniston 41 K 5
Annobón, *island* 166 D 6
An. Arkhánai 111 D 6
Áno Viánnos 111 D 6
Anóyia 111 D 6
Ansārīye, J. al, *mts.* 154 B 2
Ansbach 103 D 4
An-shan 119 H 3
An-shun 129 D 6
Anso, V. de, *valley* 91 E 1
Antakya 79 G 3
Antalaha 175 G 3
Antalya 79 F 3
Antalya Körfezi, *bay* 73 K 5
Antananarivo 175 F 3
Antarctica 27 G 5
Antarctic Pena., *peninsula* 15 R 2
Antela, Lac de, *lake* 90 B 1
Antelope I., *island* 42 D 3
Antelope Ra., *mts.* 42 C 4
Antequera 90 C 4
Anti-Atlas, *mountains* 166 C 2
Antibes 95 H 6
Antibes, C. d', *cape* 95 H 6
Anticosti I., *island* 30 G 3
Antifer, C. d', *cape* 94 E 3
Antigua 50 D 3
Antigua, *island* 31 G 5
Antioch 42 B 4
Antioche, Pertuis d', *strait* 95 D 4
Antipodes, Is., *islands* 187 H 6
Antofagasta 60 B 5
Antoing 98 B 4
Antongil, B. d', *bay* 175 F 3
Antrim 83 C 4
Antrim Mts., *mountains* 74 E 3
Antsirabe 175 F 3
Antsiranana 175 F 3
An-t'u 134 B 2
An-tung 119 H 3
Antwerpen 72 G 3
Antwerpen, *province* 98 C 3
An Uaimh 83 C 5
Anundsjö 86 Q 3
Anuradhaoura 143 D 5
Anvnvers, *see Antwerpen* 98 C 3
Anvers I., *island* 15 R 2
Anyama 166 C 5
An-yang 123 O 6
Anza, *river* 101 D 4
Anzhero-Sudzhensk 123 L 4
Anzio 106 D 4
Ao Ban Don, *bay* 147 C 7
Aogo-shima, *island* 134 D 4
Aoíz 91 E 1
Aomori 119 J 3
Aorangi Mts., *mountains* 198 F 5
Ao Sawi, *bay* 147 C 7
Aosta 106 A 2
Aosta, Valle d', *province* 101 C 4
Aotea Harb., *harbour* 198 F 3
Aouk, B., *river* 167 F 5
Aouker, *region* 166 C 4
Apalachee Bay, *bay* 41 L 5
Apalachicola 41 K 6
Apalachicola Bay, *bay* 46 C 4
Aparri 139 K 4
Apeldoorn 98 D 2
Api, *mountain* 142 D 3
Apodi, Chapado do, *region* 61 F 3
Apolda 102 D 3
Apopka, L., *lake* 46 D 4
Appalachian Mountains, *mountains* 30 F 4
Äppelbo 87 O 4
Appennini, *mountains* 72 H 4
Appenzell 101 E 2
Appleton 41 K 3
Aprilia 106 D 4
Apsheronskiy Poluostrov, *peninsula* 125 G 6
Apt 95 G 6
Apucarana, Sa. da, *mts.* 61 D 5
Apulyont Gölü, *lake* 110 F 3
Apure, *river* 60 C 2
Apuseni, Munţii, *mts.* 72 J 4
Aqaba, G. of, *gulf* 73 L 6
Aquarius Plateau, *plateau* 42 E 4
Aquidauana 60 D 5
Arabatskaya Strelka, *bay* 125 C 5
Arabian Basin, *sea feature* 13 C 2
Arabian Peninsula, *region* 27 F 3
Arabian Sea 13 C 2
Aracaju 61 F 4
Aracati 61 F 3
Aracena 90 B 4
Araçena, Sa. de, *mts.* 90 B 4
Arad 79 E 2
Arafura Sea 186 D 2
Aragats, *mountain* 79 H 3
Aragón 91 E 1
Aragón, *province* 91 E 2
Aragoncillo, *mountain* 90 D 2
Araguaia, *river* 60 D 4
Araguari, *river* 61 D 2
'Arah, Ra's al, *cape* 154 C 7
Arak 122 G 6
Arakan, *province* 146 A 4
Arakan Yoma, *mts.* 118 F 4
Araks, *river* 73 M 5
Aralar, Sa. de, *mts.* 90 D 1
Aral'sk 118 E 3
Aral'skoye More, *sea* 118 E 3
Aranda de D. 90 D 2
Aran I., *island* 82 B 4
Aran Islands, *island group* 83 B 5
Aranjuez 90 D 2
Arán, V. de, *valley* 91 F 1
Aranya Prathet 147 D 6
Arapkir 125 D 6
Araras, Sa. das, *mts.* 61 D 4
Ararat 193 H 7
Ararat, Mt., *see Büyük Ağri Daği* 73 M 5
Araripe, Sa. do, *mts.* 61 E 3
Aras, *river* 73 M 5
Arauca 60 C 2
Arauca, *river* 51 F 4
Aravalli Ra., *mountains* 138 E 3
Araxá 61 E 4
Araxes, *see Aras* 125 F 6
Arayj, Al, *region* 154 B 4
Arbatax 107 B 5
Arbay Hêre 123 N 5
Arbil 125 F 7
Arboga 87 P 5
Arbon 101 E 2
Arbroath 82 E 3
Arc, *Provence, river* 95 G 6
Arc, *Savoie, river* 95 H 5
Arcachon 95 D 5
Arc Dome, *mountain* 42 C 4
Archena 90 E 3
Archer, *river* 186 E 3
Archer Bay 193 H 2
Archidona 90 C 4
Arcis-sur-Aube 94 G 3
Arcos de la F. 90 C 4
Arcos de V. 90 A 2
Arcos, Sa. de, *mt.* 91 E 2
Arctic Bay, *trading post* 34 J 1
Arctic Ocean 26 B 1
Arda 110 D 3
Ardabil 125 G 6
Arḑ aş Şawwān, *region* 79 G 4
Ardèche, *river* 95 G 5
Ardee 83 C 5
Ard el Jabban, *region* 158 C 2
Ardennes, *mountains* 74 F 4
Ardestān 154 E 3
Ardila 90 B 3
Ardino 110 D 3
Ardnamurchan Pt., *cape* 82 C 3
Ardrossan 82 D 4
Arena, Pt., *cape* 40 C 4
Arenas de San Pedro 90 C 2
Arenberg, *region* 98 F 2
Arendal 74 G 2
Arequipa 60 B 4
Arévalo 90 C 2
Arévalo, Tierra de, *region* 90 C 2
Arezzo 78 D 2
Arga 90 E 1
Argamasilla de A. 90 D 3
Argelès-Gazost 95 D 6
Argens, *river* 95 H 6
Argenta 106 C 2
Argentan 94 D 3
Argentera, P., *mountain* 95 H 5
Argentière 101 B 4
Argentina 62 B 2
Argentino, L., *lake* 62 A 4
Argentine Basin, *sea feature* 12 C 7
Argenton-sur-Creuse 95 E 4
Argolikós Kólpos, *bay* 111 C 5
Argonne 94 G 3
Argonne, Forêt d', *forest* 98 D 5
Árgos 111 C 5
Arguello, Pt., *cape* 42 B 5
Argun', *river* 119 G 3
Argyll, *region* 82 D 3
Ariakeno-umi, *bay* 134 B 4
Ariake-wan, *bay* 134 B 5
Ari Atoll, *island* 143 C 6
Arica 60 B 4
Arid, C., *cape* 192 D 6
Ariège, *river* 95 E 6
Arima 51 G 3
Aripuanã, *river* 60 C 3
Arivonimamo 175 F 3
Ariza 90 D 2
Arizona, *state* 40 E 5
Arjeplog 86 Q 2
Arjona 90 C 4
Arjonilla 90 C 4
Arkabutla Res., *reservoir* 46 B 3
Arkagala 123 R 3
Arkansas, *river* 30 E 4
Arkansas, *state* 41 J 4
Arkansas City 41 H 4
Arka Tagh, *mountains* 142 E 2
Arkhangel'sk 73 M 2
Arklow 83 C 5
Árkoi, *island* 111 E 5
Arkoúdhi, *island* 111 B 4
Arlanzón, *river* 90 C 1
Arlberg, *mountains* 101 F 2
Arlbergpass, *pass* 101 F 2
Arles 78 C 2
Arlon 94 G 3
Arly, *river* 101 B 4
Armagh 83 C 4
Armagnac, *region* 72 F 4
Armançon, *river* 94 G 4
Armatnhiá, *island* 111 E 6
Armavir 79 H 2
Armenia 60 B 2
Armentières 94 F 2
Armidale 193 K 6
Armstrong 34 F 3
Armutçuk D., *mountain* 111 E 3
Armyanskaya S.S.R., *republic* 122 G 5
Arnedo 90 D 1
Arnes 86 B 2
Arnhem 74 F 3
Arnhem, C., *cape* 186 D 3
Arnhem Land, *region* 186 D 3
Arno, *river* 106 C 3
Arnøy, *island* 86 Q 1
Arnsberg 102 C 3
Arnstadt 102 D 3
Aro, P. de, *mountain* 90 D 1
Aroánia Óri, *mountain* 79 E 3
Aroche, Picos de, *mt.* 90 B 3
Arolsen 102 C 3
Aron, *river* 95 F 4
Arona 106 B 2
Arosa 101 E 3
Arosa, Ria de, *inlet* 90 A 1
Arowhana, *mountain* 198 G 4
Ar Rachidiya 166 C 2
Arraiolos 90 B 3
Ar Ramādī 154 C 3
Arran, *island* 82 D 4
Arras 74 F 3
Arrée, Mt. d', *mt.* 94 C 3
Ar Rihāb, *region* 73 M 6
Ar Rimāl, *region* 118 D 5
Arronches 90 B 3
Arrowsmith, Mt., *mt.* 199 D 6
Arrowtown 199 C 7
Arroyo de la Luz 90 B 3
Arruda dos V. 90 A 3
Arsen'ev 134 C 1
Arta, *Greece* 110 B 4
Arta, *Spain* 91 G 3
Artem 134 C 2
Artemovskiy 75 N 3
Artesa de S. 91 F 2
Artesia 40 G 5
Arthur's Pass, *mt. pass* 199 D 6
Arti 75 N 3
Artois, *province* 94 E 2
Artois, Collines d', *region* 94 F 2
Ar-tsagan Nor, *lake* 128 E 3
Aru, Kep., *island group* 119 H 6
Arua 167 G 5
Aruba, *island* 31 G 5
Arudy 91 E 1
Arunachal Pradesh, *state* 142 F 3
Arunta, *see Simpson Desert* 186 D 4
Aruppukkottai 143 D 5
Arusha 175 E 2
'Arvat Sedom 158 B 4
Arve, *river* 101 B 3
Arvida 35 K 4
Arvidsjaur 86 Q 3
Arvika 87 O 5
Arys' 122 J 5
Arzew 91 E 5
Arzew, G. d', *gulf* 91 E 5
Arzúa 90 A 1
Ås 102 E 3
Asahi, *river* 134 C 4
Asahi-d., *mountain* 134 E 2
Asahigawa 119 J 3
Asama y., *mountain* 134 D 3
Asan Man, *bay* 128 H 4
Asansol 139 F 3
Åsarna 86 O 4
Asbest 75 N 3
Ascalon, *ancient site* 158 A 3
Ascension I., *island* 12 E 5
Aschaffenburg 102 C 4
Aschersleben 102 D 3
Ascoli 106 D 3
Ascoli Satriano 106 E 4
Aseda 87 P 5
Asedjrad, *mountains* 166 D 3
Asekrem, *mountain* 166 D 3
Åsele 86 P 3
Asenovgrad 111 D 3
Ashburton, *New Zealand* 199 D 6
Ashburton, *river* 186 B 4
Ashburton Ra., *mts.* 186 D 3
Ashdod 158 A 3
Asheville 41 L 4
Ashford 83 G 6
Ashfork 42 D 5
Ashikaga 134 D 3
Ashizuri-saki, *cape* 134 C 4
Ashkhabad 118 D 4
Ashland, *U.S.A., Kentucky* 46 D 2
Ashland, *U.S.A., Oregon* 42 B 3
Ashmore Reef, *reef* 192 D 2
Ashqelon 158 A 3
Ash Sharqāţ 125 E 7
Ash Shihr 154 D 7
Ashton 42 E 2
Ashuanipi L., *lake* 35 L 3
'Āsi, *river* 79 G 3
Asia, Kep., *island group* 151 E 3
Asinara, Golfo Dell', *gulf* 106 B 4
Asino 122 L 4
Asīr 118 D 5
Asi T., *mountain* 110 F 4
Askersund 87 O 5
Askja 86 D 3
Asmara 167 G 4
Asopós, *river* 111 C 4
Asosa 167 G 4
Asoteriba, J., *mountain* 167 G 3
Asinara, *island* 78 D 3
Aspiring, Mt., *mountain* 199 C 7
Aspromonte, *mountains* 107 E 5
Assab 118 D 5
Assab B., *bay* 154 F 6
Aş Şaḩn, *region* 154 C 3
Assale, L., *lake* 154 C 7
Assam, *state* 142 F 3
As Samāwah 154 D 3
Assateague I., *island* 46 F 2
Assen 98 E 2
Assens 87 N 6
Assinara, *island* 106 B 4
Assiniboine, *river* 34 H 4
Assiniboine, Mt., *mt.* 30 E 3
Assisi 106 D 3
Aş Şummān, *region* 154 D 4
Aş Şummān, *rocky plateau* 154 D 5
Assumption, *island* 175 F 2
As Suwaydā' 154 B 3
Aş Şuwayrah 154 C 3
As Suways 166 G 3
Astakidha, *island* 111 E 6
Asterabad, *region* 154 E 2
Asti 106 B 2
Astipálaia, *island* 111 E 5
Astola I., *island* 142 B 3
Astorga 90 B 1
Astoria 40 C 2
Astove I., *island* 175 F 3
Astrakhan' 73 M 4
Åsträsk 86 Q 3
Asturias, *province* 90 B 1
Asunción 60 D 5
Asuncion, *island* 151 F 2
Aswān 167 G 3
Aswan Dam, *dam* 167 G 3
Asyūt 167 G 3
Atacama, Desierto de, *desert* 60 C 5
Atacama, Puna de, *mts.* 60 C 5
Atakora, Chaîne de l', *mountains* 166 D 4
Atakpamé 166 D 5
Atalayas de Alcalá, *region* 91 F 2
Atar 166 B 3
Atascadero 42 B 5
Atbara 167 G 4
Atbara, *river* 167 G 4
Atbasar 122 J 4
Atchafalaya B., *bay* 46 B 4
Ateca 90 E 2
Ateibe, B. el, *lake* 158 C 1
Atessa 106 E 3
Ath 94 F 2
Athabasca, *river* 34 F 3
Athabasca, L., *lake* 30 E 3
Athens, *U.S.A., Georgia* 46 D 3
Athens, *U.S.A., Ohio* 46 D 2
Atherton 193 J 3
Atherton Plateau, *plateau* 186 E 3
Athínai 72 J 5
Athlit 158 A 2
Athlone 83 C 5
Athos, *mountain* 72 K 5
Athy 83 C 5
Ati, J., *mountains* 166 E 3
Atienza 90 D 2
Atikonak L., *lake* 35 L 3
Atka 123 S 3
Atkarsk 75 L 3
Atlanta 30 F 4
Atlantic-Antarctic or Atlantic-Indian Ridge, *sea feature* 12 E 7
Atlantic City 41 N 4
Atlantic-Indian Antarctic Basin, *sea feature* 15 B 2
Atlantic Ocean 14 O 3
Atlas Saharien, *mts.* 166 C 2
Atlixco 50 D 3
Átokos, *island* 111 B 4
Atrak, *river* 154 E 2
Aţ Ţā'if 138 B 3
Attáviros, *mountain* 111 E 5
Attawapiskat, *river* 34 J 3
At Taysīyah, *region* 154 C 4
Atter See, *lake* 103 E 5
At Tih, *region* 79 G 4

C

Cachi-Celebes

Cachi, Nos. de, *mountain* 60 C 5
Cachimbo, Sa. do, *mts.* 60 D 3
Cachoeira do Sul 62 C 2
Cactus Ra., *mountains* 42 C 4
Cader Idris, *mountain* 83 E 5
Cadi, Sa. del, *mountains* 91 F 1
Cadiz, *Spain* 72 F 5
Cadiz, B. de, *bay* 90 B 4
Cadiz, Golfo de, *gulf* 90 B 4
Cadiz L., *lake* 42 D 5
Caen 74 E 4
Caernarvon 83 D 5
Caernarvon Bay, *bay* 83 D 5
Caesarea, *ancient site* 158 A 2
Caesarea Philippi, *ancient site* 158 B 1
Cagayan 119 H 5
Cagayan, *river* 150 D 2
Cagliari 72 H 5
Caguas 51 G 3
Caha Mts., *mountains* 83 B 6
Cahore Pt., *cape* 83 C 5
Cahors 95 E 5
Caiapó, Sa. do, *mts.* 61 D 4
Caibarién 46 E 6
Caicos Is., *island group* 51 F 2
Caicos Passage, *strait* 41 N 7
Caillou Bay, *bay* 46 B 4
Caird Coast, *region* 15 A 2
Cairngorm Mts., *mts.* 82 E 3
Cairns 186 E 3
Cairntoul, *mountain* 82 E 3
Cairo, *Egypt* 167 G 2
Cairo, *U.S.A.* 41 K 4
Cajamarca 60 B 3
Čakovec 106 F 1
Calabar 174 B 1
Calabozo 51 G 4
Calabria, *province* 107 F 5
Cala, Emb. de, *lake* 90 B 4
Calahorra 90 E 1
Calais 72 G 3
Calalaste, Cord. de, *mountains* 62 B 1
Calamar 51 F 3
Calamian Group, *island group* 139 J 4
Calamocha 91 E 2
Cala Moral, Pta. de, *cape* 90 C 4
Calañas 90 B 4
Calanda 90 E 2
Călânda, *region* 101 E 3
Calapan 139 K 4
Calarasi 116 E 4
Calar del Mundo, *mts.* 90 D 3
Calasetta 107 B 5
Calasparra 90 E 3
Calatayud 90 E 2
Calatrava, Campo de, *region* 90 D 3
Calavà, C., *cape* 107 E 5
Calayan I., *island* 129 G 8
Calcutta 118 F 4
Caldas da Rainha 90 A 3
Caldeirão, Sa. do, *mts.* 90 A 4
Calderina, Sa. de la, *mountains* 90 D 3
Caldwell 40 D 3
Caldy I., *island* 83 D 6
Calexico 42 D 5
Calf of Man, *island* 83 D 4
Calğal Dag, *mountain* 79 G 3
Calgary 30 E 3
Cali 60 B 2
Caliente 42 D 4
California, *state* 40 C 4
California, Golfo de, *gulf* 31 E 4
Calimere, Pt., *cape* 143 D 5
Calipatria 42 D 5
Calispell Peak, *mountain* 42 C 1
Callabonna, L., *lake* 193 H 5
Callander 82 D 3
Callao 60 B 4
Callosa de Ensarriá 90 E 3
Caltagirone 78 D 3
Caltanissetta 107 E 6
Calvi 106 B 3
Calvia 91 G 3
Calvinia 174 C 5
Calvitero, *mountain* 90 C 2
Calw 103 C 4
Camacupa 174 C 3
Camagüey 31 G 4
Camagüey, Archo. de, *island group* 51 F 2
Camarasa, Emb. de, *lake* 91 F 2
Camarat, C., *cape* 78 C 2
Camargues, *region* 95 G 6
Camariñas 90 A 1
Camas 90 B 4
Ca Mau, Pte. de, *cape* 119 G 5
Cambados 90 A 1
Cambay, G. of, *gulf* 118 E 4
Cambrai 74 F 3
Cambre 90 A 1
Cambria 42 B 5
Cambrian Mts., *mts.* 74 E 3
Cambridge, *England* 83 G 5
Cambridge, *New Zealand* 198 F 3
Cambridge Bay 34 G 2
Camden 41 M 4
Cameron Mts., *mts.* 199 B 8
Cameroons Mt., *mt.* 166 D 5
Cameroun 166 E 5
Caminha 90 A 2
Camino, C. di, *mountain* 90 F 4
Camiri 60 C 5
Camoghe, *mountain* 101 E 3
Camonica, Val, *valley* 101 F 4
Camoniche, Alpi, *mts.* 101 F 4
Camooweal 193 G 3
Camorta I., *island* 143 F 5
Campagna, *region* 78 D 2
Campania, *province* 107 E 4
Campanquix, Cerros, *mountains* 60 B 3
Campanario 90 C 3
Campbell, C., *cape* 198 F 5
Campbell I., *Burma, island* 147 C 7
Campbell I., *New Zealand, island* 15 L 3
Campbell, Mt., *mountain* 34 D 2
Campbellton 35 L 4
Campbeltown 82 D 4
Camp de Châlons, *region* 98 C 5
Camp de Villa, *region* 90 C 1
Campeche 50 D 3
Campeche, Bahía de, *bay* 31 F 5
Campeche Bank, *sea feature* 31 F 4
Cam-pha 119 G 4
Campilhas, Barr., *lake* 90 A 4
Campillos 90 C 4
Câmpina 116 E 4
Campiña, La, *region* 90 C 4
Campina Grande 61 F 3
Campinas 61 E 5
Campoalegre 51 F 4
Campobasso 106 E 4
Campo de Cariñena, *reg.* 90 E 2
Campo de Dalías, *region* 90 D 4
Campo Grande 60 D 5
Campo Maior 90 B 3
Campos 61 E 5
Campos, *E. Brazil, reg.* 61 E 4
Campos, *Spain, region* 90 C 2
Campos, Tierra de, *reg.* 90 C 1
Campsie Fells, *mountains* 82 D 3
Câmpulung 116 E 4
Câmpulung Moldovenesc 116 E 3
Cam Ranh, B. de, *bay* 147 E 7
Camrose 34 F 3
Canada 30 D 3
Canadian, *river* 30 E 4
Çanakkale 110 E 3
Çanakkale Boğazi, *strait* 72 K 5
Canal Beagle, *strait* 62 B 4
Canal Casiquiare, *river* 60 C 2
Cananea 40 E 5
Canarias, Islas, *island grp.* 12 E 3
Canastra, Sa. da, *mts.* 61 E 4
Canaveral, C., *cape* 31 F 4
Canavese, *region* 101 C 4
Canberra 186 E 5
Canche, *river* 98 A 4
Candala 154 D 7
Çandarli Körfezi, *bay* 110 E 4
Candeleda 90 C 2
Candlemas I., *island* 15 A 3
Cañete 91 E 2
Canet, É. de, *lake* 91 G 1
Cangas de Narçea 90 B 1
Canicatti 107 D 6
Canigou, Mt., *mountain* 78 C 2
Canisp, *mountain* 82 D 2
Canjáyar 90 D 4
Çankiri 79 G 3
Canna, *island* 82 C 3
Cannes 78 C 2
Canning Basin, *region* 192 D 3
Cannock 83 E 5
Canosa di Puglia 106 E 4
Canouan 60 C 1
Canso, C., *cape* 30 G 3
Cantabria, Sa. de, *mts.* 90 D 1
Cantabrica, Cordillera, *mountains* 72 F 4
Cantal, Massif du, *mts.* 95 F 5
Cantal, Plomb du, *mt.* 95 F 5
Cantalapiedra 90 C 2
Cantanhede 90 A 2
Canterbury 83 G 6
Canterbury, *county* 199 D 6
Canterbury Bight, *gulf* 199 E 7
Canterbury Plains, *reg.* 199 D 7
Can Tho 119 G 5
Cantillana 90 C 4
Canton, *see Kuang-chou* 128 E 7
Canton, *U.S.A.* 41 L 3
Cantù 101 E 4
Capcir, *region* 95 F 6
Cape Barren I., *island* 193 J 8
Cape Breton I., *island* 30 G 3
Cape Coast 166 C 5
Cape Dorset, *trading post* 35 K 2
Cape Girardeau 41 K 4
C. Hallet, *scientific base* 15 L 2
Cape Hope's Advance, *trading post* 35 L 2
Cape I., *island* 46 E 3
C. Johnson Depth, *sea feature* 11 A 2
Capella, *mountain* 151 F 4
Capernaum, *ancient site* 158 B 2
Cape Town 174 C 5
Cape Verde Basin, *sea feature* 12 D 3
Cape Verde Is., *island group* 12 D 4
Cape Verde Plateau, *sea feature* 12 D 4
Cape York Peninsula, *peninsula* 186 E 3
Cap-Haïtien 31 G 5
Capoompeta, *mountain* 193 K 5
Capraia, *island* 106 B 3
Capri, *island* 78 D 3
Capricorn Chan., *channel* 187 F 4
Capricorn Group, *reefs* 193 K 4
Caprino 106 C 2
Caprivi Strip, *region* 174 D 3
Cap St. Jacques 139 H 4
Capua 106 E 4
Capulin Mt., *mountain* 40 G 4
Caquetá, *river* 60 B 3
Carabaya, Cord. de, *mountains* 60 B 4
Caracal 110 D 1
Caracas 60 C 1
Carajás, Sa. dos, *mts.* 61 D 3
Caramulo, Sa. do, *mts.* 90 A 2
Caransebeş 116 D 4
Caratasca, Laguna, *lake* 51 E 3
Caravaca 90 E 3
Caravaggio 101 E 4
Caravelas 60 F 4
Carballino 90 A 1
Carballo 90 A 1
Carbonara, C., *cape* 107 B 5
Carboneras, *mountain* 90 C 3
Carcagente 91 E 3
Carcans, Étang de, *lake* 95 D 5
Carcar, Monti, *mountain* 167 H 5
Carcassonne 78 C 2
Carcross 34 D 2
Cardamon Hills, *mts.* 143 D 5
Cardamones, Chaine des, *mountains* 147 D 6
Cárdenas 50 D 2
Cardiff 72 F 3
Cardigan 83 D 5
Cardigan Bay, *bay* 83 D 5
Cardoner, *river* 91 F 2
Carei 116 D 3
Carentan 83 F 7
Carey, L., *lake* 186 C 4
Cariaco Trench, *sea feature* 51 G 3
Caribbean Sea 31 F 5
Cariboo Mts., *mountains* 30 D 3
Caribou 34 H 3
Caribou Mt., *mountain* 42 E 3
Cariñena 91 E 2
Carinhanha 61 E 4
Caripito 60 C 1
Carlisle 74 E 3
Carlit, Pic., *mountain* 95 E 6
Carlow 83 C 5
Carlsbad 40 G 5
Carlsberg Ridge, *sea feature* 13 B 2
Carlyle Res., *reservoir* 46 B 2
Carmarthen 83 D 6
Carmarthen Bay, *bay* 83 D 6
Carmel, Cape, *cape* 158 A 2
Carmel Hd., *cape* 83 D 5
Carmel Mt., *mountain* 158 A 2
Carmen, *Colombia* 51 F 4
Carmen, *Mexico* 50 D 3
Carmen, *island* 40 E 6
Carmona 90 C 4
Carnarvon Ra., *mountains* 192 D 5
Carnegie, L., *lake* 186 C 4
Carnegie Ridge, *sea feature* 12 A 5
Carniche, Alpi, *mts.* 106 D 1
Car nicobar, *island* 143 F 5
Carnsore Pt., *cape* 83 C 5
Carolina 61 E 3
Caroline Islands, *island group* 11 A 2
Caroline-Solomon Ridge, *sea feature* 11 B 2
Caroní, *river* 51 G 4
Carpathians, *mountains* 72 J 4
Carpatii Meridionali, Mti., *mountains* 72 J 4
Carpentaric, Gulf of, *gulf* 186 D 3
Carpenter Ridge, *sea feature* 13 D 2
Carpentras 95 G 5
Carpi 106 C 2
Carrantuohill, *mountain* 83 B 6
Carranza, C., *cape* 62 A 2
Carrara, *town* 106 C 2
Carrascoy, Sa. de, *mts.* 91 E 4
Carriacou, *island* 60 C 1
Carrick-on-Suir 83 C 5
Carrión 90 C 1
Carson City 40 D 4
Carson Sink, *region* 40 D 4
Cartagena, *Colombia* 60 B 1
Cartagena, *Spain* 78 B 3
Cartago 51 F 4
Cartelle 90 A 1
Carterpuri 142 D 3
Carterton 198 F 5
Carthage, *ancient site* 107 C 6
Cartier I., *island* 192 D 2
Cartwright 35 M 3
Caruaru 61 F 3
Carupano 61 C 1
Carvin 98 A 4
Carvoeira, C., *cape* 90 A 3
Caryapundy Swamp, *swamp* 193 H 5
Casablanca, *see El-Dar-el-Beida* 166 C 2
Casa Grande 42 E 5
Casale Monferrato 106 B 2
Casalmaggiore 106 C 2
Casas Ibáñez 91 E 3
Casavieja 90 C 2
Cascade 42 C 2
Cascade Dam Res., *res.* 42 C 2
Cascade Range, *mts.* 30 D 3
Cascais 90 A 3
Caserta 78 D 3
Cashel 83 C 5
Casino 193 K 5
Čáslav 102 F 4
Caso 90 C 1
Caspe 91 E 2
Casper 40 F 3
Caspian Sea 73 N 4
Cassai, *river* 174 D 3
Cassiar Mts., *mountains* 34 D 2
Cassino 106 D 4
Castejon, Montes de, *mountains* 91 E 2
Castellammare del Golfo 107 D 5
Castellammare di Stabia 107 E 4
Castellammare, G. di, *gulf* 107 D 5
Castellane 95 H 6
Castellar 90 D 3
Castellar, El, *region* 91 E 2
Castellón de la Plana 78 C 3
Castellote 91 E 2
Castelltallat, Sa. de, *mountains* 91 F 2
Castelnaudary 95 E 6
Castelo Branco 90 B 3
Castelo de Vide 90 B 3
Castelsarrasin 95 E 5
Castelvetrano 107 D 6
Castiglione 91 G 4
Castiglione di Stiviere 101 F 4
Castilla la Nueva, *prov.* 90 C 3
Castilla la Vieja, *prov.* 90 C 2
Castillejo, Sa. de, *mts.* 90 C 3
Castillo, Pampa del, *pampas* 62 B 3
Castlebar 83 B 5
Castle Rock, *mountain* 199 C 7
Castres 78 C 2
Castries 51 G 3
Castro del Rio 90 C 4
Castrojeriz 90 C 1
Castropol 90 B 1
Castro-Urdiales 90 D 1
Castro Verde 90 A 4
Castrovillari 107 F 5
Catalca 110 F 3
Çatal Daği, *mountain* 110 F 4
Cataluña, *province* 91 F 2
Catamarca 62 B 1
Catanduva 61 E 5
Catania 72 H 5
Catania, Golfo di, *gulf* 107 E 6
Catanzaro 107 F 5
Catarroja 91 E 3
Catastrophe, C., *cape* 186 D 5
Cat I., *island* 31 G 4
Catoche, C., *cape* 31 F 4
Catskill Mts., *mountains* 30 G 3
Cauca, *river* 60 B 2
Caucasus Mts., *see Bol'shoy Kavkaz* 73 M 4
Caudete 90 E 3
Cau Hai, Lagune de, *lake* 147 E 5
Cauquenes 62 A 2
Caura, *river* 51 G 4
Cauvery, *river* 143 D 5
Caux, *region* 94 E 3
Cávado, *river* 90 A 2
Cavaignac 91 F 4
Cavaillon 95 G 6
Cavan 83 C 5
Caviana, I., *island* 61 D 2
Caxias 61 E 3
Caxias do Sul 62 C 1
Caxine, C., *cape* 91 G 4
Cayenne 61 D 2
Cayman Is., *island group* 31 F 5
Cayman Trench, *sea feature* 12 A 4
Cay Sal Bank, *sea feature* 51 E 2
Cazalla de la Sierra 90 C 4
Cazaux et de Sanguinet, É. de, *lake* 95 D 5
Cazin 106 E 2
Cea, *river* 90 C 1
Cebollera, *mountain* 90 D 2
Cebollera, Sa., *mountains* 78 B 2
Cebreros 90 C 2
Cebu 119 H 5
Cebu, *island* 119 H 5
Ceclavín 90 B 3
Cedar City 40 E 4
Cedar Falls 41 J 3
Cedar I., *N. Carolina, island* 46 E 3
Cedar I., *Virginia, island* 46 F 2
Cedar L., *lake* 34 G 3
Cedar Rapids 41 J 3
Cedeira 90 A 1
Cedros, *island* 31 E 4
Ceduna 192 F 6
Cefalù 107 E 5
Cega, *river* 90 C 2
Cegléd 116 C 3
Celanova 90 B 1
Celaya 50 C 2
Celtic Sea 72 F 4
Celebes, *see Sulawesi* 139 J 6

Celebes Sea-Chorol Tsho

Celebes Sea 119 H 5
Celje 116 B 3
Celle 102 D 2
Čemerna Plan., *mountains* 110 B 2
Central African Republic 167 E 5
Central Arctic, *district* 34 F 1
Central Brahui Ra., *mts.* 142 C 3
Central, Cord., *Bolivia, mountains* 60 C 4
Central, Cordillera, *Colombia, mountains* 60 B 2
Central, Cord., *Dominican Rep., mts.* 51 F 3
Central, Cord., *Peru, mountains* 60 B 3
Central, Cordillera, *Philippines, mountains* 129 G 8
Central Hwy. 193 J 5
Centralia 41 K 4
Central Makran Range, *mountains* 142 B 3
Central, Massif, *mts.* 72 G 4
Central Ra., *mountains* 186 E 2
Central Valley 42 B 3
Cerbere, C., *cape* 91 G 1
Cerdaña, La, *region* 91 F 1
Ceret 91 G 1
Cerignola 106 E 4
Cerknica 106 E 2
Cernavoda 116 F 4
Cerrato, Valles de, *valley* 90 C 2
Cerro Pinacate, *mt.* 42 D 6
Cerro de Pasco 60 B 4
Cervati, M., *mountain* 107 E 4
Cervera, *Spain, Cataluña* 91 F 2
Cervera, *Spain, Navarra* 91 E 1
Cervera, C., *cape* 91 E 3
Cervera de Pisuerga 90 C 1
Cervera, P. de, *mountain* 90 D 2
Cervione 106 B 3
Cesena 106 D 2
Česká Lípa 102 F 3
České Budějovice 78 D 2
Ceskezeme, *province* 102 F 4
Českomoravská Vysočina, *mountains* 103 F 4
Český Krumlov 103 F 4
Cess, *river* 166 C 5
Cessnock 193 K 6
Cetinje 116 C 4
Cetraro 107 E 5
Ceuta 78 B 3
Cevedale, M., *mountain* 101 F 3
Cevennes, *mountains* 72 G 4
Ceyhan, *river* 79 G 3
Ceylon, *island* 143 D 6
Ceylon Rise, *sea feature* 13 D 2
Chablais, *region* 101 B 3
Chacabuco 62 B 2
Chachoengsao 147 C 6
Chaco Austral, *region* 62 B 1
Chaco Boreal, *region* 60 C 5
Chaco Central, *region* 60 D 5
Chad 166 E 4
Chad Lake, *lake* 166 E 4
Chagai Hills, *mountains* 118 E 4
Chagos Archipelago, *island group* 118 E 6
Chaiyaphum 147 C 6
Chala Shan, *mountains* 139 G 2
Chaleurs, B. des, *bay* 35 L 4
Chalky Inlet, *inlet* 199 B 8
Challans 95 D 4
Challenger Depth, *sea feature* 11 B 2
Chalmy Varre 86 W 2
Châlons-sur-Marne 78 C 2
Chalon-sur-Saône 78 C 2
Cham 103 E 4
Chaman 142 C 3
Chamao, Kh., *mountain* 147 C 6
Chamartin de la Rosa 90 D 2
Chambal, *river* 139 E 3
Chambéry 78 C 2
Chamdo 118 F 4
Chamdo, *province* 146 A 2
Chamo, L., *lake* 167 G 5
Chamonix 95 H 5
Champa 142 E 4
Champagne, *province* 94 G 3
Champagne, *region* 94 E 4
Champagne Charentaise, *region* 95 D 5
Champagnole 101 A 3
Champlain, L., *lake* 30 G 3
Champsaur, Mts., *mts.* 95 H 5
Chamusca 90 A 3
Chance I., *island* 147 B 7
Chan-chiang 119 G 4
Chandausi 142 D 3
Chandeleur Is., *island group* 46 B 4
Chandeleur Sd., *inlet* 46 B 4
Chandigarh 138 E 2
Chandigarh, *state* 142 D 3
Chandrapur 118 E 4
Ch'ang Ch., *river* 119 G 4
Ch'ang-chih 128 E 4
Chang-chou 119 G 4
Ch'ang-ch'un 119 H 3
Chang Ho, *river* 128 E 4
Chang-hua 129 G 7
Ch'ang-li 128 F 4
Chang-p'ai Shan, *mts.* 118 H 4
Ch'ang-p'u 129 F 7
Changsangot, *cape* 128 G 4
Ch'ang-sha 119 G 4
Ch'ang-shan Lieh-tao, *island group* 128 G 4
Ch'ang-shu 128 G 5
Chang Tång, *mountains* 128 B 5
Chang Tang, *plateau* 118 F 4
Ch'ang-te 139 J 3
Ch'ang-t'ing 129 F 6
Chang-yeh 123 M 6
Channel Islands, *island group* 72 F 4
Channel Rock, *island* 46 E 6
Chantada 90 B 1
Chanthaburi 139 H 4
Chantonnay 95 D 4
Chanza, *river* 90 B 4
Ch'ao-an 129 F 7
Chao-an Wan, *island* 129 F 7
Ch'ao Hu, *lake* 128 F 5
Chao-t'ung 129 C 6
Chaowula Shan, *mts.* 142 F 2
Chao-yang 129 F 7
Ch'ao-yang-chen 128 H 3
Chapada dos Parecis, *mountains* 60 C 4
Chapala, L., de, *lake* 50 C 2
Chaparral 51 F 4
Chapayevsk 75 M 3
Chaplina, M., *cape* 119 L 2
Chapra 138 F 3
Chaqui 60 C 4
Charchan Darya, *river* 142 E 2
Charcot I., *island* 15 R 2
Chard 83 E 6
Chardzhou 118 E 4
Charente, *river* 95 E 4
Chari, *river* 166 E 4
Charleroi 94 G 2
Charles, C., *cape* 30 G 4
Charles I., *island* 35 K 2
Charles Pk., *mountain* 192 D 6
Charleston, *U.S.A., S. Carolina* 30 G 4
Charleston, *U.S.A., West Virginia* 41 L 4
Charleston Pk., *mountain* 42 D 4
Charleville 193 J 5
Charleville-Mézières 95 G 3
Charlotte 41 L 4
Charlotte Amalie 51 G 3
Charlotte Harb., *inlet* 46 D 5
Charlottenberg 87 O 5
Charlottesville 46 E 2
Charlottetown 30 G 3
Charolles 95 G 4
Charters Towers 193 J 4
Chartres 94 E 3
Chartreuse, Gde., *mts.* 95 G 5
Chasseral, *mountain* 101 C 2
Chatal Balkan, *mountains* 110 E 2
Châteaubriant 94 D 4
Château-Chinon 94 F 4
Château d'Oex 101 C 3
Châteaudun 94 E 3
Château-Gontier 94 D 4
Châteaulin 94 B 3
Château, Pte. de, *cape* 94 C 3
Châteauroux 95 E 4
Château Salins 94 H 3
Château Thierry 94 F 3
Châteleu, Mt., *mountain* 101 B 3
Châtellerault 95 E 4
Chatham, *Canada, New Brunswick* 35 L 4
Chatham, *England* 83 G 6
Chatham Is., *island group* 187 J 6
Chatham Rise, *sea feature* 11 B 4
Chatham Str., *strait* 34 D 3
Châtillon 101 C 4
Châtillon-sur-Seine 94 G 4
Chatkal'skiy Khr., *mts.* 142 C 1
Chatrapur 143 E 4
Chattahoochee, *river* 41 K 5
Chattanooga, *river* 41 K 4
Chau Doc 147 D 7
Chaumont 94 G 3
Chaunskaya Guba, *bay* 123 T 3
Chaves 90 B 2
Chayatyn, Khr., *mts.* 123 Q 4
Chayul 142 F 3
Cheaha Mt., *mountain* 46 C 3
Cheb 102 E 3
Cheboksary 73 M 3
Chech, Erg, *sand dunes* 166 C 3
Cheduba I., *island* 143 F 4
Chehalis 42 B 2
Cheju 128 H 5
Cheju Do, *island* 123 P 6
Cheju Haehyŏp, *strait* 128 H 5
Chekiang, *province* 128 F 6
Chela, Sa. da, *mountains* 174 C 3
Che-lang-piao, *cape* 129 F 7
Chelan, L., *lake* 42 B 1
Ch'e-li 129 C 7
Chéliff, *river* 72 G 5
Chelkar 122 H 5
Chellala 91 G 5
Chelm 116 D 2
Chelmno 116 C 2
Chelmsford 83 G 6
Cheltenham 83 E 6
Chelva 91 E 3
Chelyabinsk 73 O 3
Chelyuskin 123 N 2
Chelyuskin, Mys, *cape* 118 G 2
Chemnitz 102 E 3
Chenab, *river* 142 D 2
Chen-chiang 139 J 2
Ch'eng-chiang 139 H 3
Cheng-chou 119 G 4
Ch'eng-hai 129 F 7
Ch'eng-mai 129 D 8
Chengshan Tow, *cape* 139 K 2
Ch'eng-te 128 F 3
Cheng-ting 128 E 4
Ch'eng-tu 118 G 4
Chen-hai 128 G 6
Chen-hsi 123 M 5
Ch'en-hsien 119 G 4
Chen-yüan, *China, Kweichow* 128 D 6
Chen-yuan, *China, Yunnan* 129 C 7
Cher, *river* 94 E 4
Cherangani Hills, *mts.* 167 G 5
Cherbourg 74 E 4
Cherchel 166 D 2
Chercher, *region* 167 H 5
Cherdyn 75 N 2
Cheremkhovo 118 G 3
Cherepovets 73 L 2
Cheriyam I., *island* 143 C 5
Cherkassy 79 F 2
Cherkessk 125 E 5
Chernigov 72 K 3
Chernigovka 134 C 1
Chernikovsk 75 N 3
Cherni Vrŭkh, *mountain* 110 C 2
Chernovtsy 79 F 2
Chernyakhovsk 116 D 1
Chernysheva, Kryazh, *mountains* 73 O 1
Cherokee 41 H 3
Cherokee Pt., *cape* 46 E 5
Cherokees, L. O'The, *lake* 41 H 4
Cherry Creek Mt., *mt.* 42 D 3
Cherskogo, Khrebet, *mountains* 119 H 2
Cherven Brya 110 D 2
Chesapeake B., *bay* 30 G 4
Cheshskaya Guba, *bay* 75 L 1
Cheste 91 E 3
Chester 83 E 5
Chesterfield 83 F 5
Chesterfield, Îles, *reefs* 187 F 3
Chesterfield Inlet 34 H 2
Chetlat I., *island* 143 C 5
Chetumal 51 E 3
Cheviot Hills, *mountains* 74 E 3
Cheviot, The, *mountain* 82 E 4
Cheyenne 40 G 3
Cheyenne, *river* 40 G 3
Chhindwara 142 D 4
Chhuikhadan 142 D 4
Chia-hsing 128 G 5
Chia-Ling Chiang, *river* 128 D 5
Chia-mu-ssu 123 Q 5
Chi-an, *China, Kiangsi* 129 E 6
Chi-an, *China, Liaoning* 128 H 3
Chiang-ling 129 E 5
Chiang Mai 118 F 5
Chiang Saen 146 C 4
Chiang-tu 139 J 2
Chiao-chou Wan, *bay* 128 G 4
Chiao-hsien 128 F 4
Chiao-tso 128 E 4
Chiari 101 E 4
Chiasso 101 E 4
Chiavari 106 B 2
Chiavenna 101 E 3
Chia Wang 128 F 5
Chiba 119 J 4
Chicago 30 F 3
Chichagof I., *island* 30 D 3
Chichester 83 F 6
Ch'i-ch'i-ha-erh 119 H 3
Chickamauga L., *lake* 46 C 3
Chickmagalur 143 D 5
Chiclana de la Frontera 90 B 4
Chiclayo 60 B 3
Chico, *C. Argentina, river* 62 B 3
Chico, *S. Argentina, river* 62 B 3
Chico, *U.S.A.* 42 B 4
Chicoutimi 35 K 4
Chidley, C., *cape* 30 G 2
Chieh-shih Wan, *bay* 129 F 7
Chiem See, *lake* 103 E 5
Chienchang 128 F 3
Ch'ien-ch'eng 129 D 6
Chien-ou 139 J 3
Chien-p'ing 128 F 3
Chien Shan, *mountains* 129 C 6
Chien-shih 129 F 7
Chien-shui 129 C 7
Chien-yang 129 F 6
Chierh Shan, *mountains* 122 L 5
Chieti 106 E 3
Chih-chiang 129 D 6
Ch'ih-feng 123 O 5
Chihli, Gulf of, *see* Po 'Hai 128 F 4
Ch'ih-Shui Ho, *river* 146 D 2
Chihuahua 31 E 4
Chilas 142 D 2
Chilcott I., *island* 193 K 3
Childers 193 K 5
Chile 62 A 3
Chi-lin 119 H 3
Chilka Lake, *lake* 118 F 5
Chillán 62 A 2
Chillicothe 46 D 2
Chiloé, I. de, *island* 62 A 3
Chilpancingo de los Bravos 50 D 3
Chilterns, *hills* 74 E 3
Chi-lung 139 K 3
Chilwa, L., *lake* 175 E 3
Chiman Tagh, *mountains* 142 E 2
Chimay 98 C 4
Chimbay 122 H 5
Chimborazo, *mountains* 60 B 3
Chimbote 60 B 3
Chimbu 151 F 4
Chimkent 118 E 3
Chimmo Pt., *cape* 129 F 7
Chimtarga, *mountain* 142 C 2
Chin, *province* 146 A 4
China 118 F 4
China Lake 42 C 5
Chi-nan 119 G 4
Chinandega 51 E 3
Chin-chiang 119 G 4
Chin Chiang, *river* 129 E 6
Chinchilla 193 K 5
Chinchilla, Altos de, *mountains* 91 E 3
Chinchilla de Monte Aragón 90 E 3
Chinchón 90 D 2
Chin-chou 119 H 3
Chin-chou Wan, *bay* 128 G 4
Chin-chu Shan, *mountains* 129 D 7
Chincoteague Bay, *bay* 46 F 2
Chinde 175 E 3
Chin-do, *island* 128 H 5
Chindru 142 F 3
Chindwin, *river* 139 G 3
Ch'ing Chiang, *river* 129 E 5
Ch'ing Hai, *lake* 118 G 4
Ching Ho, *river* 128 D 4
Ching-hsing 128 G 2
Ching-ku 139 H 3
Chingleput 143 D 5
Chingola 174 D 3
Ching-po Hu, *lake* 128 H 3
Ch'ing-p'u 128 G 5
Ching Shan, *mountains* 128 E 5
Ching-shih 129 E 6
Ch'ing-tao 119 H 4
Ching-tung 129 C 7
Ch'ing-yang 128 D 4
Ch'ing-yüan 129 E 7
Ch'ing-yü Hu, *lake* 128 C 4
Ch'in-hsien 129 D 7
Chin-hua 139 J 3
Ch'in-huang-tao 123 O 6
Chi-ning, *China, Inner Mongolia* 128 E 3
Chi-ning, *China, Shantung* 128 F 4
Chinju 128 H 4
Chink Kaplankyr, *mts.* 73 O 5
Chin-ling Shan, *mountains* 119 G 4
Chin-men Chiang, *bay* 129 F 7
Chin-men Tao, *island* 129 F 7
Chinon 94 E 4
Chioggia 106 D 2
Chipata 175 E 3
Chippenham 83 E 6
Chirchik 142 C 1
Chiriquí, Golfo de, *gulf* 51 E 4
Chirripó, *mountain* 31 F 5
Chirpan 110 D 2
Chisimayu, *see Kismaayo* 167 H 6
Chistopol' 125 G 2
Chita 119 G 3
Ch'i-t'ai 123 L 5
Chitradurga 143 D 5
Chitral 122 K 6
Chittagong 118 F 4
Chittagong, *province* 142 F 4
Chittoor 143 D 5
Chiu-chang 139 J 3
Chiu-ch'uan 118 F 4
Chiung-cho-hsiao Ho, *river* 146 E 3
Ch'iung-chou Hai-hsia, *strait* 139 H 3
Chiung-hsia Shan, *mts.* 118 G 4
Ch'iung-shan 139 J 3
Chiu-shan Lieh-tao, *island* 128 G 6
Chiusi 106 C 3
Chivasso 106 A 2
Chivilcoy 62 B 2
Ch'i-yao Shan, *mountains* 139 H 3
Chloride 42 D 5
Chlumec 102 F 3
Cho-chou 139 J 3
Chocolate Mts., *mts.* 42 D 5
Choctawhatchee B., *bay* 46 C 4
Ch'o-do, *island* 128 G 4
Ch'o-erh Ho, *river* 128 G 2
Choiseul I., *island* 186 F 2
Chojna 102 F 2
Chojnów 102 F 3
Chōkai san, *mountain* 134 E 3
Choke Mts., *mountains* 167 G 4
Cholet 94 D 4
Chomdo Dz 146 B 2
Chomen Swamp, *swamp* 154 B 8
Chomutov 102 E 3
Chon Buri 147 C 6
Chongjin 123 Q 5
Chŏngju 123 P 6
Chonju 123 P 6
Chonos, Archipiélago de los, *island group* 62 A 3
Cho Oyo, *mountain* 142 F 3
Chorita, Sa. del, *mts.* 90 C 3
Chorol Tsho, *lake* 142 D 2

D

E

G

H

J

Kiryu-Kure

Kiryu 134 D 3
Kisamou, Kolpos, *bay* 111 C 6
Kisangani 166 F 5
Kiselevsk 123 L 4
Kishangarh 142 D 3
Kishb, Ḥarrat al, *lava flow* 154 C 5
Kishinev 72 K 4
Kishiwada 134 C 4
Kisir D., *mountains* 79 H 3
Kiskomárom 106 F 1
Kiskunfélegyháza 116 C 3
Kiskunhalas 116 C 3
Kislovodsk 79 H 2
Kismaayu 167 H 6
Kiso, *river* 134 D 4
Kiso samm., *mountains* 134 D 4
Kissaraing, *island* 147 C 7
Kistrand 86 S 1
Kisumu 167 G 6
Kiswe 158 C 1
Kitakami, *river* 134 E 3
Kitakyūshū 119 H 4
Kitale 167 G 5
Kitami 134 E 2
Kitami sammyaku, *mts.* 134 E 1
Kita-ura, *lake* 134 E 3
Kitchener 35 J 4
Kitega 174 D 2
Kíthira 111 C 5
Kíthira, *island* 79 E 3
Kíthnos, *island* 111 D 5
Kitimat 34 E 3
Kittilä 86 S 2
Kitwe 174 D 3
Kitzbühel 103 E 5
Kitzbühler A., *mountains* 103 E 5
Kitzingen 102 D 4
Kiulin Shan,*mountains* 129 E 7
Kivu, L., *lake* 167 F 6
Kiyev 72 K 3
Kizel 75 N 2
Kizil Adalar, *island group* 110 F 3
Kizil Irmak, *river* 73 L 5
Kizlyar 79 H 2
Kizyl-Arvat 122 H 6
Kjelvik 86 S 1
Klagenfurt 78 D 2
Klaipeda 74 H 3
Klamath, *river* 40 C 3
Klamath Falls, *falls* 34 E 4
Klamath Mts., *mountains* 30 D 3
Klamono 151 E 4
Klappan Ra., *mountains* 34 D 3
Klar, *river* 72 H 2
Klatovy 103 E 4
Klausenpass, *pass* 101 D 3
Klin 125 D 2
Klingkang Ra., *mountains* 150 C 3
Klinovec, *mountain* 102 E 3
Klintehamn 87 Q 5
Klintsy 75 K 3
Klisura 110 D 2
Kljuc 106 F 2
Kłodsko 116 C 2
Klöfta 87 N 4
Klosterneuburg 103 G 4
Klostertal, *valley* 101 E 2
Klötze 102 D 2
Klövsjö 86 O 4
Kluczbork 116 C 2
Klyuchevskaya Sopka, *mountain* 119 K 3
Klyuchi 123 T 4
Knin 106 F 2
Knjaževac 110 C 2
Knockmealdown Mts., *mountains* 83 C 5
Knokke 94 F 2
Knox, C., *cape* 34 D 3
Knox Coast, *region* 15 H 2
Knoxville, *U.S.A., Iowa* 41 J 3
Knoxville, *U.S.A., Tennessee* 41 L 4
Knysna 174 D 5
Kobarid 103 E 5
Kobe 119 H 4
København 72 H 3
Koblenz 74 F 3
Kobrin 116 E 2
Kobroör, *island* 151 E 4
Koca, *river* 110 E 4
Kocabaş, *river* 110 E 3
Kocakatran Daği, *mts.* 110 E 4
Kočani 110 C 3
Koçarli 111 E 5
Kočevje 106 E 2
Ko Chang, *island* 147 D 6
Kōchi 123 Q 6
Ko-chiu 139 H 3
Koch Mt., *mountain* 42 E 2
Kodiak I., *island* 30 C 3
Ko-do, *island* 128 H 5
Kodzha Balkan, *mts.* 110 E 2
Koegras, *canal* 98 C 2
Kofa Mts., *mountains* 42 D 5
Koforidua 166 C 5
Kofu 134 D 4
Koga 134 D 3
Køge 87 O 6
Kohat 138 E 2
Koh-i-baba, *mountains* 122 J 6
Kohima 146 B 3
Koh-i-Patandar, *mountain* 142 B 3
Koitere, *lake* 86 U 4
Kōje-do, *island* 128 H 5
Kojonup 192 C 6
Kokand 122 K 5
Kokas 151 E 4
Kokchetav 118 E 3
Kokhanovo 116 F 1
Kokhtla Yarve 87 T 5
Kokkola 74 H 2
Kokoda 151 F 4
Koko Nor, *see Ch'ing Hai* 128 B 4
Kokopo 151 G 4
Ko Kram, *island* 147 C 6
Kokshaal-tau, Khr., *mts.* 142 D 1
Koksoak, *river* 35 K 3
Kokstad 174 D 5
Kök Teke Tau, *mountains* 142 E 1
Ko Kut, *island* 147 D 7
Kola, *India* 138 E 4
Kola, *U.S.S.R.* 86 V 2
K'o-lan 128 E 4
Kolari 86 R 2
Kolding 74 G 3
Kolea 91 G 4
Kolepom, *island* 119 H 6
Kolguyev, O., *island* 14 J 2
Kolhapur 138 E 4
Kolín 102 F 3
Kolka, Mys, *cape* 87 R 5
Kolleru L., *lake* 143 D 4
Köln 72 G 3
Kolo 116 C 2
Kolobrzeg 102 F 1
Kołomna 75 K 3
Kolomyya 74 J 4
Kolpakovskiy 123 S 4
Kolpashevo 122 L 4
Kolpino 87 U 5
Kol'skiy P-ov., *peninsula* 72 K 2
Kolvereid 86 N 3
Kolwa, *river* 142 B 3
Kolwezi 174 D 3
Kolyma, *river* 119 J 2
Kolymskaya Nizmennost', *plain* 119 J 2
Kolymskiy Khrebet, *mts.* 119 J 2
Kom, *mountain* 110 C 2
Komadugu Gana, *river* 167 E 4
Komandorskiye O-va., *island group* 119 K 3
Komarno 116 C 3
Komarom 116 C 3
Komatsu 134 D 3
Kommunarsk 125 D 4
Kommunizma, Pik, *mountain* 118 E 4
Komodo, *island* 150 C 4
Komotiní 110 D 3
Kompong Som, B. de, *bay* 147 D 7
Komrat 116 F 3
Komsomolets, Zaliv, *bay* 122 H 5
Komsomolets, O., *island* 123 M 1
Komsomol'sk 119 H 3
Konam Dz 146 A 2
Konare, Gol., *lake* 110 D 2
Kondopoga 86 V 4
Kong Christian den IX's Land, *region* 130 J 2
Kong Frederik den VI's Kyst, *region* 30 H 2
Kong Frederik den VIII's Land, *region* 30 J 2
Kongolo 174 D 2
Kongsberg 87 N 5
Kongsvinger 87 O 4
Königs B., *mountain* 98 F 5
Könkämä älv, *river* 86 R 2
Konos 151 G 4
Konosha 75 L 2
Konotop 75 K 3
Konstanz 101 E 2
Kontovoúnia, *mountains* 111 B 5
Kontum 147 E 6
Kontum, Plateau du, *plateau* 147 E 6
Konya 73 L 5
Konya Ovasi, *plateau* 73 L 5
Konzhakovskiy Kamen', G., *mountain* 73 O 2
Kootenai, *region* 40 D 2
Ko Pai, *island* 147 C 6
Kopäis, *lake* 111 C 4
Kopaonik, *mountains* 72 J 4
Kópasker 86 D 2
Koper 106 D 2
Kopervik 87 L 5
Kopet Dag, Khr., *mts.* 73 O 5
Kopeysk 75 N 3
Ko Phangan, *island* 147 C 7
Köping 87 P 5
Kopparberg, *county* 87 O 4
Koprivnica 106 F 1
Korab, *mountains* 110 B 3
Korana, *river* 106 E 2
Korçe 79 E 3
Korčula 116 C 4
Korea B., *bay* 119 H 4
Korea Str., *strait* 139 K 2
Korf 123 T 3
Korinthiakós Kólpos, *bay* 79 E 3
Kórinthos 79 E 3
Koritnik, *mountain* 110 B 2
Kóriyama 134 E 3
Korkino 75 N 3
Kornat, *island* 106 E 3
Korónia, L., *lake* 110 C 3
Koropí 111 C 5
Korosten 75 J 3
Korpilombolo 86 R 2
Korsakov 123 R 5
Korsør 87 N 6
Kortrijk 98 B 4
Koru Dagi, *mountains* 110 E 3
Koruteva, Sa., *mountains* 174 C 3
Koryakskiy Khr., *mts.* 119 K 2
Kos, *island* 111 E 5
Ko Samui, *island* 147 C 7
Koscian 102 G 2
Kosciusko, Mt., *mountain* 186 E 5
Koshiki-kaikyō, *strait* 134 B 5
Koshiki-rettō, *island group* 134 B 5
Kosice 74 H 4
Ko Si Chang, *island* 147 C 6
Kosovo i Metohija, *region* 110 B 2
Kosovska Mitrovica 116 D 4
Kostajnica 106 F 2
Kosti 167 G 4
Kostroma 73 M 3
Kostrzyn 74 G 3
Koszalin 116 C 1
Koszalin, *province* 116 B 2
Kota 138 E 3
Kota Bharu 118 G 5
Kota Kinabalu 119 G 5
Kota Kota 175 E 3
Kotari 151 F 4
Kotel 110 E 2
Kotel'nich 75 M 2
Kotel'nikovskiy 125 E 4
Kotel'nyy, O., *island* 123 Q 2
Köthen 102 D 3
Kothi 142 D 3
Kotka 74 J 2
Kotlas 75 L 2
Koto Syo, *island* 129 G 7
Kotovsk 116 F 3
Ko-tse 128 F 4
Kottagudem 143 D 4
Kotto, *river* 174 D 1
Kotuy, *river* 123 N 3
Koudougou 166 C 4
Koufonísi, *island* 111 E 6
Kounoúpoi, *island* 111 E 5
Kouroussa 166 C 4
Kovd Ozero, *lake* 86 U 2
Kovel' 74 J 3
Kovroy 75 L 3
Kovzha, *canal* 86 W 4
Kowloon 139 J 3
Koyp, G., *mountain* 73 O 2
Koyukuk, *river* 30 C 2
Kozani 110 B 3
Kozhikode 118 E 4
Kozhva 75 N 2
Kozlovets 110 D 2
Kozuchów 102 F 3
Kōzu-sh., *island* 134 D 4
Kra, Isthmus of, *isthmus* 139 G 5
Krabi 150 A 3
Krâchéh 119 G 5
Kragerø 87 N 5
Kragujevac 79 E 2
Krakatoa, *see Anak Krakatau* 139 H 6
Kraków 72 J 3
Kraków, *province* 116 D 2
Kralovice, *West Czechoslovakia* 102 E 4
Královice, *Central Czechoslovakia* 102 F 4
Kramatorsk 79 G 2
Kramis, C., *cape* 91 F 4
Kranj 106 E 1
Krapina 103 F 5
Krasnoarmeyskoye 123 U 3
Krasnodar 73 L 4
Krasnokamsk 75 M 2
Krasnoslobodsk 125 F 4
Krasnotur'insk 75 N 2
Krasnoufimsk 75 N 3
Krasnovishersk 75 N 2
Krasnovodsk 118 D 3
Krasnovodskiy Zaliv, *bay* 154 E 2
Krasnoyarsk 118 F 3
Krasnyy Chikoy 128 D 1
Krefeld 102 B 3
Kremenchug 79 G 2
Kremenets 116 E 2
Krems 103 F 4
Krestovyy Pereval, *pass* 79 H 2
Kretinga 87 R 6
Kreuzlingen 101 E 2
Kriens 101 D 2
Krimml 103 E 5
Krios, Akr., *cape* 111 C 6
Krishna, *river* 118 E 5
Krishna, Mouths of the, *river mouths* 143 D 5
Krishnagiri 143 D 5
Krishnanagar 142 E 4
Krishnaraja Sagara, *reservoir* 143 D 5
Kristel 91 E 5
Kristiansand 74 F 2
Kristianstad 87 O 6
Kristianstad, *county* 87 O 6
Kristiansund 86 M 3
Kristiinankaupunki 86 R 4
Kristinehamn 74 G 2
Kríti, *island* 72 K 5
Kritsá 111 D 6
Krivoy Rog 73 L 4
Krk 106 E 2
Krk, *island* 106 E 2
Krka 106 E 2
Krkonose, *mountains* 102 F 3
Krnov 116 C 2
Kronoberg, *county* 87 O 6
Kronotskiy P-ov., *peninsula* 123 T 4
Kronprinsesse Märtha Kyst, *region* 15 B 2
Kronprins Olav Kyst, *region* 15 E 2
Kronštadt 75 J 2
Kroonstad 174 D 4
Kropotkin 79 H 2
Krosno 102 F 2
Krottenkopf, *mountain* 101 G 2
Kroussónas 111 D 6
Krrab, *mountain* 110 A 2
Krrabë, *mountains* 110 A 3
Krugersdorp 174 D 4
Krujë 110 A 3
Krummel Deep, *sea feature* 60 B 4
Krumovgrad 110 D 3
Krung Thep 118 G 5
Kruševac 110 B 2
Krušovo 110 B 3
Kryazh Chernysheva, *mountains* 75 N 1
Kryazh Polousnyy, *mts.* 119 H 2
Krym, *peninsula* 73 L 4
Krymskiye Gory, *mts.* 72 L 4
Krzyż 102 G 2
Ksar el Boukhari 78 C 3
Ksour Essaf 166 E 2
Ksour, Mts. des, *mts.* 166 D 2
Ksours, Mts. des, *mts.* 72 G 6
Kuala Lumpur 118 G 5
Kuala Trengganu 150 B 3
Ku-an 128 F 4
Kuang-chou 119 G 4
Kuang-hua 128 E 5
Kuang-nan 139 H 3
Kuan-hsien 139 H 2
Kuantan 119 G 5
Kuba 79 J 3
Kuban', *river* 73 L 4
Kubor, Mt., *mountain* 151 F 4
Kubrat 110 E 2
K'u-ch'e 118 F 3
Kuchen Sp., *mountain* 101 F 2
Kuching 119 G 5
Kuchino-sh., *island* 134 B 5
Küçük Menderes, *river* 111 E 4
Kudat 139 J 5
Kudus 139 J 6
Küdzüpchi Sands, *region* 128 D 3
Kuei Chiang, *river* 129 E 7
Kuei-lin 139 J 3
Kuei-p'ing 139 H 3
Kuei-shan-ting, *mountain* 129 E 6
Kuei-yang 119 G 4
Kufra Oasis, *region* 167 F 3
Kufstein 103 E 5
Kuhanbokano, *mountain* 142 E 3
Kuhhā-ye Zagros, *mts.* 118 D 4
Kūhrān, Kūh-e, *mountain* 154 F 4
Kuiling Shan, *mountains* 129 E 6
Kuito 174 C 3
Kuju zan, *mountain* 134 B 4
Kukālār, Kūh-e, *mountain* 73 N 6
Kukës 110 B 2
Kulal, Mt., *mountain* 167 G 5
Kulaly, O., *island* 125 G 5
Kuldiga 87 R 6
Kulgera 192 F 5
Kulmbach 102 D 3
Kulon, Ug., *cape* 150 B 4
Kul'sary 75 M 4
Kulumadau 151 G 4
Kulundinskaya Step , *steppe* 118 E 3
Kulyab 142 C 2
Kuma, *river* 79 H 2
Kumagaya 134 D 3
Kumamoto 119 H 4
Kumanovo 110 B 2
Kumara 199 D 6
Kumasi 166 C 5
Kumba 167 D 5
Kumbakonam 143 D 5
Kumbetsu-yama, *mts.* 134 E 2
Kum Darya, *river* 142 E 1
Kumon Ra., *mountains* 139 G 3
Kunashir, *island* 123 R 5
Kundelungu Mts., *mts.* 174 D 2
Kungalv 87 N 5
Kung-chu-ling 128 H 3
Kungey Alatau, Khr., *mts.* 142 D 1
Kung-lung Shan, *mts.* 129 B 7
K'ung-ming 146 D 3
Kungsbacka 87 O 5
Kungur 75 N 3
Kun Lun Plains, *region* 142 D 2
Kun-lun Shan, *mountains* 118 F 4
K'un-ming 118 G 4
Kunsan 128 H 4
Kuntsevo 75 K 3
Kuolayarvi 86 T 2
Kuo-lo Shan, *mountains* 128 C 5
Kuopio 74 J 2
Kuopio, *county* 86 T 3
Kupa, *river* 106 E 2
Kupang 119 H 6
Kura, *river* 73 N 5
Kurashiki 134 C 4
Kurayoshi 134 C 4
Kurbah Bank, *sea feature* 107 C 6
Kürdzhali 110 D 3
Kure 123 Q 6

Leiria-Lora

Leiria 90 A 3
Lei Shui, *river* 129 E 6
Leisler, Mt., *mountain* 192 E 4
Leith 82 E 4
Leith Hill, *hill* 83 F 6
Lek, *river* 98 C 3
Lekáni 110 D 3
Leksand 87 O 4
Leksozero, Oz., *lake* 86 U 3
Leksvik 86 N 3
Le Locle 101 B 2
Le Madonie, *mountain* 107 E 6
Léman, L., *lake* 72 G 4
Le Mans 78 C 2
Lemhi Range, *mountains* 42 D 2
Lena, *river* 118 H 2
Lendery 86 U 3
Lengerich 98 F 2
Lengua de Vaca, Pta., *cape* 62 A 2
Leninabad 122 J 5
Leninakan 79 H 3
Lenina, Pik, *mountain* 122 K 6
Leningrad 72 K 2
Leninogorsk, *R.S.F.S.R.* 122 L 4
Leninogorsk, *West R.S.F.S.R.* 125 H 2
Leninski-Kuznetskiy 123 L 4
Lenkoran 122 G 6
Lens 94 F 2
Lenvik 86 Q 1
Lenya', *river* 147 C 7
Leominster 83 E 5
León, *Mexico* 31 E 4
León, *Nicaragua* 31 F 5
León, *Spain* 78 B 2
León, *province* 90 C 2
Léon, *region* 94 B 3
León, Monts. de, *mts.* 90 B 1
Leone, M., *mountain* 101 D 3
Leopold II, L., *see Mai-Ndombe* 174 C 2
Lepel' 116 F 1
Lèpontine, Alpi, *mts.* 106 B 1
Le Puy 95 F 5
Lercara Friddi 107 D 6
Lérida 78 C 3
Lerma 90 D 1
Lermoos 103 D 5
Léros, *island* 111 E 5
Lerwick 74 E 2
les Andelys 94 E 3
Les Cayes 51 F 3
les Heumis 91 F 4
Lesima, M., *mountain* 106 B 2
Leskovac 110 B 2
Lesnoy 86 V 2
Lesotho 174 D 4
Lesozavodsk 123 Q 5
Lesparre 95 D 5
Les Raimeux, *mountain* 101 C 2
les Rousses 101 B 3
Les Sables-d'Olonne 95 D 4
Lesse, *river* 98 D 4
Lesser Antilles, *island group* 31 G 5
Lesser Slave L., *lake* 34 F 3
Lesser Sunda Is., *island group* 119 H 6
Lésvos, *island* 72 K 5
Leszno 116 C 2
Letha Ra., *mountains* 142 F 4
Lethbridge 34 F 4
Leticia 60 C 3
Leti, Kep., *island group* 186 C 2
Letniy Bereg, *region* 86 W 3
Leucate, C., *cape* 95 F 6
Leucate, É. de, *lake* 95 F 6
Leuk 101 C 3
Leuser, G., *mountain* 150 A 3
Leuven 98 C 4
Leuze 98 B 4
Levádhia 110 C 4
Levanger 86 N 3
Levelland 40 G 5
Leven, L., *lake* 82 E 3
Leventina, Valle, *valley* 101 D 3
Lévêque, C., *cape* 186 C 3
Levice 116 C 3
Levier, B. du, *bay* 166 B 3
Le Vigan 95 F 6
Levin 198 F 5
Levítha, *island* 111 E 5
Levká Óri, *mountains* 111 C 6
Levkás 110 B 4
Levkás, *island* 111 B 4
Levski 110 D 2
Lewes 83 G 6
Lewis, *island* 82 C 2
Lewis, *river* 42 B 2
Lewis Range, *mountains* 34 F 4
Lewiston, *U.S.A., Idaho* 40 D 2
Lewiston, *U.S.A., Maine* 41 N 3
Lexington, *U.S.A., Kentucky* 41 L 4
Lexington, *U.S.A., N. Carolina* 46 D 3
Leyte, *island* 139 K 4
Lezhë 110 A 3
Lézignan 91 G 1
Lhasa 118 F 4
Liang-ho-chai 128 E 5
Liant, C., *cape* 146 C 6
Liao-ch'eng 128 F 4
Liao Ho, *river* 128 G 3
Liaoning, *province* 128 G 3
Liao-Tung Wan, *bay* 128 G 3
Liao-yang 123 P 5
Liao-yüan 128 G 3
Liard, *river* 34 E 2
Libar, Sa. de, *mountains* 90 C 4
Libenge 167 E 5
Libby 42 D 1
Liberal 40 G 4
Liberec 116 B 2
Liberia 166 B 5
Libnan, Jebel, *mountains* 79 G 4
Libohovë 110 B 3
Libourne 95 D 5
Libreville 166 D 5
Libya 166 E 3
Libyan Desert, *desert* 167 F 3
Libyan Plateau, *plateau* 167 F 2
Licata 107 D 6
Li-chiang 139 H 3
Lichinga 175 E 3
Lichtenburg 174 D 4
Lichtenfels 102 D 3
Licking, *river* 46 D 2
Licosa, Punta, *cape* 107 E 4
Lida 116 E 2
Lidingo 87 Q 5
Lidköping 74 G 2
Lido di Roma 106 D 4
Liebig Ra., *mountains* 199 D 6
Liechtenstein 72 H 4
Liège 74 F 3
Liège, *province* 98 D 4
Liene, *region* 86 O 3
Lien-hsien 129 E 7
Lienhua Shan, *mountains* 129 F 7
Lien-p'ing 129 E 7
Lien-yün-kang 129 J 2
Lienz 103 E 5
Liepāja 74 H 3
Lier 98 C 3
Liestal 101 C 2
Lieuvin, *region* 94 E 3
Liévin 94 F 2
Liffey, *river* 83 C 5
Lifi Mahuida, *mountain* 62 B 3
Lighten, L., *lake* 142 D 2
Ligonha, *river* 175 E 3
Ligure, Appno., *mts.* 106 B 2
Liguria, *province* 106 B 2
Ligurian Sea 72 H 4
Lihir Group, *island group* 151 G 4
Lihou Reef and Cays, *reefs* 187 F 3
Li-hsien 129 E 6
Likasi 174 D 3
L'Ile Rousse 106 B 3
Lille 74 F 3
Lille Bælt, *strait* 87 N 6
Lillebonne 94 E 3
Lillehammer 74 G 2
Lillesand 87 M 5
Lillhärdel 86 O 4
Lillo, Altos de, *mountains* 90 D 3
Lilongwe 175 E 3
Lim 110 A 2
Lima 60 B 4
Lima, *river* 90 A 2
Limah 154 F 4
Limassol 79 G 3
Limavady 82 C 4
Limay, *river* 62 B 2
Limbe, *Malawi* 175 E 3
Limbe, *Nigeria* 166 D 5
Limburg, *Belgium, prov.* 98 D 3
Limburg, *Netherlands, province* 98 D 4
Limburg an der Lahn 102 C 3
Limenária 110 D 3
Limerick 83 B 5
Limfjorden, *channel* 72 H 3
Limmen Bight, *gulf* 186 D 3
Límní Xiniás, *lake* 110 C 4
Límnos, *island* 72 K 5
Limoges 78 C 2
Limogne, Causse de, *limestone region* 95 E 5
Limón 51 E 3
Limousin, *province* 95 E 4
Limousin, Monts du, *mts.* 95 E 5
Limoux 95 F 6
Limpopo, *river* 174 D 4
Limu Ling, *mountains* 129 D 8
Linares, *Chile* 62 A 2
Linares, *Mexico* 50 D 2
Linares, *Spain* 78 B 3
Lin-ch'ing 128 F 4
Lin-ch'uan 139 J 3
Lincoln, *England* 83 F 5
Lincoln, *U.S.A., California* 42 B 4
Lincoln, *U.S.A., Nebraska* 40 H 3
Lincoln Edge, *region* 83 F 5
Lincoln Sea 14 P 1
Lincoln Wolds, *region* 83 F 5
Lindau 101 E 2
Lindesay, Mt., *mountain* 41 E 4
Lindesberg 87 P 5
Lindesnes, *cape* 72 G 3
Lindi 175 E 2
Líndos 111 F 5
Line Islands, *island group* 11 C 2
Lin-fen 139 J 2
Lingayen 150 D 2
Lingayen G., *gulf* 150 D 2
Lingen 102 B 2
Lingga, *island* 150 B 4
Lingga, Kep., *island group* 139 H 5
Ling-ling 139 J 3
Língos, *mountains* 110 B 3
Ling Shan, *mountain* 128 F 3
Ling Shui Wan, *bay* 129 D 8
Lingsugur 143 D 4
Ling-yün 129 D 7
Lin-hai 129 G 6
Lin-hsi 123 O 5
Lin-hsia 128 C 4
Lin-i 128 F 4
Linköping 74 G 2
Linn, Mt., *mountain* 42 B 3
Linsell 86 O 4
Lin-t'an 128 C 5
Lin-tao 139 H 2
Linth, *river* 101 E 3
Linthal 101 D 3
Lin-tien 128 G 2
Linz 74 G 4
Lion, Golfe du, *gulf* 72 G 4
Lipari 107 E 5
Lipari, *island* 107 E 5
Lipari, Isole, *island group* 72 H 5
Lipetsk 73 L 3
Lípez, Cord. de., *mts.* 60 C 5
Lipiany 102 F 2
Li-p'ing 129 D 6
Lippe, *river* 102 B 3
Lippstadt 102 C 3
Lipsói, *island* 111 E 5
Liri, *river* 106 D 4
Liria 91 E 3
Lisala 167 F 5
Lisān, El, *region* 158 B 3
Lisboa 72 E 5
Lisbon, *see Lisboa* 90 A 3
Lisburn 83 C 4
Lisburne, C., *cape* 30 B 2
Lisieux 94 E 3
Li-she Ho, *river* 129 C 7
Li-shih 128 E 4
Li-shui' 129 F 6
Liski 75 K 3
l'Isle-sur-le-Doubs 101 B 2
Lismore, *Australia* 193 K 5
Listowel 83 B 5
Lit 86 O 3
Litāni, *river* 158 B 1
Litera, La, *region* 91 F 2
Lithgow 193 K 6
Líthinon, Akr., *cape* 110 D 6
Litija 103 F 5
Litoměřice 116 B 2
Litomyšl 102 G 4
Litovskaya S.S.R., *rep.* 74 H 3
Little Abaco, *island* 46 E 5
Little Aden 154 C 7
Little America V, *scientific base* 15 M 2
Little Andaman, *island* 143 F 5
Little Bahama Bank, *sea feature* 41 M 6
Little Barrier I., *island* 198 F 3
Little Basses, *island group* 143 D 6
Little Belt Mts., *mts.* 34 F 4
Little Coco I., *island* 143 F 5
Little Colorado, *river* 40 E 4
Little Halibut Bank, *sea feature* 82 F 2
Littlehampton 83 F 6
Little Karroo, *region* 174 D 5
Little Minch, *channel* 82 C 3
Little Missouri, *river* 40 G 2
Little Nicobar, *island* 143 F 6
Little Rann of Kutch, *flood region* 142 C 4
Little Rock 41 J 5
Liu-chou 119 G 4
Liu-heng Tao, *island* 128 G 6
Liulaka, *river* 167 F 6
Liu Ling, *mountains* 128 E 5
Liu-pan Shan, *mountains* 128 D 4
Livermore 42 B 4
Liverpool, *Australia* 193 K 6
Liverpool, *England* 72 F 3
Liverpool Bay, *bay* 34 E 1
Liverpool Plains, *region* 186 F 5
Liverpool Ra., *mountains* 186 F 5
Livingston 40 E 2
Livingstone I., *island* 15 R 2
Livingstone Mts., *mts.* 175 E 2
Livno 106 F 3
Livojoki, *river* 86 S 3
Livorno 106 C 3
Livramento 62 C 2
Lizard Pt., *cape* 74 E 4
Ljubljana 78 D 2
Ljuboten, *mountain* 110 B 2
Ljubuški 106 F 3
Ljungby 87 O 6
Ljusdal 86 P 4
Ljusnan, *river* 86 O 4
Llanberis Pass, *pass* 83 D 5
Llandrindod Wells 83 E 5
Llandudno 83 E 5
Llanelly 83 D 6
Llanes 90 C 1
Llano de los Caballos Mesteños, *region* 50 C 2
Llano Estacado, *region* 30 E 4
Llanos, *region* 60 C 2
Llanos de Cardiel, *region* 91 F 2
Llanos de Mojos, *region* 60 C 4
Llanos de Urgel, *region* 91 F 2
Llena, Sa. de la, *mts.* 91 F 2
Llerena 90 B 3
Lleyn Pena., *peninsula* 83 D 5
Lloydminster 34 F 3
Lluchmayor 91 G 3
Llullaillaco, Vol., *mt.* 60 C 5
Lobatse 174 D 4
Löbau 102 F 3
Łobez 102 F 2
Lobito 174 C 3
Lobos Cay, *reef* 46 E 6
Lobstick L., *lake* 35 L 3
Locarno 101 D 3
Lochaber, *region* 82 D 3
Lochem 98 E 2
Loches 94 E 4
Lo-ch'ing Ho, *river* 129 D 7
Lochnagar, *mountain* 82 E 3
Lod 158 A 3
Lodève 95 F 6
Lodeynoye Pole 75 K 2
Lodi, *Italy* 106 B 2
Lodi, *U.S.A.* 40 C 4
Lodosa 90 D 1
Łódź 72 J 3
Łódź, *province* 116 C 2
Lofoten, *island group* 72 H 1
Lofty Ra., *mountains* 192 C 4
Logan 40 E 3
Logan, Mt., *Canada, mt.* 30 C 2
Logan, Mt., *U.S.A., mt.* 42 B 1
Logan Mts., *mountains* 34 E 2
Logansport 46 C 1
Logone, *river* 166 E 4
Logroño 78 B 2
Logrosán 90 C 3
Loharu 142 D 3
Lo Ho, *river* 128 D 4
Loikaw 146 B 5
Loi Lan, *mountain* 146 B 5
Loing, *river* 94 F 4
Loipyet Hills, *mountains* 146 B 3
Loir, *river* 94 E 4
Loire, *river* 72 G 4
Loja, *Ecuador* 60 B 3
Loja, *Spain* 90 C 4
Lokeren 98 B 3
Lokilalaki, G., *mountain* 150 D 4
Løkken 86 N 3
Loko 166 E 5
Loks Land, *island* 35 L 2
Lola, Mt., *mountain* 42 B 4
Lolland, *island* 87 N 6
Lom, *river* 110 C 2
Loma de Chiclana, *mts.* 90 D 3
Lomami, *river* 167 F 6
Lomas Coloradas, *mts.* 62 B 3
Lomas de Zamora 62 C 2
Lombardia, *province* 106 B 2
Lombard, Serra, *mts.* 61 D 2
Lombez 95 E 6
Lomblen, *island* 150 D 4
Lombok, *island* 119 G 6
Lombok, Selat, *strait* 150 C 4
Lomé 166 D 5
Lomela, *river* 174 D 2
Lomond, Loch, *lake* 82 D 3
Lomonosov (Harris) Ridge, *sea feature* 14 O 1
Lomont, Montagne du, *mountain* 101 B 2
Lompoc 42 B 5
Lomseggja, *mountain* 86 M 4
Łomza 116 D 2
London, *Canada* 35 J 4
London, *England* 72 F 3
Londonderry 74 E 3
Londonderry, C., *cape* 186 C 3
Londrina 61 D 5
Lone Pine 42 C 4
Longa, Proliv, *strait* 119 K 2
Long Bay, *bay* 41 M 5
Long Beach 30 E 4
Long Branch 46 F 1
Longfellow, Mt., *mt.* 199 E 6
Longford 83 C 5
Long Forties, *sea feature* 72 F 3
Long I., *New Zealand, island* 199 B 8
Long I., *Territory of New Guinea, island* 151 F 4
Long I., *U.S.A.* 30 G 3
Longmont 40 F 3
Long, P., *mountain* 95 E 6
Long Pt., *New Zealand, cape* 199 C 8
Long Ra. Mts., *mountains* 30 H 3
Longreach 193 H 4
Longs Pk., *mountain* 30 E 3
Longuyon 94 G 3
Longview 40 C 2
Longwy 94 G 3
Long Xuyen 147 D 7
Lons-le-Saunier 95 G 4
Lookout, C., *cape* 30 G 4
Lookout Mt., *mountain* 46 C 3
Lookout Pass, *pass* 42 D 2
Lookout Pt., *cape* 199 C 8
Lookout Ridge, *mts.* 34 B 2
Loop Hd., *cape* 83 B 5
Lopatka, Mys, *cape* 119 J 3
Lop Buri 147 C 6
Lopera 90 C 4
Lopez, C., *cape* 166 D 6
Lop Nor, *seasonal lake* 118 F 3
Lopphavet, *channel* 86 R 1
Lora del Río 90 C 4
Lorain 41 L 3
Lora, La, *region* 90 C 1

M

Malbork-Mazar-i-Sharif

Malbork 116 C 2
Malchin 102 E 2
Maldegem 98 B 3
Malditos, Montes, *mts.* 91 F 1
Maldive Islands, *island group* 13 C 2
Maldive Ridge, *sea feature* 13 C 2
Maldonado 62 C 2
Maldonado, Pta., *cape* 50 D 3
Maléa, Akr., *cape* 79 E 3
Male 118 E 5
Male Atoll, *reef* 143 C 6
Malebo, Pool, *lake* 174 C 2
Malegaon 138 E 3
Malekula, *island* 187 G 3
Malen'ga 86 W 3
Malgomaj, *lake* 86 P 3
Malhão, Sa. do, *mts.* 90 A 4
Malheur Lake, *lake* 42 C 3
Mali, *state* 166 C 4
Mali Hka, *river* 146 B 3
Malik Naro, *mountain* 142 B 3
Målilla 87 P 5
Malindi 175 F 2
Maling, G., *mountain* 150 D 3
Malin Hd., *cape* 72 F 3
Ma-li-p'o 129 C 7
Malkapur 142 D 4
Malkara 110 E 3
Malkhanskiy, Khrebet, *mountains* 128 D 1
Malko Tŭrnovo 110 E 3
Mallaig 82 D 3
Mallani, *region* 142 C 3
Mallorca, *island* 72 G 5
Mallow 83 B 5
Malmberget 86 Q 2
Malmédy 98 E 4
Malmesbury 174 C 5
Malmköping 87 P 5
Malmö 72 H 3
Malmöhus, *county* 87 O 6
Malmyzh 125 G 2
Malosmadulu Atoll, *reef* 143 C 6
Malozoemel'skaya Tundra, *region* 73 N 1
Malpartida de C. 90 B 3
Malpelo 11 E 2
Målselv 86 Q 1
Malta, *island* 72 H 5
Malta Chan., *channel* 72 H 5
Maluku, *island group* 119 H 6
Maluku, Laut, *sea* 119 H 6
Malung 87 O 4
Malwy Taung Hills, *mountains* 147 C 6
Malyy Kavkaz, *mts.* 79 H 3
Malyy Yenisey, *river* 123 M 4
Mamaia 116 F 4
Mamanovo 116 C 1
Mamberamo, *river* 150 E 4
Mamers 94 E 3
Mamonovo 87 Q 6
Mamoré, *river* 60 C 4
Mamou 166 B 4
Mampodre, *mountain* 90 C 1
Man 166 C 5
Manacor 78 C 3
Manado 119 H 5
Managua 31 F 5
Managua, L. de, *lake* 51 E 3
Manakara 175 F 4
Mānasarowar L., *lake* 138 F 2
Manaslu, *mountain* 142 E 3
Manaus 60 C 3
Manawatu, *river* 198 F 5
Manawatu Gorge, *gorge* 198 F 5
Mancha, La, *region* 78 B 3
Mancha Real 90 D 4
Manchester, *England* 72 F 3
Manchester, *U.S.A.* 41 N 3
Manchouli, *see Lu-pin* 123 O 5
Manchuria, *region* 119 H 3
Mandal 74 F 2
Mandalay 118 F 4
Mandalay, *province* 146 B 4
Mandalya Körfezi, *gulf* 111 E 5
Mandan 34 G 4
Mandar, Teluk, *bay* 150 C 4
Mandara Mts., *mts.* 166 E 4
Mandasor 142 D 3
Mandav Hills, *mountains* 142 C 4
Manding, *region* 166 C 4
Mandla 142 D 4
Mandra, *river* 110 E 2
Manduria 107 F 4
Manfredonia, Golfo di, *gulf* 106 F 4
Manga, *region* 166 E 4
Mangabeiras, Sa. das, *mountains* 61 E 4
Mangakino 198 F 4
Mangalia 110 F 2
Mangalore 118 E 5
Mangaweka, *mountain* 198 G 4
Mangoky, *river* 175 F 4
Mangole, *island* 151 D 4
Mangrol 142 C 4
Mangsahan 147 D 6
Mangualde 90 B 2
Mangueni, Hamada, *plateau* 166 E 3
Mangyshlak P-ov, *peninsula* 73 N 4
Maní, *region* 111 C 5
Manika, Plat. de la, *plateau* 174 D 3
Manila 119 H 5
Manindjau, D., *lake* 150 B 4
Manipur, *state* 142 F 3
Manipur, *river* 146 A 3
Manirang, *mountain* 142 D 3
Manisa 79 F 3
Man., I. of, *island* 72 F 3
Manitoba, *province* 34 H 3
Manitoba, L., *lake* 30 F 3
Manitoulin I., *island* 35 J 4
Manizales 60 B 2
Manjimup 192 C 6
Manlleu 91 G 2
Manmad 142 D 4
Mannar 143 D 5
Mannar, G. of, *gulf* 118 E 5
Mannheim 72 H 4
Mannu 107 B 5
Manokwari 119 H 6
Manono 174 D 2
Manosque 95 G 6
Mano-w., *bay* 134 D 3
Manresa 78 C 3
Mansel I., *island* 30 F 2
Mansfield, *England* 83 F 5
Mansfield, *U.S.A.* 41 L 3
Manso, *river* 61 D 4
Manta 60 A 3
Mantanzas 46 D 6
Mantap San 128 H 3
Manteca 42 B 4
Mantes-Gassicourt 94 E 3
Manti 42 E 4
Mantiqueira, Sa. da, *mountains* 61 E 5
Mantova 106 C 2
Manukau Harb., *harbour* 198 F 3
Manus I., *island* 151 F 4
Manych-Gudilo, Ozero, *lake* 79 H 2
Manychskaya Vpadina, *region* 79 H 2
Manzanares 90 D 3
Manzanillo, *Cuba* 51 F 2
Manzanillo, *Mexico* 50 C 3
Manzano Mts., *mountains* 40 F 5
Manzil 158 C 3
Manzini 174 E 4
Mao-mao Shan, *mts.* 128 C 4
Mao-ming 129 E 7
Maouin Pena., *peninsula* 72 H 5
Mapia, Kep., *island group* 151 E 3
Maple Creek 34 G 4
Mappi 151 E 4
Maprik 151 F 4
Mapuera, *river* 60 D 3
Maputo 175 E 4
Maqueda 90 C 2
Mar del Plata 62 C 2
Mar, Sa. do, *mountains* 61 E 5
Maracá, I. de, *island* 60 D 2
Maracaibo 60 B 1
Maracaibo, L. de, *lake* 60 B 2
Maracajú, Sa. de, *mts.* 60 D 5
Maracay 60 C 1
Maradi 166 D 4
Marāgheh 125 F 7
Marahuaca, Co., *mt.* 51 G 4
Marajó, I. de, *island* 61 E 3
Maramba 174 D 3
Marand 125 F 6
Marañón, *river* 60 B 3
Marão, *mountain* 90 B 2
Marapi, G., *mountain* 150 B 4
Maraş 79 G 3
Marau Pt., *cape* 198 H 4
Marbella 90 C 4
Marble Bar 192 C 4
Marble Canyon, *gorge* 42 E 4
Marburg 102 C 3
Marca, Pta. da, *cape* 174 C 3
Marçal D., *mountains* 111 E 5
Marcali 106 F 1
Marche, *France, province* 95 E 4
Marche, *Italy, province* 106 D 3
Marchena 90 C 4
Marche-en-Famenne 98 D 4
Marche, Plateau de la, *plateau* 95 E 4
Mar Chiquita, *lake* 62 B 2
Marco Polo Ra., *see Bukalik Tagh* 142 F 2
Marcus I., *island* 119 J 4
Marcus-Necker Rise, *sea feature* 11 B 2
Mardan 138 E 2
Mardin 79 H 3
Maree, Loch, *lake* 82 D 3
Mareeba 193 J 3
Marengo 91 G 4
Marennes 95 D 5
Marettimo, *island* 107 D 6
Margaret, *river* 192 E 3
Margarita I. de, *island* 51 G 3
Margate 83 G 6
Marguerite, Mts. de la, *mountains* 95 F 5
Marguerite Bay, *bay* 15 R 2
Margungu, *mountain* 174 D 2
Maria Augustina Bank, *sea feature* 13 E 3
María Elena 60 C 5
Maria I., *island* 192 G 2
Marianao 51 E 2
Marianas, *island group* 11 B 2
Marianas Ridge, *sea feature* 11 B 2
Marianas Tr., *sea feature* 11 B 2
Mariánské Lázně 102 E 4
Marias, *river* 42 D 1
Maria, Sa. de, *mountains* 90 D 4
Marias Pass, *pass* 42 D 1
Maria van Diemen, C., *cape* 187 H 5
Maribo 102 D 1
Maribor 116 B 3
Mariefred 87 P 5
Marie Galante, *island* 51 G 3
Mariental 174 C 4
Mariestad 87 O 5
Marietta 46 C 3
Mariinsk 123 L 4
Marília 61 D 5
Marimas, Las, *region* 78 B 3
Marin 90 A 1
Marinha Grande 90 A 3
Marion, *U.S.A., Illinois* 41 K 4
Marion I., *island* 15 D 3
Marion, L., *lake* 41 L 5
Marion Reef, *reef* 187 F 3
Maritimes, Alpes, *mts.* 95 H 5
Maritsa 110 D 2
Maritsa, *river* 72 K 4
Marittime, Alpi, *mts.* 72 G 4
Mark, *river* 98 C 3
Markaryd 87 O 6
Marken, *island* 98 D 2
Markerwaard, *polder* 98 D 2
Marlin 41 H 5
Marmande 95 E 5
Marmara, *island* 110 E 3
Marmara Gölü, *lake* 111 E 4
Marmara, Sea of, 72 K 5
Marmaris 111 F 5
Mar Menor, *lake* 91 E 4
Marmolada, *mountain* 103 D 5
Marmoleja 90 C 3
Marne, *river* 94 G 3
Maroantsetra 175 F 3
Maroua 166 E 4
Marquesas, *island group* 11 D 3
Marquesa's Keys, *island group* 46 D 5
Marquette 41 K 2
Marquina 90 D 1
Marra, Jebel, *mountains* 167 F 4
Marrakech 166 C 2
Marree 193 G 5
Marroquí, Pta., *cape* 90 C 4
Marsala 78 D 3
Marsdiep, *strait* 98 C 1
Marseille 72 G 4
Marseilles, *see Marseille* 95 G 6
Marsh I., *island* 46 B 4
Marshall Islands, *island group* 11 B 2
Martaban 147 B 5
Martaban, G. of, *gulf* 118 F 5
Martes, *mountain* 91 E 3
Martha's Vineyard, *island* 30 G 3
Martigny-Ville 101 C 3
Martina 107 F 4
Martinborough 198 F 5
Martinique, *island* 31 G 5
Martinique Pass., *strait* 51 G 3
Martin L., *lake* 46 C 3
Martinsville 46 E 2
Martin Vaz, *island* 12 D 5
Marton 198 F 5
Martorell 91 F 2
Martos 90 D 4
Marungu, *mountains* 174 D 2
Marvejols 95 F 5
Marvine, Mt., *mountain* 42 E 4
Mary 142 B 2
Maryborough, *Australia, Queensland* 193 K 5
Maryborough, *Australia, Victoria* 193 H 7
Maryland, *state* 41 M 4
Marysville 42 B 4
Masada, *ancient site* 158 B 3
Masai Steppe, *steppe* 175 E 2
Masaka 175 E 2
Masan 123 P 6
Masaya 51 E 3
Masbate 119 H 5
Mascara 78 C 3
Mascarene Basin, *sea feature* 13 B 3
Mascarene Ridge, *sea feature* 13 B 3
Maseru 174 D 4
Mashâbih, J., *island* 167 G 3
Mashhad 118 D 4
Mashonaland, *region* 174 E 3
Masindi 167 G 5
Maşirah, J., *island* 118 D 4
Masirah Chan., *channel* 154 F 5
Masjed Soleymān 154 D 3
Mask, L., *lake* 83 B 5
Masoala, C., *cape* 175 G 3
Massa 106 C 2
Massachusetts, *state* 41 N 3
Massanutten Mt., *mt.* 46 E 2
Massawa 167 G 4
Massif Central, *mts.* 78 C 2
Massif de l'Oisans, *mts.* 95 H 5
Massif de l'Ouarsenis, *mountains* 78 C 3
Massif des Maures, *mts.* 95 H 6
Massif du Diois, *mts.* 95 G 5
Massif du Tsaratanana, *mountains* 175 F 3
Masterton 198 F 5
Mástikho, Akr., *cape* 111 D 4
Masuda 134 B 4
Masvingo 175 E 4
Mata, Sa. de, *mountains* 60 C 2
Matabeleland, *region* 174 D 3
Matebele Plain, *region* 174 D 3
Matadi 174 C 2
Matagalls, *mountain* 91 G 2
Matagalpa 51 E 3
Matagorda I., *island* 41 H 6
Mataimoana, *mountain* 198 F 4
Matakana I., *island* 198 G 3
Matale 143 D 6
Matama 154 B 7
Matamata 198 F 3
Matamoros, *Central Mexico* 50 C 2
Matamoros, *East Mexico* 50 D 2
Matanzas 30 F 4
Matanzas Inlet, *inlet* 46 D 4
Matapozuelos 90 C 2
Matara 143 D 6
Mataram 139 J 6
Mataró 91 G 2
Mataura 199 C 8
Matehuala 50 C 2
Matera 107 F 4
Matese, *mountain* 106 E 4
Mátészalka 116 D 3
Mateur 107 B 6
Mathura 138 E 3
Matifou, C., *cape* 91 G 4
Matjan, Kep., *island group* 150 D 4
Matochkin Shar, Proliv, *strait* 118 D 2
Mato Grosso, Planalto do, *plateau* 60 D 4
Matopo Hills, *mountains* 174 D 4
Matozinhos 90 A 2
Maţraḩ 154 F 5
Matsang Tsangpo, *river* 142 E 3
Matsudo 134 D 4
Matsue 123 Q 6
Matsumoto 134 D 3
Matsusaka 134 D 4
Ma-tsu Tao, *island* 129 F 6
Matsuyama 119 H 4
Mattamuskeet L., *lake* 46 E 3
Mattancheri 143 D 5
Matterhorn, *Switzerland, mountain* 72 G 4
Matterhorn, *U.S.A., mountain* 40 D 3
Matthew, *island* 187 H 4
Mattmar 86 O 3
Maturín 60 C 2
Mauberme, P. de, *mt.* 91 F 1
Maubeuge 94 F 2
Maubin 147 B 5
Maudheim, *scientific base* 15 B 2
Maud Seamount, *sea feature* 15 C 2
Mauges, Les, *region* 94 D 4
Mauk Mai 146 B 4
Mauléon-Licharre 95 D 6
Maumere 139 K 6
Maungahaumi, *mountain* 198 G 4
Maungamangero, *mt.* 198 F 4
Maungataniwha, *mt.* 198 G 4
Maungmagan I., *island group* 147 B 6
Mau Ra., *mountains* 167 G 6
Maurepas, L., *lake* 46 B 4
Mauriac 95 F 5
Maurice, L., *seasonal lake* 192 F 5
Maurienne, *river* 95 H 5
Mauritania 166 B 4
Mauritius, *island* 13 B 4
Mauritius Basin, *sea feature* 13 B 4
Mava 151 F 4
Mavrovoúni Pílion, *mt.* 110 C 4
Mawang Gangri, *mt.* 142 D 2
Mawlaik 146 B 4
Mawson, *scientific base* 15 F 2
Mawson Coast, *region* 15 F 2
Mayadin 79 H 3
Mayaguana, *island* 31 G 4
Mayaguana Passage, *strait* 51 F 2
Mayagüez 51 G 3
Maya Mts., *mountains* 31 F 5
Mayenne 94 D 3
Mayenne, *river* 94 D 3
Maykop 79 G 2
Maymyo 146 B 4
Mayo Landing 34 D 2
Mayo, Mts. of, *mountains* 83 B 4
Mayor, C., *cape* 90 D 1
Mayor I., *New Zealand, island* 198 G 3
Mayor I., *Spain, island* 91 E 4
Mayor, Isla, *interfluve* 90 B 4
Mayotte, *island* 175 F 3
Mayoumba 174 C 2
May Pen 51 F 3
May Pt., C., *cape* 41 N 4
Mayuram 143 D 5
Mazagan, *see El-Jadida* 16 C 2
Mazamet 95 F 6
Mazandaran, *region* 73 N 5
Mazara del Vallo 107 D 6
Mazari, C., *cape* 90 C 5
Mazarin, Forêt de, *region* 98 C 5
Mazar-i-Sharif 138 D 2

Mittelland-Muroto-saki

Mittelland, *region* 101 C 3
Mittweida 102 E 3
Mitumba, Chaîne des, *mountains* 174 D 2
Mitumba, Mts., *mts.* 174 D 2
Miyako 134 E 3
Miyake-jima, *island* 134 D 4
Miyakonojō 134 B 5
Miyazaki 134 B 5
Mizen Hd., *cape* 83 B 6
Mizoram, *state* 142 F 4
Mladá Boleslav 102 F 3
Mlanje, Mt., *mountain* 175 E 3
Mlawa 116 D 2
Mljet, *island* 106 F 3
Mo 74 G 1
Mo, *island* 151 D 4
Moab, *region* 158 B 3
Mobaye 167 F 5
Mobile 41 K 5
Mobile Bay, *bay* 41 K 5
Mobutu Sese Seko, L., *lake* 167 G 5
Moçambique 175 F 3
Mocha, I., *island* 62 A 2
Modane 101 B 4
Modena 78 D 2
Modesto 42 B 4
Modica 107 E 6
Mödling 116 C 3
Moers 98 E 3
Moeting 151 F 4
Moffat 82 E 4
Moffat Pk., *mountain* 199 C 7
Mogadishu, *see Muqdisho* 167 H 5
Mogami 134 D 3
Mogaung 146 B 3
Mogilev 72 K 3
Mogilev-Podol'skiy 79 F 2
Mogocha 123 O 4
Mogok 146 B 4
Mogollon Mesa, *tableland* 40 E 5
Moguer 90 B 4
Mohács 116 C 4
Mohaka, *river* 198 G 4
Mohave Mts., *mountains* 42 D 5
Mohawk, *river* 41 N 3
Mohammadia 91 F 5
Mohomeru, G., *mt.* 150 C 4
Mohon Pk., *mountain* 42 D 5
Moissac 95 E 5
Mojave 42 C 5
Mojave Desert, *desert* 30 E 4
Mojo, *island* 150 C 4
Mojokerto 139 J 6
Mokau, *river* 198 F 4
Mokmer 151 E 4
Mokokchung 146 B 3
Mokolo 166 E 4
Mokpo 123 P 6
Mokra Pl., *mountains* 110 B 2
Mol 98 D 3
Moldavskaya S.S.R., *rep.* 79 F 2
Molde 74 F 2
Molepolole 174 D 4
Molfetta 106 F 4
Molina 90 E 3
Molina de A. 90 E 2
Molins 91 G 2
Mollendo 60 B 4
Mölndal 87 O 5
Molodechno 116 E 1
Molopo, *river* 174 D 4
Molsheim 94 H 3
Molu, *island* 151 E 4
Moluccas, *see Maluku* 186 C 2
Mombasa 175 E 2
Mombetsu 134 E 1
Momchilgrad 110 D 3
Mompós 51 F 4
Momskiy Khr., *mountains* 119 J 2
Møn 87 O 6
Monach, S. of, *inlet* 82 C 3
Monaco 78 C 2
Monaco, *state* 72 G 4
Monadhliath Mts., *mts.* 82 D 3
Monåfjärd, *fjord* 86 R 3
Monaghan 83 C 4
Mona, I., *island* 51 G 3
Monarch Mt., *mountain* 34 E 3
Monas Pass., *strait* 31 G 5
Monashee Mts., *mts.* 30 E 3
Monastir 78 D 3
Moncada 91 E 3
Monção 90 A 1
Mon Cay 129 D 7
Moncayo, *mountain* 90 E 2
Mönch, *mountain* 101 D 3
Monchegorsk 86 U 2
Mönchengladbach 102 B 3
Monchique 90 A 4
Monchique, S. de, *mts.* 90 A 4
Monclova 40 G 6
Moncton 35 L 4
Mondego, *river* 90 A 2
Mondego, C., *cape* 90 A 2
Mondoñedo 90 B 1
Mondovi 106 A 2
Mondúber, *mountain* 91 E 3
Monegros, Los, *region* 91 E 2
Monesterio 90 B 3
Monfalcone 106 D 2
Monforte 90 B 3
Monforte de Lemos 90 B 1
Monga Gangri, *mountain* 142 E 2
Monger, L., *seasonal lake* 192 C 5
Möng Hsu 146 C 4
Monghyr 142 E 3
Möng Mit 146 B 4
Mongo, *mountain* 91 F 3
Mongolia 118 F 3
Mongos, Massif des, *mountains* 167 F 5
Möng Pai 146 B 5
Möng Sit 146 B 4
Möng Yai 146 C 4
Monitor Ra., *mountains* 42 C 4
Monmouth 83 E 6
Mono, *river* 166 D 5
Mono L., *lake* 40 D 4
Monopoli 106 F 4
Monreal del C. 91 E 2
Monroe 41 J 5
Monrovia 166 B 5
Mons 98 B 4
Monselice 106 C 2
Montafon, *river* 101 E 2
Montagu I., *island* 15 A 3
Montalbán 91 E 2
Montalegre 90 B 2
Montana, *state* 40 E 2
Montana, La., *region* 60 B 4
Montánchez 90 B 3
Montargis 94 F 4
Montauban 78 C 2
Montbéliard 94 H 4
Montblanch 91 F 2
Montbozon 101 B 2
Montbrison 95 G 5
Montcalm, L., *lake* 142 E 2
Mont-de-Marsan 95 D 6
Montdidier 94 F 3
Mont-Doré, le, 95 F 5
Montealegre 90 E 3
Monte Bello Is., *island group* 186 B 4
Monte Carlo 95 H 6
Monte Caseros 62 C 2
Montecristo, *island* 106 C 2
Montego Bay 51 F 3
Montehermoso 90 B 2
Montélimar 95 G 5
Montellano 90 C 4
Montemor-o-Novo 90 A 3
Montemuro, *mountain* 90 B 2
Montenotte 91 F 4
Móntepescali 106 C 3
Montepulciano 106 C 3
Monterey 40 C 4
Monterey B., *bay* 30 D 4
Montería 60 B 2
Montero 60 C 4
Monterrey 31 E 4
Montesano 42 B 2
Monte Sant'Angelo 106 E 4
M. Santu, C. di, *cape* 107 B 4
Montes Claros 61 E 4
Montevideo 62 C 2
Montfort-sur-Meu 94 D 3
M. Genèvre, Col de, *pass* 95 H 5
Montgomery, *Pakistan* 142 C 3
Montgomery, *U.S.A.* 30 F 4
Montgomery, *Wales* 83 E 5
Monthey 101 B 3
Montiel, Campo de, *region* 90 D 3
Montijo, *Portugal* 90 A 3
Montijo, *Spain* 90 B 3
Montluçon 78 C 2
Montmédy 94 G 3
Montmorillon 95 E 4
Monto 193 K 4
Montoro 90 C 3
Montpelier 41 N 3
Montpellier 78 C 2
Montreal 30 G 3
Montreuil 94 E 2
Montreux 101 B 3
Montrichard 94 E 4
Montrose, *Scotland* 82 E 3
Montrose, *U.S.A.* 40 F 4
Mont St. Michel, B. du, *bay* 94 D 3
Montsant, Sa. de, *mts.* 91 F 2
Montsech Sa. de, *mts.* 91 F 1
Montseny, Sa. de, *mts.* 91 G 2
Montserrat, *island* 51 G 3
Montserrat, Sa., *mts.* 91 F 2
Monywa 146 B 4
Monza 106 B 2
Monzón 91 F 2
Monzur Dağlari, *mts.* 73 L 5
Mookhorn, *island* 46 F 2
Moonta 193 G 6
Moora 192 C 6
Moore, L., *seasonal lake* 186 B 4
Moorfoot Hills, *hills* 82 E 4
Moosburg 103 D 4
Moose Jaw 34 G 3
Moose Lake, *lake* 34 G 3
Moosomin 34 G 3
Moosonee 41 L 1
Mopti 166 C 4
Mora, *Portugal* 90 A 3
Mora, *Spain* 90 D 3
Mora, *Sweden* 87 O 4
Moradabad 138 E 3
Moradal, Sa. do, *mts.* 90 A 3
Mora de Rubielos 91 E 2
Moral de C. 90 D 3
Moramanga 175 F 4
Moraña, La, *cape* 90 C 2
Morant Pt., *cape* 51 F 3
Morar, L., *lake* 82 D 3
Morás, C., *cape* 90 B 1
Moratalla 90 E 3
Morava, *river* 79 E 2
Moravia, *region* 116 C 3
Moray Firth, *firth* 72 F 3
Moray Ra., *mountains* 192 F 3
Morbier 101 B 3
Morbihan, G. du, *gulf* 94 C 4
Morecambe Bay, *bay* 83 E 4
Moree 193 J 5
Morelia 50 C 3
Morella, *Spain* 91 E 2
Morena, Sierra, *mts.* 73 F 5
Morenci 40 F 5
Møre og Romsdal, *county* 86 M 4
Moresby I., *island* 30 D 3
Mores I., *island* 46 E 5
Moreton I., *island* 193 K 5
Morges 101 B 3
Moriarty's Ra., *mts.* 193 J 5
Morioka 123 R 6
Morlaix 94 C 3
Mornington I., *island* 193 G 3
Mórnos, *river* 111 B 4
Morobe 151 F 4
Morocco 166 C 2
Morogoro 175 E 2
Moro Gulf, *gulf* 119 H 5
Moroleón 50 C 2
Morón 46 E 6
Morondava 175 F 4
Moroni 175 F 3
Morotai, *island* 151 D 3
Moroto, *mountain* 167 G 5
Morpeth 82 F 4
Morrinsville 198 F 3
Morris I., *island* 46 E 3
Morshansk 75 L 3
Morskaya 86 V 3
Mortagne-au-Perche 94 E 3
Mortain 94 D 3
Mortara 106 B 2
Morteau 101 B 2
Morungole 167 G 5
Morvan, *region* 78 C 2
Morvan, Mts. de, *mts.* 94 F 4
Morven, *region* 82 D 3
Morvi 142 C 4
Moschchnyy O., *island* 87 T 4
Moscow 42 C 2
Mosel, *river* 102 B 3
Moselle, *river* 94 H 3
Moses L., *lake* 42 C 2
Mosgiel 199 D 7
Moshi 175 E 2
Mosi-Oa-Toenja, *falls* 174 D 3
Mosjøen 86 O 3
Moskenesøy, *island* 86 O 2
Moskva 73 L 3
Mosquitia, *region* 51 E 3
Mosquito Lagoon, *lake* 46 D 4
Mosselbaai 174 D 5
Mossoró 61 F 3
Most 102 E 3
Mostaganem 166 D 2
Mostar 116 C 4
Mota 154 B 7
Mota del Marqués 90 C 2
Motala 87 P 5
Motere, *mountain* 198 F 4
Motherwell 82 D 4
Motien Ling, *mountains* 128 C 5
Motihari 142 E 3
Motilla del P. 90 E 3
Motiti I., *island* 198 G 3
Motovskiy Zaliv, *bay* 86 U 1
Motril 90 D 4
Motueka 198 E 5
Motuhora, *island* 198 G 3
Mouchoir Pass., *strait* 51 F 2
Moúdhros 110 D 4
Moudon 101 B 3
Moukance, Mts., *mts.* 174 C 2
Moulins 95 F 4
Moulmein 119 F 5
Moulouya, *river* 166 C 2
Moultrie 46 D 4
Moultrie, L., *lake* 46 D 3
Moúnda, Akr., *cape* 111 B 4
Moundou 166 E 5
Mt. Barker 192 C 6
Mt. Cenis, Col du, *pass* 95 H 5
Mt. Gambier 193 H 7
Mounth, *region* 82 E 3
Mount Hagen 151 F 4
Mount Isa 193 G 4
Mt. Lofty Ra., *mts.* 186 D 5
Mt. Magnet 192 C 5
Mount Maunganui 198 G 3
Mt. Morgan 193 K 4
Mount's Bay, *bay* 83 D 6
Mt. Vernon, *U.S.A., Illinois* 41 K 4
Mount Vernon, *U.S.A., Washington* 42 B 1
Moura, *Portugal* 90 B 3
Mourão 90 B 3
Mourdi, Depression de, *region* 167 F 4
Mourne Mts., *mountains* 82 C 4
Mouscron 98 B 4
Moussaou Salah, Dj., *mt.* 78 B 4
Mouthier 101 B 2
Moutier 101 C 2
Moutiers 95 H 5
Moy, *river* 83 B 4
Moyen Atlas, *mountains* 166 C 2
Moyobamba 60 B 3
Mozambique 175 E 4
Mozambique Channel, *channel* 175 E 4
Mozyr' 75 J 3
M'Sila 166 D 2
Msta, *river* 87 U 5
Mtwara 175 F 3
Mu, *mountain* 90 A 4
Mu, *river* 146 B 4
M. Chainat 147 C 6
M. Chiang Rai 118 F 5
Muang Khon Kaen 147 D 5
M. Lampang 139 G 4
Muang Lamphun 146 C 5
Muang Nan 146 C 5
M. Phayao 146 C 5
M. Phetchabun 147 C 5
M. Phichit 147 C 5
M. Phitsanulok 147 C 5
Muang Phrae 146 C 5
Muang Sakhon Makhon 147 D 5
M. Samut Prakan 147 C 6
M. Ubon 119 G 5
M. Uthai Thani 147 C 6
Muar 150 B 3
Muari, Ras, *cape* 142 C 3
Mubrak, J., *mountain* 158 B 4
Muchinga Mts., *mts.* 174 D 3
Much Wenlock 83 E 5
Muck, *island* 82 C 3
Mudanya 110 F 3
Mudhol 143 D 4
Mud L., *lake* 42 C 3
Mudugh, *region* 167 H 5
Muela, Sa. de la, *mts.* 91 E 2
Mufu Shan, *mountains* 129 E 6
Muge 90 A 3
Mugia 90 A 1
Muğla 79 F 3
Mugodzhary, *mountains* 73 O 4
Muhajjah 158 C 2
Muḥammad, Râ's., *cape* 79 G 4
Mühldorf 103 E 4
Mui Ron Ma, C., *cape* 146 E 5
Muir Seamount, *sea feature* 12 B 3
Mūjib, *river* 158 B 3
Mukachevo 116 D 3
Mukallā 138 B 4
Mukden, *see Shen-yang* 128 G 3
Mukoshima-retto, *island group* 134 E 6
Muktinath 142 E 3
Mukur 142 C 2
Mula 90 E 3
Mulata Mts., *mountains* 154 C 8
Mulde, *river* 102 E 3
Mu-leng Ho, *river* 134 C 1
Mulgrave 35 L 4
Mulgrave I., *island* 151 F 5
Mulhácen, C. de, *mt.* 78 B 3
Mülhausen 102 D 3
Mülheim (*Rhein*) 102 B 3
Mülheim (*Ruhr*) 102 B 3
Mulhouse 78 C 2
Mull, *island* 74 E 3
Mullaittivu 143 D 5
Mullan 42 D 2
Mullardoch, L., *lake* 83 D 3
Müller Geb., *mountains* 139 J 5
Mullewa 192 C 5
Mullingar 83 C 5
Multan 118 E 4
Mu-miao Ling, *mountain* 128 E 5
Muna, *island* 150 D 4
Müncheberg 102 D 3
Münchberg 102 F 2
München 72 H 4
Münden 102 C 3
Munella, *mountain* 111 B 3
Mungaroona Ra., *mts.* 192 C 4
Munia, Pico de la, *mt.* 95 E 6
Munich, *see München* 103 D 4
Münster 78 C 1
Münsterland, *region* 98 F 3
Muonio 86 R 2
Muonio älv, *river* 74 H 1
Muqdisho 167 H 5
Mur, *river* 103 F 5
Murallón, C., *mountain* 62 A 3
Murat 95 F 5
Murat, *river* 73 M 5
Murchison, *river* 186 B 4
Murchison Mts., *mts* 199 D 6
Murchison Mts., 199 B 7
Murcia 72 F 5
Murcia, *province* 90 D 3
Mureş, *river* 72 J 4
Muret 95 E 6
Murgab, *river* 142 B 2
Murgon 193 K 5
Muriaé 61 E 5
Murias de Paredes 90 B 1
Müritz See, *lake* 102 E 2
Murmansk 72 L 1
Murmanskiy Bereg, *region* 86 W 2
Murnau 101 G 2
Muro 91 G 3
Murom 75 L 3
Muroran 123 R 5
Muros 90 A 1
Muros y Noya, Ria de, *inlet* 90 A 1
Muroto-saki, *cape* 134 C 4

N

Q

Ripon-St. Helier

Ripon	83	F 4
Rishiri-suidô, *strait*	134	E 1
Rishiri-tô, *island*	134	E 1
Rishon le Zion	158	A 3
Risle, *river*	94	E 3
Risør	87	N 5
Risoux, Mts. du, *mts.*	101	B 3
Ritchie's Archo., *island group*	143	F 5
Ritter, Mt., *mountain*	42	C 4
Ritter Ra., *mountains*	142	F 2
Riva-del-Garda	106	C 2
Rivera	62	C 2
Riverina, *region*	186	E 5
Riversdale	174	D 5
Riverside	42	C 5
Riverton	199	C 8
Riviera, *region*	78	C 2
Riyadh	118	D 4
Rize	125	E 6
Rizhskiy Zaliv, *bay*	72	J 3
Rizzuto, C., *cape*	107	F 5
Rjukan	87	M 5
Rjuven, *mountains*	87	M 5
Rkiz, L., *lake*	166	B 4
Roa	90	D 2
Road Town	51	G 3
Roan Mt., *mountain*	41	L 4
Roanne	78	C 2
Roanoke	41	M 4
Roanoke, *river*	41	M 4
Roanoke I., *island*	46	F 3
Robbio	101	D 4
Robertsfors	86	Q 3
Roberts, Mt., *mountain*	193	K 5
Robinson Ras., *mts.*	186	B 4
Roboredo, Sa. de, *mts.*	90	B 2
Robson, Mt., *mountain*	30	E 3
Roca Partida, *island*	51	B 3
Rocas, *island*	61	F 3
Rocas Alijos, *island group*	50	B 2
Roccastrada	106	C 3
Roc d'Enfer, *mountain*	101	B 3
Rocha	62	C 2
Rochdale	83	E 5
Rochechouart	95	E 5
Rochefort	78	B 2
Rochester, *U.S.A., Minnesota*	41	J 3
Rochester, *U.S.A., New York*	41	M 3
Rockall Deep, *sea feature*	72	E 3
Rockall Oceanic Bank, *sea feature*	72	E 3
Rock & Pillar Ra., *mts.*	199	C 7
Rockford	41	K 3
Rockhampton	186	F 4
Rock Hill	46	D 3
Rock Island	46	B 1
Rock L., *lake*	42	C 2
Rock Pt., *cape*	198	E 5
Rock Springs	40	F 3
Rocky Mount	46	E 3
Rocky Mt., *mountain*	42	D 2
Rocky Mountains, *mts.*	30	D 3
Rocroi	94	G 3
Rødby	102	D 1
Rodez	95	F 5
Ródhos	29	F 3
Ródhos, *island*	72	K 5
Rodniki	125	E 2
Rodopi Planina, *mts.*	72	J 5
Rodriguez I., *island*	199	C 3
Roebourne	192	C 4
Roen, M., *mountain*	101	G 3
Roermond	94	G 2
Roeselare	98	B 4
Roes Welcome Sd., *inlet*	34	J 2
Rogachev	116	F 2
Rogagua, Lago, *lake*	60	C 4
Rogaland, *county*	87	L 5
Rogers L., *lake*	42	C 5
Rogoaguado, Lago, *lake*	60	C 4
Rogozna, *mountains*	110	B 2
Rogue, *river*	42	A 3
Rohtak	142	D 3
Roignais, Le, *mountain*	101	B 4
Roi, Pont du, *pass*	95	E 6
Rojo, C., *Mexico, cape*	50	D 2
Rojo, C., *Puerto Rico, cape*	51	G 3
Røldal	74	F 2
Roma, *Australia*	193	J 5
Roma, *Italy*	72	H 5
Roma, *island*	186	C 2
Romagnano	101	D 4
Roman	116	E 3
Romania	72	J 4
Romanche Gap, *sea feature*	12	E 4
Romano, C., *cape*	46	D 5
Romano, C., *island*	46	E 6
Romano di Lom	101	E 4
Romanshorn	101	E 2
Romans-sur-Isère	95	G 5
Romanzof, C., *cape*	30	B 2
Romblon	150	D 2
Rome, *Italy, see Roma*	106	D 4
Rome, *U.S.A., Georgia*	46	C 3
Romorantin	94	E 4
Roncador Cay, *reef*	51	E 3
Roncador, Sa. do, *mts.*	60	D 4
Ronciglione	106	D 3
Ronda	90	C 4
Ronda, Sa. de, *mountains*	78	B 3
Rondane, *region*	86	N 4
Rondeslottet, *mountain*	86	N 4
Rongklang Ra., *mts*	146	A 4
Rønne	74	G 3
Ronneby	87	P 6
Ronne Entrance, *channel*	15	R 2
Ronse	98	B 4
Roosendaal	98	C 3
Roosevelt I., *island*	15	M 2
Roper, *river*	186	D 3
Roquetas	91	F 2
Rora Hd., *cape*	82	E 2
Roraima, Mt., *mountain*	60	C 2
Røros	86	N 4
Rorschach	103	C 5
Rosa, C., *cape*	107	B 6
Rosalind Bank, *sea feature*	51	E 3
Rosa, Monte, *mountain*	72	H 4
Rosamund L., *lake*	42	C 5
Rosanna, *river*	101	F 2
Rosario	62	B 2
Rosarito, Emb. de, *lake*	90	C 2
Rosas, G. de, *gulf*	91	G 1
Roscommon	83	B 5
Roscrea	83	C 5
Roseau	51	G 3
Roseburg	40	C 3
Rose I., *island*	46	E 5
Rosemary Bank, *sea feature*	72	E 2
Rosenberg	41	H 6
Rosenheim	103	E 5
Roşiorii de Vede	110	D 1
Roskilde	74	G 3
Roslavl'	75	K 3
Rossano	107	F 5
Ross Dependency, *territory*	15	M 2
Rossel I., *island*	193	K 2
Ross Ice Shelf	15	M 1
Ross I., *Burma, island*	147	C 6
Ross I., *Ross Dependency, island*	15	L 2
Ross River	34	D 2
Ross Sea	15	M 2
Rostock	74	G 3
Rostov	75	K 3
Rostov-na-Donu	73	L 4
Rösvatn, *lake*	86	O 3
Roswell	40	G 5
Rota	90	B 4
Rota, *island*	151	F 2
Rotenburg	102	C 2
Rote Wand, *mountain*	101	E 2
Roth	103	D 4
Rothaar Geb., *mountains*	102	C 3
Rothenburg	103	D 4
Rother, *river*	83	G 6
Rotherham	83	F 5
Rothesay	82	D 4
Roth Hn., A., *mountain*	101	E 3
Roti, *island*	119	H 6
Rotoiti, *lake*	198	G 4
Rotoma, *lake*	198	G 4
Rotondo, M., *mountain*	78	D 2
Rotondo, P., *mountain*	101	D 3
Rotoroa, L., *lake*	198	E 5
Rotorua	198	G 4
Rotorua, *lake*	198	G 4
Rotterdam	72	G 3
Rottnest I., *island*	192	B 6
Rottumeroog, *island*	98	E 1
Rottumerplaat, *island*	98	E 1
Rottweil	103	C 4
Rotuma I., *island*	187	H 3
Roubaix	94	F 2
Rouen	78	C 2
Rouge, *river*	129	C 7
Rough Ridge, *mountains*	199	C 7
Round Mt., *mountain*	187	F 5
Roussillon, *province*	95	F 6
Roussillon, Plaine de, *region*	95	F 6
Rouyn	35	K 4
Rovaniemi	74	J 1
Rovato	101	E 4
Rovereto	106	C 2
Rovigo, *Algeria*	91	G 4
Rovigo, *Italy*	106	C 2
Rovinj	106	D 2
Rovno	79	F 1
Rowley Shoals, *reefs*	186	B 3
Roxburgh	199	C 7
Royale, I., *island*	41	K 2
Royan	95	D 5
Rtanj, *mountains*	110	B 2
Ruahine Range, *mts.*	198	G 5
Ruapehu Vol., *mountain*	187	H 5
Ruapuke Island, *island*	199	C 8
Rub' al Khālī, *desert*	118	D 5
Rubha Reidh, *cape*	82	D 3
Rubí	90	G 2
Rubial, Sa. de, *mountains*	91	E 3
Rubio	51	F 4
Rubtsovsk	122	L 4
Ruby Mts., *mountains*	40	D 3
Ruda Śląska	116	C 2
Rūd-e Atrak, *river*	73	N 5
Rudnik, *mountain*	110	B 1
Rudok	142	D 2
Rudoka Plan., *mountains*	110	B 3
Rudolf, Lake, *see Turkona, Lake*	167	G 5
Rudolstadt	102	D 3
Ruffec	95	E 4
Rufiji, *river*	175	E 2
Rufino	62	B 2
Rufisque	166	B 4
Rugby	83	F 5
Rügen, *island*	72	H 3
Ruhr, *river*	102	B 3
Rujen, *mountain*	110	C 2
Rujm es Sakhiri	158	B 3
Ruki, *river*	174	C 3
Rukwa, Lake, *lake*	175	E 2
Ruma	116	C 4
Rumblar, Emb. del, *lake*	90	D 3
Rumoi	134	E 2
Runanga	199	D 6
Runaway, C., *cape*	198	G 3
Rungwe Mt., *mountain*	175	E 2
Rupat, P., *island*	150	B 3
Rupert	42	D 3
Ruppert Coast, *region*	15	N 2
Rur, *river*	98	E 3
Ruse	79	F 2
Russell	198	F 2
Russell Ra., *mountains*	186	C 5
R.S.F.S.R., *republic U.S.S.R.*	122	K 4
Rustavi	79	H 3
Rustenburg	174	D 4
Rute	90	C 4
Ruth	42	D 4
Rüti	101	D 2
Rutland I., *island*	143	F 5
Ru'ūs al Jibāl, *region*	154	F 4
Ruvuma, *river*	175	E 3
Ruwenzori Ra., *mts.*	167	G 5
Ruzayevka	125	F 3
Ružomberok	116	C 3
Ruz, Val de, *valley*	101	B 2
Rwanda	167	F 6
Ryan, L., *lake*	83	D 4
Ryan Pk., *mountain*	42	D 3
Ryazan'	73	L 3
Rybachiy, Poluostrov, *peninsula*	72	L 1
Rybach'ye	142	D 1
Rybinsk	75	K 2
Rybinskoye Vdkhr., *res.*	73	L 2
Rybnitsa	116	F 3
Ryfylke, *region*	87	L 5
Ryn-Peski, *desert*	73	N 4
Ryūkyū Rettō, *island group*	119	H 4
Rzepin	102	F 2
Rzeszów	116	D 2
Rzeszów, *province*	116	D 3
Rzhev	75	K 3

S

Saale, *river*	102	D 3
Saane, *river*	101	C 3
Saanen	101	C 3
Saar, *river*	103	B 4
Saarbrücken	78	C 2
Saarburg	102	B 4
Saare, *river*	94	H 3
Saaremaa *Island*	72	J 2
Saariselkä, *mountains*	74	J 1
Saarland, *länder*	103	B 4
Saarlautern	103	B 4
Saarmin Uula, *mountains*	142	E 1
Saba Bank, *sea feature*	51	G 3
Sabac	116	C 4
Sabadell	78	C 3
Sabah, *province*	139	J 5
Sabana, Archo. de, *island group*	51	F 2
Sabanalarga	51	F 3
Sabderat	154	B 6
Sabinal, Pta. del, *cape*	90	D 4
Sabinas	50	C 2
Sabine, *river*	41	J 5
Sabini, Mti., *mountains*	106	D 3
Sable, C., *Canada, cape*	30	G 3
Sable, C., *U.S.A., cape*	31	F 4
Sable I., *island*	30	H 3
Sablé-sur-Sarthe	94	D 4
Sablon, Pte. du, *cape*	95	G 6
Sabor, *river*	90	B 2
Sabrina Coast, *region*	15	H 2
Sabtang I., *island*	129	G 7
Sabugal	90	B 2
Sabyā	154	C 6
Sabzevār	154	F 2
Sacajaewae Pk., *mountain*	42	C 2
Sacavem	90	A 3
Sacecorbo, *mountain*	90	D 2
Sacedón	90	D 2
Sachsen, *länder*	102	E 3
Sachsen Anhalt, *länder*	102	D 2
Sachs Harbour, *trading post*	34	E 1
Säckingen	101	C 2
Sacramento	40	C 4
Sacramento, *river*	30	D 3
Sacramento Mts., *mts.*	30	E 4
Sacramento Valley, *valley*	42	B 4
Sacratif, C., *cape*	90	D 4
Saddle L., *island*	147	C 7
Saddle Pk., *mountain*	143	F 5
Saddle, The, *mountain*	82	D 3
Sadec	147	D 7
Sadiya	139	G 3
Sa'diyah, Hawr as, *lake*	154	D 3
Sado, *island*	119	H 4
Sado, *river*	90	A 3
Safad	158	B 2
Sāfājah, *region*	154	B 4
Säffle	87	O 5
Saffron Walden	83	G 5
Safi, *Jordon*	158	B 3
Safi, *Morocco*	166	C 2
Safier Tal, *valley*	101	E 3
Safonovo	125	C 2
Saga	134	B 4
Sagaing	146	B 4
Sagaing, *province*	146	B 4
Sagami-nada, *island*	134	D 4
Sagar	138	E 3
Sagauli	142	E 3
Sagi H., *mountain*	158	A 4
Saginaw Bay, *bay*	35	J 4
Saglouc	35	K 2
Sagra, La, *mountain*	90	D 4
Sag Sag	151	F 4
Sagua la Grande	46	D 6
Saguenay, *river*	41	N 2
Saguia el Hamra, *river*	166	B 3
Sagunto	91	E 3
Sahand, Kūh-e, *mountain*	154	D 2
Sahara Desert, *desert*	166	C 4
Saharanpur	138	E 3
Şahrā'al, Hijārah, *region*	154	C 3
Saḥrā ash Sharqiyah, *plateau*	79	F 4
Sahuayo	50	C 2
Sahul Shelf, *sea feature*	186	C 3
Sahyadriparvat, *mts.*	142	D 4
Saïda	96	F 5
Sa'īdābād	138	C 3
Saidpur	118	F 4
Saigon, *see Ho Chi Min City*	139	H 4
Saijō	134	C 4
Sailana	142	D 4
Saileen	151	E 4
Saimaa, *lake*	72	K 2
Sā'īn Dezh	154	D 2
St. Abbs Hd., *cape*	82	E 4
Saint-Affrique	95	F 6
St. Albans	83	F 6
St.-Amand	94	F 2
Saint-Amand-Montrond	95	F 4
St. André, C., *cape*	175	F 3
St. André, Plaine de, *plain*	94	E 3
St. Andreas, Cape, *cape*	79	G 3
St. Andrews	82	E 3
St. Andrews Sound, *inlet*	46	D 4
St. Andrija, *island*	106	E 3
St. Anthony, *Canada*	35	M 3
St. Anthony, *U.S.A.*	42	E 3
St. Augustine	46	D 4
St. Austell	83	D 6
St. Barthélemy, *island*	51	G 3
St. Bathans, Mt., *mt.*	199	C 7
St. Bees Hd., *cape*	83	E 4
St. Boniface	34	H 4
St. Bride's Bay, *bay*	83	D 6
St. Brieuc	78	B 2
St. Brieuc, B. de, *bay*	94	C 3
Saint-Calais	94	E 4
St. Catherines I., *island*	46	D 4
St. Christopher, *island*	51	G 3
St. Clair, L., *lake*	30	F 3
Saint-Claude	95	G 4
St. Cloud	41	J 2
St. Croix, *island*	51	G 3
St. David's Hd., *cape*	75	E 3
St.-Denis	175	G 4
Saint-Dié	94	H 3
Saint-Dizier	94	G 3
Ste. Catherine, Pte., *cape*	166	D 6
Sainte-Croix	101	B 3
St. Elias, Mt., *mountain*	30	C 2
St. Elias, Mts., *mountains*	30	C 2
Sainte-Menehould	94	G 3
Saintes	95	D 5
St.-Étienne	78	C 2
St. Flour	95	F 5
St. Francis, *river*	46	B 2
St. Francois Mts., *mts*	41	J 4
St. Gallen	103	C 5
St. Gallen, *canton*	101	E 2
St. Gaudens	95	E 6
St. George	42	D 4
St. George, C., *cape*	35	M 4
St. George I., *island*	41	L 6
St. George, Pt., *cape*	42	A 3
St. George's	51	G 3
St. George's Chan., *British Isles, channel*	72	F 3
St. George's Chan., *Territory of New Guinea, channel*	187	G 2
Saint-Germain-en-Laye	94	F 3
St. Gildas, Pte. de, *cape*	94	C 4
St. Gingolph	101	B 3
Saint-Girons	95	E 6
St. Gotthard P., *pass*	101	D 3
St. Govan's Hd., *cape*	83	D6
St. Helena, *island*	12	E 5
St. Helena B., *bay*	174	C 5
St. Helena Sd., *inlet*	46	D 3
St. Helens, *England*	83	E 5
St. Helens, *U.S.A.*	42	B 2
St. Helens, Mt., *mountain*	42	B 2
St. Helier	83	E 7

T

W

X

Y

Z

Geographical terms

Bay — B.
Baie — B.
Bahía — B.
Bucht — B.
Bugt — B.
Bukten
Flói
Ghubbat
Guba
Khalij
Kólpos
Nada
Teluk — Tel.
Wan
Zaliv
Zatoka

Cape — C.
Akra — Akr.
Burnu — Br.
Cabo — C.
Cap — C.
Chiao
Head — Hd.
Kapp — K.
Misaki
Mys — M.
Piao
Point — Pt.
Pointe — Pte.
Ponta — Pta.
Punta — Pta.
Ras
Rås
Ra's
Saki
Tandjung — Td.

Desert
Dasht
Gobi
Hamada
Kum
Peski
Sha-mo

Gulf — G.
Golfe — G.
Golfo — G.
Körfezi — K.

Island — I.
Do
Île — Î.
Ilha — I.
Isla — I.
Isola — I.
Jazira — Jaz.
Jima
Ostrov — O.
Shima
Tao
Tō

Islands — Is.
Eilanden — Eil.
Gugusan
Guntō
Îles — Îs.
Ilhas — Is.
Islas — Is.
Isole — I.
Kepulauan — Kep.
Ostrova — O-va
Rettō

Lake — L.
Buhayrah
Chott
Danau
Daryächeh — D.
Embalse — Emb.
Étang — É.
Gölü — G.

Hawr
Hu
Jezioro — Jez.
Ko
Köl
Kul'
Lac — L.
Lacul — L.
Lago — L.
Lagôa — L.
Laguna — L.
Loch — L.
Lough — L.
Nor
Nür
Nuur
Ozero — Oz.
See — S.
Tscho

Mountain — Mt.
Ballon
Beinn
Ben
Cerro — Co.
Dägh — D.
Daği — D.
Gunung — G.
Horn
Jabal — J.
Küh
Mont — M.
Monte — M.
Montagne — Mgne.
Nevos — Nev.
Peak — Pk.
Peña
Pico — P.
Pik — P.
Piz — P.
San
Tor
Volcano — Vol.
Yama — Y.

Mountains — Mts.
Alin
Alpen — A.
Alpi — A.
Altos
Cerros
Cordillera — Cord.
Dağlari — D.
Gebirge — Geb.
Gory
Khrebet — Khr.
Massif
Melkosopochnik
Montagnes — Mgnes.
Montes — Mts.
Monti — Mti.
Óri — Ó.
Óros — Ó.
Planina — Plan.
Range — Ra.
Sammyaku — Samm.
Sanchi
Serra — Sa.
Serranía
Shan
Shan-mo
Sierra — Sa.
Slieve — Sl.
Tagh
Úla
Uula
Yoma

Peninsula — Pena.
Hantō
Khersónisos
Pan-tao
Presqu'île
Poluostrov — Po-v
Yarimada — Yar.

Plain
Nizmennost'
Ténéré

Plateau — Plat.
Planalto — Plan.
Plato
Tassili
Vozvyshennost' — Vozvysh.

Reservoir — Res.
Dam
Sagara
Vodokhrcnilishche — Vdkhr.

River — R.
Älv
Bahr — B.
Bü
Chiang — Ch.
Chu
Creek — Cr.
Dar'ya
Gol
Hka
Ho
Mae

Sand dune region
Edeyin
Erg
Ghurd

Sea
Laut
More
Nada

Strait — Str.
Baelt
Bocche
Gat
Hai-hsia
Passage — Pass.
Proliv
Selat — Sel.
Stenón
Suidō

Swamp
Aydar
Bañados
Uvaly
Zalew

Index

Index